INTRODUCTION TO INFORMATION TECHNOLOGY

Second Edition

EFRAIM TURBAN
City University of Hong Kong

R. KELLY RAINER, Jr.
Auburn University

RICHARD E. POTTER
University of Illinois, Chicago

JOHN WILEY & SONS, INC.

ACQUISITIONS EDITOR	Beth Lang Golub
DEVELOPMENT EDITORS	Ann Torbert, Johnna Barto
SUPPLEMENTS EDITOR	Cynthia Snyder
EDITORIAL ASSISTANT	Lorraina Raccuia
MARKETING MANAGER	Gitti Lindner
SENIOR PRODUCTION EDITOR	Norine M. Pigliucci
COVER DESIGN	Harry Nolan
ILLUSTRATION EDITOR	Anna Melhorn
PHOTO EDITOR	Sara Wight
PHOTO RESEARCHER	Elyse Rieder
PRODUCTION MANAGEMENT SERVICES	Suzanne Ingrao
COVER PHOTOGRAPH	© Richard Price/FPG/Getty Images

This book was set in Times Ten by UG / GGS Information Services, Inc. and printed and bound by Von Hoffmann Corporation. The cover was printed by Von Hoffmann Corporation.

This book is printed on acid-free paper.

L.C. Card No.
ISBN 0-471-07380-6

Printed in the United States of America

10 9 8 7 6 5 4 3 2

Efraim Turban (right in photo) is currently on the faculty of the City University of Hong Kong. He obtained his MBA and Ph.D. degrees from the University of California, Berkeley. His industry experience includes eight years as an industrial engineer, three of which were spent at General Electric Transformers Plant. He also has extensive consulting experience to small and large corporations as well as to foreign governments. In his 30 years of teaching, Dr. Turban has served as Distinguished Professor at Eastern Illinois University, and as Visiting Professor at Nanyang Technological University in Singapore. He has also taught at UCLA, USC, Simon Fraser University, and California State University, Long Beach.

Dr. Turban was a co-recipient of the 1984/85 National Management Science Award (Artificial Intelligence in Management). In 1997 he received the Distinguished Faculty Scholarly and Creative Achievement Award at California State University, Long Beach. He was the co-chair of the 1999 International Conference of Electronic Commerce. Dr. Turban has published over 100 articles in leading journals. He has also published 21 books, including *Fundamentals of Electronic Commerce* (2002).

R. Kelly Rainer, Jr. (center in photo), is George Phillips Privett Professor of Management Information Systems at Auburn University, Auburn, Alabama. He received his BS degree in Mathematics from Auburn and his Doctor of Dental Medicine (DMD) from the University of Alabama in Birmingham. After practicing dentistry for ten years, Professor Rainer returned to school and received his Ph.D. at the University of Georgia. He has published numerous articles in leading journals and is currently investigating various aspects of virtual organizations and application service providers.

Richard E. Potter (left in photo) is Assistant Professor of Information and Decision Sciences in the College of Business Administration at the University of Illinois at Chicago. He received a bachelors degree in psychology from California State University–Hayward, and an MS in Management degree and Ph.D. degree in Management and Management Information Systems from the University of Arizona. Dr. Potter was a Postdoctoral Fellow at the University of Michigan's School of Public Health and Visiting Scholar and Adjunct Professor of MIS at the University of Arizona's Keller School of Management. He also served Mexico's ITESM system as Director of Research and Doctoral Programs at their Mexico City Graduate School of Business.

Dr. Potter's current research interest is cognition and behavior in the electronic environment, with emphasis on performance assessment and intervention with electronically supported groups, and cultural effects on collaborative technology use. He has published in a number of leading scientific journals, has authored numerous book chapters, and has presented his work in academic conferences around the world.

PREFACE

As we enter the digital revolution, successful organizations must deal effectively with intense global competition, a heightened focus on the bottom line, and an increasingly rapid pace of change. For an organization to thrive in today's Internet economy, managers and functional specialists in all areas—accounting, finance, marketing, production and operations management, and human resources—must perform their jobs even more effectively and efficiently. Information technology provides the tools that enable all organizational personnel to solve increasingly complex problems and to capitalize on opportunities that contribute to the success, or even the survival, of the organization.

This book is based on the fundamental premise that the major role of information technology (IT) is to support organizational personnel, regardless of their functional area or level in the organization. IT supports business processes that enable companies to operate in the digital era by quickly and properly reacting to changes. In many cases, IT is the basis for aggressive proactive strategies that can radically alter the competitive landscape of an industry. We aim here to teach all undergraduate business majors how to use IT to master their current or future jobs and to help ensure the success of their organization. Our focus is not on merely *learning* the concepts of information technology but rather on *applying* those concepts to facilitate business processes.

KEY FEATURES

Recognizing the challenges of teaching an introductory MIS course to students of varied backgrounds and interests, we have been guided by the following goals that we believe will enhance the teaching and learning experience.

Assume an Active Approach to Learning. We recognize the need to actively involve the students in problem solving, creative thinking, and capitalizing on opportunities. We enable students to actually do something with the concepts they learn, such as how to create a small business on the Web, to configure products, and to use spreadsheets to facilitate problem solving. Every chapter includes many hands-on exercises, activities, and minicases.

Show How IT Can Help Individuals in All Functional Areas Be More Effective and Efficient. We show why IT is important by calling attention in each chapter to how that chapter's IT topic relates to students in each major. Special icons guide readers to relevant issues for their specific functional area. In addition, chapters end with a summary of how the concepts relate to each functional area ("What's in IT for Me?").

Provide Diversified and Unique Examples from Different Disciplines and Industries. Extensive use of vivid examples from large corporations, small businesses, and government and not-for-profit agencies helps to enliven concepts by showing students the capabilities of IT, its cost and justification, and innovative ways that real corporations are using IT in their operations. Each chapter constantly highlights the integral connection between IT and business. This is especially evident in the special "IT's About Business" boxes.

Highlight Creativity and Innovation. In today's rapidly changing environment, creativity and innovation are necessary for a business to operate effectively and profitably. Throughout the book we show how these concepts are facilitated by IT. We provide success stories as well as examples of IT failures.

Include Numerous International Examples. The importance of global competition, partnerships, and trading is rapidly increasing throughout the business world. We discuss how IT facilitates export and import, managing multinational companies, and electronic trading around the globe.

Emphasize Use of the World Wide Web and e-Commerce. In addition to teaching the fundamentals of the Internet, we present a comprehensive chapter on electronic commerce (Chapter 9). We also include Web-based real-world applications and Internet exercises in each chapter. Internet addresses (URLs) for organizations cited in examples are provided so students can further explore the issues. "Virtual Company" assignments included in the book direct students to a special Web site.

Stress New and "Cutting-Edge" Applications. The book discusses the importance of integrated systems both internal (e.g., SAP R/3 and customer resource management) and external (e.g., EDI and extranets). We relate the integrated systems to enterprise resource planning (ERP), supply chain management, and multinational corporations.

WHAT'S NEW IN THE SECOND EDITION
We have made a special effort to update and reorganize the second edition to reflect how IT is used in today's business environment. Some of the major changes include:

- The new Chapter 10 addresses supply chain management and IT's role in integration and coordination up and down the supply chain.
- The electronic commerce chapter has been moved forward to Chapter 9, reflecting its crucial importance to modern organizations.
- Topics addressing interorganizational IT and global IT have been integrated throughout the text, particularly in the supply chain management chapter and in the real-world examples in all chapters.
- All examples and real-world cases in the text are new and/or updated to reflect the rapidly changing nature of IT.
- A CD, packaged with the text, provides video clips, cases, and interactive hands-on exercises for students, reflecting the major learning objectives of each chapter.
- Interactive Learning Sessions have been included at the end of every chapter. These refer students to the CD or Web site where interactivities help them apply and understand concepts they've studied in the chapter.
- The Virtual Company case, which runs throughout the text referring students to the Web site, has been updated to reflect the rapidly changing nature of IT.
- To stay abreast of rapid changes in IT, the authors provide weekly IT updates that may be accessed on the book's Web site (*www.wiley.com/college/turban*). These updates include topics such as technological advances and real-world examples and cases. These updates provide current, interesting material for students.
- The technology chapters (3, 4, 5, 6, and 7) have built-in flexibility for the professor. The basic concepts are covered in the text, and more detailed, technical information is available on the book's Web site (*www.wiley.com/college/turban*). Concepts on the Web site are denoted with a Web icon in the margin for ease of access.

www.wiley.com/
college/turban

- The latest technology topics are addressed, including mobile commerce and the wireless Web, application service providers, peer-to-peer networking, middleware, XML, on-line storage service providers, and many others.

PEDAGOGICAL STRUCTURE

In addition to presenting the material in an easy-to-read manner with a logical flow of ideas, we have crafted a strong pedagogical structure to motivate students and guide their learning experience. Other pedagogical features provide a learning system that reinforces the concepts through chapter organizers, section reviews, frequent applications, and hands-on exercises and activities.

Chapter Opening Organizers include:

- A *chapter preview*, which shows how the chapter fits with other topics in the book.
- *Chapter outlines*, which preview the major concepts covered in the chapter.
- *Learning objectives*, which tell what students can expect to learn in the chapter.
- A *real-world case*, which identifies a business problem of an actual company, gives the solution and results, and summarizes what was learned from the case.

Study Aids are provided throughout each chapter:

- Tables list key points or summarize different concepts.
- *Managers' checklists* review the advantages/benefits and disadvantages/limitations of important systems and processes.
- *IT's About Business* are special sections that provide real-world applications, with questions that relate to concepts covered in the text. Special icons key these sections to the specific functional areas.
- Highlighted *examples* show the use and misuse of IT by real-world organizations and help illustrate the conceptual discussion.
- End-of-section reviews (*Before You Go On*) give students an opportunity to test their understanding of concepts before moving on to the next section.

End-of-Chapter Study Aids provide extensive opportunity for readers to review and actually "do something" with the concepts they have just studied:

- *What's in IT for Me?* is a special chapter summary section that shows the relevance of topics for different functional areas (e.g., accounting, finance, marketing, production/operations management, human resources management).
- *Chapter Summary* is keyed to learning objectives that were listed at beginning of chapter and allow students to review the major concepts covered in the chapter.
- *Interactive Learning Sessions* refer students to the CD or Web site where they will find exercises and cases to apply the concepts they have learned.
- *Discussion Questions, Problem-Solving Activities, Internet Activities, and Team Assignments* provide practice through active learning. These exercises are hands-on opportunities to use the concepts discussed in the chapter.
- The *Real-World Case* is organized around a business problem and how IT helped to solve it; questions relate it to concepts discussed in the chapter.
- The *Virtual Company Assignment* gives the student an assignment as an intern for Extreme Descent Snowboards and refers readers to the book's Web site (*www.wiley.com/college/turban*) for support information.

SUPPLEMENTS

This book also facilitates the teaching of an Introduction to IT course by providing extensive support materials for instructors and students.

Instructor's Manual prepared by Russell Casey, Delaware State University. The *Instructor's Manual* includes a chapter overview, teaching tips and strategies, answers to all end-of-chapter questions, supplemental minicases with essay questions and answers, experiential exercises that relate to particular topics, and war stories for each chapter. This manual also includes a feature called "What's Next" within each chapter, which provides a glimpse of what is to come in the next chapter. Finally, a Video Guide with three to five viewing questions that relate to chapter topics, relevant Web links wherever possible, and a case correlation guide that provides a correlation of each case the text authors have provided with the related chapters from the text are also included.

Test Bank prepared by Kelly Rainer, Auburn University. The *Test Bank* is a comprehensive resource for test questions. It contains approximately 125 questions per chapter consisting of multiple choice, true/false, fill-in-the blanks, matching, and short answer questions.

PowerPoint Presentations prepared by Roberta Roth, University of Northern Iowa. The *PowerPoint Presentations* consist of a series of slides for each chapter of the text that is designed around the text content, incorporating key points from the text and all text illustrations as appropriate. These slides are intended to further enhance the instructor's classroom lectures.

BusinessExtra with *Wall Street Journal* articles keyed to every chapter. An ongoing timely series of on-line newspaper articles relating to the various topics within the text that are accessible through the text Web site so that students and instructors can have access to this collection of current and relevant articles as they become available. By including these articles and readings on-line, this course becomes more real-world, research, and analysis based for students. The primary source for these articles is the *Wall Street Journal/Dow Jones Publications,* through the wsj.com, with whom Wiley has an exclusive partnership.

www.wiley.com/
college/turban

Web Quizzes prepared by Jeff Stewart, Macon State College. These practice tests, which are designed to help prepare for class tests, are provided as an on-line resource within the text Web site. These on-line quizzes have been created to serve as an interactive study guide for students. Once students have completed a particular quiz they can submit it electronically and receive feedback regarding their incorrect responses. The feedback provides helpful hints about where they can find material in the text that relates to the correct answer.

Nightly Business Report Videos. This comprehensive video compilation offers selections from the highly respected business news program, "Nightly Business Report" (NBR). The segments within this video package tie directly to the core topics of the text and bring to life real-world examples of information technology in practice. Each segment is approximately three to seven minutes long and can be used to introduce topics to the students, enhance lecture material, and provide real-world context for related concepts.

NBR Video Guide prepared by Ed Glantz, Pennsylvania State University. The video guide provides the instructor with a brief overview of each video clip, along with relevant topic points and discussion questions. The Guide also includes suggestions for which chapters each clip can be used with.

Instructor's Resource CD includes all the electronic files for the Instructor's Manual, Test Bank, PowerPoint Presentations, and NBR Video Guide. It also includes a computerized version of the Test Bank that enables instructors to customize their own quizzes and tests for their students.

Course Management. New WebCT and Blackboard courses are available with this text. WebCT and Blackboard are tools that facilitate the organization and delivery of course materials via the Web. They provide powerful communication, loaded content, easy and flexible course administration, sophisticated on-line self-tests and diagnostic systems, and ease of use for both students and instructors.

ACKNOWLEDGMENTS

Creating, developing, and producing a new text for the introduction to information technology course is a formidable undertaking. Along the way, we were fortunate to receive continuous evaluation, criticism, and direction from many of our colleagues who regularly teach this course. We would like to acknowledge the contributions made by the following individuals.

Second Edition Reviewers: Omar Benli, *California State University–Long Beach,* Warren Boe, *University of Iowa*; Russell Casey, *Delaware State University*; Debra Chapman, *University of Southern Alabama*; Eli Cohen, *Kozminski Academy of Entrepreneurship and Management*; Mohamad Dadashzadeh, *Witchita State University*; Tony Kendall, *Naval Postgraduate School*; Brian Kovar, *Kansas State University*; Patricia Logan, *Weber State University*; Rajiv Sabherwal, *University of Missouri, St. Louis*; Linda Salchenberger, *Loyola University–Chicago*; David Schaefer, *California State University–Sacramento*; Rod Sink, *Northern Illinois University*; Cheri Speier, *Michigan State University*; Zachary Wong, *Sonoma State University*; Haw Jan Wu, *Whittier College*; and Marie Wright, *Western Connecticut State University*.

First Edition Reviewers: Murugan Anandarajan, *Drexel University*; Bay Arizne, *Drexel University*; Boris Baran, *Concordia University–Montreal*; Jack Becker, *University of North Texas*; Bill Bistline, *St. John's University*; Alan Brandyberry, *University of Minnesota–Duluth*; Dan Davis, *Rowan University*; Lauren Eder, *Rider University*; Vipul Gupta, *St. Joseph's University*; Dale Gust, *Central Michigan State University*; Joan Hoopes, *Marist College*; Chang-Tseh Hsieh, *University of South Mississippi*; Edward Kaplan, *Bentley College*; Donald Kaufman, *Maryville University–St. Louis*; Dennis Kira, *Concordia University–Montreal*; Douglas Lavery, *Sir Sandford Fleming College*; Douglas Leif, *Bemidji State University*; James Linderman, *Bentley College*; Pat Logan, *Weber State University*; Jane Mackay, *Texas Christian University*; Jack Marchewka, *Northern Illinois University*; Anne Massey, *Indiana University*; Suzanne McClure, *Bowling Green State University*; Gordon McCray, *Wake Forest University*; Enrique Mu, *University of Pittsburgh*; Barin Nag, *Towson State University*; Maggie O'Hara, *Eastern Carolina University*; Sasan Rahmatian, *California State University–Fresno*; Stephanie Robbins, *University of North Carolina–Charlotte*; Linda Salchenberger, *Loyola University of Chicago*; Tom Seymour, *Minot State University*; Jae P. Shim, *Mississippi State University*; Cheri Speier, *Michigan State University*; Amita Suhrid, *Keller Graduate School*; Jack Van Deventer, *Washington State University*; Marie Wright, *Western Connecticut State University*; Vincent Yen, *Wright State University*; and Dale Young, *Miami University (Ohio)*.

Focus Group Participants: Carl Adams, *University of Minnesota*; Anil Aggarwal, *University of Baltimore*; Jay Aronson, *University of Georgia*; Snehamay Banerjee, *Rutgers University–Camden*; Jack Becker, *University of North Texas*; Bill Bistline, *St. John's University*; Warren Boe, *University of Iowa*; Christer Carlssen, *Abo Akademi University, Finland*; Tom Case, *Georgia Southern University*; Jae Hwa Choi, *Dankook University Chonan, Korea*; Eli Cohen, *Grand Valley College*; Kevin Crowston, *Syracuse University*; Nancy Davidson, *Troy State University*; Bob DeMichiell, *Fairfield University*; David Feinstein, *University of South Alabama*; Bill Friedman, *Louisiana Tech University*; Merrill Friedman, *Northeastern University*; Jeff Harper, *Indiana State University*; Tony Hendrickson, *Iowa State University*; Charlotte Hiatt, *California State University–Fresno*; Dan Joseph, *RIT*; Chang E. Koh, *University of North Texas*; Paula Ladd, *University of Central Arkansas*; Matthew Lee, *City University of Hong Kong*; John Lehman, *University of Alaska*; Jack Marchewka, *Northern Illinois University*;

Anne Massey, *Indiana University*; Gordon McCray, *Wake Forest University*; Pat Mc-Quaid, *California Polytechnic State University*; Barin Nag, *Towson State University*; Maggie O'Hara, *Eastern Carolina University*; Diane Parente, *University of Buffalo*; Roger Pick, *University of Missouri–Kansas City*; Janet Renwick, *University of Arkansas*; Ralph Ruby, *Arkansas State University*; Cynthia Ruppel, *University of Toledo*; Asghar Sabbaghi, *Indiana University–South Bend*; Sam Seward, *Sonoma State University*; Jae P. Shim, *Mississippi State University*; Rod Sink, *Northern Illinois University*; Janice Sipior, *Villanova University*; Sandy Slaughter, *Carnegie-Mellon University*; Pirkko Walden, *Abo Akademi University, Finland*; Kent Walstrom, *Illinois State University*; Joseph Wen, *New Jersey Institute of Technology*; and Ralph Westfall, *California State University–Long Beach.*

Survey Respondents and Focus Group Attendees: Joe Brooks, *Western Connecticut State University*; Mike Crews, *University of Texas Pan American*; Vinod Lall, *Minnesota State University–Moorhead*; Douglas Leif, *Bemidji State University*; William Leigh, *University of Central Florida*; Les Rydl, *University of Texas Pan American*; Roger Pick, *University of Missouri–Kansas City*; Daniel Power, *University of Northern Iowa*; Jae P. Shim, *Mississippi State University*; David Smith, *Cameron University*; Sandy Staples, *Queen's University*; Sai Vemulakonda, *George Brown College*; Shouhong Wang, *University of Massachusetts–Dartmouth*; Sidne Ward, *University of Missouri–Kansas City;* and Bruce White, *Quinnipiac College.*

Supplements Authors: We are especially grateful to Marc Miller, Augusta State College, who developed the CD that accompanies this book; to Jack Marchewka, Northern Illinois University, who created the Virtual Company case that is on the book's Web site; and Bobbie Hyndman, Amarillo College, who revised the Virtual Company exercises that are integrated throughout the book. In addition, we would like to thank the following professionals who worked to produce a variety of support materials for both instructors and students: Russell Casey, Delaware State University, who prepared the Instructor's Manual; Roberta Roth, University of Northern Iowa, who helped create the PowerPoint presentations; Jeff Stewart, Macon State College, who compiled the Web quizzes; and Ed Glantz, Pennsylvania State University, who prepared the NBR Video Guide.

Efraim Turban
Kelly Rainer
Richard Potter

BRIEF CONTENTS

CONTENTS

PART IV: ACHIEVING INFORMATIONAL AND ORGANIZATIONAL GOALS

INTRODUCTION: BUSINESS AND INFORMATION TECHNOLOGY

1

CHAPTER PREVIEW

This chapter will introduce the fundamental and powerful roles that information technologies play in the modern global business environment. Along the way, we introduce basic concepts about information, information technologies, and information systems. We tell you what they can do and where we think they are headed. The chapter also explains how to formulate questions on the strategic roles of information technologies. Throughout, the chapter provides a number of real-world examples of how information technologies solve (and sometimes cause) business problems and how they create competitive advantage. We finish up the chapter with an explanation of this book's approach and layout.

CHAPTER OUTLINE

1.1 Business in the Information Age: Pressures and Responses
1.2 Reality Check I: Why You Need to Know About Information Technology
1.3 What Is an Information System?
1.4 Reality Check II: Strategic Questions, IT Answers
1.5 The Plan of This Book

LEARNING OBJECTIVES

1. Discuss business pressures and responses in today's Information Age.
2. Differentiate among data, information, and knowledge, and describe the characteristics of high-quality data.
3. Name and describe the components of an information system.
4. Describe the capabilities expected of information systems in modern organizations.
5. Describe opportunities for strategic use of information systems.

AUSTRALIAN TENNIS OPEN PROVIDES A BOX SEAT ON THE WEB

ausopen.org

The Business Problem

The popularity of many sports events is increasing, along with the world's population and the proportion of that population that wants tickets to the events. But the number of seats at many events around the world remains limited by the physical capacity of the stadium or arena that hosts the event. Since a great deal of money is made through sales of event- and team-related merchandise, promoters are searching for ways to increase these sales in ways that overcome the natural limitations on attendance. A good example of such an event is the Australian Tennis Open, whose managers have discovered a way to use information technology (IT) to provide greater access to the event and to boost merchandise sales.

The IT Solution

Tennis fans around the world can get a head start on the Australian Open tennis tournament by visiting the official Web site (*ausopen.org*)—designed, developed, and hosted by IBM. The site provides fans with a "virtual box seat" by allowing them access to real-time scores and images from Melbourne Park, the site of the tournament, plus other information and photos. Tennis fans also can buy Australian Open merchandise from the online store. "The Web site adds depth to the overall experience of the Australian Open and significantly expands the tournament's reach for a global audience," said Paul McNamee, Australian Open chief executive. "Technology has helped increase international interest in the Australian Open as one of the world's great sporting events, thanks to increased access for fans in different time zones across Asia, North America, and Europe."

Winners and runners up in the 2001 Australian Open Women's Doubles tournament.

The Results

During the 2001 tournament, 543,843 tennis fans attended and another 975,000 visited the Web site and generated 48 million page views, an increase of 152 percent over the previous year. IBM is the official information technology and Internet supplier to Tennis Australia for the Australian Open. The company provides equipment and services for results and statistics collection; supplies information and graphics to television broadcasters and media; and distributes tournament data through information terminals around Melbourne Park.

Source: ibm.com/news/us/2001.

What We Learned from This Case

Information technologies are now in some sense overcoming the laws of physics, particularly as they relate to marketing products and services and transacting business. A customer's physical presence is now optional for conducting myriad business activities ranging from perusing a catalog, purchasing, and arranging shipping, to contributing feedback to a provider, interacting with other consumers, searching the world for the desired commodity, and many other related activities. No segment of the world's economy remains untouched by the revolutionary power of electronic commerce. For all the powerful advantages to the product or service provider in using the Internet, there is a counterbalancing force that gives consumers much greater ability to enjoy a much broader range of available products and services and to comparison shop for that product or service. In short, the floodgates of information have opened, and many traditional business relationships and principles have been upended.

1.1 BUSINESS IN THE INFORMATION AGE: PRESSURES AND RESPONSES

We're in the Information Age, where fortunes spring from innovative ideas and the clever use of information. Businesses in the Information Age must compete in a challenging marketplace—one that is rapidly changing, complex, global, hypercompetitive, and customer focused. Companies must rapidly react to problems and opportunities arising from this modern business environment. The *business environment* refers to the combination of social, legal, economic, physical, and political factors that affect business activities.

The pace and magnitude of change affecting organizations continue to accelerate, causing increased uncertainty in company operations and strategies. Therefore, companies must operate under increased pressures to produce more with fewer resources. For example, large corporations such as IBM, AT&T, General Electric, and General Motors have restructured their organizations, eliminating hundreds of thousands of jobs, in an attempt to remain competitive in the global marketplace.

Pressures

The business environment in the Information Age places many pressures on companies. Organizations may respond *reactively* to a pressure already in existence, or *proactively* to an anticipated pressure. Company responses are typically facilitated by **information technology (IT)**, which in a broad sense is a collection of the individual technology components that are typically organized into computer-based information systems (ISs). (Note that the two terms—IT and IS—are not precisely synonymous, although they are used interchangeably in common practice.) In some cases, IT is the only solution to business pressures. The pressures on organizations at the beginning of the twenty-first century include the following.

Global competition for trade and for labor. The reasonably stable world political environment at the end of the twentieth century and the moves toward market economy by many countries (including China and Russia) created the foundation necessary for a *global economy*. In a global economy, trade is much less constrained by traditional barriers such as borders, language, currency, or politics. Goods and services are produced profitably as dictated by competitive advantages that any nation might hold (e.g., expertise with certain technologies, or low labor costs). Advanced telecommunications networks helped facilitate the creation of a global economy. A particularly influential force for globalization in recent years has been the **Internet**, the electronic telecommunications network connecting computers around the world. Regional agreements such as the North American Free Trade Agreement (United States, Canada, and Mexico), the European Union, and the World Trade Organization (WTO) also contribute to increased world trade through reduction of trade barriers.

Low labor costs make Chinese firms attractive as partners in joint manufacturing ventures.

Labor costs differ widely from one country to another. While the hourly industrial wage rate (excluding benefits) is over $15 in some Western countries, it is only $1 to

$2 in many developing countries, including those in Asia, South America, Eastern Europe, and Africa. The lowest labor cost for industrial employees is in China, where the hourly wage rate is less than $1.

In addition, companies in developed countries usually pay high fringe benefits and environmental protection costs. Therefore, they have difficulty competing in labor-intensive industries with developing countries. As a result, companies are moving their manufacturing facilities to countries with low labor costs. Such a global strategy requires extensive communications, frequently in several languages and under several cultural, ethical, and legal conditions. The complexity of the communication system may greatly hinder global competition unless it is properly supported by IT.

Global competition is especially intensified when governments become involved through the use of subsidies, tax policies, import/export regulations, and incentives. Rapid and inexpensive communication and transportation modes increase the magnitude of international trade even further.

Need for real-time operations.   Companies in the Information Age no longer have the luxury of "information float," which is the time between when a business event occurs and when information captured about that event reaches the necessary decision makers. High-performance telecommunications technologies can reduce this time lag to near zero. Similarly, these same technologies permit financial transactions to be nearly instantaneous. For many businesses, slow, paper-based, mail-based transactions and processes are a thing of the past. Orders now can occur instantly, as can electronic payment transfers and documentation of transactions.

Changing workforce.   The workforce, particularly in developed countries, is changing rapidly and becoming more diversified. An increasing number of females, single parents, minorities, and physically challenged persons work today in all types of positions. More employees than ever before prefer to defer retirement. IT is easing the integration of these various employees into the traditional workforce. In addition, as more organizations become transnational, managerial complexity accompanies growing cultural complexity.

Customer orientation.   Customer sophistication and expectations increase as customers become more knowledgeable about the availability and quality of products and services. They are also more knowledgeable about competing products. These expectations translate into the need for organizations to demonstrate a customer orientation.

Customers are demanding ever-more detailed information about products and services. They want to know what features are available, what warranties they will receive, what financing is available, and so on, and they want to know immediately. Companies must be able to deliver information quickly to satisfy their customers, or risk losing them. Advances in the use of the Internet and electronic commerce (e-commerce) bring customers information about thousands of products, including cost and quality comparisons. (For example, see Edmund's automotive Web site at *edmunds.com*, which provides comparative information on all types of automotive products.)

Customers also want customized products, with high quality and low prices. Information technology enables vendors to respond through *mass customization*. Customers are finding that information technology, when used effectively, can tip the balance of power decidedly in their favor, as illustrated in IT's About Business Box 1.1.

Technological innovation and obsolescence.   Pressures to produce goods and services efficiently (quickly and at low cost) cause organizations to look for technological

IT's About Business

Box 1.1:   Reverse Auction Saves University Money

Purchasing officials at a large university saved a surprising amount of money on their latest large purchase—a big order of lighting equipment. They used a type of electronic auction called a *reverse auction,* which makes use of the Internet to bring all parties together for the bidding. In a reverse auction, there is one buyer and many would-be sellers. The buyer invites sellers to bid on a proposal, and the lowest bidder wins. The university paid $5,000 for the auction service but saved more than $30,000 on the purchase.

In the past, buying large quantities of electronic-lighting equipment would have involved only two or three bidders and would have taken a week or two to complete. The reverse auction attracted 16 bidders and took place in 30 minutes.

Source: "Reverse Auctions Can Save Colleges Money on Big-Ticket Purchases, Users Say," *The Chronicle of Higher Education,* August 10, 2001.

Questions

1. What other categories of products might be targets for this type of buying behavior?

2. What other impacts do you see the Internet having on the traditional purchasing process?

---

breakthroughs that will give them an advantage over their competitors. Technology is playing an increased role in both manufacturing and service organizations. New and improved technologies such as computer-integrated manufacturing enable organizations to produce superior products, to customize products more easily, and to quickly alter manufacturing processes as the market dictates.

However, continuing innovation with computer technologies means faster obsolescence of products, shorter life cycles, and increasing quality standards. In addition, advances in information technologies allow customers to be aware of innovations sooner, forcing companies to respond more quickly or risk losing market share. Thus organizations feel the pressure of increasing customer expectations and an increasing ability to respond rapidly with improved products and services. Although this cycle benefits consumers, for many organizations the result is quicker product obsolescence, shorter product life cycles, and higher costs for investment in new technologies.

Information overload.   The Internet and other telecommunications networks increase the amount of information available to organizations and individuals. The amount of information available on the Internet more than doubles every year, and most of it is free. The information and knowledge generated and stored inside organizations are also increasing exponentially. Managers are at risk of "analysis paralysis"—bombarded with so much potentially useful information that they feel compelled to consider vast amounts of it before taking action. But of course, only some of the information is truly relevant. Therefore, the accessibility, navigation, and management of information necessary for managerial decision making is becoming critical.

"Every two years the speed doubles and the size decreases. They'll soon be infinitely fast, but so tiny we won't be able to use them."

EXAMPLE

Too much of a good thing.   Some researchers say that 5 to 10 percent of Internet users have the potential for an addiction problem. In the words of one subscriber to an Internet-addiction support mailing list, "My marriage is breaking up because of my husband's addiction, which seems to have destroyed not only our marriage but my husband's personality, his values, his morals, his behavior, and his parenting." In another case, a therapist tells of one man who threw his wife's modem out the window in disgust at her refusal to log off, only to have her beat him in retaliation. The research firm Jupiter Communications, Inc. claims there will be more than 116 million Americans online by 2002. If a 5 percent addiction estimate is accurate, more than 5 million Americans—along with their families and friends—will experience the downside of too much available information. ●

Social responsibility.   Social issues affecting organizations range from the state of the physical environment, to nondiscriminatory employment practices, to the spread of infectious diseases and other health concerns. Organizations are feeling the pressure of such social issues as they, and the public, are becoming more aware of these problems. Some businesses are taking active measures to respond to social issues and to contribute toward social improvements. Such activities are known as organizational **social responsibility**. Failure to accept social responsibility can result in employee dissatisfaction and turnover, a tarnished corporate reputation with the public, and in some cases, governmental sanctions. Organizations can be proactive in their social responsibility, finding innovative ways to advance any number of human causes.

EXAMPLE

Simputer to bridge language "digital divide."   The new Simputer is pretty plain, just a small gray box the size of a digital organizer, with four buttons and a black-and-white screen. But the handheld device might solve the most pressing problem of the Internet age: how to get developing countries online. The Simputer (short for "simple computer") promises to have a profound impact on communication in the developing world, giving users access to the Internet for around $200. Developed by a group of Indian scientists, the Simputer does not need household voltage, but instead runs reliably on three AAA batteries. Its most important feature, however, is that it eliminates the single biggest barrier to computer use in the third world: illiteracy.

Engineers at the Indian Institute of Sciences in Bangalore and the software company Encore created what they call Illiterate Markup Language software. It not only translates English text into a variety of Indian languages in the Simputer, but also reads aloud the information to the user in his or her chosen language (including Hindi, Kannada, and Tamil). The Simputer is designed to allow one device to be easily shared by a community. For the equivalent of $1, individual users can buy a smart card onto which all their personal information is saved. Each time the user plugs in, the Simputer is customized to his or her needs. (*Source:* Stuart Miller, Dawn/The Guardian News Service, *dawn.com/2001/07/10/int16htm.*) ●

Government regulation and deregulation.   When companies and industries generally fail to address certain social responsibility issues that come to be important to the general public, governments sometimes step in with regulations to protect their citizens. In the twentieth century, both federal and state governments in the United States expanded government regulation in the areas of health, safety, environmental control, and equal opportunity. For example, companies that change the oil in your car must dispose of the used oil in an environmentally safe manner, a process that adds operating costs to the business. Other government regulations, created ultimately from mandates of the citizenry, exist to safeguard the ethical and safe treatment of employees. Compliance with governmental regulations costs companies money, and these additional costs are eventually passed along to consumers in the form of higher prices. In an environment in which all companies face the same regulations, the added costs could be seen as the price the public pays for the greater social good that regulation is intended to ensure. But for global companies, regulations create an uneven playing field—they make it more difficult to compete with companies from countries that lack such regulation.

Because business organizations tend to view government regulations as expensive constraints, they usually lobby for the removal of rules and regulations involving business competition. Such *deregulation* can be a blessing to one company and a curse to another company previously protected by the regulation. In the United States, deregulation since the 1980s has changed the landscape of several industries—especially transportation, telecommunications, and financial services. In general, deregulation increases competition. But remaining competitive requires innovation and investment in technologies that can bring competitive advantage. As will become clear as you read this book, information technology brings competitive advantage in many industries.

Ethical issues.   Organizations must deal with ethical issues of their employees, customers, and suppliers. *Ethics* in a business context refers to standards and values for judging whether particular conduct in the workplace is right or wrong. Ethical issues are very important because they can damage the image of an organization as well as destroy the morale of the employees. What makes ethics difficult is that what is ethical to one person may not seem so to another. Similarly, what is ethical in one country may be considered unethical in another.

The use of information technology is raising many new ethical issues, ranging from the surveillance of electronic mail to the potential invasion of privacy of millions of customers whose data are stored in private and public databases. Governments around the world are considering legislation related to information privacy. But because IT is new and rapidly changing, there is little experience or agreement on how to deal with related ethical issues.

EXAMPLE

Tampa uses cameras to scan for wanted faces.   A computer software program linked to 36 cameras recently began scanning crowds in Tampa, Florida's nightlife district, Ybor City. The images taken are matched against a database of mug shots of people with outstanding arrest warrants. European cities and U.S. government offices, casinos, and banks are already using the so-called face-printing system, but Tampa is the first U.S. city to install a permanent system on public streets. A similar system was used at Super Bowl XXXV, which was held in Tampa in January 2001.

The technology has raised concerns over privacy, ethics, and government intrusion. "This is Big Brother actually implemented," said Jack Walter of the Tampa chapter of the American Civil Liberties Union. "I think this just opens the door to it being everywhere."

But Tampa Detective Bill Todd says the surveillance technology is no different from having a police officer standing on a street holding a mug shot and looking for the wanted person. The system used at the Super Bowl spotted 19 people at the crowded stadium with outstanding warrants for minor offenses, but no arrests were made. With the sheer volume of people, it was very difficult to get to the suspects to make an arrest. (*Source:* CNN.com/sci-tech, *cnn.com/2001/TECH/ptech/0702/high. tech.security.ap/.*) ●

To summarize, the modern global business environment is transnational and culturally complex. Its diversity brings different competitive advantages and challenges to each country, to each industry, and to each business. These advantages and challenges appear and disappear as fast as world events occur and as fast as generations of new technologies are created and become obsolete. The business world is increasingly "transparent": information moves so rapidly around the world that industrial secrets, technical advantages, and managerial innovations can evaporate with the speed of e-mail. This speed of change and global dispersion of information also accelerates the rate of social change across the globe. The pressures produced by these factors affect all organizations to some degree.

Organizational Responses

Organizations respond in many ways to the business pressures of competition in the Information Age. Many of their responses are facilitated or enhanced by information technologies. The major responses fall in one of five categories, discussed below and pictured in Figure 1.1.

Strategic systems.   Organizations seek to implement systems that will significantly impact the organization's operations, success, or survival. Such **strategic systems** provide organizations with strategic advantages in meeting organizational objectives, enabling them to increase their market share, to better negotiate with their suppliers, or to prevent competitors from entering their markets. There are a variety of IT-supported strategic systems. The Sabre reservation system, originally developed by American Airlines and now spun off as an independent company, and the package tracking systems developed by Federal Express are good examples. Market

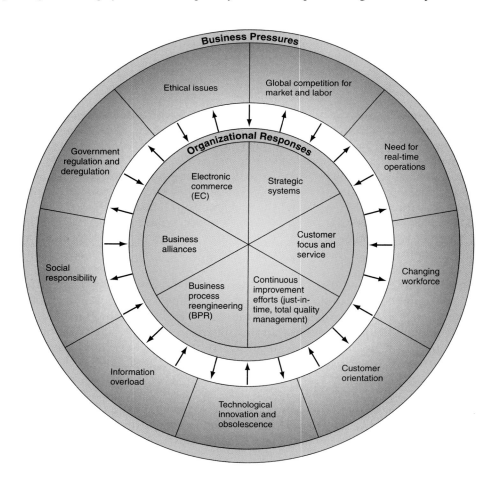

Figure 1.1 *Business pressures and organizational responses.*

share increased dramatically for these firms when they offered these systems to their clientele. As is typical in the Information Age, however, such IT-based competitive advantages decrease over time as competitors adopt similar technologies. The need for constant innovation is the only part of the competitive landscape that does not change.

Customer focus and service.   The increased power of customers and stiff competition in many industries and markets force organizations to adopt a **customer-focused approach**. In other words, they must pay more attention to customers and their preferences. Sometimes such an approach even involves reengineering the organization to better meet consumer demands. This can be done in part by changing manufacturing processes from mass production to mass customization. In mass production, a company produces a large quantity of identical items. In **mass customization**, the company produces a large quantity of items that are manufactured to fit the desires of each customer. Information technology supports mass customization.

Similarly, IT plays a major role in supporting the traditional activities of customer service, such as providing troubleshooting advice or help lines. One major new factor in improved communications is the ability of organizations to communicate with existing and potential customers via information on their Web sites. In addition, organizations are developing other innovative ways to use IT to support customer service.

Continuous improvement efforts.   In response to business pressures, many firms also make continuous efforts to improve their productivity and quality. *Productivity* is the ratio of outputs to inputs. Companies can improve productivity by increasing output, reducing costs, increasing output faster than cost, or a combination of these. IT is used extensively for both productivity and quality improvement.

One effort at reducing costs that has been very successful and widely adopted in manufacturing industries is the **just-in-time (JIT)** inventory approach. JIT attempts to reduce costs and improve work flow by scheduling materials and parts to arrive at a workstation exactly when they are needed. JIT minimizes in-process inventories and waste and saves inventory space and cost. Information technology makes it easier to implement large and complex JIT systems.

A widely used organizational improvement tool is **total quality management (TQM)**. TQM is a corporatewide organized effort to improve quality wherever and whenever possible. Information technology can enhance TQM by improving data monitoring, collection, analysis, and reporting. IT can also increase the speed of inspection, raise the quality of testing, and reduce the cost of performing various quality-control activities. Finally, IT can help avert quality problems before they arise.

Another aspect of continuous improvement is the need for better decision making at all organizational levels. Appropriate decision making attempts to select the best, or at least a good enough, alternative course of action. This task becomes difficult in a frequently changing environment, when the number of alternative choices can be very large and the impacts of a decision can be far reaching as well as difficult to forecast. The complexity of organizations—that is, their diversity and the large number of constraints, such as governmental regulations—complicates decision making. Also, the cost of making wrong decisions can be very high. Decisions require information that is timely and accurate. Organizations need to build appropriate IT infrastructures and use effective methods to store, access, navigate, and properly use their vast amounts of knowledge and information. It is obvious that IT plays a major role in providing such information, as well as in supporting difficult decision-making processes.

But developing systems that improve information access and decision making is no easy task. Sometimes an effort to improve productivity or quality just doesn't work, as the IT's About Business Box 1.2 demonstrates. Occasional failures are an unavoidable "fact of life" with information technologies.

IT's About Business   *irs.gov*   MIS

Box 1.2:   Is the Third Time the Charm for the IRS?

During the past 25 years, the IRS has twice failed to modernize its information systems. In 1978, President Jimmy Carter halted a project to network the IRS's central databases because the agency could not protect taxpayer privacy. In 1995, Congress stopped a second effort, after the IRS had spent 10 years and over $2 billion on the project with little to show for the money.

The IRS has begun a $10 billion, 10-year IT modernization program to streamline interactions with taxpayers and tax professionals. This program includes a secure Web portal, a public information site, and an intranet to help the 90,000 IRS employees quickly gain access to technical, legal, procedural, and record information.

For the program to succeed, the IRS must master secure transactions over the Web, standardize data from a huge number of legacy databases, and overcome its history of failed information technology projects. For example, the agency must integrate data collected over the last 45 years that resides in virtually every storage format technology.

In addition to taking a public-relations beating in recent years for overzealous auditing practices, the IRS has also been downsized, making it more difficult to collect taxes and catch tax evaders. Information technology that automates taxpayers interactions would let the IRS redeploy resources now dedicated to customer service.

Source: "Taxing Overhaul," *Internet Week,* April 23, 2001, pp. 50–51.

Questions

1. What factors make a government bureaucracy more or less susceptible to systems development failure compared to a private, for-profit organization? Why?

2. What should be the primary motive for developing a new information system in a government bureaucracy? In a private for-profit organization? Why?

Business process reengineering.   However, organizations may discover that even continuous improvement efforts have limited effectiveness in an environment full of strong business pressures. In such cases, a new approach called **business process reengineering (BPR)** may be called for. BPR introduces a *major* innovation in an organization's structure and the way it conducts its business. In the process, technological, human, and organizational dimensions of a firm may all be changed. Management realignments, mergers, consolidations, operational integration, and/or reoriented distribution practices may take place as part of BPR. Over 70 percent of all large U.S. companies claim to be doing reengineering of some sort.

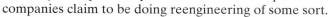

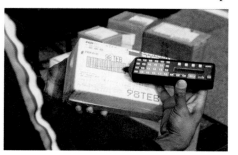

Cutting-edge IT helps FedEx compete.

IT plays a major role in BPR. It provides automation; allows business to be conducted in different locations; provides flexibility in manufacturing; permits quicker delivery to customers; and supports rapid and paperless transactions among suppliers, manufacturers, and retailers. Reducing the business process time (*cycle time*) is extremely important for increasing productivity and competitiveness. Similarly, reducing the time from the inception of an idea until its implementation (*time to market*) is important because those who can be first on the market with a product, or who can provide customers with a service faster than competitors, enjoy a distinct competitive advantage. IT can be used to expedite the various steps in the process of development, testing, and implementation of new products or services.

Empowering employees and fostering collaborative work.   Giving employees the authority to act and make decisions on their own is a strategy used by many organizations as part of their BPR. Management delegates authority to self-directed teams who can execute the work faster and with fewer delays than were possible in the traditional organizational structure. IT allows the decentralization of decision making and authority but simultaneously supports centralized control. For example, empowered employees are able to access data, information, and knowledge they need for making good decisions quickly by using the Internet, *intranets* (corporate networks that use Internet technologies), or *extranets* (secured networks that allow business partners to access portions of each other's intranets). In addition, computer networks allow team members to communicate with each other effectively as well as to communicate with other teams in different locations.

Changing organizational structures and empowered employees in BPR can alter organizational relationships and responsibilities.

EXAMPLE

Revving up employees' financial engines.   In recent years, many employers have shifted the burden for managing retirement funds to employees. But the employers have not often given their employees sufficient means to accomplish that task. Financial Engines (*financialengines.com*) provides a service for companies that want to give their employees sophisticated analytical tools to plan and manage their retirement funds over the Internet. The service consists of a Web site and database of daily price and performance information for all U.S. stocks and mutual funds. Users can retrieve from the database current figures for their portfolio holdings and make projections on how their portfolio will do under various hypothetical economic scenarios.   ●

Business alliances.   In response to some of the competitive pressures of the global economy, many firms are realizing that alliances with other firms, even competitors, can be very beneficial.

There are several types of alliances: sharing resources, establishing permanent supplier–company relationships, and creating joint research efforts. One of the most interesting types of alliance is the temporary *joint venture*, in which companies form a special company for a specific, limited-time mission. A more permanent type of alliance that links manufacturers, suppliers, and finance corporations is known as *keiretsu* (a Japanese term). Business alliances can be heavily supported by IT ranging from electronic data interchange to electronic transmission of maps and drawings.

Various alliances can result from careful **supply chain management**, the management of every step of the logistics involved in supplying a manufacturing firm. Supply chain management seeks to make every step in the chain as efficient as possible, emphasizing communication and coordination between the various parties involved. It is therefore heavily reliant on computer-based communication technologies.

A similar process known as **enterprise resource planning (ERP)** focuses on coordinating all material, production, and management resources within a company, often linking together all functional areas that contribute in some way to the production of a particular good. ERP systems are very sophisticated information systems that extend to all parts of the organization, and may even extend to allied organizations such as key suppliers.

Electronic commerce.   Doing business electronically is the newest, and perhaps the most promising, business strategy that many companies can pursue. **Electronic commerce (e-commerce, or EC)** is a multifaceted concept involving the exchange of products, services, information, or money with the support of computers and networks. Applications of e-commerce range from electronic transfer of funds between buyers and suppliers, to Internet-based marketing, to intranet and extranet-based information networks for both inter- and intraorganizational support. The amount of business done electronically is very significant. Some $80 billion changes hands over the Internet annually. By 2030 it is estimated that this flow will total $4 trillion, or one-quarter of the world's industrial economy. Obviously, information technology is an essential component of the growing phenomenon of e-commerce.

Before you go on . . .

1. Describe some of the pressures that characterize the modern global business environment.

2. What are some of the organizational responses to these pressures?

1.2   REALITY CHECK I: WHY YOU NEED TO KNOW ABOUT INFORMATION TECHNOLOGY

No one seriously contemplating a career in business can afford to be ignorant of the powerful and revolutionary roles that information technologies play in their chosen industry. The same goes for almost all other areas of human endeavor, from the fine arts to medicine to archeology to warfare. These technologies first enable great advances in human work, and then the world immediately demands that all enterprises perform at this new, higher level. And that is necessary just to survive and compete. Superiority comes from imagining and enacting a future that is increasingly built on leveraging information technologies. The stark reality is that effective people must understand information technologies and develop insights into what these technologies can do. To remain ignorant is surely to be ineffective and of little potential value to the vast majority of modern organizations. That is the central reason for everyone to know about information technology these days. Some other reasons are discussed in this section.

IT Is Generally Interesting

The upside of the responsibility to be educated about information technologies is that their effects on the world are fascinating. We do not expect every student to be thrilled with every aspect of this diverse topic. Some will revel in the beauty and the brilliance of the technologies, appreciating them as forms of engineering art. Others will be amazed at their profound power to transform traditional organizational practices. Still others will be energized by the fabulous new entrepreneurial opportunities that the technologies themselves and their innovative uses generate. Some will recognize how the technologies can be used to change the political and social world for the better.

But none of this can occur without knowledge. Both the complexity and the power of information technologies are profound. Fortunately, most people easily find the motivation to understand the complexities when they can be shown examples of the power. In fact, the two domains reinforce each other: The more you know about the power of the technologies, the more you will want to know about how they work. The more you learn about how they work, the more you will be able to see how they can accomplish what they do.

IT Facilitates Work in Organizations

But there are additional reasons for learning about information technology beyond simply augmenting your knowledge. Information technologies and business systems

that use IT allow us to work more intelligently and efficiently. They also often
change how we structure and manage
our organizations and processes—that
is, *how* we work and *how* we interact
and transact. Information technology is
a facilitator of organizational activities
and processes. Therefore, it is very important for every manager and professional staff member to learn about IT
from the standpoint of his or her specialized field, and also from the stand-

point of IT across the entire organization and in interorganizational settings such as
the supply chain. IT is important not only for its supporting role, but also for its impacts on people, organizational structure, organizational strategy, and business and
management processes.

Every manager and staff member should know how to build, use, and manage
successful systems based on information technology. He or she also should know how
to avoid unsuccessful systems and failures.

IT Offers Career Opportunities

Finally, you should learn about IT because of the many employment opportunities in
the field. It is important to note that although information technology eliminates some
jobs, it creates many others. The demand for traditional information technology
staff—programmers, systems analysts, and systems designers—is huge. In addition,
there are large numbers of well-paid opportunities appearing in emerging areas such
as the Internet (e.g., Web page design and operation), e-commerce, network security,
systems development, telecommunications, multimedia design, artificial intelligence,
and document management.

The U.S. Department of Commerce says that the information technology industry
has doubled the growth rate of the U.S. economy, accounting for more than a quarter
of the country's economic growth over the last five years. Commerce says that IT now
makes up 8 percent of the economy, employing 7.5 million workers, who typically are
paid significantly higher salaries than non-IT workers. IT workers average a salary of
almost $50,000 annually. The nationwide private-sector average is $28,000.

Commerce says that despite the higher salaries, the industry still lacks the people
to fill IT jobs, with almost 1.5 million IT positions needing to be filled in the next 10
years. IT growth has been pushed in part by the rapid growth of the Internet, which
has doubled in traffic every 100 days and is expected to reach one billion users by the
year 2005, up from three million users in 1994. Commerce says it expects $300 billion
in Internet commerce by 2002.

IT Is Used by All Departments

Further, information technology is vital for every functional area of an organization,
and IT systems are integral to every functional area. In *finance* and *accounting*, for example, managers use such systems to forecast revenues and business activity, determine the best sources and uses of funds, manage cash and other financial resources,
analyze investments, and perform audits to ensure that the organization is fundamentally sound and that all financial reports and documents are accurate.

In *sales* and *marketing*, managers use information technology to develop new
goods and services (product analysis), determine the best location for production and

distribution facilities (site analysis), determine the best advertising and sales total revenues (promotion analysis), and set product prices to get the highest total revenues (price analysis). Marketing managers also use information technology to manage the customer relationship.

EXAMPLE

Using IT to increase efficiency.   Paul's Hauling, Ltd. is a group of companies specializing in bulk handling and general freight transportation. It operates more than 1,000 tractors and 3,500 trailers out of 12 major terminals across Canada and the U.S. as well as a maintenance and service facility. Paul's is privately owned and employs 2,000 people across the companies. With several companies within its enterprise, Paul's was experiencing an undesirable situation: The services of member companies were overlapping in some geographic areas, creating apparent competition. Paul's hoped to find a solution that would help it align the member companies with corporate processes and would provide better access to crucial product and fleet data.

Paul's chose a new IBM database program and data warehouse to serve as a foundation for future technology directions. Paul's upgraded its infrastructure, replacing a number of computers and modernizing its networks for greatly improved connectivity. Data were pulled from each company and then manipulated, combined, summarized, and placed in a corporate data warehouse.

With this solution all member companies use the same data source and user tools, which offers users a common view of the data and improves data integrity and business process checking. This integration of the data and the technology that handles it allows Paul's to reduce redundancy and overlap of the marketing efforts of its various member companies. Paul's sees improvements in customer service and the internal benefits of effective teaming and information sharing. In addition, the time associated with processing and analyzing reports manually is greatly reduced, increasing productivity and lowering costs for the company. (*Source: 2.software.ibm.com/casestudies. swcs.nsf/topstories.*) ●

In *manufacturing*, managers use IT to process customer orders, develop production schedules, control inventory levels, and monitor product quality. In addition, these managers use information technology to design products (computer-assisted design, or CAD), manufacture items (computer-assisted manufacturing, or CAM), and integrate multiple machines or pieces of equipment (computer-integrated manufacturing, or CIM).

Managers in *human resources* use IT to screen job applicants, administer performance tests to employees, and monitor employee productivity. These managers also use legal IT to analyze product liability and warranties and to develop important legal documents and reports.

EXAMPLE

Using IT to manage human resources.   Since its founding in Forrest City, Arkansas, in 1979, AutoZone has emerged as the largest do-it-yourself auto parts provider in the United States, in 2001 breaking into the Fortune 500 ranks as its retail network reached 2,700 stores with 40,000 employees in 40 states. That's not bad for a company that had only 900 stores and 12,000 employees four years before. But this rapid growth had made it increasingly difficult for AutoZone to manage all of its human resources paperwork, and so the retailer introduced content management technology from IBM.

With this technology, the company has moved from relying on paper files and microfiche to using an online document management system that makes documents available instantaneously from desktop computers across its enterprise. In the process, the company has integrated the IBM content management software with its existing PeopleSoft enterprise resource planning (ERP) system, enabling its human resources department to further increase its efficiency.

AutoZone also uses IBM's software to create and archive digital images of W-4 forms, employment applications, résumés, and other documents, making them easily accessible to authorized employees. The software indexes the documents by content, enabling human resources personnel to conduct dynamic searches of the database for the documents they need. After only one year of digitizing its paper documents, AutoZone has stored more than half a terabyte of data. "Currently, we are imaging 10,000 documents each day," says Jeff Mitchell of AutoZone's document management group. "This two-tiered architecture gives us the unlimited storage capacity we need." (*Source: 2.software.ibm.com/casestudies/swcs.nsf/.*) ●

These are just a few examples of the roles of information technology in the various functional areas. We think it is important for students from the different functional areas to see the value of the information systems in their field. To help do this, we have included at the end of every chapter a section called **What's in IT for Me?** that discusses the chapter's relevance to the various business functions.

Before you go on . . .

1. Is information technology as vital to modern global business as money? Why or why not?

2. Why might it benefit you to read this book and learn more about IT in the modern global business environment?

1.3   WHAT IS AN INFORMATION SYSTEM?

An **information system (IS)** collects, processes, stores, analyzes, and disseminates information for a specific purpose. Like any other system, an information system includes *inputs* (data, instructions) and *outputs* (reports, calculations). It processes the inputs and produces outputs that are sent to the user or to other systems. A feedback mechanism that controls the operation may be included. Like any other system, an information system operates within an environment.

In studying information systems, it is important to note the differences between data, information, and knowledge. **Data** are raw facts or elementary descriptions of things, events, activities, and transactions that are captured, recorded, stored, and classified, *but not organized* to convey any specific meaning. Examples of data would include grade point averages, bank balances, or the number of hours employees worked in a pay period.

Information is a collection of facts (data) organized in some manner so that they are meaningful to a recipient. For example, if we include student names with grade point averages, customer names with bank balances, and employee wages with hours worked, we would have useful information. In other words, information comes from data that have been processed.

Knowledge consists of information that has been organized and processed to convey understanding, experiences, accumulated learning, or expertise as it applies to a current business problem or process. Information that is processed to extract critical implications and to reflect past experience and expertise provides the recipient with *organizational* knowledge, which has a high value. This value may prevent a manager from making the same mistakes that another manager made or save a manager the need to "reinvent the wheel."

To be useful to managers and the organization, information should exhibit a variety of characteristics. It should be accurate, complete, flexible, reliable, relevant, timely, verifiable, accessible, and secure. Information that is not of high quality can lead to poor decisions, costing the organization a great deal of money.

What Is a Computer-based Information System?

A **computer-based information system (CBIS)** is an information system that uses computer and telecommunications technology to perform its intended tasks. An *information technology* is a particular component of a system (e.g., a personal computer, a printer, or a network). But few information technologies are used alone. Rather, they are most effective when combined into information systems. The basic components of information systems are the following.

- *Hardware:* a set of devices such as a processor, monitor, keyboard, and printer that accepts data and information, processes them, and displays them
- *Software:* a set of computer programs that enables the hardware to process data
- *Database:* an organized collection of related files or records that stores data and the associations among them
- *Network:* a connecting system that permits the sharing of resources among different computers
- *Procedures:* the strategies, policies, methods, and rules for using the information system
- *People:* the most important element in information systems; includes those persons who work with the information system or use its output

These components are pictured in Figure 1.2. IT's About Business Box 1.3 describes the combination of some of these components in a computer-based information system.

In addition, all CBISs have a similar *purpose*: to provide a solution to a business problem. The successful application of a CBIS requires an understanding of the business and its environment, as well as an understanding of the business problem to which the CBIS is to be applied. For example, to build a CBIS that supports an airline reservation system, it is necessary to understand how the airline operates: its schedules, routes, type of planes, fare structure, number and type of seats on each type of plane, and so on. CBISs also must be developed to reflect their social context—the values and beliefs that determine what is admissible and possible within the culture of the people and groups involved.

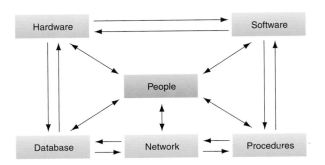

Figure 1.2 *Components of a computer-based information system.*

IT's About Business

Box 1.3:   Information Technology at the Olympic Games

When skiers, skaters, hockey players, and other world-class athletes competed at the 2002 Winter Olympics in Salt Lake City, a large, behind-the-scenes IT infrastructure from SchlumbergerSema enabled information to flow smoothly and quickly. The $300 million Olympics IT network accommodated applications such as the provision of credentials and maintaining the latest information on competitors, contests, and results.

Building the giant Olympics IT network, which had to host all the latest and historical information on the Games, was a huge effort. The Games featured 10 sporting venues, a main media center for broadcasters and the press, and the Olympic village. Included in the IT network were 4,000 Windows PCs, 145 Sun Microsystems UNIX servers, 1,500 fax machines and copiers, and more than 1,000 printers. Some 50 applications ran on the system.

The most high-profile part of the Olympic IT system was the "Commentator Information System," or CIS. When a broadcaster was sitting in his or her booth, he or she had a television and the CIS. As soon as the athlete was going through the final gate, the software went through all the processes of finding where he or she ranked. The CIS consisted of a proprietary application and multiple layers of hardware and software. The CIS used a central repository, a huge database that stored all the data including biographies, data from previous games, and event information.

The Olympic IT network also included various feeds to the outside world. Some of these feeds included one to the Olympic Web site and a results data feed to the World News Press Agency, which supplied information to sites around the globe within minutes after each event.

Interestingly, SchlumbergerSema did not participate in the Olympics Web site (*saltlake2002.com*). The Salt Lake Olympic committee produced the combined site with the MSNBC broadcasting network. During the Olympics, the site featured the official results of the games as well as biographies of more than 2,400 athletes and feature stories on top participants. Also, Web viewers could take virtual visits to venues, such as taking a bobsled ride via a QuickTime application.

Source: "Olympic IT," *InfoWorld*, November 5, 2001, pp. 42–44.

Questions

1. What are some of the various types of information technology that SchlumbergerSema used in developing the Olympic IT network?

2. What advantages did the Olympic IT network provide for the television network broadcasting the games?

CBISs come in a great variety. One way to categorize them is by the level in the organization in which they are used. For example, at the lower levels of an organization we find many *transaction processing systems (TPSs)*. As their name implies, TPSs handle the basic *transactions* of the firm. These systems are found in all functional areas of a company, and they not only process transactions but also collect data on each transaction. At the middle (managerial) level of the firm, *management information systems (MISs)* are used by managers to analyze the data from the TPS (and other sources) to create reports and other types of information that can be used to support managerial decision making. More specialized CBISs such as *decision support systems* and *executive information systems* are used at higher levels in the organization.

Capabilities of Information Systems

In order to be able to compete successfully in the modern business environment, organizations expect their information systems to have many powerful capabilities. Information systems must be able to do the following.

Provide fast and accurate transaction processing.   Every event that occurs in a business is called a *transaction*. Transactions include the sale of a unit of goods, a paycheck issued, a bank deposit, a course grade registered, and so on. Clearly, organizations can produce millions of transactions per day. (Think about the number of transactions worldwide for a large bank, for example.) Each transaction generates data. These data must be captured accurately and quickly. This process is called *transaction processing*, and information systems that capture, record, store, and update these data are called *transaction processing systems*. A good example of a transaction processing system is a point-of-sale (POS) computer technology linked to other computers that store these data. These POSs are the computerized cash registers and bar code readers that are found in the vast majority of modern retail stores, restaurants, and other consumer businesses.

Provide large-capacity, fast-access storage.   Information systems must provide both enormous storage for corporate data, and also fast access to those data. IT's About Business Box 1.4 shows a new way to gather and analyze corporate data.

Provide fast communications (machine to machine, human to human).   Networks enable organizational employees and computers to communicate almost instantly, around the world. High-transmission-capacity networks (those with high bandwidths) make fast communications possible. In addition, they allow data, voice, images, documents, and full-motion video to be transmitted simultaneously. Networks also provide nearly instantaneous access to information for decision makers, thereby reducing information float.

IT's About Business   *llbean.com*   MKT

Box 1.4:   Business Intelligence at L. L. Bean

A crucial element of e-commerce is the creation of a unified, single view of the customer. That is, a customer's online, catalog, and store-based retail activities are tracked, stored, and consolidated in one place, resulting in a better understanding of buying patterns.

L. L. Bean, the privately held 87-year-old company, is best known for its mail-order catalog business and "outdoorsy" product line. Top management at L. L. Bean decided that e-commerce was a necessary channel to reach customers. As a result, Bean launched *llbean.com*, through which customers can choose from nearly 1,000 of the 16,000 products that Bean offers in its print catalog.

L. L. Bean wanted the new sales channel to augment rather than cannibalize existing business. Bean developed a business intelligence (BI) system to understand the precise impact of the Web site on its sales and customer base. To apply the BI system, Bean had to consolidate data from three sources—catalog, retail, and e-commerce—in one place, the company's data warehouse.

All customer, order, and purchasing information is forwarded to the data warehouse. The company keeps track of such things as how many times customers have been contacted, from which retail source orders originate, the number of promotions received, and, of course, the items ordered.

The business intelligence system and the data warehouse have given L. L. Bean knowledge of the synergies between its e-commerce site and catalog business.

Source: "House Business Intelligence Bridges Retail to E-Tail," *Knowledge Management Magazine*, June 2, 2000.

Questions

1. Identify the benefits of the business intelligence system to L. L. Bean.

2. How important is a unified, single view of the customer? Why? How do data warehouses contributed to such a view?

Reduce information overload. Information systems (particularly networks) have contributed to managers having too much information. For example, the amount of information available on the Internet doubles approximately every 100 days. As a result, managers can feel drowned in information and unable to make decisions efficiently and effectively. Information systems can be designed to reduce this information overload. For example, *executive information systems* (*EISs*) provide structured information that is tailored to each executive according to his or her critical success factors. Another example is software that prioritizes managers' e-mails, according to criteria that they set.

Span boundaries. Information systems span boundaries inside organizations as well as between organizations along the entire supply chain. Inside the organization, such *boundary spanning* facilitates decision making across functional areas, business process reengineering, and communications. Along the supply chain, boundary spanning facilitates shorter cycle times for product delivery, reduces inventory, and increases customer satisfaction.

Provide support for decision making. Decision support systems help decision makers across an organization and at all levels of the organization. Executive information systems, for example, support executive decision making. Interestingly, as information systems make information available to all employees, decision making is often pushed down the organization. Therefore, employees at lower organizational levels have the authority and responsibility to make more and larger decisions than ever before.

Provide a competitive weapon. In the past, information systems were viewed primarily as an expense. Today, information systems are being viewed as a profit center and are expected to give the organization an advantage over its competitors. The classic examples of information systems being used for competitive advantage are the early airline reservation systems of the 1970s. Today, information systems are being linked across entire supply chains to give competitive advantage to networked organizations. For example, Wal-Mart integrates its information systems with those of its suppliers to coordinate rapid inventory replenishment.

General Technological Trends for IT

As computer technology continues to leapfrog forward, computer-based information systems are changing rapidly. These changes are having enormous impact on the capabilities of organizational information systems. As a consumer, you are already aware of many of the technological trends that are affecting information technology. For example, you've probably observed over your years in school that personal computers have become more powerful, at lower cost, every year. You probably have seen evidences of portable computing—from people on your campus or businesspeople at airports who have laptops or personal digital assistants (PDAs), to FedEx and UPS delivery personnel with handheld computers that scan package information, to advertisements for global positioning devices in new luxury cars. And you most likely have had experiences of some sort with the Internet and the world of e-commerce that it has opened up.

Portability and connectivity equal increased productivity for many.

    These technological trends, and many others, are affecting how organizations do business. As we've seen elsewhere in the chapter, new computing technologies make possible innovations that contribute to business competition. These trends will be the subject matter of this book. Table 1.1 provides an overview of the most significant

Table 1.1   Overview of General IT Trends

Trend	What It Is	Benefits
Constantly improving cost–performance ratio	Computer processing speed and memory capacity are improving, while computer costs continue to decrease. As labor costs increase, the ratio of cost to performance of computers versus manual work improves dramatically.	Computers will have increasingly greater comparative advantages over people; more and more routine tasks will be economically done by computers.
Storage and memory	CD-ROMs and other storage devices will increase storage of data and information.	Large memory capacities will support the use of multimedia and other emerging computer technologies.
Graphical and other user-friendly interfaces	A *graphical user interface (GUI)* is a set of software features that provide users with direct control of visible objects on the screen. Thus they can use icons, pull-down menus, windows, and a mouse, rather than complex command syntax.	GUIs improve user-friendliness by making the human–machine interface as simple as possible.
Client/server architecture	This *architecture* links personal computers (*clients*) to specialized, powerful computers (*servers*), which they share via local or global networks.	Allows interconnection of different types of hardware and software. Is used to support the Internet and intranets.
Network computers ("thin clients")	Computers that do not have a hard drive but, rather, are served from a central computer through a network.	Provide the benefits of desktop computing without the high cost of regular personal computer hardware.
Enterprisewide computing	An extension of computing infrastructure that links all of an organization's functions and sometimes even those of its business partners.	Improves relationships with suppliers, other business partners, and customers. Enables organizations to bring products and services to market more quickly when the product design process is online.
Intranets and extranets	*Intranets* are networks within an organization that use Internet technologies to link organizational communications. *Extranets* are secured networks that connect the intranets of several business partners.	Intranets improve organizational communications. Extranets create powerful interorganizational communication and collaboration systems.
Data warehousing	Gigantic computer warehouses (storage) of large amounts of data.	Data warehouses organize data for easy access by end users of the data. When integrated with the Internet, they can be accessed from any location at any time.
Data mining	A sophisticated analysis technique that automatically discovers previously undetected relationships among data.	Enables managers to see relationships and dynamics in data elements that they had not foreseen (e.g., how the sales of one product might drive the sales of another).
Object-oriented environment	A type of software development that emphasizes the construction and use of self-contained units of software instructions and data (*objects*) that can be used and reused as components of software developed for a variety of purposes across the organization.	Can significantly reduce the cost of both building and maintaining computer-based information systems.

Table 1.1   Overview of General IT Trends (Continued)

Trend	What It Is	Benefits
Electronic document management	A technique that converts paper-based documents to digital electronic form via scanning and related technologies.	Greatly reduces storage requirements and allows the documents to be organized and manipulated like any other type of electronic data.
Multimedia and virtual reality	*Multimedia* is the integration of various types of media—voice, text, graphics, full-motion video, and animation. *Virtual reality* uses 3-D graphics to allow users to enter an artificial representation of some environment.	Provide interesting graphic images, which can be used to improve educational, training, advertising, communication, and decision-making materials.
Intelligent systems and agents	Automated rules that execute pre-programmed decisions or tasks when encountering specified conditions in data. Use expert or knowledge-based components to mimic human thought processes in decision making.	Increase productivity and ease the execution of complex tasks. Intelligent agents help users navigate the Internet, access databases, and conduct e-commerce.
Portable computing	Use of compact computers in cars, machines, and consumer products.	Can be carried almost anywhere. Reduce the time between data collection and processing.
Expansion of the Internet and completion of information superhighways	The integration of television and computers over a national fiber-optic-based network could connect more than 750 million Internet users worldwide in less than 10 years.	Completion of information superhighways will allow the Internet to reach every networked home, business, school, and other organization and will change how we live, learn, and work.
Electronic commerce (EC)	Business done online; the exchange of products, services, and money with the support of computers and computer networks.	Can provide a competitive edge and could change organizational structure, processes, procedures, culture, and management.
Integrated home computing	Integration of home computing, television, telephone, and home security systems in one unit.	Will facilitate telecommuting and the use of the Internet.

trends for information technology. Take a general look at these now, but don't worry about absorbing all the details at this point. We'll come back to these trends throughout the book. Like a song you eventually know from having heard it multiple times, by the end of this book you'll know and understand what these trends are and the impact they have on information technology in organizations.

Before you go on . . .

1. What are the basic components of an information system?

2. What capabilities do we expect of an information system?

3. What are some of the trends in IT development? Which are of particular interest to you?

1.4   REALITY CHECK II: STRATEGIC QUESTIONS, INFORMATION TECHNOLOGY ANSWERS

The previous section introduced some basic definitions and concepts about information and information systems. Here we will challenge your knowledge about information technologies by posing a series of questions about the strategic use of these technologies. The questions represent the kind of strategic thinking about information technologies and organizational objectives that goes on in boardrooms around the world every day. Rest assured that few people can answer most of the questions well. That's because every industry is different, every technology is different, and information technologies are "moving targets"—the state of the art today is passé tomorrow, and competitive advantage is just as fleeting. The good news is that this book will give you a very good start on how to understand the questions, and how to find the answers.

This book is not designed as a course on business strategy, and it assumes that you have some familiarity with that subject. But the fact is that information technology and organizational strategy are inseparable. This will become very clear as you read through this text.

Harvard professor Michael Porter's *strategic analysis model* is popular for understanding the strategic forces that affect organizations in particular industries. These include the relative power of buyers and suppliers, threats from substitute products and services, the ease or difficulty with which new competitors can enter the industry, and the amount of rivalry between industry competitors. Porter and others provide basic competitive strategies that emphasize cost reduction and product differentiation.

A related strategic concept is the *value chain*. The value chain refers to the discrete steps involved in the manufacture of a product or the provision of a service. In manufacturing, for example, the value chain stretches from the suppliers of each component, through the manufacturing process, to the after-sale support of the product. Companies strive to understand and optimize every part of the value chain so as to add value to their products by improving quality and efficiency at every step.

These two concepts—Porter's strategic analysis model and the value chain—are useful because they can be used to generate a series of questions about information technology whose answers can shape an organization's competitive strategy.

Strategic Questions

Take the time to consider the questions in Table 1.2. Bear in mind that the answer to every single one is "yes." The question that naturally follows this answer is, "How"? You will be able to begin to answer that key question after reading this book.

Information Technology Answers

These questions are very general, but they reflect the kind of strategic thinking that is necessary to lead organizations now and in the future. There are also many other similar questions that strategic thinkers ask. Another goal of this book is to get you prepared to understand and formulate these types of questions and to provide useful answers. Our basic strategy is to give you fundamental information about the technologies and systems, and to augment that information with insight into their strategic management and use. We provide this insight through real-world examples in the forms of cases at the beginning and end of each chapter and in our **IT's About Business**

Table 1.2   Strategic Analysis Questions

1. Can we use IT to gain leverage over our suppliers?
   To improve our bargaining power?
   To reduce their bargaining power?

2. Can we use IT to reduce purchasing costs?
   To reduce our order processing costs?
   To reduce suppliers' billing costs?

3. Can we use IT to identify alternative supply sources?
   To locate substitute products?
   To identify lower-price suppliers?

4. Can we use IT to improve the quality of products and services we receive from suppliers?
   To reduce order lead times?
   To monitor quality?
   To leverage supplier service data for better service to our customers?

5. Can we use IT to give us access to vital information about our suppliers that will help us reduce our costs?
   To select the most appropriate products?
   To negotiate price breaks?
   To monitor work progress and readjust our schedules?
   To assess quality control?

6. Can we use IT to give our suppliers information important to them that will in turn yield a cost, quality, or service reliability advantage to us?
   To conduct electronic exchange of data to reduce their costs?
   To provide master production schedule changes?

7. Can we use IT to reduce our customers' costs of doing business with us?
   To reduce paperwork for ordering or paying?
   To provide status information more rapidly?
   To reduce our costs and prices?

8. Can we provide some unique information to our customers that will make them buy our products/services?
   Can we provide better billing or account status data?
   Can we provide options to switch to higher-value substitutes?
   Can we be first with an easy-to-duplicate feature that will provide value simply by being first?

9. Can we use IT to increase our customers' costs of switching to a new supplier?
   Can we provide proprietary hardware or software?
   Can we make customers dependent upon us for their data?
   Can we make our customer service more personalized?

10. Can we use external database sources to learn more about our customers and discover possible market niches?
    To relate buying from us to buying other products?
    To analyze customers' interactions with us and questions to us in order to develop customized products/services or methods of responding to customer needs?

11. Can we use IT to help our customers increase their revenues?
    To provide proprietary market data to them?
    To support their access to their markets through our channels?

12. Can we use IT to raise the entry barriers of new competitors into our markets?
    To redefine product features around IT components?
    To provide customer services through IT?

13. Can we use IT to differentiate our products/services?
    To highlight existing differentiations?
    To create new differentiations?

14. Can we use IT to make a preemptive move over our competition?
    To offer something new because we have proprietary data?

15. Can we use IT to provide substitutes?
    To simulate other products?
    To enhance our existing products?

16. Can we use IT to match an existing competitor's offerings?
    Can we match competitor' product/services based on unique IT capabilities or technologies and capabilities?

boxes that you will find throughout each chapter. We also provide many additional examples integrated into the text. They illustrate a variety of business, organizational, and consumer challenges that information technology can address (or sometimes cause). You probably won't understand all the technical, strategic, or ethical issues when you read through the examples in this first chapter, but you will understand the issues by the time you finish this book. IT's About Business Box 1.5 illustrates the ongoing efforts of established companies to deploy IT strategically through e-commerce.

IT's About Business

Box 1.5:   "Bricks and Clicks" Are Proving To Be a Good Fit

Not too long ago, forecasters predicted that Internet companies selling everything from books to pet food would put traditional retailers out of business. After all, why would anybody drive to the mall when they could shop online at any time of day? These predictions have not turned out to be correct.

Giants such as Wal-Mart and Home Depot are expanding and refining their Internet offerings. Federated Department Stores and Staples are combining Internet operations with their catalog businesses. These firms are using an integrated, multichannel marketing model where people can shop online and then walk into the stores as educated consumers.

For example, Target Stores *(target.com)* considers its Internet presence to be more valuable for marketing and customer relations than for sales. At Target's Web site *(target.com)*, the most popular area is its bridal registry, where visitors can print out prenuptial shopping lists, then go to their local Target and pick up the goods. About 10 percent of all visitors to Target's Web site simply want to find directions to a store.

Home Depot *(homedepot.com)* was criticized on Wall Street when the company did not quickly develop a full-scale Internet business. Instead of offering all its products for sale online nationwide, Home Depot ties its Internet shopping and order fulfillment to existing stores in only a few markets. Internet orders in these markets can be filled by a store's regular staff during slow times. Home Depot says its objective is not to maximize Internet sales, but to maximize the relationship with its customers.

At Borders *(borders.com)*, executives are hoping that customers will use its Web site and the 335 superstores and the 900 Waldenbooks stores it manages interchangeably. For instance, a customer might go online to see if her local Borders store has a book she wants, reserve it, then drive down to the store to pick it up and pay for it—sitting in on a poetry reading and buying a latte while she is in the store.

Source: "Bricks and Clicks Make a Good Fit," *The Atlanta Journal-Constitution*, April 14, 2001.

Questions

1. What appears to be the dominant strategy for established businesses that want to enter electronic commerce?

2. Electronic commerce can be conducted by virtual companies that exist only as an organized network of order-filling suppliers and a Web-based transaction entity—almost no "brick-and-mortar" infrastructure. Are the values of brand names more or less important to such companies compared to traditional companies?

Before you go on . . .

1. Give an example of a strategic question about the role of IT in a particular functional business area (e.g., production, marketing).

2. What functional business areas or processes have not yet received any strategic benefit from using IT? Why?

1.5   THE PLAN OF THIS BOOK

As we stated above, a major objective of this book is to bring you to the point where you will understand the roles of information technologies today. Another objective is to prepare you to think strategically about information systems—to be able look into the future and see how these tools can help you, your organization, and your world. A third objective is to demonstrate how information technology supports all of the functional areas of the organization.

The book is divided into four parts. The content of each part is as follows.

Part I: The operation of organizations in the modern hypercompetitive business environment is so complex and events occur so rapidly that the support of information systems is critically important (Chapter 1). However, there are many configurations of information systems and several ways that they can be classified. We also take a look at the types of people and career paths found in professional IS management (Chapter 2).

Part II: The technologies that form the information technology infrastructure are introduced in the next five chapters: hardware (Chapter 3), software (Chapter 4), organizational data and information management (Chapter 5), telecommunications and networks (Chapter 6), and the Internet, intranets, and extranets (Chapter 7).

Part III: Technologies and systems do not solve problems or give competitive advantage until people understand how to apply them. This part of the book shows information technologies and systems in action, solving organizational problems and creating competitive advantage. Chapters 8, 11, and 12 focus on different systems and their roles in business organizations. Chapters 9 and 10 focus on broader applications of integrated systems—e-commerce and supply chain management.

Part IV: Information systems—when used effectively—can bring great competitive advantage. They can also foment great changes in how an organization functions internally and how it relates to the rest of the world. We now revisit IT as a driver of strategy both within and between organizations (Chapter 13), the complex issues involved in creating information systems (Chapter 14), and how new systems can impact a host of management issues such as ethics, organizational culture, and security (Chapter 15).

www.wiley.com/
college/turban

FOR THE ACCOUNTING MAJOR

Data and information are the lifeblood of the accounting function. Information systems capture, organize, analyze, and disseminate data and information throughout modern organizations. Virtually no companies in the modern business world handle their accounting without support from information systems. And accounting information systems commonly integrate with other information systems in other parts of a large organization, so that transactional information from a sales or marketing information system becomes input for the accounting system.

FOR THE FINANCE MAJOR

The modern financial world turns on speed, volume, and accuracy of information flow, all facilitated by advanced information systems and telecommunications. As with accounting, very few firms would attempt to manage their finances without the aid of information systems that can monitor world financial markets, support financial decision making (for portfolio management, for example), provide quantitative analyses (for cash flow projections, for example), and support a host of other financial functions.

FOR THE MARKETING MAJOR

The Internet and the World Wide Web have opened an entirely new channel for marketing from business to business and business to consumer. They have also dramatically increased the amount of information available to customers, allowing rapid and thorough product and price comparisons. The Internet also provides for much closer contact between the consumer and the supplier. The e-commerce venue continues to grow in size and sophistication, so that everyone contemplating a career in marketing must be thoroughly trained in its unique technologies and techniques.

 FOR THE PRODUCTION/OPERATIONS MANAGEMENT MAJOR

Every process in a product or service's value chain can be enhanced by the proper use of computer-based information systems. In manufacturing, these processes occur everywhere from supplier production and logistics, through the manufacturing process, through outbound logistics, and after the sale of the product. The value chains in service industries are also a series of processes that benefit from information systems support. From computer-aided design and computer-integrated manufacturing, through Internet-based order systems, information systems have transformed the competitive landscape.

HRM **FOR THE HUMAN RESOURCES MANAGEMENT MAJOR**

Human resources management is changing radically as it is increasingly supported by information systems. Record keeping is greatly improved in terms of speed, convenience, and accuracy. Dissemination of HR information throughout the company via private company intranets means that employees can handle much of their personal business (configuring their benefits, for example) themselves, without direct intervention by HR personnel. The Internet makes a tremendous amount of information available to the job seeker, increasing the fluidity of the labor market. Finally, information systems skills are rapidly becoming imperative in many careers; HR professionals must have an understanding of these systems and skills to best support hiring, training, and retention.

SUMMARY

❶ **Discuss business pressures and responses in today's Information Age.**
   The main business pressures in the Information Age are: global competition for trade and labor, the need for real-time operations, the changing workforce, customer orientation, technological innovation and obsolescence, information overload, social responsibility, government regulations and deregulation, and ethical issues. Major organizational responses are: strategic systems, customer focus and service, continuous improvement efforts, business process reengineering, enterprise resource planning and supply chain management, business alliances, and e-commerce.

❷ **Differentiate among data, information, and knowledge, and describe the characteristics of high-quality data.**
   Data are raw facts or elementary descriptions of things, events, activities, and transactions that are captured, recorded, stored, and classified, but not organized to convey any specific meaning. Information is a collection of facts organized in some manner that is meaningful to a recipient. Knowledge is information that has been organized and processed to convey understanding, experiences, accumulated learning, and expertise as it applies to a current business problem or process. Desirable characteristics of high-quality information include accuracy, completeness, flexibility, reliability, relevance, timeliness, verifiability, accessibility, and security.

❸ Name and describe the components of an information system.
The components of an information system are hardware, software, databases, networks, procedures, and people. Hardware is a set of devices such as a processor, monitor, keyboard, and printer that accept data and information, process them, and display them. Software is a set of computer programs that enable the hardware to process data. A database is an organized collection of related files and records that stores data and the associations among them. A network is a connecting system that permits the sharing of resources among different computers. Procedures are the strategies, policies, methods, and rules for using the information system. The most important element in information systems is people, those persons who work with the information system or use its output.

❹ Describe the capabilities expected of information systems in modern organizations.
Information systems in modern organizations provide fast and accurate transaction processing, large-capacity, fast-access storage, and fast communications (machine to machine, human to human). They also reduce information overload, span boundaries within and between organizations, provide support for decision making, and provide a competitive weapon in the marketplace.

❺ Describe opportunities for strategic use of information systems.
The forces that shape the level and type of competition in any industry include the relative power of buyers and suppliers, threats from substitute products and services, and the ease or difficulty with which new competitors can enter the industry. Basic competitive strategies emphasize cost reduction and product differentiation. In addition, the value chain enables companies to understand and optimize the discrete steps involved in the manufacture of a product or the provision of a service, so as to add value to their products by improving quality and efficiency at every step. These business concepts can be used to generate a series of questions about IT whose answers can shape an organization's competitive strategy. In general, IT gives strategic competitive advantage through addressing and sometimes altering the nature of strategic forces in industry, as well as advancing strategies based on cost and product differentiation.

INTERACTIVE LEARNING SESSION

Go to the CD and access Chapter 1: Introduction: Business and IT. There you will find a video clip from the "Nightly Business Report" about the outlook for information technology in the twenty-first century. The video includes a lot of information about the increased need for high-speed transmission and other telecommunications. You will be asked to watch the video and answer questions about it.

www.wiley.com/
college/turban

For additional resources, go to the book's Web site for Chapter 1. There you will find Web resources for the chapter, including links to organizations, people, and technology; "IT's About Business" company links; "What's in IT for Me?" links; and a self-testing Web quiz for Chapter 1.

DISCUSSION QUESTIONS

1. Why is the study of information systems important to you, regardless of your major?

2. "One person's data is another person's information." Explain this statement with an example.

3. What does it mean that we live in an Information Age?

4. What are the capabilities of information systems that businesses must have to compete (and survive) in the Information Age?

5. Discuss the general technological trends for information technology.

PROBLEM-SOLVING ACTIVITIES

1. Search through several business publications (*Business Week*, *Fortune*, *Forbes*, *Forbes ASAP*, *Wall Street Journal*) for recent articles that discuss the use of information technology to deliver significant business benefits to an organization. Then go to the Web sites of these organizations and find additional recent articles.

2. Develop a list of occupations or human endeavors that you believe cannot benefit from using information technology. Keep this list and refer back to it at the end of the course or after you have finished reading this book. Then revise the list in light of what you have learned, coming up with examples of how to apply IT to these areas.

INTERNET ACTIVITIES

1. Enter a Web site that offers employment opportunities in IT (such as *recruitersonline.com*). Note IT job availability and salaries. Compare job availability and salaries to other professions.

2. Access the Web site of your university. Note the functionality and ease of use of your school's Web site. Access the Web sites of universities that are your school's main competitors, and assess their functionality and ease of use. Now access the Web sites of Harvard University, Massachusetts Institute of Technology, and Stanford University. Assess the sites' functionality and ease of use. Draw implications from your findings.

TEAM ACTIVITIES AND ROLE PLAYING

At the beginning of the semester, the class will be divided into investment groups. Each group will have $200,000 to "invest" in the stock of any 10 technology companies and any 5 nontechnology companies. The minimum investment is $5,000 in each company chosen. As the semester progresses, each group may buy stock in additional companies, buy additional stock in currently held companies, or sell stock in currently held companies.

Before your group invests in any company, you must research the firm's stock. You may go to company home pages or access free online brokers for the information. Your group must prepare an initial report containing the research that led to the investment.

Each group must track each stock daily and each trade as it is made. The group with the most money at the end of the semester wins.

REAL-WORLD CASE   *circleintl.com*

The Harper Group Collaborates With Honda in International Trade

The Business Problem   The Harper Group, a subsidiary of Circle International, is an international freight-moving company. It uses information technology to support the services it provides to its clients who export and import goods. International trade is complex because it involves buyers and sellers of goods and services in different countries, customs services, sea or air shipping and receiving ports, storage companies, and transportation companies. Harper operates in a highly competitive environment in which hundreds of freight-moving companies in the United States and abroad serve an international market. In this market, large amounts of information flow among several trading partners and support services. This information includes bids, orders, billings, status queries, contracts, payments, and so on. Harper manages this information for its customers, the exporters and importers. The problem faced by Harper is how to effectively manage the information and do it at competitive prices.

The IT Solution   To improve information flow so that it will move more consistently, freely, and rapidly, and thus to expedite the movement of cargo, the Harper Group uses information technology that links the computers of involved organizations, resulting in a paperless flow of routine information. Harper has an IT arrangement with 500 of its largest customers, one of which is Honda Motor Company of Japan. Honda ships over 300,000 cars and trucks to the United States each year. Harper takes care of all the necessary arrangements, including those involving the U.S. Customs. Harper can also tap into Honda's database to deposit or retrieve information required by U.S. Customs.

The electronic transaction begins when Honda sends a shipment of cars from Japan to the United States. Honda sends its export documents electronically from its headquarters in Japan to the American Honda offices in Los Angeles. The information is then transferred electronically to Harper's mainframe computer in San Francisco. The complete files (one order may include several hundred pages of data) are then transferred electronically to U.S. Customs several days before the ship carrying the cars docks in a U.S. port. Customs agents calculate the duty fees and send them to Harper electronically. Honda's duty payment for each shipment is then transferred electronically from a bank to the U.S. Customs' bank. Finally, Harper bills Honda electronically for its services and is paid via an electronic transfer of funds.

The Results   This electronic communication system allows cheaper, faster, and more reliable information to flow among all business partners and support Harper's global business. IT enables Harper to maintain its position as the second-largest importer in the United States. In addition, although Harper operates in an industry with thin profit margins, its profit margins are substantially above the industry's average due to its sophisticated information systems.

The Harper Group case illustrates the realities of doing business as we enter the twenty-first century. The transactions surrounding each shipment of cars are complex, involving several trading partners in Japan and the United States as well as government officials. Therefore, Honda hired a vendor that specializes in global transactions to do the job. The Harper Group must be effective and efficient, or Honda will select a competing vendor. The solution is an information system through which large amounts of transactional information can flow among several business partners around the globe.

Questions

1. What are some of the complexities of international manufacturing and shipping?

2. How does Harper use information technology for competitive advantage?

VIRTUAL COMPANY ASSIGNMENT

wiley.com/college/turban

Extreme Descent Snowboards

Background   Congratulations! You have been hired as an IS intern by Extreme Descent Snowboards (EDS)—a relatively new company that manufactures and sells custom-crafted snowboards. As an IS intern, you will

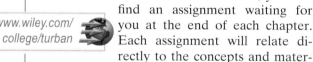

www.wiley.com/
college/turban

find an assignment waiting for you at the end of each chapter. Each assignment will relate directly to the concepts and material that you read in the chapter. You will then apply these concepts just as if you were working on a real assignment for the company. Jacob March, the vice president of information systems at EDS, will be your mentor and supervisor during your internship. To start, he suggests you do the following.

Assignment

Management at EDS is very interested in the further development of its Web site and corporate intranet. EDS's electronic commerce Web presence and corporate intranet can be found at *www.wiley.com/college/turban*. Click on the hyperlink *To the Student Companion site*. Then click on the hyperlink *Virtual Company* to enter the EDS Web site. You will need Internet access to enter this site.

You need to become familiar with the company and its Internet and intranet sites. Briefly study the company overall. Then prepare and submit a report that addresses the following questions and issues.

1. Briefly describe the history of the company.

2. What are the company's goals?

3. Who founded the company, and how was it founded?

4. How does a customer order a snowboard?

5. What is the EDS warranty policy?

6. What employment opportunities are at EDS?

7. What is your "boss's" e-mail address?

8. What type of financial reports can you get?

9. What training classes are available for employees? How can employees register for more than one class?

10. How long does it take for EDS to reimburse travel expenses? (Only if you use the online travel expense form.)

11. How can using the travel planner help you make travel arrangements? Are any of the links obsolete? How do obsolete links affect a Web site? What would be involved in keeping the links up-to-date? Should EDS consider hiring someone to keep links current?

2

INFORMATION TECHNOLOGIES IN THE MODERN ORGANIZATION

CHAPTER PREVIEW

Now that you are acquainted with how business is done at the beginning of the twenty-first century and the supporting role of IT in general, we turn attention to the foundations of information systems in organizations and how they help organizations solve problems and seize opportunities.

The two major determinants of IT support are organizational structure and the functions that employees perform within organizations. As this chapter shows, information systems tend to follow the structure of the organization, and they are based on the needs of individuals and groups.

Information systems are scattered throughout organizations, often in several locations and sometimes in two or more organizations. For example, suppliers and customers may allow each other access to their databases, so as to better coordinate inventory and logistics. Such diversity of information systems creates difficulty in managing them. This chapter looks at the types of support that information technologies give to various workers in organizations, at how IT systems are managed in organizations, and at the careers available in IT.

CHAPTER OUTLINE

2.1 Basic Concepts of Information Systems
2.2 Organizations: Structure and IT Support
2.3 IT Support at Different Organizational Levels
2.4 Managing Information Technology in Organizations
2.5 IT People and Careers

LEARNING OBJECTIVES

1. Discuss major information systems concepts such as architecture and infrastructure
2. Describe the hierarchical structure of organizations and the corresponding information systems.
3. Describe the support provided to different types of employees in an organization.
4. Describe how information resources are managed.
5. Describe IT careers and personnel.

INFORMATION SYSTEMS AT BURLINGTON COAT FACTORY

The Business Problem

Burlington Coat Factory Warehouse Corporation operates over 310 clothing retail stores, five subsidiaries, and two distribution centers in 46 states of the United States. In addition to being the largest retailer of coats in the United States, Burlington sells clothes, linens, luggage, jewelry, and baby furniture. The competition in all these lines is extremely strong. Burlington's major strategy is to offer a large selection of the world's leading manufacturers, at savings up to 60 percent off department store prices.

Burlington must receive daily sales information, by item sold, from its stores, so that it can order merchandise from its suppliers and its own factories, in rapid response to sales. The company must communicate with store managers, suppliers, and customers quickly and effectively. Burlington looks to IT to reduce expenses, improve operations, and boost customer spending.

The IT Solution

Burlington's information system uses a Web-based architecture. The point-of-sale terminals and other PCs in each store are networked to an in-store server. All in-store servers are connected via communication gateways to the corporate mainframe computers using the TCP/IP protocol. Sales data are transferred every night over the Internet. At headquarters, data are processed, stored, and if needed, sent to external destinations such as the VISA/MasterCard system. Managers at individual stores can access information in corporate databases for end-user computing and decision support. Burlington communicates over the Internet with its suppliers and its customers.

Burlington recently deployed a customer relationship management (CRM) system. The CRM system collects and stores customer information in a central repository, so Burlington representatives at its call center, on the Web, and in stores, can view a customer's history while responding to an inquiry.

Burlington Coat Factory uses IT to manage worldwide manufacturing and distribution.

The Results

Burlington's information system has reduced expenses, improved operations, improved communications with suppliers and customers, and increased customer spending. As a result, Burlington has enjoyed steady growth in number of stores, sales, and profits.

Source: "Burlington Coat Factory Warehouse Corporation," *Computerworld,* March 11, 2002; "CRM One Step at a Time," *Computerworld,* December 19, 2001.

What We Learned from This Case

This opening case illustrates a networked corporate information system with characteristics that can be found in many organizations:

- Several different information systems exist in one organization. Burlington's information system contains hundreds of smaller information systems. Thus, a *collection* of a number of information systems is also referred to as an *information system.*

- Information systems are connected by means of electronic networks. If the entire company is networked and people can communicate with each other and access information throughout the organization, the arrangement is known as an *enterprisewide system.*

- The information system is composed of large and small computers and other hardware connected by different types of networks (the Internet, as well as networks that connect hardware within stores, between individual stores, and the entire company).

These characteristics point to the complexities involved in organizing and managing information systems, which are issues we address in this chapter.

2.1 BASIC CONCEPTS OF INFORMATION SYSTEMS

Before we discuss in detail IT and its management, we need to define some major concepts and organize them in a logical way. We look first, therefore, at the concepts of information infrastructure and architecture, and follow with descriptions of common types of information systems.

Information Infrastructure

An **information infrastructure** consists of the physical facilities, services, and management that support all computing resources in an organization. There are five major components of infrastructure: computer hardware, general-purpose software, networks and communication facilities (including the Internet), databases, and information management personnel. Infrastructures include these resources as well as their integration, operation, documentation, maintenance, and management. The infrastructure also tells us how specific computing resources are arranged, operated, and managed. Specific components of infrastructures are further discussed in Chapters 3 through 7.

Architecture

An **information architecture** is a high-level map or plan of the information requirements in an organization and the manner in which these requirements are being satisfied. It is a guide for current operations and a blueprint for future directions. It helps ensure that the organization's IT meets the organization's strategic business needs. Therefore, it must tie together the information requirements, the infrastructure, and the applications. Note that *information architecture* is different from *computer architecture*, which describes the hardware needs of a computer system. For example, the architecture for a computer may involve several processors, or special features to increase speed. Our interest here is in *information* architecture only.

Information architecture is similar to the conceptual planning of a house. When preparing a conceptual high-level drawing of a house, the architect needs to know the purpose of the house, the requirements of the dwellers, and the building constraints (time, money, materials, etc.). In preparing the information architecture, the designer needs similar information, which can be divided into two parts:

1. The business needs for information—that is, the organizational objectives and problems, and the contribution that IT can make. The potential users of IT must play a critical role in this part of the design process.

2. The existing and planned information infrastructure and applications in the organization. This information includes how the planned system and its applications can

be combined among themselves or with future systems to support the organization's information needs.

Transaction Processing Systems

Organizations perform routine, repetitive tasks. For example, employees are paid at regular intervals, customers place purchase orders and are billed, and expenses are monitored and compared to budgets. Table 2.1 presents a partial list of routine business transactions in a manufacturing organization.

The information system that supports such tasks is called a **transaction processing system (TPS)**. A TPS supports the monitoring, collection, storage, processing, and dissemination of the organization's basic business transactions. It also provides the input data for many other applications, including computerized decision making. Frequently, several transaction processing systems exist in one company. They are considered critical to the success of any organization because they support the core business operations, such as purchasing of materials, billing customers, preparing a payroll, and shipping goods to customers. The repetitive number-crunching systems introduced in the 1950s were transaction processing systems. Such systems are as useful to organizations today as they were then. The difference is that today's transaction processing systems are much more sophisticated and complex. (We will study TPSs in further detail in Chapter 8.)

Management Information Systems

As the cost of computing decreased and computer capabilities increased, it became possible to justify using information technology for more analytical tasks than transaction processing. In the 1960s, a new breed of information system started to develop. These systems accessed, organized, summarized, and displayed information for supporting routine *decision making* in the functional areas. Such systems are called functional **management information systems (MISs)** and are geared toward middle managers.

Functional information systems are put in place to ensure that business activities (functions) are done in an efficient manner. Typically a functional MIS provides periodic reports about such topics as operational efficiency, effectiveness, and

Table 2.1   Routine Business Transactions in a Factory

Payroll
- Monitor employee time cards
- Track employee pay and deductions
- Issue payroll checks

Purchasing
- Issue purchase orders
- Accept and record deliveries
- Pay accounts payable

Sales
- Keep sales records
- Issue invoices and billings
- Track accounts receivable
- Record and credit sales returns
- Keep shipping records

Manufacturing
- Prepare production reports
- Prepare quality-control reports

Finance and Accounting
- Prepare and issue financial statements
- Maintain tax records
- Monitor and pay expense accounts

Inventory Management
- Track materials usage
- Monitor inventory levels
- Reorder inventory as needed

productivity. It prepares these reports by extracting information from the corporate database and processing it according to the needs of the user. For example, an organization's TPS records every order as it is generated, and its marketing MIS can generate from these records weekly and monthly summaries by product, customer, or salesperson.

Initially, management information systems had a *historical orientation;* they described events after they occurred. Later, they also came to be used to support routine decisions, to provide answers to queries, and to forecast trends. Today, MIS reports might also include summary reports for the current period or for any number of previous periods. MISs are used for monitoring, planning, and control. For example, the accounting department might produce a weekly report on the status of delinquent accounts receivable. Or, a sales forecast by region, as shown in Figure 2.1, could help the marketing manager make better decisions regarding advertising and pricing of products. Besides being useful in making routine decisions, MISs also enable managers to detect possible problems in their early stages. Table 2.2 summarizes some of the major outputs of a functional MIS. (We'll discuss MISs in more detail in Chapter 8.)

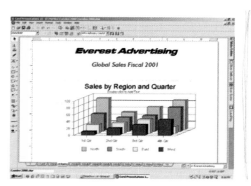

Figure 2.1   *Sales forecast by region.*

Support Systems

Managers are not the only organizational employees who can benefit from information systems. Support systems for *office employees* began to emerge in the late 1960s and early 1970s when networked computing and electronic communication became more prevalent. Airline reservation systems are perhaps the best example of this development. Electronic communication is only one aspect of what is now known as an **office automation system (OAS)**. Another form of OAS, word processing systems, spread to many organizations in the late 1970s and early 1980s. Later on, document management and other productivity software was added as part of office automation support. Since the 1970s, computers have also been introduced to the manufacturing environment. Applications range from robotics to computer-aided design and manufacturing (CAD/CAM) to inventory and logistics management.

By the early 1970s, the demand for all types of information technology, for all levels of workers, had begun to accelerate. Increased capabilities and reduced costs

Table 2.2 Major Outputs of a Functional MIS	
Output	*Description*
Statistical summaries	Summaries of raw data such as daily production, and weekly and monthly usage of electricity.
Exception reports	Highlights of data items that are larger or smaller than designated levels.
Periodic reports	Statistical summaries and exception reports provided at scheduled, regular periods.
Ad-hoc reports	Special, unscheduled reports provided on demand.
Comparative analysis	Performance comparision to that of competitors, past performance, or industry standards.
Projections	Advance estimates of trends in future sales, cash flows, market share, etc.

justified computerized support for a growing number of nonroutine and even one-time applications, and the **decision support system (DSS)** concept was born. The basic objective of a DSS is to provide computerized support for complex, sometimes nonroutine decisions, as illustrated in IT's About Business Box 2.1. (Chapter 11 will provide more detail on DSSs.)

At first, the high cost of building DSSs constrained their widespread use. However, the microcomputer (personal computer) revolution, which started around 1980, changed that. The availability of desktop computers made it possible for someone who knows little about programming to build DSS applications. This was the beginning of the era of **end-user computing**, in which the principal users of a system's output—analysts, managers, many other professionals, and their staffs—build their own systems.

Decision support expanded in two directions. First, **executive information systems (EISs)** were designed to support senior executives. These were later expanded to support all levels of managers around the organization. The second direction was the support of people working in groups. **Group support systems (GSSs)** initially supported people working in a special decision-making situation or meeting, in a single location. As network computing developed, GSSs became able to support decision makers working in different locations. The various commercial software products that support people working in groups is called **groupware**. Groupware is designed for use with all types of networks because it supports employees in different locations.

IT's About Business

a-dec.com

Box 2.1:   Decision Support System Helps Manufacturing Company

A-dec, Inc. is one of the largest dental equipment manufacturers in the world. The company designs and builds most of what you see in your dentist's office, then markets its products through a worldwide network of authorized dealers. The company's growth over its 36-year history resulted in a large management information problem.

Regional managers, responsible for about 75 territory managers around the world, would meet annually to estimate sales revenue for the next year. Then they would guess at what that meant in terms of actual production. They were not even in the ballpark when forecasting the product mix needed, costing the company much more money to respond to customers' needs. A-dec needed a decision support system to help solve the problem.

Using Comshare Decision as its decision support system, A-dec was able to solve its sales forecasting and production scheduling problem. The system was Web-based and was compatible with A-dec's mainstream database technology. Also, A-dec managers were able to use the system interactively as a reporting and information gathering and deployment tool. A-dec territory managers can now communicate their sales forecasts, the product mix they need, and when they need it, to finance and manufacturing via the Web. In addition, the system shows trends that can help the managers identify how to help dealers boost sales.

The system enables A-dec to manufacture the products that its customers need when they need them, while saving the company time and money, and increasing customer satisfaction. The net effect of the new system is increased sales. The new system also cut overtime pay by almost $1 million, by making the manufacturing planning process easier and more accurate.

Source: comshare.com, a-dec.com

Questions

1. Why was a DSS needed in this case?
2. Identify the different decisions supported by the DSS.

"WE DIGITIZED OUR COPY, WE DIGITIZED OUR PICTURES, AND NOW WE'RE BEGINNING TO DIGITIZE OUR STAFF."

Intelligent Systems

By the mid-1980s, managerial applications of so-called artificial intelligence began, creating **intelligent systems** that seem able to replicate the thought processes of humans. Of special interest are **expert systems (ESs)**, which are advisory systems that provide the stored knowledge of experts to nonexperts, so that the latter can solve difficult problems. For example, expert systems are frequently used to capture the knowledge of bank loan officers and enable a less experienced employee to make a complex loan decision.

Later, by the beginning of the 1990s, a new breed of intelligent systems emerged, systems with *learning capabilities*. This capability enables computers to incorporate new information or feedback and update their knowledge. This type of artificial intelligence excels at processing vague or incomplete information, recognizing subtle patterns in data, and making predictions or recognizing patterns or profiles in situations where the logic or rules are not known. For example, IT's About Business Box 2.2 describes several uses of an intelligent system called an *artificial neural network (ANN)*. (Chapter 12 will provide more information on intelligent systems.)

IT's About Business

Box 2.2:   Applications of Artificial Neural Networks

Artificial neural networks (ANNs) have proven useful in a variety of real-world applications that deal with complex, often incomplete, data. The earliest of these were in visual pattern recognition and speech recognition. More recently, programs for text-to-speech have utilized ANNs. Many handwriting analysis programs (such as those used in popular PDAs) are powered by ANNs. Automated and robotic factories are now being monitored by ANNs that control machinery, adjust temperature settings, and diagnose malfunctions.

Large financial institutions have used ANNs to improve performance in such areas as bond rating, credit scoring, target marketing, and evaluating loan applications. ANNs are now used to analyze credit card transactions to detect likely instances of fraud. The personnel office of the Chicago Police Department uses ANNs to try to root out corruption among police officers.

Since 1993, the U.S. Federal Aviation Administration (FAA) has used ANNs to improve bomb detection effectiveness. The ANN is exposed to a set of historical cases; i.e., it is shown pictures obtained by gamma rays. It is also told whether each specific piece of luggage contains an explosive or not. Once trained, the ANN is

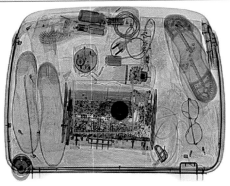

Not much can remain hidden from modern security technology.

used to predict the existence of explosives in new instances.

Source: "Artificial Neural Networks," *Computerworld*, February 12, 2001.

Question

1. It is said that two heads are better than one. Can the addition of ANN be considered an extra head? Why?

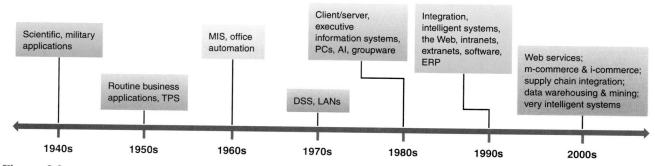

Figure 2.2   *The evolutionary path of computer-based information systems.*

Integrating Support (and Other) Systems

Within an organization, information can flow among the various computer systems. For example, an MIS might extract information from a TPS, and an EIS might receive information from both a TPS and an MIS. However, providing a computerized solution to a business problem may require *integrating* two or more of the information systems described in this section. For example, a decision support system combined with an expert system can be built to support a marketing promotion program.

As we enter the twenty-first century, various computerized systems are being integrated to increase their functionalities. One popular form of integrated system is *enterprise resources planning (ERP)*. ERP plans and manages all of an organization's resources and their use, including contacts with business partners. An example of ERP software is SAP R/3, which can integrate more than 70 departmental TPS, MIS, and DSS components. (Details are provided in Chapter 8.)

The evolution of computer-based information systems just described is shown in Figure 2.2.

Before you go on . . .

1. Distinguish between the terms *information infrastructure* and *information architechure*.

2. Describe a TPS and its major functions.

3. Define MIS and list three of its major characteristics.

4. Briefly define DSS, groupware, and expert systems.

2.2   ORGANIZATIONS: STRUCTURE AND IT SUPPORT

To better understand how IT supports organizations and their activities, it is useful to see how companies are organized and what roles managers and other employees play in them. First, it is important to understand that organizations can be classified by various characteristics. One characteristic is whether they are intended to make a profit. Nike, Microsoft, and Budget Car Rental, for example, are organized as *profit-making* businesses. *Not-for-profit* organizations like the United Way, the U.S. Army, and most churches, on the other hand, contribute (in a broad sense) to the public good. Organizations also can be classified by whether they manufacture *goods* (computers, cars, tools, food, and so forth) or produce *services* (insurance companies, universities, banks, and hospitals). The nature of organizations determines their activities, the information support they need, and the type of information systems provided.

Other important factors are the size of an organization and its location. Two extreme types can be distinguished:

1. Companies that are located in *one place*, from which they conduct all their operations. These are usually small to medium-sized companies.

2. Companies that are located in several places, sometimes in several countries. We refer to these as *global* or *multinational organizations*. They are usually medium-sized to large organizations.

Size and number of locations are the major determinants of an organization's structure.

Organizational Structure

Organizations typically have a centralized headquarters and divisions at different locations. These *divisions* can be independent subsidiaries or integral parts of one corporation. Depending on the organization and its size, a division may be further divided into units (such as plants), each of which is in a different location. Alternatively, each division may represent a plant or another organizational entity (for example, a warehouse). A plant is usually composed of departments and other operating units.

Departmental structure is most widely used in business organizations. It is also referred to as a *functional* structure. As discussed in Chapter 1, a *functional department* specializes in the delivery of a certain function, such as manufacturing or marketing. Most organizations have, at minimum, the following departments:

- Accounting
- Finance
- Marketing and Sales
- Production or Operations Management (POM)
- Human Resources Management
- Information Systems

Note that these functions correspond to the departments in most business schools.

In addition, other, smaller units in organizations provide specialized services such as legal, engineering, or purchasing.

The hierarchical structure.   The most widely used organizational structure is a *hierarchical* one. A typical hierarchical structure is shown in Figure 2.3.

Project management and matrix organization.   In some cases, organizations have found the hierarchical structure to be inflexible or nonresponsive. To increase flexibility it is customary to add teams, temporary or permanent, to this structure. Some of these teams are cross-functional, and they are responsible for an entire business process. An example would be a team assembled to work on a new and urgent business problem.

When cross-functional teams are temporary, and their members return to their regular functional departments when the team's task is completed, the structure is

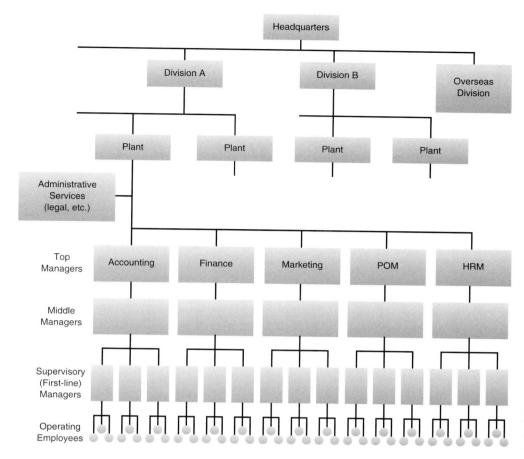

Figure 2.3 *Typical hierarchical organizational structure.*

called *project management.* When the teams are a permanent collection of people from different departments assigned to work on a series of special projects, the structure is called a *matrix organization.* As shown in Figure 2.4 (on page 40), a cross-functional organizational structure in effect creates teams with representatives from each relevant business function. Matrix organization tends to work well in high-tech industries and with firms that develop many new products.

Regardless of its format, organizational structure is a major driver of information systems arrangements in organizations.

Mapping Information Systems to Organizational Structure

One way to classify information systems is by the part of the organizational structure they support. Although some organizations are reengineering themselves into cross-functional teams, the vast majority still have a traditional hierarchical structure. Therefore, the most common arrangement of information systems is one that follows the hierarchical structure. This arrangement provides a match between the needs of organizational entities and the support provided by IT.

Information technology provides support in three major areas: *communication, collaboration,* and *data processing and access* (including knowledge sharing). Specific types of support are usually given by an **application program** (or, more simply, an *application*). An application is a system developed for a specific purpose, such as facilitating a production schedule, expediting a financial forecast, or executing the weekly

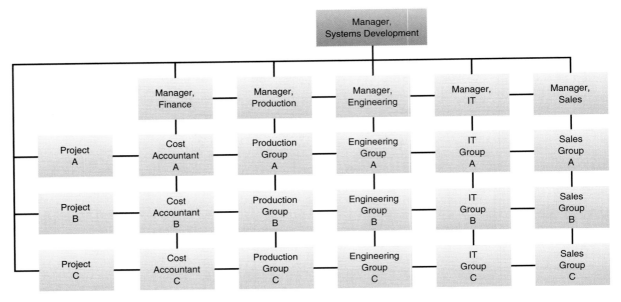

Figure 2.4 *Typical matrix organization.*

payroll. It is usually a software program built on existing infrastructure, although some applications require specialized hardware.

Thus, we can categorize information systems by their breadth. Systems and applications can be built for headquarters, for divisions, for departments, for specific teams (e.g., quality-assurance teams), and even for individuals. Other systems are: enterprisewide, interorganizational, and global (international). Such systems are typically interconnected. Brief descriptions of some of these systems follow.

Departmental information systems.   Frequently, *departmental information systems* are named to reflect the department they support, such as accounting information systems or human resources information systems. In practice, each functional information system is composed of several specific application programs. For instance, in managing human resources, the HR department might use one application program for recruiting and another for monitoring employee turnover. The collection of the various application programs in the human resources area would be called the human resources information system. Some of the applications might be completely independent of each other; others might be integrated.

Plant information systems.   Whereas a departmental information system is usually related to a functional area, the collection of all departmental applications combined with the applications of other business units comprises the *plant information system*. The plant information system provides the necessary communication and collaboration among the departmental entities of the plant as well as access to data for all authorized people.

Divisional information systems.   The *divisional information system* connects all of a plant's systems with information systems of other business units in the same division. It permits communication and collaboration among the plants and other units in the division, including access to headquarters and the business environment.

Enterprisewide information systems. In a similar manner, an *enterprisewide information system* connects all divisions and other units of an organization. Burlington's system described at the beginning of the chapter is an enterprisewide system.

Interorganizational information systems. Some information systems connect two or more organizations. For example, a worldwide airline reservation system is composed of several information systems belonging to different airlines, of which American Airlines' SABRE system is one of the largest. Such **interorganizational information systems (IOSs)** are common among business partners. These systems may provide for communication at the plant, divisional, or enterprisewide level, depending on the needs of the organizations involved. A special instance of an IOS is an international or multinational corporation whose computing facilities are located in two or more countries. Such an IOS is called a **global information system (GIS)**. Interorganizational information systems play a major role in e-commerce, as well as in supply chain management support.

Before you go on . . .

1. Describe the hierarchical structure of organizations.

2. List and briefly describe the major types of information systems that correspond to the hierarchical structure.

3. Define interorganizational and global information systems.

2.3 IT SUPPORT AT DIFFERENT ORGANIZATIONAL LEVELS

Individuals in organizations are supported by different types of information systems, depending on the roles and the tasks they perform:

- *Strategic decisions* are usually made by top management; these are relatively long-term planning decisions that deal with the organization's objectives as a whole and the allocation of resources to achieve these objectives. Top management may rely on executive information systems for some of their decision making and forecasting.

- *Tactical* or *managerial decisions* are made by middle managers, who prepare short-term plans, procedures, and policies with which to begin implementing the organization's long-term strategies. MISs provide the primary support at this level, along with some types of DSS.

- *Operational decisions* are made by line managers and operators. These are the day-to-day decisions that aim to keep the organization's operations moving smoothly. TPSs typically capture the operational information relevant for decision making at this level.

    The relationships between information systems and the people they support in organizations are shown in Figure 2.5 (on page 42). Organized as a triangle, the figure also illustrates the number of employees involved at the various levels of decision making. Top managers are few, and they sit at the top of the triangle.

    As you can see in the figure, an additional level of employees is introduced between top managers and middle managers. These are professional people who act as advisors to both top and middle management. Many of these professionals can be

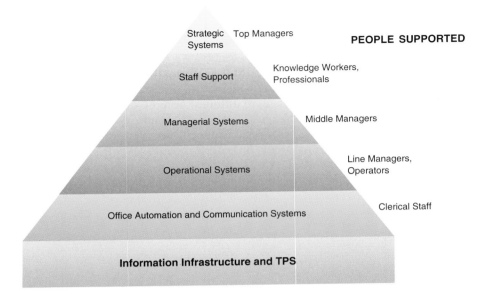

Figure 2.5 *The information systems support of people in organizations.*

thought of as **knowledge workers**—people who create information and knowledge and integrate it into the business. Knowledge workers are engineers, financial and marketing analysts, production planners, lawyers, and accountants, to mention just a few. They are responsible for finding or developing new knowledge for the organization and integrating it with existing knowledge. Therefore, they must keep abreast of all developments and events related to their profession. They also act as advisors and consultants to the members of the organization. Finally, they act as change agents by introducing new procedures, technologies, or processes. In many developed countries, 60 to 80 percent of all workers are knowledge workers.

Knowledge workers can be supported by a large variety of information systems. These range from Internet search engines that help them find information, to expert systems that support information interpretation, to computer-aided design, and even to hyperlinks that help them increase their productivity and the quality of their work. Within most organizations, knowledge workers are the major users of the Internet. They need to learn what is new, to communicate regularly with corporate managers and colleagues, and frequently to collaborate with knowledge workers in other organizations.

One way that IT can integrate the expertise of knowledge workers into an organization and assist in improving worker performance is through the use of intelligent systems. These systems contain the knowledge of super-experts and can disseminate that knowledge to all employees who need it. An example of how expert systems can be used is shown in IT's About Business Box 2.3.

However, knowledge workers do not have an exclusive right to an organization's knowledge. Knowledge should be accumulated by *all employees* in organizations. IT can facilitate not only the creation of knowledge by all workers but also its preservation and use. The reserve of accumulated knowledge in organizations is called an organizational *knowledge base*. Besides that developed from within, the knowledge base may also contain knowledge generated by people outside the organization, such as that provided by consultants. This outside knowledge is known as *best global practices*, or *benchmarks*. The process of acquiring, maintaining, and disseminating organizational knowledge is called **knowledge management**. It is supported by several types of information systems, as will be shown in Chapters 11 and 12.

IT's About Business

 ford.com   **POM**

Box 2.3: An expert system increases productivity at Ford Motor

On production lines at Ford Motor Company, manufacturing processes are achieving major productivity increases through the adoption of a computer-integrated manufacturing (CIM) strategy. CIM provides access to the information flowing from robots and other machines and allows all of the resources of the plant to be combined into a unified network.

Cadiz Electronica of Spain, a subsidiary of Ford Motor Company, employs about 480 people on two production lines. The first line produces electronic engine control modules. The second builds the antilock brake system modules. This subsidiary has installed an information system called the System for Diagnosis and Repair (SEDYR). This expert system detects and diagnoses printed circuit malfunctions by analyzing the CIM system information flow and assisting repair operations on-line during the production process. Each component is automatically diagnosed, in real time, while it is still on a manufacturing line. The system also provides access to the manufacturing-process history located on a database.

It maintains a real-time connection with the main CIM computer, informing it about failures in processing. The failed boards are eventually separated from the boards that pass the functional tests and sent to the repair zone.

Besides being able to visualize the boards and identify failed components, the expert system also links a graphical representation of the problem with appropriate comments and provides tips for the treatment of the failures. This ability has drastically lowered the time needed to repair a board. Another benefit provided by this approach of manufacturing supervision is the ability to use the system as a realistic and cost-effective simulation-training tool.

Questions

1. How is productivity increased by use of the expert system at Cadiz Electronics?

2. Why is a real-time connection necessary?

Another class of employees who need IT support is *clerical workers*, who support managers at all levels. Among clerical workers, those who use, manipulate, or disseminate information are referred to as *data workers*. These include bookkeepers, assistants who work with word processors, electronic file clerks, and insurance claim processors. Clerical employees are supported by office automation and groupware, including document management, workflow, e-mail, and other personal productivity software.

The IT support provided to managers and other employees, by the type of information system, is summarized in Table 2.3.

Table 2.3   Main Types of IT Support Systems

System	Employees Supported	Detailed Discussion in
Office automation	Office workers	Chapters 7, 8
Communication	All employees	Chapters 6, 8
Group support	People working in groups	Chapter 11
Decision support	Decision makers, managers	Chapter 11
Executive information	Executives, top managers	Chapter 11
Intelligent systems	Knowledge workers	Chapters 8, 12
TPS	Line managers and employees	Chapter 8
MIS	Middle management	Chapter 8

Before you go on . . .

1. Relate organizational levels to transaction processing systems, executive information systems, and management information systems.

2. What are knowledge workers?

2.4 MANAGING INFORMATION TECHNOLOGY IN ORGANIZATIONS

A modern organization possesses a considerable amount of information resources. As described in Chapter 1, the major categories of information resources are: hardware (all types of computers, servers, and other devices), software (development tools, languages, and applications), databases, networks (local, wide, the Internet and intranets, and supporting devices), procedures, and physical buildings. These resources are scattered throughout the organization; some of them change frequently. Therefore, it may be rather difficult to manage IT resources.

Information systems have enormous strategic value, and firms rely on them heavily. In some cases, when one information system is not working, even for a short time, an organization cannot function. Furthermore, the acquisition, operation, and maintenance of these systems may cost a considerable amount of money. Therefore, it is essential to manage information systems properly. The planning, organizing, implementing, operating, and controlling of the infrastructures and other information resources must be done with great skill.

The responsibility for the management of information resources is divided between a usually centralized information systems department (ISD) and the end users, who are scattered throughout the organization. This division of responsibility raises some important interrelated questions: Which resources are managed by whom? What is the role of the ISD? Who runs the ISD and to whom should the department report? What are the relationships between the ISD and end users? Brief answers to these questions are provided below.

Which Resources Are Managed by Whom?

Generally speaking, the information systems department is responsible for corporate-level and shared resources, and the end users are responsible for departmental resources. Regardless of who is managing what, there are several activities that must be done. These range from planning and purchasing of both hardware and software to application development and maintenance. Frequently, the ISD and the end users will divide such activities. For example, the ISD may acquire or build systems, and the end users will operate and maintain them.

Because of interdependencies of information resources, it is important that the ISD and the end users work closely together and cooperate, regardless of who is doing what.

What Is the Role of the Information Systems Department?

The role, structure, and place of the ISD in the organization's hierarchy vary considerably, as does the department's leadership in the organization. These characteristics of the ISD depend upon the amount and importance of information resources to be managed, the extent to which IT is outsourced by the organization, and the role that

Table 2.4   The Changing Role of the Information Systems Department

Traditional Major IS Functions

- Managing systems development and systems project management
- Managing computer operations, including the computer center
- Staffing, training, and developing IS skills
- Providing technical services

New (Additional) Major IS Functions

- Initiating and designing specific strategic information systems
- Infrastructure planning, development, and control
- Incorporating the Internet and e-commerce into the business
- Managing systems integration including the Internet, intranets, and extranets
- Educating the non-IS managers about IT
- Educating the IS staff about the business
- Supporting end-user computing
- Partnering with the executive level that runs the business
- Actively participating in business process reengineering
- Proactively using business and technical knowledge to "seed" the line managers with innovative ideas about IT
- Creating business alliances with vendors and IS departments in other organizations

end users play. Here, we provide only some major observations about the role of the ISD.

The role of the ISD has been changing from purely technical to more managerial and strategic. Table 2.4 shows the ISD's changing functions in recent years. As a result of its changing role, the position of the ISD within the organization tends to be elevated from a unit reporting to a functional department, to a unit reporting to a senior vice president of administration or to the CEO. The role of the director of the ISD is changing from a technical manager to a senior executive, sometimes referred to as the *chief information officer (CIO)*. The internal structure of the ISD is changing to reflect its new role—perhaps emphasizing vendor relations over software programming as outsourcing becomes more strategically efficient than internal development of systems. The ISD must frequently work closely with external organizations such as vendors, business partners, research institutions, universities, and consultants.

The key issues in information systems management change over time. Changing issues reflect progress made in achieving organizational IT goals and objectives as well as new opportunities made possible by new technologies. Recent important IT issues are the need to improve productivity, develop strategic applications, cut costs, enhance customer relationships, improve supply chains, and manage data. All of these issues are covered in many places throughout this book.

Who Runs the ISD and to Whom Does the Department Report?

The centralized ISD is run by a director who may have a title such as MIS director, manager of computing services, manager of information technology, or **chief information officer (CIO)**. The latter title indicates the importance of the IS area in any organization that uses it. The title "chief" is usually reserved for the top managers in an organization, such as the chief financial officer (CFO), chief operating officer (COO), or chief executive officer (CEO). You can find CIOs in organizations that are heavily dependent on IT, such as banks or airlines.

A position related to the CIO is that of **chief knowledge officer (CKO)**—the director assigned to capture and make effective use of knowledge for an organization. The same person may assume the roles of the CIO and CKO, especially in smaller companies. The major challenges facing CIOs are summarized in Manager's Checklist 2.1.

Information technology has become a strategic resource for many organizations. Coordinating this resource requires strong IT leadership and genuine cooperation between the ISD and end users within the organization. Therefore, the positive professional relationships among the CIO and other members of the top management group are crucial for effective, successful utilization of IT, especially in organizations that greatly depend on IT.

In many large organizations, the chief information officer (or whatever other title the top information executive holds) generally is a member of the corporate *executive committee*, which has responsibility for strategic business planning and response. The executive committee is the most important committee in any organization. Its members include the chief executive officer and the senior vice presidents. The executive committee provides the top-level oversight for the organization's information resources. It guides the IS *steering committee*, which is usually chaired by the CIO.

 Manager's Checklist 2.1

Major Questions and Challenges for the Chief Information Officer

- Do I understand the complexity inherent in doing business in a competitive, global environment?
- Am I managing the accelerating pace of technological change?
- Do I understand that IT may reshape organizations that could become technology driven?
- Do I realize that IT often is the primary enabler of business solutions?
- How well do I know the business sector in which the organization is involved?
- Do I understand the organizational structure and operating procedures?
- Am I using business, not technology, terms when communicating with corporate management?
- Am I gaining acceptance as a member of the business management team?
- Am I establishing the credibility of the IS department?
- Am I increasing the technological maturity of the company?
- Am I creating a vision of the future of IT and selling it to upper management?
- Am I implementing IT architecture that will support the vision?
- Am I maintaining sufficient technology competency?
- Do I understand networking on a global basis?
- Am I able to facilitate change within the department and the organization?
- Am I managing IT safety and security?
- Am I providing education to other executives?
- Do I understand industry standards?
- Is our organization setting industry standards?
- Am I balancing priorities?

What Are the Relationships Between the ISD and End Users?

The ISD and the end-user units must be close partners. Some mechanisms that provide the required cooperation are:

- A *steering committee* that represents all end users and the ISD. This committee sets IT policies, provides for priorities, and coordinates IS projects.
- *Joint ISD/end-user project teams* for planning, budgeting, application development, and maintenance.
- ISD representation on the *top corporate executive committee.*
- *Service agreements* that define computing responsibilities and provide a framework for services rendered by the ISD to end users.
- *Technical and administrative support* (including training) for end users.
- A *conflict resolution unit* established by the ISD to handle end-user complaints quickly and resolve conflicts as soon as possible.
- An *information center* that acts as a help center to end users regarding purchase, operations, and maintenance of hardware and software.

Before you go on . . .

1. List the major information resources in an organization. Which of these are managed by the ISD?

2. Describe the role of the ISD in an organization.

3. List five major challenges of the CIO.

2.5   IT PEOPLE AND CAREERS

People rarely begin a career in information systems management at the CIO level. Rather, there are a number of career paths that can lead to that position. Most require a fair amount of technical training and experience. Some place a greater emphasis on business and strategic knowledge, while others emphasize almost purely technical knowledge, similar to an engineering position. The various career paths are described below.

Programmer

Programmers are IS professionals who modify existing computer programs or write new computer programs to satisfy user requirements. Programmers typically can specialize in one or more programming languages, and be trained in universities or technical schools. On large development projects, programmers often work in teams. Although knowledge of business processes is a plus, a programmer's focus is primarily technical. This is a common entry-level IS position.

Jobs in IT require technical training and experience. Some place a greater emphasis on business and strategic knowledge, while others emphasize almost purely technical knowledge.

Systems Analyst/Developer

Systems analysts are information systems professionals who specialize in analyzing and designing information systems. They usually have some programming skills that are augmented by greater knowledge of business processes. In addition, analysts use a variety of specialized analysis and design tools. This job also places a premium on communication skills, as systems analysts must spend a great deal of time with users to determine how best to meet their needs.

Telecommunications/Network Specialist

Telecommunications/network specialists have a greater technical orientation. At higher levels, these specialists often hold electrical engineering degrees, although some network specialists may have technical training only in their particular area. Given the mission-critical nature of networks and telecommunications in most organizations, this career path is both demanding and in demand.

Systems Operations Specialist

Systems operations specialists keep systems up and running, and may have subspecializations with particular types of computing hardware (e.g., mainframes) and their related software, as well as some aspects of the telecommunications and networks involved. There are entry-level positions where training may be provided by the organization or contracted out to a training company. As with other areas, ongoing training is always necessary to keep pace with advances in technology.

Business Analyst

A *business analyst* has IT experience and an in-depth knowledge of the organization's business processes. He or she is often heavily involved with the development of new information systems and acts as a "translator" between IS developers and users. This role enables a clearer understanding of business problems and appropriate IT solutions, and ensures that the strategic goals and the user requirements are understood and appropriately addressed by the technical IT people.

Database Administrator

Data are an extremely valuable organizational asset for both day-to-day operations and strategic objectives. Organizational data reside in databases that must be designed and managed for maximum efficiency and effectiveness. *Database administrators* typically have considerable experience and training in one or more types of database software and hardware. Like many other IT positions, this position requires strong communication skills as well as technical training so that the databases can be as useful as possible to users.

Webmaster/E-Commerce Specialist

This new area encompasses programming skills as well as strong knowledge of an organization's processes. With the advent of the Internet and e-commerce there has been a high demand for people who have professional command of the languages and packages used for Web site development. For many organizations, the Web site is designed to transact business, and this requires some very advanced programming skills to link what a client sees to many other areas within the company, particularly databases and other IT-supported parts of the supply chain.

This chapter illustrates that information systems vary in breadth and specialization. They can be suitable for supporting different numbers of users, from the stand-alone personal computer through the group system, to the enterprisewide system. They can be designed to support users at different levels in the organization, from the transaction processing systems used by operational managers and lower-level employees, to executive information systems used by top management teams. Because of their strategic importance, information resources, technologies, and systems require professional management. Also, the relationships between the ISD and those who rely on it for support—from the operational to the strategic—must receive high priority. Finally, we see that a career in information systems management can begin in different ways and follow different technical and managerial directions.

Before you go on . . .

1. List the major career paths in IT.

2. Which career path is most appealing to you at this point? Why?

www.wiley.com/
college/turban

FOR THE ACCOUNTING MAJOR

The accounting department in organizations regularly interfaces with the ISD. Many of the transactions handled in a TPS—such as billing customers, preparing payrolls, and purchasing and paying for materials—are data that the accounting department needs to record and track.

FOR THE FINANCE MAJOR

Enterprisewide information systems have moved from focusing primarily on manufacturing to integrating finance and other functional areas. These are important changes. The interfaces between IT and finance are getting stronger, and reliance of finance on IT is rapidly increasing. Finance departments, for example, often use a specialized DSS for forecasting and portfolio management. An understanding of the fundamentals of information systems is, therefore, a must for finance people.

FOR THE MARKETING MAJOR

It is said that marketing without IT is not modern marketing. Marketing now uses such IT-related concepts as customer databases, marketing decision making, and sales automation. To better understand such basic concepts, marketers need to understand how information systems are structured, what they support, and how they are managed.

FOR THE PRODUCTION/OPERATIONS MANAGEMENT MAJOR

Organizations are competing on price, quality, time (speed), and customer service—all of which are concerns of production and operations management, and all of which are enhanced and supported by IT. Purchasing, inventory, quality control, logistics, and other aspects of operations each receive considerable integrated IT support in modern manufacturing firms, each often a complex system of its own.

FOR THE HUMAN RESOURCES MANAGEMENT MAJOR

As we begin the twenty-first century, the "new" human resources department is taking full advantage of IT, especially intranets, to disseminate throughout the organization relevant information such as job opportunities, benefits information, and educational materials. Critical IT knowledge for the HRM professional includes what kind of systems are available, what their capabilities are, and how they are utilized in HRM.

SUMMARY

❶ Discuss major information systems concepts such as architecture and infrastructure.
An information architecture is the "blueprint" that provides the conceptual foundation for building the information infrastructure and specific applications. It maps the information requirements as they relate to information resources. The information infrastructure refers to the physical shared information resources (such as a corporate database) and their linkages, operation, maintenance, and management. The major categories include: (a) the transaction processing system (TPS), which covers the core repetitive organizational transactions such as purchasing, billing, or payroll; (b) management information systems (MISs) that support managers in the major functional areas; (c) the general support systems, including office automation, decision support, group support, and executive support; (d) intelligent systems such as expert systems and artificial neural networks; and (e) the integrated systems that link the entire organization, such as enterprise resource planning (ERP) systems.

❷ Describe the hierarchical structure of organizations and the corresponding information systems.
Most organizations are structured vertically in what is known as hierarchical structure, from headquarters down to departments and operating units. Information systems follow this structure closely. For example, an organization typically would have divisional information systems, plant information systems, and departmental information systems.

❸ Describe the support provided to different types of employees in an organization.
Information systems are also categorized by the support they provide to certain individuals in organizations, particularly to managers at different levels, to knowledge workers, and to data workers (clerical, office employees). Knowledge workers are those who find, develop, integrate, and maintain organizational knowledge. They are usually the experts in the functional areas.

❹ Describe how information resources are managed.
Information resources are extremely important to an organization, and they must be properly managed by both the ISD and end users. In general, the ISD manages shared enterprise information resources such as networks, while end users are responsible for departmental information resources, such as PCs. The role of the ISD is becoming more managerial, and its importance is rapidly increasing. Steering committees, service agreements, and conflict-resolution units are some of the mechanisms used to facilitate the cooperation between the ISD and end users.

❺ Describe IT careers and personnel.
There are a number of IS management career paths that begin with positions such as programmer, systems analyst/developer, database administrator, Webmaster, or network specialist. Most require a fair amount of technical training and experience. Some place a greater emphasis on business and strategic knowledge, while others emphasize almost purely technical knowledge.

INTERACTIVE LEARNING SESSION

Go to the CD and access Chapter 2: IT in the Modern Organization. There you will find a video clip from the "Nightly Business Report" of an interview of Peter Solvik, the CIO of Cisco System, in which he discusses IT management issues. You will be asked to watch the video and answer questions about it.

For additional resources, go to the book's Web site for Chapter 2. There you will find Web resources for the chapter, including links to organizations, people, and technology; "IT's About Business" company links; "What's in IT for Me?" links; and a self-testing Web quiz for Chapter 2.

www.wiley.com/ college/turban

DISCUSSION QUESTIONS

1. Discuss the logic of building information systems in accordance with the organizational structure.

2. Discuss the characteristics and roles of knowledge workers.

3. Discuss the relationship between TPS, MIS, and DSS.

4. Describe how the importance of issues in IS management can change over time.

5. Discuss how one might decide among career paths in information systems management.

PROBLEM-SOLVING ACTIVITIES

1. Classify each of the following systems as one (or more) of these types: TPS, DSS, EIS, GSS, ES, CAD/CAM.

   a. A student registration system in a university

   b. A system that advises farmers about which fertilizers to use

   c. A hospital patient admission system

   d. A system that provides a marketing manager with demand reports regarding the sales volume of specific products

   e. A robotic system that paints cars in a factory.

2. Prepare a list of what you think, based on your reading and experience, are key IT issues.

   a. Present these issues to IT managers in an organization to which you have access. (You may want

   to develop a questionnaire.) Have the managers vote on the importance of these items in their organization. (Instruct them that they can also add items, if appropriate.)

   b. Report the results. Try to explain the differences between this and the published studies.

3. Review the following systems in this chapter, and classify each system according to the triangle in Figure 2.5.

   Burlington Coat Factory Warehouse

   A-dec, Inc.

   Ford Motor Company

   Hershey Foods

INTERNET ACTIVITIES

1. Surf the Internet for information about airport security via bomb-detecting devices. Examine the available products, and comment on the IT techniques used.

2. Visit the site of American Airlines (*AA.com*). Find out how the Internet is being used for advertising, auctions, etc.

3. Enter the site of Hershey (*hersheys.com*). Examine the information about the company and its products and markets. Explain how an intranet helps such a company compete in the global market.

TEAM ACTIVITIES AND ROLE PLAYING

1. Observe a supermarket checkout counter that uses a scanner. Find some material that describes how the scanned code is translated into the price that the customers pay.

   a. Identify the following components of the system: inputs, processes, outputs, feedback.

   b. What kind of a system is this (TPS, DSS, EIS, MIS, etc.)? Why?

   c. Having the information about a product filed electronically in the system may provide opportunities for additional managerial uses. Identify such uses.

   d. Research and report on how such systems will be operating in the future. Describe them.

REAL-WORLD CASE   *hersheys.com*

Hershey Foods Enhances Group Work with an Intranet

The Business Problem   Hershey bars and kisses can be found on the shelves of convenience stores and supermarkets in about a hundred countries, competing with both local brands and brands from other countries. But the transportation cost and the low labor cost in many foreign countries are factors that reduce the competitiveness of Hershey in overseas markets.

The IT Solution   Hershey's use of a corporate intranet is helping compensate for the disadvantages imposed by transportation and labor costs. Recognizing the importance of group work, internal communication, and collaboration, the company set up a Director of Corporate Communications position. The director initiated a Web site as early as 1994 and also created a comprehensive corporate intranet in 1996. Since then, Hershey has developed the following intranet applications: Most corporate internal communications are now paperless, training materials are delivered to the desktops of employees, and the intranet includes e-mail and software to support the work of groups (such as video teleconferencing). In addition to training, the HRM department uses the intranet extensively to manage its fringe benefits, broadcast available job openings to all employees, and publish an electronic newsletter about corporate people and events.

The Results   Hershey now runs one of the most efficient food-processing businesses in the world. By 1999, more than 4,000 key employees were on the intranet. Corporate information such as annual reports, press re-

leases, information on quality, and internal newsletters are published electronically, saving paper and delivery cost. All departments have their own home pages. This enables improved communications and collaboration within and among departments.

John Long, Director of Corporate Communications, said that to him the corporate intranet is much more exciting than the Internet since there is a greater opportunity to defray costs and measure the system's worth. All in all, Hershey's intranet helps the company produce high-quality products at a low cost, easing its competitiveness problem and enabling it to capitalize on new markets worldwide.

Questions

1. How does the intranet-based system support the human resources management function at Hershey?

2. How is collaborative (group or team) work hindered by having group members in different locations and/or time zones?

3. Who is communicating with whom at Hershey? That is, what kinds of groups or teams might be assembled for what kinds of projects or problems?

4. What is it about the Internet that makes *intranets* popular as a basis for groupware? (*Hint:* How many people do you know who are comfortable using a common Internet browser and other functionalities of the Internet, like search engines? What about the perceived reliability of the Internet?)

VIRTUAL COMPANY ASSIGNMENT

wiley.com/college/turban

Extreme Descent Snowboards

Background Jacob March summons you to his office. Jacob greets you with a smile and a handshake. He asks you to take a seat at the small conference table.

After a brief period of small talk, Jacob reviews your preliminary report about Extreme Descent Snowboards (EDS). He asks if you have any further questions. Jacob commends you on a job well done. He further explains that your IS internship should provide you with valuable insight concerning the role and use of information technology throughout the functional areas of an organization.

Jacob wants you to gain an appreciation for the interdisciplinary nature of the information systems field and how the various functional areas within an organization are related and depend on each other.

*www.wiley.com/
college/turban*

Assignment

Prepare and submit a report that addresses the following questions and issues.

1. Define TPS, MIS, DSS.

Visit the EDS Web site and corporate intranet site to answer the following questions.

2. Identify TPS, MIS, and DSS systems of the EDS Corporation.

3. Who are the users for each type of information system?

3

COMPUTER HARDWARE

CHAPTER PREVIEW

Understanding the fundamentals of the technical components of information systems is an essential first step in understanding the strategic role of information systems in modern organizations. An obvious technical component is the physical computing machinery, known as hardware. In this chapter we will see that hardware is more than just the computer itself—it includes a variety of related technologies involved with getting data into and out of the computer. The information in this chapter not only will provide a foundation for understanding the rest of the text, but it also will help you make informed decisions about personal and professional computing technology.

CHAPTER OUTLINE

3.1 The Significance of Hardware
3.2 The Central Processing Unit
3.3 Computer Memory
3.4 Computer Hierarchy
3.5 Input Technologies
3.6 Output Technologies
3.7 Strategic Hardware Issues

LEARNING OBJECTIVES

1. Identify the major hardware components of a computer system.
2. Describe the design and functioning of the central processing unit.
3. Discuss the relationships between microprocessor component designs and performance.
4. Describe the main types of primary and secondary storage.
5. Distinguish between primary and secondary storage along the dimensions of speed, cost, and capacity.
6. Define enterprise storage and describe the various types of enterprise storage.
7. Describe the hierarchy of computers according to power and their respective roles.
8. Differentiate the various types of input and output technologies and their uses.
9. Describe what multimedia systems are and what technologies they use.
10. Discuss strategic issues that link hardware design and innovation to competitive business strategy.

COMBINING MAINFRAMES AND E-COMMERCE

The Business Problem

ABF Freight System, Inc.® (ABF) is a less-than-truckload (LTL) transportation company in Fort Smith, Arkansas. LTL carriers such as ABF® and competitor Roadway Express fill the niche between parcel carriers like Federal Express and full-truckload carriers like JB Hunt that specialize in huge shipments. Competition also comes from virtual companies, such as Freightquote.com and Transportation.com.

LTL carriers ship general commodities. Their core customers are businesses, not consumers. These carriers calculate prices for each shipment using variables such as weight, volume, distance, and the number of boxes. LTL carriers typically offer discounts on most shipments, often making custom quotes to win jobs. ABF® wanted to leverage the Internet to be able to keep up with rapidly changing business conditions and to offer an accurate price to customers without reinventing mainframe applications.

ABF Freight Systems® trucks can be tracked via a new e-commerce infrastructure.

The IT Solution

ABF Freight System, Inc.® built an e-commerce infrastructure that runs on its IBM S/390 mainframe. The same mainframe applications that ABF® had used to calculate pricing, trace shipments, schedule routes, and review freight bills are now accessible via the e-commerce Web site, the intranet, devices enabled by Wireless Application Protocol (WAP), imaging software, and an interactive voice response (IVR) system.

At ABF®'s self-service Web site, dubbed eCenter®, customers map routes, trace shipments, schedule a pickup, and create a bill of lading (the formal document required for shipments). ABF® customers generate price quotes that include discounts, view images of shipment documents, and review damage claim status. The eCenter® also provides predictive e-mail alerts that offer progress reports of a shipment in transit and alert the customer if the shipment will be late.

eCenter® has several innovative features. The Shipment Planner™ displays pending shipments in a calendar format. A feature called Transparent Links lets ABF® customers incorporate shipping data from ABF®'s mainframe into their own systems via XML. ABF® Anywhere lets users communicate with ABF® with a Palm handheld device or mobile phone equipped with Internet access. Dynamic Rerouting lets customers change the destination of an in-transit shipment or recall a shipment by accessing ABF®'s Web site. ABF® then e-mails a confirmation of the new destination and revised charges.

Drivers en route check in at ABF® service stations in 311 locations until they arrive at the destination terminal, where the shipment is scheduled for delivery to the consignee's address. At each checkpoint, drivers submit documents (each with a bar code), such as the bill of lading, for scanning. The scanned images are uploaded via FTP over the wide area network (WAN) to a database on the mainframe located at company headquarters. This process creates a visual record.

The Results

ABF®'s e-commerce infrastructure has more than 23,000 registered users from more than 17,000 ABF® customers. These customers generate more than 70 percent of ABF®'s annual revenue and shipment volume. ABF®'s new e-commerce infrastructure enhances customer service, and has created a new business line and opened new markets for the company. The infrastructure also has revamped virtually everyone's job at ABF®, from how a regional vice president builds customer loyalty to how a customer service representative spends the day.

Source: Network World (February 26, 2001); abfs.com.

Selecting the right IT infrastructure for any business is a complex decision. Such a decision often entails "out of the box" thinking—that is, imagining how business processes could be ideally configured and supported—rather than incremental improvement of an outdated process. Indeed, ABF®'s e-commerce infrastructure is an outstanding example of old-to-new economy transformation. The company had a tremendous amount riding on its IT decision. In the LTL industry, superior system performance translates very quickly into customer satisfaction.

The same basic issues confront all organizations that use computing technology. Such decisions about information technology usually focus on three interrelated factors: capability (power and appropriateness for the task), speed, and cost. A computer's hardware design drives all three factors, and all three factors are interrelated and are much more complex than you might imagine.

The incredible rate of innovation in the computer industry further complicates IT decisions. The ABF® executives in this case had a difficult decision to make, because ABF® was already a going concern with an information technology already in place. Computer technologies can become obsolete much more quickly than other organizational technologies. Yet, regardless of industry, computer hardware is essential to survival, and the most modern hardware may be essential to sustaining advantage over competitors. Evaluating new hardware options and figuring out how to integrate them with existing (legacy) systems is an ongoing responsibility in most organizations.

Finally, almost any time an organization makes major changes in its computer infrastructure, much of its software needs to be rewritten to run on the hardware's new operating system. In some cases, all the data that a company has accumulated may have to be put into a different format. Personnel may have to be retrained on the new computers. These are very lengthy and expensive undertakings, often dwarfing basic hardware acquisition costs by tenfold. Therefore, computer hardware choices are generally made only after careful study. Many of the issues in such decision making involve employees from all functional areas and are the topics of this chapter.

3.1 THE SIGNIFICANCE OF HARDWARE

Most businesspeople rightly suspect that knowing how to use computer technology is more important to their personal productivity and their firm's competitive advantage than knowing the technical details of how the technology functions. But some basic understanding of computer hardware design and function is essential because organizations frequently must assess their competitive advantage in terms of computing capability. Important decisions about computing capability have to be made, and to a large degree these decisions turn on an understanding of hardware design. In this chapter you will learn the basics of hardware design and understand the sources of this capability.

Our objective is to demonstrate how computers input, process, output, and store information. We will also look at the hierarchy of computer hardware, from the super computer down to the handheld microcomputer and even some smaller technologies. Finally we will consider the dynamics of computer hardware innovation and the effects it has on organizational decision making.

An important benefit from reading this chapter will be that not only will you better understand the computer hardware decisions in your organization, but also your personal computing decisions will be much better informed. Many of the design principles presented here apply to any size computer, as do the dynamics of innovation and cost that affect personal as well as corporate hardware decisions.

As we noted in Chapter 1, computer-based information systems (CBISs) are composed of hardware, software, databases, telecommunications, procedures, and people. The components are organized to input, process, and output data and information. Chapter 3 focuses on the hardware component of the CBIS. *Hardware* refers to the physical equipment used for the input, processing, output, and storage activities of a computer system. It consists of the following:

- Central processing unit (CPU)
- Memory (primary and secondary storage)
- Input technologies
- Output technologies
- Communication technologies

The first four of these components are discussed in the following sections. Communication technologies is the subject of Chapter 7.

3.2   THE CENTRAL PROCESSING UNIT

The **central processing unit (CPU)** performs the actual computation or "number crunching" inside any computer. The CPU is a **microprocessor** (for example, a Pentium 4 by Intel) made up of millions of microscopic transistors embedded in a circuit on a silicon wafer or *chip*. (Hence, microprocessors are commonly referred to as chips.) Examples of specific microprocessors are listed in Table 3.1.

As shown in Figure 3.1 (on page 58), the microprocessor has different parts, which perform different functions. The **control unit** sequentially accesses program instructions, decodes them, and controls the flow of data to and from the ALU, the registers, the caches, primary storage, secondary storage, and various output devices. The **arithmetic-logic unit (ALU)** performs the mathematic calculations and makes logical comparisons. The **registers** are high-speed storage areas that store very small amounts of data and instructions for short periods of time. (For a more technical overview of the components of modern chips, see Modern Chip Components on the Web site.)

Intel's Pentium 4 microprocessor.

www.wiley.com/
college/turban

How the CPU Works

The CPU, on a basic level, operates like a tiny factory. Inputs come in and are stored until needed, at which point they are retrieved and processed and the output is

Table 3.1   Examples of Microprocessors

Name	Manufacturer	Word Length	Clock Speed (MHz)	Application
Pentium III	Intel	32	1000+	PCs and workstations
Pentium 4	Intel	64	2000+	PCs and workstations
PowerPC	Motorola, IBM, Apple	32	1000+	High-end PCs and workstations
Alpha	Compaq	64	1500+	PCs and workstations
Athlon	Advanced Micro Devices	32	1000+	PCs and workstations

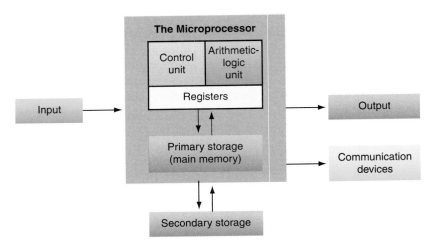

Figure 3.1   *Parts of a microprocessor.*

stored and then delivered somewhere. Figure 3.2 illustrates this process, which works as follows:

- The inputs are data and brief instructions about what to do with the data. These instructions come from software in other parts of the computer. Data might be entered by the user through the keyboard, for example, or read from a data file in another part of the computer. The inputs are stored in registers until they are sent to the next step in the processing.

- Data and instructions travel in the chip via electrical pathways called *buses*. The size of the bus—analogous to the width of a highway—determines how much information can flow at any time.

- The control unit directs the flow of data and instructions within the chip.

- The arithmetic-logic unit (ALU) receives the data and instructions from the registers and makes the desired computation. These data and instructions have been translated into **binary form**, that is, only 0s and 1s. The CPU can process only binary data.

- The data in their original form and the instructions are sent to storage registers and then are sent back to a storage place outside the chip, such as the computer's hard

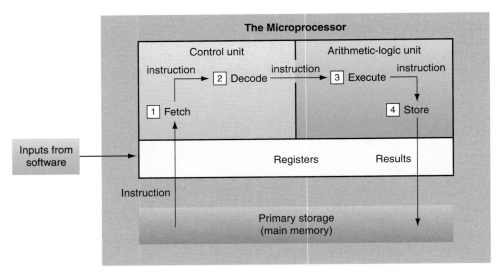

Figure 3.2   *How the CPU works.*

drive (discussed below). Meanwhile, the transformed data go to another register and then on to other parts of the computer (to the monitor for display, or to be stored, for example).

(For a more technical overview of CPU operations, see CPU Operations on the Web site.)

www.wiley.com/ college/turban

This cycle of processing, known as a **machine instruction cycle**, occurs millions of times per second or more. It is faster or slower, depending on the following four factors of chip design:

1. The preset speed of the clock that times all chip activities, measured in megahertz (MHz), millions of cycles per second, and gigahertz (GHz), billions of cycles per second. The faster the **clock speed**, the faster the chip. (For example, all other factors being equal, a 1.0 GHz chip is twice as fast as a 500 MHz chip.)

2. The **word length**, which is the number of bits (0s and 1s) that can be processed by the CPU at any one time. The majority of current chips handle 32-bit word lengths, and the Pentium 4 is designed to handle 64-bit word lengths. Therefore, the Pentium 4 chip will process 64 bits of data in one machine cycle. The larger the word length, the faster the chip.

3. The **bus width**. The wider the *bus* (the physical paths down which the data and instructions travel as electrical impulses), the more data can be moved and the faster the processing. A processor's *bus bandwidth* is the product of the width of its bus (measured in bits) times the frequency at which the bus transfers data (measured in megahertz). For example, Intel's Pentium 4 processor uses a 64-bit bus that runs at 400 MHz. That gives it a peak bandwidth of 3.2 gigabits per second.

4. The physical design of the chip. Back to our "tiny factory" analogy, if the "factory" is very compact and efficiently laid out, then "materials" (data and instructions) do not have far to travel while being stored or processed. We also want to pack as many "machines" (transistors) into the factory as possible. The distance between transistors is known as **line width**. Historically, line width has been expressed in microns (millionths of a meter), but as technology has advanced, it has become more convenient to express line width in nanometers (billionths of a meter). Currently, most CPUs are designed with 180-nanometer technology (0.18 microns), but chip manufacturers are moving to 130-nanometer technology (0.13 microns). The smaller the line width, the more transistors can be packed onto a chip, and the faster the chip.

These four factors make it difficult to compare the speeds of different processors. As a result, Intel and other chip manufacturers have developed a number of benchmarks to compare processor speeds. (For a discussion of these benchmarks, see the section on Processor Benchmarks on the Web site.)

www.wiley.com/ college/turban

Advances in Microprocessor Design

Innovations in chip designs are coming at a faster and faster rate, as described by **Moore's Law**. Gordon Moore, an Intel Corporation co-founder, predicted in 1965 that microprocessor complexity would double approximately every two years. As shown in Figure 3.3 (on page 60), his prediction was amazingly accurate.

The advances predicted from Moore's Law come mainly from the following changes:

- Increasing miniaturization of transistors.
- Making the physical layout of the chip's components as compact and efficient as possible (decreasing line width).

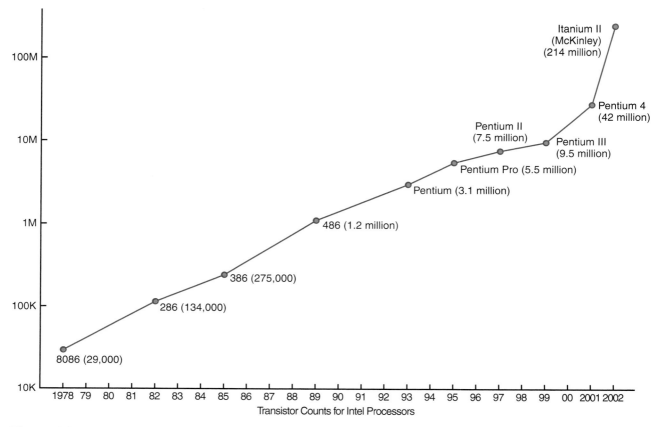

Figure 3.3 *Moore's Law as it relates to transistor counts in Intel microprocessors.*

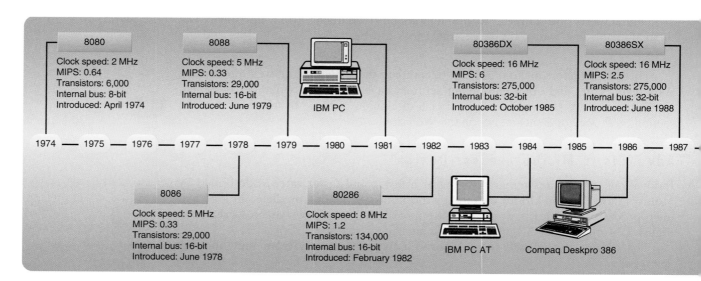

Figure 3.4 *The lineage of Intel microprocessors. [Diagram and content displayed from 1974–1993 reprinted from* PC Maga- *zine (April 27, 1993), with permission. Copyright (c) 1993, ZD, Inc. All rights reserved. Diagram and content displayed for dates beyond 1993 based on data from Intel, added by the authors to show Intel microprocessing trends through 2001.]*

- Using materials for the chip that improve the *conductivity* (flow) of electricity. The traditional silicon is a semiconductor of electricity—electrons can flow through it at a certain rate. New materials such as *gallium arsenide* and *silicon germanium* allow even faster electron travel and some additional benefits, although they are more expensive to manufacture than silicon chips.

- Targeting the amount of basic instructions programmed into the chip. There are four broad categories of microprocessor architecture: *complex instruction set computing (CISC), reduced instruction set computing (RISC), very long instruction word (VLIW)*, and the newest category, *explicitly parallel instruction computing (EPIC)*. Most chips are designated as CISC and have very comprehensive instructions, directing every aspect of chip functioning. RISC chips eliminate rarely used instructions. Computers that use RISC chips (for example, a workstation devoted to high-speed mathematical computation) rely on their software to contain the special instructions. VLIW architectures reduce the number of instructions on a chip by lengthening each instruction. With EPIC architectures, the processor can execute certain program instructions in parallel. Intel's Pentium 4 is the first implementation of EPIC architecture. (For a more technical discussion of these architectures, see Microprocessor Architectures on the Web site.)

www.wiley.com/college/turban

In addition to increased speeds and performance, Moore's Law has had an impact on costs. For example, in 1998, a personal computer with a 16 MHz Intel 80386 chip, one megabyte of RAM (discussed later in this chapter), a 40-megabyte hard disk (discussed later in this chapter), and a DOS 3.31 operating system (discussed in Chapter 4), cost $5,200. In 2002, a personal computer with a 2 GHz Intel Pentium 4 chip, 512 megabytes of RAM, an 80-gigabyte hard disk, and the Windows XP operating system, cost less than $1,000 (without the monitor).

Although organizations certainly benefit from microprocessors that are faster, they also benefit from chips that are less powerful but can be made very small and inexpensive. **Microcontrollers** are chips that are embedded in countless products and technologies, from cellular telephones to toys to automobile sensors. Microprocessors and microcontrollers are similar except that microcontrollers usually cost less and

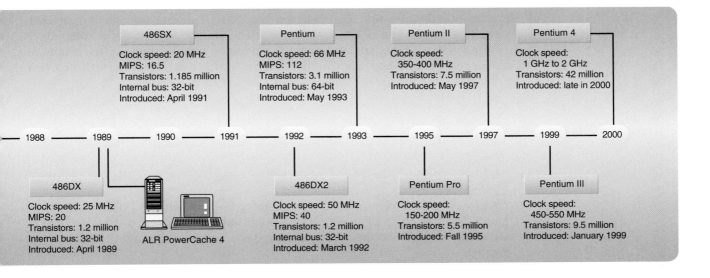

work in less-demanding applications. Thus, the scientific advances in CPU design affect many organizations on the product and service side, not just on the internal CBIS side.

Figure 3.4 (on pages 60–61) illustrates the historical advancement of Intel microprocessors. New types of chips continue to be produced. (For a discussion of advanced chip technologies, see Advanced Chip Technologies on the Web site.)

www.wiley.com/
college/turban

Before you go on . . .

1. Briefly describe how a microprocessor functions.

2. What factors determine the speed of the microprocessor?

3. How are microprocessor designs advancing?

3.3 COMPUTER MEMORY

The amount and type of memory that a computer possesses has a great deal to do with its general utility, often affecting the type of program it can run and the work it can do, its speed, and both the cost of the machine and the cost of processing data. There are two basic categories of computer memory. The first is *primary storage*, so named because small amounts of data and information that will be immediately used by the CPU are stored there. The second is *secondary storage*, where much larger amounts of data and information (an entire software program, for example) are stored for extended periods of time.

Memory Capacity

As already noted, CPUs process only 0s and 1s. All data are translated through computer languages (covered in the next chapter) into series of these binary digits, or **bits**. A particular combination of bits represents a certain alphanumeric character or simple mathematical operation. Eight bits are needed to represent any one of these characters. This 8-bit string is known as a **byte**. The storage capacity of a computer is measured in bytes. (Bits are used as units of measure typically only for telecommunications capacity, as in how many million bits per second can be sent through a particular medium.) The hierarchy of byte memory capacity is as follows:

- *Kilobyte.* *Kilo* means one thousand, so a kilobyte (KB) is approximately one thousand bytes. Actually, a kilobyte is 1,024 bytes (2^{10} bytes).

- *Megabyte.* *Mega* means one million, so a megabyte (MB) is approximately one million bytes (1,048,576 bytes, or 1,024 × 1,024, to be exact). Most personal computers have hundreds of megabytes of RAM memory (a type of primary storage, discussed in a later section).

- *Gigabyte.* *Giga* means one billion; a gigabyte (GB) is actually 1,073,741,824 bytes (1,024 × 1,024 × 1,024 bytes). The storage capacity of a hard drive (a type of secondary storage, discussed shortly) in modern personal computers is often many gigabytes.

- *Terabyte.* One trillion bytes (actually, 1,078,036,791,296 bytes) is a terabyte.

To get a feel for these amounts, consider the following examples. If your computer has 256 MB of RAM (a type of primary storage), it can store 268,435,456 bytes of data. A written word might, on average, contain 6 bytes, so this translates to approximately 44.8 million words. If your computer has 20 GB of storage capacity on the hard drive (a type of secondary storage) and the average page of text has about 2,000 bytes, your hard drive could store some 10 million pages of text.

Primary Storage

Primary storage, or *main memory*, as it is sometimes called, stores for very brief periods of time three types of information: data to be processed by the CPU, instructions for the CPU as to how to process the data, and operating system programs that manage various aspects of the computer's operation. Primary storage takes place in chips mounted on the computer's main circuit board (the *motherboard*), located as close as physically possible to the CPU chip. (See Figure 3.5.) As with the CPU, all the data and instructions in primary storage have been translated into binary code.

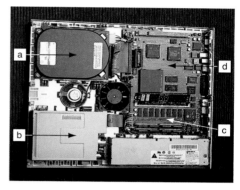

There are four main types of primary storage: (1) register, (2) random access memory (RAM), (3) cache memory, and (4) read-only memory (ROM). To understand their purpose, consider the following analogy: You keep a Swiss Army knife handy in your pocket for minor repairs around the house. You have a toolbox with an assortment of tools in the kitchen cabinet for bigger jobs. Finally, in the garage you have your large collection of tools. The amount and type of tools you need, how often you need them, and whether you will use them immediately determines how and where you store them. In addition, one type of storage area—like a fireproof wall safe—must be completely safe, so that its contents cannot be lost. The logic of primary storage in the computer is just like the logic of storing things in your house. That which will be used immediately gets stored in very small amounts as close to the CPU as possible. Remember, as with CPU chip design, the shorter the distance the electrical impulses (data) have to travel, the faster they can be transported and processed. That which requires special protection will be stored in an exceptionally secure manner. The four types of primary storage, which follow this logic, are described next.

Figure 3.5 *Internal workings of a common personal computer. (a) Hard disk drive; (b) floppy disk drive; (c) RAM; (d) CPU board with fan.*

Registers.   As indicated earlier in the chapter, **registers** are part of the CPU. They have the least capacity, storing extremely limited amounts of instructions and data only immediately before and after processing. This is analogous to your pocket in the Swiss Army knife example.

Random access memory.   **Random access memory (RAM)** is analogous to the kitchen toolbox. It stores more information than the registers (your pocket) and is farther away from the CPU, but it stores less than secondary storage (the garage) and is much closer to the CPU than is secondary storage. When you start most software programs on your computer, the entire program is brought from secondary storage into RAM. As you use the program, small parts of the program's instructions and data are sent into the registers and then to the CPU. Again, getting the data and instructions as close to the CPU as possible is key to the computer's speed, as is the fact that the RAM is a type of microprocessor chip. As we shall discuss later, the chip is much faster (and more costly) than are secondary storage devices.

RAM is temporary and *volatile*; that is, RAM chips lose their contents if the current is lost or turned off (as in a power surge, brownout, or electrical noise generated by lightning or nearby machines). RAM chips are located directly on the computer's main circuit board or in other chips located on peripheral cards that plug into the main circuit board.

The two main types of RAM are *dynamic RAM (DRAM)* and *static RAM (SRAM)*. DRAM memory chips offer the greatest capacities and the lowest cost per bit, but are relatively slow. SRAM costs more than DRAM but has a higher level of performance, making SRAM the preferred choice for performance-sensitive applications, including the external L2 and L3 caches (discussed next) that speed up microprocessor performance.

Cache memory.   **Cache memory** is a type of high-speed memory that a processor can access more rapidly than main memory (RAM). It augments RAM in the following way: Many modern computer applications (Microsoft XP, for example) are very complex and have huge numbers of instructions. It takes considerable RAM capacity (usually a minimum of 128 megabytes) to store the entire instruction set. Or you may be using an application that exceeds your RAM. In either case, your processor must go to secondary storage (similar to a lengthy trip to the garage) to retrieve the necessary instructions. To alleviate this problem, software is often written in smaller blocks of instructions. As needed, these blocks can be brought from secondary storage into RAM. This process is still slow, however.

Cache memory is a place closer to the CPU where the computer can temporarily store those blocks of instructions used most often. Blocks used less often remain in RAM until they are transferred to cache; blocks used infrequently stay stored in secondary storage. Cache memory is faster than RAM because the instructions travel a shorter distance to the CPU. In our tool analogy, cache memory might represent an additional box with a selected set of needed tools from the kitchen toolbox and the garage.

There are two types of cache memory in the majority of computer systems—Level 1 (L1) cache is located in the processor, and Level 2 (L2) cache is located on the motherboard but not actually in the processor. L1 cache is smaller and faster than L2 cache. Chip manufacturers are now designing chips with L1 cache and L2 cache in the processor and Level 3 (L3) cache on the motherboard.

Read-only memory.   In our previous example, we alluded to the need for greater security when storing certain types of critical data or instructions. (This was represented by the wall safe.) Most people who use computers have lost precious data at one time or another due to a computer "crash" or a power failure. What is usually lost is whatever is in RAM, cache, or the registers at the time. This loss occurs because these types of memory are **volatile**. Whatever information they may contain is lost when there is no electricity flowing through them. The cautious computer user frequently saves his or her data to **nonvolatile** memory (secondary storage). In addition, most modern software applications have autosave functions. Programs stored in secondary storage, even though they are temporarily copied into RAM when used, remain intact because only the copy is lost and not the original.

"Oops! I just deleted all your files. Can you repeat everything you've ever told me?"

Read-only memory (ROM) is the place (a type of chip) where certain critical instructions are safeguarded. ROM is nonvolatile and retains these instructions when the power to the computer is turned off. The read-only designation means that these instructions can be read only by the computer and cannot be changed by the user. An example of ROM instructions are those needed to start or "boot" the computer once it has been shut off. There are variants of ROM chips that can be programmed (PROM), and some that can be erased and rewritten (EPROM). These are relatively rare in mainstream organizational computing, but are often incorporated into other specialized technologies such as video games (PROM) or robotic manufacturing (EPROM).

Another form of rewritable ROM storage is called **flash memory**. This technology can be built into a system or installed on a personal computer card (known as a *flash card*). These cards, though they have limited capacity, are compact, portable, and require little energy to read and write. Flash memory via flash cards is very popular for small portable technologies such as cellular telephones, digital cameras, handheld computers, and other consumer products.

Secondary Storage

Secondary storage is designed to store very large amounts of data for extended periods of time. Secondary storage can have memory capacity of several terabytes or more and only small portions of that data are placed in primary storage at any one time. Secondary storage has the following characteristics:

- It is nonvolatile.
- It takes much more time to retrieve data from secondary storage than it does from RAM because of the electromechanical nature of secondary storage devices.
- It is much more cost effective than primary storage (see Figure 3.6).
- It can take place on a variety of media, each with its own technology, as discussed next.
- The overall trends in secondary storage are toward more direct-access methods, higher capacity with lower costs, and increased portability.

Magnetic media.   **Magnetic tape** is kept on a large open reel or in a smaller cartridge or cassette. Although this is an old technology, it remains popular because it is the cheapest storage medium and can handle enormous amounts of data. The downside is that it is the slowest for retrieval of data, because all the data are placed on the tape sequentially. **Sequential access** means that the system might have to run through the majority of the tape, for example, before it comes to the desired piece of data. Magnetic media store information by giving tiny particles of iron oxide embedded on the tape a positive or negative polarization. Recall that all data that a computer understands are binary. The positive or negative polarization of the particles corresponds to a 0 or a 1.

Magnetic tape storage often is used for information that an organization must maintain, but uses rarely or does not need immediate access to. Industries with huge numbers of files (e.g., insurance companies), use magnetic tape systems. Modern versions of magnetic tape systems use cartridges and often a robotic system that selects and loads the appropriate cartridge automatically. There are also some tape systems,

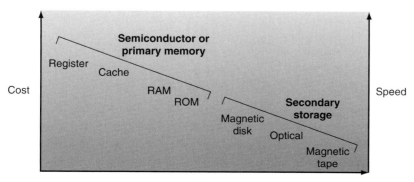

Figure 3.6 *Primary memory compared to secondary storage.*

like digital audio tapes (DAT), for smaller applications such as storing copies of all the contents of a personal computer's secondary storage ("backing up" the storage).

Magnetic disks come in a variety of styles and are popular because they allow much more rapid access to the data than does magnetic tape. Magnetic disks, called *hard disks* or fixed disk drives, are the most commonly used mass storage devices because of their low cost, high speed, and large storage capacity. Fixed disk drives read from, and write to, stacks of rotating magnetic disk platters mounted in rigid enclosures and sealed against environmental or atmospheric contamination. These disks are permanently mounted in a unit that may be internal or external to the computer.

All disk drives (including removable disk modules, floppy disk drives, and optical drives) are called **hard drives** and store data on platters divided into concentric tracks. Each track is divided further into segments called *sectors*. To access a given sector, a read/write head pivots across the rotating disks to locate the right track, calculated from an index table, and the head then waits as the disk rotates until the right sector is underneath it. (For a more technical discussion of hard disk drives, see Hard Disk Drives on the Web site.)

Every piece of data has an address attached to it, corresponding to a particular track and sector. Any piece of desired data can be retrieved in a nonsequential manner, by **direct access** (which is why hard disk drives are sometimes called *direct access storage devices*). The read/write heads use the data's address to quickly find and read the data. (See Figure 3.7.) Unlike magnetic tape, the system does not have to read through all the data to find what it wants.

The read/write heads are attached to arms that hover over the disks, moving in and out (see Figure 3.8). They read the data when positioned over the correct track and when the correct sector spins by. Because the head floats just above the surface of the disk (less than 25 microns), any bit of dust or contamination can disrupt the device. When this happens, it is called a disk crash and usually results in catastrophic loss of data. For this reason, hard drives are hermetically sealed when manufactured.

A modern personal computer typically has many gigabytes (some more than 100 gigabytes) of storage capacity in its internal hard drive. Data access is very fast, measured in milliseconds. For these reasons, hard disk drives are popular and common. Because they are somewhat susceptible to mechanical failure, and because users may need to take all their hard drive's contents to another location, many users like to back up their hard drive's contents with a portable hard disk drive system, such as Iomega's Jaz.

Disk drive interfaces. To take advantage of the new, faster technologies, disk drive interfaces must also be faster. Most PCs and workstations use one of two

www.wiley.com/
college/turban

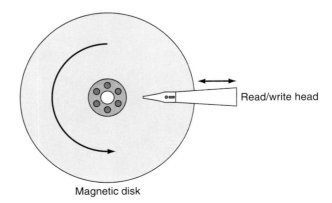

Figure 3.7 *Magnetic disk drive.*

Read/write head

Magnetic disk

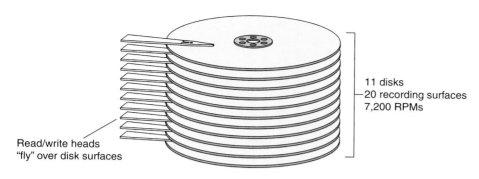

11 disks
20 recording surfaces
7,200 RPMs

Read/write heads
"fly" over disk surfaces

Figure 3.8   *Read/write heads.*

high-performance disk interface standards: **Enhanced Integrated Drive Electronics (EIDE)** or **Small Computer Systems Interface (SCSI)**. EIDE offers good performance, is inexpensive, and supports up to four disks, tapes, or CD-ROM drives. SCSI drives are more expensive than EIDE drives, but they offer a faster interface and support more devices. SCSI interfaces are therefore used for graphics workstations, server-based storage, and large databases. (For discussions of other interfaces, including fibre channel, firewire, Infiniband, and the universal serial bus, see Other Interfaces on the Web site.)

www.wiley.com/
college/turban

Magnetic diskettes.   **Magnetic diskettes**, or *floppy disks* as they are commonly called, function similarly to hard drives, but with some key differences. The most obvious is that they are not rigid, but are made out of flexible Mylar. They are much slower than hard drives. They have much less capacity, ranging from 1.44 megabytes for a standard high-density disk to 250 megabytes for a disk formatted for a Zip drive (on which the data are compressed). Further, although they are individually inexpensive, floppy disks are less cost-efficient than hard drive storage. However, the big advantage of floppy disks has been that they are portable. Hard disk drives are usually permanently installed in a computer, but the small, removable diskette (installed in its thin plastic housing) can fit into a shirt pocket and can be easily mailed.

Optical storage devices.   Unlike magnetic media, **optical storage devices** do not store data via magnetism. As shown in Figure 3.9, to record information on these devices, a pinpoint laser beam is used to burn tiny holes into the surface of a reflective plastic platter (such as a compact disk). When the information is read, another laser, installed in the optical disk drive of the computer (such as a compact disk drive), shines on the surface of the disk. If light is reflected, that corresponds to one binary state. If the light shines on one of the holes burned by the recording laser, there is no reflection

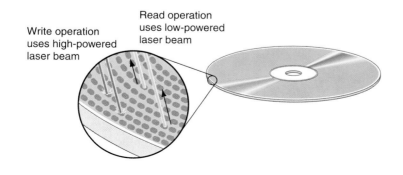

Write operation
uses high-powered
laser beam

Read operation
uses low-powered
laser beam

Figure 3.9   *Optical storage device.*

and the other binary state is read. Compared to magnetic media, optical disk drives are slower than magnetic hard drives. On the other hand, they are much less susceptible to damage from contamination and are also less fragile.

In addition, optical disks can store much more information, both on a routine basis and also when combined into storage systems. Optical disk storage systems can be used for large-capacity data storage. These technologies, known as **optical jukeboxes**, store many disks and operate much like the automated phonograph record changers for which they are named.

Types of optical disks include compact disk read-only memory (CD-ROM), digital video disk (DVD), and fluorescent multilayer disk (FMD-ROM).

Compact disk, read-only memory (CD-ROM) storage devices feature high capacity, low cost, and high durability. However, because it is a read-only medium, the CD-ROM can be only read and not written on. Compact disk, rewritable (CD-RW) adds rewritability to the recordable compact disk market, which previously had offered only write-once CD-ROM technology.

The **digital video disk (DVD)** is a five-inch disk with the capacity to store about 135 minutes of digital video. DVD provides sharp detail, true color, no flicker, and no snow. Sound is recorded in digital Dolby, creating clear "surround-sound" effects. DVDs have advantages over videocassettes, including better quality, smaller size (meaning they occupy less shelf space), and lower duplicating costs. DVDs can also perform as computer storage disks, providing storage capabilities of 17 gigabytes. DVD players can read current CD-ROMs, but current CD-ROM players cannot read DVDs. The access speed of a DVD drive is faster than a typical CD-ROM drive.

A new optical storage technology called **fluorescent multilayer disk (FMD-ROM)** greatly increases storage capacity. The idea of using multiple layers on an optical disk is not new, as DVDs currently support two layers. However, by using a new fluorescent-based optical system, FMDs can support 20 layers or more. FMDs are clear disks; in the layers are fluorescent materials that give off light. The presence or absence of these materials tells the drive whether there is information there or not. All layers of an FMD can be read in parallel, thereby increasing the data transfer rate.

Memory cards.   PC **memory cards** are credit-card-size devices that can be installed in an adapter or slot in many personal computers. The PC memory card functions as if it were a fixed hard disk drive. The cost per megabyte of storage is greater than for traditional hard disk storage, but the cards do have advantages. They are less failure-prone than hard disks, are portable, and are relatively easy to use. Software manufacturers often store the instructions for their programs on a memory card for use with laptop computers. The Personal Computer Memory Card International Association (PCMCIA) is a group of computer manufacturers who are creating standards for these memory cards.

Expandable storage.   **Expandable storage devices** are removable disk cartridges. The storage capacity ranges from 100 megabytes to several gigabytes per cartridge, and the access speed is similar to that of an internal hard drive. Although more expensive than internal hard drives, expandable storage devices combine hard disk storage capacity and diskette portability. Expandable storage devices are ideal for backup of the internal hard drive, as they can hold more than 80 times as much data and operate five times faster than existing floppy diskette drives.

www.wiley.com/
college/turban

Advanced storage technologies.   (For an overview of advanced storage technologies, see the section on Advanced Storage Technologies on the Web site.)

Enterprise Storage Systems

The amount of digital information is doubling every two years. As a result, many companies are employing enterprise storage systems.

An **enterprise storage system** is an independent, external system with intelligence that includes two or more storage devices. These systems are an alternative to allowing each host or server to manage its own storage devices directly. Enterprise storage systems provide large amounts of storage, high-performance data transfer, a high degree of availability, protection against data loss, and sophisticated management tools. (For a technical discussion of enterprise storage systems, see the section on Enterprise Storage Systems on the Web site.)

 www.wiley.com/college/turban

There are three major types of enterprise storage systems: redundant arrays of independent disks (RAIDs), storage area networks (SANs), and network-attached storage (NAS).

Redundant array of independent disks.   Hard drives in all computer systems are susceptible to failures caused by temperature variations, head crashes, motor failure, controller failure, and changing voltage conditions. To improve reliability and protect the data in their enterprise storage systems, many computer systems use **redundant arrays of independent disks (RAID)** storage products.

RAID links groups of standard hard drives to a specialized microcontroller. The microcontroller coordinates the drives so they appear as a single logical drive, but they take advantage of the multiple physical drives by storing data redundantly, thus protecting against data loss due to the failure of any single drive.

Storage area network.   A **storage area network (SAN)** is an architecture for building special, dedicated networks that allow rapid and reliable access to storage devices by multiple servers. **Storage over IP**, sometimes called *IP over SCSI* or *iSCSI*, is a technology that uses the Internet Protocol to transport stored data between devices within a SAN. **Storage visualization software** is used with SANs to graphically plot an entire network and allow storage administrators to view the properties of, and monitor, all devices from a single console.

Network-attached storage.   A **network-attached storage (NAS)** device is a special-purpose server that provides file storage to users who access the device over a network. The NAS server is simple to install (i.e., plug-and-play), and works exactly like a general-purpose file server, so no user retraining or special software is needed.

Table 3.2 (on page 70) compares the advantages and disadvantages of the various secondary storage media.

Storage Service Providers

Storage service providers (SSPs), also called storage-on-demand or storage utilities, provide customers with the storage capacity they require as well as professional services including assessment, design, operations, and management. Services offered by SSPs include primary online data storage, backup and restorability, availability, and accessibility.

SSPs offer the advantages of implementing storage solutions quickly and managing storage around-the-clock, even if the storage devices are located at the customer's data center. However, there is some increased security risk associated with moving an enterprise's data off-site.

Table 3.2   Secondary Storage

Type	Advantages	Disadvantages	Application
Magnetic storage devices:			
Magnetic tape	Lowest cost per unit stored	Sequential access means slow retrieval speeds	Corporate data archiving
Hard drive	Relatively high capacity and fast retrieval speed	Fragile; high cost per unit stored	Personal computers through mainframes
RAID	High capacity; designed for fault tolerance and reduced risk of data loss; low cost per unit stored	Expensive, semipermanent installation	Corporate data storage that requires frequent, rapid access
SAN	High capacity; designed for large amounts of enterprise data	Expensive	Corporate data storage that requires frequent, rapid access
NAS	High capacity; designed for large amounts of enterprise data	Expensive	Corporate data storage that requires frequent, rapid access
Magnetic diskettes	Low cost per diskette, portability	Low capacity; very high cost per unit stored; fragile	Personal computers
Memory cards	Portable; easy to use; less failure prone than hard drives	Expensive	Personal and laptop computers
Expandable storage	Portable; high capacity	More expensive than hard drives	Backup of internal hard drive
Optical storage devices:			
CD-ROM	High capacity; moderate cost per unit stored; high durability	Slower retrieval speeds than hard drives; only certain types can be rewritten	Personal computers through corporate data storage
DVD	High capacity; moderate cost per unit stored	Slower retrieval speeds than hard drives	Personal computers through corporate data storage
FMD-ROM	Very high capacity; moderate cost per unit stored	Faster retrieval speeds than DVD or CD-ROM; slower retrieval speeds than hard drives	Personal computers through corporate data storage

Before you go on . . .

1. Describe the four main types of primary storage.

2. Describe different types of secondary storage.

3. How does primary storage differ from secondary storage in terms of speed, cost, and capacity?

4. Describe the three types of enterprise storage systems.

3.4　COMPUTER HIERARCHY

The traditional way of comparing classes of computers is by their processing power. Analysts typically divide computers (called the *platform* in the computer industry) into six categories: supercomputers, mainframes, midrange computers (minicomputers and servers), workstations, notebooks and desktop computers, and appliances. Recently, the lines between these categories have blurred. This section presents each class of computer, beginning with the most powerful and ending with the least powerful. We describe the computers and their respective roles in modern organizations. IT's About Business Box 3.1 gives an example of several different types of computers used in Formula One auto racing.

A supercomputer.

Supercomputers

The term **supercomputer** does not refer to a specific technology, but to the fastest computing engines available at any given time. Supercomputers generally address computationally demanding tasks on very large data sets. Rather than transaction processing and business applications—the forte of mainframes and other multiprocessing platforms—supercomputers typically run military and scientific applications, although their use for commercial applications, such as data mining, has been increasing. Supercomputers generally operate at 4 to 10 times faster than the next most powerful computer class, the mainframe. (For

---

IT's About Business

Box 3.1: Where the computers meet the road

Formula One racing is big business. Each racing team has a multimillion-dollar budget each season. The cars are high-tech, but the real high-tech machines are the computers and other information technologies that go into designing—and increasingly, controlling—the race cars. Formula One racing is perhaps the most technologically advanced sport in the world.

In 1991, the Williams British racing team introduced a revolutionary car combining a computer-controlled, semiautomatic gearbox with electronic traction control. That computerized car won the 1992 world championship.

For today's top Formula One racing teams, engineers draft car designs on numerous Sun workstations running computer-aided design software (discussed in Chapter 4). The car models are run through virtual wind tunnels simulated on a high-end Sun server.

On race day, roughly 120 sensors in the car monitor everything from engine temperature to the position of each wheel. The data from the sensors are relayed by microwave radio to servers that each team keeps trackside; about 1.2 gigabytes of information are recorded on each

lap. Engineers study the data and make instant decisions about when to bring the car in for a pit stop and what adjustments to make. The crew and the engineers can relay advice to the driver. Formula One teams have installed controls on the steering wheel that let the driver make mid-race changes to the car's transmission and power train.

The race data from the trackside servers is sent via high-speed Internet or satellite links to team headquarters. At the headquarters lab, laps are recorded and later replayed on a mainframe computer—or with a real car mounted on a *chassis dynamics rig*—to fine-tune the car's engineering. During races, the lab can send tips for tweaking a car's configuration to crews at the track.

Source: Business 2.0 (October 2001).

Questions

1. Identify the different types of computers used by Formula One racing teams.

2. Does what is learned in Formula One racing transfer to regular automobiles? Give examples.

www.wiley.com/
college/turban

a more technical overview of supercomputers, see the section on Supercomputers on the Web site.)

EXAMPLE

Supercomputers help analyze the Earth's crust.   Scientists know that the Earth's continental plates are constantly moving at a glacial pace over the planet's surface, but the complicated internal dynamics that cause this movement are unresolved. The Earth rids itself of the intense heat within its core through a massive circulation system of molten earth and solidified crust, powering the movement of the continental plates. Earlier computer models viewed the process in two dimensions—depth and horizontal extension—which is not a full 3-D representation of the Earth.

The scale is so huge that, until recently, scientists could not assemble computers powerful enough to process the immense amount of data necessary to realistically simulate the movement of the plates. Now, using a massively parallel supercomputer (4 gigaflops—4 billion floating point operations per second—of processing power) and specially designed modeling software, researchers at Princeton University in New Jersey have been moving toward the answer. They are working to understand the cycle of convection occurring deep inside the planet. The researchers' work could someday help scientists accurately predict earthquakes and volcanic eruptions. ●

Mainframe Computers

Although mainframe computers are increasingly viewed as just another type of server, albeit at the high end of the performance and reliability scales, they remain a distinct class of systems differentiated by hardware and software features. **Mainframes** remain popular in large enterprises for extensive computing applications that are accessed by thousands of users. Examples of mainframe applications include airline reservation systems, corporate payroll, and student grade calculation and reporting. Analysts predict that Internet-based computing will lead to continued growth in the mainframe market.

Mainframes are less powerful and generally less expensive than supercomputers. In 2000, mainframe capacity was priced at approximately $2,260 per MIP (millions of instructions per second), down significantly from $9,410 in 1997. Prices are expected to fall to $490 per MIP by 2004. This pricing pressure has forced two vendors of mainframe systems, Amdahl and Hitachi, out of the mainframe market, leaving only IBM as a vendor of traditional mainframe systems. IBM calls its mainframe computer series the eServer zSeries.

A mainframe system may have up to several gigabytes of primary storage. Online and offline secondary storage (see the discussion of Enterprise Storage Systems on page 69) may use high-capacity magnetic and optical storage media with capacities in

A mainframe computer.

the terabyte range. Typically, several hundreds or thousands of online computers can be linked to a mainframe. Today's most advanced mainframes perform at more than 2,500 MIPs and can handle up to one billion transactions per day.

Some large organizations that began moving away from mainframes toward distributed systems now are moving back toward mainframes because of their centralized administration, high reliability, and increasing flexibility. This process is called *recentralization*. The reasons for the shift include supporting the high transaction levels associated with e-commerce, reducing the total cost of ownership of distributed systems, simplifying administration, reducing support-personnel requirements, and improving system performance. In addition, host computing provides a secure, robust computing environment in which to run strategic, mission-critical applications. (Distributed computing and related topics are discussed in detail in Chapter 6.) (For a more technical discussion of mainframes, see the section on Mainframes on the Web site.)

www.wiley.com/ college/turban

EXAMPLE

Merrill Lynch's online information and customer service.   Merrill Lynch, with total client assets of more than $1.5 trillion, has a long history of mainframe computing for providing innovative client services. A new mainframe system plays a key role in delivering information via the company Web site, satisfying nearly 750,000 requests daily. To run its Web presence and to provide support for online Internet trading, Merrill Lynch uses an IBM mainframe with 8 gigabytes of random access memory. The mainframe also supports market data capture, feedback pages from customers, and secure portfolio downloads. Mainframe workloads at Merrill Lynch have increased 30 percent over the last few years. Internet activity, extended trading hours, and moving to stock-pricing decimalization are expected to further increase workloads. ●

Midrange Computers

There are two types of midrange computers, minicomputers and servers. **Minicomputers** are relatively small, inexpensive, and compact computers that perform the same functions as mainframe computers, but to a more limited extent. These computers are designed to accomplish specific tasks such as process control, scientific research, and engineering applications. Larger companies gain greater corporate flexibility by distributing data processing with minicomputers in organizational units instead of centralizing computing at one location. Minicomputers meet the needs of smaller organizations that would rather not utilize scarce corporate resources by purchasing larger, less scalable computer systems. IBM is the market leader in minicomputers with its eServer iSeries (formerly the AS/400).

EXAMPLE

Automated Training Systems moves to the Internet.   Automated Training Systems (ATS) produces training products for midrange computer users, which consist of audiocassette media and workbooks. ATS packages, developed for in-house training, allow learning when convenient for students, and they virtually eliminate many of the problems normally associated with training new users (time away from the job, scheduling, and travel). ATS uses an IBM iSeries minicomputer to run its Web site. The company modified its order-entry application with a browser interface to provide its customers with information and the ability to place orders over the Internet. Since the implementation of its Internet project, ATS is receiving orders and inquiries from all over the world. In response to demand, ATS is currently working to translate its courses into Japanese and Chinese. ATS has significantly improved its customer service and support while reducing its overall costs. The company's president notes that ATS received enough orders in one day over the Internet to recover its entire investment in hardware. ●

Smaller types of midrange computers, called **servers**, typically support computer networks, enabling users to share files, software, peripheral devices, and other network resources. Servers have large amounts of primary and secondary storage and powerful CPUs.

Servers provide the hardware for e-commerce. They deliver Web pages and process purchase and sales transactions. Organizations with heavy e-commerce requirements and very large Web sites are running their Web and e-commerce applications on multiple servers in **server farms**. Server farms are large groups of servers maintained by an organization or by a commercial vendor and made available to customers.

As companies pack greater numbers of servers in their server farms, they are using pizza-box-size servers called *rack servers* that can be stacked in racks. These computers run cooler, and therefore can be packed more closely, requiring less space. To further increase density, companies are using a server design called a blade. A *blade* is a card about the size of a paperback book on which memory, processor, and hard drives are mounted.

EXAMPLE

Immunet: Using the Web to combat AIDS.   Immunet uses the Web to help fight HIV and AIDS. Because HIV and AIDS research evolves so rapidly, medical personnel must rely on accredited Continuing Medical Education (CME) courses to keep on top of the latest developments, medications, and treatment protocols. Immunet offers accredited CME courses online.

In addition, while AIDS treatment is covered by health plans, many of these do not specify which doctors specialize in AIDS. Patients are often required to seek referrals from multiple doctors before finding the right one. In some cases, these issues must first be discussed with human resources personnel who administer health benefit plans—an uncomfortable option for many seeking help. Immunet provides automated searches and matches between patients and doctors.

Having acquired two new domain names, *aids.edu* and *aids.org*, Immunet chose IBM Netfinity servers because they provided reliability and availability to enable the company to manage its Web sites. Immunet now has a comprehensive Web site that monthly serves more than 80,000 visitors from more than 155 countries. ●

Workstations

Computer vendors originally developed desktop engineering workstations, or *workstations* for short, to provide the high levels of performance demanded by engineers. That is, workstations run computationally intensive scientific, engineering, and financial applications. **Workstations** are typically based on *RISC* (reduced instruction set computing) *architecture* and provide both very high-speed calculations and high-resolution graphic displays. These computers have found widespread acceptance within the scientific community and, more recently, within the business community. Workstation applications include electronic and mechanical design, medical imaging, scientific visualization, 3-D animation, and video editing. By the second half of the 1990s, many workstation features were commonplace in PCs, blurring the distinction between workstations and personal computers.

Microcomputers

Microcomputers (also called *micros*, **personal computers**, or **PCs**) are the smallest and least expensive category of general-purpose computers. They can be subdivided into four classifications based on their size: desktops, thin clients, notebooks and laptops, and mobile devices.

Desktop PCs.   The **desktop personal computer** has become the dominant method of accessing workgroup and enterprisewide applications. It is the typical, familiar microcomputer system that has become a standard tool for business, and, increasingly, the home. It is usually modular in design, with separate but connected monitor, keyboard, and CPU. In general, modern microcomputers have between 64 megabytes and 512 megabytes of primary storage, one 3.5-inch floppy drive, a CD-ROM (or DVD) drive, and up to 100 gigabytes or more of secondary storage.

Most desktop systems currently use Intel 32-bit technology (but are moving to 64-bit technology), running some version of Windows. The exception is the Apple Macintosh, which runs Mac OS (operating system) on a PowerPC processor. Apple offers two desktop Macintosh systems, the high-performance Power Mac G4 series and the entry-level iMac series.

Thin-client systems.   **Thin-client systems** are desktop computer systems that do not offer the full functionality of a PC. Compared to a PC, thin clients are less complex, particularly because they lack locally installed software, and thus are easier and less expensive to operate and support than PCs. The benefits of thin clients include fast application deployment, centralized management, lower cost of ownership, and easier installation, management, maintenance, and support. Disadvantages include user resistance and the need to upgrade servers and buy additional server applications and licenses. One type of thin client is the *terminal*, allowing the user to only access an application running on a server.

Another type of thin client is a **network computer**, which is a system that provides access to Internet-based applications via a Web browser and can download software, usually in the form of Java applets. With PC vendors lowering their systems costs and simplifying maintenance, NCs remain niche products. However, vendors continue to manufacture thin-client systems for use at retail stations, kiosks, and other sites that require access to corporate repositories but little desktop functionality. Industry experts predicted that the PC would give way to network computers, but as IT's About Business Box 3.2 (on page 76) shows, that has not been the case. Table 3.3 (on page 76) compares the classes of computers discussed so far.

Laptop and notebook computers.   As computers become much smaller and vastly more powerful, they become portable, and new ways of using them open up. **Laptop and notebook computers** are small, easily transportable, lightweight microcomputers that fit easily into a briefcase. They are designed for maximum convenience and transportability, allowing access to processing power and data outside an office environment. Manager's Checklist 3.1 (on page 77) compares the trade-offs between desktop and portable PCs.

A notebook computer.

IT's About Business   MIS

Box 3.2: Predictions of the death of PCs were exaggerated

Conventional wisdom says that the personal computer is a $1,000 commodity with too much processing power, too much memory, too much storage, and an unhealthy dependence on Windows and a Web browser. But in a survey, three-quarters of IT executives said that the PC will remain their main desktop computer for the next five years.

The GartnerGroup (a marketing research group that often studies IT trends) predicted that 20 percent of the desktop market would be thin clients by the end of 2002, a figure that in June 2001 actually was about 1 percent. Instead, the differences between PCs and thin clients are blurring. Analysts stated that thin clients could save up to 39 percent on PC total cost of ownership (TCO), but that has not happened. IT executives say they do not measure TCO simply as PC versus thin client. They note that the cost of thin clients is not so low that it is worth reengineering, retraining, and running a mixed environment. In fact, the executives said that TCO should stand for "thin clients are oversimplified."

Another problem is that if a company moves from PCs to thin clients, the new environment will require complex storage systems and higher-end servers. Also, if an application runs in only one place (i.e., the network), then the network must always be up and running. One executive said that his firm could just buy PCs, or it could spend twice as much on the communications network in order to keep the client thin.

Source: CIO Magazine (June 1, 2001).

Questions

1. What are the advantages and disadvantages of network PCs?

2. What is the biggest reason for staying with desktop PCs?

A personal digital assistant (PDA).

Mobile Devices.   Emerging platforms for computing and communications include such **mobile devices** as handheld computers, often called **personal digital assistants (PDAs)** or *handheld personal computers*, and mobile phone handsets with new wireless and Internet access capabilities formerly associated with PDAs. Other emerging platforms (game consoles and cable set-top boxes) are consumer electronics devices that are expanding into computing and telecommunications. Mobile devices are be-

Table 3.3   Comparing Computers (Desktop and Larger)

Type	Processor Speed	Amount of RAM	Physical Size	Common Role/Use
Supercomputer	60 billion to 3 trillion FLOPs	8,000 MB+	Like a small car	Scientific calculation, complex system modeling, and simulation
Mainframe	500–4,500 MIPS	256–4,096 MB	Like a refrigerator	Enterprisewide systems, corporate database management
Midrange Computers Minicomputer	250–1,000 MIPS	256–2,048 MB	Like a file cabinet	Department-level or small company; dedicated to a particular system (e.g., e-mail)
Server	100–500 MIPS	256–1,024 MB	Fits on desktop	Supports computer networks; e-commerce
Workstation	50–250 MIPS	128–1,024 MB	Fits on desktop	Engineering/CAD software development
Microcomputer	10–100 MIPS	64–512 MB	Fits on desktop	Personal/workgroup productivity, communication

Desktop Personal Computer	Portable Personal Computer
Impractical for mobile computing	Designed for mobile computing
Lower cost	Higher cost
Easily expanded	Difficult to expand
Comfortable ergonomics	Uncomfortable ergonomics (small keyboard, often with inconvenient placement of function keys)*
Easy-to-use mouse or other pointing device	Awkward pointing devices (some allow traditional mouse to be connected)
High-resolution/brightness monitor	Lower resolution, less bright*
High RAM and hard-drive capacity	Somewhat less RAM and hard-drive capacity
Easy serviceability	More difficult to service/repair
Can utilize all current PC chips	Some models cannot use some chips, due to cooling problems

* Most portable PCs can be used with a conventional desktop monitor and keyboard when connected to them through a docking station (a popular option).

Manager's Checklist 3.1

Desktop or Portable PC? The Tradeoffs

coming more popular and more capable of augmenting, or even substituting for, desktop and notebook computers.

Table 3.4 (on page 78) describes the various types of mobile devices. In general, mobile devices have the following characteristics:

- They cost much less than PCs.
- Their operating systems are simpler than those on a desktop PC.
- They provide good performance at specific tasks but do not replace the full functions of a PC.
- They provide both computer and/or communications features.
- They offer a Web portal that is viewable on a screen.

The following example describes an application of PDAs in the U.S. Navy.

EXAMPLE

PDAs in the U.S. Navy. The U.S. Navy recently realized that its aircraft carrier flight-grading system was not effective. Officers spent all day recording flight evaluations in spiral notebooks, then sat for up to two hours each night reentering that data into a computer.

Using application development software and Palm handheld devices, the Navy created a flight-recording program, PASS, for devices running the Palm operating system. The results were immediate. PASS is now in official use by more than 50 landing-signal officers—pilots who grade flight landings—on two of the Navy's 12 aircraft carriers.

The application is simple to use. Using custom menus and the Palm's built-in handwriting recognition software, officers input information on each flight, including the plane ID number, pilot name, which wire helped catch the plane, a grade for the

Table 3.4   Mobile Devices and Their Uses

Device	Description and Use
Handheld companions	Devices with a core functionality of accessing and managing data; designed as supplements to notebooks or PCs
PC companions	Devices primarily used for personal information management (PIM), e-mail, and light data-creation capabilities
Personal companions	Devices primarily used for PIM activities and data-viewing activities
Classic PDAs	Handheld units designed for PIM and vertical data collection.
Smart phones	Emerging mobile phones with added PDA, PIM, data, e-mail or messaging creation/service capabilities
Vertical application devices	Devices with a core functionality of data access, management, creation, and collection; designed for use in vertical markets*
Pen tablets	Business devices with pen input and tablet form for gathering data in the field or in a mobile situation
Pen notepads	Pen-based for vertical data collection applications
Keypad handhelds	Business devices with an alphanumeric keypad used in specialized data-collection applications

*Vertical markets refer to specific industries, such as manufacturing, finance, healthcare, etc.

landing, and additional evaluation comments. After completing notes on a day's worth of flights, the pilot synchronizes his PDA with a desktop computer. The PASS software flags any evaluations where data are missing or the comments do not mesh with the flight grade, then it enters the evaluations into the computer's database. Data are backed up on Zip disks and periodically sent to the Pacific Fleet's central data repository in San Diego.

The program has freed up more than 100 man-hours a month on each of the ships. Those extra hours are time the officers can spend doing more meaningful training. PASS has also increased the accuracy of flight evaluations. Thanks to the Palm's ability to time-stamp records, landing-signal officers can precisely record landing intervals. (With flights coming in every 45 seconds at peak times, precision is crucial.) PASS's shortcut keys for entering comments take the guesswork out of deciphering notebook scribbles. ●

Computing Devices

As technology has improved, ever-smaller computing/communication devices have become possible. Technology such as wearable computing/communication devices (à la *Star Trek*)—which for generations seemed like science fiction—has now become reality. This section briefly looks at some of these new computing devices.

Wearable computing.   **Wearable computers** are designed to be worn and used on the body. This new technology has so far been aimed primarily at niche markets in industry rather than at consumers. Industrial applications of wearable computing include systems for factory automation, warehouse management, and performance support, such as viewing technical manuals and diagrams while building or repairing something. The technology is already widely used in diverse industries such as freight delivery, aerospace, securities trading, and law enforcement. Governments have been examining such devices for military uses.

Embedded computers are placed inside other products to add features and capabilities. For example, the average mid-sized automobile has more than 3,000 embedded computers that monitor every function from braking to engine performance to seat controls with memory.

Active badges can be worn as ID cards by employees who wish to stay in touch at all times while moving around the corporate premises. The clip-on badge contains a microprocessor that transmits its (and its wearer's) location to the building's sensors, which send it to a computer. When someone wants to contact the badge wearer, the phone closest to the person is identified automatically. When badge wearers enter their offices, their badge identifies them and logs them on to their personal computers.

Memory buttons are nickel-sized devices that store a small database relating to whatever it is attached to. These devices are analogous to a bar code, but with far greater informational content and a content that is subject to change. The U.S. Postal Service is placing memory buttons in residential mailboxes to track and improve collection and delivery schedules.

Active badges worn by employees.

An even smaller form of computer is the **smart card**. Similar in size and thickness to ordinary plastic credit cards, smart cards contain a small processor and memory that allow these "computers" to be used in everyday activities such as personal identification and banking.

Uses for smart cards are appearing rapidly. People are using them as checkbooks; a bank ATM (automated teller machine) can "deposit money" into the card's memory for "withdrawal" at retail stores. Many states and private health maintenance organizations are issuing smart health cards that contain the owner's complete health history, emergency data, and health insurance policy data. Smart cards are being used to transport data between computers, replacing floppy disks. Adding a small transmitter to a smart card can allow businesses to locate any employee and automatically route phone calls to the nearest telephone.

Before you go on . . .

1. Describe the computer hierarchy from the largest to the smallest computers.

2. What type of desktop PC has the least amount of processing power?

3. Give examples of the uses of supercomputers and handheld computers.

3.5   INPUT TECHNOLOGIES

Input technologies allow people and other technologies to put data into a computer. We begin with human data-entry devices.

Human Data-Entry Devices

Human data-entry devices allow people to communicate with the computer. Some of these devices are very common, such as the keyboard and the mouse. Others, such as the touch screen, stylus, trackball, joystick, and microphone, are used for somewhat more specialized purposes.

Keyboards.   **Keyboards** are the most common input device. The keyboard is designed like a typewriter but with many additional function keys. Most computer users utilize keyboards regularly. However, excessive use of keyboards can lead to repetitive stress injuries like carpal tunnel syndrome. This type of injury is thought to be caused by improper placement of the hands and wrists when typing at the computer keyboard. As a result, a new generation of keyboards has been designed to encourage the proper hand and wrist positions by splitting and angling the keypad and by incorporating large wrist rests.

A more radical keyboard redesign is the DataHand keyboard from DataHand Systems of Phoenix, Arizona. The DataHand keyboard consists of two unattached pads, and rather than a conventional array of keys, the device has touch-sensitive receptacles (or finger wells) for the fingers and thumbs. Each finger well allows five different commands, which are actuated by touching one of the sides or the bottom of the finger wells. Complex commands can be programmed so that a single flick of the finger can be used to enter frequently used sequences of commands or chunks of data. The DataHand Web site has an excellent demonstration of the company's ergonomic keyboard (see *datahand.com*).

The "split" keyboard has improved ergonomics.

Mice and trackballs.   A **mouse** is a handheld device used to point a cursor at a desired place on the screen, such as an icon, a cell in a table, an item in a menu, or any other object. Once the arrow is placed on an object, the user clicks a button on the mouse, instructing the computer to take some action. The use of the mouse reduces the need to type in information or use one of the function keys.

A variant of the mouse is the **trackball**, which is often used in graphic design. The user holds an object much like a mouse, but rather than moving the entire device to move the cursor (as with a mouse), he or she rotates a ball that is built into the top of the device. Portable computers have some other mouselike technologies, such as the glide-and-tap pad, used in lieu of a mouse. Many portables also allow a conventional mouse to be plugged in when desired.

Another variant of the mouse, the **optical mouse**, replaces the ball, rollers, and wheels of the mechanical mouse with a light, lens, and a camera chip. It replicates the action of a ball and rollers by taking photographs of the surface it passes over, and comparing each successive image to determine where it is going.

The **pen mouse** resembles an automobile stick shift in a gear box. Moving the pen and pushing buttons on it perform the same functions of moving the cursor on the screen as a conventional pointing device. But the pen mouse base stays immobile on the desk. With a pen mouse, the forearm rests on the desk, saving wear and tension. Because the mouse is not lifted or moved, the fingers, not the arm, do the work.

Other human data-entry devices.   **Touch screens** are a technology that divides a computer screen into different areas. Users simply touch the desired area (often buttons or squares) to trigger an action. These are common in computers built into self-service kiosks such as ATM machines and even bridal registries.

A **stylus** is a pen-style device that allows the user either to touch parts of a predetermined menu of options (as with a wearable computer, discussed above) or to handwrite information into the computer (as with some PDAs). (See the photo of the PDA and stylus on page 76.) The technology may respond to pressure of the stylus, or the stylus can be a type of light pen that emits light that is sensed by the computer.

A **joy stick** is used primarily at workstations that display dynamic graphics. It is also used to play video games. The joy stick moves and positions the cursor at the desired place on the screen.

A **microphone** is becoming a popular data-input device as voice-recognition software improves and people can use microphones to dictate to the computer. These are also critical technologies for people who are physically challenged and cannot use the more common input devices.

Source Data Automation

The object of **source data automation** is to input data with minimal human intervention. These technologies speed up data collection, reduce errors, and gather data at the source of a transaction or other event. Below are the common types.

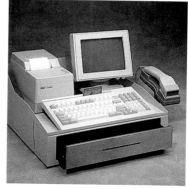

A POS terminal.

Cash-transaction devices.   Various input devices are common in association with cash transactions. The most common are ATMs and POS terminals.

Automated teller machines (ATMs) are interactive input/output devices that enable people to make bank transactions from remote locations. ATMs utilize touch screen input as well as magnetic card readers.

Point-of-sale (POS) terminals are computerized cash registers that also often incorporate touch screen technology and bar-code scanners (described below). These devices allow the input of numerous data such as item sold, price, method of payment, name or Zip code of the buyer, and so on. Some inputs are automated; others may be entered by the operator.

Optical scanners.   Bar-code scanners, ubiquitous in retail stores, scan the black-and-white bar code lines typically printed on labels on merchandise. In addition, bar-code scanners are very popular for tracking inventory and shipping.

An **optical mark reader** is a special scanner for detecting the presence of pencil marks on a predetermined grid, such as multiple-choice test answer sheets. Similarly, **magnetic ink character readers (MICRs)** are used chiefly in the banking industry. Information is printed on checks in magnetic ink that can be read by the MICR technology, thus helping to automate and greatly increase the efficiency of the check-handling process.

Optical character recognition (OCR) software is used in conjunction with a scanner to convert text into digital form for input into the computer. Although the scanner can digitize any graphic, the OCR software can recognize the individual characters, so that they can be manipulated. As a practical example, the scanner by itself could "take a picture" of this page of text and convert it into digital information that the computer could store as a picture of the text. But you would not be able to decompose the "picture" file into individual words that could be further modified (manipulated by a word-processing program, for example). The OCR technology enables this last part. OCR-equipped scanning technologies are very useful when printed documents not only must be preserved but also would benefit from any manipulations or modifications. OCR technologies would enable you to scan data, process them with the OCR software, and then put them into a database, spreadsheet, or word-processing format.

As noted in the earlier section on handheld computers, OCR software is usually incorporated in stylus-input devices. Although quite sophisticated, OCR programs require training in order to be able to recognize handwriting. Even then, their accuracy in interpreting handwritten characters is less than when they are used to interpret typed text.

Other source data automation devices.   Voice-recognition systems are used in conjunction with microphones to input speech to computers. Voice-recognition software (VRS) attempts to identify spoken words and translate them into digital text. Like

OCR software used for handwriting recognition, VRS requires training to become accustomed to the user's voice and accent. These systems also leave much to be desired in terms of accuracy of word recognition, though the technology continues to improve.

Sensors are extremely common technologies embedded in other technologies. They collect data directly from the environment and input them into a computer system. Examples might include your car's airbag activation sensor or fuel mixture/pollution control sensor, inventory control sensors in retail stores, and the myriad types of sensors built into a modern aircraft.

Cameras can now operate digitally, capturing images and converting them into digital files. There are digital still-image cameras, and there are now many types of digital motion-picture cameras. Many computer enthusiasts and practical business people find it useful to attach small digital cameras to their personal computers. When linked to the Internet, and using special software such as Microsoft's NetMeeting, such a system can be used to conduct desktop videoconferencing.

Before you go on . . .

1. Distinguish between human data input devices and source data automation.

2. Describe the relationship between OCR technology and scanner technology.

3.6   OUTPUT TECHNOLOGIES

The output generated by a computer can be transmitted to the user via several devices and media. The presentation of information is extremely important in encouraging users to embrace computers. Below is a discussion of common types of output technologies.

Monitors

Monitors are the video screens used with most computers that display input as well as output. Like television sets, monitors come in a variety of sizes and color/resolution quality. And like television sets, the common desktop monitor uses **cathode ray tube (CRT)** technology to shoot beams of electrons to the screen. The electrons illuminate tiny points on the screen known as **pixels**. The more pixels on the screen, the better the resolution. That is, the less space between pixels—that is, the finer the **dot pitch**—the better the resolution. Here are some other useful facts about monitors:

- Portable computers use a flat screen that uses *liquid crystal display (LCD)* technology, not CRT.
- LCDs use less power than CRT monitors but cost six to eight times what an equivalent CRT does.
- LCD monitors may be *passive matrix*, which have somewhat less display speed and brightness compared to *active matrix monitors*, which function somewhat differently (and cost significantly more).

A comparison of an LCD (left) with an OLED display (right).

Organic light-emitting diodes.   **Organic light-emitting diodes (OLEDs)** provide displays that are brighter, thinner, lighter, and faster than liquid crystal displays (LCDs).

LCDs, invented in 1963, have become the standard display for everything from watches to laptop computers. However, LCD screens are hard to make and expensive. Compared to LCDs, OLEDs take less power to run, offer higher contrast, look equally bright from all angles, handle video, and are cheaper to manufacture.

OLEDs do face technical obstacles with color. If you leave OLEDs on for a month or so, the color becomes very nonuniform. However, OLEDs are probably good enough right now for cell phones, which are typically used for 200 hours per year and would likely be replaced before the colors start to fade. But such performance is not adequate for handheld or laptop displays, for which several thousand hours of life are required.

Retinal scanning displays. As people increasingly use mobile devices, many are frustrated with the interfaces. The interfaces are too small, too slow, and too awkward to process information effectively. As a result, Web sites become unusable, e-mails are constrained, and graphics are eliminated. One solution does away with screens altogether. A firm named Microvision (*mvis.com*) projects an image, pixel by pixel, directly onto a viewer's retina. This technology, called **retinal scanning displays (RSDs)**, is used in a variety of work situations, including medicine, air traffic control, and controls of industrial machines. RSDs can also be used in dangerous situations, for example, giving firefighters in a smoke-filled building a floor plan.

A retinal scanning display (RSD) device.

Printers

Printers come in a variety of styles for varying purposes. The three main types are impact printers, nonimpact printers, and plotters.

Impact printers.   **Impact printers** work like typewriters, using some kind of striking action. A raised metal character strikes an inked ribbon that makes a printed impression of the character on the paper. These devices cannot produce high-resolution graphics, and they are relatively slow, noisy, and subject to mechanical failure. Although inexpensive, they are becoming less popular.

Nonimpact printers.   **Nonimpact printers** come in two main styles. **Laser printers** are higher-speed, high-quality devices that use laser beams to write information on photosensitive drums, whole pages at a time; then the paper passes over the drum and picks up the image with toner (similar to ink). Laser printers produce very-high-resolution text and graphics, making them suitable for a broad range of printing needs from simple text to desktop publishing. **Inkjet printers** work differently, by shooting fine streams of colored ink onto the paper. These are less expensive than laser printers, but offer somewhat less resolution quality.

Plotters.   **Plotters** are printing devices that use computer-directed pens for creating high-quality images. They are used in complex, low-volume situations, for example, creating maps and architectural drawings. Some plotters are quite large, suited for producing correspondingly large graphics.

Voice Output

Voice output is now possible via sophisticated synthesizer software that can be installed in most personal computers. A voice output system constructs the sonic equivalent of textual words, which can then be played through speakers. Other types of software can manage spoken communication in different ways. For example, one can purchase programs that integrate telephone voice mail with the computer, so that the computer can record and make limited responses to incoming calls.

Multifunction Devices

Multifunction devices combine a variety of technologies and are particularly appropriate for home offices. The technologies include fax, printer, scanner, copy machine, and answering machine. Depending on how much one wishes to invest and one's needs, any combination can be found in a single cost-effective machine.

Multimedia

Multimedia output is the computer-based integration of text, sound, still images, animation, and digitized motion video. It merges the capabilities of computers with televisions, VCRs, CD players, DVD players, video and audio recording equipment, and music and gaming technologies. Multimedia usually represents a collection of various input and output technologies, a system unto itself, as shown in Figure 3.10. Later in the book we will discuss the business uses of multimedia technology, but for the moment, consider these useful facts:

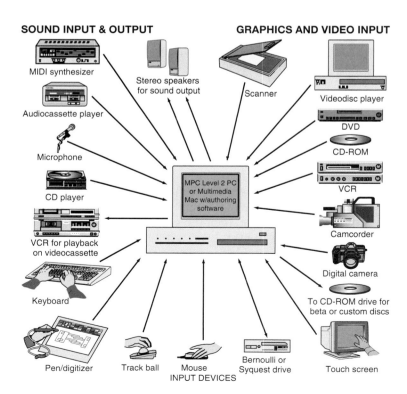

Figure 3.10 *Multimedia authoring system with a great variety of input sources and output displays. [Source: Based on illustration in* Reseller Management *(November 1993). From the 11/93 VAR Workbook Series by John McCormick and Tom Fare, Multimedia Today Supplement: VAR Workbook Series, pp. 4–5, 7.]*

IT's About Business *condopronto.com*

Box 3.3: Advertising real estate with multimedia

CondoPronto.com allows travelers to research and book online for short-term rental and vacation properties. Site visitors can see a detailed preview of each property, and obtain information on availability and cost. Before this Web site opened, there had not been any free, centralized one-stop for condo owners and travelers. CondoPronto offers a free "showcase" page to owners, which includes: one to three photos of the property, text description, reservation calendar, and online booking services. Condo-Pronto also offers a multitiered selection of services, and owners can pay for upgrades in their ads, such as full-motion-video virtual walkthroughs. Visitors to the site can also see a moving 3-D panorama of properties.

CondoPronto's IT infrastructure includes IBM's RS/6000 server running IBM's DB/2 relational database and IBM's WebSphere Commerce Suite. It took only a couple of months to get the site up and running, and visitors are providing positive feedback. Condo owners are saving time and money that they would otherwise have spent on brokers or advertisements. At the same time, owners are reaching a worldwide audience.

Source: ibm.com and *condopronto.com.*

Questions

1. What advantages does multimedia offer condo owners on CondoPronto?

2. What other multimedia functions can Condo-Pronto offer?

- High-quality multimedia processing requires the most powerful and sophisticated microprocessors available. Firms like Intel produce generations of chips especially designed for multimedia processing.

- Because of the variety of devices that can make up a multimedia system, standards such as the Multimedia Personal Computer (MPC) Council certification are important in ensuring that the devices are compliant and compatible.

- Extensive memory capacity—both primary and secondary storage—is essential for multimedia processing, particularly with video. Video typically requires using compression techniques to reduce the amount of storage needed. Even with compression techniques, those who work extensively with video processing often must augment their secondary storage with devices like writeable CD drives or external hard drives.

IT's About Business Box 3.3 discusses a multimedia application.

Before you go on . . .

1. What are the differences between various types of monitors?

2. What are the main types of printers? How do they work?

3. Describe the concept of multimedia, and give an example of a multimedia system.

3.7 STRATEGIC HARDWARE ISSUES

The majority of this chapter has explained how hardware is designed and how it works. But it is what the hardware enables, how it is advancing, and how rapidly it is advancing that are the more complex and important issues for most businesspeople.

In many industries, exploiting computer hardware is a key to competitive advantage. Successful hardware exploitation comes from thoughtful consideration of the following issues.

Productivity

Hardware technology can affect both personal and organizational productivity. Businesses need to assess whether employees' personal productivity is likely to increase as microprocessor power and speed increase. Perhaps your PC now takes 1/10th of a second to call up a program. If a new generation of chip can get your PC to call it up in 1/100th of a second, does your productivity increase by tenfold? If so, then an investment in a more powerful microprocessor might produce a competitive advantage.

Similarly, as primary storage capacity increases, what advantages come your way? A trend in software is to make each new version more complex. Consider, for example, the differences in Microsoft Office 2000. This software suite (discussed in Chapter 4) has so many more instructions that it cannot run well on machines with less than 128 MB RAM. To take advantage of the newer software, you need to upgrade machines. You also need to invest considerable time to understand whether the new innovations will help you, and then you must master them. The learning curve that comes with new machines and software typically comes with a cost to your productivity, at least in the short term. And perhaps by the time you master a new generation of technology, it will be obsolete. Multiply this decision by the number of employees who will use the new software, and you have an issue of organizational productivity to solve.

At the same time, the cost of computers is decreasing while the power is increasing. Is the workforce prepared to take advantage of these more powerful machines? How would your business measure the anticipated increases in productivity? You would need to be able to measure or somehow quantify the changes in organizational productivity in order to make a reasoned cost–benefit decision.

Changing Work Styles

Advances in miniaturization of microprocessors and memory devices are ushering in ever-smaller computing and communication devices that can assist employees in achieving a productive, nontraditional work style. This is particularly true for employees who work largely out of the office. Whether at home or on the road, employees can stay connected to the home office and keep their efforts coordinated with organizational goals via the cellular telephone, modem (discussed in Chapter 6), and portable computers of one style or another. All of these devices are enabled by advances in these technologies. The issue the organization must consider is whether these new work styles will benefit employees and the firm as a whole. In particular, does the firm know how to manage these new work styles?

New Products and Services

Because the cost of computing power continues to decline à la Moore's Law, organizations may find that supercomputers are affordable and justifiable. With a supercomputer, business organizations can tackle increasingly sophisticated problems, from forecasting to product development to advanced market research. Similarly, advances in miniaturization of microcontrollers, microprocessors, and memory devices can also drive the development of new products and services for your firm. Is the organization ready and able to take advantage of these advances? What new products and services would advances in hardware make possible for the business?

Improved Communications

Multimedia is often thought of as the basis for an entertainment system, with limited use in the business world. This is short-sighted thinking. Increasingly, organizations recognize that multimedia capability is an important aspect of knowledge management and communication (as IT's About Business Box 3.3 showed). When integrated with a firm's network and/or the Internet, multimedia technology makes possible incredibly rich communication and knowledge sharing throughout the organization, as well as with the rest of the world. Many commercial Web sites feature multimedia, making video, audio, graphic, and textual information available to all who visit. Multimedia presentations are now the standard for excellence in the business world, and anyone who has to sell a product, service, or idea benefits from exploiting this technology. Is your organization ready to do so? What multimedia applications might provide a competitive advantage for your organization?

Before you go on . . .

1. How would you explain the role of various types of computer hardware in personal productivity? In organizational productivity?

2. What are the upsides and downsides that accompany advances in microprocessor design?

www.wiley.com/college/turban

FOR ALL BUSINESS MAJORS AND NONBUSINESS MAJORS

There are practically no professional jobs in business today that do not require computer literacy and skills for personal productivity. And there are no industries that do not use computer technology for one form of competitive advantage or another.

ACC

FIN

MKT

POM

HRM

Clearly, the design of computer hardware has profound impacts for businesspeople. It is also clear that personal and organizational success can depend on an understanding of hardware design and a commitment to knowing where it is going and what opportunities and challenges innovations will bring. Because these innovations can occur so rapidly, hardware decisions at the individual level and at the organizational level are difficult.

At the *individual level*, most people who have a home or office computer system and want to upgrade it, or people contemplating their first computer purchase, are faced with the decision of *when* to buy as much as *what* to buy and at what cost.

At the *organizational level*, these same issues plague IS professionals, but they are more complex and more costly. Most organizations have many different computer systems in place at the same time. Innovations may come to different classes of computers at different times or rates, and managers must decide when old hardware *legacy systems* still have a productive role in the IS architecture, or when they should be replaced.

IS management at the corporate level is one of the most challenging careers today, due in no small part to the constant innovation in computer hardware. That may not be your career objective, but an appreciation of that area is beneficial. After all, the people who keep you equipped with the right computing hardware, as you can now see, are very important allies in your success.

SUMMARY

❶ **Identify the major hardware components of a computer system.**
Today's computer systems have six major components: the central processing unit (CPU), primary storage, secondary storage, input technologies, output technologies, and communications technologies.

❷ **Describe the design and functioning of the central processing unit.**
The CPU is made up of the arithmetic-logic unit that performs the calculations, the registers that store minute amounts of data and instructions immediately before and after processing, and the control unit that controls the flow of information on the microprocessor chip.

❸ **Discuss the relationships between microprocessor component designs and performance.**
Microprocessor designs aim to increase processing speed by minimizing the physical distance that the data (as electrical impulses) must travel, and by increasing the bus width, clock speed, word length, and number of transistors on the chip.

❹ **Describe the main types of primary and secondary storage.**
There are four types of primary storage: registers, random access memory (RAM), cache memory, and read-only memory (ROM). All are direct-access memory; only ROM is nonvolatile. Secondary storage includes magnetic media (tapes, hard drives, and diskettes) and optical media (CD-ROM, DVD, FMD-ROM, and optical jukeboxes).

❺ **Distinguish between primary and secondary storage along the dimensions of speed, cost, and capacity.**
Primary storage has much less capacity than secondary storage, and is faster and more expensive per byte stored. Primary storage is located much closer to the CPU than is secondary storage. Sequential-access secondary storage media such as magnetic tape is much slower and less expensive than direct-access media (e.g., hard drives, optical media).

❻ **Define enterprise storage and describe the various types of enterprise storage.**
An enterprise storage system is an independent, external system with intelligence that includes two or more storage devices. There are three major types of enterprise storage subsystems: redundant arrays of independent disks (RAIDs), storage area networks (SANs), and network-attached storage (NAS). RAID links groups of standard hard drives to a specialized microcontroller. SAN is an architecture for building special, dedicated networks that allow access to storage devices by multiple servers. A NAS device is a special-purpose server that provides file storage to users who access the device over a network.

❼ **Describe the hierarchy of computers according to power and their respective roles.**
Supercomputers are the most powerful, designed to handle the maximum computational demands of science and the military. Mainframes are not as powerful as supercomputers, but are powerful enough for use by large organizations for centralized data processing and large databases. Minicomputers are smaller and less powerful versions of mainframes, often devoted to handling specific subsystems. Workstations are in between minicomputers and personal computers in speed, capacity, and graphics capability. Desktop personal computers (PCs) are the most common personal and business computers. Network computers have less computing power and storage, relying on connection to a network for communication, data, processing, and storage resources.
   Laptop or notebook computers are small, easily transportable PCs. Palmtop computers are handheld microcomputers, usually configured for specific applica-

tions and limited in the number of ways they can accept user input and provide output. Wearable computers, worn on the user's clothing, free their users' movements. Embedded computers are placed inside other products to add features and capabilities. Employees may wear active badges as ID cards. Memory buttons are nickel-sized devices that store a small database relating to whatever it is attached to. Smart cards contain a small processor, memory, and an input/output device that allows them to be used in everyday activities such as personal identification and banking.

❽ Differentiate the various types of input and output technologies and their uses.
Principal input technologies include the keyboard, mouse, trackball, touch screen, stylus, joystick, ATM, POS terminal, bar-code scanner, optical mark reader, optical character reader, handwriting and voice-recognition systems, sensor, microphone, and camera. Common output technologies include the monitor, impact and nonimpact printers, plotter, voice output, multifunction devices, and multimedia.

❾ Describe what multimedia systems are and what technologies they use.
Multimedia computer systems integrate two or more types of media, such as text, graphics, sound, voice, full-motion video, images, and animation. They use a variety of input and output technologies, often including microphones, musical instruments, digitizers, CD-ROM, magnetic tape, and speakers. Multimedia systems typically require additional processing and storage capacity.

❿ Discuss strategic issues that link hardware design and innovation to competitive business strategy.
According to Moore's Law, microprocessor capability increases ever more rapidly. Miniaturization is also increasing. These advancements usher in new generations of faster, more powerful, and more compact computers, as well as new generations of microcontrollers. Organizations must continually appraise the issues of productivity work styles, new products and services, and improved communications against these new options. Adoption decisions are difficult because of heavy past, current, and future investment.

INTERACTIVE LEARNING SESSION

Go to the CD, access Chapter 3: Computer Hardware, and read the case presented. It will describe a business problem that will require you to make a decision on buying personal computers for your company. You will have to decide which variables are the most important (e.g., type of processor, processor speed, amount of RAM, hard drive capacity, etc.), and you must stay within your budget.

For additional resources, go to the book's Web site for Chapter 3. There you will find Web resources for the chapter, including additional material about hardware technologies and systems; links to organizations, people, and technology; "IT's About Business" company links; "What's in IT for Me?" links; and a self-testing Web quiz for Chapter 3.

www.wiley.com/
college/turban

DISCUSSION QUESTIONS

1. What factors affect the speed of a microprocessor?

2. If you were the chief information officer (CIO) of a firm, what factors would you consider when selecting secondary storage media for your company's records (files)?

3. What applications can you think of for voice-recognition systems?

4. Given that Moore's Law has proven itself over the past two decades, speculate on what chip

capabilities will be 10 years in the future. What might your desktop PC be able to do?

5. If you were the chief information officer (CIO) of a firm, how would you explain the workings, benefits, and limitations of a network computer–based system as opposed to using networked PCs (that is, "thin" client vs. "fat" client)?

6. How would you justify to your employer the added cost of a multimedia system over that of a nonmultimedia-capable PC?

7. Give some examples of how wearable computers might help your company.

8. What types of embedded computers can you think of in your company? In your home?

PROBLEM-SOLVING ACTIVITIES

1. Obtain back issues of *Computerworld* or other information systems magazines. (Go back 5 or 10 years.) Note the cost and functionality (e.g., size of RAM, hard drive capacity, chip speed) of computer systems listed. Compare costs and functionality year by year, and plot them on a graph.

2. Design multimedia systems for your personal use and for your professional use. Give justifications of the costs in terms of increased productivity and capability.

3. Describe what functions you would want in a PDA. Give justifications of the cost in terms of increased productivity and capability both for personal and professional use.

4. What types of computing problems justify the investment in a supercomputer for a private-sector firm?

INTERNET ACTIVITIES

1. Access the Web sites of the major hardware manufacturers, for example, IBM (*ibm.com*), Sun (*sun.com*), Apple (*apple.com*), Hewlett-Packard (*hp.com*), and Silicon Graphics (*sgi.com*), and obtain the latest information regarding hardware releases for all platforms (supercomputer, mainframe, workstation, personal computer, laptop). Prepare a table comparing cost, speed, and capacity for each product across manufacturers.

2. Access the Web sites of the major chip manufacturers, for example, Intel (*intel.com*), Motorola (*motorola.com*), and Advanced Micro Devices (*amd.com*), and obtain the latest information regarding new and planned chips. Compare performance and costs across vendors.

3. Access Intel's Web site (*intel.com*) and visit its museum and the animated microprocessor page. Prepare a presentation of each step in the machine instruction cycle.

TEAM ACTIVITIES AND ROLE PLAYING

1. Visit your campus computer center. Note each different type of computer in use and find out what types of applications are run on each type.

2. Interview your campus CIO and find out on what basis he or she decides to upgrade particular systems. What is the CIO's view of the dynamics of technology advancement, costs of new technologies, costs of in-place systems (sunk costs), and anticipated gains in productivity?

REAL-WORLD CASE   *amica.com*

Insuring Growth at Amica

The Business Problem   Amica is a $3 billion insurance company operating in 27 states. Facing increased competition in the insurance industry, Amica wanted to provide online services to its policyholders, giving them improved access to the company without compromising the company's reputation for highly personalized customer service.

Slowing market growth in the insurance industry has led to aggressive price cutting, as insurers have sought to increase their market share. With the consumer market (the segment served by Amica) increasingly willing to change providers for lower rates, the need to increase customer loyalty has become more acute.

Amica's main strategy for growth has been geographic expansion as well as a major advertising campaign designed to raise Amica's profile outside the Northeast. Amica recognized the need to expand its range of channels, and embraced the Internet as a new distribution and communications channel.

The IT Solution In response to business pressures, Amica developed a Web-based customer self-service solution that delivers rich content to policyholders as well as handles transactional services. Nonpolicyholders can visit the Web site to view information designed to support their insurance decisions as well as consumer safety information. Policyholders can access detailed billing and account history information, pay premiums, and report claims online. Policyholders can also obtain auto, homeowner, and liability insurance quotes online.

Amica's e-business solution uses multiple Windows NT servers as its Web servers, linked to a number of databases that reside on Amica's mainframe computer. The company feels that this IT infrastructure was essential for the success and smooth operation of its Web site. The mainframe provides security, reliability, and "24/7/365" availability. The Web servers provide flexibility, scalability, and rapid response time to users accessing the Web site.

The Results Amica experienced a 170 percent increase in site requests and a 145 percent increase in site visits during the Web site's first month of operation. In addition, through surveys, the company has discovered that the Web site has increased customer satisfaction. Amica has also increased new customer acquisition at lower cost via its Web site.

Source: amica.com.

Questions

1. Explain how the mainframe delivers its advantages and how the servers deliver their advantages.

2. Could Amica successfully get rid of its mainframe to save money? Why or why not?

VIRTUAL COMPANY ASSIGNMENT

wiley.com/college/turban

Extreme Descent Snowboards

Background The phone rings as you are about to start your day. You answer the

www.wiley.com/ college/turban

phone, and Jacob March, the vice president of information systems, asks if you can come to his office. You hang up the phone, grab your blazer, and head down the hall to Jacob's office.

Jacob stands up and offers his hand as you walk into his spacious office. He offers you a seat in front of his large mahogany desk. After exchanging a few pleasantries and some small talk, he asks if you are ready for another assignment. You tell Jacob excitedly that you are ready to accept the challenge.

Jacob explains that some of the PCs in the office are aging. "We need some measurement that gives us a cost-benefit analysis for acquiring new PC hardware. One measurement is the total cost of ownership model that investigates the total cost of the computer equipment," he says. You have recently studied in depth about hardware that is available. Your assignment will be to recommend a TCO model for evaluating hardware.

Assignment

1. Use a search engine to find information about TCO. What is a TCO model?

2. What are the disadvantages to the TCO model?

3. Describe how TCO could be used at EDS to determine its total computer related expenditures.

4

COMPUTER SOFTWARE

CHAPTER PREVIEW

Computer hardware is only as effective as the instructions we give it, and those instructions are contained in *software*. Software not only directs the computer to manage its internal resources, but also enables the user to tailor a computer system to provide specific business value. It is surprising to many people that at the corporate level, software expenditures (development and purchase) typically are a much larger cost than is hardware. In this chapter we learn that computer software, in its various forms and languages, can be quite complex. But these complexities must be understood in order to truly be able to exploit the power of modern information technologies. This chapter explains to the reader the concepts of what software is, how it works, and how it is created. Along the way we provide examples of software's critical role in maintaining organizational competitiveness.

LEARNING OBJECTIVES

1. Differentiate between the two major types of software.
2. Describe the general functions of the operating system.
3. Differentiate among types of operating systems and describe each type.
4. Identify three methods for developing application software.
5. Describe the major types of application software.
6. Explain how software has evolved and trends for the future.
7. Describe enterprise software.

THE SOLUTION TO SOFTWARE BUGS

A failed software upgrade left investors unable to trade shares on the New York Stock Exchange for an hour and a half in June 2001. The shutdown, the second the exchange suffered in three years, prevented many stocks from opening for trading. The shutdown made calculating market indexes like the Dow Jones Industrial Average and the Standard & Poor's Index impossible. The failed upgrade was part of the system that electronically directs orders from securities firms to the Exchange.

Software bugs are errors in a computer program that either will not let the program run (fairly easy to find), or will let the program run but will produce incorrect output (very difficult to find). Writing computer code for computer programs (i.e., producing software) unfortunately remains more an art than a science. According to the Software Engineering Institute at Carnegie Mellon University, there are about 5 to 15 bugs in every 1,000 lines of computer code.

Many software bugs arise as a result of "good-enough software"—software released by software vendors before adequate testing is performed. Software bugs have plagued new releases of Microsoft Windows and Office products, Netscape Navigator, and Intuit's Quicken, among others.

Even when individual office software products are not buggy, corporate computing environments are so complex that they are inherently unreliable. Typically, these systems are collections of mainframes, minicomputers, workstations, PCs, Macs, and mobile devices, running different operating systems that were never designed or tested in combination. Further, these systems are running thousands of different software applications, some over 50 years old.

Bugs in software can upset even the usually unflappable stock exchange trader.

Integrated enterprise resource planning software from SAP, PeopleSoft, and Oracle may remedy some aspects of the software problem, if only because they tie operations together in one suite of application modules. However, even these systems must work throughout the supply chain, raising the biggest problem to date: the interconnectedness of complex systems. Over the Internet, software now links computers that were once insulated from one another, creating additional layers of complexity.

One solution is open source software. The "open source" movement draws programmers around the world together to continuously debug major programs. With thousands of programmers pooling their skills to build and test such programs, bugs can be discovered early. The Internet provides a platform for such collaboration and an instant feedback channel.

A second solution is more rigorous software development. Governments are joining with industry to impose greater rigor on software development, hoping to transform it from art to science. The National Science Foundation wants to provide software engineers with the information to create accurate, debugged modules of code that could be used over and over to assemble all kinds of systems. The ultimate goal is a library of these modules, each with built-in intelligent agents. To produce a program, an engineer would simply specify the software's function, and then the intelligent agents would coordinate among themselves to figure out how to patch together the desired result.

The results are still unknown. The main question that remains is whether the IT solutions can keep pace with the growing complexity of the software. Another problem

93

concerns the extremely high costs of error-free software. The more that vendors test their products, the higher their costs, and the higher the prices to companies and consumers. There may be a happy medium between testing, bugs, and pricing, but as the New York Stock Exchange example above shows, any software bug can have wide-ranging and costly consequences.

Sources: "The State of Software: Quality," *InformationWeek.com*, May 21, 2001; "Software Failure Halts Big Board Trading for Over an Hour," *nytimes.com*, June 9, 2001).

What We Learned from This Case

The importance of computer software cannot be overestimated. As we noted in Chapter 3, hardware expenses have declined over the past two decades; at the same time, software costs have increased. For any business, failure to account for, and have contingency plans in place for software bugs can have devastating results. Employees from every functional area often are involved in testing software products for bugs because they are the experts in that area and can spot functional-area-specific bugs even more quickly than IT programmers can. Therefore, as you study this chapter, keep in mind that, regardless of your major, more than likely you will be involved with some aspects of software very early in your career.

4.1 SOFTWARE HISTORY AND SIGNIFICANCE

The first applications of computers in business were in the early 1950s. Software was less important (and less costly) in computer systems then, because early hardware was literally hardwired by hand for each application. Today, software comprises a much larger percentage of the cost of modern computer systems than it did in the 1950s. There are several reasons for this trend. First, the price of hardware has dramatically decreased, while the performance of hardware has exponentially increased. Second, building applications—a process called *software development*—is slow, complex, and error-prone. Software is, therefore, expensive and getting more so as its complexity grows. Finally, salaries for software developers are steadily increasing because there is an increased demand for their skills.

The Software Crisis

These factors have led to a major problem for management—the software crisis. The **software crisis** is that organizations are not able to develop new software applications fast enough to keep up with rapidly changing business conditions and rapidly evolving technologies.

Computer hardware can be designed and manufactured on automated assembly lines, and so can be turned out rather quickly, but software must be engineered by hand. Therefore, software generally lags several generations behind hardware. The result is that organizations are unable to make full use of hardware due to a lack of software to effectively exploit the hardware.

Further, organizations not only must develop new applications quickly, but they must also maintain their existing software. Often, more than 80 percent of IT personnel maintain existing software, leaving less than 20 percent to develop new applications.

The increasing complexity of software exacerbates the software crisis. This complexity naturally leads to the increased potential for errors or bugs. Large applications today may contain millions of lines of computer code, written by hundreds of people over the course of several years. Clearly, the potential for errors is huge, and testing and **debugging** software is expensive and time-consuming.

Software Fundamentals

Software consists of **computer programs**, which are sequences of instructions for the computer. The process of writing (or *coding*) programs is called *programming*, and individuals who perform this task are called *programmers*.

Unlike the hardwired computers of the 1950s, modern software uses the **stored program concept**, in which stored software programs are accessed and their instructions are executed (followed) in the computer's CPU. Once the program has finished executing, a new program is loaded into main memory and the computer hardware addresses another task.

Computer programs include **documentation**, which is a written description of the functions of the program. Documentation helps the user operate the computer system and helps other programmers understand what the program does and how it accomplishes its purpose. Documentation is vital to the business organization. Without it, if a key programmer or user leaves, the knowledge of how to use the program or how it is designed may be lost.

The computer is able to do nothing until it is instructed by software. Although computer hardware is, by design, general purpose, software enables the user to instruct a computer system to perform specific functions that provide business value. There are two major types of software: systems software and application software. The relationship among hardware, systems software, and application software is illustrated in Figure 4.1.

Systems software is a set of instructions that serves primarily as an intermediary between computer hardware and application programs, and may also be directly manipulated by knowledgeable users. Systems software provides important self-regulatory functions for computer systems, such as loading itself when the computer is first turned on, managing hardware resources such as secondary storage for all applications, and providing commonly used sets of instructions for all applications to use. *Systems programming* is either the creation or maintenance of systems software.

Application software is a set of computer instructions that provide more specific functionality to a user. That functionality may be broad, such as general word processing, or narrow, such as an organization's payroll program. An application program applies a computer to a certain need. *Application programming* is either the creation or the modification and improvement of application software. There are many different software applications in organizations today, as this chapter will discuss. For a marketing application, for example, see the Market Intelligence box at the Web site.

In summary, application programs primarily manipulate data or text to produce or provide information. Systems programs primarily manipulate computer hardware resources. The systems software available on a computer system provides the capabilities and limitations within which the application software can operate. The next two sections of this chapter look in more detail at these two types of software.

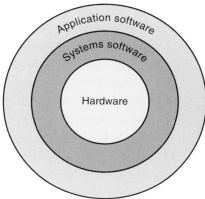

Figure 4.1 *Systems software serves as intermediary between hardware and functional applications.*

www.wiley.com/ college/turban

Before you go on . . .

1. What is the software crisis and what causes it?

2. What are differences between systems software and application software?

4.2 SYSTEMS SOFTWARE

Systems software is the class of programs that control and support the computer system and its information-processing activities. Systems software also facilitates the programming, testing, and debugging of computer programs. It is more general than application software and is usually independent of any specific type of application. Systems software programs support application software by directing the basic functions of the computer. For example, when the computer is turned on, the initialization program (a systems program) prepares and readies all devices for processing. Other common operating systems tasks are shown in Table 4.1.

Systems software can be grouped into two major functional categories: system control programs and system support programs.

System Control Programs

System control programs control the use of the hardware, software, and data resources of a computer system. The main system control program is the operating system. The **operating system** supervises the overall operation of the computer, including monitoring the computer's status and scheduling operations, which include the input and output processes. In addition, the operating system allocates CPU time and main memory to programs running on the computer, and it also provides an interface between the user and the hardware. This interface hides the complexity of the hardware from the user. That is, you do not have to know how the hardware actually operates, just what the hardware will do and what you need to do to obtain desired results. Specifically, the operating system provides services that include process management, virtual memory, file management, security, fault tolerance, and the user interface.

Process management means managing the program or programs (also called jobs) running on the processor at a given time. In the simplest case (a desktop operating system), the operating system loads a program into main memory and executes it. The program utilizes the computer's resources until it relinquishes control. Some operating systems offer more sophisticated forms of process management, such as *multitasking*, *multithreading*, and *multiprocessing*.

The management of two or more tasks, or programs, running on the computer system at the same time is called **multitasking**, or **multiprogramming**. The first program is executed until an interruption occurs, such as a request for input. While the input request is handled, the execution of a second program begins. Because switching among these programs occurs so rapidly, they appear to be executing at the same time. However, because there is only one processor, only one program is actually in execution mode at any one time. **Multithreading** is a form of multitasking that focuses on running multiple tasks within a single application simultaneously. For example, a word processor application may edit one document while another document is being spell-checked.

Table 4.1   Common Operating Systems Tasks

• Monitoring performance	• Formatting diskettes
• Correcting errors	• Controlling the computer monitor
• Providing and maintaining the user interface	• Sending jobs to the printer
• Starting ("booting") the computer	• Maintaining security and limiting access
• Reading programs into memory	• Locating files
• Managing memory allocation to those programs	• Detecting viruses
• Placing files and programs in secondary storage	• Compressing data
• Creating and maintaining directories	

Time-sharing is an extension of multiprogramming. In this mode, a number of users operate online with the same CPU, but each uses a different input/output terminal. The programs of these users are placed into partitions in primary storage. Execution of these programs rotates among all users, occurring so rapidly that it appears to each user as though he or she were the only one using the computer.

Multiprocessing occurs when a computer system with two or more processors can run more than one program, or thread, at a given time by assigning them to different processors. Multiprocessing uses simultaneous processing with multiple CPUs, whereas multiprogramming involves concurrent processing with one CPU.

Virtual memory simulates more main memory than actually exists in the computer system. It allows a program to behave as if it had access to the full storage capacity of a computer, rather than just access to the amount of primary storage installed on the computer. Virtual memory divides an application program or module into fixed-length portions called *pages*. The system executes some pages of instructions while pulling others from secondary storage. In effect, primary storage is extended into a secondary storage device, allowing users to write programs as if primary storage were larger than it actually is. This enlarged capability boosts the speed of the computer and allows it to efficiently run programs with very large numbers of instructions.

The operating system is responsible for *file management* and *security*, managing the arrangement of, and access to, files held in secondary storage. The operating system creates and manages a directory structure that allows files to be created and retrieved by name, and it also may control access to those files based on permissions and access controls. The operating system provides other forms of security as well. For example, it must typically provide protected memory and maintain access control on files in the file system. The operating system also must keep track of users and their authority level, as well as audit changes to security permissions.

Fault tolerance is the ability of a system to produce correct results and to continue to operate even in the presence of faults or errors. Fault tolerance can involve error-correcting memory, redundant computer components, and related software that protect the system from hardware, operating system, or user errors.

Although operating systems perform some of their functions automatically, for certain tasks the user interacts directly with the computer through the systems software. The ease or difficulty of such interaction is to a large extent determined by the *interface design*. Older text-based interfaces like DOS (*d*isk *o*perating *s*ystem) required typing in cryptic commands. In an effort to make computers more user-friendly, the graphical user interface was developed.

The **graphical user interface (GUI)** allows users to have direct control of visible objects (such as icons) and actions that replace complex command syntax. The GUI was developed by researchers at Xerox PARC (Palo Alto Research Center), and then popularized by the Apple MacIntosh computer. Microsoft soon introduced its GUI-based Windows operating system for IBM-style PCs. The next generation of GUI technology will incorporate features such as virtual reality, head-mounted displays, sound and speech, pen and gesture recognition, animation, multimedia, artificial intelligence, and cellular/wireless communication capabilities.

The next step in the evolution of GUIs is social interfaces. A **social interface** is a user interface that guides the user through computer applications by using cartoonlike characters, graphics, animation, and voice commands. The cartoonlike characters can be cast as puppets, narrators, guides, inhabitants, avatars (computer-generated humanlike figures), or hosts.

Types of operating systems.   As previously discussed, operating systems are necessary in order for computer hardware to function. **Operating environments**, which add features that enable system developers to create applications without directly accessing the operating system, function only with an operating system. That is, operating environments are not operating systems, but work only with an operating system. For example, the early versions of Windows were operating environments that provided a graphical user interface and worked only with MS-DOS.

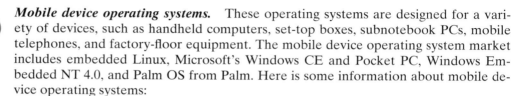

www.wiley.com/
college/turban

Operating systems (OSs) can be categorized by the number of users they support as well as by their level of sophistication (see the Operating Systems list on the Web site). *Operating systems for mobile devices* are designed to support a single person using a mobile, handheld device, or information appliance. *Desktop operating systems* are designed to support a single user or a small workgroup of users. *Departmental server operating systems* typically support from a few dozen to a few hundred users. *Enterprise server operating systems* generally support thousands of simultaneous users and millions or billions of simultaneous transactions. *Supercomputer operating systems* support the particular processing needs of supercomputers.

Supercomputer and enterprise server operating systems offer the greatest functionality, followed by departmental server operating systems, desktop operating systems, and finally mobile device operating systems. An important exception is the user interface, which is most sophisticated on desktop operating systems and least sophisticated on supercomputer and enterprise server operating systems.

www.wiley.com/
college/turban

Mobile device operating systems.   These operating systems are designed for a variety of devices, such as handheld computers, set-top boxes, subnotebook PCs, mobile telephones, and factory-floor equipment. The mobile device operating system market includes embedded Linux, Microsoft's Windows CE and Pocket PC, Windows Embedded NT 4.0, and Palm OS from Palm. Here is some information about mobile device operating systems:

- **Embedded Linux** is a compact form of Linux used in mobile devices. Both IBM and Motorola are developing Embedded Linux for mobile devices.

- **Windows CE**, a 32-bit operating system, is Microsoft's information appliance operating system. Windows CE includes scaled-down versions (known as *pocket versions*) of Microsoft Word, Excel, PowerPoint, and Internet Explorer.

- **Pocket PC** is a version of Windows CE 3.0 specifically designed for personal digital assistants and handheld computers.

- **Windows Embedded NT 4.0**, a 32-bit operating system, is aimed at embedded devices that require more operating system capabilities and flexibility than Windows CE can offer.

- The **Palm operating system** was developed by Palm for its PalmPilot handheld, pen-input PDAs. Palm OS includes a graphical user interface, and users must learn a stylized alphabet, called Graffiti, to make the device receive handwritten input.

www.wiley.com/
college/turban

(For technical discussions of Mobile Device Operating Systems, see this section on the book's Web site.)

Desktop and notebook computer operating systems.   The Windows family is the leading series of desktop operating systems. The **MS-DOS (Microsoft Disk Operating System)** was one of the original operating systems for the IBM PC and its clones. This 16-bit operating system, with its text-based interface, has now been almost totally replaced by GUI operating systems such as Windows 2000 and Windows XP. **Windows 1.0** through **Windows 3.1** (successive versions) were not operating systems, but were operating environments that provided the GUI that operated with, and extended the capabilities of, MS-DOS.

Windows 95, released in 1995, was the first of a series of products in the **Windows operating system** that provided a streamlined GUI by using icons to provide instant access to common tasks. Windows 95 is a 32-bit operating system that features multi-tasking, multithreading, networking, and Internet integration capabilities, including the ability to integrate fax, e-mail, and scheduling programs. Windows 95 also offers plug-and-play capabilities. **Plug-and-play** is a feature that can automate the installation of new hardware by enabling the operating system to recognize new hardware and install the necessary software (called device drivers) automatically.

Subsequent products in the Microsoft Windows operating system are:

- **Windows 98** was not a major upgrade to Windows 95, but did offer minor refinements, bug fixes, and enhancements to Windows 95.

- **Windows Millennium Edition (Windows ME)** is a major update to Windows 95, offering improvements for home computing in the areas of PC reliability, digital media, home networking, and the online experience.

- **Windows NT** is an operating system for high-end desktops, workstations, and servers. It provides the same GUI as Windows 95 and 98, and has more powerful multitasking, multiprocessing, and memory-management capabilities. Windows NT supports software written for DOS and Windows, and it provides extensive computing power for new applications with large memory and file requirements. It is also designed for easy and reliable connection with networks and other computing machinery, and is proving popular in networked systems in business organizations.

- **Windows 2000** is a renamed version of Windows NT 5.0. This operating system has added security features, will run on multiple-processor computers, and offers added Internet and intranet functionality.

- **Windows XP** is the first upgrade to Windows 2000 and has three versions: a 32-bit consumer version, a 32-bit business version, and a 64-bit business version. Windows XP is the first version of Windows to support Microsoft's .NET platform (discussed later in the chapter).

- Following Windows XP, Microsoft will release its first fully .NET-enabled Windows operating system, code-named **Blackcomb**. Blackcomb will feature natural interfaces, including speech recognition and handwriting support.

UNIX provides many sophisticated desktop features, including multiprocessing and multitasking. UNIX is valuable to business organizations because it can be used on many different sizes of computers (or different platforms), can support many different hardware devices (e.g., printers, plotters, etc.), and has numerous applications written to run on it. UNIX has many different versions. Most UNIX vendors are focusing their development efforts on servers rather than on desktops, and are promoting Linux for use on the desktop.

Linux is a powerful version of the UNIX operating system that is completely free of charge. It offers multitasking, virtual memory management, and TCP/IP networking. Linux was originally written by Linus Torvalds at the University of Helsinki in Finland in 1991. He then released the source code to the world (called open source software, as discussed in the chapter opening case). Since that time, many programmers around the world have worked on Linux and written software for it. The result is that, like UNIX, Linux now runs on multiple hardware platforms, can support many different hardware devices, and has numerous applications written to run on it. Linux is becoming widely used by Internet service

"I haven't the slightest idea who he is. He came bundled with the software."

providers (ISPs), the companies that provide Internet connections. The clearinghouse for Linux information on the Internet may be found at *linuxhq.com.*

The **Macintosh operating system X (ten) (Mac OS X)**, for Apple Macintosh microcomputers, is a 32-bit operating system that supports Internet integration, virtual memory management, and AppleTalk networking. Mac OS X features a new Aqua user interface, advanced graphics, virtual memory management, and multitasking.

IBM's **OS/2** is a 32-bit operating system that supports multitasking, accommodates larger applications, allows applications to be run simultaneously, and supports networked multimedia and pen-computing applications.

Sun's **Java operating system (JavaOS)** executes programs written in the Java language (described later in this chapter) without the need for a traditional operating system. It is designed for Internet and intranet applications and embedded devices. JavaOS is designed for handheld products and thin-client computing. (For a more technical discussion of the various Desktop and Notebook Computer Operating Systems—MS DOS and Windows, Linux, and Apple Macintosh—see the material on the Web.)

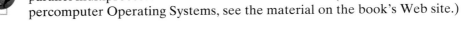

www.wiley.com/college/turban

Departmental server operating systems. The major departmental server operating systems include UNIX, Linux, Windows 2000, Windows XP, and Novell NetWare. Although some of these are also desktop operating systems, all can serve as departmental server operating systems because of their strong scalability, reliability, backup, security, fault tolerance, multitasking, multiprocessing, TCP/IP networking (Internet integration), network management, and directory services.

Enterprise server operating systems. Enterprise server operating systems (e.g., IBM's OS/390, VM, VSE, and OS/400) generally run on mainframes and midrange systems. Enterprise operating systems offer superior manageability, security, stability, and support for online applications, secure electronic commerce, multiple concurrent users, large (terabyte) databases, and millions of transactions per day. Enterprise server operating systems also offer *partitioning*, a method of segmenting a server's resources to allow the processing of multiple applications on a single system. (For a technical discussion of Partitioning, see the material on the book's Web site.)

OS/400 is IBM's operating system for the AS/400 server line, which was renamed *eServer iSeries 400.* IBM's z/Architecture (z/OS), a new 64-bit mainframe operating system, replaces all previous mainframe operating systems. The first system implementing the new architecture is the *eServer zSeries 900.* (For a technical discussion of IBM's Enterprise Server Operating Systems, see the material on the Web.)

Supercomputer operating systems. Supercomputer operating systems target the supercomputer hardware market. Examples of these systems include the Cray Unicos and IBM's AIX (both types of UNIX). These two operating systems manage highly parallel multiprocessor and multiuser environments. (For a technical discussion of Supercomputer Operating Systems, see the material on the book's Web site.)

System Support Programs

The second major category of systems software, **system support programs**, supports the operations, management, and users of a computer system by providing a variety of support services. Examples of system support programs are system utility programs, performance monitors, and security monitors.

System utilities are programs that have been written to accomplish common tasks such as sorting records, checking the integrity of diskettes (i.e., amount of storage available and existence of any damage), and creating directories and subdirectories. They also restore accidentally erased files, locate files within the directory structure, manage memory usage, and redirect output.

System performance monitors are programs that monitor the processing of jobs on a computer system. They monitor computer system performance and produce reports containing detailed statistics relating to the use of system resources, such as processor time, memory space, input/output devices, and system and application programs. These reports are used to plan and control the efficient use of the computer system resources and to help troubleshoot the system in case of problems.

System security monitors are programs that monitor the use of a computer system to protect it and its resources from unauthorized use, fraud, or destruction. Such programs provide the computer security needed to allow only authorized users access to the system. Security monitors also control use of the hardware, software, and data resources of a computer system. Finally, these programs monitor use of the computer and collect statistics on attempts at improper use.

Before you go on . . .

1. What are the two main types of systems software?

2. What are differences among mobile device, desktop, departmental server, enterprise, and supercomputer operating systems?

4.3   APPLICATION SOFTWARE

As defined earlier, application software consists of instructions that direct a computer system to perform specific information processing activities and that provide functionality for users. Because there are so many different uses for computers, there are a correspondingly large number of different application software programs available. A controversial set of software applications involves surveillance. A box on Surveillance Software on our Web site discusses the pros and cons of various types of such software.

www.wiley.com/
college/turban

Types of Application Software

Application software includes proprietary application software and off-the-shelf application software. **Proprietary application software** addresses a specific or unique business need for a company. This type of software may be developed in-house by the organization's information systems personnel or it may be commissioned from a software vendor. Such specific software programs developed for a particular company by a vendor are called **contract software**.

Alternatively, **off-the-shelf application software** can be purchased, leased, or rented from a vendor that develops programs and sells them to many organizations. Off-the-shelf software may be a standard package or it may be customizable. Special-purpose programs or "packages" can be tailored for a specific purpose, such as inventory control or payroll. The word **package** is a commonly used term for a computer program (or group of programs) that has been developed by a vendor and is available for purchase in a prepackaged form. We will further discuss the methodology involved in acquiring application software, whether proprietary or off the shelf, in Chapter 14.

Types of Personal Application Software

General-purpose, off-the-shelf application programs that support general types of processing, rather than being linked to any specific business function, are referred to as **personal application software**. This type of software consists of nine widely used packages: spreadsheet, data management, word processing, desktop publishing, graphics, multimedia, communications, speech-recognition software, and groupware. Software suites combine some of these packages and integrate their functions.

Personal application software is designed to help individual users increase their productivity. Below is a description of the nine main types.

Spreadsheets.   Computer **spreadsheet software** transforms a computer screen into a ledger sheet, or grid, of coded rows and columns. Users can enter numeric or textual data into each grid location, called a *cell*. In addition, a formula can be entered into a cell to obtain a calculated answer displayed in that cell's location. With spreadsheets, users can also develop and use **macros**, which are sequences of commands that can be executed with just one simple instruction.

Computer spreadsheet packages can be used for financial information, such as income statements or cash flow analysis. They are also used for forecasting sales, analyzing insurance programs, summarizing income tax data, and analyzing investments. They are relevant for many other types of data that can be organized into rows and columns. Although spreadsheet packages such as Microsoft's Excel and Lotus 1–2-3 are thought of primarily as spreadsheets, they also offer data management and graphical capabilities. Therefore, they may be called **integrated packages**. Figure 4.2 shows an example from a Microsoft Excel spreadsheet.

Spreadsheets are valuable for applications that require modeling and what-if analysis. After a set of mathematical relationships has been specified by the user, the spreadsheet can be recalculated instantly using a different set of assumptions (i.e., a different set of mathematical relationships).

Data management.   **Data management software** supports the storage, retrieval, and manipulation of related data. There are two basic types of data management software: *simple filing programs* patterned after traditional, manual data-filing techniques, and *database management programs* that take advantage of a computer's extremely fast and accurate ability to store and retrieve data in primary and secondary storage. File-based management software is typically very simple to use and is often very fast, but it offers limited flexibility in how the data can be searched. Database management software has the opposite strengths and weaknesses. Microsoft's Access is an example of popular database management software. In Chapter 5, we discuss data management in much more detail.

Word processing.   **Word processing software** allows the user to manipulate text rather than just numbers. Modern word processors contain many productive writing

Student Name	Exam 1	Exam 2	Exam 3	Total Points	Grade
Carr, Harold	73	95	90	258	B
Ford, Nelson	92	90	81	263	B
Lewis, Bruce	86	88	98	272	A
Snyder, Charles	63	71	76	210	C
Average	78.5	86.0	86.25	250.75	

Figure 4.2   *This Microsoft Excel spreadsheet shows a sample calculation of student grades.*

and editing features. A typical word processing software package consists of an integrated set of programs including an editor program, a formatting program, a print program, a dictionary, a thesaurus, a grammar checker, a mailing list program, and integrated graphics, charting, and drawing programs. **WYSIWYG** (an acronym for What You See Is What You Get, pronounced "wiz-e-wig") word processors have the added advantage of displaying the text material on the screen exactly—or almost exactly—as it will look on the final printed page (based on the type of printer connected to the computer). Word processing software enables users to be much more productive because the software makes it possible to create and modify the document electronically in memory.

Desktop publishing.   **Desktop publishing software** represents a level of sophistication beyond regular word processing. In the past, newsletters, announcements, advertising copy, and other specialized documents had to be laid out by hand and then typeset. Desktop software allows microcomputers to perform these tasks directly. Photographs, diagrams, and other images can be combined with text, including several different fonts, to produce a finished, camera-ready document.

Graphics.   **Graphics software** allows the user to create, store, and display or print charts, graphs, maps, and drawings. Graphics software enables users to absorb more information more quickly and to spot relationships and trends in data more easily. There are three basic categories of graphics software packages: presentation graphics, analysis graphics, and computer-aided design software.

    Presentation graphics software allows users to create graphically rich presentations. Many packages have extensive libraries of clip art—pictures that can be electronically "clipped out" and "pasted" into the finished image. Figure 4.3 demonstrates some of the capabilities of presentation graphics. One of the most widely used presentation graphics programs is Microsoft's PowerPoint.

    Analysis graphics applications additionally provide the ability to convert previously analyzed data—such as statistical data—into graphic formats like bar charts, line charts, pie charts, and scatter diagrams. Both presentation graphics and analysis graphics are useful in preparing graphic displays for business presentations, from sales results to marketing research data.

Figure 4.3 *Presentation graphics software.*

Computer-aided design (CAD) software, used for designing items for manufacturing, allows designers to design and "build" production prototypes in software, test them as a computer object under given parameters (sometimes called *computer-aided engineering*, or *CAE*), compile parts and quantity lists, outline production and assembly procedures, and then transmit the final design directly to machines. The prototype in Figure 4.4 was produced via computer-aided design.

Manufacturers of all sorts are finding uses for CAD software. *Computer-aided manufacturing (CAM)* software uses digital design output, such as that from a CAD system, to directly control production machinery. *Computer-integrated manufacturing (CIM)* software is embedded within each automated production machine to produce a product. Overall, a design from CAD software is used by CAM software to control individual CIM programs in individual machines. Used effectively, CAD/CAM/CIM software can dramatically shorten development time and give firms the advantage of economies of scope.

Figure 4.4 *Computer-aided design (CAD).*

Multimedia.   **Multimedia software** combines at least two media for input or output of data. These media include audio (sound), voice, animation, video, text, graphics, and images. Multimedia can also be thought of as the combination of *spatial*-based media (text and images) with *time*-based media (sound and video).

Communications.   Computers are often interconnected in order to share or relate information. To exchange information, computers utilize **communications software**. This software allows computers, whether they are located close together or far apart, to exchange data over dedicated or public cables, telephone lines, satellite relay systems, or microwave circuits.

When communications software exists in both the sending and receiving computers, they are able to establish and relinquish electronic links, code and decode data transmissions, verify transmission errors (and correct them automatically), and check for and handle transmission interruptions or conflicting transmission priorities. E-mail and desktop videoconferencing rely on communications software.

Speech-recognition software.   Two categories of **speech-recognition software** are available today: discrete speech and continuous speech. *Discrete speech recognition* can interpret only one word at a time, so users must place distinct pauses between words. This type of voice recognition can be used to control PC software (by using words such as "execute" or "print"). But it is inadequate for dictating a memo, because users find it difficult to speak with measurable pauses between every word and still maintain trains of thought.

Software for *continuous speech recognition* can interpret a continuing stream of words. The software must understand the context of a word to determine its correct spelling, and be able to overcome accents and interpret words very quickly. These requirements mean that continuous speech-recognition software must have a computer with significantly more speed and memory than discrete speech software.

Many firms and people use speech-recognition software when use of a mouse and a keyboard is impractical. For example, such software can provide an excellent alternative for users with disabilities, repetitive strain injuries, or severe arthritis. The following example demonstrates use of speech-recognition software.

EXAMPLE

Handling calls with speech recognition.   JetAir Belgium (*jetair.be*), a travel company, handles 3,000 calls a day from 2,000 travel agents. Before installing its voice-recognition system, JetAir lost 20 percent of its calls, because operators were busy or the calls were too complicated for tone-activated voice mail. The speech-recognition system recognizes both Flemish and French among 13 supported languages. In addition to retaining the lost calls, JetAir estimates that it handles 150 extra calls daily, worth up to $25 million in annual revenue. ●

Groupware. Groupware is a class of software products that facilitates communication, coordination, and collaboration among people. Groupware is important because it allows workgroups—people who need to interact with one another within an organization—to communicate and share information, even when they are working together at a distance. Groupware can provide many benefits to businesses, including more efficient and effective project management, location independence, increased communications capability, increased information availability, and improved workflow.

Groupware comes in many varieties. The most elaborate system, IBM's Lotus Notes/Domino, is a document-management system, a distributed client/server database, and a basis for intranet and electronic commerce systems, as well as a communication support tool. This class of groupware supplements real-time communications with asynchronous electronic connections (e.g., electronic mail and other forms of messaging). Thanks to electronic networks, e-mail, and shared discussion databases, group members can communicate, access data, and exchange or update data at any time and from any place. Group members might store all their official memos, formal reports, and informal conversations related to particular projects in a shared, online data store, such as a database. Then, as individual members need to check on the contents, they can access the shared database to find the information they need. An example of the latest type of groupware, *collaboration software*, is shown in IT's About Business Box 4.1.

IT's About Business   *pg.com*

Box 4.1:   Collaboration software helps Procter & Gamble

Procter & Gamble's computer network links 900 factories and 17 product development centers in 73 countries. The global network enables the $39 billion consumer-products company to produce and market 300 of the world's best-known brands, including Tide, Folgers, and Crest. However, it has become increasingly difficult to make such a wide variety of products with speed, efficiency, and quality.

To help solve the problem, P&G uses software from MatrixOne (*matrixone.com*) to automate P&G's product-development process. The software lets researchers comb a database of 200,000 product designs to see if they already exist in another part of the company, eliminating redundant efforts. The software has also reduced product design times by half, because it lets geographically dispersed developers produce formulas together on the Web and enables managers to measure their progress against timetables. When product development falls behind schedule, the software automatically sends an e-mail reminder to a worker when he or she needs, for example, to approve the packaging of a detergent.

Companies have been using the Web to share information and streamline purchasing, and now they are using new Web software tools to help employees and business partners work together to make products faster and more cheaply. The increase in collaboration stems partly from a dissatisfaction with the limitations of electronic marketplaces. Many public e-marketplaces are essentially auction houses. They do not offer the means to form deep business relationships online. Through online collaboration, a manufacturer can, for example, share its sales forecasts with suppliers so they can fine tune inventories, resulting in potentially enormous savings.

Source: "Simultaneous Software," *BusinessWeek*, August 27, 2001, pp. 146–147.

Questions

1. What is the relationship between corporate intranets and collaboration software? Between corporate extranets and collaboration software?

2. Can collaboration software work between companies? Give an example.

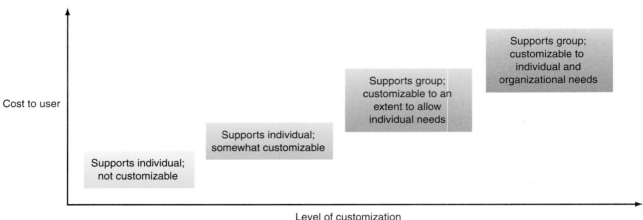

Figure 4.5   *Off-the-shelf software suites for personal productivity can be categorized according to cost and level of customization.*

Other groupware approaches focus on workflow, enhanced electronic mail (e.g., listserve), calendaring and scheduling, electronic meeting support, and videoconferencing. Microsoft's Exchange is primarily an electronic messaging server that incorporates groupware functionality for sharing information. It provides e-mail and supports workgroup activities with additional features such as interactive scheduling, built-in access to shared bulletin boards, forms design, and access to publicly shared folders on computer networks. It also offers built-in connectivity to the Internet or corporate intranets. Other leading groupware products provide functionality similar to Microsoft Exchange. These products include Netscape's SuiteSpot Servers, Novell's GroupWise, and Oracle's InterOffice. For Common Groupware Features, see the Web site.

www.wiley.com/
college/turban

Software Suites and Other Personal Application Software

Software suites are collections of application software packages that integrate some or all of the nine functions of the packages described in this section. Software suites can include word processors, spreadsheets, database management systems, graphics programs, communications tools, and other applications. Microsoft Office, Novell Perfect Office, and Lotus SmartSuite are widely used software suites for PCs. Each of these suites includes a spreadsheet program, word processor, database program, and graphics package with the ability to move documents, data, and diagrams among them. Figure 4.5 shows how software suites can be categorized according to cost and level of customization.

Surprisingly, there are even more types of personal application software that may be of interest to businesspeople. See Other Types of Personal Application Software for Businesspeople on the Web site.

www.wiley.com/
college/turban

Before you go on . . .

1. What classes of personal application software are essential for the productivity of a business or other organization with which you are familiar? Which are nonessential?

2. How can groupware add strategic advantage in that business/organization?

4.4 SOFTWARE ISSUES

The importance of software in computer systems has brought new issues to the forefront for organizational managers. These issues include software evaluation and selection, software licensing, software upgrades, open systems, and open source software.

Software Evaluation and Selection

The software evaluation and selection decision is a difficult one that is affected by many factors. Manager's Checklist 4.1 summarizes these selection factors. The first part of the selection process involves understanding the organization's software needs and identifying the criteria that will be used in making the eventual decision. Once the software requirements are established, specific software should be evaluated. An evaluation team composed of representatives from every group that will have a role in building and using the software should be chosen for the evaluation process. The team will study the proposed alternatives and find the software that promises the best match between the organization's needs and the software capabilities. Software Evaluation Criteria are shown on the Web site.

www.wiley.com/college/turban

Software Licensing

Vendors spend a great deal of time and money developing their software products. To protect this investment, they must protect their software from being copied and distributed by individuals and other software companies. A company can copyright its software, which means that the U.S. Copyright Office grants the company the exclusive

Manager's Checklist 4.1

Software Selection Factors

Factor	Considerations
Size and location of user base	Does the proposed software support a few users in a single location? Or can it accommodate large numbers of geographically dispersed users?
Availability of system administration tools	Does the software offer tools that monitor system usage? Does it maintain a list of authorized users and provide the level of security needed?
Costs—initial and subsequent	Is the software affordable, taking into account all costs, including installation, training, and maintenance?
System capabilities	Does the software meet both current and anticipated future needs?
Existing computing environment	Is the software compatible with existing hardware, software, and communications networks?
In-house technical skills	Should the organization develop software applications in-house, purchase off the shelf, or contract software out of house?

legal right to reproduce, publish, and sell that software. The Software Publisher's Association (SPA) enforces software copyright laws in corporations through a set of guidelines. These guidelines state that when IS managers cannot find proof of purchase for software, they should get rid of the software or purchase new licenses for its use. A *license* is permission granted under the law to engage in an activity otherwise unlawful. The SPA audits companies to see that the software used is properly licensed. Fines for improper software are heavy. IS managers are now taking inventory of their software assets to ensure that they have the appropriate number of software licenses.

Although many people do so routinely, copying software is illegal. The Software Publishers Association has stated that software privacy amounts to approximately $15 billion annually. Software developers, failing to recoup in sales the money invested to develop their products, are often forced to curtail spending on research and development. Also, smaller software companies may be driven out of business, because they cannot sustain the losses that larger companies can. The end result is that innovation is dampened and consumers suffer. Consumers also pay higher prices to offset the losses caused by software piracy.

As the number of desktop computers continues to increase and businesses continue to decentralize, it becomes more and more difficult for IS managers to manage their software assets. As a result, new firms have sprouted up to specialize in tracking software licenses for a fee. Firms such as ASAP Software, Software Spectrum, and others will track and manage a company's software licenses, to ensure that company's compliance with U.S. copyright laws.

Software Upgrades

Another issue of interest to organizational management is software upgrades. Software vendors revise their programs and sell new versions often. The revised software may offer valuable enhancements, or, on the other hand, it may offer little in terms of additional capabilities. Also, the revised software may contain bugs. Deciding whether to purchase the newest software can be a problem for organizations and their IS managers. It is also difficult to decide whether to be one of the first companies to buy and take strategic advantage of new software before competitors do, and take the risk of falling prey to previously undiscovered bugs.

Open Systems

The concept of **open systems** refers to a model of computing products that work together. Achieving this goal is possible through the use of the same operating system with compatible software on all the different computers that would interact with one another in an organization. A complementary approach is to produce application software that will run across all computer platforms. If hardware, operating systems, and application software are designed as open systems, the user would be able to purchase the best software for the job without worrying whether it will run on particular hardware. As an example, much Apple MacIntosh application software would not run on Wintel (Windows-Intel) PCs, and vice versa. Neither of these would run on a mainframe. Certain operating systems, like UNIX, will run on almost any machine. Therefore, to achieve an open-systems goal, organizations frequently employ UNIX on their desktop and larger machines so that software designed for UNIX will operate on any machine. Recent advances toward the open-systems goal involve using the Java language, which can be run on many types of computers, in place of a traditional operating system. Programs written in Java can then be executed by any machine (as will be explained in a later section).

Open Source Software

Open systems should not be confused with open source software. As discussed in the chapter opening case, **open source software** is software made available in source code form at no cost to developers. There are many examples of open-source software, including the GNU (GNU's Not UNIX) suite of software (*gnu.org*) developed by the Free Software Foundation (*fsf.org*); the Linux operating system; Apache Web server (*apache.org*); sendmail SMTP (Send Mail Transport Protocol) e-mail server (*sendmail.org*); the Perl programming language (*perl.com*), the Netscape Mozilla browser (*mozilla.org*); and Sun's StarOffice applications suite (*sun.com*).

Open source software is, in many cases, more reliable than commercial software. Because the code is available to many developers, more bugs are discovered, are discovered early and quickly, and are fixed immediately. Support for open source software is also available from companies that provide products derived from the software, for example, Red Hat for Linux (*redhat.com*). These firms provide education, training, and technical support for the software for a fee.

Before you go on . . .

1. What are some of the legal issues involved in acquiring and using software in most business organizations?

2. What are some of the criteria used for evaluating software when planning a purchase?

3. What is open source software and what are its advantages?

4.5   PROGRAMMING LANGUAGES

Programming languages provide the basic building blocks for all systems and application software. Programming languages allow people to tell computers what to do and are the means by which software systems are developed. This section will describe the five generations of programming languages.

Machine Language

Machine language is the lowest-level computer language, consisting of the internal representation of instructions and data. This machine code—the actual instructions understood and directly executable by the central processing unit—is composed of binary digits. Machine language is the only programming language that the machine actually understands. Therefore, machine language is considered the **first-generation language.** All other languages must be translated into machine language before the computer can run the instructions. Because a computer's central processing unit is capable of executing only machine language programs, such programs are machine dependent (nonportable). That is, the machine language for one type of central processor may not run on other types.

Machine language is extremely difficult to understand and use by programmers. As a result, increasingly more user-friendly languages have been developed. Figure 4.6 (on page 110) gives an overview of the evolution of programming languages, from the first-generation machine language to more humanlike natural language. These user-oriented

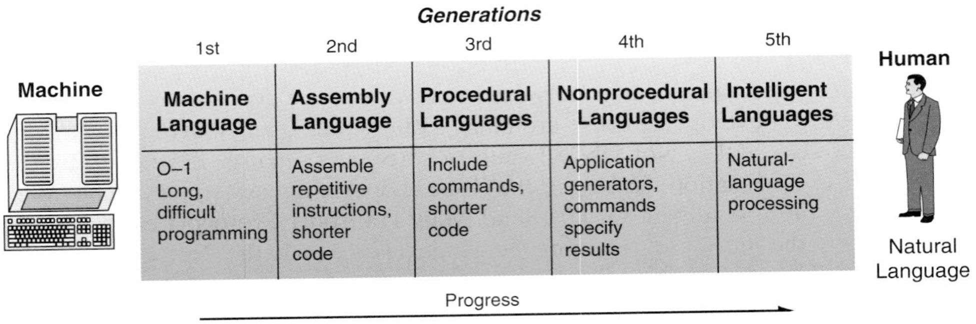

Figure 4.6 *The evolution of programming languages. With each generation, progress is made toward a humanlike natural language.*

languages make it much easier for people to program, but they are impossible for the computer to execute without first translating the program into machine language. The set of instructions written in a user-oriented language is called a **source program**. The set of instructions produced after translation into machine language is called the **object program**.

Programming in a higher-level language (i.e., a user-oriented language) is easier and less time consuming, but additional processor time is required to translate the program before it can be executed. Therefore, one trade-off in the use of higher-level languages is a decrease in programmer time and effort for an increase in processor time needed for translation.

Assembly Language

An **assembly language** is the next level up from machine language. It is still considered a lower-level language but is more user-friendly because it represents machine-language instructions and data locations in primary storage by using *mnemonics*, or memory aids, which people can more easily use. Assembly languages are considered **second-generation languages**.

Compared to machine language, assembly language eases the job of the programmer considerably. However, each statement in an assembly language must still be translated into a single statement in machine language, and assembly languages are still hardware dependent. Translating an assembly language program into machine language is accomplished by a systems software program called an **assembler**.

Procedural Languages

Procedural languages are the next step in the evolution of user-oriented programming languages. They are also called **third-generation languages**, or 3GLs. Procedural languages are much closer to so-called *natural language* (the way we talk) and therefore are easier to write, read, and alter. Moreover, one statement in a procedural language is translated into a number of machine language instructions, thereby making programming more productive. In general, procedural languages are more like natural language than assembly languages are, and they use common words rather than abbreviated mnemonics. Because of this, procedural languages are considered the first level of *higher-level languages*.

Procedural languages require the programmer to specify, step by step, exactly how the computer must accomplish a task. A procedural language is oriented toward how a result is to be produced. Because computers understand only machine language (i.e., 0s and 1s), higher-level languages must be translated into machine language prior to execution. This translation is accomplished by systems software called language

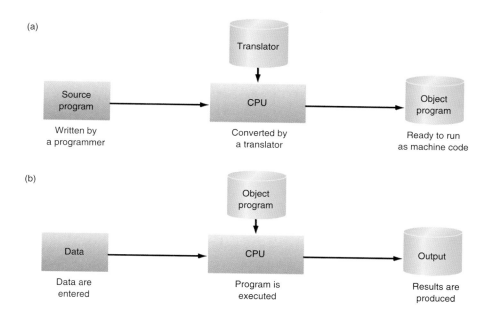

Figure 4.7   *The language translation process.*

translators. A **language translator** converts the high-level program, called *source code*, into machine language code, called *object code*. There are two types of language translators—interpreters and compilers. Figure 4.7 shows the translation process for source code.

The translation of a high-level language program to object code is accomplished by a software program called a **compiler**, which translates the entire program at once. In contrast, an **interpreter** is a compiler that translates and executes one source program statement at a time. Because this translation is done one statement at a time, interpreters tend to be simpler than compilers. This simplicity allows for more extensive debugging and diagnostic aids to be available on interpreters. For examples of FORTRAN, COBOL, and C, see Examples of Procedural Languages on the Web site.

www.wiley.com/college/turban

Nonprocedural Languages

Another type of high-level language, called **nonprocedural languages**, allows the user to specify the desired result without having to specify the detailed procedures needed for achieving the result. These languages are **fourth-generation languages (4GLs)**. An advantage of nonprocedural languages is that they can be used by nontechnical users to carry out specific functional tasks. These languages greatly simplify and accelerate the programming process, as well as reduce the number of coding errors. The 4GLs are common in database applications as query languages, report generators, and data-manipulation languages. They allow users and programmers to interrogate and access computer databases using statements that resemble natural language.

Natural Programming Languages

Natural programming languages are the next evolutionary step. They are sometimes known as **fifth-generation languages**, or **intelligent languages**. Translator programs to translate natural languages into a structured, machine-readable form are extremely complex and require a large amount of computer resources. Therefore, most of these languages are still experimental and have yet to be widely adopted by industry.

Table 4.2   Language Generations Table

Language Generation	Features				
	Portable (machine independent?)	Concise (one-to-many?)	Use of Mnemonics & Labels	Procedural?	Structured?
1st—Machine	no	no	no	yes	yes
2nd—Assembler	no	no	yes	yes	yes
3rd—High level	yes	yes	yes	yes	yes
4th—4GL	yes	yes	yes	no	yes
5th—Natural language	yes	yes	yes	no	no

We have now encountered the five generations of programming languages that communicate instructions to the computer's central processing unit. Table 4.2 summarizes the features of these five generations. But we are not finished yet; there are a handful of newer programming languages to look at before we finish this section.

Visual Programming Languages

Programming languages that are used within a graphical environment are often referred to as **visual programming languages**. These languages use a mouse, icons, symbols on the screen, or pull-down menus to make programming easier and more intuitive. Visual Basic and Visual C++ are examples of visual programming languages. Their ease of use makes them popular with nontechnical users, but the languages often lack the specificity and power of their nonvisual counterparts. Although programming in visual languages is popular in some organizations, the more complex and mission-critical applications are usually not written in visual languages.

Hypertext Markup Language

Hypertext is an approach to data management in which data are stored in a network of nodes connected by links (called **hyperlinks**). Users access data through an interactive browsing system. The combination of nodes, links, and supporting indexes for any particular topic is a **hypertext document**. A hypertext document may contain text, images, and other types of information such as data files, audio, video, and executable computer programs.

The standard language the World Wide Web uses for creating and recognizing hypertext documents is the **Hypertext Markup Language (HTML)**. HTML gives users the option of controlling visual elements such as fonts, font size, and paragraph spacing without changing the original information. HTML is very easy to use, and some modern word processing applications will automatically convert and store a conventional document in HTML. Dynamic HTML is the next step beyond HTML. **Dynamic HTML** presents richly formatted pages and lets the user interact with the content of those pages without having to download additional content from the server. This functionality means that Web pages using Dynamic HTML provide more exciting and useful information.

Enhancements and variations of HTML make possible new layout and design features on Web pages. For example, **cascading style sheets (CSSs)** are an enhancement to HTML that act as a template defining the appearance or style (such as size, color, and font) of an element of a Web page, such as a box.

English Text	HTML	XML
MNGT 3070 Introduction to MIS 3 semester hours Professor Smith	\<TITLE>Course Number\</TITLE> \<BODY> \<UL> \<LI>Introduction to MIS \<LI>3 semester hours \<LI>Professor Smith \</UL>\</BODY>	\<Department and course="MNGT 3070"> \<COURSE TITLE>Introduction to MIS\<COURSE TITLE> \<HOURS UNIT="Semester">3\</NUMBER OF HOURS> \<INSTRUCTOR>Professor Smith\<INSTRUCTOR>

Figure 4.8 *Comparison of HTML and XML.*

Extensible Markup Language (XML)

Extensible Markup Language (XML) is designed to improve the functionality of Web documents by providing more flexible and adaptable information identification. XML describes what the data in documents actually mean. XML documents can be moved to any format on any platform without the elements losing their meaning. That means the same information can be published to a Web browser, a PDA, or a smart phone, and each device would use the information appropriately. Figure 4.8 compares HTML and XML. Notice that HTML only describes where an item appears on a page, whereas XML describes what the item is. For example, HTML shows only that "Introduction to MIS" appears on line 1, where XML shows that "Introduction to MIS" is the Course Title. IT's About Business Box 4.2 shows the benefits that Fidelity has gained by standardizing on XML.

IT's About Business   *fidelity.com*   FIN

Box 4.2:   Fidelity uses XML to standardize corporate data

Fidelity Investments has made all its corporate data XML-compatible. The effort helps the world's largest mutual fund company and online brokerage eliminate up to 75 percent of the hardware and software devoted to middle-tier processing and speed the delivery of new applications.

The decision to go to XML began when Fidelity developed its Powerstreet Web trading service. At the time, Fidelity determined it would need to offer its most active traders much faster response times than its existing brokerage systems allowed. The move to XML brought other benefits as well. For example, the company was able to tie customers who have 401k plans, brokerage accounts, and IRAs under a common log-in. In the past, they required separate passwords.

Today, two-thirds of the hundreds of thousands of hourly online transactions at *fidelity.com* use XML to link the Web to back-end systems. Before XML, comparable transactions took seconds longer because they had to go through a different proprietary data translation scheme for each back-end system they retrieved data from.

Fidelity's XML strategy is most critical to bringing new applications and services to customers faster than rivals. By using XML as a common language to which all corporate data—from Web, database, transactional, and legacy systems—are translated, Fidelity is saving millions of dollars on infrastructure and development costs. Fidelity no longer has to develop translation methods for communications between the company's many systems. XML also has made it possible for Fidelity's different databases—including Oracle for its customer account information and IBM's DB2 for trading records—to respond to a single XML query.

Source: "Fidelity Retrofits All Data for XML," *InternetWeek*, August 6, 2001; *fidelity.com*.

Questions

1. What are the different ways that having all data in XML can save corporations money?

2. Could corporations standardize on other languages and also save money? Why or why not? Which languages?

Componentware

Componentware is a term used to describe component-based software applications. **Software components** are the "building blocks" of applications. They provide the operations that can be used by the application (or other applications) again and again. Any given application may contain hundreds of components, each providing specific business logic or user-interface functionality. Consider a database application as an example: The data-entry screen may contain several user-interface components for providing buttons, menus, list boxes, and so forth. There may also be business logic components to perform validation or calculations on the data, as well as components to write the data to the database. Finally, there can be components to create reports from the data, either for viewing in an on-screen chart or for printing. Component-based applications enable software developers to "snap together" applications by mixing and matching prefabricated plug-and-play software components.

Virtual Reality Modeling Language

The **Virtual Reality Modeling Language (VRML)** is a file format for describing three-dimensional interactive worlds and objects. It can be used with the World Wide Web to create three-dimensional representations of complex scenes such as illustrations, product definitions, and virtual reality presentations. VRML can represent static and animated objects, and it can have hyperlinks to other media such as sound, video, and image.

Object-Oriented Programming Languages

Object-oriented programming (OOP) languages are based on the idea of taking a small amount of data and the instructions about what to do with that data (these instructions are called **methods** in object-oriented programming) and putting both of them together into what is called an **object**. This process is called **encapsulation**. When the object is selected or activated, the computer has the desired data and takes the desired action. This is what happens when you select an icon on your GUI-equipped computer screen and click on it. That is, in object-oriented systems, programs tell objects to perform actions on themselves. For example, windows on your GUI screens do not need to be drawn through a series of instructions. Instead, a window object could be sent a message to open at a certain place on your screen, and the window will appear at that place. The window object contains the program code for opening and placing itself.

There are several basic concepts to object-oriented programming, which include classes, objects (discussed above), encapsulation (discussed above), and inheritance. For a more detailed discussion and examples of basic OOP concepts, see the Web site.

The **reusability feature** of object-oriented languages means that classes created for one purpose can be used in a different object-oriented program if desired. For example, if a class has methods that solve a very difficult computation problem, that problem does not have to be solved again by another programmer. Rather, the class is just used in the new program. This feature of reusability can represent a tremendous reduction in programming time within an organization.

A disadvantage of object-oriented programming, however, is that defining the initial library of classes is very time-consuming, so that writing a single program with OOP takes longer than conventional programming. Another disadvantage is that OOP languages, like visual programming languages, are somewhat less specific and powerful, and require more time and memory to execute than procedural languages. Popular object-oriented programming languages include Smalltalk, C++, and Java. Because Java is a powerful and popular language, we will look at it next in more detail.

www.wiley.com/
college/turban

Java.   **Java** is an object-oriented programming language developed by Sun Microsystems. The language gives programmers the ability to develop applications that work across the Internet. Java can handle text, data, graphics, sound, and video, all within one program. Java is used to develop small applications, called **applets**, which can be included in an HTML page on the Internet. When the user uses a Java-compatible browser to view a page that contains a Java applet, the applet's code is transferred to the user's system and executed by the browser.

Java becomes even more interesting when one considers that many organizations are converting their internal networks to use the Internet's TCP/IP protocol (more about this in Chapter 7). This means that with a computer network that runs the Internet protocol, applications written in Java can be stored on the network, downloaded as needed, and then erased from the local computer when the processing is completed. Users simply download the Java applets as needed, and no longer need to store copies of the application on their PC's hard drive.

Java can benefit organizations in many ways. Companies will not need to purchase numerous copies of commercial software to run on individual computers. Instead, they will purchase one network copy of the software package, made of Java applets. Rather than pay for multiple copies of software, companies may be billed for usage of their single network copy, similar to photocopying. Companies also will find it easier to set information technology standards for hardware, software, and communications; with Java, all applications processing will be independent of the type of computer platform. Companies will have better control over data and applications because they can be controlled centrally from the network servers. Finally, software management (e.g., distribution and upgrades) will be much easier and faster.

The Unified Modeling Language (UML).   Developing a model for complex software systems is as essential as having a blueprint for a large building. The **UML** is a language for specifying, visualizing, constructing, and documenting the artifacts (such as classes, objects, etc.) in object-oriented software systems. The UML makes the reuse of these artifacts easier because the language provides a common set of notations that can be used for all types of software projects.

Before you go on . . .

1. What generation of languages is popular for interacting with databases?
2. What language does a CPU actually respond to?
3. What is the difference between applications and components?
4. What are the strategic advantages of using object-oriented languages?
5. What is the Unified Modeling Language?

4.6   ENTERPRISE SOFTWARE

To respond to competitive challenges and opportunities, companies must frequently streamline their organizational processes. This kind of reorganization frequently means changing the IT infrastructure to better support the new processes. A serious difficulty that confronts most organizations as they are in the throes of change is the sheer complexity that arises from the variety of hardware and software in use. A large firm may have thousands of software programs to run its various systems, and dozens of types of hardware, with varying operating systems. Some applications may have been custom-made in-house, some specially made by vendors, and some generic off-the-shelf. Trying to get these elements to work in harmony in the first place is difficult enough. Trying to reconfigure them is often a nightmare. Firms and their IT management have to approach this new challenge differently.

Streamlining Organizational Software

Unless there are significant competitive advantages, building new custom application software has become too expensive, time consuming, and risky. Instead, many organizations are buying packaged applications. IT's About Business Box 4.3 provides an example of a customer-management software package. And organizations no longer want packages that merely automate existing processes. Rather, they want packaged applications that support integration between functional modules (i.e., human resources, operations, marketing, finance, accounting, and so on), that can be quickly changed or enhanced, and that present a common graphical look and feel, helping to reduce training and operations costs. The scope of application development projects now focuses on business processes, and therefore extends across the boundaries of the enterprise, bringing partners', suppliers', and customers' needs into the integrated business solution. This new, expanded role is filled by enterprise software.

Middleware

Internet applications designed to let one company interact with other companies are complex because of the variety of hardware and software with which they must be able to work. This complexity will increase as mobile wireless devices begin to access company sites via the Internet. **Middleware** is software designed to link application modules developed in different computer languages and running on heterogeneous platforms whether on a single machine or over a network. Middleware keeps track of the locations of the software modules that need to link to each other across a distrib-

IT's About Business

marriott.com

Box 4.3:   Customer relationship management at Marriott

Weeks in advance, Marriott planning coordinator Jennifer Rodas calls registered guests to ask them about their plans. When all is set, she faxes them an itinerary. What makes such velvet-glove treatment possible is Marriott's use of customer-management software from Siebel Systems. The hotel chain is counting on such technology to gain an edge with guests and event planners. The software lets Marriott pull together information about its customers from different departments, so that its representatives can anticipate and respond more quickly to their needs.

The biggest boost from the Siebel software is in the hotel chain's sales operations. Marriott is transforming its sales teams from order-takers for specific hotels to aggressive marketers of all Marriott properties. A salesperson in Dallas—who understands both the needs of his local customers and the chain's world inventory of hotel rooms and other facilities—can now book orders for hotels around the world. The software helped Marriott generate an additional $55 million in cross-chain sales in one year.

Source: "How Marriott Never Forgets a Guest," *Business Week,* February 21, 2000.

Questions

1. What are the various guest needs that the software can anticipate?

2. How would Marriott apply this software to first-time guests?

uted system and manages the actual exchange of information. (For a technical discussion of Middleware, see the material at the book's Web site.)

www.wiley.com/
college/turban

Organization-Wide Applications

Enterprise software consists of programs that manage the vital operations of an organization (enterprise), such as supply-chain management (movement of raw materials from suppliers through shipment of finished goods to customers), inventory replenishment, ordering, logistics coordination, human resources management, manufacturing, operations, accounting, and financial management. Some common modules of enterprise applications software are payroll, sales order processing, accounts payable/receivable, and tax accounting. For Other Common Enterprise Modules, see the Web site.

www.wiley.com/
college/turban

Enterprise software vendors are producing software that is less expensive, based on industry standards, compatible with other vendors' products, and easier to configure and install. The largest vendors—Systeme Anwendung Produkte (SAP) AG, Oracle Corporation, PeopleSoft Inc., Baan Co., Computer Associates, and J.D. Edwards—are developing software programs that make the jobs of business users and IT personnel easier. Because of the cost, complexity, and time needed to implement enterprisewide corporate applications, many companies are purchasing only the specific application (or module) required, such as manufacturing, financial, or sales force automation.

Before you go on . . .

1. What are the strategic advantages of the enterprise software approach?

2. Why is adoption of enterprise software an inherently difficult process?

 WHAT'S IN **IT** FOR ME ?

www.wiley.com/
college/turban

FOR THE ACCOUNTING MAJOR   `ACC`

Accounting application software performs the organization's accounting functions, which are repetitive and high volume. Accounting applications are data oriented rather than information oriented, and their main functions consist of data capture, storage, and manipulation. Each business transaction (e.g., a person hired, a paycheck produced, an item sold) produces data that must be captured. After capture, accounting applications manipulate the data as necessary. Accounting applications adhere to relatively standardized procedures, handle detailed data, and have a historical focus (i.e., what happened in the past).

FOR THE FINANCE MAJOR   `FIN`

Financial application software provides information to persons and groups both inside and outside the firm about the firm's financial status. Financial applications include forecasting, funds management, and control applications.

Forecasting applications predict and project the firm's future activity in the economic environment. Funds management applications use cash flow models to analyze expected cash flows. Control applications enable managers to monitor their financial performance, typically by providing information about the budgeting process and performance ratios. These applications allow managers to compare actual and budgeted expenses, produce reports, and compute ratios. Common ratios are the current ratio (current assets divided by current liabilities) and inventory turnover (cost of goods sold divided by the average inventory value).

MKT FOR THE MARKETING MAJOR

Marketing application software helps management solve problems that involve marketing the firm's products. Marketing software includes marketing research and marketing intelligence applications. Marketing intelligence applications collect information from the firm's external environment that affects marketing operations, such as information about competitors. Marketing research applications collect information on customers, prospects, and their needs.

Marketing applications provide information about the firm's products, its distribution system, its advertising and personal selling activities, and its pricing strategies. Overall, marketing applications help managers develop strategies that combine the four major elements of marketing: product, promotion, place, and price.

POM FOR THE PRODUCTION/OPERATIONS MANAGEMENT MAJOR

Managers use production/operations management applications software for production planning and as part of the physical production system. POM applications include production, inventory, quality, and cost software. These applications help management operate manufacturing facilities. Inventory applications determine the quantity of goods to reorder and when. Quality applications enable the organization to achieve product quality by monitoring the entire production process. Costing applications help managers control the costs of the production process.

Materials requirements planning (MRP) software is widely used in manufacturing. Rather than wait until it is time to reorder, MRP software identifies the materials that will be needed, their quantities, and the dates on which they will be needed, thus enabling managers to be proactive.

HRM FOR THE HUMAN RESOURCES MANAGEMENT MAJOR

Human resources management application software provides information concerning recruiting and hiring, education and training, maintaining the employee database, and termination and benefits administration. HRM applications include workforce planning, recruiting, workforce management, compensation, benefits, and environmental reporting subsystems.

Workforce planning applications allow managers to identify future personnel needs by addressing organizational charting, salary forecasting, job analysis and evaluation, planning, and workforce modeling. Recruiting applications assist managers in bringing new employees into the organization by tracking applicants and by monitoring internal and external searches. Workforce management applications include performance appraisal, training, relocation, skills and competency, succession, and disciplinary actions. Compensation applications include the functions of merit increases, payroll, executive compensation, bonus incentives, and attendance. Benefits applications encompass defined contributions, defined benefits, benefit statements, flexible benefits, stock purchase, and claims processing. Environmental reporting applications include EEO (equal employment opportunity) records and analysis, union enrollment, health records, toxic substances, and grievances.

SUMMARY

❶ Differentiate between the two major types of software.

Software consists of computer programs (coded instructions) that control the functions of computer hardware. There are two main categories of software: systems software and application software. Systems software manages the hardware resources of the computer system and functions between the hardware and the application software. Systems software includes the system control programs (operating systems) and system support programs. Application software enables users to perform specific tasks and information-processing activities. Application software may be proprietary or off-the-shelf.

❷ Describe the general functions of the operating system.

Operating systems manage the actual computer resources (i.e., the hardware). Operating systems schedule and process applications (jobs), manage and protect memory, ensure cache consistency, manage the input and output functions and hardware, manage data and files, and provide clustering support, security, fault tolerance, interapplication communications, graphical user interfaces, and windowing.

❸ Differentiate among types of operating systems and describe each type.

There are five types of operating systems: mobile, desktop, departmental, enterprise, and supercomputer. Mobile device operating systems are designed to support a single person using a mobile, handheld device or information appliance. Desktop operating systems have the least functionality and enterprise operating systems the most, with departmental operating systems in the middle. Desktop operating systems are typically designed for one user, departmental operating systems for up to several hundred users, and enterprise operating systems can handle thousands of users and millions of transactions simultaneously. Supercomputer operating systems are designed for the particular processing needs of supercomputers.

❹ Identify three methods for developing application software.

Proprietary software can be developed in-house to address the specific needs of an organization. Existing software programs can be purchased off the shelf from vendors that sell programs to many organizations and individuals. Or a combination of these two methods can be used, by purchasing off-the-shelf programs and customizing them for an organization's specific needs.

❺ Describe the major types of application software.

The major types of application software are spreadsheet, data management, word processing, desktop publishing, graphics, multimedia, communications, speech recognition, and groupware. Software suites combine several types of application software (e.g., word processing, spreadsheet, and data management) into an integrated package.

❻ Explain how software has evolved and trends for the future.

Software and programming languages continue to become more user oriented. Programming languages have evolved from the first generation of machine languages that is directly understandable to the CPU to higher levels that use more natural language and that do not require users to specify the detailed procedures for achieving desired results. This trend ensures that end users and the information systems staff will become more productive. In addition, software is becoming much more complex, expensive, and time consuming to develop. As a result, the trend is toward purchasing off-the-shelf software, often in the form of components, rather than developing it in-house. In the future, organizations will tend to buy component-based software modules to reduce costs and development time.

❼ **Describe enterprise software.**
Organizations want packaged applications that support integration between functional modules (i.e., human resources, operations, marketing, finance, accounting, etc.), that can be quickly changed or enhanced, and that present a common graphical look and feel. In addition, organizations want individual components—software modules—that can be combined as necessary to meet changing business needs. Enterprise software consists of programs that manage a company's vital operations, such as supply-chain management, inventory replenishment, ordering, logistics coordination, human resources management, manufacturing, operations, accounting, and financial management.

INTERACTIVE LEARNING SESSION

Go to the CD, access Chapter 4: Computer Software, and read the case presented. It will give case scenarios in which you will be asked to choose the best software to use for various activities. You will be presented with a list of options that will allow you to make changes if you think changes are necessary.

www.wiley.com/
college/turban

For additional resources, go to the book's Web site for Chapter 4. There you will find Web resources for the chapter, including additional material about operating systems, application software, and evaluation criteria; links to organizations, people, and technology; "IT's About Business" company links; "What's in IT for Me?" links; and a self-testing Web quiz for Chapter 4.

DISCUSSION QUESTIONS

1. You are the CIO of your company and have to develop an application of strategic importance to your firm. Do you buy an off-the-shelf application or develop it in-house? Support your answer with pros and cons of each choice.

2. You are the CIO of your company. Which computing paradigm will you support in your strategic information technology plan: the standard desktop computing model, with all the necessary functionality on the local machine, or the network computing model, where functionality is downloaded from the network as needed? Support your answer with pros and cons of each choice.

3. You have to take a programming course, or maybe more than one, in your MIS program. Which language would you choose to study? Why? Should you even have to learn a programming language?

4. What is the relationship between network computers and Java?

5. If Java and network computing become the dominant paradigm in the industry, will there be any need for in-house information systems staff? What would the staff still have to do?

PROBLEM-SOLVING ACTIVITIES

1. Research the costs and functionality of standalone personal software products such as word processing, spreadsheet, and graphics, and compare them to the costs and functionality of integrated software suites. Under what circumstances would you recommend either?

2. Different groupware products support different aspects of group work; some support many, and others only a few. With your job as an example (or one you have had in the past), determine what features you would want in your groupware. Then research the different products and identify the one most suitable for your needs.

3. Design a short program that you would like to have written in a computer language (for example, one that will calculate mortgage amortization or payroll with taxes for a small hourly workforce). Then discuss the desired program with an experienced computer programmer to determine what language should be used and why.

4. If you are not a programmer, or if you program in only one language, investigate learning how to program in conventional languages (C, for example), visual languages (e.g., Visual Basic), and object-oriented languages (e.g., Java). Which seems more intuitive and/or easier for you?

INTERNET ACTIVITIES

1. A great deal of software is available free over the Internet. Go to *shareware.cnet.com* and observe all the software available for free. Choose one and download it to your computer. Prepare a brief discussion about the software for the class.

2. Enter the IBM Web site (*ibm.com*) and search on "Software." Click on the drop box for Products and notice how many software products IBM produces. Is IBM only a hardware company? Select "Voice Recognition" and write a brief discussion of the features of IBM's voice-recognition products.

TEAM ACTIVITIES AND ROLE PLAYING

1. Go to your campus computing center and research the types of software that are available on the local area networks in the different parts of the university. Do different departments have their own stores of specialized software, or is all software centrally managed?

2. Discuss with your academic department's office director and IT support person the issue of software licensing. How does the department maintain compliance? You may also do this with the personnel at the campus computing center.

REAL-WORLD CASE   *bollingershipyards.com*

Productivity at a Shipyard

The Business Problem   Several years ago, Bollinger Shipyards was, like most shipbuilding operations, an old-economy, nontechnological, nonnetworked company. Company headquarters received information from a collection of outdated mainframe systems and in-house-developed financial software, all running separately at the company's nine shipyards. Producing the reports for basic payroll, finance, and procurement functions was a difficult, time-consuming process. And because the procurement system was nearly nonexistent, ships often sat in repair docks for weeks waiting for parts to arrive.

In the mid-1990s, Bollinger attempted to address its administrative difficulties by upgrading its computer systems. It tried two vendors of specialized enterprise resource planning software, but ended up scrapping both systems because they did not work properly.

The IT Solution   The company decided to use Oracle's e-business software suite to solve its business problems. The system, which cost $2.7 million and took eight months to build, manages every function from human resources, accounting, and finance, to procurement.

The Results   The Oracle software helped the company lower its overhead and increase its productivity. Each of the company's shipyards used to require two full-time staff members to handle administration and payroll. Now, the company uses one part-time employee per shipyard.

The Oracle software also was useful when Bollinger bought a rival, 800-person shipbuilder last year. Normally, taking on an acquired company's payroll would mean heavy overtime and many temporary employees pushing paperwork, but Bollinger's 10-person IT department just connected up the five new shipyards, loaded the new employee data into the Oracle system, and ran payroll as usual. Bollinger purchased the shipbuilder on a Tuesday, and the next week had 800 new employees on the payroll.

Bollinger's biggest gains have come from increased productivity. Each shipyard used to order its own supplies. Now shipyards send their requests to headquarters, which coordinates orders so parts and other materials arrive in a more timely manner. The company has also saved 15 percent off the time it takes to build a ship. For an 87-foot Coast Guard patrol boat that is now under construction, that savings amounts to $500,000.

But the biggest payoff for Bollinger is in procurement. By centralizing procurement, the company can now see where it is spending its money, and use that information to negotiate prices with vendors. The company expects to save as much as $5 million through procurement, twice the amount the company spent for its new information technology system.

Source: "Bollinger Shipyards," *ecompany.com*, pp. 119–120, May 2001.

Questions

1. The new information technology system cost Bollinger almost 1 percent of annual sales. Was the decision to purchase the new system risky? Why or why not?

2. Would Bollinger employees have resisted the new system, worrying about jobs being lost?

3. Now that Bollinger has a successful ERP system in place internally, what should the company do next with regard to IT in order to further reduce costs and increase efficiencies? (*Hint:* Consider the company's supply chain.)

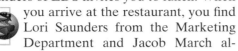

wiley.com/college/turban

Extreme Descent Snowboards

Background Matt Brandy, one of the founders of EDS invites you to lunch. When you arrive at the restaurant, you find Lori Saunders from the Marketing Department and Jacob March already seated. "Welcome," says Matt and invites you to have the seat next to him.

www.wiley.com/
college/turban

Mark introduces you to Lori Saunders. Jacob continues his conversation stating, "One of the most critical requirements for our electronic site is an excellent user interface." Lori adds, "If the company does not continually update and improve its Web presence, we risk losing our customers to our competitors. Web sites should be constructed to grab and keep the interest of a customer."

Jacob interjects his thoughts that to the end-user the software interface *is* the system. Jacob winks at you and proceeds telling everyone that he thinks this would be a good assignment for our intern to help us define what makes a good user interface.

Jacob turn to you, handing you a napkin to make your notes on.

Assignment

1. Using the World Wide Web, find two companies that have an excellent Web presence for selling a service or product. Provide the complete Web site address (URL) for each Web site. Write a report that includes an evaluation of:

- Ease of navigation from page to page
- Ease of ordering the company's product or service
- Aesthetics of the site
- Functionality of the Web site

2. Visit the EDS Web site and compare it to the two Web sites you have just evaluated. What do you like about the EDS Web site? What features from the other Web sites could be incorporated to improve the EDS Web site? How will your suggestions increase sales from the Web site? Write a report to Jacob March summarizing you findings.

MANAGING ORGANIZATIONAL DATA AND INFORMATION

5

CHAPTER PREVIEW

Our previous chapters gave us an introduction to information systems and organizational topics, as well as insights into how IT hardware and software function. These technologies and systems support organizations through their ability to handle—acquire, store, access, analyze, and transmit—electronic data. Properly managed, these data become *information*, a precious organizational resource and the basis of much competitive advantage. This chapter focuses mainly on how data are stored and accessed, with some discussion of data analysis techniques related to modern databases.

CHAPTER OUTLINE

5.1 Basics of Data Arrangement and Access
5.2 The Traditional File Environment
5.3 Databases: The Modern Approach
5.4 Database Management Systems
5.5 Logical Data Models
5.6 Data Warehouses

LEARNING OBJECTIVES

1. Discuss traditional data file organization and its problems.
2. Explain how a database approach overcomes the problems associated with the traditional file environment, and discuss disadvantages of the database approach.
3. Describe how the three most common data models organize data, and the advantages and disadvantages of each model.
4. Describe how a multidimensional data model organizes data.
5. Distinguish between a data warehouse and a data mart.
6. Discuss the similarities and differences between data mining and text mining.

HOW TO MANAGE "TONS" OF DATA

The Business Problem

Large corporations manage literally tons of data. Referring to "tons" of data may be intuitive for paper records, but it is an unusual way to describe computer-stored information, which is usually measured by gigabytes and terabytes. Still, using "tons" may give a sense of just how much data a terabyte is. Measuring data by the ton assumes that a common 20-gigabyte hard drive weighs about one pound. Figure that the weight of a shared enclosure, power supply, and electronics will roughly double the drive's weight, and we can say that 20 terabytes of data is approximately equivalent to one ton (20 GB = 1 pound; 1 TB = 1,000 GB; 40 TB = 40 GB × 1,000 = 2,000 pounds). That much storage is cumbersome and very difficult to manage.

How do enterprises deal effectively with such unwieldy mountains of information? Two data-intensive companies, Aetna and Boeing, discuss the problems they face in managing massive data stores, and how they solve them. For each company, data are a significant corporate asset resulting from huge investments of time and effort. The data are also the source of many problems for the employees who manage data.

Aetna. Aetna is responsible for 4.4 tons of data (174.6 terabytes). Most of Aetna's data is health care information. The insurance company maintains records for both health maintenance organization participants and customers covered by insurance policies. Aetna has detailed records of providers, such as doctors, hospitals, dentists, and pharmacies, and it keeps track of all the claims it has processed. Some of Aetna's larger customers send tapes containing insured employee data, but Aetna is moving toward using the Internet to collect such data.

Data integrity, backup, security, and availability are Aetna's biggest concerns. The company's data handling tools, procedures, and operations schedules have to stay ahead of not only the normal growth that results from the activities of the sales, underwriting, and claims departments, but also growth from corporate acquisitions and mergers.

Boeing. Boeing makes sure the approximately 50 to 150 terabytes (1.3 to almost 4 tons) of data the company owns remain as reliable and safe as the aircraft and spacecraft the company builds. The 50- to 150-terabyte estimate reflects Boeing's inability to know exactly how much data exist on its 150,000 desktop computers. Users do not necessarily store their data files on a server, which makes quantifying Boeing's data stores difficult. For Boeing's diverse terabytes, the firm's basic concerns are data integrity, backup, security, and availability.

Boeing's data stores are spread out across 27 states and a few overseas locations, but most computing takes place in the Puget Sound area of Washington. A major data loss has not happened yet, but the company is aware of the risks and plans to centralize the backing up and restoring of data in the future.

The IT Solutions

Aetna. Of Aetna's data, 119.2 terabytes reside on mainframe-connected disk drives, while the remaining 55.4 terabytes are on disks attached to midrange computers. Almost all of these data are located at the company's headquarters. Most of the information is in relational databases. In addition, outside customers have access to about 20 terabytes of the information. Four interconnected data centers containing 14 mainframes and more than 1,000 midrange servers process the data. It takes more than 4,100 direct-access storage devices to hold Aetna's key databases. Aetna is increasing its use of storage-area network (SAN) technology (discussed in Chapter 3) to centralize and streamline the management of its data.

124

Aetna knows the importance of maintaining large amounts of data from a logical perspective. While the physical management of large data stores is a huge effort, failing to keep the data organized leads inexorably to user workflow problems, devaluation of the data as a corporate asset, and eventually, customer complaints.

Boeing. Boeing has many mainframes and thousands of midrange servers. Much of the data exist in relational form, but across the enterprise, Boeing uses multiple file formats. Boeing uses SAN technology to manage its data.

The company currently has dozens of different backup-and-restore software utilities. Each department buys its own backup media and performs its own backup-and-restore operations. Although hard disks are inexpensive these days, data management costs on a per-disk or per-tape basis are high enough that Boeing wants to significantly reduce the amount of disk and tape "white space"—the portion of the media that Boeing does not use. In the future, Boeing wants to use a storage-on-demand model, whereby the company could simply rent whatever capacity it needed from an outside vendor and not have to worry about running out of space.

The Results

Interestingly, the results of implementing the complex blend of hardware, software, networking, and database technologies have barely enabled these two companies to stay abreast of their data management needs. The reason is that the amount of data generated by each company is growing tremendously fast. The International Data Corporation estimates that by 2003, organizations worldwide will have to manage 1.6 million terabytes of data (that is 1,600 petabytes or 1.6 exabytes of data).

(*Source:* "Managing Tons of Data," *Computerworld* (April 23, 2001); *aetna.com, boeing.com*).

What We Learned from This Case

While these companies say that good tools are important for managing terabytes of data, their IT and database administrators also agree that having a clear and comprehensive perspective on the data, via both logical and physical views, is even more critical. Security, data integrity, and data availability are not trivial concerns, they point out, and giving users easy access to the data is a never-ending job.

Boeing must manage data throughout its organizations, not just at headquarters.

Managing multiple terabytes of data is far more complex than managing gigabytes of data. You cannot simply extrapolate from experiences with small- and medium-size data stores to understand how to successfully manage "tons of data." Even backing up a database can be a major problem if the time needed to finish copying the data exceeds the time available.

Data integrity, backup, security, and availability are collectively the Holy Grail of dealing with large data stores. The sheer volume of data makes these goals a challenge, and a highly decentralized environment complicates matters even more. Developing and adhering to standardized data maintenance procedures in your organization will not only give you the best return on your data dollar investment, but will also let you sleep well at night.

Multiple terabytes of the best-maintained data in the world are just a collection of bits without accurate, meaningful data definitions and schemas. When you analyze your company's operating procedures for administering large data stores, make sure you incorporate the definitions of that information in your plan. Together, the data and their definitions are a corporate asset that contributes to your company's bottom line, and that you cannot do without.

5.1 BASICS OF DATA ARRANGEMENT AND ACCESS

Data, when properly managed, become the information upon which business decisions are based. Few business professionals are comfortable making or justifying a business decision that is not based on solid information, especially when modern data management techniques, coupled with modern hardware, software, and trained IS staff, can make access to that information rapid and easy. Certainly the managers at the two companies in the opening case would not make their marketing decisions without first conducting an extensive analysis of their data.

Organizations must be able to collect, organize, analyze, and interpret data in order to survive in hypercompetitive global markets. And data management is vital to all business functions.

The Data Hierarchy

A computer system organizes data in a hierarchy that begins with bits, and proceeds to bytes, fields, records, files, and databases (see Figure 5.1). Remember from Chapter 3 that a *bit* represents the smallest unit of data a computer can process (a 0 or a 1), and a group of eight bits, a *byte,* represents a single character, which can be a letter, a number, or a symbol. A logical grouping of characters into a word, a small group of words, or a complete number is called a **field**. For example, a student's name in a university's computer files would appear in the "name" field. A logical grouping of related fields, such as the student's name, the courses taken, the date, and the grade, comprise a **record**. A logical grouping of related records is called a **file**. For example, the student records in a single course would constitute a data file for that course. A logical grouping of related files would constitute a **database**. The student course file could be grouped with files on students' personal histories and financial backgrounds to create a student database.

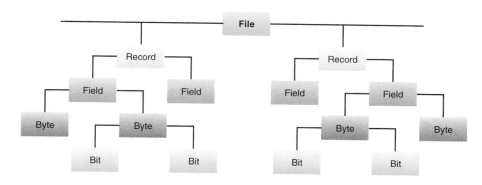

Figure 5.1 *Hierarchy of data for a computer-based file.*

A record describes an entity. An **entity** is a person, place, thing, or event about which information is maintained (such as a customer, employee, or product). Each characteristic or quality describing a particular entity is called an **attribute** (for example, customer name, employee number, product color).

Every record in a file should contain at least one field that uniquely identifies that record so that the record can be retrieved, updated, and sorted. This identifier field is called the **primary key**. For example, a student record in a U.S. college would probably use the Social Security number as its primary key. In addition, locating a particular record may require the use of secondary keys. **Secondary keys** are other fields that have some identifying information, but typically do not identify the file with complete accuracy. For example, the student's last name might be a secondary key. It should not be the primary key, as more than one student can have the same last name.

Storing and Accessing Records

Records are stored in different ways on secondary storage media, and the arrangement determines the manner in which they can be accessed. As we learned in Chapter 3, with *sequential access,* data records must be retrieved in the same physical sequence in which they are stored. In *direct, or random, access,* users can retrieve records in any sequence, without regard to the actual physical order on the storage medium. Magnetic tape utilizes sequential file organization, whereas magnetic disks use direct file organization.

Indexed sequential access method (ISAM).   The **indexed sequential access method (ISAM)** uses an index of key fields to locate individual records (see Figure 5.2 on page 128). An **index** to a file lists the key field of each record and where that record is physically located in storage. Records are stored on disks in their key sequence. A *track index* shows the highest value of the key field that can be found on a specific track. To locate a specific record, the track index is searched to locate the cylinder and the track containing the record. The track is then sequentially read to find the record.

Direct file access method.   The **direct file access method** uses the key field to locate the physical address of a record. This process employs a mathematical formula called a **transform algorithm** to translate the key field directly into the record's storage location on disk. The algorithm performs a mathematical calculation on the record key, and the result of that calculation is the record's address. The direct access method is most appropriate when individual records must be located directly and rapidly for immediate processing, when a few records in the file need to be retrieved at one time, and when the required records are found in no particular sequence.

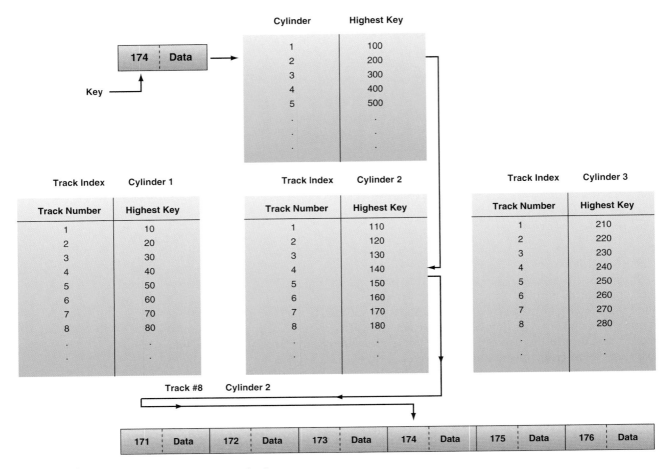

Figure 5.2 *Indexed sequential access method.*

Before you go on . . .

1. What are the smallest and largest units of the data hierarchy?

2. What is the difference between sequential and direct file access?

5.2   THE TRADITIONAL FILE ENVIRONMENT

From the time of the first computer applications in business (mid-1950s) until the early 1970s, organizations managed their data in a file environment. This environment began because organizations typically began automating one application at a time. These systems grew independently, without overall planning. Each application required its own data, which were organized in a data file.

A *data file* is a collection of logically related records. Therefore, in a *file management environment,* each application has a specific data file related to it, containing all the data records needed by the application. Over time, organizations developed

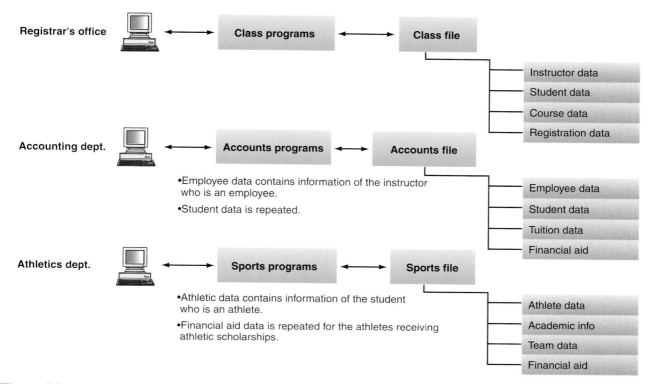

Figure 5.3   *Computer-based files in the traditional file environment cause problems such as redundancy due to partial or full duplication, inconsistency across files, and data isolation.*

numerous applications, each with an associated, application-specific data file. For example, a university has many computer-based applications involving students. These applications include course registration, fee payment, and grades, among others. In a file management environment, each of these applications would have its own student data file (see Figure 5.3). This approach to data management, where the organization has multiple applications with related data files, is considered the traditional approach.

Problems with the File Approach

The traditional file approach led to many problems. First, corporate applications typically share some common core functions, such as input, report generation, querying, and data browsing. However, these common functions typically were designed, coded, documented, and tested, at great expense, for *each* application. Moreover, users must be trained to use each application. A clerk moving from one functional area to another, for example, would likely have to be fully trained on a new application with different procedures, screen images, data formats, and detailed functionality. Traditional file environments thus often waste valuable resources creating and maintaining similar applications, as well as in training users how to use them.

Other problems also arise with the traditional file systems. The first problem is **data redundancy**. As applications and their data files were created by different programmers over a period of time, the same piece of information could be duplicated in several places. In the university example, each data file will contain records about students, many of whom will be represented in other data files. Therefore, student files in the aggregate will contain some amount of duplicate data. For example, all student records are likely to have a field for name, student identification number, address, telephone, and so on. It is not uncommon in such file environments for a new student to have to give his or her name, address, phone number, and so forth to many different campus offices—the same information over and over. This process wastes physical computer storage media, the student's time and effort, and the clerks' time needed to enter and maintain the data.

Data redundancy leads to the potential for **data inconsistency**. Data inconsistency means that the various copies of the data no longer agree. For example, if a student changes his or her address, the new address must be changed across all applications in the university that require the address.

File organization also leads to difficulty in accessing data from different applications, a problem called **data isolation**. With applications uniquely designed and implemented, data files are likely to be organized differently, stored in different formats (e.g., height in inches versus height in centimeters), and often physically inaccessible to other applications. In the university example, an administrator who wanted to know which students taking advanced courses were also starting players on the football team would most likely not be able to get the answer from the computer-based file system. He or she would probably have to manually compare printed output data from the two data files. This manual process would take a great deal of time and effort and would ignore the greatest strengths of computers—fast processing and accurate storage. Keeping data in the form of files in computer systems seriously limits the productive potential of computers and of information systems users. The file environment does not allow users to retrieve needed data conveniently and efficiently, nor does it allow for multiple users to have concurrent, simultaneous access to the data.

Not every user who has access to a computer system should have access to all the data files in the system. **Security** is difficult to enforce in the file environment, because new applications may be added to the system on an ad-hoc basis and with more applications, more people have access to data.

The file environment may also cause **data integrity** problems. Data values must often meet integrity constraints—that is, they must be accurate and fit for their intended use. For example, the students' Social Security data field should contain no alphabetic characters, and the students' grade-point-average field should not be negative. It is difficult to place data integrity constraints across multiple data files.

Finally, applications should not have to be developed with regard to how the data are stored. That is, the applications and data in computer systems should be independent—a characteristic called **application/data independence**. In the file environment, the applications and their associated data files are dependent on each other.

Storing data in data files that were tightly linked to their applications eventually led to organizations having hundreds of applications and data files, with no one knowing what the applications did or what data they required. There was no central listing of data files, data elements, or definitions of the data. The numerous problems arising from the file environment approach led to the development of databases.

Before you go on . . .

1. What other problem is often found with the problem of data redundancy?

2. How does data isolation prevent different departments, for example, from using the same data file?

5.3   DATABASES: THE MODERN APPROACH

A *database*, which is a logical group of related files, can eliminate many of the problems associated with a traditional file environment. With the database approach, all the data are typically contained in the same storage location, rather than residing in many different files across the organization. Unlike the traditional approach, in which different programs access the different data files, the database is arranged so that one set of software programs—the *database management system*—provides access to all the data. Therefore, data redundancy, data isolation, and data inconsistency are minimized, and data can be shared among all users of the data. In addition, security and data integrity are increased, and applications and data are independent of one another (see Figure 5.4).

Locating Data in Databases

A database is a collection of related files, and where those related files are located can greatly affect user accessibility, query response times, data entry, security, and cost. In general, database files can be *centralized* or *distributed*.

A **centralized database** has all the related files in one physical location. Centralized database files on large, mainframe computers were the main database platform for decades, primarily because of the enormous capital and operating costs of other alternatives. Not only do centralized databases save the expenses associated with multiple computers, but they also provide database administrators with the ability to work on a database as a whole at one location. Files can generally be made more consistent with each other when they are physically kept in one location because file changes can be made in a supervised and orderly fashion. Files are not accessible except via the centralized host computer, where they can be protected more easily from unauthorized access or modification. Also, recovery from disasters can be more easily accomplished at a central location. Like all centralized systems, however, centralized databases are vulnerable to a single point of failure. When the centralized database computer fails to function properly, all users suffer. Additionally, access speed is often a problem when users are widely dispersed and must do all of their data manipulations from great distances, thereby incurring transmission delays.

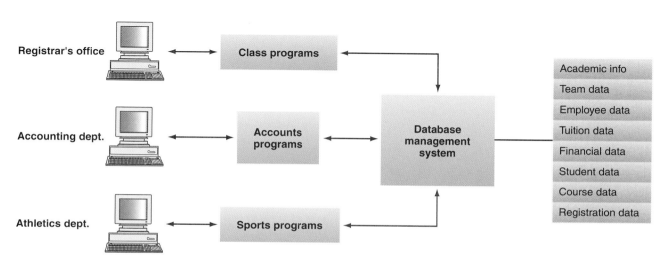

Figure 5.4   *A database management system (DBMS) provides access to all data in the database.*

A **distributed database** has complete copies of a database, or portions of a database, in more than one location, which is usually close to the user (see Figure 5.5). There are two types of distributed databases: replicated and partitioned. A **replicated database** has complete copies of the entire database in many locations, primarily to alleviate the single-point-of-failure problems of a centralized database as well as to increase user access responsiveness. There is significant overhead, however, in maintaining consistency among replicated databases, as records are added, modified, and deleted. A **partitioned database** is subdivided, so that each location has a portion of the entire database (usually the portion that meets users' local needs). This type of database provides the response speed of localized files without the need to replicate all changes in multiple locations. One significant advantage of a partitioned database is that data in the files can be entered more quickly and kept more accurate by the users immediately responsible for the data. On the other hand, widespread access to potentially sensitive company data can significantly increase corporate security problems. Telecommunications costs and associated time delays can also be major factors.

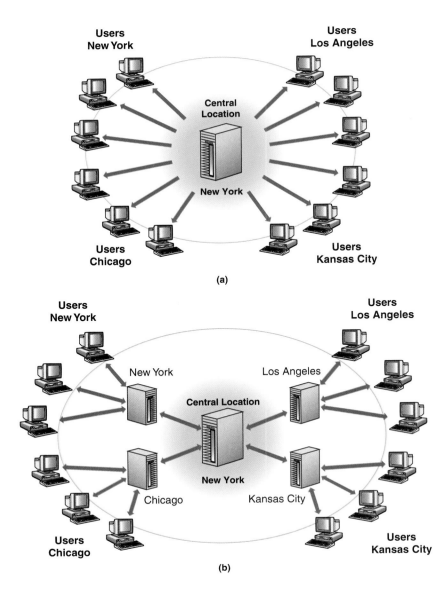

Figure 5.5 *(a) Centralized database. (b) Distributed database with complete or partial copies of the central database in more than one location.*

Creating the Database

To create a database, designers must develop a conceptual design and a physical design. The **conceptual design** of a database is an abstract model of the database from the user or business perspective. The **physical design** shows how the database is actually arranged on storage devices.

The conceptual database design describes how the data elements in the database are to be grouped. The design process identifies relationships among data elements and the most efficient way of grouping data elements together to meet information requirements. The process also identifies redundant data elements and the groupings of data elements required for specific applications. Groups of data are organized, refined, and streamlined until an overall logical view of the relationships among all of the data elements in the database appears. Entity-relationship modeling and normalization are employed to produce optimal database designs.

Entity-relationship modeling.   Database designers plan the database design in a process called **entity-relationship modeling**. They often document the conceptual data model with an **entity-relationship (ER) diagram**. ER diagrams consist of entities, attributes, and relationships; each is represented on the diagram. Entities are pictured in boxes, and relationships are shown in diamonds. The attributes for each entity are listed next to the entity, and the key field is underlined. [Fig. 5.6 (on page 134).]

As defined earlier, an *entity* is something that can be identified in the users' work environment. For example, consider student registration at a university. Students register for courses and register their cars for parking permits. In this example, STUDENT, PARKING PERMIT, COURSE, and PROFESSOR are examples of entities as shown in Figure 5.6 (on page 134).

Entities of a given type are grouped in **entity classes**. In our example, STUDENT, PARKING PERMIT, COURSE, and PROFESSOR are examples of entity classes. An **instance** of an entity class is the representation of a particular entity. Therefore, a particular STUDENT (James Smythe, 145-89-7123) is an instance of the STUDENT entity class; a particular parking permit (91778) is an instance of the PARKING PERMIT entity class; a particular course (76890) is an instance of the COURSE entity class; and a particular professor (Ted Wilson, 115-65-7632) is an instance of the PROFESSOR entity class.

Entity instances have **identifiers**, which are attributes that identify entity instances. For example, STUDENT instances can be identified with StudentIdentificationNumber; PARKING PERMIT instances can be identified with PermitNumber; COURSE instances can be identified with CourseNumber; and PROFESSOR instances can be identified with ProfessorIdentificationNumber. These identifiers are underlined on ER diagrams (see Figure 5.6).

Entities have attributes, or properties, that describe the entity's characteristics. In our example, examples of attributes for STUDENT would be StudentIdentificationNumber, StudentName, and StudentAddress. Examples of attributes for PARKING PERMIT would be PermitNumber, StudentName, StudentIdentificationNumber, and CarType. Examples of attributes for COURSE would be CourseNumber, CourseName, and CoursePlace. Examples of attributes for PROFESSOR would be ProfessorIdentificationNumber, ProfessorName, and ProfessorDepartment. (Note that each course at this university has one professor—no team teaching.)

Why are StudentName and StudentIdentificationNumber attributes of both the STUDENT and PARKING PERMIT entity classes? That is, why do we need the PARKING PERMIT entity class? If you consider all interlinked university systems, the PARKING PERMIT entity class is needed for other applications (fee payment, parking tickets, and external links) to the State Department of Motor Vehicles.

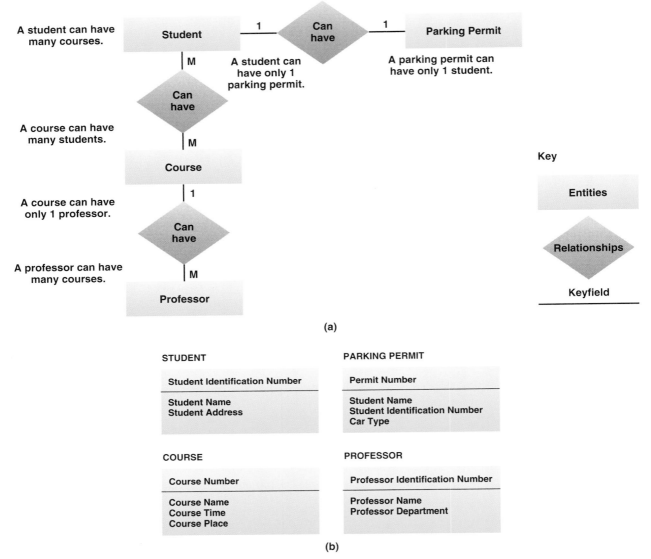

Figure 5.6 *Entity-relationship diagram model.*

Entities are associated with one another in **relationships**, which can include many entities. (Remember that relationships are noted by diamonds on ER diagrams.) The number of entities in a relationship is the degree of the relationship. Relationships between two items are common and are called *binary relationships*. There are three types of binary relationships.

- In a *1:1 (one-to-one)* relationship, a single-entity instance of one type is related to a single-entity instance of another type. Figure 5.6 shows STUDENT-PARKING PERMIT as a 1:1 relationship that relates a single STUDENT with a single PARKING PERMIT. That is, no student has more than one parking permit, and no parking permit is for more than one student.

- The second type of relationship, *1:M (one-to-many)*, is represented by the COURSE-PROFESSOR relationship in our example. This relationship means that a professor can have many courses, but each course can have only one professor. See Figure 5.6. (Remember that we have no team-teaching in our university example.)

Order	Order Number	Number of Parts	Part Number	Part Description	Unit Price	Supplier Number	Supplier Name	Supplier Address	Order Date	Delivery Date	Order Total	Customer Number	Customer Name	Customer Address

Figure 5.7   *Nonnormalized relation.*

- The third type of relationship, *M:M (many-to-many)*, is represented by the STUDENT-COURSE and SCHEDULE-COURSE relationships in our example. The first relationship means that a student can have many courses, and a course can have many students. The second relationship means that a schedule can have many courses and a course can appear on many schedules (see Figure 5.6).

Normalization.   In order to use a relational database model (discussed below) effectively, the data must be analyzed to eliminate redundant data elements. **Normalization** is a method for analyzing and reducing a relational database to its most streamlined form for minimum redundancy, maximum data integrity, and best processing performance. When data are *normalized*, attributes in the table depend only on the primary key.

As an example, consider an automotive repair garage. This business takes orders from customers who want to have their cars repaired. In this example, ORDER, PART, SUPPLIER, and CUSTOMER would be examples of entities. In this example, there are many PARTS in an ORDER, but each PART can come from only one SUPPLIER. In a nonnormalized relation called ORDER (see Figure 5.7), each ORDER would have to repeat the name, description, and price of each PART needed to complete the ORDER, as well as the name and address of each SUPPLIER. This relation contains repeating groups and describes multiple entities.

The normalization process breaks down the relation, ORDER, into smaller relations, each describing a single entity. This process is conceptually simpler and eliminates repeating groups (see Figure 5.8). For example, consider an order at the

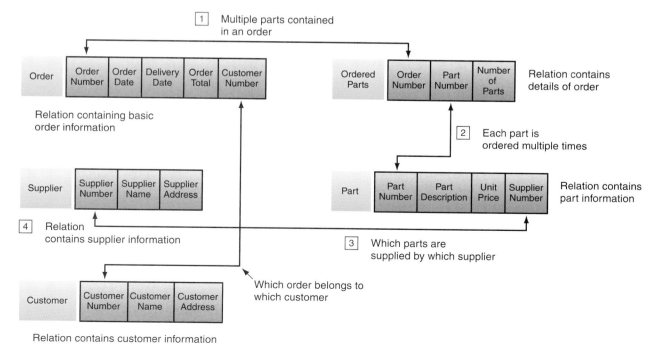

Figure 5.8   *Normalized relation.*

automobile repair shop. The normalized relations can produce the order in the following manner.

- The ORDER relation provides the OrderNumber (the key), OrderDate, Delivery-Date, OrderTotal, and CustomerNumber.
- The key of the ORDER relation (OrderNumber) provides a link to the ORDERED-PARTS relation (the link numbered 1 in Figure 5.8).
- The ORDERED-PARTS relation supplies the NumberofParts information to ORDER.
- The key of the ORDERED-PARTS relation (PartNumber) provides a link to the PART relation (the link numbered 2 in Figure 5.8).
- The PART relation supplies the PartDescription, UnitPrice, and SupplierNumber to ORDER.
- The SupplierNumber in the PART relation provides a link to the SUPPLIER relation (the link numbered 3 in Figure 5.8).
- The SUPPLIER relation provides the SupplierName and SupplierAddress to ORDER.
- The CustomerNumber in ORDER provides a link to the CUSTOMER relation (the link numbered 4 in Figure 5.8).
- The CUSTOMER relation supplies the CustomerName and CustomerAddress to ORDER. The automotive repair shop order now has all the necessary information.

Before you go on . . .

1. What are the common options for locating data in databases?

2. What tools and techniques are used to produce optimal database designs?

5.4 DATABASE MANAGEMENT SYSTEMS

The software program (or group of programs) that provides access to a database is known as a **database management system (DBMS)**. The DBMS permits an organization to store data in one location, from which it can be updated and retrieved, and it provides access to the stored data by various application programs. DBMSs also provide mechanisms for maintaining the integrity of stored information, managing security and user access, recovering information when the system fails, and accessing various database functions from within an application written in a third-generation, fourth-generation, or object-oriented language. The DBMS provides users with tools to add, delete, maintain, display, print, search, select, sort, and upgrade data. These tools range from easy-to-use natural-language interfaces to complex programming languages used for developing sophisticated database applications.

Today, DBMSs are no longer entirely the domain of the IS department, but are installed in a broad range of information systems. Some are loaded on a single user's PC and employed in an ad-hoc manner to support individual decision making. Others are located on several interconnected mainframe computers and are used to support large-scale transaction-processing systems, such as order entry and inventory control systems. Still others are interconnected throughout an organization's local area networks, giving individual departments access to corporate data. Whatever their

IT's About Business

www.lexis-nexis.com

Box 5.1:   Lexis-Nexis uses database to deal with court ruling

A Supreme Court decision is forcing electronic archive Lexis-Nexis to purge what may amount to hundreds of thousands of documents from its database. In *New York Times vs. Tasini*, a group of freelance writers sued newspaper and magazine publishers, including the *New York Times, Newsday*, and *Time*, saying that these news organizations had resold articles to online databases such as Lexis-Nexis without compensating freelance writers or gaining their permission. Most newspapers now include language in their contracts that deal with this issue, but hundreds of thousands of articles from the 1980s and 1990s were resold to Lexis-Nexis without the writers' consent.

The Supreme Court ruled that the publishers had infringed on freelancers' copyrights, and passed the case back to a lower court to determine whether the writers should receive damages. In the meantime, the news organizations and Lexis-Nexis are faced with a major data management challenge: removing all the affected stories from their databases.

A spokesman for the New York Times Co. says that the company has put together a list of more than 115,000 stories by 27,000 authors, which ran between 1980 and 1995, that could be affected by the ruling. The spokesman says the list will be passed on to Lexis-Nexis, which will have to remove the stories from its database. The *New York Times* online database, which is accessible through its Web site, will not be affected, because those stories date back only to 1996.

At the moment, Lexis-Nexis is unclear about the scope of the project it faces. "We have no way of knowing offhand how many of the 3 billion documents on our database are written by freelancers," says a spokesman. He says the company is preparing its database managers for the job as they wait to hear from publishers, who will be responsible for identifying the affected stories.

Source: "Lexis-Nexis Faces Database Purge in Wake of Copyright Ruling," *Information Week* (June 22, 2001); *nytimes.com.*

Questions

1. With three billion documents in the Lexis-Nexis database, how would you use the database management system to uncover the documents written by freelance writers? Can you do this realistically?

2. What does the Lexis-Nexis problem tell you about keeping historical data in databases?

---

purpose, database management systems are designed to be relatively invisible to the user. To interact with them as a user, however, it helps to understand how databases are structured and the procedures for interacting with them—even though much of their work is done behind the scenes and is therefore "transparent" to the end user.

As essential as databases and DBMSs are to all areas of business, they must be carefully managed. In fact, as IT's About Business Box 5.1 shows, databases can present a problem even with the most careful management.

Logical versus Physical View

A database management system provides the ability for many different users to share data and process resources. But as there can be many different users, there are many different database needs. How can a single, unified database meet the differing requirements of so many users? For example, how can a single database be structured so that sales personnel can see customer, inventory, and production maintenance data while the human resources department maintains restricted access to private personnel data?

A DBMS minimizes these problems by providing two views of the database data: a physical view and a logical view. The **physical view** deals with the actual, physical arrangement and location of data in the *direct access storage devices (DASDs)*. Database specialists use the physical view to make efficient use of storage and processing resources.

Users, however, may wish to see data differently from how they are stored, and they do not want to know all the technical details of physical storage. After all, a business user is primarily interested in using the information, not in how it is stored. The **logical view**, or user's view, of a database program represents data in a format that is meaningful to a user and to the software programs that process that data. That is, the logical view tells the user, in user terms, what is in the database.

One strength of a DBMS is that while there is only one physical view of the data, there can be an endless number of different logical views—one specifically tailored to each individual user, if necessary. This feature allows users to see database information in a more business-related way rather than from a technical, processing viewpoint. Clearly, users must adapt to the technical requirements of database information systems to some degree, but DBMS logical views allow the system to adapt to the business needs of the users.

DBMS Components

There are four main components in a database management system: the data model, the data definition language, the data manipulation language, and the data dictionary.

Data model.   The **data model** defines the way data are conceptually structured. Examples include the hierarchical, network, relational, object-oriented, object-relational, hypermedia, and multidimensional models. We will present a more detailed discussion of these models in a later section.

Data definition language.   The **data definition language (DDL)** defines what types of information are in the database and how they will be structured. The DDL defines each data element as it appears in the database before that data element is translated into the forms required by the applications. The DDL is essentially the link between the logical and physical views of the database.

A DBMS user defines views, or *schemas*, using the DDL. The **schema** is the logical description of the entire database and the listing of all the data items and the relationships among them. Each user or application program utilizes a set of DDL statements to construct a listing of those data elements that are of interest. Because there may be many users and application programs using the same database, many different "user views" or subschemas can exist. Therefore, a **subschema** is the specific set of data from the database that is required by each application.

The DDL is used to define the physical characteristics of each record, the fields within a record, and each field's logical name, data type, and character length. The DDL is also used to specify relationships among the records. Other primary functions of the DDL are to:

- Provide a means for associating related data.
- Indicate the unique identifiers (or keys) of the records.
- Set up data security access and change restrictions.

Data manipulation language.   The **data manipulation language (DML)** is used with third-generation, fourth-generation, or object-oriented languages to query the contents of the database, store or update information in the database, and develop database applications. The DML allows users to retrieve, sort, display, and delete the contents of a database.

Requesting information from a database is the most commonly performed operation. Because users cannot generally request information in a natural-language form, *query languages* form an important component of a DBMS. **Structured query lan-**

guage **(SQL)** is the most popular relational database language, combining both DML and DDL features. SQL offers the ability to perform complicated searches with relatively simple statements. Keywords such as SELECT (to specify a desired attribute), FROM (to specify the table to be used), and WHERE (to specify conditions to apply in the query) are typically used for the purpose of data manipulation. For example, a state legislator wants to send congratulatory letters to all students from her district graduating with honors from the state university. The university information systems staff would query the student relational database with an SQL statement such as SELECT (Student Name), FROM (Student Database), WHERE (Congressional District = 7 and Grade Point Average > = 3.4).

Data dictionary.   The **data dictionary** stores definitions of data elements and data characteristics such as individuals, business functions, programs, and reports that use the data elements, as well as the physical representation, responsible parties in the organization (data ownership), and security. A *data element* represents a field. Besides listing the standard data name and aliases for the element, the dictionary lists the names that reference this element in specific systems and identifies the individuals, business functions, applications, and reports that use this data element.

Data dictionaries provide many advantages to the organization. Because the data dictionary provides standard definitions for all data elements, the potential for data inconsistency is reduced. That is, the probability that the same data element will be used in different applications, but with a different name, is reduced. In addition, data dictionaries provide for faster program development because programmers do not have to create new data names. Data dictionaries also make it easier to modify data and information because programmers do not need to know where the data element is stored or what applications use the data element in order to make use of it in a program.

Database environments ensure that data in the database are defined once and consistently, and that they are used for all applications whose data reside in the database. Applications request data elements from the database and are found and delivered by the DBMS. The programmer and end user do not have to specify in detail how or where the data are to be found.

Database management systems provide many advantages to the organization:

- Improved strategic use of corporate data
- Reduced complexity of the organization's information systems environment
- Reduced data redundancy and inconsistency
- Enhanced data integrity
- Application-data independence
- Improved security
- Reduced application development and maintenance costs
- Improved flexibility of information systems
- Increased access and availability of data and information

Before you go on . . .

1. What is the difference between the logical and the physical views of the data in a database?

2. What are the main components of a DBMS?

5.5 LOGICAL DATA MODELS

Just as there are many ways to structure business organizations, so also are there many ways to structure the data those organizations need. A manager's ability to use a database is highly dependent on how the database is structured logically and physically. The DBMS separates the logical and physical views of the data, meaning that the programmer and end user do not have to know where and how the data are actually stored. In logically structuring a database, businesses need to consider the characteristics of the data and how the data will be accessed.

The three most common data models are *hierarchical*, *network*, and *relational*. Other types of data models include multidimensional, object-oriented, object-relational, and hypermedia. Using these models, database designers can build logical or conceptual views of data that can then be physically implemented into virtually any database with any DBMS. Hierarchical, network, and object-oriented DBMSs usually tie related data together through linked lists. Relational and multidimensional DBMSs relate data through information contained in the data. We'll look at most of these models in this section.

Hierarchical Database Model

The **hierarchical database model** rigidly structures data into an inverted "tree" in which each record contains two elements. The first is a single root or *master field*, often called a *key*, which identifies the type location or ordering of the records. The second is a variable number of *subordinate fields*, which define the rest of the data within a record. As a rule, while all fields have only one "parent," each parent may have many "children." An example of a hierarchical database is shown in Figure 5.9.

The hierarchical structure was developed simply because hierarchical relationships are commonly found in many traditional business organizations and processes. For example, organization charts most often describe a hierarchical relationship—top management at the highest level, middle management at lower levels, and other employees at the lowest level. Within each hierarchy, each level of management may have many employees or levels of employees beneath it, but each employee generally

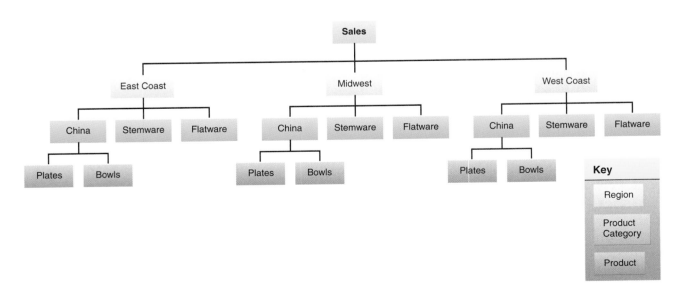

Figure 5.9   *Hierarchical database model.*

has only one manager. The hierarchical structure is characterized by this one-to-many relationship among data.

The strongest advantage of the hierarchical database approach is the speed and efficiency with which it can be searched for data. This speed is possible because so much of the database is eliminated in the search with each "turn" going down the tree. As shown in Figure 5.9, half the records in the database (East Coast Sales) are eliminated once the search turns toward West Coast sales, and two-thirds of the West Coast Sales are eliminated once the search turns toward stemware. Organizational transaction processing systems (e.g., airline reservation systems) typically use the hierarchical approach for the speed and efficiency it offers.

But the hierarchical model does have problems. Access to data in this model is predefined by the database administrator before the programs that access the data are written. Programmers must follow the hierarchy established by the data structure.

Also, in the hierarchical model, each relationship must be explicitly defined when the database is created. Each record in a hierarchical database can contain only one key field, and only one relationship is allowed between any two fields. This structure can create a problem because real-world data do not always conform to such a strict hierarchy. For example, a product like dietetic cereal might be found in a cereal section of a grocery store and in a special section for dietetic foods, a situation that would be awkward for a hierarchical structure to handle. Moreover, all data searches must originate at the top or "root" of the tree and work downward from "parent" to "child."

Network Database Model

The **network database model** creates relationships among data through a linked-list structure in which subordinate records (called *members*, not children) can be linked to more than one data element (called an *owner*). Similar to the hierarchical model, the network model uses explicit links, called *pointers*, to link members and owners. Physically, pointers are storage addresses that contain the location of a related record. With the network approach, a member record can be linked to an owner record and, at the same time, itself can be an owner record linked to other sets of members. In this way, many-to-many relationships are possible with a network database model. (See the Web site for an illustration of the Network Database Model.)

www.wiley.com/
college/turban

The network model essentially places no restrictions on the number of relationships or sets in which a field can be involved. This model, then, is more consistent with real-world business relationships where, for example, vendors have many customers and customers have many vendors. However, network databases are very complex. For every set of linked data elements, a pair of pointers must be maintained. As the number of sets or relationships increases, the work involved to expand and maintain the database becomes substantial. The network model is by far the most complicated type of database to design and implement.

Relational Database Model

While most business organizations have been organized in a hierarchical fashion, most business data—especially accounting and financial data—have been traditionally organized into simple tables of columns and rows. Tables allow quick comparisons by row or column, and items are easy to retrieve by finding the point of intersection of a particular row and column. The **relational database model** is based on the simple concept of tables in order to capitalize on characteristics of rows and columns of data.

In a relational database, these tables are called **relations**, and the model is based on the mathematical theory of sets and relations. In this model, each row of data is equivalent to a record, and each column of data is equivalent to a field. In the relational model terminology, a row is called a **tuple**, and a column is called an **attribute**. A relational database is not always, however, one big table (usually called a *flat file*) consisting of all attributes and all tuples. That design would likely entail far too much data redundancy. Instead, a database is usually designed as many related tables.

There are some basic principles involved in creating a relational database. First, the order of tuples or attributes in a table is irrelevant, because their position relative to other tuples and attributes is irrelevant in finding data based on specific tuples and attributes. Second, each tuple must be uniquely identifiable by the data within the tuple—some sort of primary key data (for example, a Social Security number or employee number). Third, each table must have a unique identifier—the name of the relation. Fourth, there can be no duplicate attributes or tuples. Finally, there can be only one value in each row-column "cell" in a table.

In a relational database, three basic operations are used to develop useful sets of data: select, join, and project. The **select operation** creates a subset consisting of all records in the file that meet stated criteria. "Select" creates, in other words, a subset of rows that meet certain criteria. The **join operation** combines relational tables to provide the user with more information than is available in individual tables. The **project operation** creates a subset consisting of columns in a table, permitting the user to create new tables that contain only the information required.

One of the greatest advantages of the relational model is its conceptual simplicity and the ability to link records in a way that is not predefined (as is the case with hierarchical and network models). This ability provides great flexibility, particularly for end users. The relational or tabular model of data can be used in a variety of applications. Most people can easily visualize the relational model as a table, although the model does use some unfamiliar terminology.

Consider the relational database example on East Coast managers shown in Figure 5.10. The table contains data about the entity called East Coast managers. Attributes or characteristics about the entity are name, title, age, and division. The tuples, or occurrences of the entity, are the four records on A. Smith, W. Jones, J. Lee, and K. Durham. The links among the data, and among tables, are implicit, as they are not necessarily physically linked in a storage device but are implicitly linked by the design of the tables into rows and columns.

This property of implicit links provides perhaps the strongest benefit of the relational model—flexibility in relating data. Unlike the hierarchical and network models, where the only links are those rigidly built into the design, in the relational model all the data in a table and between tables can be linked, related, and compared. This ability gives the relational model much more data independence than do the other two models. That is, the logical design of data into tables can be more independent of the physical implementation. This independence allows more flexibility in implementing and modifying the logical design. Of course, as with all tables, an end user needs to know only two things: the identifier(s) of the tuple(s) to be searched, and the desired attribute(s).

Name	Title	Age	Division
Smith, A.	Dir., Accounting	43	China
Jones, W.	Dir., Total Quality Management	32	Stemware
Lee, J.	Dir., Information Technology	46	China
Durham, K.	Manager, Production	35	Stemware

Figure 5.10 *Table of relational database model.*

IT's About Business   *muze.com*   MKT

Box 5.2: Relational database helps Muze grow

Some very successful sellers of books, music, and other entertainment on the Internet owe part of their success to a company called Muze. Based in New York City, Muze offers media retailers—both the click-and-modem and brick-and-mortar varieties—the type of information that influences consumers' buying decisions.

Muze aggregates and classifies millions of products from thousands of publishers in order to match contextual information and multimedia clips with the products of distributors around the world. Muze stores this massive amount of information in a relational database and licenses its database at a fraction of what it would cost sellers to compile their own information. For a retailer, the service makes the difference between putting a list of titles on the Internet and enabling shoppers to browse in an information-rich catalog environment.

The information provided by Muze enables retail customers to get in-depth information about books, CDs, and videotapes without actually having the product in hand. The shopper initiates the search using an in-store kiosk or by browsing the retailer's Web site. Muze data, such as book reviews or multimedia clips, appear as search results within the format set up by the retailer's search engine. Muze also provides classification data that help the retailer's search engine operate more efficiently. Further, Muze enables consumers to search for related music, books, and video products using a single query.

Muze's database is operable with retailers' systems, regardless of database structure. An important factor behind Muze's choice of IBM's DB2 database is that it provides support for XML structure, which enables data to be interoperable among different database systems. Amazon.com and hundreds of other Muze customers receive daily feeds from the Muze database, enabling their customers to have the latest information about their purchases.

Source: ibm.com; muze.com.

Questions

1. Are there any disadvantages for businesses using Muze's databases?

2. What is Muze's core competency, and how does database technology facilitate that core competency?

The relational model is currently the most popular of the three most common database structures because it provides the most flexibility and ease of use. But this model has some disadvantages. Because large-scale databases may be composed of many interrelated tables, the overall design may be complex and therefore may have slower search and access times (as compared to the hierarchical and network models). The slower search and access times may result in processing inefficiencies that lead to an initial lack of acceptance of the relational model. These processing inefficiencies, however, are continually being reduced through improved database design and programming. Second, data integrity is not inherently a part of this model, as it is with hierarchical and network models. Therefore, it must be enforced with good design principles.

IT's About Business Box 5.2 provides an example of how a properly designed relational database can drive the success of a business.

Advantages and Disadvantages of the Three Database Models

The main advantage of the hierarchical and network database models is processing efficiency. The hierarchical and network structures are relatively easy for users to understand because they reflect the pattern of real-world business relationships. In addition, the hierarchical structure allows for data integrity to be easily maintained.

Hierarchical and network structures have several disadvantages, though. All the access paths, directories, and indices must be specified in advance. Once specified, they are not easily changed without a major programming effort. Therefore, these designs

Model	Advantages	Disadvantages
Hierarchical database	Searching is fast and efficient.	Access to data is predefined by exclusively hierarchical relationships, predetermined by administrator. Limited search/query flexibility. Not all data are naturally hierarchical.
Network database	Many more relationships can be defined. There is greater speed and efficiency than with relational database models.	This is the most complicated model to design, implement, and maintain. Greater query flexibility than with hierarchical model, but less than with relational mode.
Relational database	Conceptual simplicity; there are no predefined relationships among data. High flexibility in ad-hoc querying. New data and records can be added easily.	Processing efficiency and speed are lower. Data redundancy is common, requiring additional maintenance.

have low flexibility. Hierarchical and network structures are programming intensive, time-consuming, difficult to install, and difficult to remedy if design errors occur. The two structures do not support ad-hoc, English-language-like inquiries for information.

The advantages of relational DBMSs include high flexibility in regard to ad-hoc queries, power to combine information from different sources, simplicity of design and maintenance, and the ability to add new data and records without disturbing existing applications.

The disadvantages of relational DBMSs include their relatively low processing efficiency. These systems are somewhat slower because they typically require many accesses to the data stored on disk to carry out the select, join, and project commands. Relational systems do not have the large number of pointers carried by hierarchical systems, which speed search and retrieval. Further, large relational databases may be designed to have some data redundancy in order to make retrieval of data more efficient. The same data element may be stored in multiple tables. Special arrangements are necessary to ensure that all copies of the same data element are updated together.

Manager's Checklist 5.1 summarizes the advantages and disadvantages of the three common database models.

Emerging Data Models

Three emerging data models are *multidimensional*, *object-oriented*, and *hypermedia*. The object-oriented and hypermedia data models are discussed here, and the multidimensional data model is discussed in the section on data warehousing, later in this chapter.

Object-oriented database model.   A recent development in databases is the **object-oriented model**. Although no common definition for this model has yet emerged, there is agreement as to some of its features. The central idea is that of an *object*—a small amount of data put together (*encapsulated*) with all the data needed in order to perform an operation with that data (as described in Chapter 4). Terminology in the object-oriented model, similar to object-oriented programming languages, consists of objects, attributes, classes, methods, and messages.

An **object** is similar to an entity in that it represents a person, place, or thing, but it also contains all of the data that the object needs in order to perform an operation. Similarly, *attributes* are characteristics that describe the state of that object—the attribute values for an object at a given period in time (for example, the age of an employee). A **method** is an operation, action, or a behavior the object may undergo (for example, a product may be sold). A message from other objects activates operations contained within the object. Once an operation is activated, it will often send another message to a third object, which, in turn, may activate methods within that object, and so on.

Every object is an *instance* of some class. An object's **class** defines all the messages to which the object will respond, as well as the way in which objects of this class are implemented. Classes are typically arranged in a tree-like structure, connecting superclasses to their subclasses. The links or relationships between a superclass and a subclass are often called *IS-A links*. For example, a "truck" class is a subclass of a "motor vehicle" class; a truck "is a" motor vehicle. The complete chain of IS-A links shows that all subclasses inherit all behaviors and attributes defined by their superclass, as well as having additional behaviors and attributes of their own.

Object-oriented databases can be particularly helpful in multimedia environments, such as in many manufacturing sites. Data from design blueprints, photographic images of parts, operational acoustic signatures, and test or quality-control data all can be combined into one object, itself consisting of structures and operations. For companies with widely distributed offices, an object-oriented database can provide users with a view of data throughout the overall system. In general, object-oriented databases allow organizations to structure their data and use them in ways that would be impossible, or at least very difficult, with other database models. Object-oriented databases can be used in some very strategic ways, as shown by the following example.

EXAMPLE

Promoting business and tourism via database. The North Cholla Provincial Government, one of eight provincial governments in Korea, will use Computer Associates' Jasmine for an Internet-based multimedia Web application designed to increase business and tourism in the province. Jasmine is a pure object-oriented database with class libraries that manage multimedia data, including bitmaps, animation, audio, and full-motion video. Using the multimedia capabilities supported by Jasmine, visitors will be able to take a virtual tour of the North Cholla Province by clicking on objects that inform and entertain using text, animation, video, and audio. Current and historical information about the Province will be accessible in such areas as weather, transportation facilities, government services, lodging, and dining. The goal is to promote and enhance the image of North Cholla Province around the world, increase business opportunities and tourism, and ultimately to improve the standard of living of North Cholla Province citizens. (*Source: cai.com.*) ●

Object-relational database model. The **object-relational database model** adds new object storage capabilities to relational database management systems. Systems based on this model integrate management of traditional fielded data, complex objects such as time-series and geospatial data (e.g., maps and photos derived from satellite transmissions), and diverse binary media such as audio, video, images, applets, and formatted and unformatted text. Object-relational database management systems include both data and processes—that is, what information the users have and what they are going to do with it.

Hypermedia database model.   The **hypermedia database model** stores chunks of information in the form of *nodes* connected by links established by the user. The nodes can contain text, graphics, sound, full-motion video, or executable computer programs. Searching for information does not have to follow a predetermined organizational scheme. Instead, users can branch to related information in any kind of relationship. The relationship between nodes is less structured than in a traditional DBMS. In most systems, each node can be displayed on a screen. The screen also displays the links between the node depicted and other nodes in the database.

Other Database Models

Because a database management system need not be confined to storing just words and numbers, firms use them to store graphics, sounds, and video as well. These capabilities have led to specialized databases, depending on the type or format of data stored. For example, a **geographical information database** may contain locational data for overlaying on maps or images. Using this type of data, users are able to spatially view customer and vendor locations instead of simply reading the actual addresses. A **knowledge database** can store decision rules used to evaluate situations and help users make decisions like an expert. A **multimedia database** can store data on many media—sounds, video, images, graphic animation, and text.

Small-Footprint Databases

Small-footprint databases enable organizations to put certain types of data in the field where the workers are. These databases offer more information, more readily available, in a form that is accessible. Where once laptops were the only portable machines capable of running a database, advances in technology such as more powerful CPUs and increased memory at lower cost are enabling handheld devices and smart phones to run some form of an SQL database and to synchronize that mobile database with a central database at headquarters.

Small-footprint databases have replication mechanisms that take into account the occasionally connected nature of laptops and handhelds, that are programmed to resolve replication conflicts among mobile users, and that ensure that data synchronization will survive a low-quality wireless or modem connection. Small-footprint database technology also runs on personal digital assistants, such as those from Palm or Psion, and embedded specialty devices and appliances, like a barcode scanner or medical tool. The following examples show applications of small-footprint databases.

EXAMPLES

Book reps with small footprints.   When Simon & Schuster (*simonsays.com*) built a sales-force automation system, the company needed to fit the software—application, presentation tools, databases, files—on the laptops of its sales representatives. The company wanted to give its salespeople enough information to take on the road and make a presentation about an upcoming title to bookstore buyers in their territories. The company knew that it could not put all the data in the firm's databases on the laptops, but salespeople needed information about the bookstore's account (order status, historical sales, and special handling and discounts for which it was eligible) as well as marketing information about new books, such as sales forecasts, cover art, and promotion plans. The key piece of technology that made the laptop project possible was a small-footprint database, one whose selective replication features allowed Simon & Schuster to put just the data relevant to each salesperson on each one's laptop and to collect the orders once the sales call was over.

Small footprints on the Palm. Bidcom's (*citadon.com*) site-inspection application places a Palm in the hands of construction company supervisors, who come to the job site to count workers, add up the materials consumed, and note safety issues. Each day, the inspectors go to a different site. The Palm has to be loaded with that day's project information. At the end of the day, the updates are sent to a central Oracle database, where they are converted into Web pages so that company executives can track each day's progress. ●

Before you go on . . .

1. What are the relative advantages and disadvantages of hierarchical, network, and relational databases?

2. How might a company use a multimedia DBMS for competitive advantage?

5.6 DATA WAREHOUSES

Access to the accurate and timely information needed for the management of daily operations and long-term strategic planning has become increasingly important in the modern global marketplace. Unfortunately, it has not always been easy to identify, access, and retrieve the required information. For that reason, for many years companies have been working to improve access to data for decision making and analysis. To date, most of these efforts have focused on enhancing or replacing the online transaction-processing systems that are the entry point for most company data. These operational systems now contain huge amounts of data, so companies are focusing their attention on making this information available to end users through efficient organization and access management.

The focus of technology has shifted from data input and capture through the firm's operational systems to information access and availability provided by the firm's data warehouse. A **data warehouse** is a relational or multidimensional database management system designed to support management decision making. Data warehouses are oriented around the major business subjects of the enterprise, such as customer, vendor, product, or activity.

The data in the "warehouse" are stored in a single, agreed-upon format even when underlying operational applications store the data differently. For example, one operational application may store the date as year-month-day, and another may store it as month-day-year. In the data warehouse, the date will have a consistent format throughout (e.g., month-day-year). The data warehouse transforms data into a more useful resource by grouping them more conveniently for end users, putting them into more usable formats, enabling them to be analyzed, and dispersing them to appropriate working groups to increase availability and accessibility (see Figure 5.11 on page 148).

Data warehouses contain current detailed data, historical detailed data, lightly summarized data, highly summarized data, and *metadata* (discussed below). Current and historical detailed data are voluminous because they are stored at the highest level of detail (the least amount of summarization). Lightly and highly summarized data are necessary to save processing time when users request them and are readily

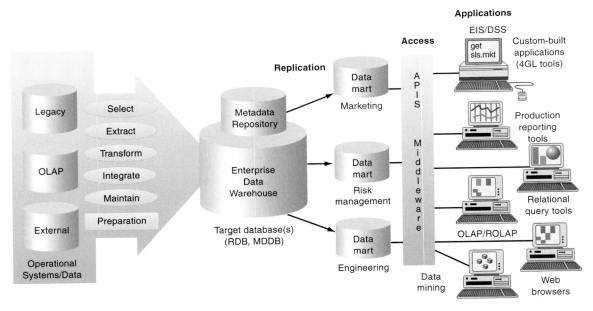

Figure 5.11 *Data warehouse framework and views. [Source: cutter.com and* Data Management Strategies, *Cutter Information Operations, February 1999.]*

accessible. For example, in a retail sales organization such as Sears, current detailed data might be the daily sales data over the last 90 days. Historical detailed data would be sales data over the last 10 years. Lightly summarized data could be weekly sales of a store or weekly sales of a particular product. Highly summarized data could be annual sales for a store, annual sales for a region, or annual sales of a product. Interestingly, older historical data are the least-used data in a data warehouse, while highly summarized data are the most used.

Metadata, which are "data about data," are important for designing, constructing, retrieving, and controlling the warehouse data. Data warehouse users need to know what data are available, what their sources are, where they are, and how to access them. *Technical metadata* include where the data come from, how the data were changed, how the data are organized, how the data are stored, who owns the data, who is responsible for the data and how to contact him or her, who can access the data, and the date of last update. *Business metadata* include what data are available, where the data are, what the data mean (description of data contents, units of measure, definitions and aliases for the data, details of how the data were calculated), how to access the data, predefined reports and queries, and how current the data are.

A data warehouse offers many business advantages:

- It provides business users with a "customer-centric" view of the company's heterogeneous data by helping to integrate data from sales, service, manufacturing and distribution, and other customer-related business systems.

- It provides added value to the company's customers by allowing them to access better information when data warehousing is coupled with Internet technology.

- It consolidates data about individual customers and provides a repository of all customer contacts for segmentation modeling, customer retention planning, and cross-sales analysis.

- It removes barriers among functional areas by offering a way to reconcile views from multiple areas, thus providing a look at activities that cross functional lines.

- It reports on trends across multidivisional, multinational operating units, including trends or relationships in areas such as merchandising, production planning, and so forth.

Table 5.1 presents some strategic uses of data warehousing in various industries, and IT's About Business Box 5.3 (on page 150) provides an example of Sprint's strategic application of its data warehouse.

Multidimensional Database Model

Multidimensional databases are often the core of data warehouses. In a **multidimensional database**, the data are intimately related and can be viewed and analyzed from different perspectives, which are called *dimensions*. A multidimensional database allows for the effective, efficient, and convenient storage and retrieval of large volumes of data. The data in such databases are analyzed by **online analytical processing (OLAP)**.

In multidimensional databases, data are stored in **arrays**, which are the fundamental elements of these databases. Similar to tables in the relational database model, arrays group related information in columns and rows. Multidimensional databases, however, typically consist of at least three dimensions. The visualization of more than three dimensions becomes increasingly complex for human beings. Therefore, most examples pertaining to multidimensional databases artificially limit the dimensions to only three, depicting the resulting database as a cube.

Dimensions are the edges of the cube, and represent the primary views of the business data. For example, sales data could be represented as a three-dimensional cube with the dimensions of product, geography (market), and time. A specific block

Table 5.1   Strategic Uses of Data Warehousing

Industry	Functional Areas of Use	Strategic Use
Airline	Operations; marketing	Crew assignment, aircraft deployment, mix of fares, analysis of route profitability, frequent-flyer program promotions
Apparel	Distribution; marketing	Merchandising and product replenishment
Banking	Product development; operations; marketing	Customer service, trend analysis, product and service promotions, reduction of IS expenses
Credit card	Product development; marketing	Customer service, new information service, fraud detection
Health care	Operations	Reduction of operational expenses
Investment and insurance	Product development; operations; marketing	Risk management, market movements analysis, customer tendencies analysis, portfolio management
Personal care	Distribution; marketing	Distribution decisions, product promotions, sales decisions, pricing policy
Public sector	Operations	Intelligence gathering
Retail chain	Distribution; marketing	Trend analysis, buying-pattern analysis, pricing policy, inventory control, sales promotions, optimal distribution channel
Steel	Manufacturing	Pattern analysis (quality control)
Telecommunications	Product development; operations; marketing	New product and service promotions, reduction of IS budget, profitability analysis

Source: Y. T. Park, "Strategic Uses of Data Warehouses," *Journal of Data Warehousing* (April 1997).

IT's About Business

sprint.com

Box 5.3:   Using a data warehouse to manage customer churn

Stiff competition in the telecommunications market is constantly tempting customers with incentives to switch providers. That makes *churn management*, the process of acquiring and retaining customers, a major challenge for the carriers.

To turn capricious service subscribers into loyal customers, Sprint's Global Markets Group relies on a 5-terabyte customer data warehouse and business intelligence system. The system's goals are to increase the amount of business Sprint does with its business customers and to identify customers who may be about to defect. Sprint says that churn management is not just about retaining a customer. It is also about retaining and growing its business. It is easier and less expensive to "up-sell" (sell new and perhaps more expensive services to existing customers) than it is to acquire new customers.

Sprint's customer-management effort comes as the range of services has expanded in recent years to include local and long-distance voice communications, Internet access, data communications, and wireless services. Understanding a customer's needs is critical. Sprint has found that customers who subscribe to two or more services are much more likely to stay with Sprint than are customers who use only one service.

Sprint's data warehouse contains information from its customer-billing and customer-service records, augmented with external, publicly available information about business customers. It is the first time that Sprint has integrated sales and customer data into one system.

Sprint uses the information to build profiles of its business customers and their service needs. That data is analyzed using SAS business-intelligence tools, allowing sales and marketing managers to see what additional services they might sell to customers. Using predictive analysis techniques, Sprint can identify customers who may be about to move to another carrier. Warning signs include reduced use of a Sprint service. That information gives Sprint the chance to correct the problem or offer incentives for users to stay put.

Sprint's customer churn rate is lower than it was before the company began using the system. Since the system went live, it has saved Sprint one million dollars in what the company used to pay outside data-analysis service providers and database marketing firms. Further, the analysis is done more quickly—in hours, rather than weeks.

Source: "Managing Customer Churn," *Information Week* (May 14, 2001); *sprint.com; sas.com.*

Questions

1. Why is it more important to retain customers than to acquire customers?

2. How does Sprint's data warehouse contribute to customer retention?

---

in this cube (at the intersection of all three dimensions) represents the sales of a specific product, to customers in a specific market, on a certain date (time).

Multidimensional databases are typically a more efficient and effective means of storing large amounts of data than relational databases. There are several reasons for these advantages over relational databases:

- Data in multidimensional databases can be presented and navigated with relative ease.

- Multidimensional databases are easier to maintain.

- Multidimensional databases are significantly faster than relational databases as a result of the additional dimensions and the anticipation of how the data will be accessed by users.

For an example to differentiate between relational and multidimensional databases, suppose your company has four products (nuts, screws, bolts, and washers), which have been sold in three territories (East, West, and Central) for the last three years (1999, 2000, 2001). In a relational database, these sales data would look like Figures 5.12a, b, and c. In a multidimensional database, these data would be represented by a three-dimensional matrix, as shown in Figure 5.13. We would say that this matrix represents sales *dimensioned by* products and regions and year. Notice that we can see

(a) 1999

Product	Region	Sales
Nuts	East	50
Nuts	West	60
Nuts	Central	100
Screws	East	40
Screws	West	70
Screws	Central	80
Bolts	East	90
Bolts	West	120
Bolts	Central	140
Washers	East	20
Washers	West	10
Washers	Central	30

(b) 2000

Product	Region	Sales
Nuts	East	60
Nuts	West	70
Nuts	Central	110
Screws	East	50
Screws	West	80
Screws	Central	90
Bolts	East	100
Bolts	West	130
Bolts	Central	150
Washers	East	30
Washers	West	20
Washers	Central	40

(c) 2001

Product	Region	Sales
Nuts	East	70
Nuts	West	80
Nuts	Central	120
Screws	East	60
Screws	West	90
Screws	Central	100
Bolts	East	110
Bolts	West	140
Bolts	Central	160
Washers	East	40
Washers	West	30
Washers	Central	50

Figure 5.12   *Relational databases.*

only sales in 1999 in Figure 5.13a. Therefore, sales in 2000 and 2001 are shown in Figures 5.13b and c. Figure 5.14 (on page 152) shows the equivalence between relational and multidimensional databases.

Data Marts

Data warehousing approaches can range from simple, called a *data mart*, to complex, the *enterprise data warehouse*. These approaches differ in scale and complexity. In practice, however, few organizations begin by implementing an enterprise data warehouse for the entire organization because the cost and time frame are prohibitive. Instead, an organization often has a cooperating collection of data marts forming a virtual data warehouse. Therefore, data marts are implemented most often, usually as the first step in proving the usefulness of the technologies to solve business problems.

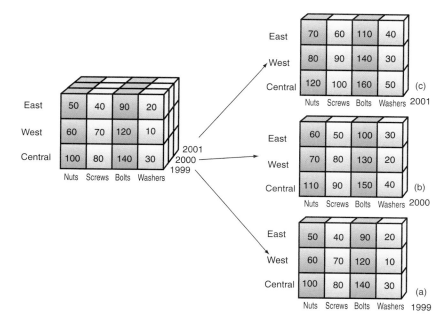

Figure 5.13   *Multi-dimensional database.*

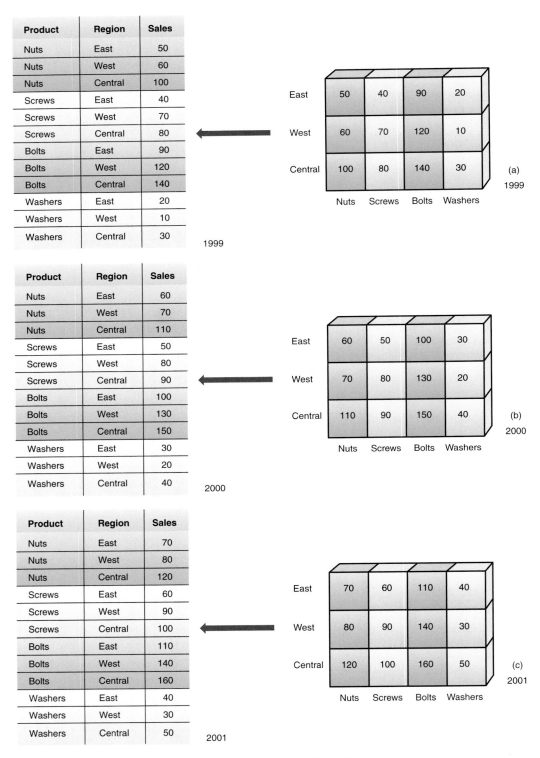

Figure 5.14 *Equivalence between relational and multidimensional databases.*

A **data mart** is a scaled-down version of a data warehouse that focuses on a particular subject area. The data mart is usually designed to support the unique business requirements of a specific department or business process. A company can have many data marts, each focused on a subset of the entire firm. The trend toward greater use of the data mart often is driven by end users and departments that want to build local data marts to meet their specific needs instead of waiting for a companywide enterprise data warehouse.

Because of its reduced scope, a data mart takes less time to build, costs less, and is less complex than an enterprise data warehouse. It is easier to agree on common data definitions for a single subject area than for an entire company. Therefore, a data mart is appropriate when a company needs to improve data access in a targeted area, such as the marketing department. However, the indiscriminate introduction of multiple data marts with no linkage to each other or to an enterprise data warehouse will cause problems. Because these data marts can proliferate quickly, they may create the same problems that earlier file management systems did, including data redundancy, data isolation, data integrity problems, and so on.

Data Mining

Data mining provides a means of extracting previously unknown, predictive information from the base of accessible data in data warehouses. Data mining tools use sophisticated, automated algorithms to discover hidden patterns, correlations, and relationships among organizational data. These tools are used to predict future trends and behaviors, allowing businesses to make proactive, knowledge-driven decisions.

For example, one typical predictive problem is targeted marketing. Data mining can use data on past promotional mailings to identify the targets most likely to maximize the return on the company's investment in future mailings. Other predictive problems include forecasting bankruptcy and other forms of default. An example of pattern discovery is the analysis of retail sales data to identify seemingly unrelated products that are often purchased together, such as milk and greeting cards at a supermarket. Another pattern discovery problem is detecting fraudulent credit card transactions.

Functions.   Data mining identifies facts or suggests conclusions based on sifting through the data to discover either patterns or anomalies. Data mining has five main functions:

- *Classification:* infers the defining characteristics of a certain group (such as customers who have been lost to competitors).
- *Clustering:* identifies groups of items that share a particular characteristic. (Clustering differs from classification in that no predefining characteristic is given in classification.)
- *Association:* identifies relationships between events that occur at one time (such as the contents of a shopping basket).
- *Sequencing:* similar to association, except that the relationship exists over a period of time (such as repeat visits to a supermarket or use of a financial planning product).
- *Forecasting:* estimates future values based on patterns within large sets of data (such as demand forecasting).

Applications.   The applications for data mining are wide-ranging. They include customer relationships (that is, customer retention); cross-selling and up-selling;

IT's About Business   eddiebauer.com   MKT

Box 5.4:   Data mining at Eddie Bauer

A division of the Spiegel Group, apparel retailer Eddie Bauer has more than 500 stores in 49 states. Bauer publishes 44 catalogs annually with a circulation of 105 million in the United States and Canada. The company is trying to build one-to-one relationships with more than 15 million retail, catalog, and Internet customers.

An average customer might have placed 20 orders in the last five years, with four items per order. Now, add to those 15 million buying histories what you know about the customer: name, age, and address, for example. The result is several terabytes of raw data—and a problem. Before implementing its data mining and data warehousing projects, the company had data in different places. So, managers decided it was time to implement data mining and data warehousing projects that could consolidate that disparate data and make them available to everyone in the company who needed them.

The company realized that it should operate from a customer-centric point of view rather than a channel-centric point of view. To do so, Bauer had to rethink the metrics it used to gauge its success and used data mining of the firm's data warehouse to determine what these metrics need to be. Metrics such as comparing annual sales figures began to give way to customer-relationship-oriented measures such as determining a customer's current value (e.g., likelihood to buy, type and quantity of product likely to buy, amount of money likely to spend, satisfaction with Bauer) and projecting his or her lifetime value.

Data mining for customer relationship management gives Eddie Bauer effective ways of analyzing customer behavior, together with the power to make projections based on that customer information. Data mining typically relates to direct-mail campaigns at Eddie Bauer—both within the catalog and retail sectors. Increasingly, such activities also focus on the Internet.

Bauer uses predictive modeling to decide who receives specialized mailings and catalogs. For example, each year Eddie Bauer features an outerwear special, and, thanks to data mining, the company can determine which customers are most likely to buy. Data mining also allows Bauer to determine seasonal buying habits. Then the company can identify people with similar characteristics and target them with mailings to bring them into the store or encourage them to buy from the catalog.

Customer loyalty is critical to Bauer, and its data mining has made tracking and maintaining the customer base easier and more efficient. Data mining helps Bauer find pieces of information that are not just common sense and use them to retain customers more effectively.

Source: sas.com; eddiebauer.com.

Questions

1. What is the difference for a company between a customer-centric point of view and a channel-centric point of view? Describe both in relation to Eddie Bauer.

2. What other metrics might Bauer use to measure its success?

---

campaign management; market, channel, and pricing analysis; and customer segmentation analysis. IT's About Business Box 5.4 provides an example of such business applications at Eddie Bauer. However, data mining applications are valuable in a variety of industries as the following examples show.

EXAMPLES

The National Basketball Association.   A data mining application, Advanced Scout, is proving very useful for NBA coaches. Coaches, like business executives, carefully study data to enhance their natural intuition when making strategic decisions. By helping coaches make better decisions, data mining applications are playing a huge role in boosting fan support and loyalty. That means millions of dollars in gate traffic, television sales, and licensing.

Before these data mining applications, the sheer volume of statistics was overwhelming, with as many as 200 possessions a game and about 1,200 games a year.

Previous applications produced only basic results—the kind of statistics anyone could find in a local newspaper.

Using the data mining software, coaches can drill down into the statistics and data and unearth comprehensible patterns that were previously hidden among seemingly unrelated statistics. Coaches are able to obtain, in real time, statistical evaluations that allow them to put in the very best players for specific points in the game. Coaches can also, in real time, ask the application which play will be the most effective relative to the time elapsed and the specific combinations of players on the court. Data mining, simply put, helps coaches make more effective decisions.

Selecting branch locations.   The Dallas Teachers Credit Union (DTCU) decided to become a full-fledged community bank, but did not know where to build branches. DTCU used data mining software to comb through demographic and customer data. One target was people who might open checking accounts, because bankers consider such accounts a way to make "cheap money." DTCU found that if a branch was within a 10-minute drive, customers had a checking account. But if the branch was a 10.5 minute drive, they did not have a checking account. Consequently, when DTCU opened a branch in north Dallas within a 10-minute drive for a large number of potential customers, it became profitable in 90 days. Normally, a branch takes a year to climb into the black. DTCU now uses data mining to select all branch locations. ●

Table 5.2 lists some other common data mining applications. We will reexamine data mining in a decision support role in Chapter 10.

Table 5.2   Common Data Mining Applications

Application	Description
Market segmentation	Identifies the common characteristics of customers who buy the same products from your company
Customer churn	Predicts which customers are likely to leave your company and go to a competitor
Fraud detection	Identifies which transactions are most likely to be fraudulent
Direct marketing	Identifies which prospects should be included in a mailing list to obtain the highest response rate
Market basket analysis	Understands what products or services are commonly purchased together (e.g., beer and diapers)
Trend analysis	Reveals the difference between a typical customer this month versus last month
Science	Simulates nuclear explosions; visualizes quantum physics
Entertainment	Models customer flows in theme parks; analyzes safety of amusement-park rides
Insurance and health care	Predicts which customers will buy new policies; identifies behavior patterns that increase insurance risk; spots fraudulent claims
Manufacturing	Optimizes product design, balancing manufacturability and safety; improves shop-floor scheduling and machine utilization
Medicine	Ranks successful therapies for different illnesses; predicts drug efficacy; discovers new drugs and treatments
Oil and gas	Analyzes seismic data for signs of underground deposits; prioritizes drilling locations; simulates underground flows to improve recovery
Retailing	Discerns buying-behavior patterns; predicts how customers will respond to marketing campaigns
Transportation	Optimizes distribution schedules and vehicle use; analyzes loading patterns for trucks and railcars

Text Mining

Text mining is the application of data mining to nonstructured or less structured text files. Data mining takes advantage of the infrastructure of stored data to extract predictive information. For example, by data mining a customer database, an analyst might discover that everyone who buys product A also buys products B and C, but does so 6 months later. Text mining, however, operates with less structured information. Documents rarely have strong internal infrastructure, and where they do, it is frequently focused on document format rather than document content. Text mining helps organizations to do the following:

- Find the "hidden" content of documents, including additional useful relationships.
- Relate documents across previously unnoticed divisions (e.g., discover that customers in two different product divisions have the same characteristics).
- Group documents by common themes (e.g., identify all the customers of an insurance firm who have similar complaints and cancel their policies).

The following example demonstrates an application of text mining.

EXAMPLE

Searching for documents at Procter & Gamble. Procter & Gamble's (*pg.com*) intranet contains increasingly large amounts of information from both inside and outside the company. Finding documents relevant to an individual's needs by utilizing traditional full-text indexing and searching is proving to be more and more difficult as the amount of information increases. Text mining's ability to organize and retrieve information based on concepts greatly reduces the number of documents returned by a search as well as increasing the relevancy of those documents. P&G's text mining software also displays a graphical depiction of closely related concepts and documents. ●

Before you go on . . .

1. What are some of the advantages of data warehousing?
2. How would a firm use data mining and text mining for competitive advantage?

www.wiley.com/
college/turban

 FOR THE ACCOUNTING MAJOR

Data gathered about each transaction (business event) in the organization is stored in its databases. Accountants access these data to create an unbroken audit trail from each transaction to the balance sheet and then to show profit and loss for the company on the transaction. The speed with which data can be accessed and searched directly affects the productivity of the accountant. Also, the flexibility with which the data can be searched, stemming from the design of the database, means that the modern accountant can investigate relationships with unprecedented ease. With the advent of modern data mining techniques, the firm can discover relationships that have not even been considered.

 FOR THE FINANCE MAJOR

Employees in the finance department make extensive use of computerized databases external to the organization, such as CompuStat or Dow Jones, to obtain financial data on organizations in their industry. They can use these data to determine if their organization meets industry benchmarks in return on investment, cash management, or other financial ratios. As for accounts, the speed and flexibility with which data can be accessed and searched bear directly on the finance professional's productivity. Modern data mining techniques are also becoming popular in finance, particularly for the automated discovery of relationships in securities and portfolio management.

FOR THE MARKETING MAJOR   `MKT`

When a customer makes a purchase from an organization, the transaction generates data that are stored in the firm's databases. Marketing personnel access this information to plan targeted marketing campaigns and to evaluate the success of previous campaigns. They also link this information to geographic databases to determine where certain products sell the best. Data mining is also uncovering many unanticipated relationships between some aspect of the buyer's "profile," the product, and the marketing and advertising campaigns, that, when identified and exploited, can increase sales substantially.

FOR THE PRODUCTION/OPERATIONS MANAGEMENT MAJOR   `POM`

Production/operations personnel access organizational databases to determine optimum inventory levels for parts in a production process. They also use information in databases to know when to perform required service on machines. Past production data enable these persons to determine the optimum configuration for assembly lines. Firms also keep quality data that inform them not only about the quality of the finished products, but also about quality issues with incoming raw materials, production irregularities, shipping and logistics, and after-sale use and maintenance of the product. Modern databases allow POM professionals to quickly identify problem areas and resolve them. Data mining automates discovery of previously undetected production issues.

FOR THE HUMAN RESOURCES MANAGEMENT MAJOR   `HRM`

Organizational databases contain extensive data on employees, including gender, race, age, current and past job descriptions, and performance evaluations. Human resources personnel access these data to provide reports for governmental agencies regarding compliance with federal Equal Opportunity guidelines. These persons also use these data to evaluate hiring practices in the organization, evaluate salary structures, and manage any discrimination grievances or lawsuits brought against the firm. Cutting-edge technologies such as data mining can help the HR professional investigate relationships in the data that bear upon the health, safety, productivity, and retention of valuable human resources.

SUMMARY

❶ Discuss traditional data file organization and its problems.

In a file management environment, each application has a specific data file related to it, containing all the data records needed by the application. Records stored in a sequential file structure may be accessed sequentially, or they may be accessed directly via an index (and then sequentially) using an indexed sequential access method. Records stored in a direct file structure may be accessed directly without using an index.

The traditional data file organization led to many problems, including data redundancy, data inconsistency, data isolation, data integrity, security, and application/data dependence. Storing data in data files that are tightly linked to their applications resulted in organizations having hundreds of applications and data files, with little or no coordination among the applications and files, and no overall plan for managing corporate data.

❷ **Explain how a database approach overcomes the problems associated with the traditional file environment, and discuss disadvantages of the database approach.**
A database, which is a logical group of related files, eliminates the problems associated with a traditional file environment. In a database, data are integrated and related so that one set of software programs provides access to all the data. Therefore, data redundancy, data isolation, and data inconsistency are minimized, and data can be shared among all users of the data. In addition, security and data integrity are increased, and applications and data are independent of one another.

The database approach does have disadvantages. Databases are expensive and require time and effort to program. Also, databases do provide security for corporate data, but once inside a database, a hacker can cause tremendous damage.

❸ **Describe how the three most common data models organize data, and the advantages and disadvantages of each model.**
The hierarchical model rigidly structures data into an inverted "tree" in which records contain a key field and a number of other fields. All records have only one "parent," and each parent may have many "children." Therefore, the hierarchical structure is characterized by one-to-many relationships among data. In the network model, records can be linked to more than one parent, allowing many-to-many relationships among the data. The relational model uses tables to capitalize on characteristics of rows and columns of data that are consistent with real-world business situations.

The main advantage of the hierarchical and network database models is processing efficiency. The hierarchical and network structures are relatively easy for users to understand because they reflect the pattern of many (but not all) real-world business relationships. In addition, the hierarchical structure allows for data integrity to be easily maintained.

Hierarchical and network structures have several disadvantages. These designs have low flexibility and are programming intensive, time-consuming, difficult to install, and difficult to remedy if design errors occur. Nor do they support ad-hoc, English-language-like inquiries for information.

The advantages of relational databases include high flexibility in regard to ad hoc queries, power to combine information from different sources, simplicity of design and maintenance, and the ability to add new data and records without disturbing existing applications. The disadvantages of relational databases include their relatively low processing efficiency.

❹ **Describe how a multidimensional data model organizes data.**
In multidimensional databases, data are stored in arrays. Similar to tables in the relational database model, arrays group related information in columns and rows. Multidimensional databases, however, typically consist of at least three dimensions. Due to problems depicting more than three dimensions, most examples artificially limit the dimensions to only three, depicting the resulting database as a cube. Dimensions are the edges of the cube, and represent the primary views of the business data.

❺ Distinguish between a data warehouse and a data mart.
Data warehousing approaches can range from simple, the data mart, to complex, the enterprise data warehouse. These approaches differ in scale and complexity.

A data mart is a scaled-down version of a data warehouse that focuses on a particular subject area. The data mart is usually designed to support the unique business requirements of a specific department or business process. Because a data mart takes less time to build, costs less, and is less complex than an enterprise data warehouse, it is appropriate when a company needs to improve data access in a targeted area, such as the marketing department.

The enterprise data warehouse provides an enterprisewide, consistent, and comprehensive view of the company, with business users employing common terminology and data standards throughout the firm. The warehouse reconciles the various departmental perspectives into a single, integrated corporate perspective.

❻ Discuss the similarities and differences between data mining and text mining.
Data mining extracts previously unknown, predictive information from data warehouses. Data mining tools use sophisticated, automated algorithms to discover hidden patterns, correlations, and relationships among organizational data. These tools are used to predict future trends and behaviors, allowing businesses to make proactive, knowledge-driven decisions.

Text mining applies data mining to nonstructured or less structured text files. Text mining helps organizations find the "hidden" content of documents, relate documents across previously unnoticed divisions, and group documents by common themes.

INTERACTIVE LEARNING SESSION

Go to the CD, access Chapter 5: Managing Organizational Data and Information, and read the case presented. It will describe a business problem that will require you to query a database for certain information. You will be able to construct SQL statements to obtain the needed information. As you construct your SQL statements, you will see what information results and decide if it meets your requirements. You may then change your SQL statements as necessary to obtain further (or different) information.

For additional resources, go to the books's Web site for Chapter 5. There you will find Web resources for the chapter, including links to organizations, people, and technology; "IT's About Business" company links; "What's in IT for Me?" links; and a self-testing Web quiz for Chapter 5.

www.wiley.com/college/turban

DISCUSSION QUESTIONS

1. You are the CIO of your company. You have just made a presentation to your CEO, proposing that the company implement a data warehouse. The CEO responds, "We already have several databases, don't we? Why do we need a data warehouse?" Prepare a response to justify your proposal.

2. As the CIO of a company, you want to implement a series of data marts. The CEO wants to know why you do not just implement one large data warehouse. Make your case to support data marts.

3. Should your university implement a data warehouse? Data marts? What types of uses would your university have for a data warehouse? For data marts?

4. In the university question above, what might the dimensions be in the multidimensional database used in the data warehouse? Give a three-dimensional example. What would each cell represent in your example?

PROBLEM-SOLVING ACTIVITIES

1. Perform a feasibility study for your university to implement a data warehouse (or data mart). Include in your study the application(s) that you would address with the data warehouse. What types of data would you include? Why?

2. Develop a simple database for your personal use, for your family's use, or for use in an organization of which you are a member. This might contain data on names, addresses, telephone numbers, birthdays, and other pertinent information.

3. Entrepreneurs can benefit from using databases and data mining by exploiting demographic data that can be purchased for any geographic region. For a startup business of your choice, what kind of data would you want to purchase, and what kinds of relationships would you want to investigate?

INTERNET ACTIVITIES

1. Access the Web sites of one or two of the major data management vendors, such as Oracle (*oracle.com*), Sybase (*sybase.com*), and IBM (*ibm.com*). What are the capabilities of their latest products? Compare these capabilities. Pay particular attention to the Web connections offered by each vendor's products.

2. Access the Web sites of one or two of the major data warehouse vendors, such as NCR (*ncr.com*),

SAS (*sas.com*), and Comshare (*comshare.com*). What are the capabilities of their latest products? Pay particular attention to the Web connection offered by each vendor's product.

3. Access the Web site of the Gartner Group (*gartner-group.com*). Examine its research papers on marketing databases, data warehousing, and data management. Prepare a report noting the most current practices in these three areas.

TEAM ACTIVITIES AND ROLE PLAYING

1. Go to your university computer center. Determine what type(s) of database(s) your university is using. Find the reasons why these type(s) of database(s) are in use, and determine the applications that run on each type of database.

2. Examine the data that your university keeps on you. (You will have to go to your university computer

center for this project.) List the fields that are included in your record. What applications would be supported by the fields in your record? Are you surprised by how much information your university keeps on students?

REAL-WORLD CASE *harrahs.com*

Harrah's Entertainment Database

The Business Problem   The difference between Harrah's and its competitors is that most companies put money into the spectacle. The prevailing wisdom in the casino industry is that it is the property's attractiveness that drives customers to one site or another. This view has propelled the spending of ever-greater amounts on increasingly lavish hotels and casinos. While its competitors continued to pour money into extravagant casinos to drum up new business, Harrah's wanted a national approach to its business.

Harrah's used to operate under the assumption that its customers were partial to one particular casino.

Its casinos around the country each operated independently and competed with one another. Each had its own player card that was valid only at the casino that issued it. None of the information systems at these individual sites were integrated with those at other casinos or could even communicate with them.

By doing marketing research, Harrah's found that customers patronized different Harrah's sites around the country. That led Harrah's to extend its card-player program so that customers could use their cards at any Harrah's casino. Extending the card-player program allowed the company to track particular customers on a national basis. Knowing customers' habits would enable Harrah's to improve service, customize the kinds of "comps" (free dinners, show tickets, and hotel rooms) it offered, and better tailor its marketing promotions. All of that would help tie customers closer to the Harrah's brand and increase the company's share of the U.S. gaming market. Harrah's was looking for a customer relationship management (CRM) program, and at the heart of such a program is an excellent database.

The IT Solution   Harrah's developed the winner's information network (WINet), the industry's first national customer database. The first step was to consolidate all its disparate IT systems, so that all the company's properties could communicate with each other and share information about customers.

Harrah's had to make its AS/400 transactional systems at each property communicate with a UNIX-based national customer database. This Patron Database contains all the company's customer information. Harrah's team used middleware and software developed in-house to enable this communication between disparate systems.

Once WINet was running, Harrah's could share information across its properties, in real time. The company's 35,000 slot machines now also connect to the AS/400 systems, and call-center representatives are linked to both the AS/400s and the UNIX Patron Database. Analysts in the marketing department access the data warehouse and use SAS software to do predictive modeling.

Real-time access is key to enabling Harrah's Total Rewards program. A customer who receives a promotion in the mail will call Harrah's to inquire about it. As soon as the customer service agent gets on the phone, a large amount of information identifying the customer pops up on the agent's computer screen. It indicates the customer's tier (platinum, gold, or diamond), where he or she usually plays, how much he or she has won or lost, and even the customer's net worth.

The agent then asks where the customer wants to make a hotel reservation and for what dates, and can bring up Harrah's reservation system to see if a room is available. The agent asks if the customer is responding to an offer. The reservation system then automatically searches the Patron Database to see if the customer has already received or redeemed the offer and if it is still valid.

WINet has the ability to drill into Harrah's extensive database, which in turn allows the company to customize its marketing and promotions to individual customers, particularly those at the lower end of the economic scale. Harrah's has been able to retain those lower-end players by calling them to ask about their trips. Retaining a customer costs one-tenth the cost of acquiring a new customer. Talk time has been reduced by an average of 12 seconds per phone call, because employees no longer have to ask for information that other employees have previously asked for, nor do they have to rekey that information.

The Results   The CRM strategy was not complete simply with the deployment of WINet. Harrah's also had to radically change its relationship with its regional properties. Before the Total Rewards program, each of Harrah's properties operated independently. Regional Harrah's managers were possessive of their markets, customers, and data and were focused almost exclusively on their own operation's bottom line. However, the parent company eventually sold the regional properties on this new strategy. It argued that customers favored the idea of extending the benefits that guests received for patronizing the casino in one area so that they could also use them at a casino in another region.

The corporate office also convinced the regional property managers that the IT capabilities and marketing tools it was developing would boost their businesses. For example, Harrah's IT systems link all its properties together for corporate promotional events.

Since Total Rewards began, Harrah's has saved $20 million a year in overall costs, while increasing same-store sales growth. At the same time, the number of Harrah's customers playing at more than one of Harrah's properties has increased by 72 percent. Harrah's has changed its relationship with its customers, gained competitive advantage, and created enterprise value.

Source: "Jackpot! Harrah's Entertainment," *CIO* (February 1, 2001); *harrahs.com.*

Questions

1. What was Harrah's bigger problem in developing its Total Rewards system—technology or people? Would this be true in developing all new systems?

2. What competitive advantage did the Total Rewards system give Harrah's?

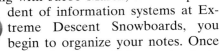

wiley.com/college/turban

Extreme Descent Snowboards

www.wiley.com/
college/turban

Background As you walk out of your meeting with Jacob March, the vice president of information systems at Extreme Descent Snowboards, you begin to organize your notes. Once you are seated at your desk, you begin to read the following notes that describe your next assignment.

Assignment 1

Develop a database application to manage the information systems training classes. The database application should be built using a database management system and must include the following features or functionality:

1. Store and retrieve information about employees who sign up for and take training classes. Information about employees should include employee ID, name, department, title, telephone number, and e-mail address.

2. Store and retrieve information about training classes. Information about training classes should include training class number, title, description, and days.

3. Store and retrieve information about employees who sign up for upcoming classes and employees that have taken classes in the past. This should include the date when the class is or was offered.

4. Reports or query capabilities that allow one to find out the courses a particular employee will take (or has attended), as well as a roster of employees who have signed up for or who have taken a particular training class.

5. An entity relationship diagram that defines the entities and the relationships between the entities. Also, list all of the attributes and associated keys for each entity and many-to-many relationship. This will document your application and allow you to transfer your design more easily to the database management system tool.

The application should be a prototype to demonstrate these capabilities or features, so you may make up data where necessary.

Assignment 2

Data mining is a relatively new concept used to predict trends and behaviors of industries, allowing businesses to make proactive, knowledge driven decisions. Visit one of the following Web sites that offers database mining software. Then answer the following questions.

www.smartdrill.com
www.angoss.com

1. What is data mining?

2. Name three benefits to EDS by incorporating a data mining service.

3. Which process would most benefit EDS?

TELECOMMUNICATIONS AND NETWORKS

6

CHAPTER PREVIEW

Computing technology is truly a modern marvel that has transformed how we do business, as well as how we manage our personal affairs. The computer's influence on today's modern competitive environment would be much diminished without the telecommunications and computer networks available today. Their development has accompanied the amazing advances in computing over the last three decades. In most firms, communication between computing technologies is just as important as the computer itself. This chapter tells us how and why competitive organizations need and support these essential telecommunications.

CHAPTER OUTLINE

6.1 The Telecommunications System

6.2 Networks

6.3 Network Communications Software

6.4 Network Processing Strategies

6.5 Telecommunications Applications

LEARNING OBJECTIVES

1. Describe the components of a telecommunications system.

2. Describe the eight basic types of communication media, including their advantages and disadvantages.

3. Classify the major types of networks.

4. Differentiate among the three types of distributed processing.

5. Identify eight telecommunications applications that can help organizations attain competitive advantage.

PEER-TO-PEER COMPUTING: WHAT TO DO WITH ALL THOSE IDLE COMPUTERS

Organizations are facing increasingly complex problems as a result of global competition; real-time, 24/7/365 operations; the explosion in information; and rapid technological change. Despite the phenomenal increases in computer processing capabilities and rapid decreases in cost, many organizations face problems that require numerous mainframes or a supercomputer to address. These computing resources remain expensive (several millions of dollars) and are complicated to manage.

A peer-to-peer community or network of computers.

At the same time, personal computer resources are greatly underutilized. Most of the time, personal computers are idle. Indeed, Pentium III and Pentium 4 computers have so much power that users typically tap only 5 percent of the processing available. Over one billion PCs, each with an average processing speed of over 1.5 gigahertz, are now connected to the Internet, representing a huge amount of underutilized processing power and storage.

The business problem for organizations is how to address their increasingly complex problems in a cost-effective manner, while making effective use of underutilized computing resources.

One solution is *peer-to-peer (P2P) processing*. P2P unlocks underused computing resources and allows a larger community to share them. Peer-to-peer computing (also called *grid computing*) is a type of distributed computing that exploits the resources of dispersed computers of a network. Instead of being clients in a client/server network, each connected device becomes a fully participating peer in the network.

Peer-to-peer computing uses the processing power of millions of individual personal computers to perform a variety of applications. Philanthropic examples of these applications include searching for extraterrestrial intelligence (*setiathome.ssl. Berkeley.edu*), exploring AIDS treatments (*fightaidsathome.org*), and researching potential cancer drugs (*ud.com*). But peer-to-peer is also about companies tapping their employees' PCs to analyze numbers or share knowledge. Examples of the P2P model providing benefits for businesses include:

- J.P. Morgan Chase & Company (*jpmorganchase.com*) uses P2P for large processing tasks such as risk management calculations.
- The law firm of Baker & McKenzie (*bakerinfo.com*) uses P2P to capture and share the knowledge of its 3,000 attorneys in 60 offices.
- Pratt & Whitney (*prattwhitney.com*) uses P2P to analyze engine turbine blades.
- Intel (*intel.com*) uses P2P to test new chip designs.
- Boeing (*boeing.com*) uses P2P to analyze the fuselages of fighter planes.
- IBM's (*ibm.com*) computing grid, known as the Distributed Terascale Facility (DTF), is capable of 13.6 trillion calculations per second. The grid enables scientists to share computing resources in search of breakthroughs in many disciplines.

P2P does have its disadvantages. Handing off sensitive corporate data to unknown PCs over the public Internet poses serious technical and security issues. PCs vary in power, operating systems, and availability. Also, if a participant shuts down his or her PC during a crucial bit of computation, that computation must be reassigned. Limited bandwidth can slow up network traffic, forcing some pieces of processing to wait in long queues.

Another disadvantage to P2P networks is how to obtain the needed numbers of machines for effective computing. With some projects, people are happy to volunteer their unused computing capacity for a good cause. However, it is unclear if people would be willing to volunteer to help businesses. As a result, some businesses are offering money to participate. For example, a company called Distributed Science (*distributedscience.com*) rents CPU cycles and network bandwidth on the public's personal computers.

(For a more technical discussion of Peer-to-Peer Computing, see the material on the book's Web site.)

www.wiley.com/
college/turban

Sources: "Peer to Peer," *BusinessWeek 50* (Spring 2001), pp. 194–196; "Five Patents to Watch," *MIT Technology Review* (May 2001), "PCs as Supercomputer," *Internet Week* (May 28, 2001), pp. 1, 45; "Peer-to-Peer Grows Up and Gets a Real Job," *New York Times* (June 13, 2001).

What We Learned from This Case

These examples of P2P computing illustrate two fundamental points about computing. First, computers do not work in isolation in modern organizations. Rather, they constantly exchange data and/or applications, either automatically or as directed by their users. Second, this exchange of data—facilitated by telecommunications technologies—brings a number of very significant advantages to companies. The P2P projects of the companies above depend on telecommunications networks as a fundamental, integral part of the IT infrastructure.

6.1   THE TELECOMMUNICATIONS SYSTEM

A **telecommunications system** consists of hardware and of software that transmits information from one location to another. These systems can transmit text, data, graphics, voice, documents, or full-motion video information. The major components of a telecommunications system include the following:

- **Hardware:** all types of computers (e.g., desktop, server, mainframe) and communications processors (such as a modems or small computers dedicated solely to communications)
- **Communications media:** the physical media through which electronic signals are transmitted, including wireless media (used with satellites and cell phones)
- **Communications networks:** the links among computers and communications devices
- **Communications software:** software that controls the telecommunications system and the entire transmission process
- **Data communications providers:** regulated utilities or private firms that provide data communications services
- **Communications protocols:** the rules for transmitting information across the system
- **Communications applications:** electronic data interchange, teleconferencing, videoconferencing, e-mail, facsimile, electronic funds transfer, and others

Figure 6.1 (on page 166) shows a typical telecommunications system. Note that such systems have two sides, the transmitter of information and the receiver of information.

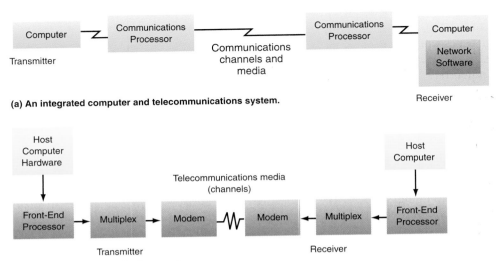

(a) An integrated computer and telecommunications system.

Figure 6.1 *Telecommunications system.*

(b) A typical telecommunications system.

To transmit and receive information, a telecommunications system must perform a number of separate functions that are *transparent* to the user (i.e., the user does not see them). The system must do all of the following: transmit information; establish the interface between the sender and the receiver; route messages along the most efficient paths; ensure that the right message gets to the right receiver; check the message for errors and rearrange the format if necessary; convert messages from one speed to another (computers are usually faster than a communications medium); ensure that the sending devices, receiving devices, and communications links are operational (in other words, maintain the network); and secure the information at all times.

Signals

Telecommunications media carry two basic types of signals, analog and digital. **Analog signals** are continuous waves that transmit information by altering the characteristics of the waves. Analog signals have two parameters, amplitude and frequency. For example, voice and all sound is analog, traveling to human ears in the form of waves. The higher the waves (or amplitude), the louder the sound; the more closely packed the waves, the higher the frequency or pitch. Radio, telephones, and recording equipment historically transmitted and received analog signals, but they are changing to digital signals.

Digital signals do not have the characteristic wave shape that analog signals do. Rather, they are discrete pulses that are either on or off. This quality allows them to convey information in a binary form that can be clearly interpreted by computers. Computers typically cannot distinguish whether an analog wave is in an "on" mode or an "off" mode. With digital signals, the signal is clearly on or off (see Figure 6.2).

Figure 6.2 *Analog versus digital signals.*

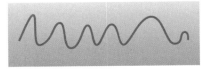

Analog data transmission
(wave signals)

Digital data transmission
(pulse signals)

Communications Processors

Communications processors are hardware devices that support data transmission and reception across a telecommunications system. These devices include modems, multiplexers, front-end processors, and concentrators.

Modem.   The U.S. public telephone system (called POTS, for "Plain Old Telephone Service") was designed as an analog network to carry voice signals or sounds in an analog wave format. In order for this type of circuit to carry digital information, that information must be converted into an analog wave pattern. The conversion from digital to analog is called *modulation*, and the reverse is *demodulation*. The device that performs these two processes is called a **modem**, a contraction of the terms *modulate/demodulate* (see Figure 6.3).

Modems are always used in pairs. The unit at the sending end converts a computer's digital information into analog signals for transmission over analog lines. At the receiving end, another modem converts the analog signal back into digital signals for the receiving computer. Like most communications equipment, a modem's transmission speed is measured in bits per second (bps). Typical modem speeds range from 14,400 to 56,600 bps.

Multiplexer.   A **multiplexer** is an electronic device that allows a single communications channel to carry data transmissions simultaneously from many sources. Multiplexers lower communication costs by allowing devices to share communications channels. Multiplexing thus makes more efficient use of these channels by merging the transmissions of several computers (e.g., personal computers) at one end of the channel, while a similar unit separates the individual transmissions at the receiving end (e.g., a mainframe).

Front-end processor.   With most computers, the central processing unit (CPU) must communicate with several computers at the same time. Routine communication tasks can absorb a large proportion of the CPU's processing time, leading to degraded performance on more important jobs. In order not to waste valuable CPU time, many computer systems have a small secondary computer dedicated solely to communication. Known as a **front-end processor**, this specialized computer manages all routing communications with peripheral devices.

The functions of a front-end processor include coding and decoding data; detecting errors; and recovering, recording, interpreting, and processing the control information that is transmitted. It can also poll remote terminals to determine if they have messages to send or are ready to receive a message. In addition, a front-end processor has the responsibility of controlling access to the network, assigning priorities to messages, logging all data communications activity, computing statistics on network activity, and routing and rerouting messages among alternative communication links.

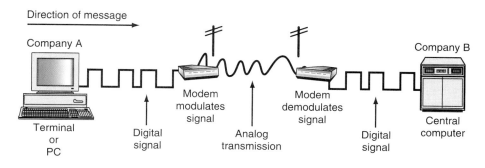

Figure 6.3   *A modem converts digital to analog signals and vice versa. (Source: Stern and Stern, Computing in the Information Age, 1996, p. 334.)*

Communications Media and Channels

For data to be communicated from one location to another, some form of pathway or medium must be used. These pathways are called **communications channels**. The communications channels, in two types of media, are shown below.

Cable Media

1. Twisted-pair wire
2. Coaxial cable
3. Fiber-optic cable

Broadcast Media

4. Microwave transmission
5. Satellite transmission
6. Radio
7. Cellular radio
8. Infrared

Cable media use physical wires or cables to transmit data and information. Twisted-pair wire and coaxial cable are made of copper, and fiber-optic cable is made of glass. However, with the exception of fiber-optic cables, cables present several problems, notably the expense of installation and change, as well as a fairly limited capacity. The alternative is communication over **wireless media**. The key to mobile communications in today's rapidly moving society is data transmissions over electromagnetic media—the "airwaves." Manager's Checklist 6.1 summarizes the advantages and disadvantages of the various communications channels. Each of the channels is discussed in this section.

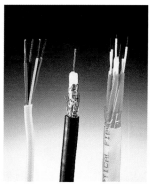

Twisted-pair telephone cable, coaxial cable, and fiber-optic cable.

Twisted-pair wire.   **Twisted-pair wire** is the most prevalent form of communications wiring; it is used for almost all business telephone wiring. Twisted-pair wire consists of strands of copper wire twisted in pairs. It is relatively inexpensive to purchase, widely available, and easy to work with, and it can be made relatively unobtrusive by running it inside walls, floors, and ceilings. However, twisted-pair wire has some significant disadvantages. It is relatively slow for transmitting data, is subject to interference from other electrical sources, and can be easily tapped for gaining unauthorized access to data by unintended receivers.

Coaxial cable.   **Coaxial cable** consists of *insulated* copper wire. It is much less susceptible to electrical interference than is twisted-pair wire and can carry much more data. For these reasons, it is commonly used to carry high-speed data traffic as well as television signals (thus the term *cable TV*). However, coaxial cable is more expensive and more difficult to work with than twisted-pair wire. It is also somewhat inflexible. Coaxial cable can cost from 10 to 20 times more than twisted-pair wire. Also, because of its inflexibility, it can increase the cost of recabling when equipment must be moved.

Data transmission over coaxial cable is divided into two basic types:

- **Baseband.** Transmission is analog, and each wire carries only one signal at a time.
- **Broadband.** Transmission is digital, and each wire can carry multiple signals simultaneously.

Fiber optics.   Fiber-optic technology, combined with the invention of the semiconductor laser, provides the means to transmit information through clear glass fibers in the form of light waves, instead of electric current. **Fiber-optic cables** consist of thousands of very thin filaments of glass fibers that conduct light pulses generated by lasers at very-high-speed transmission frequencies. The fiber-optic cable is surrounded by *cladding*, a coating that prevents the light from leaking out of the fiber.

Fiber-optic cables offer significant size and weight reductions over traditional cable media. They also provide increased speed, greater data-carrying capacity, and greater security from interference and tapping. A single glass fiber can carry more

Channel	Advantages	Disadvantages
Twisted-pair	Inexpensive Widely available Easy to work with Unobtrusive	Slow (low bandwidth) Subject to interference Easily tapped (low security)
Coaxial cable	Higher bandwidth than twisted pair Less susceptible to electromagnetic interference	Relatively expensive and inflexible Easily tapped (low-to-medium security) Somewhat difficult to work with
Fiber-optic cable	Very high bandwidth Relatively inexpensive Difficult to tap (good security)	Difficult to work with (difficult to splice)
Microwave	High bandwidth Relatively inexpensive	Must have unobstructed line of sight Susceptible to environmental interference
Satellite	High bandwidth Large coverage area	Expensive Must have unobstructed line of sight Signals experience propagation delay Must use encryption for security
Radio	High bandwidth No wires needed Signals pass through walls Inexpensive and easy to install	Create electrical interference problems Susceptible to snooping unless encrypted
Cellular Radio	Low to medium bandwidth Signals pass through walls	Require construction of towers Susceptible to snooping unless encrypted
Infrared	Low to medium bandwidth	Must have unobstructed line of sight Used only for short distances

than 50,000 simultaneous telephone calls, compared to about 5,500 calls on a standard copper coaxial cable. The capacity of fiber is doubling every 6 to 12 months. Optical fiber has reached data transmission rates of six trillion bits (terabits) per second in laboratories and, theoretically, fiber can carry up to 25 terabits per second.

Fiber optics are now installed on a scale large enough to be economically practical. Until recently, the costs of fiber and difficulties in installing fiber-optic cable slowed its growth. Although joining the ends of copper wires is fairly simple and reliable, joining fiber-optic cables with little or no loss of signal can be very difficult—especially in cable tunnels, closets, and ceilings. Communications carriers are replacing conventional copper wiring in telephone cable networks with fiber-optic cables. Fiber-optic cable is most often used as the backbone medium of a network, but not for connecting isolated devices to the backbone. That is, fiber-optic cable is used as the high-speed trunk line for a network, while twisted-pair wire and coaxial cable still are used to connect the trunk line to individual devices on the network.

Although today's fiber-optic cables are made of pure, solid glass, they distort light as it moves toward its destination. This distortion causes different wavelengths, or colors, to interfere with one another, thus limiting the number of wavelengths that can be transmitted at once.

Since the most common method of increasing cable capacity is to send more wavelengths through each fiber, attenuation is a problem for fiber transmission. *Attenuation* is the reduction in the strength of a signal, whether analog or digital. Attenuation requires manufacturers to install equipment to receive the distorted or "dirty" signals and send them out "clean." These signal regenerators can cost tens of thousands of dollars to install on land; those under water can cost one million dollars each.

In addition, fiber absorbs some of the light passing through it, making it necessary to amplify optical signals every 50 to 75 miles or so along the route. (Boosting the strength of the light so it can travel farther without amplification increases interference-causing distortion.) Eliminating optical amplifiers could save millions of dollars.

A recent advance has dramatically increased the capacity of fiber-optic cables. Scientists have replaced solid glass fibers with hollow glass tubes containing a vacuum. These tubes are lined with mirrors that reflect virtually 100 percent of the light beaming through the tube. This advance multiplies fiber capacity and reduces the need for expensive amplification equipment.

Microwave.   We now turn our attention to wireless media, which have greatly expanded telecommunications offerings. **Microwave** systems are widely used for high-volume, long-distance, point-to-point communication. Microwave towers usually cannot be spaced more than 30 miles apart because the earth's curvature would interrupt the line of sight from tower to tower. To minimize line-of-sight problems, microwave antennas are usually placed on top of buildings, towers, and mountain peaks. Long-distance telephone carriers use microwave systems because they generally provide about ten times the data-carrying capacity of wire without the significant efforts necessary to string or bury wire. Compared to 30 miles of wire, microwave communications can be set up much more quickly (within a day) at much less cost.

The fact that microwave requires line-of-sight transmission severely limits its usefulness as a practical large-scale solution to data communications needs, especially over very long distances. Additionally, microwave transmissions are susceptible to environmental interference during severe weather such as heavy rain or snowstorms. Although still widely used, long-distance microwave data communications systems are being replaced by satellite communications systems.

Satellite.   A major advance in communications in recent years is the use of communication **satellites** for digital transmissions. As with microwave transmission, satellites must receive and transmit via line of sight. However, the enormous *footprint* (the amount of the earth's surface in the line of sight for a specific satellite) of a satellite's coverage area from high altitudes overcomes the limitations of microwave data relay stations. A network of just three evenly spaced communications satellites in stationary *geosynchronous* orbit 22,300 miles above the equator is sufficient to provide global coverage. Currently, there are three types of orbits in which satellites are placed.

Geostationary earth orbit (GEO) satellites orbit 22,300 miles directly above the equator and maintain a fixed position above the earth's surface. These satellites are excellent for sending television programs to cable operators and broadcasting directly to homes. However, transmissions from GEO satellites take a quarter of a second to send and return. This brief pause, called **propagation delay**, makes two-way telephone conversations difficult. Also, GEO satellites are large and expensive, and the equatorial orbit cannot hold many more GEO satellites than the number that now orbit there.

Medium earth orbit (MEO) satellites are located about 6,000 miles above the earth's surface, in orbits inclined to the equator. While fewer satellites are needed to cover the earth than in LEO orbits, telephones need more power to reach MEO satellites than to reach LEO satellites.

Low earth orbit (LEO) satellites are located 400 to 700 miles above the earth's surface. These satellites are much closer to the earth, reducing or eliminating apparent propagation delay. They can pick up signals from weak transmitters, so handheld telephones need less power and can use smaller batteries. They consume less power and cost less to launch than GEO and MEO satellites. The footprints of LEO satellites are small, requiring many of them to cover the earth. (Multiple LEO satellites from one organization are referred to as LEO constellations.) Table 6.1 shows the differences among the three types of satellites.

Many companies are in the process of building constellations of satellites for commercial service. Teledesic (*teledesic.com*) and its partners are building a $9 billion global broadband wireless network they call the "Internet in the Sky." It will use a constellation of 288 LEO satellites. Another LEO system, SkyBridge (*skybridgesatellite.com*), will use two constellations of 40 LEO satellites each to cover the entire earth, except for the polar regions.

Global positioning systems. A **global positioning system (GPS)** is a wireless system that uses satellites to enable users to determine their position anywhere on the earth. (For a more technical discussion of how the GPS works, see the material on the Web.) GPS equipment is used for navigation by commercial airlines and ships.

GPS is supported by 24 satellites that are shared worldwide. Each satellite orbits the earth once in 12 hours, on a precise path at an altitude of 10,900 miles. At any point in time, the exact position of each satellite is known, because the satellite broadcasts its position and a time signal from its on-board atomic clock, accurate to one-billionth of a second. Receivers also have accurate clocks that are synchronized with those of the satellites. With the speed of signals (186,272 miles per second) known, it is possible to find the location of any receiving station with an accuracy of 50 feet by triangulation, using the distance from three satellites for the

www.wiley.com/
college/turban

The handheld GPS—great for hikers.

Table 6.1   Three Basic Types of Telecommunications Satellites

Type	Considerations	Orbit	Number
GEO	• Satellites remain stationary relative to point on Earth • Few satellites needed for global coverage • Transmission delay (approximately .25 second) • Most expensive to build and launch • Longest orbital life (12+ years)	22,300 miles	8
MEO	• Satellites move relative to point on Earth • Moderate number needed for global coverage • Require medium-powered transmitters • Negligible transmission delay • Less expensive to build and launch • Moderate orbital life (6–12 years)	6,434 miles	10–12
LEO	• Satellites move rapidly relative to point on Earth • Large number needed for global coverage • Require only low-power transmitters • Negligible transmission delay • Least expensive to build and launch • Shortest orbital life (as low as 5 years)	400–700 miles	many

computation. GPS software can convert the latitude and longitude computed to an electronic map.

The first dramatic use of GPS came during the Persian Gulf War, when troops relied on the technology to find their way in the Iraqi desert. GPS also played the key role in targeting for smart bombs. Since then, commercial use has become widespread, including navigation, mapping, and surveying, particularly in remote areas. Cars equipped with GPS can assist motorists in finding specific addresses. GPS is now available to hikers in the form of handheld devices.

Other countries, troubled that the Global Positioning System is run by the U.S. military and controlled by the U.S. government, are building independent satellite navigation networks. As a result, Europe is building a civil satellite system called Galileo, scheduled to be in operation by 2008. Mainland China and Russia are also constructing satellite systems.

Satellites have a number of unique characteristics. Some are advantages, while others are restrictions that render satellite use either impractical or impossible for other applications. See Manager's Checklist W6.1 "Advantages and Disadvantages of Satellites" at the book's Web site.

www.wiley.com/
college/turban

Radio.   Radio electromagnetic data communications do not have to depend on microwave or satellite links, especially for short ranges such as within an office setting. Radio is being used increasingly to connect computers and peripheral equipment or computers and local area networks. For data communications, the greatest advantage of radio is that no metallic wires are needed. Radio waves tend to propagate easily through normal office walls. The devices are fairly inexpensive and easy to install. Radio also allows for high data transmission speeds.

However, radio media can create electrical interference problems—with other office electrical equipment, and from that equipment to the radio communication devices. Also, radio transmissions are susceptible to snooping by anyone similarly equipped and on the same frequency.

Cellular radio technology.   Telephone users are increasingly employing cellular radio technology for data communications. **Cellular radio technology** works like this: The Federal Communications Commission (FCC) (*fcc.gov*) has defined geographic cellular service areas; each area is subdivided into hexagonal cells that fit together like a honeycomb to form the backbone of that area's cellular radio system. A radio transceiver and a computerized cell-site controller that handle all cell-site functions are located at the center of each cell. All the cell sites are connected to a mobile telephone switching office that provides the connections from the cellular system to a wired telephone network. As a user travels out of the cell serving one area and into another, the switching office transfers calls from one cell to another.

"I love the convenience, but the roaming charges are killing me."

Cellular service in the United States is primarily analog, like ground-based telephones, whereas in Europe it is digital. Digital transmission offers the potential of much greater traffic capacity within each cell, less susceptibility to interference, greater voice clarity, and fewer data errors. A conversion to digital is underway in the United States. The evolution of cellular transmission from analog to digital is described below.

First-generation (1G) and second-generation (2G) cellular data transmission.   1G technology was characterized by bulky handsets and adjustable antenna, and was based on analog technology. 1G allowed only limited roaming.

Second-generation (2G) cellular data transmission. 2G technology provides digital wireless transmission. 2G increases the voice capacity of earlier analog systems, and provides greater security, voice clarity, and global roaming.

2.5-generation (2.5G) cellular data transmission. 2.5G technology extends the 2G digital cellular standard and is installed as an upgrade to an existing 2G network.

Third-generation (3G) technologies. 3G technology offers increased efficiency and capacity; new services, such as wide-area networks for PCs and multimedia; seamless roaming across dissimilar networks; integration of satellite and fixed wireless access services into cellular networks; and greater bandwidth.

Mobile computing. **Mobile computing** occurs on radio-based networks that transmit data to and from mobile computers. Computers can be connected to the network through wired ports or through wireless connections. Mobile computing, especially if it is wireless, provides for many applications. For examples of mobile computing applications, refer to the material on the Web site.

www.wiley.com/ college/turban

Personal communication services. **Personal communication services (PCS)** technology uses lower-power, higher-frequency radio waves than does cellular technology. The lower power means that PCS cells are smaller and must be more numerous and closer together. The higher frequency means that PCS devices are effective in many places where cellular telephones are not, such as in tunnels and inside office buildings. PCS telephones need less power, are smaller, and are less expensive than cellular telephones. They also operate at higher, less-crowded frequencies than cellular telephones, meaning that they will have the bandwidth necessary to provide video and multimedia communication.

Emerging wireless applications. A number of wireless applications are emerging, including terrestrial fixed wireless (also called broadband wireless), ultra-wideband wireless (see *timedomain.com*), wireless local loop, multichannel multipoint distribution service (MMDS), local multipoint distribution service (LMDS), and free space laser. In general, these technologies are quick, easy, and inexpensive to deploy compared with placing wire or fiber. However, with the exception of ultra-wideband, these technologies require unobstructed lines-of-sight and their signals can be degraded by bad weather such as heavy rain or snow. Complete discussions of each of these technologies can be found on the Web site. IT's About Business Box 6.1 (on page 174) gives an example of LMDS.

www.wiley.com/ college/turban

Infrared. **Infrared** light is red light not commonly visible to human eyes. It can be modulated or pulsed for conveying information. The most common application of infrared light is in television or videocassette recorder remote control units. With computers, infrared transmitters and receivers ("transceivers") are being used for short-distance connections between computers and peripheral equipment, or between computers and local area networks. Many portable PCs can be bought with infrared ports, which are handy when cable connections with a peripheral (such as a printer or modem) are not practical.

Characteristics of Communications Media

Communications media have several characteristics that determine their efficiency and capabilities. These characteristics include the speed of transmission, the direction of transmission, the mode of transmission, and the accuracy of transmission.

IT's About Business

Box 6.1:   Wireless communications in Appalachia

Wireless networks typically debut in large metropolitan areas. Often overlooked are remote rural areas where the technology can have its greatest impact on the businesses and daily lives of inhabitants.

Virginia Polytechnic Institute and State University (*vt.edu*) wanted to use local multipoint distribution service (LMDS) to link the faculty, students, and employees to each other and the Internet. As a result, the university became the first educational institution in the United States to participate in a Federal Communications Commission spectrum auction. On the auction block were four basic trading areas (BTAs), covering large stretches of Virginia and having the university at its center.

Virginia Tech has the largest campus in the state, 2,600 acres. The school correctly anticipated that the big communications companies were interested only in bidding on licenses in the country's biggest cities and would ignore Virginia Tech's bids for licenses covering the four rural areas. Consequently, Virginia Tech won the four licenses, which cover 40 percent of Virginia. However, Virginia Tech has no aspirations of being an Internet service provider or displacing communications vendors. Rather, the school intends to develop the technology through a partnership with regional communities and businesses in the communications industry.

Having the licenses was a first step, but the actual equipment necessary to deploy an LMDS network put Virginia Tech in partnership with Harris Corporation (*harris.com*). According to Harris, this agreement is the first university/private-sector partnership for the deployment of an LMDS network. LMDS now connects Virginia Tech faculty, students, and employees to each other as well as to businesses in the entire rural area surrounding the campus.

Source: "Virginia Tech Brings Wireless to Appalachia and Beyond," *Mobile Computing & Communications* (September 2000), pp. 101–103.

Questions

1. Do you agree that communications technologies can have the greatest impact in rural areas? Why or why not?

2. Should Virginia Tech's LMDS network impact federal and state government policy? How?

3. What are the impacts that Virginia Tech's LMDS network has on local businesses?

Transmission speed.   **Bandwidth** refers to the range of frequencies available in any communications channel. Bandwidth is a very important concept in communications because the transmission capacity of any channel (stated in *bits per second* or *bps*) is largely dependent on its bandwidth. In general, the greater the bandwidth, the greater the channel capacity. For many data communications applications, a small bandwidth (2,400 to 14,400 bps) is usually adequate. On the other hand, graphical information requires a much greater bandwidth than textual data (in the range of *millions of bits per second*, or *Mbps*).

Channel capacity is subdivided into three bandwidths: narrowband, voiceband, and broadband channels. Slow, low-capacity transmissions, such as those transmitted over telegraph lines, make use of **narrowband** channels, while telephone lines utilize **voiceband** channels. The channel bandwidth with the highest capacity is **broadband**, which is used by microwave, cable, and fiber-optic lines.

The amount of data that can be transmitted through a channel is known as its **baud rate**, measured in bits per second (bps). A *baud* represents a signal change from positive to negative, or vice versa. The baud rate is not always the same as the bit rate. At higher transmission speeds, a single signal change can transmit more than one bit at a time, so the bit rate can be greater than the baud rate.

One signal change, or cycle, is necessary to transmit one or more bits per second. Therefore, the speed of a channel is a function of its frequency, the number of cycles per second that can be transmitted through a channel, measured in *hertz*.

The speeds of particular communications channels are as follows:

- Twisted-pair wire   300 bps to 10 Mbps (million bits per second)
- Microwave   256 Kbps (thousand bits per second) to 100 Mbps
- Satellite   256 Kbps to 100 Mbps
- Coaxial cable   56 Kbps to 200 Mbps
- Fiber-optic cable   500 Kbps to (theoretically) 25 Tbps (trillion bits per second)

The amount of data actually transferred from one system to another in a fixed length of time is only partially dependent on the transmission speed. Actual or effective *throughput speed* (usually measured in characters per second) varies with factors such as the use of data compression or electrical noise interference.

Transmission mode. Data transmissions may be either asynchronous or synchronous. In an **asynchronous transmission**, only one character is transmitted or received at a time. During transmission, the character is preceded by a *start bit* and followed by a *stop bit* that lets the receiving device know where a character begins and ends. Asynchronous transmission is inherently inefficient due to the additional overhead required for start and stop bits, and the idle time between transmissions. It is generally used only for relatively low-speed data transmission (up to 28,800 bps).

In **synchronous transmission**, a group of characters is sent over a communications link in a continuous bit stream, while data transfer is controlled by a timing signal initiated by the sending device. The sender and receiver must be in perfect synchronization to avoid the loss or gain of bits. Therefore, data blocks are preceded by unique characters called *sync bits* that are encoded into the information being transmitted. The receiving device recognizes and synchronizes itself with a stream of these characters. Synchronous transmission is generally used for transmitting large volumes of data at high speeds.

Transmission accuracy. An electrical communications line—whether using cable or radio—can be subject to interference from storms, signals from other lines, and other phenomena that introduce errors into a transmission. Telephone line cables may be mishandled by repair personnel, accidentally cut by construction workers, or subjected to power surges while data are being transmitted. These events might cause one bit or several bits to be "dropped" during transmission, thus corrupting the integrity of the information. Because the loss of even one bit could alter a character or control code, data transmission requires accuracy controls. These controls consist of bits called **parity bits** that are like check sums added to characters and/or blocks of characters at the sending end of the line. Parity bits are checked and verified at the receiving end of the line to determine whether bits were lost during transmission.

If transmission errors are detected, there are two general types of actions taken— backward error correction and forward error correction. **Backward error correction (BEC)** entails going back to the sender and requesting retransmission of the entire data stream or of a particular part, if it can be identified. **Forward error correction (FEC)** uses knowledge about the message stream and mathematical algorithms to allow the receiver to correct the received data stream without having to go back to the sender. BEC is much simpler and less expensive to use when there are few errors or when time delays are not crucial. FEC is more complex but may be necessary over long distances when retransmission is costly.

Telecommunications Carriers and Services

Telecommunications carriers provide the communications technology (e.g., telephone lines, satellites, and communications software) and services needed for data communications. These carriers include common carriers, other special-purpose carriers, and value-added carriers. The **common carriers** are the long-distance telephone companies. For example, AT&T, MCI, and Sprint are common carriers for long-distance service and special-purpose carriers for other services such as WATS lines. **Value-added carriers** are companies that have developed private telecommunications systems and provide services for a fee (such as microwave or satellite transmission). An example is Tymnet by MCI WorldCom.

Switched and dedicated lines.   **Switched lines** are telephone lines, provided by common carriers, that a person can access from his or her computer to transmit data to another computer; the transmission is routed or switched through paths to its destination. A *switch* is a special-purpose circuit that routes messages along specific paths in a telecommunications system.

   Dedicated lines, also called **leased lines**, provide a constant connection between two devices and require no switching or dialing. These lines are continuously available for transmission, and the lessee typically pays a flat rate for total access to the line. The lines can be leased or purchased from common carriers or private communications media vendors. These lines typically operate at higher speed than switched lines and are used for high-volume transactions.

   A dedicated line may handle digital data only, or it may be capable of handling both voice and digital data just as a standard telephone line does. When dedicated lines have been designed specifically for data transmission, they produce less static and fewer transmission errors than regular telephone lines, and they are more secure from wiretapping and other security risks. Most importantly, the central processor is always accessible through the dedicated line.

Wide-Area Telecommunications Service (WATS).   **WATS** is a method for billing customers who use voiceband media extensively. WATS uses the toll-free 800 and 888 numbers. The company you call using its WATS number pays a fee to the telephone company, depending on the level of service and usage. The fee varies, depending on the caller's geographic location within the United States and the number of incoming and outgoing calls. Companies typically use WATS services for customer service.

Telephone and dialing services.   Common carriers provide many other telephone and dialing services to homes and businesses. Many telephone systems now have **automatic number identification (ANI)**, also known as *caller ID*. ANI will identify and display the number of an incoming call, enabling people to screen unwanted calls. In a business, ANI not only can identify the caller, but also can link the caller with necessary computer-based information. For example, UPS service representatives use ANI to automatically identify the name and address of the caller, which saves time with requests for pickups.

   Other services offered by common carriers include the ability to have only one number for a business telephone, home telephone, personal computer, fax, and so on (simplifying contact for small businesses); intelligent dialing, which, if a busy signal is reached, redials the number when your line and the line of the party you are trying to reach are both free; and call priorities, which allow only certain calls to be received during certain times of the day.

Integrated Services Digital Network (ISDN).   ISDN is a high-speed data-transmission technology that allows users to transfer voice, video, image, and data simultaneously at high speed. ISDN uses existing telephone lines and provides two levels of service: basic rate ISDN and primary rate ISDN. *Basic rate ISDN* serves a single device with three channels. Two channels are B (bearer) channels with a capacity to transmit 64 Kbps of digital data. The third or D channel is a 16 Kbps channel for signaling and control information. *Primary rate ISDN* provides 1.5 Mbps of bandwidth. The bandwidth contains 23 B channels and one D channel. A second generation of ISDN is *broadband ISDN (BISDN)*, which provides transmission channels capable of supporting transmission rates greater than the primary ISDN rate. ISDN transmission is a popular upgrade with firms whose transmission requirements exceed standard telephone capacity.

Digital Subscriber Line (DSL).   Digital subscriber lines provide high-speed, digital data transmission from homes and businesses over existing telephone lines. The existing lines are analog and the transmission is digital, so modems are necessary with DSL technology. Used under similar circumstances, DSL is a popular alternative to ISDN.

As we have seen (and will see in the remainder of this chapter), there are a variety of communications alternatives available. It is difficult, however, for some customers to obtain access to broadband services. IT's About Business Box 6.2 shows one community's solution to this problem.

IT's About Business

Box 6.2:   Bringing broadband to town

Broadband can make a difference in the way the Internet enriches people's lives at work and at home. But the experience of Evanston, Illinois, shows that the transition to fast Internet connections does not happen easily or quickly. In the late 1990s, fast Internet access was not available in much of Evanston—with the exception of Northwestern University. Educators at Northwestern and local officials created a nonprofit group, e-Tropolis, to raise funds to extend Northwestern's network throughout the city, create a community Web portal (*shopevanston.com*), and market DSL service.

E-Tropolis first formed partnerships with Phoenix Networks and NorthPoint Communications to offer DSL. But Phoenix and NorthPoint ran into financial trouble during the meltdown of the telecommunications industry. As a result, Evanston switched to AT&T and Ameritech, and the market in the town became a duopoly. With less competition, the two giants raised their prices. Sprint also entered the Evanston market with fixed wireless. Although customers have to pay more, city officials have partnered with the main library and schools to allow the public to use their Internet facilities.

In the west and southeast areas of Evanston, where many of the city's low-income families live, broadband penetration is lowest. E-Tropolis has dedicated half of its resources to increasing access to broadband in poor neighborhoods. Alliances have been formed with churches and businesses to hold classes, donate PCs, and help fund an Internet community center.

Source: "Broadband and Main," *BusinessWeek* (October 8, 2001), pp. 86–91.

Questions

1. How is Evanston addressing the *digital divide*—the gap between those who have access to information technology, particularly the Internet, and those who do not?

2. What are the broadband services being offered in Evanston? Are there others that could be offered?

3. What advantages does broadband bring to Evanston's businesses?

Before you go on . . .

1. Why is the distinction between digital and analog transmission so important in telecommunications?

2. What are the common media for telecommunications? What are their respective advantages and disadvantages?

3. What are some of the common options in telecommunications service?

6.2   NETWORKS

A **computer network** consists of communications media, devices, and software needed to connect two or more computer systems and/or devices. Computer networks are essential to modern organizations for many reasons. First, networked computer systems enable organizations to be more flexible and adaptable to meet rapidly changing business conditions. Second, networks enable companies to share hardware, computer applications, and databases across the organization. Third, networks make it possible for geographically dispersed employees and workgroups to share documents, ideas, opinions, and creative insights, encouraging teamwork, innovation, and more efficient and effective interactions. Finally, the network is increasingly the link between businesses and between businesses and their customers.

Because people need to communicate over long as well as short distances, the geographic size of data communications networks is important. There are two general network sizes: local area networks and wide area networks. A "metropolitan" area network falls between the two in size.

Local Area Networks

A **local area network (LAN)** connects two or more communicating devices within 2,000 feet (usually within the same building), so that every user device on the network has the potential to communicate with every other device. A LAN allows a large number of users to share corporate resources (such as storage devices, printers, programs, and data files) and integrates a wide range of functions into a single system. In an office, a LAN can give users fast and efficient access to a common bank of information while also allowing the office to pool resources such as printers and facsimile machines. A well-constructed LAN can also eliminate the need to circulate paper documents by distributing electronic memos and other material to each worker's terminal.

LANs come in an assortment of topologies. The **topology** of a network is the physical layout and connectivity of a network. Specific protocols, or rules of communications, are often used on specific topologies, but the two concepts are different. *Topology* refers to the ways the channels connect the nodes, whereas *protocol* refers to the rules by which data communications take place over these channels. There are five basic network topologies: star, bus, ring, hierarchical, and hybrid. Figure 6.4 illustrates these different types.

Each topology has strengths and weaknesses. When systems developers choose a topology, they should consider such performance issues as delay, speed, reliability, and the network's ability to continue through, or recover after, failure in any device or connection to the network. The company should also consider such physical constraints as the maximum transmission speed of the circuit, the distances between nodes, the circuit's susceptibility to errors, and the overall system costs.

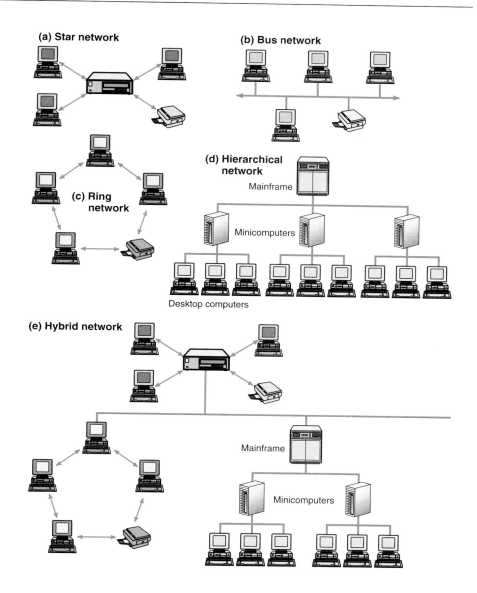

Figure 6.4 *The five main network topologies.*

LAN technology. The LAN file server is a repository of various software and data files for the network. The server determines who gets access to what and in what sequence. Servers may be powerful microcomputers with large, fast-access hard drives, or they may be workstations, minicomputers, or mainframes. The server typically houses the LAN's network operating system, which manages the server and routes and manages communications on the network.

The network *gateway* connects the LAN to public networks or other corporate networks so that the LAN can exchange information with networks external to it. A **gateway** is a communications processor that can connect dissimilar networks by translating from one set of protocols to another. A **bridge** connects two networks of the same type. A **router** routes messages through several connected LANs or to a wide area network.

A LAN consists of cabling or wireless technology linking individual devices, network interface cards (special adapters serving as interfaces to the cable), and software to control LAN activities. The LAN network interface card specifies the data transmission rate, the size of message units, the addressing information attached to each message, and network topology.

LANs employ a baseband or a broadband channel technology. In *baseband* LANs, the entire capacity of the cable is used to transmit a single digitally coded signal. In *broadband* LANs, the capacity of the cable is divided into separate frequencies to permit it to carry several signals at the same time.

Wireless local area networks (WLANs).   WLAN technologies provide LAN connectivity over short distances, typically limited to less than 150 meters, and usually within one building.

Bluetooth technology.   Bluetooth is a wireless technology that allows digital devices such as computers, printers, keyboards, cell phones, and Palm Pilots to communicate with each other via low-power radio frequencies. Bluetooth can also form a home network by linking devices like lights, televisions, the furnace and air conditioning, and the garage door. Bluetooth is not line-of-sight, which means that transmissions may occur around corners, through walls, and through briefcases. Problems with Bluetooth include security, transmission speed (Bluetooth maximum transmission speed is 720 Kbps), and cost. IT's About Business Box 6.3 provides an example of a Bluetooth application.

Private branch exchanges.   A private branch exchange (PBX) is a type of LAN. The PBX is a special-purpose computer that controls telephone switching at a company site. PBXs can carry both voice and data and perform a wide variety of functions to make communications more convenient and effective, such as call waiting, call forwarding, and voice mail. PBXs also offer functions directed at decreasing costs, such as reducing the number of outside lines, providing internal extensions, and determining least-cost routings. Automatic assignment of calls to lines reduces the required number of outside lines. Providing internal extension numbers permits people to make calls within the same site using only extension numbers and without making a chargeable outside call.

IT's About Business

Box 6.3:   Bluetooth in action

Researchers at a community college are using Bluetooth technology to monitor heart rates. The college often uses athletes in physiology research. Previously, physiologists had to attach long cords to sensors on athletes' bodies to monitor vital signs, which limited the subjects to stationary activities. The new Bluetooth system works like this: Researchers attach sensors and Bluetooth radio transmitters to the athletes' bodies. As the athletes cycle or run around a track, the transmitters send data from the sensors over radio frequencies to wireless relay devices, which are stationed at 10-meter intervals along the track. The devices forward the data over a high-speed wireless network to a server in the college's lab.

The researchers quickly have a large amount of data to analyze, and the athletes have records of their performances. The lab burns each subject's data, photo, and list of achievements onto a CD-ROM, which the athlete can take to other training facilities and hospitals. Other uses for Bluetooth include monitoring patients in hospitals, keeping track of firefighters inside burning buildings, and setting up wireless local area networks.

Sources: "Bluetooth Lets Gadgets Speak in One Language," *U.S. News & World Report* (May 15, 2000); *abcnews.com* (February 21, 2001).

Questions

1. What are other applications for Bluetooth?

2. What advantages does Bluetooth offer businesses? (*Hint:* Consider the advantages of wireless LANs.)

Wide Area Networks

Although most businesses have to transmit data throughout a LAN, most also have to send and receive data beyond the confines of the local area network. This is accomplished by connecting to one or more wide area networks. **Wide area networks (WANs)** are long-haul, broadband (analog) networks covering wide geographic areas. They generally are provided by common carriers. WANs include regional networks such as telephone companies or international networks such as global communications services providers. They usually have very-large-capacity circuits, with many communications processors that make it possible to use these circuits efficiently. WANs may combine switched and dedicated lines, microwave, and satellite communications.

Some WANs are commercial, regulated networks, while others are privately owned, usually by large businesses that can afford the costs. Some WANs, however, are "public" in terms of their management, resources, and access. One such public WAN is the Internet, the foundation of the worldwide information superhighway.

WANs can use any of the five basic types of network topologies, but they most generally use the star topology in order to more tightly control the network. A common WAN spanning the continental United States may have a dozen or more "hubs" that form a very complex star or group of stars.

Value-added networks.   **Value-added networks (VANs)** are types of WANs. They are private, data-only networks that are managed by outside third parties and used by multiple organizations to provide economies in the cost of service and in network management. VANs can add message storage, tracking, and relay services as well as teleconferencing services, thus enabling their users to more closely tailor communications capabilities to specific business needs.

VANs offer value through the telecommunications and computing services these networks provide to subscribers. Customers do not have to invest in network hardware and software or perform their own error checking, editing, routing, and protocol conversion. Subscribers realize savings in line charges and transmission costs because the costs of using the network are shared by many users.

Virtual private networks.   A **virtual private network (VPN)** is a WAN operated by a common carrier. VPNs allow an organization to leverage the robust, shared communications infrastructure of the Internet to hook up with remote users, branch offices, and business partners worldwide, without paying the distance-sensitive fees that carriers charge for conventional network links.

VPNs provide a gateway between a corporate LAN and the Internet, and they allow access to a corporate network's e-mail, shared files, or intranet, via an Internet connection. A VPN server handles the security, such as authentication, permitting access from the Internet to an intranet. The data travels over the Internet in encrypted form. VPNs are particularly effective for extranets, because they allow the use of the Internet among business partners instead of using a more expensive VAN. VPNs are also especially important for international business, where long-distance calls or VANs remain very expensive.

EXAMPLE

MasterCard's virtual private network.   MasterCard is using a VPN to upgrade its payment network. MasterCard's VPN, operated mainly by AT&T, connects 660 worldwide transaction-processing nodes. Those sites, at major banks and third-party processors that aggregate transactions from smaller banks, house MasterCard's processing systems and routers. The VPN enables those sites to communicate directly with each other without having to go through MasterCard's St. Louis headquarters.

With the VPN, member banks will have more freedom to implement their own projects, such as incentive programs or joint credit offerings with other banks. Also, resolution of disputed charges will be accelerated, addressing a costly, time-consuming process. ●

> ### *Before you go on . . .*
>
> 1. What are the main business reasons for using LANs?
> 2. What is the difference between LANs and WANs?
> 3. What are some common WAN options?

6.3 NETWORK COMMUNICATIONS SOFTWARE

Communications software provides many functions in a network. These functions include error checking, message formatting, communications logs (listings of all jobs and communications in a specified period of time), data security and privacy, and translation capabilities. These functions are performed by various parts of network communications software, which includes network operating systems, network management software, and protocols.

Network Operating Systems

A **network operating system (NOS)** is systems software that controls the hardware devices, software, and communications media and channels across a network. The NOS enables various devices to communicate with each other. NetWare by Novell and Windows NT from Microsoft are popular network operating systems for LANs.

Network Management Software

Network management software has many functions in operating a network. These functions reduce time spent on routine tasks, such as remote, electronic installation of new software on many devices across a network. They also provide faster response to network problems, greater control over the network, and remote diagnosing of problems in devices connected to the network. In short, network management software performs functions that decrease the human resources needed to manage the network.

Protocols

Computing devices that are connected to the network (often referred to as "nodes" of the network) access and share the network to transmit and receive data. These components work together by adhering to a common set of rules that enable them to communicate with each other. This set of rules and procedures governing transmission across a network is a **protocol**.

The principal functions of protocols in a network are *line access* and *collision avoidance*. Line access concerns how the sending device gains access to the network to send a message. Collision avoidance refers to managing message transmission so that two messages do not collide with each other on the network. Other functions of protocols are to identify each device in the communication path, to secure the attention of the other device, to verify correct receipt of the transmitted message, to verify that a message requires retransmission because it cannot be correctly interpreted, and to perform recovery when errors occur.

Ethernet.   The most common protocol is **Ethernet** 10BaseT. Over three-fourths of all networks use the Ethernet protocol. The 10BaseT means that the network has a speed of 10 Mbps. Fast Ethernet is 100BaseT, meaning that the network has a speed of 100 Mbps. The most common protocol in large corporations is the **Gigabit Ethernet.** That is, the network provides data transmission speeds of one billion bits per second (666 times faster than a T1 line). However, 10-gigabit Ethernet is becoming the standard (10 billion bits per second).

TCP/IP.   The **Transmission Control Protocol/Internet Protocol (TCP/IP)** is a file transfer protocol that can send large files of information across sometimes-unreliable networks with assurance that the data will arrive in uncorrupted form. TCP/IP allows efficient and reasonably error-free transmission between different systems and is the protocol of the Internet. As we will see in Chapter 7, TCP/IP is becoming very popular with business organizations due to its reliability and the ease with which it can support intranets and related functions.

Communication between protocols.   Network devices from different vendors must communicate with each other by following the same protocols. Unfortunately, commercially available data communication devices follow a number of different protocols, causing substantial problems with data communications networks.

Attempts at standardizing data communications have been somewhat successful, but standardization in the United States has lagged behind that in other countries where the communications industry is more closely regulated. Various organizations, including the Electronic Industries Association (EIA), the Consultative Committee for International Telegraph and Telephone (CCITT), and the International Standards Organization (ISO) have developed electronic interfacing protocols that are widely used within the industry.

Typically, the protocols required to achieve communication on behalf of an application are actually multiple protocols existing at different levels or layers. Each layer defines a set of functions that are provided as services to upper layers, and each layer relies on services provided by lower layers. At each layer, one or more protocols define precisely how software on different systems interacts to accomplish the functions for that layer. This layering notion has been formalized in several architectures. The most widely known is the reference model of the **International Standards Organization Open Systems Interconnection (ISO-OSI)**, which has seven layers. See the book's Web site for Table W6.1 that details the seven layers of the OSI model protocol.

www.wiley.com/
college/turban

Types of Data Transmission

For advanced computing applications, much greater bandwidth may be needed on networks. Various types of data transmission technologies address this need. These technologies include packet-switching, frame relay, fiber distributed data interface, asynchronous transfer mode, switching hubs, synchronous optical network, and the T-carrier system.

Packet-switching is used in value-added networks. **Packet switching** breaks up blocks of text into small, fixed bundles of data called *packets*. The VAN continuously uses various communications channels to send the packets. Each packet travels independently through the network. Packets of data originating at one source can be routed through different paths in the network, and then may be reassembled into the original message when they reach their destination.

Packet-switching is causing a telecommunications revolution. Telecommunications providers are transforming their infrastructure from the existing, public, circuit-switched networks designed to carry analog voice traffic to packet-switched networks designed and optimized for data that carry voice as just another data type. The main reason for this revolution is the growth of the Internet, which is a packet-switching network (discussed in Chapter 7).

Frame relay is a faster and less expensive version of packet switching. **Frame relay** is a shared network service that packages data into *frames* that are similar to packets. Frame relay, however, does not perform error correction, because modern digital lines are less error-prone than older lines, and networks are more effective at error checking. Frame relay can communicate at transmission speeds of 1.544 Mbps, although the technology can reach speeds of 45 Mbps.

Like a ring network (see Figure 6.4), **fiber distributed data interface (FDDI)** passes data around a ring, but with a bandwidth of 100 Mbps—much faster than a standard 10–13 Mbps token ring (or bus) network. Although the FDDI standard can use any transmission medium, it is based on the high-speed, high-capacity capabilities of fiber optics. FDDI can significantly boost network performance, but this technology is about 10 times more expensive to implement than most LAN networks.

Asynchronous transfer mode (ATM) networks allow for almost unlimited bandwidth on demand. These networks are packet-switched, dividing data into uniform cells, each with 53 groups of 8 bytes, eliminating the need for protocol conversion. ATM creates a virtual connection for the packet transmission, which disappears on the completion of a successful transmission. ATM offers several advantages: It makes possible large increases in bandwidth. It provides support for data, video, and voice transmissions on one communications line. It offers virtual networking capabilities, which increase bandwidth utilization and simplify network administration. ATM currently requires fiber-optic cable, but it can transmit up to 2.5 gigabits per second. On the downside, ATM is more expensive than ISDN and DSL.

Switched hub technologies are often used to boost local area networks. A switched hub can turn many small LANs into one big LAN. A network need not be rewired nor adapter cards replaced when changes are made; all that is needed is the addition of a switching hub. Switched hub technology can also add an ATM-like packet-switching capability to existing LANs, essentially doubling bandwidth.

Synchronous optical network (SONET) is an interface standard for transporting digital signals over fiber-optic links that allows the integration of transmissions from multiple vendors. SONET defines optical line rates, known as optical carrier (OC) signals. The base rate is 51.84 Mbps (OC-1), and higher rates are direct multiples of the base rate. For example, OC-3 runs at 155.52 Mbps, or three times the rate of OC-1.

The **T-carrier system** is a digital transmission system that defines circuits that operate at different rates, all of which are multiples of the basic 64 Kbps used to transport a single voice call. These circuits include T1 (1.544 Mbps, equivalent to 24 channels); T2 (6.312 Mbps, equivalent to 96 channels); T3 (44.736 Mbps, equivalent to 672 channels); and T4 (274.176 Mbps, equivalent to 4,032 channels).

Before you go on . . .

1. What is the role of telecommunications protocols?

2. What are popular data transmission options? What are their respective advantages?

6.4   NETWORK PROCESSING STRATEGIES

One of the most important issues that organizations face is sustaining network performance in light of the explosion of network-based applications and data transmission volume. The growth of client/server architectures, intranets, and the Internet has increased the attention paid to overall enterprise network performance.

Network response time and availability are widely viewed as key issues for IS managers. The performance of network operating systems and network management software has improved so that users often cannot tell the difference between accessing a computer across the room and one across the world. Thus, we say that networks are becoming *transparent* to users. Achieving this level of performance usually involves *distributed processing*. By using networks, the organization's processing demands can be distributed appropriately to different machines in different locations. This, in turn, enables faster and more efficient processing.

Types of Organizational Distributed Processing

Organizations typically use multiple computer systems across the firm. **Distributed processing** enables computers in different locations to communicate with each other via telecommunications links. There are three alternative types of distributed processing: terminal-to-host, file server, and client/server.

Terminal-to-host processing.   With terminal-to-host processing, the applications and databases reside on the host computer. The users interact with the applications with "dumb" terminals (i.e., the device has no processing capability of its own).

File server processing.   With file server processing, the applications and databases reside on the host computer, called the *file server*. The database management system runs on the user's PC. When the user needs data from the file server, the file server sends to the user the entire file with the data requested. The downloaded data can be analyzed and manipulated on the user's PC. (Data going from the file server to the user's PC are referred to as *downloaded*, and data going from the user's personal computer to the file server are *uploaded*).

Client/server architecture and processing.   As you know from earlier chapters, **client/server architecture** links two or more computers in an arrangement in which some machines (servers) perform computing functions for end-user PCs (clients). Sometimes either machine can perform processing and store applications. Usually, however, an organization has the bulk of its processing or application/data storage done on suitably powerful servers that can be accessed by less powerful client machines. The client requests applications, data, or processing from the server, which acts on these requests by "serving" the desired commodity. With client/server architecture, organizations can make their systems faster and save money, primarily by gaining the efficiency that comes from having the appropriate machine handle the appropriate measure of processing and storage.

In a client/server approach, the components of an application can be distributed over the enterprise rather than being centrally controlled. Three application components can be distributed: the presentation component, the applications (or processing) logic, and the data management component. The *presentation component* is the application interface or how the application appears to the user. The *applications logic* is the bulk of the software program, created to perform some business function. The *data management component* consists of the storage and management of the data needed by the application. The exact division of processing tasks depends on the requirements of each application, including its processing needs, the number of users, and the available resources, and may be distributed at various sites in a telecommunications network.

There are five models of client/server implementation that partition the three components between the server and the client, as shown in Figure 6.5. As you can see from the figure, the network comes in at different points in each of the five models:

- **Distributed presentation.** All three components are on the server, but the presentation logic is also found on the client.
- **Remote presentation.** Applications logic and database management are on the server, and the presentation logic is located on the client.
- **Distributed function.** Data management is on the server and presentation logic is on the client, with application logic distributed between the two.
- **Remote data management.** Database management is located on the server, with the other two components on the client.
- **Distributed data management.** All three components are on the client, with database management distributed between the client and the server.

These models lead to the ideas of "fat" clients and "thin" clients. *Fat clients* have large storage and processing power and can handle the three components of an application. *Thin clients* may have no local storage and limited processing power. This means that thin clients can handle only presentation. Network computers are popular thin clients.

The client is the user point-of-entry for the required function, and the user generally interacts directly with only the client portion of the application, typically through a graphical user interface. Clients call on the server for services rendered by the application software. When a client needs information based on files in the server, the client sends a message (or remote procedure call) requesting the information from the server.

The server has the data files and the application software. The server stores and processes shared data and performs "back-end" functions not visible to users, such as managing peripheral devices and controlling access to shared databases. When a client makes a remote procedure call, the server processes file data and provides the information, not the entire file(s), to the client. Manager's Checklist 6.2 shows the benefits and limitations of using client/server architecture in network processing.

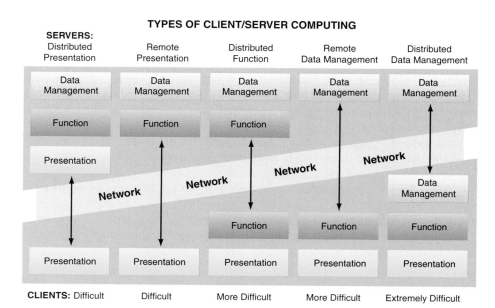

Figure 6.5 *Client/server configuration.* [*Source:* Datamation, *February 21, 1994, p. 30.*]

TYPES OF CLIENT/SERVER COMPUTING

SERVERS: Distributed Presentation	Remote Presentation	Distributed Function	Remote Data Management	Distributed Data Management
Data Management	Data Management	Data Management	Data Management	Data Management
Function	Function	Function		
Presentation				
				Data Management
		Function	Function	Function
Presentation	Presentation	Presentation	Presentation	Presentation
CLIENTS: Difficult	Difficult	More Difficult	More Difficult	Extremely Difficult

Benefits	Limitations	Manager's Checklist 6.2
• The network is not overloaded with entire files being transferred back and forth • File integrity is much easier to maintain because only the server actually updates the files. • File security is easier to maintain with server in full control of file data.	• Microcomputers with independent processing power are more difficult to coordinate and administer on a network. • There is difficulty in writing software that divides processing among clients and servers. • Specific servers can be slowed when too many clients need service.	Benefits and Limitations of Client/Server Architecture for Network Processing

Peer-to-peer processing.   As discussed in the chapter opening case, **peer-to-peer processing** is a type of client/server, distributed processing that allows two or more computers to pool their resources. Individual resources such as disk drives, CD-ROM drives, and printers become shared resources that are accessible from every computer. Unlike standard client/server networks, where network information is stored on a centralized file server and made available to many clients, the information stored across peer-to-peer networks is uniquely decentralized. Because peer-to-peer computers have their own disk drives that are accessible by all computers, each computer acts as both a client and a server. Each computer has transparent access (as assigned for security or integrity purposes) to all files on all other computers.

Popular peer-to-peer network operating systems include Microsoft's Windows 2000 and Windows XP, Novell Netware, and AppleShare. Most of these operating systems allow each computer to determine which resources will be available for use by other users. When one user's disk has been configured so that it is *sharable*, it will usually appear as a new drive to the other users.

The benefits of peer-to-peer architecture include the following:

- There is no need for a network administrator.

- The network is fast and inexpensive to set up and maintain.

- Each computer can provide backup copies of its files to other computers for security.

- It is the easiest network to build.

There are three basic types of peer-to-peer processing. The first accesses unused CPU power among networked computers, as in applications such as Napster (*napster.com*), Gnutella (*gnutella.wego.com*), and *SETI@home* (see the opening case). These applications are from open-source projects and can be downloaded at no cost.

The second form of peer-to-peer is real-time, person-to-person collaboration, such as America Online's Instant Messenger. Companies such as Groove Networks (*groove.net*) have introduced P2P collaborative applications that use buddy lists to establish a connection, then allow real-time collaboration within the application.

The third peer-to-peer category is advanced search and file sharing. This category is characterized by natural-language searches of millions of peer systems and lets users discover other users, not just data and Web pages. One example of this is Aimster (*aimster.com*), which allows searching of the major Internet file-sharing services, such as AOL and Gnutella. The search is accomplished through Aimster's integration with instant messaging tools. The following example discusses Napster and the copyright infringement issue.

EXAMPLE

Napster and its successors.   Napster, the most popular file-sharing program, was sued successfully by the music industry for copyright infringement. Whether online or offline, it is illegal to copy and distribute someone else's work in a way that deprives them of income. That means anyone getting or distributing music over the Internet is breaking the law. What made the case tricky, however, was that Napster was not buying and selling music illegally. It was simply a go-between. Though Napster did not own or distribute the music itself, it did operate the servers that enable users to search for music. Music companies sued to have those servers shut down.

In March 2001, Napster was forced to halt the exchange of copyrighted music on its Internet service. Napster remains in business and plans to launch a new membership service in early 2002 that allows the sharing of audio files while paying royalties to artists.

As Napster had 64 million users, successors emerged rapidly. These successors may not suffer Napster's fate. Napster had central servers that could be shut down, but its successors provide software for people who want to swap files, making them nearly impossible to police. For example, Aimster's audio file-sharing service allows people to evade filters by translating names of Napster files into Pig Latin. Gnutella provides software that lets its members query each other's computers directly. Gnutella has no central server and is not owned by anyone. After downloading Gnutella software, users make available whatever files they are willing to share. ●

Open Systems and Enterprise Networking

Open systems are those that allow any computing device to be seamlessly connected to and interact with any other computing device, regardless of size, operating system, or application. This has been a goal for information systems designers for many years, and it is just now becoming a (limited) reality. Open systems can provide flexibility in implementing IT solutions, optimization of computing effectiveness, and the ability to provide new levels of integrated functionality to meet user demands. Open systems require connectivity across the various components of the system.

Connectivity is the ability of the various computer resources to communicate with each other through network devices without human intervention. Connectivity allows

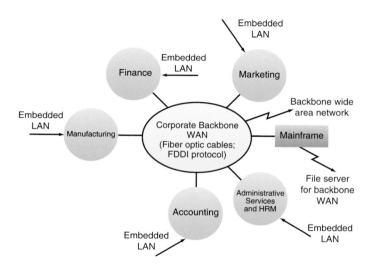

Figure 6.6 *Enterprisewide computing.*

for application portability, interoperability, and scalability. *Portability* is the ability to move applications, data, and even people from one system to another with minimal adjustments. *Interoperability* refers to the ability of systems to work together by sharing applications, data, and computer resources. *Scalability* refers to the ability to run applications unchanged on any open system, where the hardware can range from a laptop PC to a supercomputer. This saves firms money, as they can avoid having to purchase multiple copies of software.

Open systems and connectivity have enabled networks to completely span organizations. Most firms have multiple LANs and may have multiple WANs, which are interconnected to form an **enterprisewide network**. Figure 6.6 shows a model of **enterprisewide computing**. Note that the enterprisewide network in the figure has a backbone network composed of fiber-optic cable using the FDDI protocol. The LANs are called embedded LANs because they connect to the backbone WAN. These LANs are usually composed of twisted-pair wire.

Before you go on . . .

1. What are the common advantages of client/server architecture for network processing?

2. What are the goals and benefits of "open" systems?

6.5   TELECOMMUNICATIONS APPLICATIONS

The workplace of today differs drastically from the workplace of just five years ago. Within that brief span of time various telecommunications applications have been put in wide use at companies large and small. Such applications have brought new efficiencies to the workplace, and they have the potential to help businesses achieve competitive advantages.

Electronic Mail

Computer-based messages can be electronically manipulated, stored, combined with other information, and transmitted through telephone wires or wireless networks. With **electronic mail (e-mail)**, the sender inputs the message at a terminal and includes address and routing instructions to get the message to the intended recipient(s). Any other electronic objects, such as text, graphic, sound, motion, or application files, may be attached to the message. The system then automatically routes the message to the recipient(s). At the receiving end, a recipient can read the message on a computer terminal, print it, file it, edit it, and/or forward it to other recipient(s).

E-mail began as simple asynchronous communication over mainframe systems, exemplified by IBM's Professional Office System (PROFS). LAN-based systems, such as Lotus cc:Mail and Microsoft Mail, run on personal computers. Over the years e-mail has become more sophisticated by incorporating scheduling and workflow capabilities, calendaring, and threaded discussions. The market leaders in messaging software are Lotus Notes Domino and Microsoft Exchange.

Electronic mail eliminates time delays and other problems associated with physically delivered mail. E-mail users need not be concerned with the equivalent of "telephone tag" when the recipient is not physically present at the moment a message is sent. Also, recipients can read their mail when it is convenient to do so.

However, e-mail can cause problems. For example, congressional offices are coping with a flood of e-mail from Americans, a problem that threatens to worsen. Before 1995, few congressional offices had e-mail accounts, but now House offices get as many as 8,000 e-mails per month and Senate offices receive 55,000 monthly. E-mail is the biggest problem for legislators, because many congressional offices do not have the staff to handle the load. In one instance, Senator Patrick Leahy's office responded to about 50,000 people who e-mailed during the week of hearings on Napster's free Internet song-swapping service.

The benefits of e-mail far exceed its drawbacks. Today, electronic mail is assuming a larger role in many firms' information technology infrastructures. E-mail is being tied into the systems that run the business—databases, data warehouses, enterprise resource planning, manufacturing, Internet commerce, and customer support.

BlackBerry (*blackberry.net*), developed by Research in Motion (*rim.net*), is an e-mail/organizer with two-way wireless communications capabilities. BlackBerry is an extension of the user's e-mail account on the PC, which the BlackBerry software monitors. A user replies to e-mail using a small keyboard, and the reply is encrypted and routed to the BlackBerry software on the desktop PC or the server. On election night in November 2000, when Al Gore famously decided to return to his campaign headquarters rather than deliver a concession speech, what changed his mind was the message sent to him by a top advisor—via his BlackBerry—stating that Florida was suddenly too close to call.

Videoconferencing

Videoconferencing allows two or more people to have face-to-face communications with a group in another location(s) without having to be present in person. Although

Participating in a desktop videoconference.

limited by the inherent limitations of audio and video, these visual conferences save the time and expenses involved in travel. The ability to use teleconferencing technology can be key to achieving business goals.

Videoconferencing is much more expensive than audio conferencing (also called teleconferencing or conference calls), due to more expensive equipment requirements and the need for greater bandwidth. However, communications research has shown that much of the information conveyed between individuals in person is communicated by nonverbal means. Therefore, videoconferencing provides a richer means of communicating than text or audio alone.

Electronic Data Interchange

Electronic data interchange (EDI) is the electronic transmission of routine, repetitive business documents (e.g., purchase orders, invoices, approvals of credit, shipping notices, and confirmations) directly between the computer systems of separate companies doing business with each other. EDI offers both direct and indirect benefits, as shown on the Web site.

www.wiley.com/
college/turban

In the past, EDI ran on expensive value-added networks (VANs). These private, third-party-managed networks provided security and high capacity, but their use was confined to large trading partners due to their high cost. This situation is rapidly changing with the emergence of **Internet-based EDI**. For example, Duane Reade Inc., a pharmacy chain in New York, has a radio-frequency handheld application for in-store inventory management that works with its computer-assisted ordering system. These two applications link with the firm's Internet-based electronic data interchange (EDI) system that handles both Internet-based EDI with suppliers, as well as any proprietary systems that its suppliers may have in place.

Electronic Funds Transfer

Electronic funds transfer (EFT) is now widely used, electronically routing funds, debits and credits, and charges and payments among banks and between banks and customers. EFT is fast; it eliminates delays associated with sending hardcopy documents. EFT has become the only practical way to handle the large volume of financial transactions generated daily by the banking industry.

Facsimiles

Facsimile (Fax) equipment may use either analog or digital encoding. Analog encoding converts the white and black areas of a page into encoded sine waves. These modulated signals are then converted back into white and black areas for printing by the receiving facsimile machine. Digital encoding converts a page's white and black areas into binary 1s and 0s. The primary advantage of using digital encoding is that digital streams of 1s and 0s are very easy to compress, particularly with textual documents that contain large amounts of white (blank) areas. Compressing fax documents at the ratio of 20:1 is common with digitally encoded fax machines; the result is that one page can be transmitted within 5 to 10 seconds instead of the 2 to 6 minutes that it takes with analog encoding.

Telecommuting

Increasing numbers of employees are **telecommuting**—working at home, using personal computers and telecommunications technology to communicate via electronic mail with other workers and to send and receive business work. Telecommuting is popular for many reasons. It eliminates the time spent in physically commuting every day. Single parents are better able to balance family and work responsibilities. Otherwise-qualified employees who are unable to participate in the normal workforce (e.g., physically challenged persons and those who live too far from the city office to commute on a daily basis) are able to be productive workers for their companies. For organizations, telecommuting can lead to decreased needs for office space, thereby saving money. In addition, city and county governments are encouraging telecommuting as a means to reduce traffic congestion and air pollution. For more on telecommuting, see Chapter 15.

Distance Learning

Telecommunications technology is enabling many people to learn outside the classroom, a process called **distance learning**. Distance learning can be point-to-point, where students gather at a specific location and the class is transmitted to them in real time (different place, same time). The students are able to

Distance learning using videoconferencing.

IT's About Business

Box 6.4:   On-Board intelligence for your car

A picknicker realizes that he has locked his keys in his car, which is equipped with OnStar. He uses his cell phone and calls an operator, who remotely commands the vehicle to open. OnStar enables drivers not only to have their cars unlocked using wireless two-way communications but also to get roadside assistance, directions, or locations by pressing a dashboard button and making a request. OnStar also offers stolen-vehicle tracking, vehicle diagnostics, the ability to download e-mail, stock quotes, and voice-activated concierge services from the Internet, as well as real-time traffic report and navigation applications. Another service is that when a car's air bags deploy, an onboard device notifies the OnStar call center, where an operator attempts to contact the driver and passengers and calls for an ambulance. OnStar is also developing entertainment options like backseat pay-per-view movies and personal music collections beamed to the car stereo, although these features will depend on wireless broadband coming online.

Safety concerns might be a problem for telematics systems such as OnStar. A study in the *New England Journal of Medicine* in 1997 found that talking on a cell phone while driving increased by four times the chances of being involved in an accident. Many believe that the future of telematics will rely heavily on voice recognition. But the technology is not very advanced, and the car is hardly a quiet space.

Sources: gm.com; qualcomm.com; "Cars Will Let Motorists Drive and Surf," Information Week (January 8, 2001); "Wireless Delivery Drives Forward," InfoWorld (November 16, 2001).

Questions

1. Do you think OnStar can so "overload" a driver that it can cause an accident? If so, what can be done?

2. What other industries can use telematics systems?

see and hear the professor, and the professor can hear the students off-site and may be able to see them as well. The off-site locations may be around the same campus or across the world.

Distance learning may also be asynchronous (different place, different time). Many courses are offered over the Internet in prepackaged form. For example, Ziff-Davis University (*zdu.com*) and the University of Phoenix (*onl.uophx.edu*) offer an extensive list of distance learning courses and degree programs to students.

Telematics

A **telematics system** is a suite of services powered by wireless communications, global positioning systems, and onboard electronics. Telematics systems facilitate Internet and wireless cellular services, which provide services for location, navigation, traffic monitoring and control, toll collection, safety, and traveler information. The most common telematics systems are the on-board systems in automobiles. IT's About Business Box 6.4 presents OnStar from General Motors as an example of a telematics system.

Before you go on . . .

1. What competitive advantage can you imagine for EDI in your chosen field or industry?

2. Would telecommuting be a more popular option in some parts of the United States than others? Why?

FOR THE ACCOUNTING MAJOR

Corporate accountants perform cost–benefit analyses on the telecommunications infrastructure of the firm. Although it is difficult to quantify the benefits of corporate networks in hard dollars, accountants must estimate these benefits accurately in order to determine the return on these investments. Further, the accountant's chief concern is keeping track of the company's transactions. Data generated by these transactions are most often collected via electronic means (i.e., source data automation) and transmitted over the firm's networks.

FOR THE FINANCE MAJOR

Financial managers use corporate networks to transfer funds to suppliers, receive funds from customers, and complete transactions related to financing of the organization. In addition, financial managers use electronic funds transfer extensively as they manage the firm's investment portfolio and cash assets.

FOR THE MARKETING MAJOR

Modern telecommunications technologies open huge conduits of information to and from an organization, and provide great strategic advantage to the marketing function. The information can flow out from the company, for example, providing prices and production data to customers. Telecommunications also enable easy ingress of data from customers, allowing them to enter orders directly and communicate with the firm via e-mail. Corporate databases can receive transaction data directly from retailers in a timely fashion, enabling marketing managers to see the effects of marketing strategies within 48 hours or less. Intraorganizational communication also is supported by telecommunications, permitting employees to obtain data from corporate headquarters while traveling or visiting customers.

FOR THE PRODUCTION/OPERATIONS MAJOR

Telecommunications can make the linkage between the customer and the production function much more direct, making possible different manufacturing strategies such as JIT and mass customization. Transmission of transactions to and from suppliers, shippers, and others in the supply chain is enabled through EDI. LANs in the manufacturing center can transmit data sent and collected by CIM systems. This capability further enhances the firm's ability to make rapid modifications to the product or process. It allows the collection of data regarding quality, efficiency, maintenance, and general productivity of the manufacturing function.

FOR THE HUMAN RESOURCES MAJOR

Human resources managers utilize their corporate networks extensively for posting job openings. HR managers also use internal corporate networks to publish corporate policies and company newsletters. The HR department is responsible for corporate training, which may be accomplished via programmed learning, or delivered over corporate networks.

SUMMARY

❶ Describe the components of a telecommunications system.

Telecommunications systems are composed of computers (both client on the desktop and host computers, such as servers and mainframes), communications processors, communications media, and communications software.

❷ Describe the eight basic types of communications media, including their advantages and disadvantages.

The eight basic types of communications media are twisted-pair wire, coaxial cable, fiber-optic cable, microwave, satellite, radio, cellular radio, and infrared transmission. The first three media are cable media and the remaining five are broadcast media. Manager's Checklist 6.1 describes the advantages and disadvantages of each medium.

❸ Classify the major types of networks.

A local area network (LAN) connects two or more communicating devices within 2,000 feet (typically within the same building). Every user device on the network has the potential to communicate with every other device.

Wide area networks (WANs) are long-haul, broadband (analog), generally public-access networks covering wide geographic areas, provided by common carriers.

Value-added and virtual private networks are types of WANs. VANs are private, multipath, data-only, third-party-managed networks that can provide economies in the cost of service and in network management because they are used by multiple organizations. A virtual private network (VPN) is a WAN operated by a common carrier that provides what appear to be dedicated lines when used, but that actually consists of backbone trunks shared among all customers, as in a public network.

❹ Differentiate among the three types of distributed processing.

The three types of distributed processing are terminal-to-host, file server, and client/server. In terminal-to-host processing, the applications and databases reside on the host computer, and the users interact with the applications with dumb terminals. With file server processing, the applications and databases reside on the host computer, called the file server. The database management system runs on the user's PC. When the user needs data from the file server, the file server sends to the user the entire data file, and the downloaded data can be analyzed and manipulated on the user's personal computer. Client/server architecture divides processing between clients and servers. Both are on the network, but each processor is assigned functions it is best suited to perform. In a client/server approach, the components of an application (i.e., presentation, application, and data management) are distributed over the enterprise rather than being centrally controlled.

❺ Identify eight telecommunications applications that can help organizations attain competitive advantage.

The eight telecommunications applications include electronic mail, videoconferencing, electronic data interchange, electronic funds transfer, facsimiles, telecommuting, distance learning, and telematics.

Electronic mail is the transmission of computer-based messages that can be electronically manipulated, stored, combined with other information, and transmitted through telephone wires or wireless networks. Videoconferencing allows two or more people to have face-to-face communications with a group in another location(s) without having to be present in person. Electronic data interchange (EDI) is the electronic transmission of routine, repetitive business documents directly between the computer systems of separate companies doing business with each other. Electronic funds transfer (EFT) is the electronic transmission of funds, debits, credits, charges, and payments among banks and between banks and customers. Facsimile (fax) equipment encodes documents and then transmits them electronically to a receiving fax machine. Telecommuting means that employees work at home, using personal computers and telecommunications technology to communicate electronically with other workers and to send and receive business work. Distance learning is the use of telecommunications technology to connect teachers and students outside the classroom, either all at the same time or at different times. Telematics systems facilitate Internet and wireless cellular services, which provide services for location, navigation, traffic monitoring and control, toll collection, safety, and traveler information.

INTERACTIVE LEARNING SESSION

Go to the CD and access Chapter 6: Telecommunications and Networks and read the case presented. It will describe a business problem that will require you to make a decision on a telecommuting program that is being implemented in your office. You will be given various information concerning three connection choices. You will have to justify your choice as to how it will meet the needs of the organization and the end users.

www.wiley.com/college/turban

For additional resources, go to the book's Web site for Chapter 6. There you will find Web resources for the chapter, including links to organizations, people, and technology; "IT's About Business" company links; "What's in IT for Me?" links; and a self-testing Web quiz for Chapter 6.

DISCUSSION QUESTIONS

1. Is telecommuting always beneficial for an organization? For an employee? When might telecommuting not be beneficial for an organization or an employee? Do you think you would be willing to telecommute during your career? Why or why not?

2. What are the implications of having fiber-optic cable going to everyone's home?

3. Do you personally think caller ID (automatic number identification) is a good idea? Would you think it is a good idea if you were a telemarketer?

4. Would you recommend that all organizations employ client/server architectures? Why or why not? Would you recommend that all organizations employ centralized, mainframe architectures? Why or why not?

PROBLEM SOLVING ACTIVITIES

1. Develop a plan describing how you would build a telecommunications infrastructure in China. Discuss the communications media, devices, and services you would use. (Start with what China has now.)

2. Arguably, the United States has an advanced, well-developed telecommunications infrastructure in place. Develop a plan describing how you would upgrade that telecommunications infrastructure. Remember that the United States is a leading proponent of the information superhighway.

3. Create a database with all the long-distance call plans now being offered in your area. Analyze to see which is the best for personal use and which is best for use in a small business.

INTERNET ACTIVITIES

1. Prepare a report contrasting the regional Bell operating companies as to location, size, number of employees, market capitalization, strategy, and strategic alliances. You will have to access the Web to find the names of the RBOCs and then access their home pages. (Hint: To start, you might access an Internet search engine such as Google (google.com) or AltaVista (altavista.com).

2. Access the Web sites of the companies entering the satellite market and obtain the latest information regarding the status of their satellite constellations. Prepare a report for class detailing the current status of these constellations.

3. On the Web, visit an executive recruiting site for information systems personnel. What proportion of the positions offered is for network management? What are the salary ranges? What is the preferred experience? What types of networks are most commonly mentioned?

TEAM ACTIVITIES AND ROLE PLAYING

1. Your team is in charge of telecommunications and networking at a rapidly expanding manufacturing company. The company is building new manufacturing facilities in Ireland, Singapore, and Mexico to go along with three plants in the United States (South Carolina, Oregon, and Texas). The CEO wants a plan to upgrade the corporate networks. Develop a plan for the upgrade, to include the proposed type and topology of the new network. Be sure to address the networks across the enterprise as well as the networks inside the new plants.

2. With your team, visit your local police department. Prepare a report on the various ways the department uses telecommunications. (*Hint:* There are many different ways that the police use telecommunications other than radio links between headquarters and mobile units.) Be sure to address security concerns. Also, address what the police define "effective" communications to be. Make recommendations about how the department might upgrade their communications systems.

REAL-WORLD CASE

Wireless Delivers for UPS

The Business Problem   United Parcel Service Inc., the $29.8 billion logistics company, was an early adopter of wireless technology to speed its business. Prior to 1989, UPS used paper sheets to route and record all information on each package. In 1989, UPS adopted barcoded shipping labels. All the information from the device was downloaded to back-end systems at the end of each business day.

In 1992, UPS deployed a wireless transmission system within each delivery truck that used radio-frequency technology to send package information back to UPS's central network, eliminating the end-of-day downloads. UPS created its own nationwide wireless data service through an alliance with more than 100 carriers. When wireless data networks became more robust two years later, UPS switched from analog to packet-based wireless transmission. UPS realized the benefits of having wireless devices in drivers' hands and expanded the use of wireless systems in its shipping and processing centers.

Over time, UPS accumulated numerous wireless devices, applications, operating systems, and programming languages. The result was that its IT department had numerous systems that could not interoperate or be upgraded easily.

The IT Solution   UPS consolidated its wireless systems in a wireless infrastructure, called UPScan, that is based largely on Bluetooth and 802.11b, two short-range wireless transmission protocols. The company states that wireless technology is core to the business.

UPScan includes three projects. In the first project, UPScan attached fixed-mount wireless systems to walls or inside vehicles. UPScan uses wireless LANs to connect the devices to UPS's fixed networks. The second project consists of computer hardware tablets that drivers use to enter tracking numbers for each package. The third project, used by employees in UPS's routing and distribution centers, consists of a barcode scanner attached to a user's fingers that communicates via Bluetooth to a device worn on a belt or the employee's arm. Whenever the employee scans a package to gather information on a package's routing instructions, the data are transmitted from the finger scanner to the device. From there, the data are downloaded to a transmitter connected to the warehouse network so it can be sent to either of UPS's data centers for storage and assessment.

The Results   UPScan helped UPS cut equipment and repair costs by 30% and reduce spare equipment by 35%. UPS is now developing its next-generation of driver terminals, which will have a Bluetooth interface. The UPScan program consolidated separate international systems used by UPS outposts around the world that operate on different communication protocols. UPS realized the hard-dollar benefits of adopting a standardized system of emerging wireless technology to process information more rapidly. The company was able to contract out repair of the devices, decrease support costs, and provide a tangible return on investments.

Source: "The Total Package," *ecompany.com* (June 2001), pp. 91–97; "Ground Wars," *BusinessWeek* (May 21, 2001), pp. 64–68.

Questions

1. Why did UPS adopt wireless technologies?

2. What were UPS's three wireless projects and what were the advantages of each?

VIRTUAL COMPANY ASSIGNMENT

wiley.com/college/turban

Extreme Descent Snowboards

www.wiley.com/
college/turban

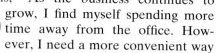

Background   Kellie Onn, Chief Executive Officer of Extreme Descent Snowboards, explains, "As the business continues to grow, I find myself spending more time away from the office. However, I need a more convenient way to keep in touch with people inside and outside the company. Now, I have to find a pay phone to call and get my messages or a virtual café to access the Internet to download my emails. Last week we almost lost a large contract because something needed my approval and my staff could not track me down until I returned to my hotel and found a message waiting for me."

Kellie continues, "I am interested in wireless or satellite connections for communicating with my staff. I have not had the time to investigate the possibility of incorporating this technology."

Assignment

Kellie has talked with Jacob March about this issue, and they would like for you to put together a proposal that will help Kellie stay in contact with the office and with her business associates outside the company. The proposal needs to include voice and e-mail type messages. They ask you to include in the proposal what telecommunication technologies are available utilizing satellite connections, as well as any other telecommunication applications that might be advantageous to the staff at EDS.

7 THE INTERNET, INTRANETS, AND EXTRANETS

CHAPTER PREVIEW

Our previous chapters have provided insight into computing technologies and how they communicate over distances. This chapter focuses on three important subareas of telecommunications—the Internet, its private organizational counterpart, *intranets*, and interorganizational telecommunications systems, *extranets*. All three of these networks support new paradigms of how business is done, from marketing to supply chain management to customer service. The possibilities are endless. These innovations put some firms at a distinct advantage and others at a great disadvantage, and are reshaping some entire industries. This chapter presents an overview of the Internet, intranets, and extranets with discussions of their development and evolution, technical underpinnings, and accompanying societal and organizational challenges. Chapter 9 will concentrate on the strategic potential of these media in the broader context of electronic commerce.

CHAPTER OUTLINE

7.1 What, Exactly, Is the Internet?

7.2 The Evolution of the Internet

7.3 The Operation of the Internet

7.4 Services Provided by the Internet

7.5 The World Wide Web

7.6 Internet Challenges

7.7 Intranets

7.8 Extranets

7.9 Enterprise Information Portals

7.10 The Mobile Internet

LEARNING OBJECTIVES

1. Describe what the Internet is, how it works (including the role of the TCP/IP protocol), and how users connect to it.

2. Describe the capabilities that the Internet offers to users.

3. Describe the World Wide Web and differentiate it from the Internet.

4. Identify and describe the tools that allow users to view and search the Web.

5. Identify and briefly describe the management challenges caused by the Internet.

6. Define the term *intranet* and discuss how intranets are used by businesses.

7. Define the term *extranet* and discuss how extranets are used by businesses.

8. Define the term *enterprise information portal* and discuss how these portals are used by businesses.

9. Define the term *mobile Internet* and discuss mobile Internet applications.

DESIGNING NEW CARS AT DAIMLERCHRYSLER WITH FASTCAR

Every automaker in the world is using the Internet to streamline the automotive development process, which can take four to six years and cost billions of dollars. There are a huge number of variables during development of a new car. The rule of thumb is that any given car has roughly 12,000 moving parts. Chrysler has 50,000 different components that it draws upon internally. Every screw, bolt, and button has detailed specifications. When other variations are introduced (e.g., 16-inch or 17-inch tires; color of paint), there are billions of permutations for Chrysler vehicles. So, Internet-based collaboration is an enormous undertaking for the automobile industry. The Chrysler Group of DaimlerChrysler is facing pressure. The group is losing money and the Germans have arrived from the parent company to supervise a turnaround.

The Internet speeds new car design at DaimlerChrysler.

The IT Solution

Part of Chrysler's answer to the pressure is FastCar, a Web-based system with 200 workstations networked in Chrysler headquarters. FastCar allows the company to link the flow of information from at least six major information systems (finance, engineering, purchasing, and so on) that had not been able to communicate seamlessly.

FastCar allows designers to go through hundreds of variations, and other units at Chrysler can understand what is changing, in real time. FastCar offers everyone what Chrysler calls a "unified data model" that they can see in three dimensions. FastCar, in effect, puts the Chrysler Development System on the Web, showing everyone each step in designing a new product.

The Results

FastCar provides designers the most time possible until they have to lock down their design. After that, only minor changes can be made without fouling up the manufacturing process. FastCar enables Chrysler to be as flexible as possible for as long as possible, in order to be able to respond to the latest trends in the marketplace and changing federal regulations. The goal of FastCar is to move from theme selection to design completion to mass manufacturing within two years, roughly half the industry standard.

FastCar targets not only Chrysler's internal processes, but also will eventually work seamlessly with Covisint, an industry consortium set up with General Motors, Ford Motor, Renault, and Nissan. Using Covisint's standards, FastCar will be able to send e-mail messages to suppliers with hyperlinks to three-dimensional renderings of the parts or systems that are changing. Suppliers so far have been leery of the automakers' Internet ambitions. Chrysler has already imposed price cuts on suppliers and is seeking more. The fear among suppliers is that FastCar and similar programs will be used to squeeze their profit margins even more.

FastCar may be able to cut the cost of each automobile by as much as $1,500. Automakers have to be able to get a concept from the design studio to the dealer's showroom in 18 months and do it for 30 percent to 35 percent less than it presently costs.

Source: "DaimlerChrysler's Net Designs," *business2.com* (April 17, 2001), pp. 26–28; *daimlerchrysler.com.*

In the automotive industry—like most other industries—having an Internet strategy is no longer just a source of competitive advantage; it is necessary for survival. However, in many industries, an innovative use of the Internet can bring competitive advantage for only so long, as competitors can often quickly duplicate it. Today's competitive advantage quickly becomes tomorrow's standard operating procedure, and the competitive bar is constantly being raised. The Internet in its various incarnations is a powerful medium whose understanding is essential for the modern business competitor.

7.1 WHAT, EXACTLY, IS THE INTERNET?

The **Internet**, which is the largest computer network in the world, is actually a network of networks. It is a collection of more than 200,000 individual computer networks owned by governments, universities, nonprofit groups, and companies. These interconnected networks exchange information seamlessly by using the same open, nonproprietary standards and protocols. They are connected via high-speed, long-distance backbone networks. Thus, the Internet forms a massive electronic communications network among businesses, consumers, government agencies, schools, and other organizations worldwide. Equally important, the Internet has opened up exciting new possibilities that challenge traditional ways of interacting, communicating, and doing business. At the same time, the Internet is raising new issues relating to culture and law.

The Internet rivals the great inventions of our time. Gutenberg's invention of the printing press took books out of ecclesiastical libraries and placed them in everyone's hands. The telephone system allows people to communicate instantaneously with each other. The Internet is now merging these two technologies. The Internet is a new communications dimension—an electronic, virtual world where time and space have almost no meaning. In 1990, in the book *Powershift*, Alvin Toffler foresaw that "electronic networks form the key infrastructure of the twenty-first century, as critical to business success and national economic development as the railroads were in Morse's era." The Internet provides this key infrastructure.

The Internet also provides a true democratic communications forum and has produced a **democratization of information**. That is, the Internet handles everyone's communications the same way, whether you are a university student or the CEO of a *Fortune 500* company. It is the *worth* of what you say that determines who is willing to listen, not your title or your bank balance. In most cases, users are free to say what they want on the Internet, and when. The Internet is an open and sharing environment that is remarkably free of censorship, a tribute to its roots in the academic and research communities.

Before you go on . . .

1. Describe the Internet.

2. What are some of the cultural implications of the Internet?

7.2   THE EVOLUTION OF THE INTERNET

The Internet began as one network, called the **ARPANET**. This network was a 1969 U.S. government experiment in packet-switched networking (see Chapter 6). ARPA was the Department of Defense Advanced Research Projects Agency. The ARPANET originally linked a largely technical audience composed of the military, government agencies, and academic researchers and scientists. The original goals of the project were to allow researchers to share computing resources and exchange information, regardless of their locations, and to create a resilient, fault-tolerant, wide area network for military communications. The original ARPANET split into two networks in the early 1980s, the ARPANET and Milnet (an unclassified military network), but connections between the two networks allowed communication to continue.

Access to the ARPANET in the early years was limited to the military, defense contractors, and universities doing defense research. Cooperative, decentralized networks such as UUCP, a worldwide UNIX communications network, and USENET (User's Network) originated in the late 1970s, initially serving the academic community and later serving commercial organizations. In the early 1980s, more networks, such as the Computer Science Network (CSNET) and BITNET, began providing nationwide networking to the academic and research communities. These networks were not part of the Internet, but special connections were made to allow the exchange of information between the networks. The National Science Foundation Network (NSFNET) originated in 1986, and linked researchers across the country with five supercomputer centers. The seamless internetworking of all these networks gave rise to the Internet we know today.

The Internet Today

The number of computers and networks connected to the Internet continues to grow rapidly. These computers and networks have been voluntarily set up to conform to the Internet's set of nonproprietary standard protocols. The power of the Internet rests in this uniform, open architecture. In 1998, less than 2 percent of the world's adults had access to the Internet. Analysts estimated that by 2001, some 500 million people worldwide were Internet users, connected to the one million networks that make up the Internet.

The Internet is international, with users on all continents, including Antarctica. Per-capita incomes limit the number of Internet users in the developing world, because the costs of personal computers and Internet connections are prohibitively high for most of the population. However, as the example below shows, the demand for Internet access exists, even if the infrastructure and per-capita income inhibit Internet usage.

EXAMPLE

Russian Internet use.   While much of the Western world jumped online in the 1990s, Russia, embroiled in political turmoil and growing poverty, missed the Internet revolution. By 2003, analysts predict that Russia will have only 11 million Internet users. As a result, e-commerce, both business-to-business and business-to-consumer, has not grown rapidly.

While Russians have access to the entire World Wide Web, most spend their time online within the Russian-language portions of the network, where e-mail addresses and Web sites are denoted by the suffix .ru—hence Runet (the name Russians call the Internet). People in Russia, regardless of location, are highly educated and want to get online and be a part of the worldwide flow of information. ●

Table 7.1 shows the top 15 countries in the world ranked by the overall number of Internet users as a percentage of population. The table also shows the total number of Internet users. By way of explanation, countries with a higher gross domestic product per person will have higher rates of personal computer ownership and higher Internet adoption rates than those with lower GDP figures. In developed countries, the ongoing cost of Internet connections does influence usage. In Germany, for example, there is a tremendous surge of online activity at 9:00 P.M., because at that time German phone rates drop by half.

In addition to relative wealth, political, cultural, and regulatory barriers have slowed the rate of Internet usage in some countries. Russia, Africa, and China have very limited numbers of Internet users, although China is in the process of connecting all the country's universities, institutions, grade schools, and research organizations. Censorship still limits content in some parts of the world. For example, in 2001, courts in France, Germany, and Italy banned Internet content in their countries that does not meet their national laws. Most notably, France prohibited the display of Nazi insignia and pro-Nazi remarks on Yahoo!'s auction site. In Australia, where the government does not censor the Internet, the Broadcasting Services Act defines forbidden online content, including specific representations of sexual acts, and information on crime, violence, and the use of certain narcotics. In France, Internet expansion has been hampered by a preference for the local Minitel system. Although not comparable to the Internet, Minitel's content is entirely in French.

Therefore, although the Internet is global, outside the United States it is still viewed as "U.S.-centric." The vast majority of sites are in English and most current software allows transmission only of characters from Western European languages. (An existing standard—*Unicode*—does allow a character set of 65,000 characters,

Table 7.1 Internet Usage in 2001

	Number of Internet Users (as percentage of population)	Number of Internet Users (in millions)
United States	49%	134.6
Sweden	49	4.4
South Korea	41	19.0
Australia	40	7.6
Canada	38	11.4
Netherlands	35	5.5
Taiwan	32	7.0
United Kingdom	28	16.8
Japan	27	33.9
Germany	24	19.9
Italy	22	12.5
France	15	9.0
Spain	14	5.6
Russia	5	7.5
China	2	22.5

which is sufficient to represent most human languages. Unicode, however, is not widely implemented on the Internet.) Similarly, the majority of content is generated in the United States.

EXAMPLE

Foreign-language versions of Web sites.   Eighty-five percent of the Web's pages are in English, but only 45 percent of the Web's users are native speakers of that language, and that percentage is dropping year by year. Companies know that if they really want to sell something to someone, they had better speak that person's language.

At Otis Elevator, monthly online sales leads increased from 130 to more than 1,000 after the company launched local-language versions of its Web site—with 70 percent of those leads coming from new customers. When Travelocity adds country-specific travel services or information to its site (such as a local customer-service phone number), sales in that country typically double.

However, it is expensive to develop a multilingual presence online. The typical cost of producing a Web site in another language is $50,000 to $100,000, with large projects costing as much as $2 million. ●

The Infrastructure of the Internet

Although the Internet began as a government project, currently the U.S. government pays only a small percentage of Internet costs. Commercial communications companies now largely provide the physical network backbone of the Internet. The U.S. government continues to contribute some funds to essential administrative processes, such as standards development and the domain name system (DNS), through contracts with private organizations that perform these functions. The National Science Foundation (NSF) also pays for certain high-performance portions of the network backbone.

The Internet infrastructure is supplied by network service providers, such as UUNET, an MCI WorldCom company, GTE Internetworking, Sprint, and others. Businesses and individual subscribers connect to the Internet through these and other, smaller Internet service providers. In some cases, the provider may be a large **backbone provider**; in other cases, it will be a smaller (often local) company connecting to the larger network service provider. Both backbone and access providers are referred to as **Internet service providers (ISPs)**. ISPs are more fully discussed later in the chapter. Service providers charge customers for various combinations of bandwidth, traffic, and access time.

Backbone providers must be connected to one another and to access providers, and this is done over **backbone networks**. The various backbone networks that make up the Internet transmit information to one another on a reciprocal basis, meaning that each carrier agrees to transport traffic originating on another carrier's network. Historically, this reciprocal transport has been done without charge. Data transmission on the backbone networks is not currently metered according to usage volume, time, or distance. However, this practice is beginning to change because of growing application demands for bandwidth and the need to finance expansions in network capacity to accommodate increasing Internet traffic. Figure 7.1 (on page 204) illustrates the global scope of the Internet. (For an interesting contrast of the Internet global network as of 2001, as shown in Figure 7.1, and the same network as of 1999, go to the book's Web site.) The following example, along with Figure 7.2, (on page 204) illustrates how the Internet works.

www.wiley.com/
college/turban

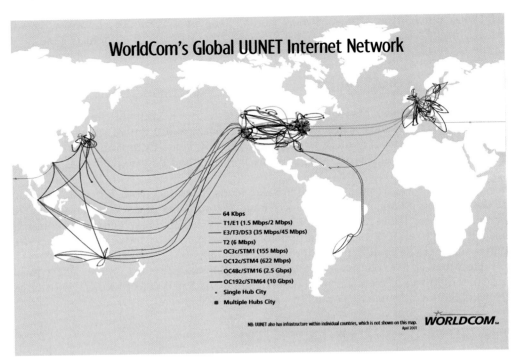

Figure 7.1   *The Internet global network as of September 2001. [Source: Courtesy of UUNET Technologies.]*

EXAMPLE

How the Internet works

Step 1: Suppose Fred in New York wants to send an e-mail to Susan across the Internet. Fred is a customer of Zip, a small Internet service provider (ISP), and Susan is a customer of another ISP. ISPs act as on-ramps to put users on the information highway.

Step 2: To connect its customers to the Internet, Zip contracts with a company that links Zip to the rest of the Internet. Zip chooses one of the smaller companies, Frontier.

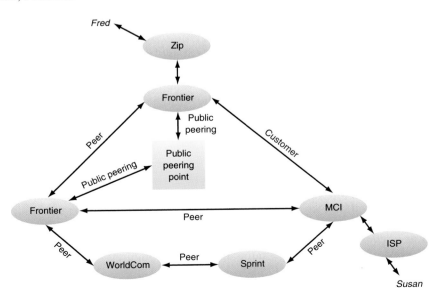

Figure 7.2   *How the Internet works.*

Step 3: Zip sends its traffic, including Fred's e-mail, to Frontier. But Frontier's network is not linked to Susan's ISP, so Frontier needs to contract with another Internet carrier to route Fred's e-mail. There are two ways that Frontier can connect to another carrier: as a *peer* or as a *customer*.

Step 4: If two Internet carriers decide that they are peers—generally of equal size—they exchange traffic with each other for free. They do this either by connecting their networks directly or by linking at a "public peering point." There are about 40 public peering points in the United States, where dozens of Internet carriers set up their communications equipment side by side and share traffic. Frontier and Verio, for example, are peers. The largest carriers—e.g., MCI WorldCom, Verio, Sprint, and Verizon—typically consider each other peers and exchange traffic without charging fees.

Step 5: If one Internet backbone provider is not accepted as a peer by another, the rejected company has to become a customer in order to send data across the other company's network. Verizon does not consider Frontier a peer, so Frontier pays "transit" fees to the larger carrier.

Step 6: Since Frontier is a customer of Verizon, the e-mail can go from Fred to Susan. ●

Internet2

The academic research community, which the Internet was originally intended to serve, found the Internet too slow for data-intensive applications such as transmitting supercomputer model data or telemedicine. Today, **Internet2** includes over 180 universities working in partnership with industry and government to develop and deploy advanced network applications and technologies. Internet2 is not a separate physical network from the Internet, but is simply a group of very high bandwidth networks on the Internet. The primary goals of Internet2 are to create a leading-edge network capability for the national research community; enable revolutionary Internet applications; and ensure the rapid transfer of new network services and applications to the broader Internet community.

Next Generation Internet (NGI).   The university-led Internet2 and the federally led Next Generation Internet (NGI) are parallel and complementary initiatives based in the United States. The NGI initiative aims to create an Internet that is fast, always on, everywhere, natural, intelligent, easy, and trusted. (For a technical description of the NGI, see "Building Blocks for the NGI" on the book's Web site.)

 *www.wiley.com/ college/turban*

Before you go on . . .

1. What are the origins of the modern Internet? What was its original purpose?

2. What factors have affected the spread of the Internet around the world?

7.3   THE OPERATION OF THE INTERNET

The set of rules used to send and receive packets from one machine to another over the Internet is known as the *Internet Protocol (IP)*, which operates at the network layer of the seven-layer ISO-OSI model discussed in Chapter 6. Other protocols are

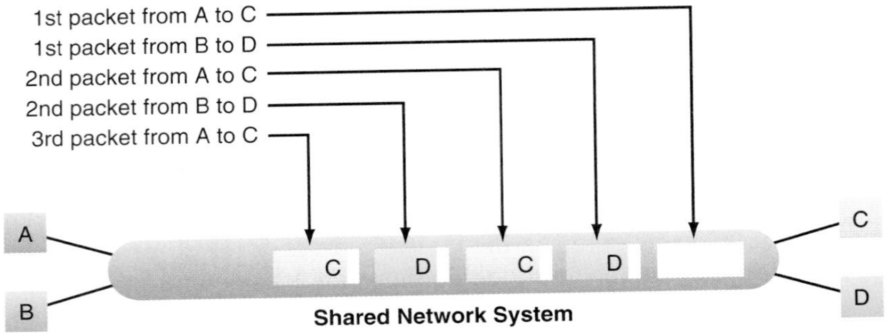

1st packet from A to C
1st packet from B to D
2nd packet from A to C
2nd packet from B to D
3rd packet from A to C

A

B

C   D   C   D

Shared Network System

C

D

Figure 7.3   *How packet switching works.* [*Source: Douglas E. Cromer,* The Internet Book, *2nd ed., Prentice-Hall, 1997. Reprinted by permission.*]

used in connection with IP, the best known of which is the *Transmission Control Protocol (TCP)*, which operates at the transport layer of the ISO-OSI model. The IP and TCP protocols are so commonly used together that they are referred to as the **TCP/IP protocol**, used by most Internet applications.

The Internet, a packet-switching network, breaks each message into packets (see Figure 7.3). Each packet contains the addresses of the sending and receiving machines, as well as sequencing information about its location relative to other packets in the message. Each packet can travel independently across various network interconnections. Therefore, packets may utilize different paths across the Internet and arrive out of sequence. When all packets arrive at the receiving computer, they are reassembled into the complete message.

Addresses on the Internet

Each computer on the Internet has an assigned address, called the **IP (Internet Protocol) address**, that uniquely identifies and distinguishes it from all other computers. The IP numbers have four parts, separated by dots. For example, the IP address of one computer might be 135.62.128.91.

Most computers also have names, which are easier for people to remember than IP addresses. These names are derived from a naming system called the **domain name system (DNS)**. Network Solutions Inc. (NSI) once had the authority to register addresses using .com, .net, or .org domain names. The company's contract ended in October 1998, as the U.S. government moved to turn management of the Web's address system over to the private sector. Currently, 82 companies, called registrars, are accredited to register domain names from the Internet Corporation for Assigned Names and Numbers (ICANN) (*internic.net*).

There are some 300,000 registered domain names, and these domain names have commercial value in themselves. This commercial value has led to the practice of *cybersquatting*—buying a potentially coveted domain name and hoping someone wants that name enough to pay for it. The practice of cybersquatting grew out of NSI's early policy of registering domain names on a first-come, first-served basis. This policy resulted in many companies or individuals registering a domain name associated with an established firm before the established firm did. The policy resulted in disputed names and legal actions. In response, Congress passed the Anti-Cybersquatting Consumer Protection Act in November 2000.

Domain names consist of multiple parts, separated by dots, and are translated from right to left. For example, consider the name software.ibm.com. "Com" is the name of the **top-level specification**, or the **zone**. The rightmost part of an Internet name is its top-level specification. "Com" indicates that this is a commercial site. There are 18 other top-level specifications, the last six of which are under consideration at this time. The 19 top-level specifications are as follows.

Zone	Used for	Zone	Used for
com	commercial sites	arts	cultural and entertainment activities
edu	educational sites	rec	recreational activities
mil	military sites	nom	individuals
gov	government sites	aero	air-transport industry
net	networking organizations	biz	businesses
org	organizations	coop	cooperatives
firm	businesses and firms	museum	museums
store	businesses offering goods for purchase	name	registration by individuals
info	information service providers	pro	accountants, lawyers, physicians
web	entities related to World Wide Web activities		

Finishing our example, "ibm" is the name of the company (IBM), and "software" is the name of the particular machine (computer) within the company to which the message is being sent.

The rightmost two letters in a domain name, if present, represent the country of the Web site. For example, "us" stands for the United States, "de" for Germany, "it" for Italy, and "ru" for Russia. In the U.S., the "us" is omitted.

Accessing the Internet

There are three main ways to connect to the Internet. These methods include connecting via a LAN server, connecting via SLIP/PPP, or connecting via an online service.

Connect via LAN server. This approach requires the user's computer to have specialized software called a *communications stack*, which provides a set of communications protocols that perform the complete functions of the seven layers of the OSI communications model. LAN servers are typically connected to the Internet at 56 Kbps or faster. This type of connection is expensive, but the cost can be spread over multiple LAN users.

Connect via Serial Line Internet Protocol/Point-to-Point Protocol (SLIP/PPP). This approach requires that users have a modem and specialized software that allows them to dial into a SLIP/PPP server through a service provider at a cost of approximately $30 per month or less. This type of connection is advantageous, for example, for employees working at home who need to access the Internet or their own company's intranet.

Connect via an online service. This approach requires a modem, standard communications software, and an online information service account with an Internet service provider. The costs include the online service fee, a per-hour connect charge, and, where applicable, e-mail service charges.

One of the first **online services (OLS)**, CompuServe, was launched in 1979. Prodigy and AOL (America Online) followed with offerings targeted toward home computer users. Services include, for example, access to specialized news sources (business, sports, etc.), market information, maps, and weather. This focus contrasted with the Internet's original orientation, which was geared to the academic and research community, and that of online research services such as Lexis-Nexis (a division of Reed Elsevier), which targets large corporations.

Originally, **Internet service providers (ISPs)** were established to provide connectivity, not content. Many ISPs now offering dial-in Internet access to consumers initially were set up to provide dedicated Internet connections to educational and commercial organizations. Others (such as NetCom) began by supplying dial-in access to Internet-connected time-sharing systems. UUNet started by providing dial-up connections for routing of e-mail and Usenet news (discussion groups devoted to specialized areas of interest) between non-Internet-connected sites. Thanks to the growth of Internet usage (as well as deregulation of the telecommunications industry), the number of ISPs has grown rapidly. Gartner Group estimates that there were approximately 13,000 ISPs worldwide at the end of 2001. Leading ISPs include America Online (*aoltimewarner.com*), MSN (*msn.com*), United Online (*unitedonline.net*), Earthlink (*earthlink.com*), and Prodigy (*prodigy.com*).

Before you go on . . .

1. What are the meanings of the different parts of an Internet address?

2. What are common ways of connecting to (accessing) the Internet?

3. What is the role of Internet service providers?

7.4   SERVICES PROVIDED BY THE INTERNET

The Internet provides four major types of services: communications, information retrieval, Web services, and the World Wide Web. *Communications services* include electronic mail, USENET newsgroups, LISTSERVs, chatting, Telnet, Internet telephony, and Internet fax. *Information retrieval services* include gophers, Archie, WAIS, File Transfer Protocol (FTP), and Veronica. *Web services* provide software applications over the Internet. The *World Wide Web*, with such great importance for e-commerce (discussed in Chapter 9), as well as for information search and retrieval, will be discussed as a separate topic.

Communications Services

The communications services available on the Internet are revolutionizing both personal and business communications. A tremendous variety of data can be accessed through the Internet. Users are no longer strictly dependent on telephony for one-to-one communication. Also, some of these services enable interactive communication with individuals and groups around the world who share personal and professional interests. "Blowing off steam" is considered a therapeutic form of communication for many employees, as shown in IT's About Business Box 7.1.

Electronic mail (e-mail).   The Internet is the most important e-mail system in the world because it connects so many people and organizations. As discussed in Chapter 6, **electronic mail (e-mail)** is an application that allows an electronic message to be sent between individuals through telephone wires or over wireless networks. E-mail is not limited to simple text messages. Users can embed sound and images in their messages, and attach files that contain text documents, spreadsheets, graphs, or executable programs. Not all networks use the same e-mail format, so a computer called a gateway translates the format of the e-mail message into the format that the next

IT's About Business

Box 7.1:   Cyberventing on gripe sites

The latest therapeutic trend among technology workers is cyberventing. The forums for this catharsis range from message boards at Vault (*vault.com*), with its Electronic Watercooler, and Yahoo! (*yahoo.com*) to company-specific sites like *untied.com* (a site for peeved United Airlines employees and customers) and *walmartyrs.com* (for employees who feel persecuted by Wal-Mart). Management, perhaps understandably, is not particularly happy about these sites. Employee discontent was once a quiet internal affair. Now such unhappiness is on display for the world to see. Some firms—Morgan Stanley for example—have gone so far as barring employees from accessing Vault in the workplace.

Instead of banning gripe sites (or "bitch boards" as they are known in executive circles), analysts say that managers would be better off logging on to these sites. Then, managers would have a free focus group and can correct misinformation, end false rumors, and set the record straight without being defensive. Analysts also say that managers should not place too much importance on individual postings, but instead look for themes that point to problems in the organization.

An interesting gripe site is *stainedapron.com*. Restaurant workers rail against skimpy tippers and meddling managers. Do not miss the revenge section. You will never stiff a waiter or waitress again.

Source: "Stop Moaning About Gripe Sites and Log On," *Fortune* (April 2, 2001) pp. 181–182.

Questions

1. Can gripe sites actually be beneficial for a business? If so, how?
2. Can managers really learn from such sites?

network can understand. Each gateway computer reads the "To" line of the e-mail message and routes the message closer to its destination.

USENET newsgroups (forums).   USENET is a protocol that delineates how groups of messages can be stored on and sent between computers. Following the USENET protocol, users send e-mail messages on a specific topic to the USENET server machine, which accrues this information. Users can log onto the server to read messages or have the computer automatically download messages to be read at the users' convenience.

USENET provides a forum for interested users on the Internet. This forum is divided into newsgroups. USENET newsgroups are international discussion groups in which people share information and ideas on a particular topic. Topics span the imagination, from medicine to college football to the space station. Approximately 30,000 newsgroups exist on the Internet. For a list of the major categories of topics on the USENET, see Table W7.1 on the book's Web site.

www.wiley.com/ college/turban

Discussion in newsgroups takes place on electronic bulletin boards, where anyone can post messages for others to read. Newsgroups are organized in a hierarchy by general topic. Each general topic has many subtopics. As members post messages and reply to messages, they create discussion threads.

Etiquette is important when participating in a newsgroup discussion or conversation (a thread). There are certain things you should do when first joining a newsgroup discussion:

- Read the Frequently Asked Questions (FAQs) for the newsgroup. Doing this will save you from asking obvious questions and wasting the time of everyone in the discussion.

- Read the discussion for some time before joining in with your comments. Doing this will give you a sense of the group and the discussion.

- Be considerate of the feelings of others by being polite. Do not use strong or inflammatory language; there could be legal implications.
- Do not offer personal information about yourself.
- Do not post copyrighted material to the newsgroup, and be extremely careful about downloading copyrighted material to your computer.

LISTSERV. Similar to a newsgroup, a **LISTSERV** is another type of public forum that allows discussions to be conducted through predefined groups. The difference is that LISTSERV uses e-mail mailing list servers instead of bulletin boards for communications. If users find a LISTSERV topic in which they are interested, they may subscribe. After that, through e-mail, they will receive all messages sent by all others concerning that topic. If users post messages to the LISTSERV, those messages will be sent to all others on that LISTSERV.

Chatting. **Chatting** allows two or more people who are simultaneously connected to the Internet to hold live (real-time), interactive, written conversations. **Internet relay chat (IRC)** is a general chat program for the Internet. Chat groups are divided into channels, each assigned its own topic of conversation. Chatting is the third-most-used Internet application, behind e-mail and search. Few services can build big audiences more quickly than chat.

Instant messaging. **Instant messaging** is online, real-time communication between two or more people who are connected to the Internet. Users can send instant text messages to other users who are logged on. A window appears on the screens of all the people engaged in the messaging. Each window displays what one person is typing, in real time. A number of companies offer instant messaging, including America Online, Yahoo!, and Microsoft. Jabber (*jabber.org*), an XML-based, open-source system for real-time messaging, makes it possible for someone on the Internet using instant messaging to communicate with someone on a cell phone anywhere in the world.

Telnet. Telnet allows users to be on one computer while doing work on another. **Telnet** is the protocol that establishes an error-free link between the two computers. Users can log on to their office computers while traveling or from their homes. Also, users can log on and use third-party computers that have been made accessible to the public, such as using the catalog of the U.S. Library of Congress.

Internet telephony. Internet vendors are providing products that emulate traditional public switched telephone network (PSTN) applications. **Internet telephony** (also called **Voice over IP** or **VoIP**) lets users talk across the Internet to any personal computer equipped to receive the call for the price of only the Internet connection.

    VoIP carries voice calls over the Internet, either partially or completely bypassing the public switched telephone network. Sound quality can be poor due to latency and jitter. *Latency* is delay during the transmission process. *Jitter* occurs when large amounts of data clog networks at certain times. When there is too much latency and jitter, callers tend to miss about one out of every four or five words.

Internet fax. The use of the Internet for real-time fax transmissions is emerging as an application that may signal a shift of traditional analog communications from the telephone companies to the packet-switched Internet. This application is useful because faxes can be sent long distances at local telephone rates, and delivery can be guaranteed through store-and-forward mechanisms.

Faxing is one of the top forms of communication in the business world. Some 800 billion pages were faxed worldwide in 2001, and that number continues to increase. With 100 million fax machines worldwide generating a telephone bill of more than $100 billion per year, companies spend a large percentage of their yearly phone bills on faxing.

Most fax machines are group resources, shared by several users. Many of these users are unhappy with some of the inconveniences of faxing: They do not like having to print out a document, pick it up at the laser printer, walk down the hall to the fax machine, and wait for the fax to go through. Faxes are not secure or encrypted, nor are they private. At the receiving end, they often lie in the fax machine or on a desktop for all to see.

An **Internet fax service** overcomes many of these drawbacks. Fax service from an Internet service provider connects desktop computers and standard fax machines to a fax server located within the ISP's network. The same service can also connect desktop e-mail to the ISP's fax servers so that faxes can be originated as easily as sending an e-mail.

Streaming audio and video.   **Streaming** allows Internet users to see and hear data as it is transmitted from the host server instead of waiting until the entire file is downloaded. For example, RealNetworks' RealAudio allows a Web site to deliver live and on-demand audio over the Internet and can work over connections as slow as 14.4 Kbps.

Streaming audio enables the broadcast of radio programs, music, press conferences, speeches, and news programs over the Internet. In the future, streaming audio and Internet telephony use will overlap and complement one another.

EXAMPLE

Radio Sonicnet offers personalized radio.   Radio Sonicnet (*sonicnet.com*) has a Web-based audio service that selects the songs it plays based in part on its users' tastes, creating customized music channels that are likely to serve up a listener's favorite song. Radio Sonicnet says that listeners decide what they want to hear.

Radio Sonicnet works like this: From the Web site, the listener selects one of 20 channels focusing on specific genres such as new rock. Using a custom tuner built on top of RealNetworks Inc.'s RealPlayer, random algorithms are used to select a song from a list of 80 songs offered on the channel. The listener rates a song on a scale of 1 to 10 while it is playing. The information is stored locally on the listener's tuner. New ratings are applied to songs the next time a selection is made from the channel. Songs ranked highly by the listener are given a heavier weight in the random sample, increasing the likelihood that they will be selected for play.

This personalization paves the way for long-term business opportunities for Radio Sonicnet by giving the company a vehicle for collecting detailed databases. These data can eventually be used for targeted advertising and also to help record companies identify potentially lucrative audience niches for their artists. ●

Streaming video has other business applications, including training, entertainment, communications, advertising, and marketing. Streaming audio and video are being used to deliver market-sensitive news and other "live" status reports to stock traders, to brief sales people on new products, to deliver corporate news to employees, and to view TV commercials for approval. Streaming audio and video vendors include Apple (QuickTime), Microsoft (ActiveMovie), and RealNetworks (RealVideo).

Real-time audio and video.   In **real-time audio** and **real-time video**, the transmission from the source is live or only slightly delayed. Real-time audio and video applications include point-to-point conversations between two people; conferences among more than two people; collaborative "white boarding" (where two or more users can interactively create graphic images) and shared hypermedia documents; live broadcasts of news, talk shows, or sporting events; and broadcasts of music and concerts. Real-time audio and video vendors include Intel (Video Phone), Microsoft (NetMeeting), and CUseeMe Networks.

Information Retrieval Services

Information retrieval allows users to access through the Internet thousands of huge online library catalogs, as well as thousands of databases that have been opened to the public by corporations, governments and government agencies, and nonprofit organizations. In addition, many users download free, high-quality software made available by developers over the Internet.

The Internet is a voluntary, decentralized collection of networks with no central listing of sites and no central listing of the data located at those sites. Therefore, users have a large problem finding what they need from the massive amounts of information available via the Internet. This section discusses five methods of accessing computers and locating files. These services are free programs available to any Internet user. (Section 7.5 on the World Wide Web discusses additional information-retrieval methods.)

File Transfer Protocol (FTP).   **File Transfer Protocol (FTP)** enables users to access a remote computer and retrieve files from it. After users have logged on to the remote computer, they can search the directories that are accessible to FTP, looking for the files they want to retrieve.

Archie.   **Archie** is a tool that allows users to search the files at FTP sites. It regularly monitors hundreds of FTP sites and updates a database (called an Archie server) on software, documents, and data files available for downloading.

If users click on a listing from an Archie server, it will take them to another computer system where relevant files are stored. Once there, the Archie server may allow users to continue their searches for files until they locate what they need. Archie database searches use subject key words, such as "Bowl Championship Series" or "network computers." The Archie database will return lists of sites that contain files on these topics.

Gophers.   Most files and digital information that are accessible through FTP are also available through gophers. A **gopher** is a computer client tool that enables users to locate information stored on Internet gopher servers through a series of hierarchical menus. Each gopher server contains its own system of menus listing subject-matter topics, local files, and other relevant gopher sites. When users access gopher software to search on a specific topic and they select an item from a menu, the server will automatically transfer them to the appropriate file on that server or to the selected server wherever it is located. Once on that server, the process continues. Users are presented with more menus of files and other gopher site servers that might be of interest. Users can move from site to site, narrowing their searches, and locating information anywhere in the world.

Veronica.   **Veronica (Very Easy Rodent-Oriented Netwide Index to Computer Archives)** provides the capability of searching for text that appears in gopher menus.

When the user enters a key word, Veronica will search through thousands of gopher sites to find titles containing that keyword. It places these files on a temporary menu on the local server, so users can browse through them.

Wide area information servers (WAIS). Wide area information servers (WAIS) also allow users to locate files around the Internet. WAIS is the most thorough way to locate a specific file, but it requires that users know the names of the databases they want to search. After users specify database names and key identifying words, WAIS searches for the key words in all the files in those databases. When the search is complete, users obtain a menu listing all the files that contain the key words.

Web Services

The next step in software evolution will have software applications provided in the form of services delivered over the Internet. Web services are unique pieces of computer code (or components) accessed through a Web site that deliver a specific type of function. Web services allow us to transparently access rich software content from any site on the Web.

The great promise of Web services is the ability to deliver applications to users at a much lower cost. As much as 30 percent of the price of traditional software is tied to the cost of distribution—pressing CDs, packaging them in boxes, and shipping them to retail outlets. Digital distribution eliminates the physical element. Some day soon, even medical services will be accessible over the Web. (See the book's Web site for an example of Potential Medical Services on the Web.)

 www.wiley.com/college/turban

Microsoft's .NET. **.NET** is Microsoft's platform for XML Web services. The .NET framework allows unrelated Web sites to communicate with each other and with programs that run on personal computers. .NET means that one click could set off a cascade of actions without requiring the user to open new programs or visit additional Web sites. C# (pronounced *C-sharp*) is Microsoft's object-oriented language that enables programmers to quickly build a wide range of applications for the .NET platform. (For technical discussions of .NET, Hailstorm, and C#, see the Web site.)

 www.wiley.com/college/turban

Before you go on . . .

1. What are the major categories of communication services provided by the Internet?

2. Which communication services are most useful for organizational use? Private use?

3. What are the major categories of information retrieval services provided by the Internet?

7.5 THE WORLD WIDE WEB

Many people believe that the World Wide Web is the same thing as the Internet, but that is not the case. The Internet functions as the transport mechanism, and the World Wide Web (called the Web, WWW, or W3) is an application that uses those transport functions. Other applications also run on the Internet, with e-mail being the most widely used.

The **Web** is a system with universally accepted standards for storing, retrieving, formatting, and displaying information via a client/server architecture. The Web handles all types of digital information, including text, hypermedia, graphics, and sound. It uses graphical user interfaces, so it is very easy to use. The technology underlying the World Wide Web was created by Timothy Berners-Lee, who in 1989 proposed a global network of hypertext documents that would allow physics researchers to work together. This work was done at the European Laboratory for Particle Physics (known by its French acronym CERN) in Geneva, Switzerland.

The Web is based on a standard hypertext language called **Hypertext Markup Language (HTML)**, which formats documents and incorporates dynamic hypertext links to other documents stored on the same or different computers. HTML was derived from the more complex **Standard Generalized Markup Language (SGML)**, a text-based language for describing the content and structure of digital documents. HTML is a simpler subset of SGML and incorporates tables, applets, text flow around images, superscripts, and subscripts. Using these hypertext links (which are typically blue, bold, and underlined), the user points at a highlighted word, clicks on it, and is transported to another document. Users are able to navigate around the Web freely with no restrictions, following their own logic, needs, or interests.

Offering information through the Web requires establishing a **home page**, which is a text and graphical screen display that usually welcomes the user and explains the organization that has established the page. (See *Wiley.com*, for example.) In most cases, the home page will lead users to other pages. All the pages of a particular company or individual are known as a **Web site**. Most Web pages provide a way to contact the organization or the individual. The person in charge of an organization's Web site is its **Webmaster**.

www.wiley.com/
college/turban

Organizations are very interested in how their Web sites serve their employees and customers. A variety of metrics can be used for this purpose. (See the discussion of Metrics for Evaluating Web Sites on the book's Web site.)

To access a Web site, the user must specify a **uniform resource locator (URL)**, which points to the address of a specific resource on the Web. For instance, the URL for Microsoft is *http://www.microsoft.com*. HTTP stands for **Hypertext Transport Protocol**, which is the communications standard used to transfer pages across the WWW portion of the Internet. HTTP defines how messages are formatted and transmitted and what actions Web servers and browsers should take in response to various commands. *www.microsoft.com* is the domain name identifying the Web server storing the Web sites. Table 7.2 offers some interesting and useful Web sites.

Browsers

Users primarily access the Web through software applications called **browsers**. At a minimum, a browser is capable of communicating via HTTP, managing HTML, and displaying certain data types, such as GIF (Graphics Interchange Format) and JPEG (Joint Photographic Experts Group) for graphics and Microsoft Windows WAV for sound.

At first, the Web was text only. Then, in 1992, researchers at the National Center for Supercomputing Applications at the University of Illinois developed Mosaic, the first graphical Web browser. The Mosaic browser provided a graphical front end that enabled users to point-and-click their way across the Web, a process called **surfing**. Web browsers became a means of universal access because they deliver the same interface on any operating system under which they run—Windows, Windows NT, OS/2, MacOS, or UNIX.

The emergence of commercial, graphical browsers that access documents written in HTML created a mass medium that allowed large numbers of people without so-

Table 7.2   Interesting and Useful Web Sites

IntelliChoice (*intellichoice.com*) Edmunds (*edmunds.com*)	Provide dealer prices and ownership costs on most car makes and models.
How Stuff Works (*howstuffworks.com*)	Tells you how almost anything works, from computers, to engines, to the human body.
Equifax (*equifax.com*)	One of the major credit-checking agencies; will provide you with a copy of your credit report for $8.
FinanceCenter/Smartcalc (*financenterinc.com*)	Will calculate your car and mortgage payments and show you how much you need to save in order to retire.
Invest-o-rama (*iclub.com*)	From the National Association of Investment Clubs, provides links to more than 2,000 investment-related sites and offers analysts' consensus reports on thousands of individual stocks, as well as how to set up and run an investment club.
The Free Site (*thefreesite.com*)	Provides a comprehensive listing and access to free software available over the Web.
Medscape (*medscape.com*)	Provides medical information and articles, news, and self-assessment tests. The site is free, but you have to register for an ID and a password.
Online Career Center (*monster.com*)	Provides listings of jobs and profiles of companies. You can search the listings by key word, and you can place resumes online.

phisticated computer skills not only to access information, but also to publish their own content on the Internet. New users could enjoy direct, interactive access to the Internet's contents without having to use system commands or contend with terminal emulators. HTML is easy to learn, and it is easy to develop authoring tools for the language. Aided by desktop publishing tools that produce HTML pages from standard documents and Internet connection kits, users set up their Web sites and communicate with millions of other Web users worldwide.

The two leading browsers are Internet Explorer from Microsoft and Netscape Navigator. The competition between them has been extremely beneficial for users, providing them with highly capable applications at almost no cost. Microsoft's strategy is to minimize the importance of the browser as a distinct application by building browser functionality directly into its latest operating systems. Netscape's strategy is to make the browser the core of a compelling suite of applications for corporate users. Netscape has pursued the approach of developing a Web-based suite of communications services, including groupware offerings for intranets.

Netscape's browser suite.   Netscape's browser suite includes Netscape Navigator, Netscape Mail, Netscape Instant Messenger, Netscape Composer, and Netscape Address Book. The suite provides functions for running Web applets, audio playback, streaming media, Web content, and Net2Phone for free PC-to-phone calls anywhere within the United States. Netscape Communicator is a comprehensive set of components that integrates e-mail, Web-based word processing, and chat to allow users to easily communicate, share, and access information.

Microsoft Internet Explorer.   Faced with the tremendous lead in the browser marketplace that Netscape established, Microsoft embarked on a strategy to gain market share and penetrate the installed base. It gave Internet Explorer away for free and bundled it with the Windows operating systems. This approach was successful but also resulted in scrutiny by the U.S. government.

In October 1997 the U.S. Justice Department filed a petition in federal court to prevent Microsoft from requiring personal computer manufacturers to bundle Microsoft's Internet browser software with Microsoft's Windows operating systems. At issue was whether Microsoft tried to monopolize the Internet browser software business by refusing to let PC makers license the Windows operating systems unless they also ship their PCs with Internet Explorer. Microsoft maintained that Internet Explorer was an enhancement of Windows, not a separate product, and that the company therefore was not violating its antitrust settlement. According to Microsoft, Internet Explorer's tight integration with Windows offers users the advantage of "one-stop computing."

In early November 2001, the Justice Department reached a settlement with Microsoft in the antitrust case. Under the settlement, a panel of three independent monitors will work onsite at Microsoft to oversee its conduct and review its accounts. Crucially, Microsoft must provide rival software firms with information to allow them to develop competing "middleware" products—in other words, software programs that interact with the computer operating system. Microsoft was prevented from retaliating against computer manufacturers and software rivals who brought out competing products, and had to deal with licensing partners on uniform terms.

Metabrowsers.   Web surfing has typically been a one-page-at-a-time experience. Then Yahoo! offered My Yahoo!, which enabled personalization of news, sports, financial data, entertainment, and other topics. Octopus (*octopus.com*) provides portal personalization by giving consumers control over what they view. Users assemble customized pages, called "views" on Octopus, choosing to start with a blank view or to use one of the sample views arranged in a menu. To add elements, users grab items from the menu and drag them onto their pages. The views are dynamically linked to the Web sites providing the content. Users who click on any page element—for example, a news headline or a stock chart—are connected directly to that site.

Users can store their views privately on Octopus, or they can "publish" them so other users can take a look. For users, the service is free. Octopus plans to make money by charging Web publishers a fee each time users click through to their sites. Other metabrowsing services include CallTheShots (*calltheshots.com*), Quickbrowse (*quickbrowse.com*), Katiesoft (*katiesoft.com*), and Yodlee (*yodlee.com*).

Offline Browsers

Offline browsers (or pull products) enable a user to retrieve pages automatically from Web sites at predetermined times, often during the night. WebWhacker (*bluesquirrel.com*) and WebCopier (*maximumsoft.com*) are offline browsers that allow users to define a group of sites by their URLs and then download text and images from those sites to their local storage. WebWhacker and WebCopier let users determine how much of a Web site to retrieve—title pages only, any linked pages, or all pages.

Search Engines

After e-mail, search is the Web's most popular function. Roughly 80 percent of surfers use search engines. **Search engines** are programs that return a list of Web sites or pages (designated by URLs) that match selected criteria. To use one of the publicly available search sites, the user navigates to the search engine's site and types in the subject of the search. Table 7.3 gives the URLs for some popular Internet search sites.

Search engines for large numbers of Web pages, such as those that attempt to cover the entire Internet, do so by maintaining databases that model the Web's struc-

Table 7.3   URLs of Popular Search Engines

AOL Search	*search.aol.com*	Lycos	*lycos.com*
Alta Vista	*altavista.com*	MSN Search	*search.msn.com*
Ask Jeeves	*askjeeves.com*	NBCi	*nbci.com*
Direct Hit	*directhit.com*	Netscape Search	*search.netscape.com*
Excite	*excite.com*	Northern Light	*northernlight.com*
FAST Search	*alltheweb.com*	Oingo	*oingo.com*
Google	*google.com*	Open Directory	*dmoz.org*
HotBot	*hotbot.lycos.com*	Yahoo!	*yahoo.com*
LookSmart	*looksmart.com*	iLOR	*ilor.com*

tures. Through a combination of information-trolling robots that collect information automatically about Web pages and developer registration, search engines select a large number of Web sites to be indexed. Their databases are then populated with information about the contents of each page deemed useful. Many Web sites have search engines embedded within them. Also, some engines search not only Web pages, but also gopher sites, FTP resources, or USENET news groups.

Search engines select pages for inclusion in their databases in two primary ways:

- **Web crawlers** traverse the Web automatically, collecting index data on one of two search principles: *depth first,* which follows only the links that are deemed relevant to a topic, or *breadth first,* which collects the entire network of links from a given starting point regardless of the page contents. Web crawlers are variously called *spiders, ants, robots, bots,* and *agents.*

- **Registration** is allowed by most search sites. Web developers can register their sites or pages by submitting a form. This process enables developers to ensure that their sites eventually will be included in the search index.

When a user enters a search query, the engine searches its database for relevant Web pages. It assembles a list of pages sorted by relevance or other, user-specified weighting factors. Some sites also remove redundant references to pages from the list. Search results are returned as a list of relevant pages that then can be retrieved via hyperlinks. Different engines can produce results that vary widely, ranging from not finding critical pages (*poor recall*) to finding hundreds of thousands of documents with few that are relevant (*poor precision ratio*).

Google is the largest search engine and the first search engine to index more than one billion pages. Google's method of searching the Web is called PageRank. The more links there are to a page, the higher it moves in Google's ranking. PageRank improves both recall and precision ratio.

"First, they do an on-line search."

Metasearch engines automatically enter search queries into a number of other search engines and return the results. Examples of metasearch engines include All4one, Metacrawler, and Starting Point. For Macintosh users, the latest operating system (Mac OS X) comes with Sherlock. Users can type in their requests, in plain English, and Sherlock accesses many other Internet search engines simultaneously. The results are returned, ranked by relevance. (For the URLs of some popular metasearch engines, see Table W7.2 on the book's Web site.)

www.wiley.com/
college/turban

Push Technology

As the amount of information available on the Internet grows, new mechanisms for delivering it to consumers are being developed. Since its inception, the Web has been based on a pull model of information access. The Web user must actively seek out information by specifying a page to be "pulled down" to the desktop by typing in a URL, following a hot link, or using the search results from a Web search site. However, passively placing content on a Web site and waiting for people to come browse is not well-suited to establishing and fostering strong relationships with customers or prospects.

Therefore, an alternative push model of information delivery has emerged. In this model, information is "pushed" to the user's desktop. **Push technology** now makes it possible to automatically supply information to users by means of a process running on either the user's desktop or a network server. With millions of Web sites available for browsing, the only way to guarantee that users receive certain content is to send or "push" it to them. Push client packages typically are given away free, and the companies that publish them rely on advertising for revenue.

One of the earliest products embodying the push model was the PointCast Network from PointCast. PointCast developed software that used the Web browser as a platform and displayed customizable news and other information on the user's screen as a screensaver. PointCast fell from favor in many organizations because the incoming broadcasts often overloaded a recipient organization's local area network. PointCast has now been incorporated into Infogate (*infogate.com*). Infogate delivers a smaller application that downloads faster and uses less system memory than earlier versions of PointCast.

Push technology is useful in the workplace, in the consumer market, and as a mechanism for software distribution. In the workplace, push technology can provide timely, prioritized distribution of information over a corporate network. For example, the software can be oriented to an organization's different departments to focus attention on important communications. In the consumer market, push technology can enhance traditional Web advertising. Users no longer need to find advertisements; instead, the users' attention can be directed to the advertisements. In addition, the quality of the presentations can be improved by tuning the software specifically to the user's platform and connection speed.

Information Filters

Information filters are automated methods of sorting relevant from irrelevant information. These filters help people access information with more precision; that is, they help people reduce information overload. As the information available over the Internet continues to grow, users increasingly need to narrow the content through which they wish to search.

The most publicized information filters are those programs that screen out adult content from Web browsers. Intended for home markets, examples of Internet screening software include SurfControl's CyberPatrol (*cyberpatrol.com*) and Net Nanny (*netnanny.com*). These programs prevent access to a list of sites deemed unacceptable by the company providing the software.

In response to public concerns and to preempt possible federal regulation, AOL, Disney, Microsoft, Netscape, and other companies are supporting the Platform for Internet Content Selection (PICS), a specification for labeling Web content. PICS embeds labels in HTML page headers to rate different Web sites by category, much like existing movie and television ratings. Microsoft's Internet Explorer browser and Netscape's Navigator browser allow parents to block categories and set a password.

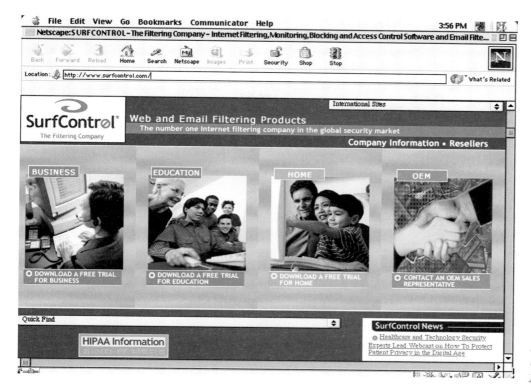

SurfControl allows parents, teachers, and businesses to filter Web content.

A more active method of filtering information uses **intelligent agents**. The goal of agents is to create applications that automatically carry out tasks for users without their intervention, other than initial configuration and updating with new requests. Intelligent agents are discussed in detail in Chapter 12.

Clipping Services

The number of publications, traditional and electronic, available online continues to increase. In digital format, publications are easily amenable to efficient or automated clipping by use of a **clipping service**. For example, Excite offers NewsTracker, a free clipping service. Through it, users can track up to 20 news topics and retrieve articles from a database of more than 300 publications. Excite generates revenue by advertising. As a marketing manager, for example, you could use a clipping service to look for information on new products or markets your company is considering. As a public relations officer of a company, for example, you could find references to your company in those publications and could also be on the lookout for references to competing companies in your industry.

Personalized Web Services

Personalized Web services offer the ability to generate Web content that is personalized for individual Web site visitors. Information about the user is gathered from activity during the current or previous visits to a Web site, the type of browser, or browser preference settings. For example, the ability to let a site visitor define how the Web page is displayed (e.g., with or without frames or Java) is a type of personalization because this home page is generated dynamically, based on the user's previous setup. This feature has become a requirement of any online news service, appearing in the Web sites of publications ranging from the *Wall Street Journal* to *Wired*.

Collaborative Filtering

Collaborative filtering is a form of personalization services exemplified by Firefly Network (bought by Microsoft). Upon registering in Firefly, users could rate films and music of various kinds. Those ratings are combined with other users' preferences to predict the new user's tastes and to offer suggestions of other music and movies he or she might like. The longer an individual used Firefly, the more accurate the predictions became, and consequently, the more personalized the information on the site.

Web Authoring

Web sites have become important creative media with the added benefits of multimedia and dynamic database-driven content. Tools for **Web authoring**—for page and site design—range from ASCII text editors to full-featured, integrated development environments.

The limiting factor that underlies all layout and design tools is what the most commonly used Web browsers can display. Standard HTML, which is constantly evolving and being extended with proprietary enhancements by browser vendors, is the common denominator. Graphics files in the CompuServe Graphics Interchange Format (GIF) are common, as are graphics in the Joint Photographic Experts Group (JPEG) format. Browsers can be extended with additional capabilities through plug-in applications and software components that are able to display other types of content, ranging from text formatted more richly than HTML allows, to animated graphics, audio tracks, and video clips. Popular Web authoring tools include Adobe's GoLive, Microsoft's FrontPage, and Netscape's Navigator Gold and Composer. Other languages that enhance Web authoring, such as Dynamic HTML and XML, are discussed in Chapter 4.

Before you go on . . .

1. What are the roles of browsers? Of search engines?

2. What are the practical differences between pull and push Web models?

3. What tools are used to author Web pages?

7.6   INTERNET CHALLENGES

Challenges facing the Internet in the next few years include making the Internet more suitable for e-commerce transactions (discussed in Chapter 9), incorporating rapidly evolving technologies, standards, and regulatory frameworks, responding to the growing need for additional bandwidth, and addressing privacy concerns. Another challenge for the Internet is providing the infrastructure for very-large-scale projects.

New Technologies

Vendors are adopting new technologies more rapidly than many users and customers can implement them. For example, the two most popular Web browsers are Netscape's Navigator and Microsoft's Internet Explorer. Many of the most innovative sites on the Web use Java applets, interactive three-dimensional graphics, and video and audio clips. To access these Web sites and take advantage of their innovative content and full functionality, users must have recent versions of Navigator and Explorer.

Internet Regulation

Technical organizations, such as the Internet Engineering Task Force and the World Wide Web Consortium, and others, have played an important role in the evolution of the Internet and the Web. These organizations are not formally charged in any legal or operational sense with responsibility for the Internet. However, they perform the important task of defining the standards that govern the Internet's functionality. Hardware and software vendors also have been instrumental in submitting specifications for consideration to standard bodies and in creating de facto standards of their own.

Recent attempts by governments in the United States and elsewhere to regulate the content of Internet-connected computers have generated concerns about privacy, security, and the legal liability of service providers. Some content providers have addressed these issues with filters, ratings, and restricted access. However, it is difficult to regulate content across international borders. Regulation of services such as gambling also has been debated.

Internet Expansion

The Internet was not designed to provide a mass-market interchange of high-density information. As a result, the massive growth of Internet traffic has strained some elements of the network. The strains manifest themselves as slowdowns in retrieval time, unreliable transmission of streamed data, and denial of service by overloaded servers.

The Internet's design, with many potential transmission paths, is in theory highly resistant to outages caused by failed links. In practice, however, the Internet often is affected by software problems.

A wide range of factors contributes to congestion or slowdowns. These problems include improperly configured networks, overloaded servers, rapidly changing Internet usage patterns, and too much traffic for available bandwidth. Approaches to solve these problems include installing high-speed transmission media to accommodate large amounts of data; bigger, faster routers and more sophisticated load balancing and management software to handle peak traffic periods; local caching (storing) of frequently requested Web pages to improve response times; and more reliable tiers of service for those willing to pay for them.

Internet Privacy

Web sites collect information with and without consumers' knowledge. One way to collect information at Web sites is through registration (as on Amazon.com). Visitors to the site enter data about themselves, and obviously know that such information is available for future use by the company that collects the data.

The most common way Web sites collect information, though, is through "clickstream" data—that is, information about where people go within a Web site and the content they see. Clickstream data are most commonly collected by cookies. A **cookie** is a small data file placed on users' hard drives when they first visit a site. This software can be used to exchange information automatically between a server and a browser without a user seeing what is being transmitted.

Cookies are useful in tracking users' actions and preferences (as noted in the previous section on personalized Web services). When a user goes back to a site, the site's computer server can read the usage data from the cookies. This background information can then be used to customize the Web content that is given to the user. That information is stored in a database and can be used to target ads or content, based on the preferences tracked. Netscape and Internet Explorer browsers support cookie technology.

The Federal Trade Commission randomly checks Web sites to see if site operators are posting privacy notices that explain how personal information—such as e-mail addresses, shopping habits, and consumer financial data—is being used and whether it is being protected from unwarranted intrusion. Privacy on the Internet at this point is not a sure thing.

There are bills in Congress related to Web privacy, ranging from laws to regulate spamming (unsolicited e-mail) to legislation restricting disclosure of subscriber information by online services. Three possibilities exist:

- The government should let groups develop voluntary privacy standards but not take any action now unless real problems arise.
- The government should recommend privacy standards for the Internet but not pass laws at this time.
- The government should pass laws now for how personal information can be collected and used on the Internet.

How Congress will resolve these issues remains to be seen.

Another aspect of the privacy issue on the Internet is transaction security, which is examined fully in Chapter 9 on electronic commerce. Although great advances have been made that ensure the security of financial transactions on the Internet, there are still gaps in the Internet's security that put personal privacy and the confidentiality of communication at risk.

Before you go on . . .

1. How do technological advances affect the spread and use of the Internet?

2. What industries should pay close attention to efforts to regulate the Internet?

3. What might be some implications of cookie software? How could you or your firm be affected?

7.7   INTRANETS

An **intranet** is a private network that uses Internet software and TCP/IP protocols. In essence, an intranet is a private Internet, or group of private segments of the public Internet network, reserved for use by people who have been given the authority to use that network. Companies increasingly are using intranets—powered by internal Web servers—to give their employees easy access to corporate information. Intranets also are an effective medium for application delivery.

Web browsers increasingly are being used to access many corporate applications because they provide a ready-made GUI client and therefore offer an inexpensive means to develop new systems. The most common applications on corporate intranets are for personnel policies and procedures; document sharing; corporate telephone directories; human resources forms; training programs; search engines; customer databases; product catalogs and various work manuals; groupware; organizational charts; IT news and updates; crisis alerts (what IT systems are down and when they will be operational); electronic bulletin board, where employees can post items for sale, items wanted to buy, and roommates wanted; and data warehouse and decision support access.

IT's About Business Box 7.2 shows a human resources management application for an intranet.

Security

With this number and variety of applications, intranet security is critically important. Companies can prevent unwanted intrusion into their intranets in several ways. **Public key security** is used to broker authorization to enter into a private intranet. It has two parts: encryption and certificate authorities. **Encryption** scrambles outgoing data, while **digital certificates** are like electronic identification cards, letting a business know that the person trying to access the intranet is a valid user. ValiCert is a leader in the

IT's About Business

HRM

Box 7.2:   Human resources management on the Web

Human resources departments are using the Web for self-service HR applications such as checking benefits, updating employee information, posting job requisitions, training, and salary reviews. For decades, HR managers have been inundated with employee queries on how to participate in the company's stock purchase program or how to change their home addresses in the corporate database. Employees often viewed the HR department as a bottleneck in resolving salary and hiring issues or completing benefits transactions.

Today, intranets are letting employees handle those processes themselves. In some cases, company intranets are linked with third-party insurance carriers and other service providers to cut out the HR middleman. In the past, companies have hired one HR staff person for every 100 employees, but Web technology reduces this ratio to one HR staff person to every 150 employees.

Many companies are also looking to the Web to seed and harvest data from thousands of job boards and recruiting services. For example, Intel gets 10 to 15 percent of its new hires over the Web. The Web has decreased hiring costs by 60 percent and the time it takes to fill open positions by 30 to 40 percent. Specialized job boards and resume-posting services, as well as the more obvious job sites such as Monster.com and Hotjobs.com, are giving companies more sources for finding people.

Today, the most aggressive HR departments are working with IT to develop links between their back-end systems, such as payroll and employee information databases, and the corporate intranet. These links let employees interface directly with HR applications and make changes or inquiries without involving HR staff members. Further, many HR organizations are using the Web to link their back-end systems with the systems of their insurance, payroll, and retirement service providers.

With the completion of the interfaces, some HR departments are adding collaborative capabilities that automate workflows, such as the approval of job requisitions or expense reports. As a result, HR staff members do not have to route forms around the company, and each process occurs much more swiftly.

Source: "Web-Powered HR," *InternetWeek* (March 12, 2001), pp. 1, 14.

Questions

1. What are some applications for other functional areas?

2. What are the implications of intranet applications for HR personnel? Could this cause a problem?

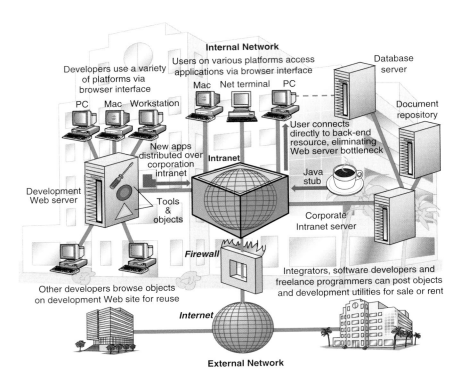

Figure 7.4 *The firewall between the intranet and its connection to the Internet.* [*Source:* Communications Week, *April 29, 1996.*]

certificate authority market with its database that checks whether a digital certificate it issued has expired. In addition, ValiCert is the only company that is able to check the validity of any other vendor's certificate.

The industries in which public key security is starting to gain momentum all have external forces driving adoption: financial securities, where regulations require encryption; legal, where the courts have said unencrypted e-mail is not covered by attorney-client privilege; and health care, where security of electronically transmitted medical records is paramount.

Another important way for companies to protect their intranets is with the use of firewalls. A **firewall** is a device located between a firm's internal network (e.g., its intranets) and external networks (e.g., the Internet). The firewall regulates access into and out of a company's network. Firewalls permit certain external services, such as Internet e-mail, to pass. Also, firewalls allow access to the Internet from internal networks. A firewall can allow access only from specific hosts and networks or prevent access from specific hosts. Firewalls can also allow different levels of access for different hosts. Figure 7.4 illustrates the position of the firewall between the intranet and the Internet.

For higher security, companies can implement assured pipelines. Whereas a firewall examines only the header information of a packet, an **assured pipeline** examines the entire request for data and then determines whether the request is valid.

Before you go on . . .

1. What are common types of corporate information and services available on intranets?

2. What security techniques are used with intranets?

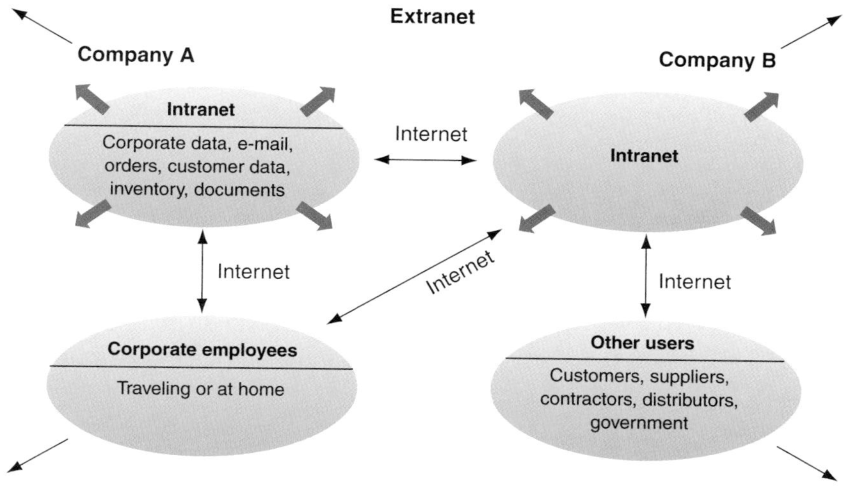

Figure 7.5   *The extranet framework.* [*Source: Toshiba America Information Services.*]

7.8   EXTRANETS

An **extranet** is a type of interorganizational information system. Extranets enable people who are located outside a company to work together with the company's internally located employees. Although extranets continue to evolve, they are generally understood to be networks that link business partners to one another over the Internet by providing access to certain areas of each other's corporate intranets. (An exception to this definition is an extranet that offers individual customers or suppliers one-way access to the intranet of a company, such as in the case of Dr. Pepper, described below.) The term *extranet* comes from "extended intranet." The main goal of extranets is to foster collaboration between business partners. An extranet is open to selected suppliers, customers, and other business partners, who access it through the Internet. It is closed to the general public.

The Components and Structure of Extranets

An extranet uses the same basic infrastructure components as the Internet, including servers, TCP/IP protocols, e-mail, and Web browsers. However, extranets use virtual private network (VPN) technology to make communication over the Internet more secure. Extranets allow the use of the capabilities of both the Internet and intranets, as shown in Figure 7.5. Using an extranet, external business partners and telecommuting employees can enter the corporate intranet via the Internet to access data, place orders, check status, and send e-mails. The Internet-based extranet is far less costly than proprietary networks. It is a nonproprietary technical tool that can support the rapid evolution of electronic communication and commerce.

Why would a company allow a business partner access to its intranet? To answer this question, let's look at Dr. Pepper in the following example.

EXAMPLE

Dr. Pepper notifies bottlers of price changes.   Dr. Pepper/Seven Up, the $1.5 billion division of Cadbury Schweppes, is using the Internet to improve efficiency for its diverse community of 1,400 independent and franchise bottlers. The Bottler Hub/ Extranet, which automates the distribution of pricing data, is made available to Dr.

Pepper's entire group of registered bottlers and retailers. The extranet has helped automate the process of communicating price changes to retailers.

Such automation was necessary for Dr. Pepper because the company depends on contract bottlers. Although the bottlers set the pricing, retailers such as Wal-Mart had complained about the bottlers' approach to faxing weekly price changes. Because many bottlers were mom-and-pop organizations and did not have the resources to modernize the process, Dr. Pepper decided to put in a centralized system that would make the information available online to retail outlets.

Dr. Pepper also uses its extranet for other purposes. The company collects case sales data online, enabling merchants to report how many cases of soda they sell. The data are used to measure sales growth and to analyze brands and packages that are sold by a bottler within a territory to the major retail chains. The information is used to help the national accounts department find opportunities to sell more Dr. Pepper/Seven Up brands within a particular account. ●

Manager's Checklist 7.1

Benefits of Extranets

Benefit	How Benefit Is Achieved
Fewer help-desk employees needed	Extranets automate inquiry systems; customers dial into databases to find information.
Improved quality	Computer-to-computer communication reduces errors in data entry.
Lower communications and travel costs	Using the Internet instead of VANs can save 50 percent or more on communications costs and can reduce travel and physical meeting costs.
Lower administrative and other overhead costs	Automation of order entry and other routine processes saves time and resulting costs.
Faster processes and information flow	By using extranets, information can flow across the supply chain rapidly, even when several tiers of suppliers are involved. Expedited processes can reduce design and production costs.
Reductions in paperwork and delivery of accurate information in a timely manner	Publishing information electronically for customers and business partners eliminates paper and assures that information is current.
Improved order entry and customer service	Many companies use extranets to simplify and improve the customer order entry process, as well as customer service and client relationships.
Better communications	Just-in-time information delivery and collaborative activities improve communications among business partners and/or customers.
Overall improvement in business effectiveness	Use of extranets enhances business opportunities, makes better use of legacy systems, promotes more effective marketing and sales, and makes available training on demand.

Types of Extranets

Depending on the business partners involved and the purpose, there are three major types of extranets.

A company and its dealers, customers, or suppliers.   Such an extranet is centered around one company. An example would be FedEx allowing its customers to track the status of a package on the Internet. To do so, customers enter a database on the FedEx intranet. When a customer checks the location of a package, FedEx saves the cost of having a human operator do that task over the phone.

An industry's extranet.   The major players in an industry may team up to create an extranet that will benefit all. The world's largest industry-based, collaborative extranet is used by General Motors, Ford, and DaimlerChrysler. The extranet, called the Automotive Network Exchange (ANX), links the carmakers with more than 10,000 suppliers. The suppliers can use the extranet to sell directly and efficiently to the carmakers, cutting communications costs by as much as 70 percent.

Joint ventures and other business partnerships.   In this type of extranet, several companies partner on a joint venture and use the extranet as a vehicle for communications and collaboration. An example would be the Bank of America extranet for commercial loans that connects many lenders, loan applicants, and the loan organizer, Bank of America. A similar case is Lending Tree (*lendingtree.com*), a company that provides mortgage quotes for your home. To obtain such a loan, you need a lender, loan broker, escrow company, title company, and others.

Benefits of Extranets

As extended versions of intranets, extranets offer benefits similar to those of intranets, as well as others. The major benefits of extranets are summarized in Manager's Checklist 7.1.

Before you go on . . .

1. Define an extranet and explain its infrastructure.

2. What is an industry-type extranet?

3. List four major benefits of an extranet.

7.9   ENTERPRISE INFORMATION PORTALS

Enterprise Information Portals (EIPs) are Web-based applications that enable companies to access internally and externally stored information, and provide users a single point of access to personalized information needed to make informed business decisions. EIPs integrate content management, business intelligence, data warehouse, data mart, and data management applications.

Content management systems capture, archive, index, manage, combine, and distribute internal and external information to create a corporate knowledge repository. *Business intelligence* software enables companies to access structured, transactional data and transform that data into business information. Business intelligence systems include software for query, reporting, online analytical processing (OLAP), data mining, and other analytical applications (see Chapter 12). *Data management systems, data warehouses*, and *data marts* and the relationships among them are discussed in Chapter 5. The following example illustrates the implementation of an EIP at 3M.

EXAMPLE

3M's data warehouse and enterprise information portal.   3M (*3m.com*) has constructed a huge global enterprise data warehouse—reaching everyone in the organization as well as channel partners and customers worldwide. Driven by a need to better understand markets and customers, 3M embarked on a mission to present one face to everyone in contact with the company.

3M, a $15 billion manufacturer, supplies products to virtually every industry, including office supplies, health care, automotive, telecommunications, electronics, and safety. With more than 50,000 products, packaged in various sizes, in all languages, total products exceed 500,000.

Previously, 50 disparate business units and 60 international subsidiaries independently tracked their customers, products, and sales without common standards. Each had independent data marts, with little cross-business unit visibility of information. Customers and suppliers dealt with each unit as if it were a separate company. 3M could not get one view of a customer to understand its global purchases across business units.

3M executives mandated a strategy to understand each customer and channel partner's business and buying habits. This strategy was the catalyst for an enterprise shift—centralizing information in a global enterprise data warehouse (GEDW), accessed by an enterprise information portal. Employees, customers, distributors, and suppliers now access one centralized source of information via the Internet and intranet.

The EIP is changing the way 3M interacts with customers, develops relationships with channel partners, and approaches enterprise strategies. Consolidating disparate business intelligence systems is yielding a multimillion-dollar return on investment by reducing IT infrastructure costs, eliminating redundant application development, and enhancing the quality and timeliness of decisions while dramatically increasing productivity. ●

Before you go on . . .

1. What is an enterprise information portal?
2. What four major applications are consolidated in enterprise information portals?
3. What are the major characteristics of enterprise information portals?

7.10   THE MOBILE INTERNET

The **mobile Internet** refers to the use of wireless communications technologies to access network-based information and applications from mobile devices. The mobile Internet is also called the **wireless Web**.

Mobile Internet applications have several interesting applications. Users can access the mobile Internet anywhere, and the mobile Internet device can know it is somewhere in particular and use that knowledge to perform services that take advantage of spatial or geographic information. These applications are called *location-based services*. The mobile Internet also provides services that are based on the type of location the mobile Internet device is in and allow the user to act in ways that make sense only in that location. These applications are called *presence-based services*. Both types of services are examples of *location-based commerce* (*l-commerce*). The following example demonstrates these applications.

EXAMPLE

How you will use the mobile Internet.   You are ready to leave for the airport. An application on your Internet-enabled smart telephone queries the airline's operations system to see if your flight is on time. Your phone tells you your plane is on time, what gate to go to, checks you in, and reminds you what seat you have. When you arrive at the airport, barcodes on your luggage identify you, and additional barcodes are added to each bag to identify the flight and destination.

You are early, so you use your phone to check your office e-mail and voice mail. Next, you use your phone to query your home network to be sure that you have turned down your heating, turned off all your appliances, and locked all your doors.

You decide to shop while you wait. As you stroll through the airport's shopping center, merchants beam specials and electronic coupons to your phone. You decide to buy a book and when you check out, your phone interacts with the bookstore computer to make the purchase and debit your credit card.

After a few minutes, your phone notifies you that your flight is delayed. It seems that you will miss your connecting flight, so your phone queries the airline operations system and books you on the next connecting flight. An application on the phone notifies your rental-car company and hotel of your new arrival time. ●

Before you go on . . .

1. What is the mobile Internet?

2. What is l-commerce?

WHAT'S IN IT FOR ME?

www.wiley.com/
college/turban

FOR THE ACCOUNTING MAJOR   ACC
Accounting personnel use corporate intranets to consolidate transaction data from legacy systems to provide an overall view of internal projects. This view contains the current costs charged to each project, the number of hours spent on each project by individual employees, and how actual costs compare to projected costs. Internet access to government and professional Web sites keeps accounting personnel informed on legal and other changes affecting their profession.

FOR THE FINANCE MAJOR   FIN
Corporate intranets can provide a risk-evaluation model so that financial analysts can evaluate the risk of a project or an investment. The analysts use two types of data in the model: historical transaction data from corporate databases via the intranet and industry data obtained via the Internet. The Web can also be a marketing and service provision channel for financial services firms.

FOR THE MARKETING MAJOR

Marketing managers use corporate intranets to coordinate the activities of the sales force. Sales personnel access the intranet for updates on pricing, promotion, rebates, customer information, or for information about competitors. Sales staff can also download presentations and customize them for their customers. The Internet, particularly the WWW, opens a completely new marketing channel for many industries. Just how advertising, purchasing, and information dispensation should occur appears to vary from industry to industry, product to product, service to service. Innovation is constant, so competitive marketers must invest the time to learn and stay abreast of development.

FOR THE PRODUCTION/OPERATIONS MANAGEMENT MAJOR

Companies are using intranets to speed product development, by providing three-dimensional models and animation for the development team. All team members can access the models for faster exploration of ideas and enhanced feedback. Intranets provide for close management of inventories and management of real-time production on assembly lines. Extranets are also proving valuable as communication formats for joint research and design efforts among companies. The Internet is also a great source of cutting-edge information for POM pros.

 FOR THE HUMAN RESOURCES MANAGEMENT MAJOR

Human resources personnel use intranets to publish corporate policy manuals, job postings, company telephone directories, and training classes. Many companies deliver online training obtained from the Internet to employees through their intranets. Via intranets, human resources departments offer employees health care, savings, and benefit plans, as well as the opportunity to take competency tests online. The Internet supports worldwide recruiting efforts, and it can be the communications platform for supporting geographically dispersed work teams.

SUMMARY

❶ Describe what the Internet is, how it works (including the role of the TCP/IP protocol), and how users connect to it.

The Internet is a network of networks, which exchange information seamlessly by using open, nonproprietary standards and protocols. It is a collection of more than one million individual computer networks owned by governments, universities, nonprofit groups, and companies. The Internet is a packet-switched network that uses the Transmission Control Protocol/Internet Protocol (TCP/IP). Users can connect to the Internet via a LAN server, via SLIP/PPP, or through an online service (an Internet service provider).

❷ Describe the capabilities that the Internet offers to users.

The Internet provides three major types of services: communications, information retrieval, Web services, and the World Wide Web. Communications services include electronic mail, USENET newsgroups, LISTSERVs, chatting, Telnet, Internet telephony, and Internet fax. Information retrieval services include gophers, Archie, WAIS, File Transfer Protocol (FTP), and Veronica. Web services are software applications delivered as services over the Internet.

❸ Describe the World Wide Web and differentiate it from the Internet.

The Web is a system with universally accepted standards for storing, retrieving, formatting, and displaying information via a client/server architecture. The Web handles all types of digital information, including text, hypermedia, graphics, and sound, and is very easy to use because it uses graphical user interfaces. The Web is not synonymous with the Internet. The Internet functions as the transport mechanism, and the Web is an application that uses those transport functions. Other applications also run on the Internet, with e-mail being the most widely used.

❹ Identify and describe the tools that allow users to view and search the Web.
Users primarily access the Web through software applications called browsers. Offline browsers (or pull methods) enable a user to retrieve pages automatically from Web sites at predetermined times, often during the night. Search engines are programs that return a list of Web sites or pages (designated by URLs) that match some user-selected criteria. Metasearch engines automatically enter search queries into a number of other search engines and return the results.

❺ Identify and briefly describe the management challenges caused by the Internet.
Internet challenges include security and all aspects of electronic commerce, the rapid evolution of new technologies, Internet regulation and expansion, and concerns about privacy. New technologies are being developed faster than they can be employed over the Internet. The Internet is not regulated by any one government or agency. The Internet Engineering Task Force and the World Wide Web Consortium have been instrumental in the development of the Internet, but are not formally charged in any legal or operational sense with responsibility for the Internet. They do, however, define the standards that govern the Internet's functionality. Recent government attempts to regulate the content of Internet-connected computers have generated concerns about privacy, security, and the legal liability of service providers. The massive growth of Internet traffic has strained some elements of the network, manifested by slowdowns in retrieval time, unreliable transmission of streamed data, and denial of service by overloaded servers. Cookie technology and Web-site registration have caused privacy concerns.

❻ Define the term *intranet* and discuss how intranets are used by businesses.
An intranet is a private network that uses Internet software and TCP/IP protocols. In essence, an intranet is a private Internet, or group of private segments of the public Internet network, reserved for use by people who have been given the authority to use that network. Companies are putting numerous applications on their intranets, including policies and procedures, document sharing, corporate telephone directories, human resources forms, training programs, search engines, customer databases, product catalogs and manuals, groupware, customer records, document routing, and data warehouse and decision support access.

❼ Define the term *extranet* and discuss how extranets are used by businesses.
An extranet is a network that links business partners to each other over the Internet by providing access to certain areas of one another's corporate intranets. An extranet is open to selected suppliers, customers, and other business partners, who access it through the Internet. Using an extranet, external business partners and telecommuting employees can enter the corporate intranet via the Internet to access data, place orders, check status, and send e-mails. The Internet-based extranet is far less costly than proprietary networks.

❽ Define the term *enterprise information portal* and discuss how these portals are used by businesses.
EIPs are Web-based applications that enable companies to unlock internally and externally stored information, and provide users a single gateway to personalized information needed to make informed business decisions. EIPs consolidate content management, business intelligence, data warehouse, data mart, and data management applications.

❾ **Define the term *mobile Internet* and discuss mobile Internet applications.**
The mobile Internet refers to the use of wireless communications technologies to access network-based information and applications from mobile devices. Mobile Internet applications include location-based services and presence-based services. Mobile Internet devices know they are somewhere in particular and use that knowledge to perform services that take advantage of geographic information. These applications are called *location-based services*. Mobile Internet devices also know the type of location they are in and allow the user to act in ways that make sense only in that location. These applications are called *presence-based services*.

INTERACTIVE LEARNING

www.wiley.com/
college/turban

Go to the CD and access Chapter 7: The Internet, Intranets, and Extranets. There you will find a video clip from the "Nightly Business Report" which presents a business problem involving the topics covered in this chapter. You will be asked to watch the video and answer questions about it.

For additional resources, go to the book's Web site for Chapter 7. There you will find Web resources for the chapter, including links to organizations, people, and technology; "IT's About Business" company links; "What's in IT for Me?" links; and a self-testing Web quiz for Chapter 7.

DISCUSSION QUESTIONS

1. Discuss the implications of the "democratization of information."
2. Should the Internet be regulated? If so, by whom?
3. Does the use of cookie technology violate the user's right to privacy?
4. Does the use of information filters violate the principle of free speech?
5. Would it be possible to deliver this book over the Internet? Do you think it would be a good idea? Support your answers.

PROBLEM-SOLVING ACTIVITIES

1. Design an e-mail policy for your college or university.
2. Evaluate your school's Web site and make suggestions for improvement.
3. Obtain permission to visit several corporate intranets. Report the types of information and services available.

INTERNET ACTIVITIES

1. Construct your own home page. You might use Netscape's Composer, for example.
2. Access The Free Site (*thefreesite.com*) and examine the free software available there. Pay particular attention to free software that can be used in constructing your home page. Use some of the available software and applets in your home page. Present your home page to the class.
3. Access the White House Web site (*whitehouse.gov*). Prepare a report on the most interesting content you find there.
4. Using a search engine, examine three Internet sites that sell cars. Pick a particular car that you would like to buy, and compare prices, features, options, etc. across the three sites. Are there differences? What are they? How do you account for any differences?
5. Examine several Web sites for auctions. Analyze the similarities and differences among the auction sites. Rank them according to ease of use.

TEAM ACTIVITIES AND ROLE PLAYING

1. The following list provides the URLs of 9 leading Internet securities (stocks and bonds) brokers. Divide the list among the members of your group. Examine each site and rate its ease of use. Determine the costs of executing various trades (e.g., small, medium, and large). Rank all 9 sites as to ease of use and costs. Are the lists identical?

   ameritrade.com   schwab.com
   discoverbrokerage.com   dljdirect.com
   etrade.com   netinvestor.com
   webstreetsecurities.com   suretrade.com
   waterhouse.com

2. Find two companies on the Web that are in the same business. For example, Amazon (*amazon.com*) and Barnes and Noble (*barnesandnoble.com*) or Dell (*dell.com*) and Gateway (*gateway.com*). Compare the Web sites of the pairs you have chosen on the basis of ease-of-use and usefulness. Pick the better Web site in each pair and explain your choice.

REAL-WORLD CASE

Web Monitoring of Pipelines

The Business Problem   Before natural gas could leak from a pipeline in South America, a warning would sound in Dayton, Ohio. Seconds after detecting where a possible leak may occur, technicians at the office of TransWave International (*transwave.com*) in Dayton would be on the phone with Buenos Aires, warning clients of the danger.

Pipeline safety is becoming a big issue in the United States, as soaring energy prices spur deployment of more natural gas lines near population centers. A rising number of domestic pipeline failures have occurred over the last few years. The government has initiated reforms, which include the use of mechanical devices that physically tour the interior of a pipe looking for corrosion or other problems. The government is also focusing on Internet technologies.

All modern pipelines, whether they are gas, oil, water, or hazardous liquids, are shielded with low doses of electricity. This electric blanket normally prevents pipes from corroding. But natural and man-made elements near pipelines—including overhead electrical transmission lines—siphon off the electricity in spots. In those places where the current "hops," pipes of all materials will begin to deteriorate. Therefore, companies maintaining pipelines have to monitor them, an expensive and time-consuming process.

The IT Solution   Using patented electronic sensors and the Web, TransWave has deployed its "intelligent pipeline" technology in buried pipes across the world. Using TransWave's technique, technicians fasten a device to a pipe's signal generator or rectifier, which emits the electric current, and then return to their headquarters. The rectifiers are linked to the Web by standard phone lines or, in remote locations, by a wireless connection. Real-time electrical data are fed back to a pipeline client as well as TransWave's headquarters, where technicians monitor for anomalies. The system can also detect "third-party" incidents, such as when city crews pierce a water main with a backhoe.

The Results   A corrosion specialist from Enron said that the company had to lower a 24-inch pipeline because the channel in Galveston Bay was being widened and the dredges were coming very close to the pipeline. Enron deployed TransWave's monitoring system in that pipeline as well as where its other pipelines run through populated and other high-risk areas. Similarly, Montgomery County in Ohio is using TransWave's technology in hopes of stemming the 450 or so water main breaks a year to its system serving the Dayton area, where annual repair bills can top $2 million—ranking it among one of the most leak-prone systems in Ohio. All TransWave monitoring devices have their own IP addresses. Therefore, TransWave personnel can even be on an airplane, plug into the phone in the seat backs, and dial up any of the pipelines.

Source: "Pipe Down," *business2.com* (May 29, 2001), pp. 38–39.

Questions

1. What are the advantages of Web monitoring of various types of pipeline?

2. What are other business applications for Web monitoring?

VIRTUAL COMPANY ASSIGNMENT

wiley.com/college/turban

Extreme Descent Snowboards

www.wiley.com/
college/turban

Background   Jacob March has been waiting for you. As you enter his office, you find two others already seated at the small conference table. Jacob introduces you to Gary Rodreiguez, Director of Marketing, and Jennifer Appletree, Director of Development. Jacob explains that both Gary and Jennifer are concerned that the marketing and development departments have no presence on the company intranet. Each department has done some research about intranets. At this time, heavy work schedules do not permit them to pursue this project.

Jacob then suggests that this would be a good assignment for you. Jennifer explains that she has done some research, and she hands you a folder. This folder contains some notes about her research, including Web page references and copies of articles from the Web relating to company intranets.

Assignment

Prepare a report addressing the following points:

1. First, choose a current intranet application at EDS. What is its business value to the EDS?

2. The following excerpt is from Jennifer's research for intranets.

   Case study of how Ford Motor Co. implemented its elaborate intranet: *http://www.cio.com/archive/ webbusiness/060197_ford.html*

Visit the Web site. After you have read the article, prepare a report answering the following questions.

a. What kinds of information need to be included in the Marketing Department's intranet site?

b. What kinds of information need to be included in the Development Department's intranet site?

c. What specific applications could best benefit EDS? Support your answers.

FUNCTIONAL, ENTERPRISE, AND INTERORGANIZATIONAL SYSTEMS

8

CHAPTER PREVIEW

In previous chapters we introduced many information technologies to show the benefits they provide to the modern organization. In this chapter we show how separate technologies are woven into systems common in today's organizations. First we introduce the most common and basic type of system, known as the *transaction processing system (TPS)*. Such systems deal with the repetitive core business processes of organizations, such as order fulfillment and payroll. The objectives of TPSs are to increase the efficiency and effectiveness of the core business processes, to reduce corporate cost, and to increase customer service. We also discuss a common system that draws from the TPS, the management information system (MIS). We then detail how TPSs are used in all functional areas. These applications can increase productivity, reduce costs, enhance customer relations, and in general, increase the efficiency and knowledge of managers in all parts of the organization. Next, we look at how the various TPSs can be integrated throughout the entire organization, in enterprise integrated systems. These systems are structured around the concepts of supply chain management (SCM) and enterprise resource planning (ERP), which provide for the optimal use of functional and integrated business processes. We end with a discussion of interorganizational systems that serve as strategic linkages between national and global business partners.

CHAPTER OUTLINE

LEARNING OBJECTIVES

1. Describe the roles of functional information systems.
2. State the objectives and operations of transaction processing and how it is supported by IT.
3. Discuss the managerial and strategic applications in the accounting and finance areas that are supported by IT.
4. Discuss marketing and sales applications provided by IT.
5. Describe how production and operations management activities are supported by IT.
6. Discuss the human resources management activities and how they can be improved by IT.
7. Discuss the need for integrating functional information systems and the role of ERP.
8. Discuss interorganizational/global information systems and their strategic importance.

235

IT TAKES SMALL BUSINESS FROM LOSS TO PROFIT WHEN ARTFULLY APPLIED

artstores.com

The Business Problem

When George Granoff bought The Art Store in 1995, the company was losing money. He had no background selling art supplies. What Granoff did have, however, was 30 years of experience managing huge retail chains. Granoff combined his knack for merchandising and customer service with information technology to manage inventory and create an efficient supply chain.

The IT Solution

Granoff worked hard to create a better shopping experience for his customers. He widened the aisles in the stores and reorganized the merchandise to make things easier to find. But the most important changes Granoff made were behind the scenes. He immediately upgraded the company's computer systems and installed retail-specific software from IBM's business partner JDA Software Group to integrate front-end point-of-sale transactions with a back-end inventory system. Granoff also worked diligently with his suppliers to get them to begin barcoding their merchandise.

Now, The Art Store keeps 26,000 product SKUs in stock with virtually no stock rooms or warehouse space. The entire inventory-control process is automated. Purchases are scanned at the checkout with an IBM/JDA POS system. Each night, the company's server polls the stores to capture sales data and to update inventory records. A JDA decision-making application is run periodically to determine when orders need to be placed with various suppliers, taking into account such factors as anticipated sales trends and the criteria to qualify for free freight. Orders are then placed at the optimum time, and products are shipped directly to the stores.

The Results

The technology investments and hard work have paid off. The business, which started out with four stores, is now thriving with twelve brick-and-mortar locations, and Granoff expects the company will just keep growing. "I can't imagine trying to keep 26,000 items in stock without this technology," Granoff says. Obviously the customers

IT enables The Art Store to efficiently track all its products.

love the new stores. They may not know how the technology is working, but they know The Art Store will have the products they need on hand whenever they visit. "We have one of the best in-stock conditions in the industry, and we do it with minimal dollar investment in inventory," says Granoff. "It's good news for us because we're managing our costs. But it's also good news for our customers because they know their trip won't be wasted."

Source: www1.ibm.com/businesscenter/us/smbusapub.nsf.

What We Learned from This Case

The Art Store case makes some interesting points about implementing information technology. First it shows that many sectors of business (in this case, retail art supply stores) are not characterized by state-of-the-art information technology. Second, those like George Granoff who can perceive this as an opportunity can greatly increase profitability and market share by instituting modern information systems. Third, the case shows that information technology extends beyond the store itself to support transactions such as inventory control and resupply. In this case, the suppliers to The Art Store were required to implement modern barcode inventory control approaches so that Granoff could more efficiently keep track of his stock. This means accurate and instant monitoring of any store's inventory, as well as facilitating rapid purchasing and resupply. And the system integrates and supports numerous business activities, for example, crossing over from inventory and logistics into marketing, enabling marketing managers to track the sales trends of each SKU, each store, at every hour of the day. Finally, the case illustrates that IT can be beneficial to a relatively small company.

8.1 INFORMATION SYSTEMS TO SUPPORT BUSINESS FUNCTIONS

The inventory, sales, logistics, and marketing *functional areas* at The Art Store are all served by the information system described above. Traditionally, functional information systems were independent from each other; they were designed to support the specific IS needs of each functional area. However, independent functional systems are usually ineffective. One remedy is an *integrated approach*, like the one used at The Art Store. To remain competitive, businesses must redesign or drastically improve operations in the individual functional areas, increasing productivity, quality, speed, and customer service, as we will see in this chapter. Before we consider integrated information systems, we will spend some time looking at more traditional functional systems.

Characteristics of Functional Information Systems

Functional information systems share the following characteristics:

1. A functional information system consists of several smaller information systems (subsystems) that support specific activities. For example, computerized truck scheduling and inventory controls support the logistics system at some companies.

2. Although some specific IS applications in any functional area can be completely independent, they often are integrated to form a coherent departmental functional

system. Alternatively, some of the applications within each module can be integrated across departmental lines to match a business process.

3. Functional information systems interface with each other to form the organization-wide information system. A specific functional information system may be used as the core of this enterprisewide system.

4. Some functional information systems interface with the environment. For example, a human resources information system can collect and transmit information to federal agencies about compliance with safety and equal-opportunity regulations and guidelines. Similarly, a manufacturing information system may be connected to the suppliers' logistics information system.

Functional Systems for Managers: Management Information Systems

Functional information systems support various types of employees, ranging from professionals to managers. Systems that support managers in the various functional areas are known as **management information systems (MISs)**. The information is provided in routine reports such as daily sales, monthly expenditures, or weekly payroll. (The term *MIS* is occasionally used as a blanket concept for all information systems combined—the same as IT by our definition. Historically, there were MIS departments in business organizations and in colleges. Today, the broad concept is referred to as IS or IT, and MIS is reserved for the specific use described above.)

The role of the MIS.   The major role of the MIS is to provide information *to managers* in the functional areas. In order to understand this role we can track the information flow as shown in Figure 8.1. Information about each and every business transaction (everything from purchase of raw materials, to hiring of employees, to paying of bills, to sale of merchandise, and much more) comes into the MIS, mainly from the various transaction processing system databases (described below). Other internal and external databases may supply additional data needed to create management reports. Each MIS generates reports in its functional area. These reports are used for applications in the specific area and in other functional areas. Notice that the MIS sends information to the corporate data warehouse and can use information from it. Notice also that functional applications include decision support systems (DSS), as will be demonstrated in Sections 8.3 through 8.6. An MIS produces routine reports, ad-hoc (on-demand) reports, and exception reports.

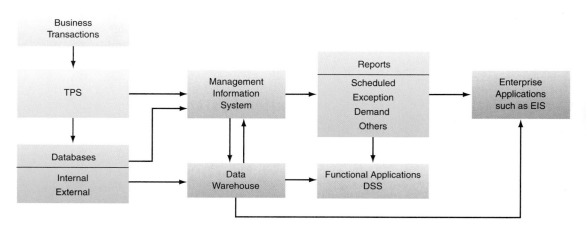

Figure 8.1   *Information flow to and from management information systems.*

Routine, scheduled reports.   Routine periodic reports are produced at scheduled intervals, ranging from hourly quality control reports to reports on monthly absenteeism rates.

Ad-hoc (demand) reports.   Managers frequently need special information, which is not included in the routine reports, or they need the same information that is included in the routine reports, but at different times ("I need the report today; I cannot wait until Friday."). Such out-of-the routine reports are called **ad-hoc (demand) reports**. They also may include requests for **drill-down reports**, which show a greater level of detail; **key-indicator reports**, which summarize the performance of critical activities; and **comparative reports**, which compare, for example, performances of different departments.

Exception reports.   Some managers favor **management by exception**. To implement such a system, management first sets standards (such as the budget). Then systems are set up to monitor performance (via the incoming data about business transactions), compare actual performance to the standards, and identify the exceptions. Management is alerted to the exceptions via **exception reports**. The exceptions themselves then need to be managed. Exception reports include only information that exceeds certain threshold standards—for example, reports on expense items that are larger than 5 percent of the budget, or sales that fall 3 percent or more short of the quota. Reporting exceptions saves managers time (since they need not read the long, complete reports) and helps them concentrate on the essentials.

Before you go on . . .

1. What is a functional information system? List its major characteristics.

2. Define a management information system (MIS) and describe its role in an organization.

3. How does the MIS system support management by exception?

8.2   TRANSACTION PROCESSING INFORMATION SYSTEMS

Tracking Business Transactions

In every organization there are major business processes that provide the mission-critical activities. *Business transactions* occur when a company produces a product or provides a service. For example, to produce toys, a manufacturer buys materials and parts, pays for labor and electricity, builds the toys, ships them to retailers (the customers in this case), bills customers, and collects money. A bank that maintains the company checking account must keep the account balance up-to-date, disperse funds to back up the checks written, accept deposits, and mail a monthly statement.

Every transaction may generate additional transactions. For example, purchasing materials will change the inventory level, and paying an employee reduces the corporate cash on hand. Because the mathematical manipulations of most transactions are simple and the volume is large and repetitive, such business transactions are fairly easy to computerize. The computerized information system that supports these

Table 8.1   The Major Characteristics of a TPS

- *Processes large amounts of data.*
- *Needs high processing speed* due to the high volume.
- *Sources of data* are mostly internal, and the output is intended mainly for an internal audience. However, trading partners may contribute data and be permitted to use TPS output directly.
- *Processes information on a regular basis:* daily, weekly, biweekly, or per transaction.
- Requires large *storage* (database) *capacity.*
- *Monitors and collects data* once generated.
- *Input and output data are structured* and are formatted in a standard fashion.
- High *level of detail,* especially in input data but often in output data as well.
- Low *computation complexity* (simple mathematical and statistical operations).
- Needs high level of *accuracy, data integrity,* and *security* (including privacy of personal data).
- Requires high *processing reliability.* Interruptions in the flow of TPS data can be fatal to the organization.
- *Ability to query* files and databases (even online and in real time) is a must.

transaction processes is called the **transaction processing system (TPS)**. The primary objective of TPSs is to collect and provide all the data needed by law and/or by organizational policies to keep the business running properly and efficiently. The major characteristics of TPS transaction processing systems are listed in Table 8.1.

A typical transaction is shown in Figure 8.2. A customer makes a purchase at a retail store. The purchase, which is recorded at the POS terminal, is then recorded in a transaction file. Inventory, sales, and payment processing (accounts payable) files then change as a result of the transaction.

Historically, TPS applications were the earliest computerized business systems, as they automated repetitive, highly structured tasks, and could produce tangible benefits. TPSs were first common in the accounting and finance functions, but are now popular for inventory, sales, personnel, and production activities as well. The transaction processing system is the backbone of an organization's information systems. It monitors, collects, stores, processes, and disseminates data for all routine core business transactions. An organization may have one integrated TPS or several, one for each specific business process. In the latter case, the systems should interface with each other.

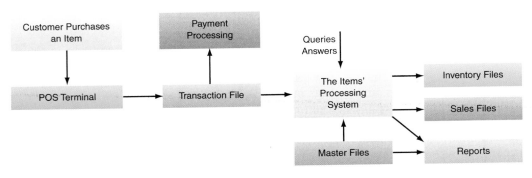

Figure 8.2   *Overview of typical transaction processing.*

The Process of TPS

Regardless of the specific data processed by a TPS, a fairly standard process occurs, whether in a manufacturer, in a service firm, or in a government organization. First, data are collected by people or sensors and entered into the computer via an *input device*. Generally speaking, organizations try to automate the TPS data entry as much as possible because of the large volume involved and to reduce errors.

Next, the system processes data in one of two basic ways: *batch* or *online processing*. In **batch processing**, the firm collects transactions as they occur, placing them in groups or batches. The system then prepares and processes the batches periodically (say, every night). In **online processing**, data are processed *as soon as* a transaction occurs. For example, when an item such as a toy is sold in a toy store, the POS terminal immediately notifies the inventory system, which triggers a change in the inventory level. The sale of the toy causes other files to be updated in real time (for example, cash on hand or a departmental sales file).

Alternatively, a *hybrid system* (a combination of batch and online processing) can collect data as they occur but process them at specified intervals. For example, sales at POS terminals are entered into the computer as they occur, but they may be processed only at a certain time (say, evenings). However, the information in the TPS database can be queried by users, downloaded, and used for routine reports; it is also used for decision support and other applications.

Modernized TPS: From Online Processing to Intranets

Client/server systems. Transaction processing systems may be fairly complex, involving customers, vendors, telecommunications, and different types of hardware and software. Traditional TPSs are centralized and run on mainframe computers usually optimized for batch processing. However, innovations such as **online transaction processing (OLTP)** created on a client/server architecture can save money by allowing suppliers to enter the TPS via an extranet and look at the firm's inventory level or production schedule. Suppliers can then assume responsibility for inventory management and ordering. This and other innovations improve TPS processing and utility, as illustrated in IT's About Business 8.1.

IT's About Business   *tommyb2b.com*

Box 8.1:   Tommy Hilfiger uses fashionable technology

Tommy Hilfiger is developing a new e-business infrastructure as the company works to expand its presence among U.S. specialty retailers, as well as its worldwide manufacturing facilities. The company created a new B2B portal that allows its specialty store retailers to view selected core and seasonal apparel products in real-time and to place, track, and ship orders. The infrastructure also supports a virtual employee store.

The Web infrastructure includes servers running Linux to handle Web-based transactions, integrated online with servers running Java that are tied to existing wholesale and warehouse management systems. The system also supports a business-to-plant Web site that links Hilfiger's production facilities around the world, which is expected to speed design-to-product time.

The manufacturing portal and employee store are producing substantial cost savings, and *tommyb2b.com* has already proved productive and efficient for retailers with limited travel budgets.

(*Source: www.tommyb2b.com.*)

Question

1. What are the advantages of Hilfiger's new e-business infrastructure for its employees? For its manufacturing plants?

Internet (intranet) transaction processing.   Rather than isolated exchanges of simple text and data over private networks, such as traditional EDI and electronic funds transfer (EFT), transaction processing is increasingly conducted over the Internet and intranets. As a result, OLTP has broadened to become interactive *Internet transaction processing.* Internet transaction processing software and servers allow multimedia data transfer, fast response time, and storage of large databases of graphics and videos—all in real time and at low cost. The Benefits of Internet Transaction Processing are listed in Manager's Checklist W8.1 at the book's Web site.

www.wiley.com/
college/turban

Typical TPS Tasks and Modules

Transaction processing includes many tasks. For example, a software application for accounting/finance areas might include standard modules for accounts receivable, accounts payable, payroll, bank reconciliation, purchase order processing, inventory management, and sales order processing. Communication and inquiry modules would support the accounting modules. The user can integrate as many of the modules as needed for the business. Other business processes that usually interface with accounting applications, and that could also be integrated as needed, include bills of materials, work order processing, job costing, point of sale, timekeeping, and billing.

The transaction processing system also provides a complete, reliable audit trail of all transactions transmitted through the network, which is vital to accountants and auditors. The data collected and managed for TPSs are input for the various functional information systems.

The major modules of a TPS are order processing, the general ledger, accounts payable and receivable, inventory management, payroll, and periodic reports. Each of these is described briefly below.

Order processing.   Orders for goods and/or services may flow to a company electronically, by phone, or on paper. Salespeople in many companies enter orders from the client's site using portable, even wireless, computers. Orders can also be internal— from one department to another. A computerized system receives, summarizes, and stores the orders.

Fast and effective order processing is recognized as a key to customer satisfaction. Using object-oriented software, for example, Sprint Inc. reduced the waiting time for hookup of commercial telephone lines from days to hours, using electronic order processing executed from the salesperson's laptop computer. In some cases, orders to warehouses and/or manufacturing are issued automatically. A traditional EDI or intranet-based EDI system can be especially useful in cases involving business partners. A computerized system can track sales by product, by zone, or by salesperson, for example, and make this information available to an executive information system. Order processing can be reengineered with innovations such as a GPS, as shown in IT's About Business 8.2.

The ledger.   A *general ledger*, a collection of all accounts in a company, contains all the assets, liabilities, and owners' equity accounts. Maintaining the general ledger requires a large number of simple transactions and is an ideal application area for computers. Use of a general ledger simplifies a company's bookkeeping procedures and makes all of the data recorded in the ledger available for various accounting uses and reports.

Accounts payable and receivable.   *Accounts payable* and *accounts receivable* record the credit, debit, and balance of each customer or vendor, generated from sales journals or purchase orders. They are updated periodically. Analysis of accounts receivable can help identify a customer's credit rating and compute the risk of an account

IT's About Business

Box 8.2:   Taxis in Singapore are dispatched by computer

Taxis in Singapore are tracked by a global positioning system (GPS) of 24 satellites originally set up by the U.S. government for military purposes. The GPS allows its users to get an instant fix on a geographical position and dispatch nearby taxis.

Customer orders for a taxi are usually received via telephone, Internet, or fax. Frequent travelers enter orders from their offices or homes by keying in a PIN number in the telephone, which automatically identifies them and their pickup point. Customers can also call for taxis from special kiosks located in shopping centers and hotels. The computerized ordering system is connected to the GPS. Once an order has been received, the GPS finds a vacant cab nearest to the caller, and a display panel in the taxi alerts the driver to the pickup address. The driver has five seconds to push a button to accept the order. If he does not, the system automatically searches out the next-nearest taxi for the job.

The system completely reengineered customer order processing. First, the transaction time for processing an order for a frequent user is much shorter, even during peak demand, since there is no need for a human operator. Second, taxi drivers are not able to pick and choose which trips they want to take, since the system will not provide the commuter's destination. This reduces the customer's average waiting time significantly, while minimizing the travel distance of empty taxis. Third, the system increases by 1,000 percent the capacity for taking incoming calls, providing a competitive edge to the cab companies that use the system. Finally, frequent customers who use the system do not have to wait a long time just to get an operator (a situation that exists during rush hours, rain, or any other time of high demand for taxis), since they are automatically identified.

Source: atip.or.jp/public/atip.reports.96/atip96.olb.html

Questions

1. What kinds of priorities can be offered to frequent customers?

2. What transactions do computers support in this system?

3. What benefits are provided to the taxi company from treating frequent travelers differently?

---

not being paid. It is also important for making decisions about when to send a reminder notice for payments, transfer the account to a collection agency, or declare a debt as a loss. Analysis of accounts payable enables a company to pay its bills on time, take any discounts offered for early payment, and maintain a good credit history.

Inventory management, receiving, and shipping of goods.   Whenever goods are received or shipped, transactions such as billing or inventory level changes are created. When items are received, a confirmation is generated to accounts payable so payments can be made and inventories updated.

In the past, companies had to count, weigh, or measure each kind of inventory on hand and record the results. Today, information technology can be used to automate and expedite these processes. For example, barcodes on packages and computerized voice technology are common computerized inventory-counting tools and are also used to track materials through all receiving and shipping processes. These technologies are often linked between purchasers and suppliers as well as with shippers to provide information on material status from origin to final destination.

Payroll.   Preparing the periodic payroll is a routine job that involves computing gross salary during a given period and determining appropriate deductions and reductions (taxes, insurance, contributions). Payroll programs calculate the net pay, and print checks or electronically transfer funds to the employee's bank.

Periodic reports and statements.   Many periodic reports and statements are generated from the TPS data. These include required external reports to the Securities and

Exchange Commission (such as K-10s), the Internal Revenue Service (IRS), and other state and federal agencies, some of which are submitted electronically. Many internal periodic reports are also produced daily, weekly, monthly, and annually. Financial statements, payroll summaries, productivity summaries, and sales figures are just a few examples.

In the next four sections of this chapter we will look at specific applications commonly used in the four main business function areas—accounting and finance, marketing and sales, production operations management, and human resources management. First, we consider accounting and finance systems because they are central to all business processes and also because they were typically the first systems computerized. Some repetitive accounting/financing activities such as payroll, billing, and inventory were computerized as early as the 1950s.

Before you go on . . .

1. Define transaction processing and list its major characteristics.

2. What are the objectives of a TPS?

3. List typical TPS tasks and explain how they are supported by IT.

4. Why were TPSs the earliest computerized business applications?

8.3 ACCOUNTING AND FINANCE SYSTEMS

The accounting and finance areas in industry are frequently organized in one department due to overlapping tasks. A primary mission of the accounting/finance functional area is to manage money flow into, within, and out of organizations. The general structure of an accounting/finance system is presented in Figure 8.3. It is divided into three levels: operational, tactical, and strategic. Information technology can support all the activities listed, as well as the communication and collaboration of accounting and finance functions with internal and external environments. Some of the key operational activities were described in Section 8.2. Here we describe selected managerial and strategic applications.

Financial Planning and Budgeting

Managers must plan for both the acquisition of financial resources and their use. Financial planning, like any other functional planning, is tied to the overall organizational planning and to other functional areas. It is divided into short-, medium-, and long-term horizons. The most well-known part is the *annual budget* that allocates the financial resources of an organization among participants and activities for the year. IT support for several related activities serves as inputs or adjuncts to budgeting.

Economic and financial forecasting.   Forecasting is a difficult task since many interrelated financial and economic indicators need to be considered. Background information about the economy, competition, government regulations, labor movements, international exchange rates, and so on are essential ingredients of a good forecast. Much of the background information is available on the Internet. Many software packages are available for conducting business, economic, and financial forecasting and planning.

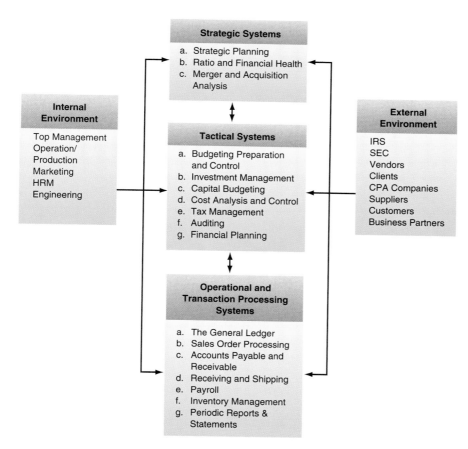

Figure 8.3 *Major activities of the accounting/finance system.*

Knowledge about the availability and cost of money is a key ingredient for successful financial planning. Especially important is the projection of cash flows, which tells organizations what money they need and when and how they will acquire it. Such analysis can be facilitated by intelligent systems such as neural computing. This function is important for companies of every size. Inaccurate cash flow projection is the major reason many small businesses go bankrupt.

Funds for organizations come from several sources, including shareholders' investments, sale of bonds, loans from banks, corporate sales, and return from investments. Using the information generated by economic and financial forecasts, the organization can build a decision support model for managing its cash and make decisions about when and how much to refinance.

Budgeting.   The budget is the financial expression of the organization's plans. It allows management to allocate resources in the way that best supports achieving the organization's mission and goals. It includes *capital budgeting*, which addresses the long-term financing of planned projects and the acquisition or disposal of major organizational assets. Capital budgeting usually includes a comparison of options, such as keep the asset, replace it with an identical new asset, replace it with a different one, or discard it. The capital budgeting process also evaluates buy-versus-lease alternatives.

Several software packages are available to support budgeting and to facilitate communication among all participants in the budget preparation (e.g., Budget 2000 from EPS Consultants and Comshare BudgetPlus from Comshare Inc.). Daily file updates can be sent via an intranet to all those who request funds and submit proposals. Software also makes it easier to build complex budgets involving multiple work

www.wiley.com/
college/turban

sites, including those in foreign countries. Budgeting software also allows various internal and external comparisons. The Benefits of Budgeting Software are listed in Manager's Checklist W8.2 at the book's Web site.

Investment Management

Organizations invest large amounts of money in stocks, bonds, real estate, and other assets. Furthermore, organizations need to pay pensions to their employees, so they need to manage the pension funds as an asset. Investment management is a difficult task for a number of reasons. For one thing, there are thousands of investment alternatives. In addition to those investments available in U.S. markets, the investment environment includes opportunities in other countries, providing both high potential rewards and risks. Computerized support can facilitate investment decisions, especially in financial institutions.

The following are the major areas of support IT can provide to investment management.

Access to financial and economic reports.   Investment decisions require managers to evaluate financial and economic reports and news provided by federal and state agencies, universities, research institutions, financial services, and corporations. There are hundreds of Internet sources for these reports, mostly free of charge. (For examples, see *sec.gov/edgar.html*.) To cope with the large amount of online financial data, investors use three supporting tools: (a) Internet meta-search engines for finding financial data, (b) Internet directories and yellow pages, and (c) software for monitoring, interpreting, and analyzing financial data, and alerting management.

Financial analysis.   Financial analysis can be executed with a spreadsheet program, or with commercially available ready-made decision support software. It can be more sophisticated, involving intelligent systems. For example, brokerage firm Morgan Stanley uses virtual reality on its intranet to display the results of risk analysis in three dimensions. Neural computing can be used in financial analysis, to analyze the financial health of corporations as possible investments, conduct risk analysis of bonds, mortgages, real estate, and other financial instruments, predict economic and financial performance, design stock market investment strategies such as arbitrage, and predict foreign exchange rates.

Financial Controls

IT also plays an important role in accounting and financial controls—specifically in budgetary control, auditing, and related financial control analyses.

Budgetary control.   Once an annual budget has been decided upon, it is divided into monthly allocations. Expenditures are then monitored and compared against the budget and operational progress of the corporate plans. Simple reporting systems summarize the expenditures and provide exception reports by flagging any expenditure that exceeds the budget by a certain percent or that falls significantly below the budget. More sophisticated software attempts to tie expenditures to program accomplishment.

Auditing.   The major purpose of auditing is to ensure the accuracy of financial reports and the financial health of an organization. Internal auditing is done by the accounting/finance department, which also prepares for external auditing by certified public accountants (CPAs). Support software ensures consistency and impartiality as well as increasing the productivity of internal and external auditors. Auditing software is especially suitable when computerized information systems are audited. More sophisticated intelligent systems can uncover fraud by finding financial transactions that deviate significantly from previous payment profiles.

Financial health analysis. Collection of data to be used as inputs for ratio analysis is done by the TPS, and computation of the ratios can be done by simple financial analysis models. However, the *interpretation* of the ratios, and especially the prediction of their future behavior, requires expertise. Such *financial health analysis* is sometimes supported by expert systems.

Profitability analysis and cost control. Companies are concerned with the profitability of individual products or services as well as with the profitability of the entire organization. Profitability analysis software allows accurate computation of profitability for individual products and for entire organizations. It also allows allocation of overhead.

One aspect of profitability analysis is product pricing. Setting the right price for each product is an important corporate decision because it determines competitiveness and profitability. A company can't exist for long if it prices products below its costs of operations, or much above the costs of its competitors. Decision support models can facilitate product pricing. Accounting, finance, and marketing can team up to jointly prepare appropriate product prices supported by integrated software and intranets.

Before you go on . . .

1. List the major planning and budgeting activities.

2. Describe some investment management decisions and explain how they are supported by IT.

3. What tasks are included in control and auditing? How is auditing facilitated by IT?

8.4 MARKETING AND SALES SYSTEMS

Earlier we emphasized the increasing importance of customer focus and the trend toward customization and consumer-based organizations. How can IT help? First we need to understand how products reach customers.

Marketing organizations get a product or service to customers and attempt to meet all other customer needs through various channels. They include manufacturers, sales representatives, wholesalers, and retailers. A **distribution channel**, as its name implies, deals with providing the good or service to the customer, and may extend through various intermediaries such as wholesalers and retailers. Some may be relatively short, as would be the case when a consumer buys produce at a farmer's market, for example. Or they may be relatively long, with products passing from a manufacturer to a wholesaler to a retailer and finally to the consumer. Other **channel systems** support other marketing linkages, such as after-sale customer support. The complexity of channel systems can be observed in Figure 8.4, where six major systems are interrelated.

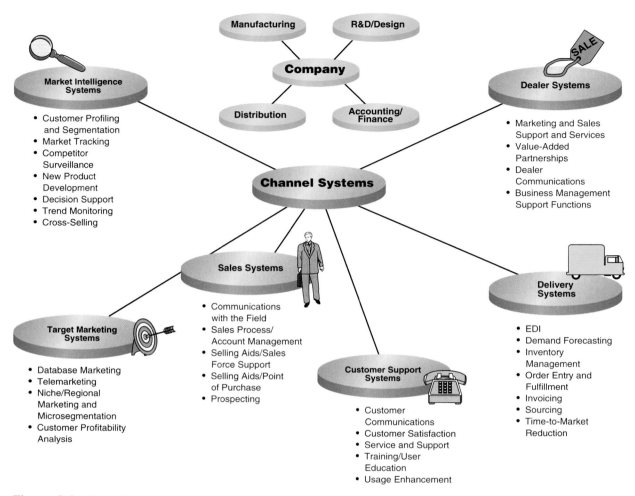

Figure 8.4   *How channel systems are composed. All activities listed in each channel can be enhanced by IT.*

Channel systems can transform marketing, sales, supply, and other activities and systems. Added market power comes from the integration of channel systems with the corporate functional areas. The problem is that a change in any of the channels may affect the other channels. Therefore, the supporting information systems must be coordinated or even integrated. We describe only a few of the many channel systems activities here, organizing them into four groups: (1) customer service, (2) telemarketing, (3) distribution channels management, and (4) marketing management.

Customer Service

It is essential for companies today to know more about their customers and to treat them well. New and innovative products and services, successful promotions, and superb customer service are becoming a necessity for many organizations. Customer service, as shown in Chapter 9, can be greatly enhanced with the Web.

Customer profiles and preference analysis.   Information about existing and potential customers is critical for success. Sophisticated information systems, ranging from intelligent agents on the Web to neural computing, collect and process data on customers, demographics (ages, gender, income level), and preferences. The data can then be analyzed and used to guide advertising and marketing efforts. Customer data are stored in a corporate database or in marketing databases for future analysis and use. IT can help create customer databases of both existing and potential customers.

Mass customization.   **Mass customization** refers to the production of large quantities of products, such as computers or cars, in which each product is customized to the customer's wishes. Mass customization is considered here a part of customer service because by using it a company provides customers with exactly what they want. An example of IT-supported mass customization would be Dell Computer, which assembles computers according the specifications of the buyers. Similarly, Continental Shoe Stores takes a digital photo of your feet and transmits it to the production floor of its shoe plant in Italy. The Web can be used to prepare customized electronic catalogs and to expedite the ordering process of customized products, even cars.

Targeted advertising on the Web.   By checking the demographics of its millions of customers and their locations, America Online and other vendors can match appropriate ads with specific groups of customers or even individual customers. The effectiveness of such ads is very high (as are the fees charged by AOL to the advertising companies).

Customer inquiry systems and automated help desk.   Organizations are flooded with inquiries from customers, sometimes thousands per day. The usual way to handle inquiries is to establish a **help desk** that answers the telephone, e-mail, faxes, and even face-to-face inquiries. However, many help desks are clogged, resulting in considerable waiting time. Information technology can provide several alternative solutions to the problem. For example, some companies use expert systems to expedite help-desk employees' search for information. A more sophisticated solution is to enable customers to find answers by themselves in the corporate database. The use of intelligent agents is expected to completely reengineer how customer inquiry systems operate. For example, intelligent agents can send automatic e-mail replies to over 90 percent of the customer queries received.

Telemarketing

Telemarketing is a process that uses telecommunications and information systems to execute a marketing program. It can be done by regular telephone calls or by telephone calls generated by computer programs, or by computer-generated messages delivered by voice technologies. A telemarketing process can be divided into five major activities: *advertising and reaching customers, order processing, customer service, sales support*, and *account management*, all of which are supported by IT.

This increases the productivity of the sales force, enables targeted marketing, reduces marketing and sales costs, and increases sales.

Distribution Channels Management

Delivery management.   Organizations can distribute their products and services through several available delivery channels. For instance, a company may use its own outlets or it may use distributors. In addition, the company needs to decide on the *transportation mode* (trains, planes, trucks). Deliveries can be accomplished by the company *itself*, by a trucker, or by a subcontractor. DSS models are frequently used to support this type of decision. Once products are shipped, firms need to monitor and track them, because only fast and accurate delivery times guarantee high customer satisfaction and repeat business. FedEx, UPS, and other large shipping companies use some of the most sophisticated tracking systems. TPSs not only support delivery management, but, along with advances in telecommunications, can fundamentally change those delivery channels.

EXAMPLE

Japanese kiosks start selling digital music.   Japan Telecom Co., Ltd. and East Japan Railway Co. have launched a music distribution service at three major train stations in Tokyo. Using the service, rail passengers can purchase and download songs onto their personal minidisk players from kiosks in the train stations. The "Digi-Break" digital music service is run by Japan Telecom, which runs a data center that distributes the music to the kiosks via high-speed optical fiber networks. The railway company plans to expand the music distribution service to eventually include other digital content, such as games and books, using the same terminals. The venture now offers approximately 500 songs, and plans to add around 40 titles per month. Each tune costs from 200 yen (US$1.61) to 500 yen, and the terminal also prints out jacket pictures and song lyrics. It takes approximately 20 to 40 seconds to record each song and about 30 seconds to print out the picture and lyrics. (Source: cnn.com/2001/TECH/ptech/06/29/music.kiosks.idg/.) ●

Improving sales at retail stores.   The home shopping alternative puts pressure on retailers to offer more products in one location and to provide better service. The increased number of products and customers' desire to get more information while at the store result in a need to add many salespeople, which increases costs. When retailers fail to add salespeople, long lines may result. Using information technology, it is possible to improve the situation by reengineering the checkout process. For example, NCR Corporation offers self-checkout counters.

Marketing Management

The marketing function must generate demand for the company's products or services and then meet that demand. Many marketing management activities are supported by computerized information systems.

Pricing of products or services.   Sales volumes are largely determined by the prices of products or services. The lower the price, the more you can usually sell. However, price is also a major determinant of profit. Pricing is a difficult decision, and prices may need to be changed frequently. Many companies are using online analytical processing to support pricing decisions.

Salesperson productivity.   Salespeople differ from each other; some excel in selling certain products, while others excel in selling to a certain type of customer or in a certain geographical zone. This information, which is usually collected in the marketing TPS, can be analyzed, using a system in which sales data by salesperson, product, region, and even the time of day can be compiled and compared to a standard. Also, current sales can be compared to historical data and to industry standards. Multidimensional spreadsheet software facilitates this type of analysis.

Salesperson productivity can be greatly increased by what is known as **sales-force automation**, namely, providing salespeople in the field with portable computers, access to databases, and so on. Sales force automation frequently empowers the sales force to close deals at the customer's office and to configure marketing strategies at home. The

Web can play a major role in automating order taking, order tracing, and customer contacts. This can be done on the Internet or on extranets (see Chapters 7 and 9).

Product-customer profitability analysis.   In deciding on advertising and other marketing efforts, managers often need to know the profit contribution of certain products, services, or customers. Profitability information can be derived from the cost-accounting system. Identification of profitable customers and the frequency with which they interact with the organization can be derived from special promotional programs, such as the frequent-flyer programs used by airlines and hotels. Both the operations and the analysis of such programs are fully computerized.

Sales analysis and trends.   The marketing TPS collects sales data that can be segregated along several dimensions for early detection of problems and opportunities, usually by searching for trends. An interesting computerized technology that can support this type of sales analysis is a geographical information system (GIS). Using pre-stored maps at various levels of detail, a marketing manager can learn a lot about the company's customers and competitors and examine potential strategies before he or she even sets foot out of the office.

New products, services, and market planning.   The introduction of new or improved products and services can be expensive and risky. An important question to ask about a new product or service is, "Will it sell?" An appropriate answer calls for careful analysis, planning, and forecasting. These can best be executed with the aid of IT because of the large number of determining factors and uncertainties that may be involved. Also, market research can be conducted on the Internet.

Ethical and Societal Issues in IT-Supported Sales Activities

IT-supported sales activities can include the use of **sales automation software**, which instructs computers to generate lists of telephone numbers and make calls to those numbers automatically. Telemarketing and the use of some sales automation software raise several ethical issues. Telephone-based telemarketing is supported by computers at its "back-end," where calls are made automatically. Similarly, e-mail lists are computer-generated and messages are sent automatically. The sometimes-annoying result is unsolicited telephone calls and junk e-mail. The latter is referred to as **spamming**. However, IT provides for several ways to stop spamming, as we'll describe in Chapter 15.

IT-supported marketing relies on marketing databases that include information about customers. This information may include personal information that might not be accurate. Furthermore, even if accurate, it may not be protected well enough while in storage or transit. Therefore, the IT-supported sales and marketing activities may cause invasion of privacy. Companies must take care of the privacy of their customers, and many organizations that do business on the Internet are taking active steps to do so. Most Web sites include a section that sets forth the company's privacy statement. Ethical issues also exist in areas other than marketing. Introducing automation to personnel systems raises the issue of privacy as well. Accessing personal data via networks may not be secured, and it is a major concern of the human resources management department.

The Next Step: CRM

The next step in customer relations is customer relationship management. In general, **customer relationship management (CRM)** is an approach that recognizes that customers are the core of the business and that the company's success depends on effectively managing relationships with them. It overlaps somewhat with the concept of *relationship marketing*, but not everything that could be called relationship marketing is in fact CRM. Customer relationship marketing is even broader, in that it includes a *one-to-one* relationship of customer and seller.

For the most part, however, being customer-oriented has always meant being oriented to the needs of the *typical* customer in the market—the average customer. In order to build enduring one-to-one relationships, a company must continuously interact with customers, *individually*. One reason so many firms are beginning to focus on CRM is that this kind of marketing can create high customer loyalty.

CRM in action.   There are five common steps in CRM:

1. Make it easy for customers to do business with you.
2. Focus on the end-customer for your products and services.
3. Redesign your customer-facing business processes from the end-customer's point of view.
4. Wire your company for profit: design a comprehensive, evolving electronic business architecture.
5. Foster customer loyalty. In e-commerce, especially, this is the key to profitability.

Table 8.2   CRM Activities and IT Support

CRM Activity	IT Support
Web-based integrated call centers; quick reply to customers' inquiries.	Facilitate help-desk activities; intelligent agents for answering FAQs.
Monitoring customers' orders inside the company.	Workflow software for planning and monitoring; intranets.
Appointment of account managers (business process redesign); creating specialized teams.	Expert systems for advice; groupware for collaboration.
Seminars and educational activities to customers (banks, hospitals, universities).	Online training, Internet.
Self-tracking of shipments, orders.	Web-based training software; workflow.
Segmenting customers.	Data mining in data warehouses.
Matching customers with products and services.	Web-based intelligent agents.
Customizing products to suit customers' specific needs.	Intelligent agents to find what customer wants; CAD/CAM to reduce cost of customization.
Customers' discussion forums.	Chat rooms, sponsored newsgroups.
Reward repeat customers (loyalty programs, e.g., frequent flyers and buyers of gas (oil) companies; airlines, retailers).	Data warehouses and data mining of customers' activities; smart cards that record purchasers' activities.
Customer participation in product (service) development.	Online surveys, newsgroups, chat rooms, e-mails.
Proactive approach to customers based on their activity level.	Data warehouse, data mining.
Customized information and services in many languages; discounts based on life style. Appointment reminders, information on doctors, research. Help center to solve member problems. Offered by medical centers, hospitals, HMOs.	E-mails (push technology), data warehouse for customer information; data mining finds relationships; intelligent translating systems. Provide search engines on the Web help center.

To accomplish these steps it is necessary to take the following actions.

- Deliver personalized services (e.g., *dowjones.com*).
- Target the right customers (e.g., *aa.com, nsc.com*).
- Help the customers do their jobs or accomplish their goals (e.g., *boeing.com*).
- Let customers help themselves (e.g., *iprint.com*).
- Stream business processes that impact the customers (e.g., *ups.com, amazon.com*).
- Own the customer's total shopping experience (e.g., *amazon.com, hertz.com*).
- Provide a 360-degree view of the customer relationship (e.g., *wells fargo.com, bellatlantic.com*).

Note that although all of these actions are Web-related, CRM does not have to be on the Web. But the trend is to move as much CRM activity to the Web as possible, because CRM generally is cheaper and/or more effective on the Web.

Typical CRM activities and their IT support are provided in Table 8.2. As the table indicates, many organizations are using the Web to facilitate CRM. (For examples, see The Enabling Role of Information Technology in CRM on the Web site.)

www.wiley.com/college/turban

Before you go on . . .

1. What are distribution channels and channel systems?

2. Describe IT-supported customer-related activities in sales and marketing.

3. List the major marketing management tasks.

4. When does marketing work best, and when it may annoy customers?

5. Describe CRM and how the Internet and related technologies contribute to it.

8.5   PRODUCTION AND OPERATIONS MANAGEMENT SYSTEMS

The production and operations management (POM) function in an organization is responsible for the processes that transform inputs into useful outputs. The POM area is very diversified in comparison to the other functional areas (see Figure 8.5 on page 254), and so are its supporting information systems. It also differs considerably across organizations. For example, manufacturing companies use completely different processes than do service organizations, and a hospital operates much differently from a university. In Chapter 2 we introduced the concept of supply chain and its management, and we devote Chapter 10 entirely to this topic. The POM function is responsible for most of the SCM activities, and we present here three such activities and their TPSs—logistics and materials management, planning production/operations, and automating design work and manufacturing.

Logistics and Materials Management

Logistics management deals with ordering, purchasing, and inbound and outbound shipping activities. Logistics activities are a good example of processes that cross several functional departments. The purchasing agent decides—in consultation with personnel from other functional areas—what, where, and when to buy. Prices are negotiated with

Figure 8.5 *A model of information systems in the production/operations functional area.*

suppliers, and materials (and parts) are ordered and received. The materials received are inspected for quality and then stored. While in storage, they need to be maintained until distributed to those who need them. Some materials are disposed of when they become obsolete or when their quality becomes unacceptable. After manufacturing creates the products, marketing and sales move them to customers.

All of these activities can be supported by information systems. For example, purchasing can use EDI to place orders. Scanners and voice technologies can support inspection, and robots can perform distribution and materials handling. Large warehouses use robots to bring materials and parts from storage whenever needed. In "intelligent buildings" in Japan, robots bring files to employees and return them for storage; in some hospitals, robots even dispense medicine.

Logistics is related to inventory management as illustrated in IT's About Business 8.3.

Inventory management. *Inventory management* determines how much inventory to keep. Overstocking can be expensive; so is keeping insufficient inventory, because of the opportunity cost of lost sales. Several inventory decisions are made by operations personnel: what to order, from whom, when to order, and how much. Because inventory scenarios can be diverse and complex, dozens of inventory models exist. Once management has made decisions about how much to order and when, an information

IT's About Business   *fedex.com*   POM

Box 8.3:   FedEx's Web shopping/shipping services

FedEx created a business-to-business service that integrates Web catalogs of various companies with order, fulfillment, and delivery functions using FedEx's own trucks and planes. This move marked a new stage for electronic commerce on the Internet: FedEx is making it possible for companies that do not want to personally deal with transactions over the Internet to sell their products there by subcontracting those services to FedEx.

The service works like this: FedEx hosts the Web pages for companies that want to put catalogs on the Internet. FedEx helps to create the online catalog if needed. The Web pages run on the FedEx secured servers, but are exclusively the selling company's branded items. When an order comes through, all of the applicable charges are calculated by the FedEx system and are sent to the buyer and to the selling company's server. Also, the system is linked to the selling company's database for real-time inventory management. The order then is routed to the selling company's product warehouses where FedEx handles the packaging and

shipping of the product. Alternatively, FedEx can even manage the inventory of the product on its own premises, usually in Memphis, the hub of its planes.

As with any other FedEx shipping, the shipment can be self-tracked by both the customer and the selling company. FedEx also provides a 24-hour Web-based technical support line for Virtual Order merchants. Finally, FedEx offers related services such as confirmations, invoicing, and after-sales service for returns and repairs.

Questions

1. List the benefits of the service to the catalog merchants (sellers) that are FedEx's customers.
2. What strategic advantage is provided to FedEx?
3. What type of customers will most likely sign up with FedEx?
4. What will be the impact on packaging companies? On wholesalers?

---

system can track the level of inventory for each item that management wants to control. When the inventory falls to a certain level, called the *reorder point*, inventory software can automatically generate a purchase order. A large number of commercial inventory software packages are available at low cost.

Quality control.   Quality-control systems provide information about the quality of incoming material and parts, as well as the quality of in-process semifinished and finished products. Quality-control software can be a standalone system or part of a total quality management (TQM) system.

Standard quality control information systems are available from several vendors for executing standard computations such as preparing control charts. After the data have been recorded, it is possible to use expert systems to make interpretations and recommend actions.

Planning Production/Operations

The extensive production and operations management (POM) planning function in many firms is supported by IT. Some major areas of planning and their computerized support are discussed below.

Materials requirement planning (MRP).   The inventory systems that use the economic order quantity (EOQ) inventory model are designed for individual items for which the demand is completely independent. When a Starbucks outlet runs below a certain level of coffee beans, for example, the EOQ model would trigger an order for *x* pounds of beans. However, in many manufacturing systems the demand for some items can be interdependent. For example, a company may make three types of chairs that all use the same legs, screws, bolts, and nuts. Thus, the company's demand for screws depends on the shipment schedule of all three types of chairs. The software that facilitates the plan for acquiring (or producing) parts, subassemblies, or materials in such a case is called **materials requirement planning (MRP)**. MRP is computerized because of the complex interrelationships among the many products and their components, and the need to change the plan each time a delivery date or the quantity ordered is changed.

Manufacturing resource planning (MRP II).   Computerized scheduling systems are frequently tied to other functional areas. **Manufacturing resource planning (MRP II)** is an *integrated* computer system that connects the regular MRP to other functional areas, especially finance and human resources. (Even greater integration can be achieved with enterprise resource planning (ERP), as will be described in Section 8.7.) MRP II determines the costs of parts and the cash flow needed to pay for parts. It also estimates costs of labor, tools, equipment repair, and energy. Finally, it provides a detailed, computerized budget.

Note that MRP II is an extension of MRP, which itself is an extension of the EOQ inventory model. Actually, over time one can trace a "family tree" succession of production operations systems and software:

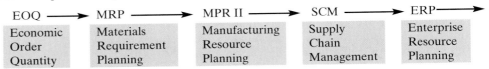

The last two topics will be described later.

Just-in-time systems.   MRP systems are conceptually related to (or can even be a part of) the just-in-time concept. **Just-in-time (JIT)** is an attempt to minimize waste of all kinds (space, labor, materials, energy, and so on). For example, if materials and parts arrive at a workstation exactly when needed, there is no need for inventory, there are no delays in production, and there are no idle production facilities. JIT systems have resulted in significant benefits. At Toyota, for example, JIT has reduced production time from 15 days to 1 day and has reduced costs by 30 to 50 percent while at the same time increasing quality.

All elements of JIT can be executed manually. However, the use of IT to support even some of the elements may result in significant enhancement, especially when complex processes are involved. For example, EDI can greatly reduce cycle time, especially when international business partners are involved. HP Manufacturing Management software (from Hewlett-Packard) supports multilocation tracking and JIT component ordering and extensive MRP and inventory control execution, and it interfaces to financial management, budgeting, and CAD/CAM applications. JIT systems are also often interrelated with computerized project management systems.

Project management.   A *project* is usually a one-time effort composed of many interrelated activities, costing a substantial amount of money, and lasting from weeks to years. The management of a project is complicated by the following characteristics: (1) Most projects are unique undertakings, and participants have little prior experience in the area. (2) Uncertainty exists due to long completion times. (3) There can be significant participation of outside vendors, which is difficult to control. (4) Extensive interaction may occur among participants. (5) Projects often carry high risk but also high profit potential.

The management of projects is enhanced by project management tools such as the program evaluation and review technique (PERT) and critical path method (CPM). These tools generally identify key activities in a project upon which other activities depend and schedule activities in an optimal sequence. They are easily computerized, and there are dozens of commercial packages on the market that offer these project management tools.

Short-term schedules.   Operations managers schedule jobs and employees on a daily or weekly basis, with the support of information systems. For example, bar or Gantt charts that show scheduled and actual production times can be computerized, and complex scheduling situations can be supported by DSS or by expert systems.

Automated Design Work and Manufacturing

IT has been very successfully used in cutting the time required for the design of products, services, or processes. Following are descriptions of three important representative applications.

Computer-aided design.   **Computer-aided design (CAD)** is a system that enables drawings to be constructed on a computer screen and subsequently stored, manipulated, and updated electronically. The ability to rotate or create movement in the design allows testing for clearances and frequently reduces the cost of prototyping the products.

Having access to a computerized design database makes it easy for a designer to quickly modify an old design to meet new design requirements—an event that occurs quite frequently. This capability enhances

Designer using CAD software.

designers' productivity, speeds up the design process, reduces design errors resulting from hurried copying, and reduces the number of designers needed to perform the same amount of work. These advantages can provide a significant competitive edge.

Computer-aided manufacturing.   **Computer-aided manufacturing (CAM)** uses computer-aided techniques to plan and control a production facility. Such techniques include computer-aided process planning, numerical control part programming, robotics programming, computer-generated work standards, MRP II, capacity requirements planning, and shop-floor control. When CAD feeds design and testing information to a CAM system, the combined system is referred to as *CAD/CAM*.

Computer-integrated manufacturing.   Computer-integrated manufacturing (CIM) is a concept or philosophy about the implementation of various integrated computer systems in factory automation. CIM has three basic goals:

1. *Simplification* of all manufacturing technologies and techniques.
2. *Automation* of as many of the manufacturing processes as possible by the integration of many information technologies. Typical technologies include flexible-manufacturing systems (FMS), JIT, MRP, CAD, and computer-aided engineering (CAE).

3. *Integration and coordination*, via computer hardware and software, of all aspects of design, manufacturing, and related functions.

The major advantages of CIM are its comprehensiveness and flexibility. It results in considerable cost savings and improved quality.

Before you go on . . .

1. List the logistics activities supported by IT.

2. Describe MRP and MRP II.

3. Explain the role of IT in product design.

8.6   HUMAN RESOURCES MANAGEMENT SYSTEMS

Managing human resources (HR) is an important job that starts with the hiring of an employee and ends with his or her departure or retirement. It includes several tasks, the most important of which are recruitment, development, and planning, as described below.

Recruitment

Recruitment is finding employees, testing them, and deciding which ones to hire. Some companies are flooded with applicants, while others have a difficulty in finding the right people. Information systems can be helpful in both cases. Here are some examples of how IT can be used in recruitment activities.

Position inventory.   Organizations maintain a file that lists all open positions by job title, geographical area, task content, and skills required. Like any other inventory, this position inventory is updated each time a transaction (a hiring or termination, for example) occurs.

A computerized position inventory system keeps the job listings current and matches openings with available personnel. If an intranet is available, employees can view job listings from any location at any time. Outsiders can view openings via the Internet. HR personnel can analyze the position inventory and its changes over time. For example, they can find those jobs with high turnover. Information from such analysis can support decisions about promotions, salary administration, and training plans.

Recruitment using the Internet.   As indicated above, many companies advertise position openings on the Internet and intranets. In addition, several thousand employment agencies on the Internet attempt to match job seekers and positions. Intelligent agents help companies find relevant resumes on the Internet, initially to screen applications and then to match applicants with jobs (see *resumix.com*).

Employee selection.   The human resources department is responsible for screening job applicants, evaluating, testing, and selecting them in compliance with state and federal regulations. Interviews can be conducted using video teleconferencing, which saves both time and money. To expedite the testing and evaluation process and ensure consistency in selection, companies use information technologies such as expert systems, sometimes online, as shown in IT's About Business 8.4.

IT's About Business

cydsa.com, nike.com   **HRM**

Box 8.4:   CYDSA and Nike use IT to assess future performance of job candidates

The human resources department of CYDSA, a large company in Mexico, administers a behavioral profile test to measure the capabilities of individuals under consideration for employment. The test results were analyzed manually by experts and divided into three categories: candidate style, candidate values, and candidate thought preferences. Due to the large number of applicants, the many locations of the corporation, and the high level of expertise required for the analysis, it was very difficult to execute a quality analysis in a timely manner. To overcome these problems, a computerized test system with an expert system was developed.

The basic objective of CYDSA's system is to assess the candidates' directional initiative, potential performance problems, and supervision effectiveness. Analysis of an average applicant, which takes an hour when done manually, can be performed in about five minutes when supported by the expert system. The system was initially available via satellites to all corporate sites. In 1998 it was placed on the corporate intranet.

Nike Inc. had more than 6,000 applicants for 250 positions for its Las Vegas Niketown store. Using automatic computerized interactive voice response, the company screened the employees over the telephone,

asking them for information about themselves and their skills. This process reduced the number of applicants to 2,500. Then, remaining job candidates filed a standard detailed application online. The answers were analyzed by a computer, which resulted in reducing the number of candidates to 600, who were invited for face-to-face interviews. The human interviewers had all the previous information on the screen during the interview, expediting the interview and making it more meaningful. The process cut interview costs by over 50 percent, expedited the recruiting process by over 100 percent, and increased the quality of the recruitees so turnover was reduced by 21 percent.

Questions

1. What were the benefits to CYDSA of its expert system?

2. How would you feel if your job application were assessed by a machine for a yes-or-no decision?

3. Is CYDSA's approach superior or inferior to that of Nike?

4. What is the role of the satellites and the intranet in recruitment and selection?

Human Resources Maintenance and Development

Once recruited, employees become part of the corporate human resources pool, which needs to be maintained and developed. Some of these activities supported by IT are described here.

Training and human resources development.   Employee training and retraining is an important activity of the human resources department. Sophisticated human resources departments build a career development plan for each employee. IT can support these activities by using several technologies, including training over the Web. For examples of companies that conduct such training, see Table W8.1 on the Web site. Also there you can find Intranet Applications in HR Management.

www.wiley.com/
college/turban

Performance evaluation.   Most employees are evaluated by their immediate supervisors periodically or at the completion of certain projects. Peers or subordinates may also evaluate others. Evaluations can be keyed or scanned into the information system. Once digitized, evaluations can be used to support many decisions, ranging from rewards to transfers to layoffs. HR managers can analyze employees' performances with the help of expert systems, which provide an unbiased and systematic interpretation of performance over time.

Wage and salary review is related to performance evaluation and can also be handled by IT applications. For example, Hewlett-Packard has developed a paperless wage review (PWR) system that uses intelligent agents to deal with quarterly reviews of HP's 11,000 employees. Via software agents, the PWR system sends wage review forms to first-level managers by e-mail or fax every quarter, reminding them about the appropriate evaluation dates, and it speeds up all the administrative tasks and improves the accuracy of the information throughout the entire process.

Turnover, tardiness, and absenteeism analyses.   Replacing a skilled employee may cost a company as much as $25,000 in recruiting, selection, and training costs. Therefore, it is important to learn why employees leave. In addition, tardiness and absenteeism hurt productivity and morale and may indicate deeper individual or systemic problems. Data on these topics are collected in the payroll system and personnel files. By using DSS models and/or neural computing, for example, it is possible to identify causes and patterns as well as to assess the impact of programs that aim to reduce turnover, tardiness, and absenteeism.

Human Resources Management and Planning

Managing human resources in large organizations requires extensive record-keeping as well as planning. Here are some examples of how IT can help in both HR management and planning.

Personnel files and skills inventory.   All information about an employee is contained in an HRM personnel file. The information includes his or her skills and experience, the tests taken and passed, and performance evaluations and compensation over time. In addition, the file may include the employee's preferences for relocation and for changing his or her current job. When the personnel files are computerized, it is easy to identify qualified employees within the company for open positions, promotion, transfer, special training programs, and layoffs. Many companies allow employees to electronically update parts of their own personal files (for example, to change an address), saving clerical labor and reducing errors in data entry.

A few words about privacy: Companies must take strict measures to protect the privacy of their employees' records. The issue of privacy becomes even more important when records are transmitted electronically. Oracle, for example, allows employees to enroll in benefits programs over the Web, but the information is then encrypted and sent to the headquarters over a secure T1 line. Breaches of confidentiality can be damaging to the firm as well as to the employee. Beyond incurring significant legal and punitive costs, the firm risks damage to its public image.

Benefits administration.   Managing the benefits system can be a complex task, due to its many components (health care plans, pensions, and so on) and the tendency of organizations to allow employees to choose and trade-off benefits ("cafeteria style"). In some organizations, employees can learn about benefits and/or register for specific benefits using networks and voice technology or intranets. The system specifies the value of each benefit and the available benefits balance of each employee. Some companies use intelligent agents to assist the employees and monitor their actions.

Government reports.   The human resources department is responsible for the completion of several routine state and federal reports that indicate compliance with laws and regulations. Both scheduled and ad-hoc reports go to agencies such as the Equal Employment Opportunity Commission (EEOC), Occupational Safety and Health Administration (OSHA), Immigration and Naturalization Service (INS), and Employment Standards Administration (ESA). Availability of computerized personnel records greatly eases the reporting process.

Personnel planning. The human resources department forecasts requirements for people and skills over both the short term (one year) and longer terms (five years or more). In some geographical areas and for overseas assignments it may be difficult to find particular types of employees. Large companies develop qualitative and quantitative workforce planning models. Such models can be enhanced if IT is used to collect, update, and process the information.

Succession planning and implementation. Replacement of top managers can be a difficult, lengthy, and expensive process. Therefore, prudent corporations prepare long-range plans for replacing departing managers, especially those who are due to leave soon. Expert systems and personnel databases have been successfully used to support succession planning. Also, IT is used in case of an emergency, such as after the World Trade Center disaster on September 11, 2001, when IT was utilized to implement the succession plan that involved shifting many employees from their jobs to others.

Labor-management negotiations. Labor-management negotiations can take several months, during which time employees and management need to make concessions and trade-offs. Large companies have developed computerized DSS models that support such negotiations. The models can simulate financial and other impacts of fulfilling any demand made by employees, and they can provide answers to queries in a matter of seconds.

Another information technology that has been used successfully in labor-management negotiations is group decision support systems, which have helped improve the negotiation climate and considerably reduced the time needed for reaching an agreement.

Before you go on . . .

1. List the major activities of the HRM department.

2. Describe how IT facilitates recruiting, training, and personnel development and labor planning.

3. Describe how the Web facilitates recruiting, benefits management, training, and dissemination of information.

8.7   INTEGRATED INFORMATION SYSTEMS AND ENTERPRISE RESOURCE PLANNING

Functional information systems such as those described in the previous sections are useful. However, they may not be sufficient in providing management with timely information, effectively and efficiently. The solution is to integrate two or more functional information systems within an organization and with the information systems of business partners.

Why Integrate?

Information systems integration tears down barriers between and among departments and corporate headquarters and reduces duplication of effort. A sample structure for

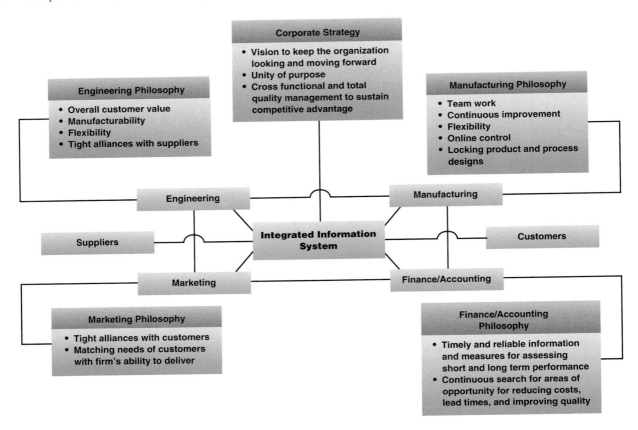

Figure 8.6   *Integrated information systems—sharing data and business processes across functional lines.* [*Source: M. Yakhou and B. Rahali, "Integration of Business Functions: Roles of Cross-Functional Information Systems," APICS, December 1992, p. 36.*]

an integrated information system is shown in Figure 8.6. There is data sharing as well as joint execution of business processes across functional areas, allowing individuals in one area to quickly and easily provide input to another area. Various functional managers are linked together in an *enterprisewide system*.

How to Integrate

There are several approaches to integrating functional systems into an enterprisewide system. Here we present three of them: connect existing systems, use supply chain management software, and use enterprise resource planning software.

Connect existing systems.   The basic concept of this approach is to maximize the use of existing systems and minimize the changes in them. Good integration allows the addition of new applications to existing ones and the connection of systems to intranets and the Internet. This approach extends the life of applications and saves tremendous amounts of money.

However, connecting existing systems may be difficult and/or expensive in many cases. The difficulty with this approach is that old systems were built over a number of years. Some were "home-grown," and others were purchased and possibly modified. Although connecting and integrating existing systems may help improve operations, some systems may need to be replaced with newer ones. Therefore other approaches may be called for.

Use supply chain management software.   The basic idea of this approach is to use one integrated package in one or several functional areas. A frequently used integrated package is a comprehensive manufacturing system that supports many of the managerial and strategic tasks of *supply chain management (SCM)*. Such software enables companies to collaborate with suppliers and customers, forecast with greater accuracy, shorten product life cycle, and reduce inventories.

SCM software may be viewed as an evolution of MRP, MRP II, and logistics systems described in Section 8.5, with added functionality and interactivity. Using sophisticated modeling techniques and business rules, SCM software helps companies plan, source, manufacture, and deliver their products in cost-effective and integrated ways. Its functionality includes order and inventory management, demand planning and forecasting deployment, distribution-center operations, and transportation management.

The basic objective of SCM software is to help companies provide one-stop information access to sales, purchasing, manufacturing, distribution, and transportation planners, so that various departments use the *same data*. This overcomes the isolation of the traditional departmental structure where the functional areas are separated from one another—and are motivated, at times, by conflicting incentives and interests.

The major advantage of SCM is its ability to achieve an excellent fit with the company's needs. However, most SCM software deals with *decision support*; such systems are not effective for repetitive transactions. Therefore, to handle the processing of transactions, a company needs to add TPS software, which complicates the task of integration and can lengthen the software development process. This is where ERP enters the picture as a third integration approach.

Use enterprise resource planning and SAP software.   The advance of enterprisewide client/server computing now makes it possible to control *all* major business processes with a single software architecture in *real time*. This integrated solution, known as **enterprise resource planning (ERP)**, promises benefits from increased efficiency to improved quality, productivity, and profitability. For example, improved order entry allows immediate access to inventory, product data, customer credit history, and prior order information. The leading software vendor for ERP is SAP AG with its product **SAP R/3**. Oracle, J.D. Edwards, Computer Associates, PeopleSoft, and Baan Company make similar products. Many of these products include Web modules.

The ERP software such as SAP crosses functional departments and can be extended along the supply chain to both *suppliers* and *customers*. Companies have been successful in integrating several hundred applications into SAP, saving millions of dollars and significantly increasing customer satisfaction. For example, Mobil Oil consolidated 300 different systems by implementing SAP R/3 in its U.S. petrochemical operations alone. The SAP concept is shown in Figure 8.7 (on page 264).

SAP R/3 is comprised of four major parts: accounting, manufacturing, sales, and human resources—containing more than 70 smaller modules. R/3 is a totally integrated system, allowing companies to automate or eliminate many costly and error-prone manual communication procedures. R/3 can work for multinational corporations, since it can handle different currencies, different languages, different tax laws and regulations, and different requirements of several countries. SAP can be used to support interorganizational activities along the supply chain. SAP forces organizations to operate along business processes. By doing so it not only supports

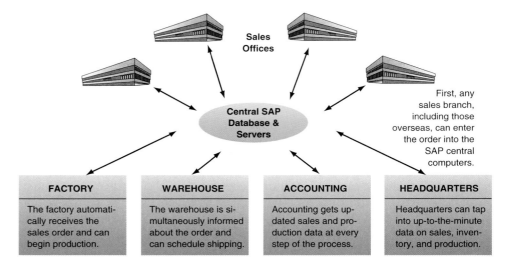

Figure 8.7 *With SAP software, a company can keep different departments updated with crucial product information. If, say, the sales department enters an order, it goes to a central computer system where others can access it.* [*Source: Lieber, 1995, p. 122.*]

business process reengineering but also permits organizations to grow globally and operate effectively and efficiently.

Implementing SAP is a difficult process, especially for large corporations. Not only is it necessary to modify business processes to conform to SAP's strict integration requirements, but SAP implementation is very complex and consequently very expensive (up to $200 million for a large company). For example, there are over 8,000 tables in the SAP database containing both user data and system data. These complicated tables direct the users through many menus and screens. Implementing these tables in a multilanguage, multicurrency, multifunction, multiproduct environment can take two to four years. Interfacing SAP's client/server architecture with legacy systems adds to the complexity. As a result, introducing SAP means significant changes in organizational structure, job descriptions, business processes, and organizational strategy.

SAP has proved to be ideal for medium-sized corporations of about $500 million annual sales. For large companies the problems cited above could be difficult, yet successful implementation can be very rewarding. SAP also now offers special variations of R/3 geared to small businesses. Other variations are geared toward certain industries (banking, hospitals, retailing, etc.).

Extreme Integration: Putting it All Together

ERP plays a critical role in improving or reengineering outdated infrastructures, gaining tighter control over internal operations, and driving down costs. Yet some companies are taking integration of functional systems even further—they are undertaking what we will call **extreme integration**. These companies are paying attention to integration issues beyond the corporate walls by integrating ERP with supply chain management and sales-force automation systems. Their aim is to better connect their processes with those of customers and business partners to further increase profits.

As one version of extreme integration, SCM software can be nested inside an ERP system. The SCM system links data from order entry to manufacturing and to accounts payable. The ERP system transacts processes, typically replacing old mainframe back-office TPSs. SCM serves as a decision support tool, using the ERP data to help answer what-if and other questions. SCM can be viewed as the brain, and ERP as the strong body. Both are needed to achieve a total solution. The benefits of extreme integration are shown in Manager's Checklist W8.3 at the book's Web site.

www.wiley.com/
college/turban

Before you go on . . .

1. Discuss the need for information systems integration.
2. Describe the different approaches of integration.
3. List the benefits of an extreme integration.

8.8 INTERORGANIZATIONAL/GLOBAL INFORMATION SYSTEMS

An **interorganizational information system (IOS)** involves information flow among two or more organizations. Its major objective is efficient processing of transactions, such as transmitting orders, bills, and payments. A major characteristic of an IOS is that the customer-supplier relationship is determined in advance, with the expectation that it will be ongoing. Advance arrangements result in agreements between organizations on the nature and format of business documents and payments that will be exchanged. Both parties also know which communication networks will be integral to the system. Interorganizational systems may be built around privately or publicly accessible networks. When IOSs use telecommunications companies for communication, they typically employ *value-added networks (VANs)*. These are *private*, third-party networks that can be tailored to specific business needs. However, use of publicly accessible networks is growing with the increased use of the Internet. See the Web site for a list of the Business Drivers of IOSs.

www.wiley.com/college/turban

Types of Interorganizational Systems

Interorganizational information systems include a variety of business activities, from data interchange to messaging services to funds transfers. The most prominent types of interorganizational systems are:

- *Global systems:* information systems connecting two or more companies in two or more countries
- *Electronic data interchange (EDI):* the electronic movement of business documents between business partners
- *Electronic funds transfer (EFT):* the transfer of money using telecommunication networks
- *Extranets:* extended intranets that link business partners
- *Shared databases:* databases that can be shared by trading partners, often used to reduce time in communicating information between parties as well as arranging cooperative activities
- *Integrated messaging:* delivery of electronic mail and fax documents through a single transmission system that can combine electronic mail and electronic business documents

Global Information Systems

Interorganizational systems can operate in one country or can connect companies located in two or more countries. In the latter case they are referred to as **global**

information systems. Several types of companies need global information systems. They are multinational companies, international companies, and virtual global companies.

Multinational companies are those that operate in several countries. Examples would be Coca-Cola, McDonald's, IBM, and SAP/AG (a German company). Multinational organizations may have sales offices in several countries or may conduct operations in locations where factory workers are plentiful and inexpensive, where highly skilled employees are available at low salaries, or where there is a need to be close to the market. SAP/AP, for example, has a large research and development division in Silicon Valley, California, and distribution and sales offices in dozens of countries.

International companies are those that do business with other companies in different countries. For example, Toyota Motor Company (Japan) works with many suppliers in the United States. Boeing Corporation solicits bids from and does contract work with manufacturers in over 40 countries.

Virtual global companies are joint ventures whose business partners are located in different countries. The partners form a company for the specific purpose of producing a product or service. Such companies can be temporary, with a one-time mission (such as building an oil pipeline), or they can be permanent. (Details are provided in Chapter 13.)

Let's look at an example of a global venture. (For another example and a listing of Benefits of Global Information Systems, see the Web site.)

www.wiley.com/
college/turban

EXAMPLE

europcar.com

Integrated client/server system at Europcar. Major reengineering of Europcar Internet, the largest European-based car rental agency, changed the structure of the entire organization, as well as its everyday work processes and methods. To support these changes, the company combined 55 different mainframe and minicomputer systems into a single client/server center known as Greenway. Located at corporate headquarters near Paris, the $500 million system combines data from nine different countries within Europe.

The 55 independent systems used various data types, many of which were incompatible. Europcar wanted to integrate its business practices, customer preferences, and related data into a single system. To complicate matters, the company had to develop at the same time a uniform set of business practices, or corporate standards, to support the new single business entity. Furthermore, Europcar had to consider the variety of languages spoken in the nine countries involved, as well as different currencies and cultures.

Key business processes—including reservations, billing, fleet management, cost control, and corporate finance—were all integrated into Greenway. Customer-related benefits of the new global information system include (1) fast service, since clerks no longer have to verify credit cards or calculate bills manually, (2) reservation desks linked to airline reservation systems, like SABRE or Amadeus, for fast communication, and (3) handling of corporate customers from one location, which results in consistent and faster service. Several thousand Europcar employees at about 1,000 offices throughout the continent utilize Greenway. ●

Issues in Interorganizational/Global IS Design

The task of designing any effective interorganizational information system is complicated. It is even more complex when the IOS is a global system, because of differences in cultures, economies, and politics among parties in different countries.

Cultural differences.   *Culture* consists of the objects, values, and other characteristics of a particular society. It includes many different aspects ranging from legal and ethical issues to what information is considered offensive. When companies plan to do business in countries other than their own, they must consider the cultural environment. An example is GM's car Nova. *No va* means "no go" in Spanish. GM did not pay attention to this issue, and the model's sales in Spanish-speaking countries suffered as a result.

Many companies use different names, colors, sizes, and packaging for their overseas products and services. This practice is referred to as *localization*. In order to maximize the benefits of global information systems, the localization approach should also be used in the design and operation of such systems.

Economic and political differences.   Countries also differ considerably in their economical and political environments. One result of such variations is that the information infrastructures may differ from country to country. For example, many countries own the telephone services; others control communications very tightly. France, for example, insisted for years that French should be the sole language on French Web sites. Additional languages are now allowed, but French must also appear in every site. China controls the content of the Internet, blocking some Web sites from being viewed in China.

Compliance with software copyright is also a major issue. Gross violations are reported in several countries where billions of potential revenue dollars are lost by software companies due to illegal copying and use of software.

Transfer of data across international borders.   The impact of economic and political differences on the design and use of global information systems can be seen in the issue of **cross-border data transfer**. Several countries, such as Canada and Brazil, impose strict laws to control the flow of corporate data across their borders. These countries usually justify their laws as protecting the privacy of their citizens, since corporate data frequently contain personal data. (Other justifications are intellectual property protection and keeping jobs within the country by requiring that data processing be done there.)

The transfer of information in and out of a nation raises an interesting legal issue: Whose laws have jurisdiction when records are in a different country for reprocessing or retransmission purposes? For example, if data are transmitted by a Polish company through a U.S. satellite to a British corporation, whose laws control what data, and when? Governments are developing laws and standards to cope with the rapidly increasing rate of information technology in order to solve some of these issues, and international efforts to standardize these are underway (e.g., see *www.oecd.org*). Some issues of cross-border data transfer are shown in Table W8.2 on the Web site.

www.wiley.com/
college/turban

Although the potential for a global economy certainly exists, some countries are erecting artificial borders through local language preference, local regulation, and access limitations. In addition, barriers of various sorts must be dealt with before global information systems can achieve their potential.

Before you go on . . .

1. Describe an interorganizational information system (IOS).

2. List the major types of IOSs and global information systems.

3. Describe the challenges provided by a global information system.

ACC

FOR THE ACCOUNTING MAJOR

The large CPA companies employ thousands of people in implementing ERP integrated solutions. To excel in this area, it is necessary to understand the various activities of all functional areas and how they are interconnected. Furthermore, by studying this chapter, you can learn some innovations that can be used to improve the operations of the accounting area. Finally, executing TPSs effectively is a major concern of any accountant.

FIN

FOR THE FINANCE MAJOR

One of the major areas in SCM is securing the financing required for smooth operations. The use of IT helps financial analysts and managers perform their difficult tasks better. ERP software is extremely important in supporting global transactions involving different currencies and fiscal regulations. For example, credit approval can be greatly expedited with the support of extranets, thereby boosting both local and global sales.

MKT

FOR THE MARKETING MAJOR

Marketing and sales are usually a target in a cost-reduction program. This chapter provides examples of how to reduce these costs through IT yet keep strong marketing and sales capabilities. Sales force automation not only improves salespeople's productivity (and thus reduces costs) but also makes possible improved customer service. Finally, by understanding how ERP software operates, marketing people can greatly improve the software utilization by developing challenging corporate applications.

POM

FOR THE PRODUCTION/OPERATIONS MANAGEMENT MAJOR

Supply chain management and ERP are critical today for medium and large manufacturing companies as well as for service organizations such as hospitals and banks. Execution of the production tasks, materials handling, and inventories in short time intervals, at a low cost and high quality, is critical for competitiveness and can be achieved only if properly supported by IT. Also, interaction with other functional areas, especially sales, can be greatly improved by IT.

HRM

FOR THE HUMAN RESOURCES MANAGEMENT MAJOR

The HRM major can benefit from understanding how to improve the efficiency and effectiveness of the HRM activities by using IT. The HRM department needs to understand the flow of information to and from the HRM department to the other functional areas. Finally, the ERP concept and implementation have a major impact on skills requirements, scarcity of employees, and the need to deal with resistance to change, all of which are related to the tasks performed by the HRM department.

SUMMARY

❶ **Describe the role of functional information systems.**
   Functional information systems are designed to support functional areas such as accounting, marketing, and finance. They are comprised of several subsystems for specialized applications, and they interface with each other. A major portion of functional systems is made up of MISs, whose major role is to provide routine and demand reports to functional area managers.

❷ State the objectives and operations of transaction processing and how it is supported by IT.

The core operations of organizations involve transactions such as ordering and billing. The information system that handles these transactions is called the transaction processing system (TPS). The TPS must provide all the information needed for effective operations in an efficient manner. The major transactions processed are preparing and maintaining order processing, ledger, accounts payable and receivable, and generating periodic reports and statements.

❸ Discuss the managerial and strategic applications in the accounting and finance areas that are supported by IT.

Accounting information systems cover applications in the areas of cost control, tax, and auditing. In industry, accounting and finance are frequently in the same department. Financial information systems deal with topics such as investment management, financing operations, raising capital, risk analysis, and credit approval.

❹ Discuss marketing and sales applications.

Channel systems deal with all activities related to customer orders, sales, advertising and promotion, market research, customer service, and product and service pricing. IT can assist marketing personnel in planning, advertising, and pricing decisions, and sales activities such as ordering, telemarketing, and efficient retailing.

❺ Describe how POM activities are supported by IT.

POM activities are very diversified, ranging from materials management and quality control to capacity planning and just-in-time management. The major area of IT support to production/operations management is in logistics and inventory management, quality control, and planning: MRP, MRP II, JIT, project management, CAD, CAM, and CIM.

❻ Discuss the human resources management activities and how they can be improved by IT.

All tasks related to human resources acquisition and development can be supported by human resources information systems. These tasks include employee selection, hiring, performance evaluation, salary and benefits administration, training and development, labor negotiations, and work planning. Web technologies and especially intranets are helpful in improving training, dissemination of information, fringe benefits management, recruitment and testing, and managing health benefits and insurance.

❼ Discuss the need for integrating functional information systems and the role of ERP.

Integrated information systems are necessary to ensure effective and efficient execution of activities that cross functional lines or require functional cooperation. While supply chain software integrates several tasks in a functional area, or in a few areas, enterprise resource planning (ERP) software integrates all the tasks along the supply chain, frequently extending the integration to business partners. SAP software is designed to integrate across functional areas so that whatever resource or information is required from any functional area, it can be gathered and coordinated with all other inputs (for example, integrating HRM with supply chain management, so that human resources as well as materials for production can be ensured).

❽ Discuss interorganizational/global information systems and their strategic importance.

An interorganizational and/or global information system (IOS) involves information flow among two or more organizations, which may or may not be located in the same country. Its major objective is efficient processing of transactions. Interorganizational systems have developed in direct response to two business pressures (drivers): the growing desirability to reduce costs and to improve the effectiveness and timeliness of business processes. IOSs enable effective communication at a reasonable cost, and collaboration to overcome differences in distance, time, language. They provide partners with access to each other's databases and frequently enable them to work on the same projects while their members are in different locations.

INTERACTIVE LEARNING SESSION

www.wiley.com/
college/turban

Go to the CD and access Chapter 8: Functional, Enterprise, and Interorganizational Systems. You will be given a simulation in which you must interact with an ERP and CRM system. You will be given objectives for several decisions, and must decide what information will be relevant to use in the ERP/CRM system. The program will give you feedback on how well the particular information would help in making business decisions.

For additional resources, go to the book's Web site for Chapter 8. There you will find Web resources for the chapter, including links to organizations, people, and technology; "IT's About Business" company links; "What's in IT for Me?" links; and a self-testing Web quiz for Chapter 8.

DISCUSSION QUESTIONS

1. Can MIS exist without TPS? Would it make sense to have a TPS without MIS?

2. Why is it logical to organize IT applications by functional areas?

3. Discuss how IT facilitates the budgeting process, why risk management is so important, and how it can be enhanced by IT.

4. Explain how IT can "make the customer king (queen)," and why information systems are critical to sales order processing.

5. Discuss the need for software integration. Compare the integrated software used by The Art Store (at the beginning of the chapter) to an integrated system using ERP software.

6. Identify some of the major HRM tools and discuss the benefits of using a computerized support system.

7. Analyze the cross-border data issues. Which are likely to limit the spread of global trade?

PROBLEM-SOLVING ACTIVITIES

1. The introduction of software like SAP/R3 transforms the way business is done and the organizational culture. Review some clients' success stories (try *sap.com* and *peoplesoft.com*). Prepare a report on the major impacts.

2. Argot International (a fictitious name) is a medium-sized company in Peoria, Illinois, with about 2,000 employees. The company manufactures special machines for farms and food processing plants, buying materials and components from about 150 vendors in six different countries. It also buys special machines and tools from Japan. Products are sold either to wholesalers (about 70) or directly to clients (from a mailing list of about 2,000). The business is very competitive.

The company has the following information systems in place: financial/accounting, marketing (primarily information about sales), engineering, research and development, and manufacturing

(CAM). These systems are independent of each other, and only the financial/accounting systems are on a local area network.

Argot is having profitability problems. Cash is in high demand and short supply, due to strong competition from Germany and Japan. The company wants to investigate the possibility of using information technology to improve the situation. However, the vice president of finance objects to the idea, claiming that most of the tangible benefits of information technology are already being realized. You are hired as a consultant to the president. Respond to the following:

a. Prepare a list of 10 potential applications of information technologies that you think could help the company. Prioritize them.

b. From the description of the case, would you recommend any telecommunications arrangements?

Be very specific. Remember, the company is in financial trouble.

c. How can the Internet help Argot?

3. Conduct some research on the succession of EOQ→MRP→MRP II→SCM→ERP. Evaluate the role of IT in this succession process.

INTERNET ACTIVITIES

1. Surf the Net and find free accounting, sales, or other functional software (try *shareware.com*). Download the software and try it. Comment on its benefits.

2. Enter the site of Federal Express (*fedex.com/usa*) and learn how to ship a package, track the status of a package, and calculate the shipping cost online.

3. Finding a job on the Internet is challenging; there are almost too many places to look. Visit the following sites: *careermosaic.com, http://vertical.worklife.com/onlines/careermag/, jobcenter.com,* and *monster.com*. Can they be useful to you? Why?

4. Enter the Web site *tandem.com* and find information about Tandem's iTP solutions. Identify the software that allows Internet transaction processing. Prepare a report about the benefits of iTP.

5. Enter the Web site *peoplesoft.com* and identify products and services in the area of HRM integrated software. E-mail PeopleSoft to find out whether their product can fit the organization where you work or one with which you are familiar.

6. Examine the capabilities of the following financial software packages: Comshare BudgetPlus (from Comshare), Financial Analyzer (from Oracle), and CFO Vision (from SAS Institute). Prepare a table or report comparing their capabilities.

7. Surf the Internet and find information on sales-force automation (try *sybase.com/products/*). Prepare a report on the state of the art. What are the capabilities and benefits of such products?

TEAM ACTIVITIES AND ROLE PLAYING

1. Visit a large company in your area and identify its marketing channel systems. Before you go, prepare a diagram that shows the six components of Figure 8.4. Then during your visit find how IT supports each of those components. Finally, suggest improvements in the existing channel system that can be supported by IT technologies that are not in use by the company today.

2. Divide the class into groups of four. Each member represents a major functional area. Prepare several examples of processes that cross several functional areas and may require the *integration* of functional information systems in a company of your choice.

3. Divide the class into three groups. One will investigate SCM vendors, the second will investigate ERP vendors, and the third will deal with all integration issues. Check the ERP/SCM integration and compare it to integration of existing information systems.

4. With the class divided into teams of three or four, go to the Web sites of three or four well-known companies (including at least one retailer), and read their privacy statements. Prepare a report for the class detailing what common threads you found among the statements, and what was unique. If you were writing a privacy statement for a company run by your team, what would it include, and why?

REAL-WORLD CASE

CRM in Action at Mercedes-Benz

The Business Problem   Firms that produce luxury items in any market are in fierce competition to attract and retain customers. Many of them, such as DaimlerChrysler's Mercedes-Benz (M-B) division, find that along with maintaining competitive products, the key to this effort is innovating via customer relationship management (CRM). In the case of M-B, part of the CRM strategy involves linking end-customers directly to the production systems. The Mercedes-Benz brand has always been known as a high-quality, upscale vehicle, and DaimlerChrysler has firmly established itself as a company that delivers superior customer service. One of the high-touch services offered by the company is a delivery option in which the customer may take delivery at the U.S. factory where their M-Class SUV is built. The company can provide such perquisites as transportation to and from the airport, child care, private factory tours, and even a ride on the factory test track in their new vehicle. To make the program, called the Factory Delivery

Reservation System (FDRS), work, DaimlerChrysler had to come up with a method that would coordinate the logistics in an effective manner. It wouldn't do to have multiple customers vying for a limited number of delivery slots.

The IT Solution   DaimlerChrysler chose Baan ERP software for its manufacturing operations and IBM Global Services to assist in defining the enterprise business processes and their interfaces to the Mercedes-Benz supply chain, extending all the way from initial design to development, manufacture, marketing, and distribution of the M-class vehicle. The CRM solution that makes the FDRS possible is driven by IBM's Lotus Domino. By creating direct links from the Web into the underlying Baan manufacturing system, the FDRS allows retailers to show customers available delivery dates and time slots at the factory. The retailer selects a date and time, then FDRS creates an itinerary for the customer. FDRS immediately coordinates this reservation with all other Mercedes-Benz U.S. computer systems so that the vehicle is ready on time at the right location. It also completes all internal record keeping.

The Results   Thanks to the efficiency of the system, Mercedes-Benz U.S. International can create and validate 1,800 orders per hour and automatically generate material requirements and bills of material for 35,000 vehicles per hour. Keeping the customer in the loop with its innovative use of Lotus Domino, Mercedes has managed not only to improve its customer relations by providing a top-flight service, but also to demonstrate its commitment to customers by making them an integral part of the process. The customer is, in a sense, tied directly into the factory floor, which has proved to be a powerful sales tool.

Questions

1. Describe how Mercedes-Benz links its CRM strategy to its ERP strategy.

2. If you were a competitor of Mercedes-Benz, what additional features or services would you incorporate into your CRM strategy?

3. Do you think that lower-cost brands in Daimler-Chrysler's organization (e.g., Dodge) will enhance their CRM services along these lines? Why or why not?

VIRTUAL COMPANY ASSIGNMENT

wiley.com/college/turban

Extreme Descent Snowboards

www.wiley.com/
college/turban

Background   You have received an e-mail message from Jacob March, vice president of information systems. Upon reading the e-mail, you find you next assignment.

Assignment

I will be out of town on business for the next few days. I have outlined your next assignment.

Setsu Kiawa, Department Manager of Accounting, believes the accounting department could benefit from an enterprise resource-planning (ERP) package. This solution package software is new to EDS. I would like for you to do some preliminary investigation.

The ability for supply chain members to view the fulfillment status increases efficiency. EDS could better serve its customers by knowing the exact status of each order. Changepoint offers a hosted supply chain solution. Its Web site shows a full tour with all its service features.

1. Visit the *Changepoint* site (*www.changepoint.com*)

2. Identify three ERP vendors. (Your book lists several vendors and each has a Web site.) Provide a URL (Web page address) and a short description of what each vendor can offer EDS.

3. Recommend one ERP vendor who can provide the best solution for EDS. Support your recommendation.

4. In your opinion, would a small company like EDS benefit more from componentization? (Refer to your book, if necessary.) Support your answer.

Thank you,
Jacob

ELECTRONIC COMMERCE

9

CHAPTER PREVIEW

One of the most profound changes currently transpiring in the world of business is the introduction of electronic commerce. The impact of electronic commerce (e-commerce, or EC) on procurement, shopping, business collaboration, and customer services as well as on delivery of various services is so dramatic that almost every organization is affected. E-commerce is changing all business functional areas and their important tasks, ranging from advertising to paying bills. The nature of competition is also drastically changing, due to new online companies, new business models, and the diversity of EC-related products and services. EC provides unparalleled opportunities for companies to expand worldwide at a small cost, to increase market share, and to reduce costs. In this chapter we will explain the major applications of EC, the issues related to its successful implementation and to its failures, and what services are necessary for its support. We look at business-to-consumer (B2C) commerce, business-to-business (B2B) commerce, intrabusiness commerce, and e-government. Also, we will demonstrate the impact on the various functional areas of organizations.

CHAPTER OUTLINE

9.1 Overview of E-Commerce
9.2 Business-to-Consumer Applications
9.3 Market Research, Advertising, and Customer Service
9.4 B2B and Collaborative Commerce Applications
9.5 Innovative Applications of E-Commerce
9.6 Infrastructure and E-Commerce Support Services
9.7 Legal and Ethical Issues in E-Commerce

LEARNING OBJECTIVES

1. Describe electronic commerce, its scope, benefits, limitations, and types.
2. Describe the major applications and issues of business-to-consumer commerce, service industries in e-commerce, and electronic auctions.
3. Discuss the importance and activities of B2C market research, advertising, and customer service.
4. Describe business-to-business and collaborative commerce applications.
5. Describe emerging EC applications such as e-government and mobile commerce.
6. Describe the e-commerce infrastructure and support services, including payments and logistics.
7. Discuss legal and other implementation issues.

273

INTEL CORPORATION EMBRACES THE WEB

intel.com

The Business Problem

Intel Corporation, the world's largest producer of microprocessor chips, sells its products to thousands of manufacturers. Much of its business is in the personal computer market, in which companies such as Dell computer use Intel's chips ("Intel Inside" logo). Competition in the chip market is intense. Intel creates customized catalogs and sends them to its potential customers together with information on product availability. Until 1997 it was all done on paper. Orders from Intel's thousands of customers, distributors, and business partners worldwide were received by fax and phone, making the distribution process slow, expensive, and frequently error-prone. During 1997, a number of departments launched their own electronic order handling that resulted in incompatible and inefficient systems.

The IT Solution

So, in 1998, Intel established its e-business program, which is focused on selling online and on customer support for a range of products, including microprocessors, motherboards, embedded chips, chipsets, and flash memory.

Order placing is only part of what Intel is doing online. The site also features self-service order tracking and a library of product documentation and roadmaps that replace the work of customer service representatives, who previously sent information manually to customers. In 1999, Intel moved to a broad program of electronic procurement of products and services. Finally, Intel is using electronic commerce to improve its internal operations, such as interdepartmental collaboration.

Intel first specifically targeted small and midsize customers, the majority of which operate outside the United States. These companies had previously communicated with Intel mostly by phone and fax. Intel also moved 11 of its larger customers, which previously were connected to Intel on *electronic data interchange (EDI)* networks, to a system called Supply Line Management. This system lets Intel link to customers' plants across the Internet to track usage of parts. Intel is also using online systems to deliver personalized information to its customers and employees. Intel claims that it is doing more e-business than any other company in the world.

The Results

Intel's e-business initiatives enhance its competitive advantage by giving its customers better tools for managing transactions. At the same time they bring substantial tangible savings to Intel. For example, the company has been able to eliminate 45,000 faxes per quarter to Taiwan alone.

Sources: Compiled from *InternetWeek* (November 23, 1998), pp. 1, 98, "Intel Goes E-Business" (*intel.com/eBusiness/enabling/ebusiness.htm*, December 28, 1999), and *intel.com/ebusiness* (August 2001).

What We Learned from This Case

The Intel case illustrates a new and effective way for conducting business—selling and buying products on the Internet. This is an example of *business-to-business electronic commerce,* one of the most exciting and fastest-growing business phenomena of our times. The case demonstrates that electronic commerce not only involves electronic buying and selling, but also provides *customer service* and improves the *organization's internal business processes.*

This chapter will explore what electronic commerce is, how it works, what issues are involved in its implementation, and how it creates new business models that change the world of business. It also will show that while large companies such as Intel can benefit from electronic commerce, so too can very small companies successfully capitalize on the opportunities created by electronic commerce.

9.1 OVERVIEW OF E-COMMERCE

Electronic commerce (e-commerce, or EC) describes the buying, selling, and exchanging of products, services, and information via computer networks, primarily the Internet. Some people view the term *commerce* as describing transactions conducted between business partners. To them, the term *electronic commerce* seems fairly narrow, so many use the term **e-business** (electronic business) instead. It refers to a broad definition of EC, not just buying and selling, but also servicing customers, collaborating with business partners, and conducting electronic transactions within an organization. According to Lou Gerstner, IBM's former CEO, "e-business is all about time, cycle, speed, globalization, enhanced productivity, reaching new customers, and sharing knowledge across institutions for competitive advantage." In this book we use the term electronic commerce in its broadest scope, as basically equivalent to e-business.

E-commerce is a very diverse and interdisciplinary topic, with issues ranging from e-technology, addressed by computer experts, to consumer behavior, addressed by behavioral scientists and marketing research experts.

Types of E-Commerce

The opening case shows an example of **business-to-business (B2B) EC**, in which two or more businesses make transactions or collaborate electronically. Although B2B is the major current type of electronic commerce (as measured by monetary volume), there are several other important types of EC:

- *Collaborative commerce (c-commerce).* In this type of EC, business partners collaborate electronically. Such collaboration frequently occurs between and among business partners along the supply chain.
- *Business-to-consumers (B2C).* In this case the sellers are organizations, the buyers are individuals.
- *Consumers to businesses (C2B).* In this case consumers make known a particular need for a product or service, and organizations *compete* to provide the product or service to consumers. (An example would be Priceline.com, where the customer names the price and suppliers try to fulfill it.)
- *Consumer-to-consumer (C2C).* In this case an individual sells products (or services) to other individuals.
- *Intrabusiness (intraorganizational) commerce.* In this case an organization uses EC internally to improve its operations. A special case of this is known as **B2E** (business to its employees) EC.
- *Government-to-citizens (G2C) and to others.* In this case the government provides services to its citizens via EC technologies. Governments can do business with other governments (G2G) as well as with businesses (G2B).
- *Mobile commerce (m-commerce).* When e-commerce is done in a wireless environment, such as using cell phones to access the Internet, we call it *m-commerce.*

Each of the above types of EC may have several business models. For example, in B2B one can sell from catalogs or in auctions. Buying can be done in several models such as reverse auctions, group purchasing, or negotiations.

History and Scope

E-commerce applications began in the early 1970s with such innovations as electronic transfer of funds. However, the applications were limited to large corporations and a

few daring small businesses. Then came electronic data interchange (EDI), which added other kinds of transaction processing and extended participation to all industries. Since the commercialization of the Internet and the introduction of the Web in the early 1990s, EC applications have rapidly expanded.

The field of e-commerce is broad. There are many applications of EC, such as home banking, shopping in electronic malls, buying stocks, finding a job, conducting an auction, collaborating electronically with business partners around the globe, and providing customer service. The implementation of various EC applications depends on four major support categories, shown in Figure 9.1: people, public policy, marketing/advertising, and supply chain logistics. In addition, there is infrastructure support (shown at the bottom of the figure). The EC management within each organization coordinates the applications and infrastructure. Figure 9.1 can

"First of all—you need a Web site."

be used as a framework for understanding the relationships among the EC components. In this book we concentrate mainly on the applications, on issues related to support categories, and on EC management topics.

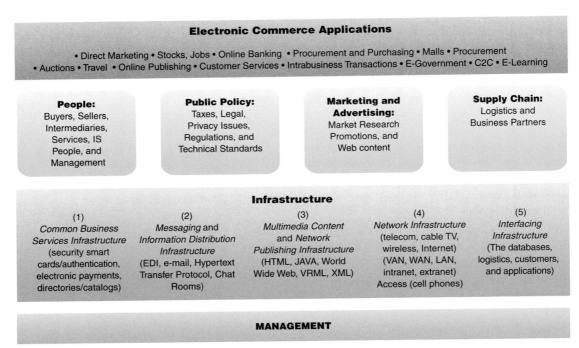

Figure 9.1 *A framework for e-commerce. [Sources: Modified from R. Kalakota and A. B. Whinston,* Electronic Commerce: A Manager's Guide *(Reading, MA: Addison-Wesley, 1997), p. 12; and from a list provided by V. Zwass, "Electronic Commerce: Structures and Issues,"* International Journal of Electronic Commerce, *Fall 1996, p. 6.]*

Benefits of E-Commerce

Few innovations in human history encompass as many benefits to *organizations, individuals,* and *society* as does e-commerce. These benefits have just begun to materialize, but they will increase significantly as EC expands. The major benefits are listed in Table 9.1.

Limitations and Failures of E-Commerce

Counterbalancing its many benefits, EC has some limitations, both technical and nontechnical, which have slowed its growth and acceptance. Those limitations are listed in Table 9.2, and some have been contributing factors in the *failures* of many EC projects and dot-com companies in recent years. As time passes, the limitations, especially the technical ones, will lessen or be overcome. In addition, appropriate planning can minimize the impact of some of them. Despite its limitations and failures, e-commerce has made very rapid progress. Also, various B2B activities, e-government, and some B2C activities are ballooning. As experience accumulates and technology improves, the ratio of EC benefits to cost will increase, resulting in an even greater rate of EC adoption.

Table 9.1   Benefits of E-Commerce

To Organizations

- Expands a company's marketplace to national and international markets. With minimal capital outlay, a company can quickly locate more customers, the best suppliers, and the most suitable business partners worldwide.
- Enables companies to procure material and services from other companies, rapidly and at less cost.
- Shortens or even eliminates marketing distribution channels, making products cheaper and vendors' profits higher.
- Decreases (by as much as 90 percent) the cost of creating, processing, distributing, storing, and retrieving information by digitizing the process.
- Allows lower inventories by facilitating pull-type supply chain management. This allows product customization and reduces inventory costs.
- Lowers telecommunications costs because the Internet is much cheaper than value-added networks (VANs).
- Helps small businesses compete against large companies.
- Enables very specialized niche markets.

To Customers

- Frequently provides less expensive products and services by allowing consumers to conduct quick online comparisons.
- Gives consumers more choices than they could easily locate otherwise.
- Enables customers to shop or make other transactions 24 hours a day, from almost any location.
- Delivers relevant and detailed information in seconds.
- Enables consumers to get customized products, from PCs to cars, at competitive prices.
- Makes it possible for people to work and study at home.
- Makes possible electronic auctions.
- Allows consumers to interact in *electronic communities* and to exchange ideas and compare experiences.

To Society

- Enables individuals to work at home and to do less traveling, resulting in less road traffic and lower air pollution.
- Allows some merchandise to be sold at lower prices, thereby increasing people's standard of living.
- Enables people in developing countries and rural areas to enjoy products and services that are otherwise not available. This includes opportunities to learn professions and earn college degrees, or to receive better medical care.
- Facilitates delivery of public services, such as government entitlements, reducing the cost of distribution and chance of fraud, and increasing the quality of social services, police work, health care, and education.

Table 9.2   Limitations of E-Commerce

Technical Limitations

1. Lack of universally accepted standards for quality, security, and reliability.
2. Insufficient telecommunications bandwidth.
3. Still-evolving software development tools.
4. Difficulties in integrating the Internet and EC software with some existing (especially legacy) applications and databases.
5. Need for special Web servers in addition to the network servers.
6. Expensive and/or inconvenient Internet accessibility for many would-be users.

Nontechnical Limitations

1. Unresolved legal issues (see Section 9.7 and Chapter 15).
2. Lack of national and international government regulations and industry standards.
3. Lack of mature methodologies for measuring benefits of and justifying EC.
4. Many sellers and buyers waiting for EC to stabilize before they take part.
5. Customer resistance to changing from a real to a virtual store. People do not yet sufficiently trust paperless, faceless transactions.
6. Perception that EC is expensive and unsecured.
7. An insufficient number (critical mass) of sellers and buyers exists for profitable EC operations.

Before you go on . . .

1. Define e-commerce and distinguish it from e-business.

2. List the major types of EC.

3. Distinguish among business-to-consumer, business-to-business, and intra-business EC.

4. List some organizational, societal, and consumer benefits of EC (five each).

5. List the major technical and nontechnical limitations of EC (three each).

9.2   BUSINESS-TO-CONSUMER APPLICATIONS

Forrester Research Institute and others predict that online B2C will be in the range of $300 billion to $800 billion in 2004, up from $515 million in 1996 (see *cyberatlas.com* and *emarketer.com*). For 2004, the total of B2C and B2B is estimated to be in the range of $2,500 billion to $7,000 billion. Some EC applications grew by 10 percent per *month*. Here we will look at some of the major categories of business-to-consumer applications.

Electronic Retailing, Storefronts, and Malls

For generations, home shopping from catalogs has flourished, and television shopping channels have been attracting millions of shoppers for more than a decade. However, these methods have drawbacks: Paper catalogs are sometimes inaccurate, and television shopping is limited to what is shown on the screen. Also, many people are troubled by the waste of paper used in catalogs that just get tossed out.

Like any mail-order shopping experience, e-commerce enables you to buy from home, 24 hours a day, 7 days a week. But EC overcomes some of the limitations of the other forms of home shopping. It offers a wide variety of products and services, including the most unique items, usually at lower prices. Furthermore, within seconds, you can get very detailed information on products, and you can easily search for and compare competitors' products and prices. **Electronic retailing** (e-tailing) is the direct sale of products through electronic storefronts or electronic malls, usually designed around an electronic catalog format and/or auctions.

Electronic storefronts.   Hundreds of thousands of solo storefronts can be found on the Internet, each with its own Internet name and Web site. **Electronic storefronts** may be an extension of physical stores such as Home Depot, The Sharper Image, or Wal-Mart. Others are new businesses started by entrepreneurs who saw a niche on the Web. Examples of these are Amazon.com, CDNow, Peapod, and Virtual Vineyards now *Evineyard*, (described in Box W9.1 at the book's Web site).

 www.wiley.com/college/turban

There are two types of storefronts, *general* and *specialized*. The latter sell one or a few products (e.g., flowers, wines, or dog toys). The general storefronts sell many products. Goods that are bought most often are computers and computer-related items, books and magazines, CDs, cassettes, movies and videos, clothing and shoes, toys, and food. Services that are bought most often online include travel services, stocks and bonds trading, electronic banking, insurance, and job matching. (Services will be presented as a separate topic later in this section.) Directories and hyperlinks from other Web sites and intelligent search agents help buyers find the best stores and products to match their needs. Storefronts may or may not be affiliated with electronic malls.

Electronic malls.   An **electronic mall**, also known as a **cybermall** or **e-mall**, is a collection of individual shops under one Internet address. The basic idea of an electronic mall is the same as that of a regular shopping mall—to provide a one-stop shopping place that offers many products and services. Representative cybermalls are Downtown Anywhere (*da.awa.com*), HandCrafters Mall (*rocksworld.com*), America's Choice Mall (*mall.choicemall.com*), and Shopping 2000 (*shopping2000.com*).

As is true for vendors that locate in a physical shopping mall, a vendor that locates in an e-mall gives up a certain amount of independence. Its success depends on the popularity of the mall, as well as on its own marketing efforts. On the other hand, malls generate streams of prospective customers who otherwise might never have stopped by the store. Each cybermall may include thousands of vendors. For example, *shopping.yahoo.com* and *eshop.msn.com* include tens of thousands of products from thousands of vendors.

Issues in e-tailing.   The following are the major issues faced by e-tailers.

- *Channel conflict.* If the seller is a click-and-mortar company, it may face a conflict with its regular distributors when it sells directly online. Known as **channel conflict**, this situation can alienate the regular distributors and has forced some companies (e.g., *lego.com*) to limit their B2C efforts; others (e.g., automotive companies) have decided not to sell direct online. However, a better approach is to try to collaborate in some way with the existing distributors, whose services may be restructured.

- *Order fulfillment.* E-tailers face a difficult problem of shipping very small quantities to a large number of buyers. This can be expensive, especially when returned items need to be handled. This topic is discussed in Section 9.6.

- *Viability of online e-tailers.* Most of the purely online e-tailers (excluding service industries) were unable to survive and folded in 2000–2002. Companies had problems with customer acquisition, order fulfillment, and forecasting demand. Online competition, especially in commodity-type products such as CDs, toys, books, or groceries, became very fierce, due to the ease of entry to the marketplace.

- *Conflicts within click-and-mortar organizations.* When an established company decides to sell direct online, on a large scale, it may create a conflict within its existing operation. Conflict may arise in areas such as pricing of products and services, allocation of resources (e.g., advertising budget), and logistics services provided to the online activities by the offline activities (e.g., handling of returned items purchased online). As a result of these conflicts, some companies have completely separated the "clicks" (the online portion of the organization) from the "mortars" (the traditional brick-and-mortar part of the organization). This may increase expenses and reduce the synergy between the two.

- *Lack of funding.* The so-called dot-com companies enjoyed almost unlimited funding between 1995 and 1998. After "burning" lots of money and being unable to generate profits quickly, the sources of funding dried up, resulting in many bankruptcies.

- *Incorrect revenue models.* Many dot-com companies were selling at or below cost with the objective of attracting many customers as well as advertisers to their sites. The idea was to generate enough revenue from advertising. This model did not work. Too many dot-com companies were competing on too few advertising dollars, which went mainly to a small number of well-known sites such as AOL and Yahoo!

Service Industries Online

Selling books, toys, computers, and most other products on the Internet may reduce vendors' selling costs by 20 to 40 percent. Further reduction is difficult to achieve because the products must be delivered physically. Only a few products (such as software or music) can be digitized to be delivered online for additional savings. On the other hand, delivery of services, such as buying stocks or insurance online, can be done 100 percent electronically, with considerable cost reduction. Therefore, delivery of services online is growing very rapidly, with millions of new customers added annually. The major online services to be discussed here are banking, trading of securities (stocks, bonds), job matching, travel, and real estate.

Cyberbanking.   **Electronic banking**, also known as **cyberbanking**, virtual banking, home banking, and online banking, includes various banking activities conducted from home, a business, or on the road instead of at a physical bank location. Electronic banking has capabilities ranging from paying bills to securing a loan. It saves time and is convenient for customers. For banks, it offers an inexpensive alternative to branch banking (for example, about 2 cents cost per transaction versus $1.07 at a physical branch) and a chance to enlist remote customers. Many banks are beginning to offer home banking, and some use EC as a major competitive strategy. One such bank is Wells Fargo (see IT's About Business 9.1).

Electronic banking offers several of the benefits listed in Section 9.1, such as expanding the customer base and saving the cost of paper transactions. In addition to regular banks with added online services, we are seeing the emergence of *virtual banks*, dedicated solely to Internet transactions, such as *sfnb.com* and *netbank.com*.

International and multiple-currency banking.   International banking and the ability to handle trading in multiple currencies are critical for international trade. Although some international retail purchasing can be done by giving a credit card number, other transactions may require cross-border banking support. Transfers of electronic funds and letters of credit are other important services in international banking.

IT's About Business

wellsfargo.com

Box 9.1: Cyberbanking at Wells Fargo

Wells Fargo is a large California Bank. At one time it had more than 1,700 branch banks. It has been known for generations for its financial services, dating back to the days of the Wild West. Wells Fargo's declared competitive strategy is cyberbanking. It is moving millions of customers to the Internet and closing hundreds of branches. A visit to the Wells Fargo Web site indicates the richness of services available.

The services are divided into five major categories: online (personal) banking, personal finance services, small business, commercial banking, and international trade. In addition, there are employment opportunities listed, and even a virtual mall in which you can buy from the Wells Fargo Museum Store or be linked to several virtual stores such as Amazon.com. The bank offers many services in all categories. Most interesting are the services that cover all the needs of small businesses. These are extremely user friendly and can run even on an old computer system.

Sources: Communications Week (May 27, 1997), p. 44; *Datamation* (June 1997), pp. 91–93; and *wellsfargo.com* (November 2001).

Questions

1. What services cannot be performed by electronic banking?

2. Can a small bank offer similar electronic banking services?

3. Why would a bank get involved in cybershopping?

EXAMPLES

Hong Kong Bank grows without branches. Hong Kong and Shanghai Bank (*hsbc.com.hk*) has developed a special system (called HEXAGON) to provide electronic banking in 60 countries. Using this system, the bank has leveraged its reputation and infrastructure in the developing economies of Asia to become a major international bank rapidly, without developing an extensive new branch network.

hsbc.com.hk

Supporting foreign currency trading. The company Oanda provides conversion of over 160 currencies. International traders can be assisted by many online services (see *financialsupermarket.com* and *foreign-trade.com*). ●

Electronic bill payments. In August 1998, 90 percent of people surveyed in the San Francisco Bay area indicated a desire to pay bills on the Internet. Mostly, people prefer to pay monthly bills, such as telephone, utilities, credit cards, and cable TV, online. The recipients of such payments are even more enthusiastic about such service than the payers, since online payments enable them to significantly reduce processing costs. The following are the major existing payment systems in common use: automatic payment of mortgages; automatic transfer of funds to pay monthly utility bills; paying bills from online banking account; merchant-to-customer direct billing; and use of an intermediary to aggregate bills into one payable Web site.

Online securities trading. It is estimated that by the year 2004, about 35 million people in the United States will be using computers to trade stocks, bonds, and other financial instruments. In Korea, more than 65 percent of stock traders are using the Internet. Why? Because it makes a lot of dollars and "sense." An online trade typically costs between $3 and $30, compared to an average fee of $100 from a full-service broker and $35 from a discount broker. There is no waiting on busy telephone lines. Furthermore, the chance of making mistakes is small because there is no oral communication with a securities broker in a frequently very noisy physical environment.

Orders can be placed from anywhere, any time, and you can find on the Web, by yourself, a considerable amount of information regarding investing in a specific company or in a mutual fund.

How does online trading work? Let's say you have an account with Charles Schwab. You access Schwab's Web site (*schwab.com*), enter your account number and password, and click on stock trading. Using a menu, you enter the details of your order (buy or sell, margin or cash, price limit, market order, etc.). The computer tells you the current "ask" and "bid" prices, much as a broker would do on the telephone, and you can approve or reject the transaction. Some well-known companies offer only online trading. Examples are E*Trade, Ameritrade, and Suretrade.

The online job market.   The Internet offers a perfect environment for job seekers and for companies searching for hard-to-find employees. The online job market is especially effective for technology-oriented jobs. However, there are thousands of companies and government agencies that advertise available positions in all types of jobs, accept resumes, and take applications via the Internet. The online job market is used by:

1. *Job seekers.* Job seekers can reply to employment ads online. Or they can take the initiative and place resumes on their own home pages or on others' Web sites, send messages to members of newsgroups asking for referrals, and use recruiting firms such as Career Mosaic (*careermosaic.com*), Job Center (*jobcenter.com*), and Monster Board (*monster.com*). For entry-level jobs and internships for newly minted graduates, job seekers can use *jobdirect.com*. Need help writing your resume? Try *resume-link.com* or *jobweb.com*.

2. *Job offerers.* Many organizations advertise openings on their Web site. Others use sites ranging from Yahoo! to bulletin boards and recruiting firms.

3. *Recruiting firms.* Hundreds of job-placement brokers and related services are active on the Web. They use their own Web pages to post available job descriptions and advertise their services in electronic malls and on others' Web sites. Recruiters use newsgroups, online forums, bulletin boards, and chat rooms. Job-finding brokers help candidates write their resumes and get the most exposure. Matching of candidates and jobs is done by companies such as *discoverme.com*.

4. *Newsgroups.* Job finding is of interest to many newsgroups. Jobs in a certain category or location are posted, discussions are conducted, and resumes can be sent.

In addition to low cost and wide exposure, participants in the online job market cite the ease of transmitting information and documents (resumes and job descriptions) and the speed of the recruiting process as motivators for using the Internet. Also, the recruiting companies save time on data entry by using electronic forms for taking applications. Finally, the ability to widen an employee's search geographically is an advantage to both the recruiter and the recruitee. Hot Jobs (*hotjobs.com*) provides links to many sources for further research, for accessing job listings, and for finding for-fee counselors. Manager's Checklist W9.1 at the Web site lists the benefits and limitations of the online job market.

www.wiley.com/
college/turban

Travel.   The Internet is an ideal place to plan, explore, and economically arrange almost any trip. Potential savings are available through special sales, comparisons, use of auctions, and the elimination of travel agents. Examples of comprehensive travel online services are Expedia.com, Travelocity.com, and Travelweb.com. Services are also provided online by all major airline vacation services, large conventional travel agencies, car rental agencies, hotels, and tour companies. Online travel services allow you to purchase airline tickets, reserve hotel rooms, and rent cars. Most sites also support an itinerary-based interface, including a fare-tracker feature that sends you e-mail messages about low-cost flights to your favorite destinations. Finally, Price-line.com allows you to set a price you are willing to pay for an airline ticket or hotel accommodations and Priceline then attempts to find a vendor that will match your price.

Real estate.   Real estate transactions are an ideal area for e-commerce, for the following reasons. First, you can view many properties on the screen, saving time for you and the broker. Second, you can sort and organize properties according to your criteria and preview the exterior and interior designs of the properties, shortening the search process. Finally, you can find detailed information about the properties and frequently get even more detail than brokers will provide. In some locations brokers allow the use of such databases only from their offices, but considerable information is now available on the Internet. For example, Realtor.com allows you to search a database of over one million homes across the United States. The database is composed of local "multiple listings" of all available properties and properties just sold, in hundreds of locations.

In another application, homebuilders now use virtual reality technology on their Web sites to demonstrate three-dimensional floor plans to potential home buyers. They use virtual models that enable buyers to walk through mockups of homes.

Auctions

An **auction** is a market mechanism by which sellers place offers and buyers make sequential bids. Auctions are characterized by the competitive nature by which a final price is reached. Auctions have been an established method of commerce for centuries, and they are especially suited to deal with products and services for which conventional marketing channels are ineffective or inefficient. Auctions can expedite the disposal of items that need liquidation or a quick sale, and they ensure prudent execution of contracts.

The Internet provides an infrastructure for executing auctions at lower cost, and with many more involved sellers and buyers. Individual consumers and corporations alike can participate in this rapidly growing form of e-commerce. There are several types of auctions, each with its motives and procedures. Auctions are divided here into two major types: *forward* auctions, and *reverse* auctions.

Forward auctions.   **Forward auctions** are used mainly as a selling channel. A single seller auctions item(s) to many potential buyers. The specific alternative mechanisms in a forward auction are as follows.

- *English auctions.* Buyers bid on one item at a time. The bidding price increases with additional bids. The highest bidder wins (if price is the only criterion).

- *Yankee auctions.* These are similar to English auctions, but multiple identical items are offered. You can bid on any number of items. Bidding prices are escalating.

- *Dutch auctions.* These are usually for multiple, identical items (e.g., flowers). Prices are set high and are reduced as the auction clock runs down until a bid for a specific quantity is submitted. The first bidder wins. (You can see the auction clock at *aquarius-flora.com*).

Reverse auctions.   In **reverse auctions**, there is one buyer, who wants to buy a product or a service. Suppliers are invited to submit bids. The supplier that submits the lowest bid wins. Several rounds may take place if the lowest bid is not satisfactory to the seller.

Auctions are used in B2C, B2B, C2B, e-government, and C2C commerce, and they are becoming popular in many countries. Benefits are derived for sellers, buyers, and auctioneers as shown in Manager's Checklist 9.1.

Electronic auctions started in the 1980s on private networks, but their use was limited. The Internet opens many new opportunities for e-auctions, and millions of sellers and buyers participate. Auctions can be conducted from the seller's site or from a third-party site. For example, eBay (*ebay.com*) offers hundreds of thousands of different items in several types of auctions. Over 300 other major companies, including Amazon.com, offer online auctions as well. B2B auctions are discussed in Section 9.4.

Bartering.   Related to auctions is **electronic bartering**, the *exchange* of goods or services without a monetary transaction. In addition to the individual-to-individual bartering ads that appear in some newsgroups, bulletin boards, and chat rooms, there are several intermediaries that arrange for corporate bartering (e.g., *barterbrokers.com*). These intermediaries try to find partners to a barter.

Not all e-commerce applications are Internet based. For an example of a B2C non-Internet EC service, see the description of the Highway 91 project at our Web site.

Manager's Checklist 9.1

Benefits of Electronic Auctions

> ### Benefits to Sellers
>
> - Increased revenues from broadening customer base and shortening cycle time
> - Optimal price setting, determined by the market (more buyers)
> - Saves on the commission to intermediaries. (Physical auctions' fees are very expensive compared to e-auctions.)
> - Can liquidate large quantities quickly
> - Improved customer relationship and loyalty (in the case of specialized B2B auction sites and electronic exchanges).
>
> ### Benfits to Buyers
>
> - Opportunities to find unique items and collectibles
> - Chance to bargain, instead of buying at a fixed price
> - Entertainment. Participation in e-auctions can be entertaining and exciting.
> - Anonymity. With the help of a third party, buyers can remain anonymous.
> - Convenience. Buyers can trade from anywhere, even with a cell phone; they do not have to travel to an acution place.
>
> ### Benefits to Auctioneers
>
> - High "stickiness" of the Web site (customers stay at "sticky" sites longer and come back more often); generates more ad revenue to auctioneer
> - Expansion of the auction business

Before you go on . . .

1. Describe electronic storefronts and malls.

2. List the benefits of cyberbanking.

3. Describe electronic securities trading.

4. Describe the online job market.

5. Explain how electronic auctions work and list their benefits.

9.3   MARKET RESEARCH, ADVERTISING, AND CUSTOMER SERVICE

Conducting successful B2C commerce requires several support activities. Most notable are advertising, customer service, and understanding of consumers and their behavior.

Consumers and Their Behavior

To successfully conduct B2C it is important to find out who are the actual and potential customers. Several research institutions collect Internet usage statistics (e.g., *emarketer.com*), look at factors that inhibit shopping, and more. Merchants then can prepare their marketing and advertising strategies, based on this information.

Online purchasing constitutes a fundamental change for customers. If the customer has previously used mail-order catalogs or television shopping, the change will not be so drastic. But moving away from a physical shopping mall to an electronic mall may not be simple. Furthermore, shopping habits keep changing as a result of innovative marketing strategies. Finding out what specific groups of consumers (such as teenagers or residents of certain geographical zones) want is a major role of market research. This dividing of customers into specific groups is called **segmentation**. However, even if we know what groups of consumers in general want, each individual consumer is very likely to want something different. Some like classical music while others like jazz. Some like brand names, while price is more important to many others. A major advantage of EC is its ability to *customize* products, services, advertisements, and customer service at a reasonable cost. This is referred to as **personalization**.

Learning about customers is extremely important for any successful business, especially in cyberspace. Such learning is facilitated by market research.

Market Research

Market research has been conducted offline for years in order to find out what motivates consumers to buy. The key for e-tailers is to understand the consumer decision-making process on the Web. To do that, we developed a model for explaining consumer buying decisions on the Internet, as shown in Figure 9.2 (on page 286). The model starts on the left, showing factors that stimulate a consumer to think about buying. Then, two types of factors influence the buying decision-making process, individual (personal) factors (top left) and environmental factors (top right). In EC there are additional factors that influence shoppers' decision making—these are shown at the bottom, in the vendor-controlled box. The model shows us that cybershopping is a

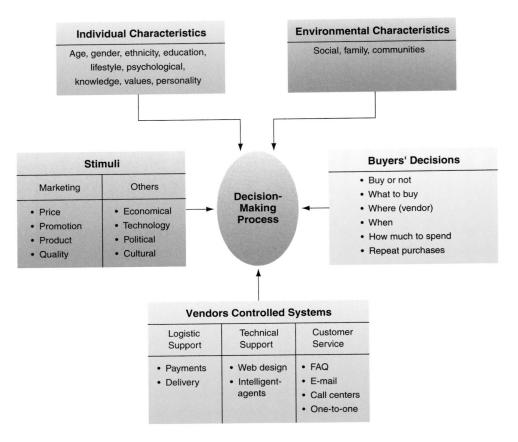

Figure 9.2   *E-commerce consumer behavior model.*

complex process. It is also clear from this figure that there is much that sellers need to know about customers, since the seller controls all the online (vendor-controlled) systems shown at the bottom of the figure, as well as being able to influence some of the stimulus factors (for example, through advertising). Such knowledge is provided by market research.

The Internet is a powerful and cost-effective tool for conducting market research about consumer behavior, for identifying new markets, for investigating competitors and their products, and for testing consumer interest in new products. There are basically two ways to find out what customers want. The first is to ask them, and the second is to infer what they want by observing what they do in cyberspace.

Asking customers what they want.   The Internet provides easy, fast, and relatively inexpensive ways for vendors to find out what customers want by interacting directly with them. The simplest way is to ask potential customers to fill in electronic questionnaires. To do so, vendors need to provide some inducements. For example, in order to play a free electronic game or participate in a sweepstakes, you are asked to fill in an online form and answer some questions about yourself. Marketers not only learn what you want from the direct answers, but also try to infer from your preferences of music, for example, what type of books, clothes, or movies you may be likely to prefer.

In some cases, asking customers what they want may not be feasible. Or customers may refuse to answer questionnaires, or they may provide false information (as is done in about 40 percent of the cases, according to studies done at Georgia Tech University). Also, questionnaires can be lengthy and costly to administer. Therefore, a different approach may be needed—observing what customers do in cyberspace.

Tracking customer activities on the Web.   Today it is possible to learn about customers by observing their behavior on the Internet. Many companies offer site-tracking services, based on *cookies* or other approaches. For example, Nettracker (from *sane.com*) collects data from client/server logs and provides periodic reports that include demographic data such as where customers come from or how many customers have gone straight from the home page to ordering. The company translates Internet domain names into real-company names and includes general and financial corporate information. One of the most interesting tools for tracking customers on the Internet as well as helping them to shop is intelligent agents.

E-Commerce Intelligent Agents

Agents are computer programs that conduct routing tasks, search and retrieve information, support decision making, and act as domain experts. These agents sense the environment and act autonomously without human intervention. This results in a significant savings of users' time (up to 99 percent in some cases). There are various types of agents, ranging from **software agents**, which are those with no intelligence, to *learning agents* that exhibit some intelligent behavior (see Chapter 12).

Agents are used to support many tasks in EC. It will be beneficial to distinguish between search engines and the more intelligent type of agents. A **search engine**, which is usually a software agent, is a computer program that can automatically contact other network resources on the Internet, search for specific information or key words, and report the results. Unlike search engines, an **intelligent agent** uses expert, or knowledge-based, capabilities to do more than just "search and match." For example, it can monitor movement on a Web site to check whether a customer seems lost or ventures into areas that may not fit his profile, and the agent can notify the customers and even provide assistance. Depending on their level of intelligence, agents can do many other things. In this section we will concentrate on intelligent agents for assisting customers.

Search and filtering agents.   Intelligent agents can help customers determine what to buy to satisfy a specific need. This is achieved by looking for specific product information and critically evaluating it. An agent helps consumers decide what product best fits their profile and requirements.

Product- and vendor-finding agents.   Once the consumer has decided what to buy, a *comparison agent* will help in doing comparisons, usually of prices from different vendors. A pioneering intelligent agent for online price comparison was Bargainfinder from Accenture. This agent was used only in online shopping for CDs. The agent queried the price of a specific CD from a number of online vendors and returned the list of vendors and prices. Today much more sophisticated agents such as Mysimon.com help with comparisons.

An interesting agent worth mentioning is Kasbah (*kasbah.com*). This experimental agent from MIT media lab was sent out to actively seek buyers or sellers. In creating the agent, users had to specify requirements, including desired price, highest (or lowest) acceptable price, and a date by which to complete the transaction. The agent's goal was to complete an acceptable transaction based on these requirements. Kasbah agents were expected to be able to negotiate with each other, following specific strategies assigned by their creators, using a number of different parameters: price, warranty, delivery time, service contracts, return policy, loan options, and other value-added services.

Profiling customers using intelligent agents.   Some companies collect information about consumers for the purpose of creating a customer's profile. With this profile, the company can tailor ads to the specific customers or offer them product information. Use of this type of intelligent agent is called *product brokering*. To build a customer profile, an agent uses a *collaborative filtering* process. The consumer is asked to rate a number of products; the system then matches these ratings with the ratings of other consumers, and, relying on the ratings of other consumers with similar tastes, recommends products that the consumer has not yet rated.

EXAMPLE

fujitsu.com

Fujitsu's agents profile consumers.   Fujitsu, a major Japanese vendor of consumer products, is using an agent-based technology called Interactive Marketing Interface (iMi) that allows advertisers to interact directly with targeted customers (*magazine. fujitsu.com*). Consumers submit a personal profile to iMi, indicating such characteristics as product categories of interest, hobbies, travel habits, and the maximum number of e-mail messages per week they are willing to receive. In turn, via e-mail, customers receive product announcements, advertisements, and marketing surveys based on their personal profile. By answering the marketing surveys or acknowledging receipt of advertisements, consumers earn iMi points, redeemable for gift certificates and phone cards. Consumers remain anonymous to the advertisers. ●

The information collected by market research and intelligent agents is used for advertising strategies and for customer service, the topics we discuss next.

Advertising Online

Advertising is an attempt to disseminate information in order to influence a buyer–seller transaction. Traditional advertising on TV or newspaper is impersonal, one-way mass communication. Direct-response marketing contacts individuals by means of direct mail or by telephone calls and requires them to respond in order to make a purchase. The direct-response approach personalizes advertising and marketing, but it can be expensive, slow, and ineffective. Internet advertising redefines the process, making it media-rich, dynamic, and interactive. It improves on traditional forms of advertising in a number of ways: Internet ads can be updated any time at minimal cost, and therefore can always be timely. They can reach a very large number of potential buyers all over the world. Online ads are sometimes cheaper in comparison to print (newspaper and magazine), radio, or television ads. Ads in these other media are expensive because they are determined by space occupied (print ads), by how many days (times) they are run, and by the number of local and national stations and print media that run them. Internet ads can be interactive and targeted to specific interest groups and/or to individuals. Finally, the use of the Internet itself is growing very rapidly, and it makes sense to move advertising to the Internet, where the number of viewers is growing. Nevertheless, the Internet as an advertising medium does have some shortcomings, most of which relate to measurement of effectiveness. For one thing, it is difficult to measure the actual results of placing a banner ad, and the audience is still relatively small (compared to television, for example). For a summary of the benefits and the limitations of Internet advertising, see Manager's Checklist W9.2 at our Web site.

www.wiley.com/
college/turban

Advertising methods.   The most common advertising methods online are banners and e-mail, which we look at first.

Banners.   As you drive along a highway you see countless billboards on the sides of the road. **Banners** are electronic billboards, and banner advertising is the most commonly used form of advertising on the Internet. Typically, a banner contains a short text or graphical message to promote a product or a vendor. It may even contain video clips and sound. When customers click on the banner, they are transferred to the advertiser's home (ordering) page. Advertisers go to great lengths to design banners that catch consumers' attention.

There are two types of banners: **Keyword banners** appear when a predetermined word is queried from the search engine. It is effective for companies who want to narrow their target to consumers interested in particular topics. **Random banners** appear randomly and might be used to introduce new products to the widest possible audience, or to keep a well-known brand, such as Amazon.com or IBM, in the public eye.

A major advantage of using banners is the ability to customize them to the target audience. Keyword banners can be customized to a market segment or even to an individual. If the computer system knows who you are, or what your profile is, you may be sent a banner that is supposed to match your interests. However, one of the major drawbacks of using banners is that limited information is allowed. Hence advertisers need to think of creative but short messages to attract viewers. Another drawback is that banners, which were a novelty in late 1990s and so were noticed by viewers, are ignored by many viewers today. Therefore some question their cost effectiveness and instead recommend e-mail advertising.

E-mail advertising.   E-mail is emerging as an Internet advertising and marketing channel that affords cost-effective implementation and a better and quicker response rate than other advertising channels (such as print ads). Marketers develop or purchase a list of e-mail addresses, place them in a customer database, and then send advertisements via e-mail. A list of e-mail addresses can be a very powerful tool because the marketer can target a group of people or even individuals. However, there is potential for misuse of e-mail advertising. A major issue related to unsolicited e-mail advertising is *spamming*, the practice of indiscriminate distribution of electronic messages (electronic junk mail) without permission of the receiver.

What will happen when many marketers start inundating prospects and customers with electronic mail? How will consumers deal with it? What areas must marketers focus on to ensure e-mail marketing success? The answers to these and similar questions will determine the success of e-mail advertising. Unfortunately, the answers to these questions are not always known. Market research may help provide some answers to these questions.

Other forms of Internet advertising.   Online advertising can be done in several other forms, including non-banner ads or posting advertisements in chat rooms, to newsgroups, and on online kiosks. Advertising on Internet radio is just beginning, and soon advertising on Internet television will commence. Of special interest is advertising to members of *Internet communities*. Community sites are gathering places for people of similar interests and are therefore a logical place to promote products related to those interests. Advertising at a community site (such as at *geocities.com*) might include direct advertising and, frequently, a chance to buy the advertised products at a discount.

Some advertising issues and approaches.   There are many issues related to the implementation of Internet advertising: how to design ads for the Internet, where and when to advertise, and how to integrate online and offline ads. Most of such decisions require the input of marketing and advertising experts. We present several illustrative issues: permission marketing, viral marketing, customizing ads, interactive marketing, and attracting visitors to a site.

Permission marketing.   Traditional telemarketers contact consumers without their permission, frequently when the consumers are busy or are eating dinner. This does not leave consumers with a positive feeling, nor does it put them in the mood to buy the product or service being marketed. As consumers gain more control of information, marketers must find ways to cleverly communicate their brand messages. **Permission marketing** is one answer. It offers consumers incentives to accept advertising and e-mail voluntarily. How does it work? Ask people what they are interested in, ask permission to send them marketing information, and then do it in an entertaining, educational, and interesting manner.

Permission marketing is the basis of many Internet marketing strategies. For example, some 1.7 million Net users receive e-mails each week from airlines such as American and Southwest. Users of this marketing service can ask for notification of low fares to exotic (or not-so-exotic) places. In addition, users can easily unsubscribe at any time. Permission marketing is also extremely important for market research (e.g., see *mediametrix.com*).

In one particularly interesting form of permission marketing, MyPoints.com, Getpaid4i12.com, and Surf-to-get-paid.com built customer lists of millions of people who are happy to receive advertising messages whenever they are on the Web. These customers are paid $0.50 an hour to view messages while they do their normal surfing. They may also be paid $0.10 an hour for the surfing time of any friends they refer to the above sites. The sites charge advertisers for space in the view bar on the user screens, but instead of pocketing all the money they collect, they split it with customers.

Viral marketing.   The customer referrals at AllAdvantage are an example of one type of viral marketing. **Viral marketing** refers to online word-of-mouth marketing. The main idea in viral marketing is to have people forward messages to friends, asking them, for example, to "check this out." A marketer can distribute a small game program, for example, that comes embedded with a sponsor's e-mail that is easy to forward. By releasing a few thousand copies, vendors hope to reach many more thousands. Word-of-mouth marketing has been used for generations, but its speed and reach are multiplied manyfold by the Internet. Viral marketing is one of the new models being used to build brand awareness at a minimal cost. It has long been a favorite strategy of online advertisers pushing youth-oriented products.

Examples abound: Viral marketing was used by the founder of Hotmail, which grew from zero to 12 million subscribers in just 18 months. It also was successfully used by Blueskyfrog.com to give away five free SMS cell phone messages for every friend you bring in. Within a few months, this Australian company had over a million subscribers.

Unfortunately, though, several e-mail hoaxes have spread via viral marketing. Also, a danger of viral advertising is that a destructive virus can be added to an innocent advertisement, related game, or message. However, when used properly, the innovative approach of viral marketing, known also as *advocacy marketing*, can be both effective and efficient.

Customizing ads.   There is too much information on the Internet for customers to view. So filtering the irrelevant information by providing customized ads can be beneficial to customers and advertisers alike. BroadVision's Web site (*broadvision.com*) is an example of a customized ad service platform. Software there enables a marketing manager to customize display ads based on users' profiles. (For an example of how to customize ads see *Bcentral.com*) For even better reach to their intended audience, customized ads can be interactive.

Interactive advertising and marketing.   Conventional advertising is passive, targeted to mass audiences, and for that reason it may be ineffective. Therefore, all advertisers, whether online or not, attempt to customize their ads to special groups and, if possible, to individuals. A good salesperson is trained to interact with sales prospects, asking questions about the features they are looking for and handling possible objections as they come up. Online advertising comes closer to supporting this selling process than more traditional advertising media possibly can.

Ideally, in **interactive marketing**, advertisers present customized, one-on-one ads. The term *interactive* points to the ability to address an individual, to gather and remember that person's responses, and to serve that customer based on his or her previous, unique responses. When the Internet is combined with marketing databases, interactive marketing becomes a very effective and affordable competitive strategy. See Figure W9.1 which shows the keys to successful interactive marketing, on the book's Web site.

Attracting visitors to a site.   The following are examples of ways to attract visitors to a Web site.

www.wiley.com/
college/turban

- ***Making the top of the list of a search engine.*** Web sites submit their URLs to *search engines*. The search engine's intelligent program (called a spider) crawls through the submitted site, indexing all related content and links. Some lists generated by search engines include hundreds or thousands of items. Users typically start by clicking on the first 10 or so items, and soon get tired. So, for best exposure, advertisers like to make the top of the list. How do they do it? A company can get to the top of a search engine's list merely by adding, removing, or changing a few sentences on its Web pages. By doing so, the Web designer may alter the way a search engine's program ranks its findings.

- ***Online events, promotions, and attractions.*** People generally like the idea of something funny or something free, or both. Contests, quizzes, coupons, and free samples are an integral part of e-commerce as much as, or even more than, they are in offline commerce. Running promotions on the Internet is similar to running off-line promotions. These mechanisms are designed to attract visitors and to keep their attention. Examples include games, contests, monetary payments, and even free Internet access. For some specific examples of innovative ideas for online promotions and attractions, see Table W9.1 on the Web site.

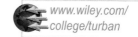
www.wiley.com/
college/turban

Electronic catalogs.   Printed catalogs have been a medium of advertising for a long time. Recently electronic catalogs on CD-ROMs and on the Web have been gaining popularity. The merchant's objective in using **online catalogs** is to advertise and promote products and services. From the customer's perspective, online catalogs offer a source of information that can be searched quickly with the help of special search engines. Also, comparisons involving catalog products can be made very effectively.

In the early days of online catalogs, most were replications of the text and pictures of printed catalogs. Today, electronic online catalogs are dynamic, customized, and integrated with selling and buying features such as electronic order taking and payment. The benefits and limitations of online catalogs are contrasted with those of paper catalogs in Manager's Checklist W9.3 at the book's Web site.

www.wiley.com/
college/turban

Customized catalogs.   A *customized catalog* is a catalog assembled specifically for a particular company, usually a regular customer of the catalog owner. It can even be tailored to individual consumers, in some cases. One way of doing this is to let the customers identify the parts of the public catalog that interest them; then, they do not have to deal with items they consider irrelevant.

Coupons online.   Finally, just as in offline advertising, shoppers can get discounts via coupons. You can gather any discount coupons you want by accessing sites like *hotcoupons.com* or *coupons.com*, selecting the store where you plan to redeem the coupons, and printing them. In the future, transfer of coupons directly to the virtual supermarket (such as *peapod.com* or *netgrocer.com*) will be available so that you can receive discounts on the items you buy there. Coupons also can be distributed via wireless devices, based on your location. As you approach a restaurant you may be offered a 15 percent discount electronic coupon to show to the proprietors when you arrive.

Customer Service

Whether an organization is selling to organizations or to individuals, in many cases a competitive edge is gained by providing superb customer service. In e-commerce, customer service becomes even more critical, since customers and merchants do not meet face-to-face.

Phases in the customer service life cycle.   Customer service should be approached as a business life cycle process, with the following four phases:

Phase 1. *Requirements.* Assist the customer to determine needs by providing photographs of a product, video presentations, textual descriptions, articles or reviews, sound bites on a CD, and downloadable demonstration files. Also use intelligent agents to make requirements suggestions.

Phase 2. *Acquisition.* Help the customer to acquire a product or service (online order entry, negotiations, closing of sale, and delivery).

Phase 3. *Ownership.* Support the customer on an ongoing basis (interactive online user groups, online technical support, FAQs and answers, resource libraries, newsletters, and online renewal of subscriptions).

Phase 4. *Retirement.* Help the client to dispose of a service or product (online resale, classified ads).

Many activities can be conducted in each of these phases. For example, when an airline offers information such as flight schedules and fare quotes on its Web site, it is supporting phases 1 and 2. Similarly, when computer vendors provide electronic help desks for their customers, they are supporting phase 3. Dell will help you to auction your obsolete computer, and Amazon.com will help you to sell used books, activities that support phase 4.

EXAMPLE

fidelity.com

Fidelity Investments offers financial information and news.   Fidelity Investments provides investors with "the right tools to make their own best investment decisions." The site has several sections, which include daily updates of financial news, information about Fidelity's mutual funds, material for interactive investment and retirement planning, and brokerage services. This is an example of support given to phase 1 in the online selling of services. The site also helps customers buy Fidelity's products (phase 2), handle their accounts (phase 3), and sell the securities (phase 4). ●

Facilitating customer service.   Several tools are available for facilitating online customer service:

- ***FAQs.*** Companies provide online answers to questions customers ask most.
- ***E-mail.*** Companies can send confirmations, product information, and instructions to customers. They can also take orders, complaints, and other inquiries.

- **Tracking capabilities.** Customers can track the status of their orders, services (such as FedEx shipments, banking or stock-trading activities), or job applications.
- **Personalized Web pages.** Customers build individualized pages at the vendor's site; customized information can be provided there.
- **Chat rooms.** Customers can interact with each other and with the vendor's personnel, who monitor the chat room.
- **Web-based call centers.** A comprehensive communication center takes customers' inquiries in any form they come (fax, telephone, e-mail, letters) and answers them quickly and automatically, whenever possible. Customers can also interact with the vendor and get quick problem resolution.

An application of Web-based call centers is becoming very popular, as shown in IT's About Business 9.2 about Canadian Tire's integrated call center.

IT's About Business   *canadiantire.com*   **MKT**

Box 9.2: Canadian Tire provides superb customer service via integrated call center

Canadian Tire Acceptance Ltd. (CTAL), the financial services division of the $5 billion Canadian Tire Corp., Ltd., serves over four million of Canadian Tire's credit card holders. In 1998, CTAL became the primary call center of the company, handling telephone, fax, e-mail, and Internet contacts. It increased sales, enhanced customer retention, and eliminated annoying and time-consuming call transfers, ensuring that customers are treated on an individual basis. "The call center is a strategic asset," says Mary Turner, vice president of customer services at CTAL. "This is our main point of contact with the customer. We have to maximize it."

Canadian Tire's call center is actually 10 call centers, each dealing with a different area (general information, retail, wholesale, service, etc.), or with a geographical zone. The demands are heavy. CTAL's 10 call centers operate 24 hours a day, 7 days a week, and they respond to more than 16 million calls each year. Call center representatives are expected to provide personalized service while handling a diverse set of customer needs—dealing with more than 200 types of customer requests, for example. CTAL's new system ensures that any representative can resolve any customer need without handing it off to another department.

CTAL has several key business objectives:

- Greater customer loyalty to Canadian Tire as a result of enhanced service
- Personalized customer attention and fewer transfers from one service agent to another
- Rapid introduction of new products or changes to existing business services

- Reduced training requirements for customer-service representatives
- Integration of all customer touch points via a single system capable of handling Web, e-mail, and call center interactions

"When we began the project, we took a look at our operations and saw too many independent call centers," Turner continues. "It seemed that every time we introduced a new product or services, we set up a new call center. We decided to streamline operations to make it possible for customers to reach the right representative whenever they called."

One of the call center's major capabilities is to build customer profiles and act on them when needed, providing one-to-one relationships. The call center can be viewed as an *interaction center* that immediately recognizes the individual customer and integrates data that reflect on the relationship. While the Web-based call center is still new, it is expected to pay for itself quickly.

Sources: Compiled from D. Peppers et al., *The One to One Fieldbook* (New York: Currency & Doubleday, 1999) and *canadiantire.ca* (2001).

Questions

1. Why does the company have several call centers?
2. What are the capabilities of the Web-based system?
3. What are the advantages of the Web-based system?

Before you go on . . .

1. Describe the EC consumer behavior model.

2. Describe EC market research and its tools.

3. Describe the major support areas of intelligent agents in EC.

4. Describe online advertising, its methods, and benefits.

5. List the phases of the customer service cycle.

9.4 B2B AND COLLABORATIVE COMMERCE APPLICATIONS

In business to business (B2B) applications, the buyers, sellers, and transactions involve only organizations. Business-to-business comprises the majority of EC volume. It covers a broad spectrum of applications that enable an enterprise to form electronic relationships with its distributors, resellers, suppliers, customers, and other partners. By using B2B, organizations can restructure their supply chains and partnerships.

There are several business models for B2B applications. The major ones are sell-side marketplace, buy-side marketplace, and electronic exchanges.

Sell-Side Marketplace

In the **sell-side marketplace** model, organizations attempt to sell their products or services to other organizations electronically. This model is similar to the B2C model in which the buyer is expected to come to the seller's site (or to an electronic mall), view catalogs, and place an order. In this case, however, the buyer is an organization that may be a regular customer of the seller.

The key mechanisms in the sell-side model are: (1) electronic catalogs that can be customized for each large buyer *(dell.com)*, and (2) forward auctions. Dell Computer also uses auctions extensively *(dellauction.com)*. In addition to auctions from their Web site, organizations can use auction sites, such as eBay, to liquidate items. Companies such as freemarkets.com are helping organizations to auction obsolete and old assets and inventories (asset recovery programs).

The sell-side model is used by thousands of companies and is especially powerful for companies with superb reputations. Examples are major computer companies such as Cisco, IBM, and Intel. The seller in this model can be either a manufacturer, a distributor (e.g., *bigboxx.com* and *avnet.com*), or a retailer. In this model EC is used to increase sales, reduce selling and advertising expenditures, increase delivery speed, and reduce administrative costs. An example is provided in an IT's About Business box W9.2 (about Cisco Systems) at our Web site.

www.wiley.com/
college/turban

Buy-Side Marketplace

The **buy-side marketplace**, also known as **e-procurement**, is a model in which EC technology is used to streamline the purchasing process in order to reduce the cost of items purchased, the administrative cost of procurement, and the purchasing cycle time. A major method of e-procurement is a reverse auction. Here, a company that wants to buy items places a *request for quotation (RFQ)* on its Web site or in a bidding marketplace. Once RFQs are posted, suppliers (usually preapproved ones) submit bids electronically. The bids are routed via the buyer's intranet to the engineering and finance departments for evaluation. Clarifications are made via e-mail, and the winner is notified electronically. Such auctions attract larger pools of willing suppliers. General Electric (*gegxs.com*), for example, saves 10 to 15 percent on the cost of the items placed for bid and up to 85 percent on the administrative cost; in addition, cycle time is reduced by about 50 percent. The seller in the buy-side model can be either a manufacturer, a distributor, or a retailer.

Procurements using a third-party buy-side marketplace model are especially popular for medium and small organizations. However, General Electric has organized a market for small companies that use GE's Global Exchange Services (GXS) to post the small companies' RFQs (*gegxs.com*). These companies pay GE a fee for this service and for handling support services like payments. In this capacity, GE acts as an intermediary.

Another option of e-procurement that is popular with small companies is **group purchasing**. In group purchasing, the requirements of many buyers are aggregated so that they make up a large volume. Once buyers' orders are aggregated, they can be placed on a reverse auction, or a volume discount can be negotiated. The orders of small buyers usually are aggregated by a third-party vendor, such as *shop2gether.com*.

Buyer's internal marketplace.   In this variation of the buy-side model, suppliers' catalogs are aggregated in a master catalog on the buyer's server, so that the company's purchasing agents can shop more conveniently. In the *buyer's internal marketplace* model, a company has many suppliers, but the quantities purchased are relatively small. This model is most appropriate for large companies and for government entities. It is mostly suitable for indirect *maintenance, replacement, and operations (MRO)* items, such as office supplies, as shown in the following example.

EXAMPLE

MasterCard charges supplies in company catalog.   MasterCard International buys large numbers of MRO items from many vendors. Once prices are agreed upon, the items are placed on MasterCard's internal procurement system. About 10,000 items, from dozens of vendors, are listed in the company's e-catalog. Over 2,300 purchasers at various MasterCard offices around the world can view the catalog, select the appropriate products, electronically place orders, and pay with a MasterCard procurement card. Use of the buyer's internal marketplace model enabled MasterCard to consolidate buying activities from many corporate locations and to reduce administrative processing costs. Also, procurement cycle time was reduced in many cases from 20 days to just one. Since MasterCard now has a smaller supplier base from which to buy, the quantities purchased from each vendor are larger, so MasterCard has been able to negotiate larger purchase discounts. Finally, the system can be used to control the budget of each corporate buyer. ●

*mastercardinternational
.com*

Electronic Exchanges

Electronic exchanges (in short, **exchanges**) refer to e-marketplaces in which there are many sellers and many buyers. Sometimes these are referred to as *e-hubs*, or *portals*. There are basically four types of exchanges:

- *Vertical distributors.* These are B2B marketplaces where *direct materials* (materials that are inputs to manufacturing) are traded in an environment of long-term relationship, known as **systematic sourcing**. Examples are *plasticsnet.com* and *plasticscommerce.com*. Both fixed and negotiated prices are common in this type of exchange.

- **Vertical exchanges.** Here direct and indirect materials in one industry are purchased on an as-needed basis. Buyers and sellers may not even know each other. *ChemConnect.com* and *e-steel.com* are online examples. In vertical exchanges, prices are continually changing, based on the matching of supply and demand. This is called **dynamic pricing**. Auctions are typically used in this kind of B2B marketplace, sometimes done in private trading rooms, as shown in IT's About Business 9.3.

- **Horizontal distributors.** These are many-to-many e-marketplaces for indirect (MRO) materials, when systematic sourcing is used. Prices are fixed or negotiated. Examples are *globalsources.com* and *alibaba.com*.

- **Functional exchanges.** Here, needed *services* such as temporary help or extra space are traded on an as-needed basis. Prices can be negotiated, and they vary depending on supply and demand.

All types of exchanges offer diversified services, ranging from payments to logistics. Vertical exchanges are frequently owned and managed by a group of big players in an industry. For example, Marriott and Hyatt own a procurement consortium for the hotel

IT's About Business   *chemconnect.com*   **POM**

Box 9.3: Chemical companies "bond" at ChemConnect

Buyers and sellers of chemicals and plastics today can meet electronically in a large Internet marketplace called ChemConnect (*chemconnect.com*). Using this marketplace, global industry leaders such as British Petroleum, Dow Chemical, BASF, Hyundai, Sumitomo, and many more can reduce trading cycle time and cost, and can find new markets and trading partners around the globe.

ChemConnect provides a *public trading marketplace* and an information portal to more than 12,000 members in 125 countries. In 2001, over 60,000 products were traded in this public e-marketplace. This is an unbiased, third-party-managed market that offers three trading places:

- A *public exchange floor*. Here, members can post items for sale or bid anonymously for all types of products, at market prices. A large catalog displays by category offers to sell and requests to buy, including starting prices and shipping terms. If the prices are not established, buyers can bid by changing the starting prices.

- The *commodities floor*. This space allows the more than 200 top producers, intermediaries, and buyers to buy, sell, and exchange commodity products online, in real time, through regional trading hubs.

- *Corporate trading rooms*. In these ChemConnect-managed private online virtual rooms, members can conduct private auctions and negotiate long-term contracts or spot deals (one-time, as-needed

purchases), in real time. The trading room allows companies to make money-saving deals in 30 minutes that might take weeks or months with a manual method. Companies can host a private auction in a trading room as they negotiate simultaneously online with suppliers or buyers on the public exchange floor.

In all three of the trading mechanisms, up-to-the-minute market information is available and can be translated into 30 different languages. Members pay transaction fees only for successfully completed transactions. Business partners provide several support services, such as financial services for the market members.

The marketplace works with certain rules and guidelines that ensure an unbiased approach to the trades. There is full disclosure of all legal requirements, payments, trading rules, etc. (Click on "Policy, Fees & Legal info and privacy issues" at their Web site.) ChemConnect is growing rapidly, adding members and trading volume.

Source: *chemconnect.com*.

 www.wiley.com/college/turban

Questions

1. What are the advantages of such exchange?
2. Why are there three trading places?
3. Why does the exchange provide information portal services?
4. Why are the rules needed?

industry, and Texaco and Chevron own an energy e-marketplace. The vertical e-marketplaces offer services particularly suited to the particular e-community they serve.

Since B2B activities involve many companies, specialized network infrastructure is needed. Such infrastructure works either as an EDI or as extranets. (We will return to the topic of EC infrastructure in Section 9.6.)

In addition, business-to-business EC can involve much more than buying and selling between companies. One area of considerable activity is collaborative commerce.

Collaborative Commerce

Collaborative commerce (c-commerce) refers to non-selling/buying EC transactions between and among organizations. An example would be a company that it is collaborating electronically with a vendor that is designing a product or part for this company. C-commerce implies communication, information sharing, and collaboration, done electronically by means of tools such as groupware (Chapter 4) and specially designed EC collaboration tools. Let's look at some areas of collaboration.

* *Retailer-suppliers.* Large retailers, such as Wal-Mart, collaborate with their major suppliers to conduct production and inventory planning and forecasting of demand. Such collaboration enables the suppliers to improve their production planning as well.

* *Vendor-managed inventory.* This is a service provided by large suppliers, such as Procter & Gamble, to large retailers, such as Wal-Mart, in which the vendor monitors and replenishes the inventory for the retailer. In some cases, vendor-managed inventory programs now are available to small retailers as well

* *Product design.* All the parties that are involved in a specific product design share data and use special tools. One such tool is *screen sharing,* in which several people can work on the same screen while they are in different locations. This enables suppliers to provide quick feedback when they see the drawing of a product the customer wants made. Changes made in one place are visible to others instantly. Documents that can be processed through collaborative product design include blueprints, bills of material, accounting and billing documents, and joint reports and statements.

* *Collaborative manufacturing.* Manufacturers can create dynamic collaborative networks. For example, Original Equipment Manufacturers outsources components and subassemblies to suppliers, which in the past often created problems in coordination, work flows, and communication. Collaborative tools have improved the outsourcing process, and are especially useful during changes, which may be initiated by any partner of the supply chain.

Various business activities and functions lend themselves to collaborative processes: (1) **planning and scheduling:** material position, visibility forecasts, advanced planning, forecasting, and capacity management; (2) **design:** mechanical, electrical, test, and others; also component selection and design of and for the supply chain; (3) **new product information:** design validation, bill-of-material management, prototyping, production validation, and testing; (4) **product content management:** generating changes, change impact assessment, and phase-in of changes; (5) **order management:** order capture and configuration, order tracking, and delivery arrangements; and (6) **sourcing and procurement:** approving vendors, reverse auctions (tendering), supplier selection, strategic sourcing, and component selection. Specialized tools for c-commerce applications are provided by vendors such as *glyphica.com, allegis.com, lotus.com,* and *ca.com.*

The major benefits of c-commerce are smoothing the supply chain, reducing inventories along the supply chain, reducing operating costs, increasing customer satisfaction, and increasing a company's competitive edge. The challenges faced by the collaborators are software integration issues, technology selection, trust and security, and resistance to change and collaboration.

Before you go on . . .

1. Briefly describe the sell-side marketplace.

2. Describe the various methods of e-procurement.

3. Describe how forward and reverse auctions are used in B2B commerce.

4. Describe the role of exchanges in B2B.

5. Describe c-commerce and its various activities.

9.5   INNOVATIVE APPLICATIONS OF E-COMMERCE

While B2C and B2B received most of the media attention since 1995, several other EC innovative applications are starting to play a major role in e-commerce. These are e-government, mobile commerce, consumer-to-consumer e-commerce, and intrabusiness and business-to-employees e-commerce, and e-learning.

E-Government

As e-commerce matures and its tools and applications improve, greater attention is given to its use to improve the business of public institutions and governments (country, state, county, city, etc).

    E-government is the use of Internet technology in general and e-commerce in particular to deliver information and public services to citizens, business partners and suppliers, and those working in the public sector. It is also an efficient way of conducting business transactions with citizens and businesses and within the governments themselves. E-government can make government more transparent to citizens and improve delivery of public services. For other potential benefits of e-government, see Manager's Checklist W9.4 at our Web site.

    E-government applications can be divided into three major categories: *government-to-citizens (G2C)*, *government-to-business (G2B)*, and *government-to-government (G2G)*. Government agencies are increasingly using the Internet to provide various services to citizens. An example would be **electronic benefits transfer (EBT),** in which government transfers Social Security, pension, and other benefits directly to recipients' bank accounts or to smart cards. Governments also are using the Internet to conduct business with businesses (sell to or buy from). For example, electronic tendering systems, using reverse auctions, are becoming mandatory. Many governments are moving public services online. For an example, see Hong Kong Offers G2C Services, on our Web site.

www.wiley.com/ college/turban

M-Commerce

M-commerce (mobile commerce) refers to the conduct of e-commerce via wireless devices. The number of mobile devices in use worldwide, according to the Gartner-Group, is projected to top 1.3 billion by 2004. Furthermore, these devices can be connected to the Internet, making it possible for users to conduct transactions from anywhere. In addition, many corporate employees are mobile, namely working at home, on clients' sites, or on the road. GartnerGroup projected that 30 to 50 percent of all employees in developed countries will be mobile by 2010. These employees need to collaborate and communicate with office employees and to access corporate data, rapidly and conveniently. Such a capability is provided by m-commerce.

The advantages of m-commerce.   Two main characteristics are driving the interest in m-commerce: mobility and reachability. *Mobility* implies that the Internet access travels with the customer. M-commerce is appealing because wireless offers customers information from any location. This enables employees to contact the office from anywhere they happen to be or customers to act instantly on any shopping impulse. *Reachability* means that people can be contacted at any time, which most people see as a convenience of modern life. (Of course, you can block certain times or certain messages.) These two characteristics—mobility and reachability—break the geographic and time barriers. As a result, mobile terminals such as a PDA (personal digital assistant) or a cell phone with Internet access can be used to obtain real-time information and to communicate from anywhere, at any time.

In addition, mobile devices make possible location-based commerce, also known as **l-commerce.** L-commerce delivers information about goods and services based on where you (and your mobile device) are located. For example, in San Francisco, NextBus service knows, by the use of global positioning systems (GPSs), where the buses are, in real time; when you call on your cell phone from a particular bus stop, the system will compute when the bus will actually arrive there. Other localization systems will find where you are located, and based on this information will send you advertisements for nearby vendors. For some representative applications, see Applications of M-Commerce, on the book's Web site.

www.wiley.com/
college/turban

EXAMPLE

I-MODE spreads m-commerce.   I-MODE is a pioneering wireless service that took Japan by storm in 1999 and 2000. With a few clicks of a handset, I-MODE users can conduct a large variety of m-commerce activities ranging from online stock trading and banking to purchasing travel tickets and booking karaoke rooms. You can also send and receive color images via I-MODE. The service was launched in February 1999, and it had over 29 million users by the end of 2001. I-MODE users can access train and bus timetables, guides to shopping areas, and automatic notification of train delays; get discount coupons for shopping and restaurants; purchase music online; send or receive photos; buy airline tickets; find information about best-selling books and then buy the books; and even receive Tamagotchi's characters, every day, for only $1 per month. I-MODE was taken international in late 2000. ●

nttdocomo.com/imode

Technology and limitations.   The implementation of m-commerce requires a multitude of infrastructures: hardware (cell phones, PDAs, screen phones, etc.), software (microbrowsers, operating systems, application software), and wireless transmission media (e.g., satellites). Some of the major limitations of m-commerce relating to these technologies are insufficient bandwith, lack of standard security protocols, high cost of 3G licenses, high power consumption, and possible health hazards.

Consumer-to-Consumer E-Commerce

An increasing number of individuals are using the Internet to conduct business or to collaborate with others. Auctions are by far the most popular C2C e-commerce activity. Some other C2C activities are:

- *Classifieds.* Individuals used to sell items by advertising in the classified section of the newspaper. Today, they are using the Internet for this purpose. Some classified services are provided free (see *classifieds2000.com*).

- *Personal services.* A variety of personal services are offered on the Internet, ranging from tutoring and astrology to legal and medical advice. Personal services are advertised in the classified areas, in personal Web pages, on Internet communities' bulletin boards, and more. *Be very careful before you buy any personal services.* You need to be sure of the quality of what you buy.

- *Peer-to-peer (P2P) and file exchanges.* An increasing number of individuals are using the P2P services of companies such as Napster.com. Individuals can exchange online digital products, such as music and games.

Intrabusiness and Business-to-Employees E-Commerce

E-commerce can be done not only between business partners, but also within organizations. Such activity is referred to as *intrabusiness EC* or, in short, **intrabusiness**. Intrabusiness can be done between a business and its employees (B2E); among units within the business (usually done as c-commerce); and among employees in the same business (usually done as c-commerce).

Business to its employees (B2E) commerce.   Companies are finding many ways to do business with their own employees electronically. They disseminate information to employees over the intranet, for example. They also allow employees to manage their fringe benefits and take training classes, electronically. In addition, employees can buy discounted insurance, travel packages, and tickets to events on the corporate intranet, and they can electronically order supplies and material needed for their work. And many companies have electronic corporate stores that sell a company's products to its employees, usually at a discount.

E-commerce between and among units within the business.   Large corporations frequently consist of independent units, or *strategic business units* (SBUs), which "sell" or "buy" materials, products, and services to and from each other. Transactions of this type can be easily automated and performed over the intranet. An SBU can be considered as either a seller or a buyer. An example would be company-owned dealerships.

E-learning. E-learning is the online delivery of information for purposes of education, training, knowledge management, or performance management. It is a Web-enabled system that makes knowledge accessible to those who need it, when they need it—any time, anywhere. E-learning is useful both for facilitating learning at schools and for efficient and effective corporate training.

Before you go on . . .

1. Describe e-government and its benefits.

2. What makes m-commerce so appealing?

3. Describe some C2C activities.

4. Describe intrabusiness and B2E commerce.

9.6 INFRASTRUCTURE AND E-COMMERCE SUPPORT SERVICES

For e-commerce applications to succeed, it is necessary to provide them with all the needed support, as shown in Figure 9.1 (p. 276). This is not a simple task because of the large number of issues to be considered and the large number of companies and government agencies that may be involved. Here we present some major issues in e-commerce support. First, an infrastructure must be in place. E-commerce transactions must be executable worldwide, without any delay or mistake. Some transactions involve several trading partners, requiring a more complex infrastructure. Second, electronic payment issues must be addressed. Payments need to be secure, convenient, fast, and inexpensive to process. Third, order fulfillment and related logistics must be in place. Several other services ranging from Web site content to security are needed. An example is a clearinghouse for paying royalties on intellectual property. Finally, appropriate planning and strategy that considers legal, technological, and other requirements is necessary. Some of these topics are the subject of this section.

E-Commerce Infrastructure

E-commerce infrastructure requires a variety of hardware, software, and networks. The major components are networks, Web servers, Web server support and software, electronic catalogs, Web page design, construction software, transactional software, and Internet access components. In addition, special software and sometimes hardware is needed for conducting auctions, e-procurement, and m-commerce. The key infrastructures that are needed to support electronic transactions, communication, and collaboration include: networks; Web servers and supporting software; electronic catalogs; Web page design software; transactional software; and Interent access components. For further description of these infrastructure components, see Table W9.2 on our Web site.

 www.wiley.com/
college/turban

Electronic Payments

Payments are an integral part of doing business, whether in the traditional way or online. Unfortunately, in most cases traditional payment systems are not effective for EC.

Limitations of traditional payment instruments. Nonelectronic payment methods such as using cash, writing a check, sending a money order, or giving your credit card number over the telephone have several limitations in EC. First, cash cannot be used because there is no face-to-face contact. Second, if payment is sent by mail, it takes time for it to be received. Even if a credit card number is provided by phone or fax, it takes time to process it. Nor is it convenient to have to switch from the computer to the phone to complete a transaction. Also, not everyone accepts credit cards or checks, and some buyers do not have credit cards or checking accounts. Finally, contrary to what many people believe, it is less secure for the buyer to use the telephone or mail to arrange or send payment, especially from another country, than to finish a secured transaction on a computer.

Another issue is that many EC transactions are valued at only a few dollars or cents. The cost of processing such **micropayments** needs to be very low; you would not want to pay $5 to process a purchase valued at only a few dollars. The cost of making micropayments offline is too high. For all of these reasons, a better way is needed to pay in cyberspace. This better way is electronic payment systems.

Electronic payment systems.   As in the traditional marketplace, so too in cyberspace, diversity of payment methods allows customers to choose how they wish to pay. The following instruments are acceptable means of payment: electronic checks, electronic credit cards, electronic cash, smart cards, person-to-person payments, electronic funds transfer (EFT), e-wallets, and purchasing cards. Here we will look at each of these payment mechanisms. Later on we will see how to make them secure.

Electronic checks.   **Electronic checks (e-checks)** are similar to regular checks, and they are used mostly in B2B. Here is how they work:

Step 1. The customer establishes a checking account with a bank.

Step 2. The customer contacts a seller, buys a product or a service, and e-mails an encrypted electronic check.

Step 3. The merchant deposits the check in his or her account; money is debited from the buyer's account and credited to the seller's account.

Like regular checks, e-checks carry a signature (in digital form) that can be verified. Properly signed and endorsed e-checks are exchanged between financial institutions through electronic clearinghouses.

Electronic credit cards.   **Electronic credit cards** make it possible to charge online payments to one's credit card account. It is easy and simple for a buyer to e-mail her or his credit card number to the seller. The risk here is that hackers will be able to read the credit card number. Sender authentication is also difficult. Therefore, for security, only cards with *encrypted* information should be used. The data associated with such cards are scrambled so that only those recipients with a key to the coding can retrieve the data. Credit card details can be encrypted by using the SSL protocol (described later) in the buyer's computer, which is available in standard browsers. When you buy a book from Amazon your credit card information and purchase amount are encrypted in your browser. When this information arrives at Amazon, it will be transferred automatically (encrypted) to VISA, Mastercard, and so forth, for authorization.

An enhanced credit card security system uses an intermediary for additional encryption. Unfortunately, this additional layer of protection adds to both the cost and the processing time. Also, a more secure protocol, called *SET*, can be used at a higher cost. (SET is described in detail later.)

Electronic cash.   Cash is the most prevalent consumer payment instrument. Traditional brick-and-mortar merchants prefer cash since they do not have to pay commissions to credit card companies and they can put the money to use as soon as it is received. Also, some buyers pay with cash because they do not have checks or credit cards, or because they want to preserve their anonymity. It is logical, therefore, that EC sellers and some buyers may prefer **electronic cash (e-cash)**. Electronic cash appears in two forms.

1. *Electronic cash in a PC.* The use of this approach involves a six-step process:

Step 1. The customer opens an account with a bank and receives special software for his or her PC.

Step 2. The customer buys "electronic money" from the bank by using the software. The customer's bank account is debited accordingly.

Step 3. The bank sends a secured electronic money note to this customer.

Step 4. The money is stored on the buyer's PC and can be spent in any electronic store that accepts e-cash.

Step 5. The software is also used to transfer the e-cash from the buyer's computer to the seller's computer.

Step 6. The seller can deposit the e-cash in a bank, crediting his or her regular or electronic account, or the seller can use the e-cash to make a purchase elsewhere.

2. ***Electronic payment cards with e-cash.*** Electronic payment cards have been in use for several decades. The best known are credit cards, which use magnetic strips that contain limited information, such as the card's ID number. A more advanced form of payment card, known as a stored-value money card, is the one that you use to pay for photocopies in your library, for transportation, or for telephone calls. It allows a fixed amount of prepaid money to be stored in quantities that can be decreased and sometimes increased. Each time you use the card, the amount is reduced. One successful example is used by the New York Metropolitan Transportation Authority (MTA), which operates buses, trains, interstate toll bridges, and tunnels. Nearly 5 million customers present cards to card reader machines on buses, subways, and road tollbooths each day. The Chicago Transit Authority (CTA) uses similar cards. Some of these cards are reloadable, and some are discarded when the money is depleted.

An electronic payment card from the Chicago Transit Authority (CTA).

Cards with stored-value money also can be purchased for Internet use. You enter a third-party Web site and you provide an ID number and a password, much as you do when you use a prepaid phone card. The money can be used only in participating stores.

Smart cards.   Although some people refer to stored-value cards as smart cards, they are not really the same. True **smart cards** contain a microprocessor (chip) and can store a considerable amount of information (more than 100 times that of a stored-value card) and can conduct processing. Such cards are multipurpose, as shown in the Takashimaya Inc. example at our Web site.

www.wiley.com/
college/turban

Advanced smart cards have the ability to transfer funds, pay bills, buy from vending machines, or pay for services such as those offered on television or PCs. Money values can be loaded at ATMs, kiosks, or from your PC. For example, the VISA Cash Card allows you to buy goods or services at participating gas stations, fast-food outlets, pay phones, discount stores, post offices, convenience stores, coffee shops, and even movie theaters. Smart cards are ideal for micropayments. Smart cards can also be used to transfer benefits from companies to their employees, as when retirees get their pension payments, and from governments that pay citizens different entitlements. The money is transferred electronically to a smart card at an ATM, kiosk, or PC.

Person-to-person (P2P) payment   **Person-to-person (P2P) payments** is one of the newest and fastest-growing payment schemes. They enable the transfer of funds between two individuals for a variety of purposes like repaying money borrowed from a friend, sending money to students at college, paying for an item purchased at an on-line auction, or sending a gift to a family member. One of the first companies to offer this service was PayPal (*paypal.com*). PayPal claimed, in late 2001, to have 8 million customer accounts, handling 25 percent of all eBay transactions and funneling $5 billion in payments through its servers annually. Although PayPal had not made a profit by fall 2001, this kind of business activity has drawn the attention of a number of other companies who are trying to get in on the action. Citibank C2IT (*c2it.com*), AOL QuickCash (*aol.com*), One's Bank eMoneyMail, Yahoo! PayDirect, and WebCertificate (*webcertificate.com*) are all PayPal competitors.

Virtually all of these services work in a similar way. Assume you want to send money to someone over the Internet. First, you select a service and open up an account with the service. Basically, this entails creating a user name, a password, giving them your e-mail address, and providing the service with a credit card or bank account number. Next, you add funds from your credit card or bank account to your P2P account. Once the account has been funded you're ready to send money. You access PayPal (for example) with your user name and password. Now you specify the e-mail address of the person to receive the money, along with the dollar amount that you want to send. An e-mail is sent to the payee's e-mail address. The e-mail will contain a link back to the service's Web site. When the recipient clicks on the link, he or she will be taken to the service. The recipient will be asked to set up an account to which the money that was sent will be credited. The recipient can then credit the money from this account to either his or her credit card or bank account. The payer pays a small amount (around $1) per transaction.

Electronic funds transfer.   **Electronic funds transfer (EFT)** is the electronic transfer of money to and from financial institutions using telecommunication networks. EFT is now widely used—with funds, debits and credits, and charges and payments electronically routed via clearinghouses among banks and between banks and customers. Examples of EFT include: interbank transactions around the globe; payment of university tuition using an ATM; direct deposit of salaries in employees' accounts; and payment of mortgages, utility bills, and car payments through monthly bank account deductions.

EFT is fast; it reduces delays associated with sending hardcopy documents, and it eliminates returned checks. It has become the only practical way to handle the large volume of financial transactions generated daily in the banking industry. EFT-based ATMs are increasingly available in shopping centers and business areas, allowing individuals to make deposits, withdrawals, and money transfers 24 hours a day.

Electronic wallets.   Most of the time when you make a purchase on the Web you're required to fill out a form with your name, shipping address, billing address, credit card information, and so on. Doing this a few times is fine, but having to do it every time you shop on the Web is an annoyance. Some merchants solve the problem by having you fill out a form once and then saving the information stored on their servers for later use. For instance, this is what Amazon.com has done with its "one-click" feature. Of course, even if every merchant provides a "one-click" feature, you would still have to set up an account with every merchant.

One way to avoid the problem of having to repeatedly fill out purchase information, while at the same time eliminating the need to store the information on a merchant's server, is to use an **electronic wallet (e-wallet)**. An e-wallet is a software component that is downloaded to a user's PC and in which the user stores credit card numbers and other personal information. When the user shops at a merchant who accepts the e-wallet, the user can perform one-click shopping, with the e-wallet automatically filling in the necessary information. Credit card companies like Visa and MasterCard offer e-wallet services, as do Yahoo!, America Online (called Quick Checkout), and Microsoft (Passport). Of these, Yahoo! has the largest number of merchant participants (over 12,000). As of 2001, many banks around the world offer e-wallet service.

Purchasing cards.   In some countries, such as the U.K., United States, and Hong Kong, companies are paying other companies by means of *purchasing cards*. Unlike credit cards, where credit is provided for 30 to 60 days for free before payment is made to the merchant, payments made with purchasing cards are settled within a week. Purchasing cards are used for unplanned B2B purchases, and corporations generally limit the amount per puchase (usually $1,000 to $2,000). Purchasing cards can be used on the Internet much like regular credit cards.

Security in Electronic Payments

Two main issues need to be considered under the topic of payment security: what is required in order to make EC payments safe, and the methods that can be used to do it.

Security requirements.   Security requirements for conducting EC are:

1. ***Authentication.*** The buyer, the seller, and the paying institutions must be assured of the identity of the parties with whom they are dealing.
2. ***Integrity.*** It is necessary to ensure that data and information transmitted in EC, such as orders, reply to queries, and payment authorization, are not accidentally or maliciously altered or destroyed during transmission.
3. ***Non-repudiation.*** Merchants need protection against the customer's unjustified denial of placing an order. (Such denial is called *repudiation.*) On the other hand, customers need protection against merchants' unjustified denial of payments made.
4. ***Privacy.*** Many customers want their identity to be secured. They want to make sure others do not know what they buy. Some prefer complete anonymity, as is possible with cash payments.
5. ***Safety.*** Customers want to be sure that it is safe to provide a credit card number on the Internet.

Security protection.   Several methods and mechanisms can be used to fulfill the security requirements. One of the primary mechanisms is encryption, which is often part of the most useful security schemes.

Encryption.   **Encryption** is a process of making messages indecipherable except by those who have an authorized decryption key. The key is a code composed of a very large collection of letters, symbols, and numbers. For example, the letter "A" might be coded as: ABQ8iF 1 73 Rjbj / 83 ds 1 22 m 3 3 SP 5 Qqm2z. Every letter and number in the encrypted data would have similarly complex coding, which may include as many as 128 characters for each letter or number. The newer types of keys include graphics as well. Two basic encryption methods exist—those that use one key and those that use two keys. A third method combines the two.

- ***Single-key encryption.*** In early encryption technologies only one key was used. The sender of the electronic message (or payment) encrypted the information with a key. The receiver used an identical key to decrypt the information to a readable form. Therefore, the same code had to be in the possession of both the sender and the receiver. This created problems. For example, if a key were transmitted electronically and intercepted illegally, it could have been used to read all encrypted messages or to steal money. Since keys are changed frequently, the problem becomes repetitive.
- ***Two-key encryption.*** This method uses two different keys. One of the keys is called *public*, the other one, *private*. Many people may know the **public key** (it may be posted on a Web site, for example), but only its owner knows the **private key**. Every user of the system (which might be an individual or a business) has one private key and one public key. Encryption and decryption can be done with either key. However, if encryption is done with the public key, the decryption can be done only with the private key, and vice versa. For example: Amanda wants to be sure that Brian

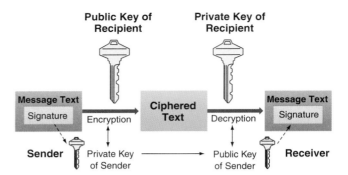

Figure 9.3 *Public key infrastructure: a message and digital signature.*

will be the only one able to read her message. Amanda encrypts the message with Brian's public key. He decrypts it with his private key. There are several public key encryption algorithms; the most well known is RSA (*rsa.com*).

- **Public key infrastructure.** A **public key infrastructure (PKI)** is a security system based on use of the two keys, and also including a digital signature and a certificate. Let's look at an example: Clarissa (C) wants to assure David (D) that she is the author of a message. She encrypts the message with D's public key. In addition, C encrypts a signature with her own private key. The signature, called a **digital signature**, is attached to the original message (see Figure 9.3). D uses C's public key to decrypt the signature and his private key to read the message.

We still face one problem: How do we assure Clarissa that the public key she uses really belongs to David? And how can David be sure that the public key he has used to verify Clarissa's signature really belongs to Clarissa? Such assurances are provided by *electronic certificates.*

Electronic certificates.   **Electronic certificates** are issued by a trusted third party, called a *certificate authority (CA)*, in order to verify that a specific public key belongs to a specific individual (or organization). In addition to a name, a certificate may verify age, gender, and other attributes of the individual to whom the public key belongs. Also, if the CA is not well-known to the recipient of the certificate, it may be necessary to certify the CA by another, more trustworthy legal entity. Thus, there could be several levels of certification. Certificates are signed by the CA and are valid until an expiration date. A major issuer of certificates is VeriSign, Inc. (*verisign.com*). In many countries, especially where retail transactions are handled in association with the national postal system (called a *giro system*), a highly trusted certificate authority is the post office.

The PKI is the backbone of the various payment mechanisms described earlier, including e-check, e-cash, and wireless payments. However, to ensure the acceptance of payments anywhere in the world, it is necessary to have some universal protocols.

Protocols.   As discussed in Chapter 6, a *protocol* is a set of rules and procedures that governs the transfer of information on the Internet. It is the software that also helps in authentication, security, and privacy. Two major payment protocols are used in e-commerce: SSL and SET.

- *Secure Socket Layer (SSL).* The SSL is the most common protocol used in EC. Its main capability is to encrypt messages. For example, any time you order merchandise from Wal-Mart, Amazon.com, and most other large vendors on the Internet, your order is encrypted automatically by the SSL in your computer browser *before* being sent over the Internet.

- *Secure Electronic Transaction (SET) protocol.* A more comprehensive protocol for credit card processing is SET. It is not used much due to its cost and complexity. However, it is designed to allow consumers to shop anywhere as conveniently and securely as possible by incorporating digital signatures, certification, encryption, and an agreed-upon payment gateway (to banks). While SSL protects only integrity and safety, SET can provide protection against all security hazards.

Order Fulfillment

When a company sells direct to individual customers it is involved in various order fulfillment activities. It must:

1. Quickly find the products to be shipped, and pack them.
2. Arrange for the packages to be delivered speedily to the customer's door.
3. Collect the money from every customer, either in advance, by COD, or by individual bill.
4. Handle the return of unwanted or defective products.

It is very difficult to accomplish these activities both effectively and efficiently since a company may need to ship small packages to many customers, and do so quickly. For this reason, both online companies and click-and-mortar companies have difficulties in their B2C supply chain. Here we provide only a brief overview; a more detailed discussion is provided in Chapter 10.

    Order fulfillment refers not only to providing customers with what they ordered and doing it on time, but also to providing all related customer service. For example, the customer must receive the assembly and operation instructions to a new appliance. (A nice example is available at *livemanuals.com.*) In addition, if the customer is not happy with a product, an exchange or return must be arranged. Order fulfillment is basically a part of the *back-office* operations.

    During the last few years, e-tailers have faced continuous problems in order fulfillment, especially during the holiday season. The problems resulted in inability to deliver on time, delivery of wrong items, high delivery costs, and the need to heavily compensate unhappy customers. Several factors can be responsible for delays in deliveries. They range from inability to forecast demand accurately to ineffective supply chains. Some such problems exist also in offline businesses. One factor that is typical of EC, though, is that it is based on the concept of "pull" operations, which begin with an *order*, frequently a customized one. This is in contrast with traditional retailing that begins with a production to inventory, which is then "pushed" to customers. In the pull case it is more difficult to forecast demand, due to unique demands of customized orders and lack of sufficient years of experience. For solutions to order fulfillment problems, see Chapter 10. For many e-tailers, taking orders over the Internet could well be the easy part of B2C e-commerce. Fulfillment to customers' doors is the sticky part.

Before you go on . . .

1. List the major infrastructure items in EC.
2. List the various electronic payment mechanisms.
3. List the security requirements for EC.
4. Explain encryption for EC.
5. Describe the issues in EC order fulfillment.

9.7   LEGAL AND ETHICAL ISSUES IN E-COMMERCE

Ethical standards and their incorporation into law frequently trail technological innovation. As with advancements in genetic medicine, for example, e-commerce is taking new forms and enabling new business practices that may bring numerous risks—particularly for individual consumers—along with their advantages. We encourage you to develop an awareness of the issues discussed in this section, and to carefully assess the risks involved in future e-commerce developments. Before we present these specific issues, we discuss the issues of market practices and consumer/seller protection.

Market Practices and Consumer and Seller Protection

When buyers and sellers do not know each other and cannot even see each other (they may even be in different countries), there is a chance that dishonest people will commit fraud and other crimes over the Internet. During the first few years of EC, the public witnessed many of these, ranging from the creation of a virtual bank that disappeared along with the investors' deposits, to manipulation of stock prices on the Internet. Unfortunately, fraudulent activities on the Internet are increasing.

Fraud on the Internet.   Internet fraud and its sophistication have grown as much and even faster than the Internet itself. As one example, in fall 1998 the SEC brought charges against 44 companies and individuals who illegally promoted stocks on computer bulletin boards, online newspapers, and investment Web sites. (You can see details on both settled and pending cases at *sec.gov*.) The scheme is to increase demand for the stock and drive up prices. They sell the stock, pocket their profit, and leave the investors with the overvalued stock. In most of these cases, stock promoters falsely spread positive rumors about the prospects of the companies they touted. In other cases, the information provided might have been true, but the promoters did not disclose that they were paid to talk up the companies. Stock promoters specifically target small investors who are lured by the promise of fast profits.

Stocks are only one of many areas where swindlers are active. Auctions are especially conducive to fraud, by both sellers and buyers. Other areas of potential fraud include selling bogus investments and phantom business opportunities. Financial criminals now have access to far more people, mainly due to the availability of electronic mail. The U.S. Federal Trade Commission has published a list of 12 scams most likely to arrive via e-mail, which is shown in Table W9.3 on the book's Web site.

There are several ways buyers can be protected against EC fraud. Representative methods are described next.

www.wiley.com/
college/turban

Buyer protection.   Buyer protection is critical to the success of any commerce where buyers do not see the sellers, and this is especially true for e-commerce. Some tips for safe electronic shopping are shown in Table 9.3. In short, do not forget that you have shopper's rights. Consult your local or state consumer protection agency for general information on your consumer rights.

Seller protection.   Sellers, too, may need protection. They must be protected against consumers who refuse to pay or who pay with bad checks, and from buyers' claims that the merchandise did not arrive. They also have the right to protect against the

Table 9.3   Tips for Safe Electronic Shopping

- Look for reliable brand names at sites like Wal-Mart Online, Disney Online, and Amazon.com. Make sure that the sites are authentic before purchasing, by entering the site directly and not from an unverified link.
- Search any unfamiliar selling site for the company's address and phone and fax numbers. Call up and quiz the employees about the sellers.
- Check out the vendor with the local Chamber of Commerce or Better Business Bureau (*bbbonline.org*). Look for seals of authenticity such as TRUSTe.
- Investigate how secure the seller's site is by examining the security procedures and by reading the posted privacy notice.
- Examine the money-back guarantees, warranties, and service agreements.
- Compare prices to those in regular stores. Too-low prices are too good to be true, and some "catch" is probably involved.
- Ask friends what they know. Find testimonials and endorsements in community sites and well-known bulletin boards.
- Find out what your rights are in case of a dispute.
- Consult the National Fraud Information Center (*fraud.org*).
- Check *consumerworld.org* for a listing of useful resources.

use of their name by others as well as use of their unique words and phrases, slogans, and Web address (trademark protection). Another seller protection applies particularly to electronic media: Sellers have legal recourse against customers who download without permission copyrighted software and/or knowledge and use it or sell it to others.

Ethical Issues

Many of the ethical and global issues related to IT apply also to e-commerce. These will be discussed in Chapter 15. Here we touch on issues particularly related to e-commerce.

Privacy.   Most electronic payment systems know who the buyers are; therefore, it may be necessary to protect the buyers' identities. Another privacy issue may involve tracking of Internet user activities by intelligent agents and Web tracking with cookies (see below). A privacy issue related to employees also involves tracking: Many companies monitor employees' e-mail and have installed software that performs in-house monitoring of Web activities; many employees don't want to feel like they are under the watchful eye of "Big Brother," even while at work.

Web tracking.   By using tracking software, companies can track individuals' movements on the Internet. Programs such as "cookies" raise a batch of privacy concerns. The tracking history is stored on your PC's hard drive, and any time you revisit a certain Web site, the computer knows it. Programs such as Cookie Cutter are designed to allow users to have some control over cookies. (For further discussion see *commerceNet.com*.)

Disintermediation.   The use of EC may result in the elimination of some of a company's employees as well as brokers and agents. This result is called **disintermediation**—that is, "eliminating the intermediary." The manner in which these unneeded workers, especially employees, are treated may raise ethical issues, such as how to handle the displacement.

Legal Issues Specific to E-Commerce

Domain name.   Internet addresses are known as **domain names**. Domain names appear in levels. A top-level name is *wiley.com*, or *stanford.edu*. A second-level name will be *wiley.com/turban* or *ibm.com.hk* (for IBM in Hong Kong). Top-level domain names are assigned by central nonprofit organizations that check for conflicts and possible infringement of trademarks. Obviously, companies who sell goods and services over the Internet want customers to be able to find them easily, so the URL must match the company's name. Problems arise when several companies that have similar names compete over a domain name. For example, if you want to book reservations at a Holiday Inn hotel and you go to *holidayinn.com*, you get the Web site for a hotel at Niagara Falls, New York; to get to the hotel chain's Web site, you have to go to *holiday-inn.com*. Several cases of disputed names are already in court. An international arbitration organization is available as an alternative to the courts. The problem of domain names was alleviated somewhat in 2001 after several upper-level names were added to "com" (such as "info" and "corp").

Taxes and other fees.   Federal, state, and local authorities are scrambling to figure out how to get a piece of the revenue created electronically. The problem is particularly complex for interstate and international commerce. For example, some claim that even the state in which a server is located deserves to receive some sales tax from an e-commerce transaction. Others say that the state in which the seller is located deserves the entire sales tax (or value-added tax, VAT, in some countries).

In addition to sales tax, there is a question about where (and in some case, whether) electronic sellers should pay business license tax, franchise fees, gross-receipts tax, excise tax, privilege tax, and utility tax. Furthermore, how should tax collection be controlled? Legislative efforts to impose taxes on e-commerce are opposed by an organization called the Internet Freedom Fighters. Their efforts have been successful so far: At the time this edition was written, there was a ban on taxing business done on the Internet in the United States and many other countries (sales tax only), which could remain valid until fall 2006.

Copyright.   Intellectual property, in its various forms, is protected by copyright laws and cannot be used freely. Copyright issues and protection of intellectual property are discussed in detail in Chapter 15.

www.wiley.com/
college/turban

For other issues that are emerging as challenges to the existing legal system, see the book's Web site.

Before you go on . . .

1. Describe some of the potential fraud on the Internet.

2. Describe buyer protection in EC.

3. List some ethical issues in EC.

4. List the major legal issues of EC.

FOR THE ACCOUNTING MAJOR

Accounting personnel will be involved in several EC activities. Designing the ordering system and its relationship with inventory management requires accounting attention. Billing and payments also are accounting-related, as are determining cost and profit allocations. The implications of replacing paper documents by electronic means affect many of the accountants' tasks, especially the auditing of EC activities and systems. Finally, building a cost–benefit and justifications system of what products/ services to take online and the creation of a chargeback system are critical to the success of EC.

FOR THE FINANCE MAJOR

The worlds of banking, securities and commodities markets, and other financial services are being reengineered due to EC. Online securities trading and its supporting infrastructure are growing more rapidly than any other EC activity. Many innovations already in place are changing the rules of economic and financial incentives for financial analysts and managers. Online banking, for example, does not recognize state boundaries and may create a new framework for financing global trades. Public financial information is accessible in seconds. All this changes the manner in which finance personnel will operate and excel.

FOR THE MARKETING MAJOR

A major revolution in marketing and sales is taking place due to EC. In addition to moving from a physical to a virtual marketplace, a radical transformation to one-on-one advertising and sales and to customized and interactive marketing is happening. This revolution is affecting several marketing theories, ranging from consumer behavior to advertising strategies. Marketing channels are being combined, eliminated, or recreated. The EC revolution is creating new products and markets and significantly altering others. Digitization of products and services has many implications for marketing and sales. The direct producer-to-consumer channel is expanding rapidly, and with it the nature of customer service. As the battle for customers intensifies, the role of marketing and sales employees and managers is becoming the most critical success factor in many organizations. Online marketing can be a blessing to one company and a curse to another.

FOR THE PRODUCTION/OPERATIONS MANAGEMENT MAJOR

EC is changing the manufacturing system from *product-push* mass production to *order-pull* mass customization. This change requires a robust supply chain, information support, and reengineering of processes that frequently involve suppliers and other business partners. Extranets are mushrooming, sometimes involving entire industries, and completely changing the logistics systems. In addition, the Internet and intranets help significantly reduce cycle times. Many production/operation problems that have persisted for years, such as complex scheduling and coordination as well as excess inventories, are being solved rapidly with the use of Web technologies. Using extranets, suppliers monitor and replenish inventories without the need for constant reorders. External and internal networks also provide for improved quality, and companies can now find and manage manufacturing operations in other countries much more easily. Also, the Web is reengineering procurement, by helping companies conduct electronic bids for parts and subassemblies, thus reducing cost. All in all, the job of the progressive production/operations manager is closely tied in with e-commerce.

FOR THE HUMAN RESOURCES MANAGEMENT MAJOR

Every activity and task performed by the HRM department may be affected by e-commerce. Recruiting, for example, is becoming Web-based for many companies, and benefits management and employee training are rapidly moving to intranets. And both collaborative commerce and e-government have the potential to break down traditional job descriptions and change job responsibilities.

SUMMARY

❶ Describe electronic commerce, its scope, benefits, limitations, and types.

E-commerce can be conducted on the Web, by e-mail, and on other networks. It is divided into the following major types: business-to-consumer, consumer-to-consumer, business-to-business, e-government, collaborative commerce, and intra-business. In each type you can find several business models. E-commerce offers many benefits to organizations, consumers, and society, but it also has limitations (technical and nontechnical). The current technical limitations are expected to lessen with time.

❷ Describe the major applications and issues of business-to-consumer commerce, service industries in e-commerce, and electronic auctions.

The major application areas of B2C commerce are in direct retailing, banking, securities trading, job markets, travel, and real estate. Several issues slow the growth of B2C, notably channel conflict, order fulfillment, and customer acquisition. B2C e-tailing can be pure (such as Amazon.com), or part of a click-and-mortar organization. Direct marketing is done via solo storefronts, in malls, and by using electronic auctions. The Internet provides an infrastructure for executing auctions at lower cost, and with many more involved sellers and buyers, including both individual consumers and corporations. *Forward* auctions and *reverse* auctions are the two major types.

❸ Discuss the importance and activities of B2C market research, advertising, and customer service.

Understanding consumer behavior is critical to e-commerce. Finding out what customers want can be done by asking them, in questionnaires, or by observing what they do online. Other forms of market research can be conducted on the Internet by using intelligent agents. Like any commerce, EC requires advertising support, much of which can be done online by methods such as banner advertisements and customized ads. Permission marketing, interactive and viral marketing, electronic catalogs, and online coupons offer ways for vendors to reach more customers. Customer service occurs before, during, and after purchasing, and during disposal of products.

❹ Describe business-to-business and collaborative commerce applications.

The major B2B applications are selling from catalogs and by forward auctions, buying in reverse auctions and in group purchasing, and trading in exchanges. In addition, most organizations employ collaborative commerce, usually along the supply chain.

❺ Describe emerging EC applications such as e-government and mobile commerce.

E-government commerce can take place between government and citizens or between businesses and governments. It makes government operations more effective and efficient. Using a wireless environment allows new mobile commerce applications as well as more convenient access to the Internet. EC also can be done between consumers (C2C), but should be undertaken with caution. Finally, EC can be done within organizations (intrabusiness).

❻ Describe the e-commerce infrastructure and support services, including payments and logistics.

The major EC infrastructure components are networks, Web servers, Web tools, electronic catalogs, programming languages, transactional software, and security devices. Traditional, nonelectronic payment systems are insufficient or inferior for doing business on the Internet. Therefore, electronic payment systems are used. Electronic payments can be made by e-checks, e-credit cards, e-cash, smart cards, and EFT. Order fulfillment is especially difficult in B2C.

❼ Discuss legal and other implementation issues.

Protection of customers, sellers, and intellectual property is a major concern, but so are the value of contracts, domain names, and how to handle legal issues in a multicountry environment. Implementing e-commerce is not simple, and multiple financial, organizational, technological, and managerial issues must be addressed.

INTERACTIVE LEARNING SESSION

Go to the CD and access Chapter 9: Electronic Commerce. You will follow an Internet transaction and make choices and decisions about the path as the transactions moves from one point to another. The program will give you feedback on your choices and decisions.

www.wiley.com/
college/turban

For additional resources, go to the book's Web site for Chapter 9. There you will find Web resources for the chapter, including links to organizations, people, and technology; "IT's About Business" company links; "What's in IT for Me?" links; and a self-testing Web quiz for Chapter 9.

DISCUSSION QUESTIONS

1. Discuss the major limitations of e-commerce. Which of them are likely to disappear? Why?

2. Why is the electronic job market popular, especially among the high-tech professions?

3. Discuss the relationship between digital signature, certification, and PKI.

4. Distinguish between business-to-business forward auctions and buyers' bids for RFQs.

5. Some say that the major benefit of EC occurs in c-commerce. Why?

6. What is interactive advertising? What are its major benefits?

7. Discuss the benefits to sellers and buyers of a B2B exchange.

8. What are the major benefits of e-government?

9. Why is m-commerce attracting a great deal of attention?

10. Why are online auctions becoming popular?

PROBLEM-SOLVING ACTIVITIES

1. Assume you're interested in buying a car. You can find information about cars at *carpoint.com*. Go to *autoweb.com* or *autobytel.com* for information about financing and insurance. Decide what car you want to buy. Configure your car by going to the car manufacturer's Web site. Finally, try to find the car from *autobytel.com*. Write a report about your experience.

2. To find information about how to start a new EC business, go to *cio.com/forums/ec*, and to *financehub.com*. Also try e-business at the Netscape main menu, at "Starting EC business" at *google.com*, and *sellitontheweb.com*. Prepare a report.

3. Find information on the Web on:
   a. Getting an MBA degree at a virtual university.
   b. Going public on the Internet with stocks (IPO).

c. Business credit verification.

d. Electronic letter of credit.

4. Describe how public and private keys can be used in the following instances:

a. Person A wants to send a secure message to many people.

b. Person B received an e-check from person C. How can he be sure it is real?

c. You want to make sure that the credit card number you give to an e-tailer is secured. How can a PKI system help? If it cannot help, why not? What other approach can you use?

INTERNET ACTIVITIES

1. Access *etrade.com* and register for the Internet stock game. You will be bankrolled with $100,000 in a trading account every month. Try to win the game!

2. Access *hsbc.com.hk/hk/hexagon.default.htm* and *us.hsbc.com/business/payments/hexagon*, and find information about Hexagon. What are its advantages to the bank? To the customers?

3. Select one of the following destinations you want to visit: Australia, Nepal, Israel, Thailand, or Finland. Access *expedia.com* and *google.com*.

a. Find the lowest airfare.

b. Examine a few hotels by class.

c. Get suggestions of what to see.

d. Find out about local currency, and convert $1,000 to that currency with an online currency converter.

e. Compile travel tips.

f. Prepare a report.

4. Access *realtor.com*. Prepare a list of services available on this site. Then prepare a list of advantages derived by the users and advantages to realtors. Are there any disadvantages? To whom?

5. You can customize your own CD from existing music. Look at *musicmatch.com* or *cductive.com*. Examine the process, payments, etc. Try your own CD. Write a report.

6. Enter *alibaba.com*. Identify the site's capabilities. Look at the site's private trading room. Write a report.

7. Try to find a unique gift on the Internet for a friend. Several sites help you do it. (You might try *shopping.com* and *amazon.com*, for example.) Describe your experience with such a site.

8. Access the sites of Pizza Hut (*pizzahut.com*) and Domino's (*dominos.com*) to find what they are doing in your area with respect to take-home orders. Also check their distribution of coupons and any other strategic activities.

9. Access *peapod.com* and *netgrocer.com*. Compare and contrast the two companies.

10. Access *info.gov.hk* and find the major e-government initiatives. Look also at *ets.com.hk*.

11. Enter *campusfood.com*. Explore the site. Why is the site so successful? Could you start a competing one? Why or why not?

TEAM ACTIVITIES AND ROLE PLAYING

1. Have each team study a major bank with extensive EC strategy. For example, Wells Fargo Bank is well on its way to being a cyberbank. Hundreds of brick-and-mortar branch offices are being closed. In late 2001, the bank served more than a million cyberaccounts (see *wellsfargo.com*). Other banks are Citicorp, Netbank, and HSBC (Hong Kong). Each team should attempt to convince the class that its bank offers the best online services.

2. Find 10 real-world applications of the major business-to-business models listed in the chapter. (Try success stories of vendors and EC-related magazines.) Find at least one in each category. Examine the problems they solve or the opportunities they exploit.

3. Amazon.com, the giant Internet bookstore, lists close to 10 million books. Its major competitor is Barnes & Noble online (*bn.com*). Assign one team to each company.

a. Find out how the company administers its book logistics.

b. Evaluate the customer services the site offers.

c. Examine how comparison agents such as *bestbookbuys.com* work.

d. Search press releases regarding the corporate strategy.

e. Convince the class that your company is better.

REAL-WORLD CASE   *woolworths.com.au*

Supermarket Keeps It Fresh

The Business Problem   Perishable goods such as fruit, vegetables, meat, and milk are significant in any retail marketplace, including online grocers such as start-up companies like Peapod.com (U.S.), and Green-grocer.com (Australia), which have found new ways to satisfy customers.

How is a well-established major grocer to respond? With huge investments in bricks-and-mortar stores, Woolworths of Australia found itself dealing with just this question. The grocery market in Australia is dominated by three major players: Coles-Meyers, Woolworths, and Franklins. Between them they control some 80 percent of the market. Franklins, which is Hong Kong–owned, takes a low-cost minimum service approach. The others, both Australian-owned, provide a full range of products, including fresh foods and prepared meals.

The IT Solution   Woolworths' initial approach was to set up a standard Web site offering a limited range of goods, but excluding perishable items. This idea was tested in areas near major supermarkets, in response to the newly emerging approaches from entrepreneurs. If those organizations were allowed to take over a sizeable segment of the market, regaining market share could be difficult. It was not long before management realized that this was not an attractive approach. Woolworths' staff had to walk the aisles, fill the baskets, pack the goods, and deliver them. For an organization that had optimized its supply chain in order to cut costs, here was a sudden explosion in costs. When gross margins are only 10 percent and net margins around 4 percent, it is very easy to become unprofitable. Furthermore, Woolworths had established its place in public perception as "the fresh-food people" by heavily promoting fruit and vegetables, freshly baked bread, meat, and prepared meals. If home shopping were to ignore these, Woolworths would be avoiding its strengths.

Woolworths' Homeshop, the second-generation home shopping site (*woolworths.com.au*), is designed with freshness in mind, and all the fresh food is available for delivery. Deliveries are arranged from major regional warehouses, rather than from every local store. There is a A$50 ($50 Australian) minimum order, a 7.5 percent surcharge for home delivery, and a A$6 delivery charge. These charges help in recovering the additional costs, but an average order around A$200 still returns little profit.

New users can register only if deliveries are possible to their postal address. On first use of the system, the customer is guided to find the products that they want, with suggestions from the list of best-selling items. Alternatively the customer can browse for items by category or search by keyword. Items are accumulated in the "shopping trolley" (cart). The first order can form a master list for future orders, as can subsequent orders.

After the customer has selected the required items, he or she selects "checkout," where the total value is computed and the customer confirms that delivery is required. Payment is made only at time of delivery using a mobile (cellular) electronic funds transfer (EFTPOS) terminal, and either a credit card or a debit card. In this way, precise charges can be made based on weight of meat or fish, as well as allowing for out-of-stock items. The customer has to set the delivery time, and will bear an additional charge if there is no one at home to accept the delivery.

The Results   By the end of 2001, the competitive position of Woolworths against the pure online grocers had been strengthened. The company was still losing money on its online endeavor, but its market share had increased significantly.

Source: Prof. Ernie Jordan, Macquarie Graduate School of Management, Sydney, Australia.

Questions

1. Vist the Woolworths' Homeshop site (*woolworths .com.au*) and find new capabilities not mentioned above.

2. Who would be the target customers for an online grocer?

3. How easy is it to order regularly used items from this site? Suggest some improvements to the design.

4. How does this service disrupt the previously highly tuned supply chain?

5. Compare the advantages and disadvantages of the EFTPOS payment mechanism used with the more usual "credit card at time of order" payment method.

6. Should the newer startups such as greengrocer.com and peapod be threatened by this service? How about the traditional local grocery stores, such as Dewsons Wembley (*dewsons.com.au*)?

VIRTUAL COMPANY ASSIGNMENT

wiley.com/college/turban

Extreme Descent Snowboards

www.wiley.com/
college/turban

Background   Kellie Onn, CEO, looks up from her paperwork just as you are about to knock on the door. Kellie walks across the office to meet and greet you. She says, extending her hand, "I hope you are doing well." Jacob March pops into the office and greets each of you. You take a seat across from Jacob and the meeting begins.

Kellie explains that the company has developed a strong regional sales base but has expanded it sales globally using the Internet. She continues that Jacob and his staff have been working on EDS's e-commerce, along with the company's intranet. Kellie wants to be sure that the e-commerce site has friendly user interface and conveys the marketing environment strategy that is used in EDS's brick-and-mortar store.

Jacob suggests this would be a good research project for "our new intern." The meeting is quickly adjourned. Jacob walks out with you, and hands you a piece of paper on which are outlined the questions your research should answer.

Jacob asks if you have any questions. "Not at this time," you reply. Jacob says to call if you do, and he leaves your cubicle to let you get started on your new assignment.

Assignment

You will prepare and submit a report to your instructor that addresses the following questions and issues. (Hint: You might want to use a spreadsheet to answer question 2.)

1. Define electronic commerce (EC). How does the EDS Internet site fit your definition?

2. Use a search engine to find the Web sites of three companies that are in the same industry. Provide the Web site address (URL) and comparison of each site based on the following:

   a. Ease of navigation of the Web site. Is the site user friendly? How does a customer order a snowboard? What is the company's warranty policy? How does a customer return a snowboard?

   b. What is each Web site's major function?

   c. How well does each site support the company's business strategy?

   d. How does each company's site compare to the EDS site? What improvements can be made to the EDS e-commerce site?

3. Which company do you think has the most effective Web site for selling its product or service? Discuss your rationale for choosing this company.

COMPUTER-BASED SUPPLY CHAIN MANAGEMENT AND INFORMATION SYSTEMS INTEGRATION

10

CHAPTER PREVIEW

The success of many organizations, private, public, and military, depends on their ability to manage the flow of materials, information, and money into, within, and out of the organization. Such a flow is referred to as a *supply chain*. Because supply chains may be long and complex and may involve many different business partners, we frequently see problems in the operation of the supply chains. These problems may result in delays, in customers' dissatisfaction, in lost sales, and in high expenses of fixing the problems once they occur. World-class companies, such as Dell Computer, attribute much of their success to effective supply chain management (SCM), which is largely supported by IT.

In this chapter we describe the nature and types of supply chains and explain why problems occur there. Then we outline the IT-based solutions, most of which are provided by integrated software such as MRP and ERP. Next we show you how EC can cure problems along the supply chain. Finally we describe the problems of fulfilling orders in e-commerce systems and some of the solutions used.

CHAPTER OUTLINE

LEARNING OBJECTIVES

1. Understand the concept of the supply chain, its importance, and its management.
2. Describe the various types of supply chains.
3. Describe the problems in managing supply chains.
4. Describe the major categories of supply chain solutions.
5. Explain the need for software integration and describe the available software.
6. Explain how EC improves supply chain management.
7. Describe EC order-fulfillment problems and solutions.

HOW DELL MANAGES ITS SUPPLY CHAIN

> **The Business Problem**

Michael Dell started his business as a student, from his university dorm, by using a mail-order approach for selling PCs. This changed the manner by which PCs were sold. The customer did not have to come to a store to buy a computer, and Dell was able to customize the computer to the customer's specifications. The direct-mail approach enabled Dell to underprice his rivals, who were using distributors and retailers, by about 10 percent. For several years the business grew, and Dell constantly captured market share. In 1993, Compaq, the PC market leader at that time, decided to drastically cut prices in order to drive Dell out of the market. As a result of the price war, Dell Computer Corporation had a $65 million loss from reduced sales and inventory writedowns in the first six months of 1993 alone. The company was on the verge of bankruptcy.

> **The IT Solution**

Dell realized that the only way to win the marketing war was to introduce fundamental changes along the supply chain, from its suppliers all the way to its customers. Among the innovations used to restructure the business were the following.

- Most orders from customers and to suppliers were moved to the Web. Customers configure what they want, and find the cost and the deliverability in seconds, all online.

- Dell builds most computers only after they are ordered. This is done by using just-in-time manufacturing, which also enables quick deliveries, low inventories, little or no obsolescence, and lower marketing and administrative costs. This is an example of mass customization cited previously in the text.

- Some component warehouses, which are maintained by Dell's major suppliers, are located within 15 minutes of Dell factories. Not only does Dell get components quickly, but those components are up to 60 days newer than the ones acquired by major competitors.

- Shipments, which are done by UPS and other carriers, are all arranged electronically.

- Dell collaborates electronically with its buyers to pick their brains for new product ideas.

- Dell's new PC models are tested at the same time as the networks that they are on are tested. This collaboration reduces the testing period from 60 or 90 days to 15.

In addition to competing on *price* and *quality*, Dell started competing on *speed*. Since 2000, if you order a customized PC on any working day in the United States, the computer will be on the delivery truck the next day. A complex custom-made PC will be delivered in no more than 5 days.

In 2001, Dell was selling more than $4 million worth of computers each day on its Web site, and this amount was growing by 6 percent per month! In 1999, Dell added electronic auctions (*dellauction.com*) as a marketing channel. Eventually, Dell is aiming to sell most of its computers and servers from its Web site (*dell.com*).

In addition, Dell created customized home pages for its biggest corporate customers, such as Eastman Chemical, Monsanto, and Wells Fargo. At these sites, customers' employees use configuration tools and work-flow software to design computers, get the order approved inside the client organization, and place the order quickly and easily. The electronic ordering by both larger and smaller customers enables Dell to collect payments very quickly, even before it starts to assemble the computers.

Once orders are received they are transferred electronically to the production floor. Intelligent systems prepare the required parts and component list for each computer, and check availability. If not in stock, components and parts are automatically and electronically ordered directly from suppliers, who sometimes deliver in less than 60 minutes. Computerized manufacturing systems tightly link the entire demand and supply chains from suppliers to buyers. These systems are the foundation on which the build-to-order strategy rests.

Dell also electronically passes along to its suppliers data about its defect rates, engineering changes, and product enhancements. Since Dell and its suppliers are in constant communication, the margin for error is reduced. Dell employees collaborate electronically with business partners in real time on product designs and enhancements. Also, suppliers are required to share sensitive information with Dell, such as their own quality problems. Suppliers follow Dell's lead because they also reap the benefits of faster cycle times, reduced inventory, and improved forecasts.

Dell is using several other information technologies, including e-mail, EDI, videoteleconferencing, electronic procurement, computerized faxes, an intranet, DSS, a Web-based call center, and more. Dell also uses the Internet to create a community around its supply chain. Dell's corporate portal has links to bulletin boards where partners from around the world can exchange information about their experiences with Dell's products, logistics, and customer service.

The Results

By 1999, Dell had become the world's number-two PC seller, and in 2001 it became number one. It is considered one of the world's best-managed and most profitable companies.

Sources: Compiled from articles in *Business Week* (1997–2001), *Information Week* (1998–2001), *cio.com* (2001), and *us.dell.com/dell/media*.

What We Learned from This Case

The Dell case demonstrates that the new build-to-order business model changed the manner in which business is done in the PC industry (and later, in the computer server industry). To implement such a model on a large scale (mass customization), Dell built superb supply chain management that includes both suppliers and customers. A major success factor in Dell's operation was the improvements made by using IT along the *entire* supply chain. Dell created flexible and responsive IT-based manufacturing systems that are integrated with the supply chain. In addition, Dell is able to collect payments before it starts to assemble computers, thus shortening the corporate cash flow cycle. Dell successfully implemented the concepts of *supply chain management, enterprise resource planning, supply chain intelligence*, and *customer-relationship management*. The first three topics are the subject of this chapter. (CRM is described in Chapter 8.)

10.1 SUPPLY CHAINS AND THEIR MANAGEMENT

Definitions and Benefits

Initially, the concept of a *supply chain* referred to the flow of materials from their sources (suppliers) to the company, and then inside the company for processing. Then, finished products were moved to customers. Today the concept is much broader.

Definitions.   A **supply chain** refers to the flow of materials, information, payments, and services, from raw material suppliers, through factories and warehouses, to end customers. A supply chain also includes the *organizations* and *processes* that create and deliver products, information, and services to the end customers. It includes many tasks such as purchasing, payment flow, materials handling, production planning and control, logistics and warehousing inventory control, and distribution and delivery. The function of **supply chain management (SCM)** is to plan, organize, coordinate, and control all the supply chain's activities.

Benefits.   The goals of modern SCM are to reduce uncertainty and risks in the supply chain, thereby positively affecting inventory levels, cycle time, business processes, and customer service. All these benefits contribute to increased profitability and competitiveness. The benefits of supply chain management have long been recognized both in business and in the military. As early as 401 B.C., Clerchus of Sparta said, that the survival of the Greek army depended not only upon its discipline, training, and morale, but also upon its supply chain. The same idea was later echoed by famous generals such as Napoleon and Eisenhower.

The Components of Supply Chains

The term *supply chain* comes from a picture of how partnering organizations in a specific supply chain are linked together. Figure 10.1 shows a relatively simple supply chain, which links a company with its suppliers (on the left) and its distributors and

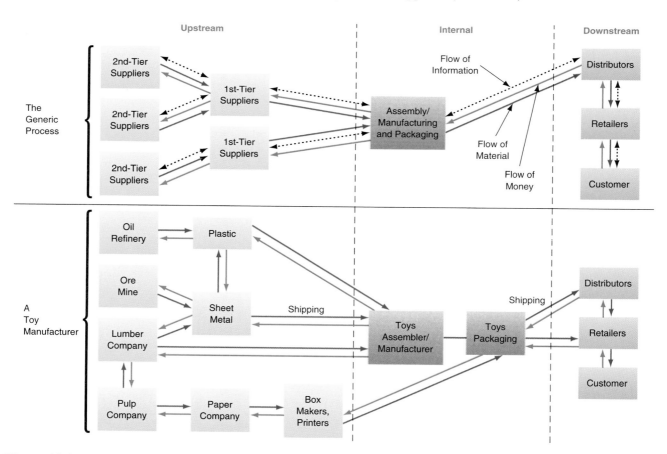

Figure 10.1   *A linear supply chain.*

customers (on the right). The upper part of the figure shows a generic supply chain; the lower part shows the chain of a toy manufacturer. Notice that suppliers may have their own (second-tier) suppliers, and so on. In addition to flow of material there is a flow of information (shown only in the upper part of the figure) and money as well. The flow of money usually goes in the direction opposite to the flow of materials.

Note that the supply chain is *linear* and it involves three basic segments:

1. *Upstream supply chain segment.* This segment includes the organization's *first-tier* suppliers (which themselves can be manufacturers and/or assemblers) and their suppliers. Such a relationship can be extended, to the left, in several tiers, all the way to the origin of the material (e.g., mining ores, growing crops). Here the major activities are purchasing and shipping.

2. *Internal supply chain segment.* This segment includes all the processes used by an organization in *transforming* the inputs shipped by the suppliers into outputs, from the time materials enter the organization to the time that the finished product goes to distribution, outside the organization. Activities here include materials handling, inventory management, manufacturing, and quality control.

3. *Downstream supply chain segment.* This segment includes all the processes involved in distributing and delivering the products to final customers. Looked at very broadly, the supply chain actually ends when the product reaches its after-use disposal—presumably back to "Mother Earth" somewhere. Activities here include packaging, warehousing, and shipping. These activities may be done by using several tiers of distributors (e.g., wholesalers and retailers).

Supply chains come in all shapes and sizes and may be fairly complex, as shown in Figure 10.2 (page 322). As can be seen in the figure, the supply chain for a car manufacturer includes hundreds of suppliers, dozens of manufacturing plants (for parts) and assembly plants (assembling cars), warehouses, dealers, direct business customers (buying fleets), wholesalers (some of which are virtual), customers, and support functions such as product engineering, purchasing agents, banks, and transportation companies.

Notice that in this case the chain is not strictly linear as it was in Figure 10.1. Here we see some loops in the process. In addition, sometimes the flow of information and even goods can be bidirectional, as it would be, for example, for the *return* of products (known as **reverse logistics**). For an automaker, that would be cars returned to the dealers in cases of defects or recalls by the manufacturer. Also notice that the supply chain is much more than just physical. It includes both information and financial flows. As a matter of fact, the supply chain of a service such as obtaining a mortgage or delivering music or other digitizable product may not include *any* physical materials. (See Problem-Solving Activity 4 for an example.)

Types of Supply Chains

The supply chain shown in Figure 10.1 is typical for a manufacturing company. If the company is a traditional one, it will produce items that will be stored in warehouses and other locations, making the supply chain more complex. If the company uses a make-to-order business model, there will be no need for storing finished products, but there will be need to store raw materials and components. Therefore, it is clear that supply chains depend on the nature of the company. The following four types are very common.

Integrated make-to-stock.   The **integrated make-to-stock** supply chain model focuses on tracking customer demand in real time, so that the production process can restock the finished-goods inventory efficiently. This integration is often achieved through use

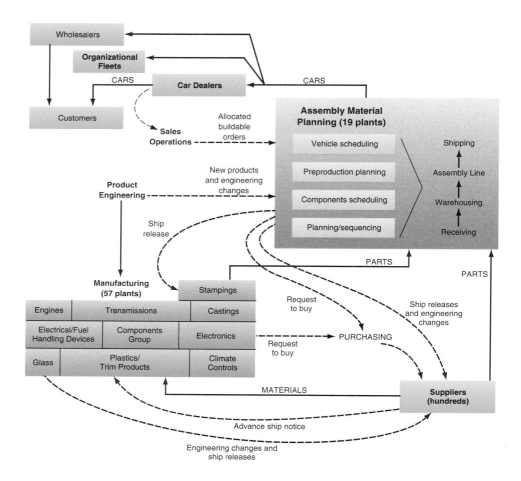

Figure 10.2   *An automotive supply chain. [Source: Modified from R. B. Handfield and E. L. Nichols, Jr.,* Introduction to Supply Chain Management, *Upper Saddle River, NJ: Prentice-Hall, 1999.]*

of an information system that is fully integrated (an enterprise system, described in Section 10.4). Through application of such a system, the organization can receive real-time demand information that can be used to develop and modify production plans and schedules. This information is also integrated further down the supply chain to the **procurement** function, so that the modified production plans and schedules can be supported by input materials.

EXAMPLE

Starbucks matches supply and demand using IT.   Starbucks Coffee (*starbucks.com*) uses several distribution channels, not only selling coffee drinks to consumers, but also selling beans and ground coffee to businesses such as airlines, supermarkets, department stores, and ice-cream makers. Sales are also done through direct mail, including the Internet. Starbucks is successfully integrating all sources of demand and matching it with the supply by using Oracle's automated information system for manufacturing (called GEMMS). The system does distribution planning, manufacturing scheduling, and inventory control (using MRP). The coordination of supply with multiple distribution channels requires timely and accurate information flow about demand, inventories, storage capacity, transportation scheduling, and more. The information systems are critical in doing all the above with maximum effectiveness and reasonable cost. Finally, Starbucks must work closely with hundreds of business partners. ●

Continuous replenishment.   The idea of the **continuous replenishment** supply chain model is to constantly replenish the inventory by working closely with suppliers and/or intermediaries. However, if the replenishment process involves many shipments, the cost may be too high, causing the supply chain to collapse. Therefore very tight integration is needed between the order-fulfillment process and the production process. Real-time information about demand changes is required in order for the production process to maintain the desired replenishment schedules and levels. This model is most applicable to environments with stable demand patterns, as is usually the case with distribution of prescription medicine. The model requires intermediaries when large systems are involved. Such a distribution channel is shown in Figure 10.3a, for McKessen Co. (whose case is described in Section 10.5 in detail).

Build-to-order.   Dell Computer (opening case) is best known for its application of the **build-to-order** model. The concept behind the build-to-order supply chain model is to begin assembly of the customer's order almost immediately upon receipt of the order. This requires careful management of the component inventories and delivery of needed supplies along the supply chain. A solution to this potential inventory problem is to utilize many common components across several production lines and in several locations.

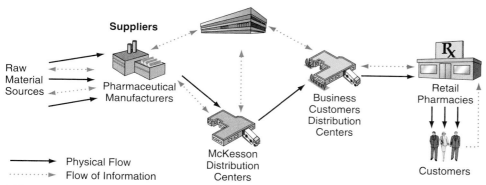

(a) **Integrated pharmaceutical supply chain. (Flow of payments not shown.)**

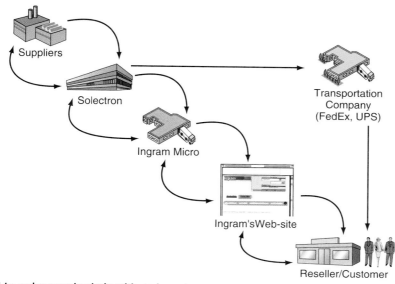

(b) **Build-to-order supply chain with no inventory.**

Figure 10.3   *Types of supply chains. [Source for part b: R. Kalakota and M. Robinson,* E-Business 2.0, *Reading, MA, Addison Wesley, 2000, p. 301, Fig. 9.10.]*

One of the primary benefits of this type of supply chain model is the perception that each customer is receiving a personalized product. In addition, the customer is receiving it rapidly. This type of supply chain model supports the concept of *mass customization*.

Channel assembly.   A slight modification to the build-to-order model is the **channel assembly** supply chain model. In this model, the parts of the product are gathered and assembled as the product moves through the distribution channel. This is accomplished through strategic alliances with *third-party logistics (3PL)* firms. These services sometimes involve either physical assembly of a product at a 3PL facility or collection of finished components for delivery to the customer. For example, a computer company would have items such as the monitor shipped directly from its vendor to a 3PL facility, such as at Federal Express and UPS. The customer's computer order

IT's About Business

lego.com

Box 10.1:   Lego struggles with global issues

Lego Company of Denmark is a major producer of toys, including electronic ones. In 1999, the company decided to market its Lego Mindstorms on the Internet. Mindstorms' users can build a Lego robot using more than 700 traditional Lego elements, program it on a PC, and transfer the program to the robot.

Lego sells its products in many countries using several regional distribution centers. When the decision to do global e-commerce was made, the company had the following concerns:

- Choice of countries. It did not make sense to go to all countries, since sales are very low in some countries, and some countries offer no logistical support services.
- A supportive distribution and service system would be needed.
- Merging the offline and online operations or creating a new centralized unit seemed to be a complex undertaking.
- Existing warehouses were optimized to handle distribution to commercial buyers, not to the individual customers who would be the buyers over the Internet.
- It would be necessary to handle returns around the globe.
- Lego products were selling in different countries in different currencies and at different prices. Should the product be sold on the Net at a single price? In which currency? How would this price be related to the offline prices?
- The company would need a system to handle the direct mail and to track individual shipments.

- Invoicing must comply with the regulations of many countries.
- Should Lego create a separate Web site for Mindstorms? What languages should be used there?
- Some countries have strict regulations regarding advertising and sales to children. Also laws on consumer protection vary among countries. How would the company ensure compliance with these regulations and laws?
- How to handle restrictions on electronic transfer of individuals' personal data.
- How to handle the tax and import duty payments in different countries.

In the rush to get its innovative product to market, Lego did not solve all of these issues before the direct marketing was introduced. The resulting problems forced Lego to close the Web site for business. It took almost a year to solve all global trade-related issues and eventually reopen the site. By 2001 Lego was selling online many of its products, priced in U.S. dollars, but the online service was available in only 15 countries.

Questions

1. Visit Lego's Web site (*lego.com*). What are the company's latest EC activities?
2. Investigate what Lego's competitors are doing.
3. Do you think the Web is the best way for Lego to go global? Why or why not?
4. Contact Lego and find out how they will ship to you. Draw the supply chain.

would therefore only come together once all items were placed on a vehicle for delivery. A channel assembly may have low or zero inventories, and it is popular in the computer technology industry. An example is shown in Figure 10.3b (page 323) with a large distributor, Ingram Micro, at the center of the supply chain.

Global Supply Chains

Supply chains that involve suppliers and/or customers in other countries are referred to as **global supply chains**. The major reasons why companies go global in their supply chains are: lower prices of materials, services, and labor; availability of products or technology that are unavailable domestically; high quality of products available in global markets; the firm's global sales strategy; intensification of global competition, which drives companies to cut costs; the need to develop a foreign presence; and fulfillment of counter trade. The introduction of e-commerce has made it much easier and cheaper to find suppliers in other countries (e.g., by using electronic bidding) and to reach many customers.

Global supply chains are usually longer than domestic ones, and they may be complex. Therefore, additional uncertainties and problems are likely. Information technologies are extremely useful in supporting global supply chains. For example, TradeNet in Singapore connects sellers, buyers, and government agencies via electronic data interchange (EDI). (TradeNet's case is described in detail on the Web site of this book.) A similar network, TradeLink, operates in Hong Kong, using both EDI and EDI/Internet to connect thousands of trading partners. Some of the issues that may create difficulties in global supply chains are legal issues, customs fees and taxes, language and cultural differences, fast changes in currency exchange rates, and political instabilities. Such difficulties can be seen in IT's About Business 10.1 (page 324).

www.wiley.com/
college/turban

Before you go on . . .

1. Define supply chain and describe its benefits and its management.

2. Describe the components of a supply chain.

3. Define reverse logistics.

4. Describe the major types of supply chains.

5. Describe a global supply chain and its difficulties.

10.2   SUPPLY CHAIN PROBLEMS AND SOLUTIONS

A large number of problems may develop along supply chains. Here we demonstrate the most recurrent ones.

Background

Supply chain problems have been recognized both in the military and in business operations for generations. Some even caused armies to lose wars or companies to go out of business. The problems are most evident in complex or long supply chains and in cases where many business partners are involved. In the business world there are numerous examples of companies that were unable to meet demand, had too large and expensive inventories, and so on. On the other hand, some world-class companies such as Wal-Mart, Federal Express, and Dell have superb supply chains with many innovative features.

EXAMPLE

Problems with "Santa's 1999" supply chain.　A recent example of a supply chain problem was the difficulty of fulfilling orders received electronically for toys during the 1999 holiday season. During the last months of 1999 online toy retailers, including Amazon.com and Toys 'R' Us, conducted a massive advertising campaign for Internet ordering. This included $20–$30 discount vouchers for shopping online. The retailers underestimated the overwhelming customer response and were unable to get some of the necessary toys from the manufacturing plants and warehouses and deliver them to the customers' doors by Christmas Eve. As compensation to those whose toys did not arrive on time, Toys 'R' Us offered unhappy customers a $100 store coupon. Despite its generous offer, over 40 percent of the unhappy Toys 'R' Us customers said they would not shop online at Toys 'R' Us again. ●

In the remaining portion of this section we will look closely at some of the major problems in managing the supply chain and at some proposed solutions, many of which are supported by IT.

Problems Along the Supply Chain

The problems along the supply chain stem mainly from two sources: (1) from uncertainties, and (2) from the need to coordinate several activities, internal units, and business partners.

A major source of supply chain uncertainties is the *demand forecast*, as demonstrated by the Santa's 1999 toy example. The demand forecast may be influenced by several factors such as competition, prices, weather conditions, technological development, and customers' general level of confidence. Other supply chain uncertainties are delivery times, which depend on many factors ranging from machine failures in the production process to road conditions and traffic jams that interfere with shipments. Quality problems with materials and parts may create production delays.

Coordination problems occur when a company's departments are not well connected, when messages to business partners are misunderstood or lost, and when parties are not informed, are misinformed, or are informed too late on what is needed or is occurring.

A major symptom of ineffective supply chain management is poor customer service, which hinders people or businesses from getting products or services when and where needed, or gives them poor-quality products. Other symptoms are high inventory costs, loss of revenues, extra cost of expediting shipments, and more. One of the most persistent SCM problems is known as the bullwhip effect.

The bullwhip effect.　The **bullwhip effect** refers to erratic shifts in orders along the supply chain. This effect was initially observed by Procter & Gamble (P&G) in connection with its disposable diapers product (Pampers). Although actual sales in stores were fairly stable and predictable, orders from wholesalers and distributors to P&G (the manufacturer) had wild swings, creating production and inventory problems for P&G. An investigation revealed that distributors' orders were fluctuating because of poor demand forecast and lack of coordination and trust among the supply chain partners. If each distinct entity along the supply chain makes ordering and inventory decisions with an eye to its own interests (fear of product outages) above those of the chain, stockpiling may occur simultaneously at as many as seven or eight places across the supply chain. Such stockpiling can lead in some cases to as many as 100 days of inventory (instead of the usual 10 to 15 days)—inventory that is waiting, "just in case." Keeping such large inventory can be very expensive for supply chain members, costing as much as 24 percent of the value of the items stocked, each year.

The bullwhip effect is not unique to P&G. Firms ranging from Hewlett-Packard in the computer industry to Bristol-Myers Squibb in the pharmaceutical field have experienced a similar phenomenon. A 1998 grocery industry study projected that simply by sharing information, $30 billion in savings could materialize in the grocery industry supply chains alone. To avoid the "sting of the bullwhip," companies must *share information*. Such sharing is facilitated by EDI, extranets, and groupware technologies, and it is now part of collaborative commerce as it is done by P&G with its major customers, as the following example shows.

EXAMPLE

Information sharing between two giants.   One of the most notable examples of information sharing is between Procter and Gamble (P&G) and Wal-Mart. Wal-Mart provides P&G access to sales information about every P&G product that Wal-Mart sells. The information is collected electronically by P&G on a daily basis, from every Wal-Mart store. By monitoring the inventory level of each P&G item in every store, P&G knows when the inventories fall below the threshold that requires a shipment. This way, P&G is able to manage the inventory replenishment for Wal-Mart. All this is done electronically. The benefit for P&G is accurate demand information. P&G has similar agreements with other major retailers. Thus, P&G can plan production more accurately, avoiding some of the problem of the bullwhip effect. In fact, P&G implemented a Web-based "Ultimate-Supply System," which replaced 4,000 different EDI links to suppliers and retailers in a more cost-effective way. ●

Other problems along the supply chain.   Many other supply chain problems exist. One major problem is known as **phantom stockouts**. Such a problem occurs when customers are told that a product they want is *not available*, though in fact the product *is available* (e.g., when the product is misplaced, or the count of in-stock is inaccurate). According to *Harvard Business Review* (May 2001), phantom stockouts cut one company's profitability by 25 percent.

Solutions to Supply Chain Problems

Over the years organizations have developed many solutions to supply chain problems. One of the earliest solutions was *vertical integration*. For example, Henry Ford purchased rubber plantations in South America in order to control tire production for his cars. Today, many companies whose success depends on tight coordination of all the parts use vertical integration. For example, Starbucks Coffee owns coffee-processing plants, warehouses, and distribution systems, all tied together by software programs.

Undoubtedly, the most common solution used by companies is *building inventories* as insurance against supply chain uncertainties. This way products and parts flow smoothly through the production processes. The main problem with this approach is that it is very difficult to correctly determine inventory levels for each product and part. If inventory levels are set too high, the cost of keeping the inventory will be very large. If the inventory is too low, there is no insurance against high demand or slow delivery times, and revenues (and customers) may be lost. In either event the total cost, including inventory holding cost and the cost of sales opportunities lost and bad reputation, can be very high. Thus, companies make major attempts to control inventory, usually with the aid of inventory control software or supply chain software that includes inventory modules.

Manager's Checklist 10.1

IT Solutions to Supply Chain Problems

- Use outsourcing rather than do-it-yourself during demand peaks.
- Similarly, "buy" rather than "make" production inputs whenever appropriate.
- Configure optimal shipping plans.
- Create strategic partnerships with suppliers.
- Use the *just-in-time approach* to purchasing, in which suppliers deliver small quantities whenever supplies, materials, and parts are needed. (See the Dell opening case.)
- Reduce the lead time for buying and selling.
- Use fewer suppliers.
- Improve supplier-buyer relationships.
- Manufacture only after orders are in, as Dell does with its custom-made computers.
- Achieve accurate demand by working closely with suppliers to forecast demand.

Effective supply chain and inventory management requires coordination of all activities and links of the supply chain. Successful coordination enables materials and goods to move smoothly and on time from suppliers to manufacturers to customers, which enables firms to keep inventories low and costs down. For example, computerized point-of-sale (POS) information can be transmitted once a day, or even in real time, to distribution centers, suppliers, and shippers. This enables firms to achieve optimal inventory levels. Other solutions for solving SCM problems are provided in Manager's Checklist 10.1.

In conclusion, in today's competitive business environment, the efficiency and effectiveness of supply chains in most organizations are critical for the organization's survival and are greatly dependent upon the supporting information systems. In the next section, we will show you how IT is used to support supply chains.

Before you go on . . .

1. Describe typical problems along the supply chain.
2. Define the bullwhip effect.
3. Describe some solutions to supply chain problems.

10.3   IT SUPPLY CHAIN SUPPORT AND SYSTEMS INTEGRATION

Effective solutions to supply chain problems have been provided by IT for decades. Indeed, the concept of the supply chain is interrelated with the computerization of its activities, which has evolved over 50 years. Some examples of how IT solves recurrent supply chain problems are provided in Table 10.1. (Some of the supporting technologies mentioned in this table are described in Chapters 11 and 12.)

Table 10.1   Some Supply Chain Problems and Their IT Solutions

Supply Chain Problem	IT Solution
Linear sequence of processing is too slow.	Parallel processing, using workflow software.
Waiting times between chain segments are excessive.	Identify reason (using decision support software) and expedite communication and collaboration (intranets, groupware).
Existence of non-value-added activities.	Value analysis (SCM software), simulation software.
Slow delivery of paper documents.	Electronic documents and communication system (e.g., EDI, e-mail).
Repeat process activities due to wrong shipments, poor quality, etc.	Electronic verifications (software agents), automation, eliminating human errors, electronic control systems.
Batching; accumulate work orders between supply chain processes to get economies of scale (e.g., save on delivery).	SCM software analysis; digitize documents for online delivery.
Learn about delays after they occur, or learn too late.	Tracking systems, anticipate delays, trend analysis, early detection (intelligent systems).
Excessive administrative controls such as approvals (signatures). Approvers are in different locations.	Parallel approvals (workflow), electronic approval system, analysis of need.
Lack of information, or too slow flow.	Internet/intranet, software agents for monitoring and alert, barcodes, direct flow from POS terminals.
Lack of synchronization of moving materials.	Workflow and tracking systems, synchronization by software agents.
Poor coordination, cooperation, and communication.	Groupware products, constant monitoring, alerts, collaboration tools.
Delays in shipments from warehouses.	Use robots in warehouses, use warehouse management software.
Redundancies in the supply chain. Too many purchasing orders, too much handling and packaging.	Information sharing via the Web, creating teams of collaborative partners supported by IT.
Obsolescence of parts and components that stay too long in storage.	Reducing inventory levels by information sharing internally and externally, using intranets and groupware.
Scheduling problems, manufacturing lack of control.	Intelligent agents for B2B modeling (see *gensym.com*).

The Evolution of Computerized Aids

Historically, many of the supply chain activities were managed with paper transactions, which can be very inefficient. Therefore, since the time when computers first began to be used for business, people have wanted to automate the processes along the supply chain. The first software programs, which appeared in the 1950s and early 1960s, supported short segments along the supply chain. Typical examples are inventory management systems, production scheduling, and billing. The major objectives were to reduce costs, expedite processing, and reduce errors. Such applications were developed in the functional areas, independent of each other, and they became more and more sophisticated with the passage of time. But it was difficult to combine them.

In a short time it became clear that interdependencies exist among some of the supply chain activities. One early realization was that production schedule is related to inventory management and purchasing plans. As early as the 1960s, the **material**

requirements planning (MRP) model was devised. This model essentially integrates production, purchasing, and inventory management of interrelated products (see Chapter 8). It became clear that computer support could greatly enhance the use of this model, which may require daily updating. This resulted in commercial MRP software packages coming on the market.

MRP packages were useful in many cases, and they are still in use today, helping to drive inventory levels down and streamlining portions of the supply chain. However, some of the MRP applications failed. One of the major reasons for such failure was that schedule-inventory-purchasing operations are closely related to both financial and labor resources, but were not included in the MRP models. The realization of this failure resulted in an enhanced MRP methodology and software called **manufacturing resource planning (MRP II)**, which adds labor and financial planning to the simpler MRP model.

This evolution continued, leading to the **enterprise resource planning (ERP)** concept, which expanded MRP II to consider other activities in the entire enterprise. ERP was confined initially to include internal suppliers and customers, but later it incorporated external suppliers and customers in what is known as *extended ERP software*. (We look at ERP again in more detail in Section 10.4.)

The above evolution of computerized integrated systems is shown in Figure 10.4. The next step in this evolution, which is just beginning to make its way into business use, is the inclusion of markets and communities. (See *mySAP.com* for details.)

Notice that throughout this evolution there have been more and more integrations along several dimensions (more functional areas, combining transaction processing and decision support, inclusion of business partners). The question is—why?

Why Systems Integration?

Creating the twenty-first-century enterprise cannot be done effectively with twentieth-century computer technology, which is *functionally* oriented. Functional systems may not let different departments communicate with each other in the same language. Worse yet, crucial sales, inventory, and production data often have to be painstakingly entered manually into separate computer systems every time they need to be

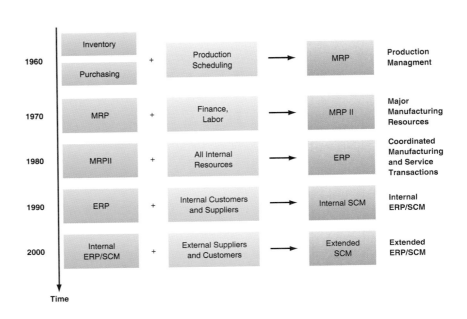

Figure 10.4 *The evolution of integrated systems.*

processed together. In many cases employees simply do not get the information they need, or they get it too late.

The following are the major tangible and intangible benefits of systems integration (in order of importance):

- *Tangible benefits:* Inventory reduction, personnel reduction, productivity improvement, order management improvement, financial-close cycle improvements, IT cost reduction, procurement cost reduction, cash management improvements, revenue/profit increases, transportation and logistics cost reduction, maintenance reduction, and on-time delivery improvement

- *Intangible benefits:* Information visibility, new/improved processes, customer responsiveness, standardization, flexibility, globalization, and business performance

Notice that in both types of benefits many items are directly related to improved supply chain management.

Supply Chain and Value Chain Integration

The integration of the segments in the supply chain has been facilitated by the need to streamline operations in order to meet customer demands in the areas of product and service cost, quality, delivery, technology, and cycle time brought by increased global competition. This requires flexibility of the integrated systems.

Types of integration: from supply to value and system chains.   The most obvious integration is of the segments of the supply chain and/or of the information that flows among the segments. But there is another type of integration, related to what are called value chains. The term **value chain** (Chapter 13) describes the primary activities of an organization (inbound logistics, operations, etc.), along with its support activities (infrastructure, human resources, technology, etc.), and the net value that is added to the organization's product or service by each primary activity, sequentially.

Traditionally, we thought of the value chain in terms of one organization's primary activities such as purchasing, transportation, warehousing, and logistics. However, when the value chain is extended to include suppliers, customers, and so forth, it becomes a **value system**, or **integrated value chain**. The integrated value chain is a more encompassing concept. It is the process by which *multiple* enterprises within a shared market channel collaboratively plan, implement, and manage (electronically as well as physically) the flow of goods, services, and information along their entire joint chain in a manner that increases customer-perceived value (**value proposition**). This process optimizes the efficiency of the chain, creating competitive advantage for all stakeholders in their own value chains.

Another way of defining value chain integration is as a *process of collaboration* that optimizes all internal and external activities involved in delivering greater perceived value to the ultimate customer. A supply chain is transformed into an integrated value chain when it:

- Extends the chain all the way from subsuppliers (tier 2, 3, etc.) to customers
- Integrates back-office operations with those of the front office
- Becomes highly customer-centric, focusing on demand generation and customer service as well as demand fulfillment and logistics
- Is proactively designed by chain members to compete as an extended enterprise, creating and enhancing customer-perceived value by means of cross-enterprise collaboration
- Seeks to optimize the value added by information and utility-enhancing services

Box 10.2:   How Warner-Lambert applies an integrated supply chain

One of Warner-Lambert's major products is Listerine antiseptic mouthwash (now a division of Pfizer). The materials for making Listerine come from eucalyptus trees in Australia and are shipped to the Warner-Lambert (W-L) manufacturing plant in New Jersey, USA. Listerine is distributed by wholesalers and by thousands of retail stores, some of which are giants such as Wal-Mart. The problem that W-L faces is to *forecast the overall demand* in order to determine how much Listerine to produce. A wrong forecast will result either in high inventories, or in shortages. Inventories are expensive to keep, and shortages may result in loss of revenue and reputation.

Warner-Lambert forecasts demand with the help of Manugistics Inc.'s Demand Planning Information System. (Manugistics is a vendor of IT software for SCM.) Then the system analyzes manufacturing, distribution, and sales data against expected demand and business climate information. Its goal is to help W-L decide how much Listerine (and other products) to make and distribute and how much of each raw ingredient is needed, and when. The sales and marketing group of W-L enters the expected demand for Listerine into another SCM software, which schedules the production of Listerine in the amounts needed and generates electronic purchase orders for W-L's suppliers.

W-L's supply chain excellence stems from the Collaborative Planning, Forecasting, and Replenishment (CPFR) program. This is a retailing-industry project for which piloting was done at W-L. In the pilot project W-L shared strategic plans, performance data, and market insight with Wal-Mart over private networks (see the figure). The company realized that it could benefit from Wal-Mart's market knowledge, just as Wal-Mart could benefit from W-L's product knowledge. In CPFR, trading partners collaborate on demand forecast. The project includes major SCM and ERP vendors such as SAP and Manugistics. During the CPFR pilot, W-L increased its products' shelf-fill rate—the extent to which a store's shelves are fully stocked—from 87 percent to 98 percent, earning the company about $8 million a year in additional sales for much less investment. W-L is now using the Internet to expand the CPFR program to all its suppliers and retail partners.

Warner-Lambert is involved in another collaborative retail-industry project, the Supply-Chain Operations Reference (SCOR), an initiative of the Supply-Chain Council in the United States. SCOR divides supply chain operations into parts, giving manufacturers, suppliers, distributors, and retailers a framework with which to evaluate the effectiveness of their processes along the same supply chains.

Questions

1. Can you identify other industries, besides retailing, for which a similar collaboration would be beneficial?

2. Why was Listerine a target for the pilot SCM collaboration?

In a pilot project, Wal-Mart has used the CPFR to link up with one of its key suppliers, Warner-Lambert. Through CPFR workbenches (spreadsheet-like documents with ample space for collaborative comments), Wal-Mart buyers and Warner-Lambert planners are able to jointly develop product forecasts.

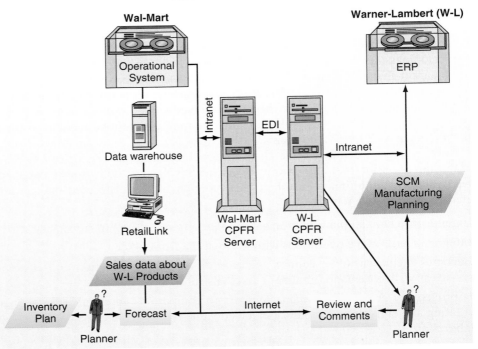

Presently only a few large companies are successfully involved in a comprehensive collaboration to reengineer the value system. One such effort is described in IT's About Business 10.2, a case about Warner-Lambert, manufacturer of consumer products like Listerine (page 332).

Through CPFR workbenches (spreadsheet-like documents with ample space for collaborative comments), Warner-Lambert (W-L) planners and buyers from Wal-Mart, a giant buyer of W-L products, are able to jointly develop forecasts of overall product demand. Such forecasts help guide W-L's production planning for its manufacturing plants. This kind of collaboration is referred to as **collaborative commerce networks**, a type of *collaborative commerce* (see Chapter 9).

Another example of supply chain integration is *product development systems* that allow suppliers to dial into a client's intranet, pull product specifications, and view illustrations and videos of a manufacturing process. Finally, one should distinguish between integration inside a company (integrating the information systems of departments, connecting to database, connecting the ordering system to the back-end production activities), and interorganizational system integration (connecting systems of different organizations).

Before you go on . . .

1. Trace the evolution from MRP to ERP.

2. Describe the need for software integration.

3. Define value chain and value system.

10.4   ENTERPRISE RESOURCE PLANNING (ERP)

With the advance of enterprisewide client/server computing comes a new challenge: how to control all major business processes with a single software architecture in real time. The integrated solution known as **enterprise resource planning (ERP)** is a process of managing all resources and their use in the entire enterprise in a coordinated manner. ERP's major objective is to *integrate all departments and functions across a company* onto a single information system that can serve all of the enterprise's needs. For example, improved order entry allows immediate access to inventory, product data, customer credit history, and prior order information. This availability of information raises productivity, quality, and profitability, and it increases customer satisfaction. The implementation of ERP is done by commercial software available from companies such as SAP, Oracle, and PeopleSoft. An ERP implementation is illustrated in IT's About Business 10.3 (on page 334).

ERP software crosses functional department lines. It includes dozens of integrated modules such as sales, procurement, inventory control, manufacturing scheduling, accounts payable, accounts receivable, payroll, monthly financial statements, and systems management. An ERP suite provides a single interface for managing all the routine activities performed in manufacturing—from entering sales orders to coordinating shipping and after-sales customer service. As of the late 1990s, ERP systems have begun to be extended along the supply chain to suppliers and customers, incorporating functionality for customer interaction and for managing relationships with suppliers and vendors.

IT's About Business

colgate.com

www.wiley.com/
college/turban

Box 10.3:   Colgate-Palmolive uses ERP to smooth its supply chain

Colgate-Palmolive is the world leader in oral-care products (mouthwashes, toothpaste, and toothbrushes) and a major supplier of personal-care products (baby care, deodorants, shampoos, and soaps). In addition, the company's Hill's Health Science Diet is a leading pet-food brand worldwide. Foreign sales account for about 70 percent of Colgate's total revenues.

To stay competitive, Colgate continuously seeks to streamline its supply chain, where thousands of suppliers and customers interact with the company. At the same time, Colgate faces the challenges of new-product acceleration, which has been a factor in driving faster sales growth and improved market share. Also, Colgate is devising ways to offer consumers a greater choice of better products at a lower cost to the company, which creates complexities in the manufacturing and the supply chains. To better manage and coordinate its business, Colgate embarked on an ERP implementation to allow the company to access more timely and accurate data, and reduce costs.

An important factor for Colgate was whether it could use the ERP software across the entire spectrum of the business. Colgate needed the ability to coordinate globally and act locally. Colgate's U.S. division installed SAP R/3 for this purpose. (See description of SAP R/3 on the book's Web site.)

Questions

1. Draw the supply chain of Colgate's toothpaste. (To do so, you need to find how the product is made and distributed.)
2. What role does the ERP software play?
3. What benefits can customers, like yourself, derive from the ERP?

But ERP was never meant to fully support supply chains. ERP solutions are centered around *business transactions*. As such, they do not provide the computerized decision support needed to respond rapidly to real-time changes in supply, demand, labor, or capacity. This deficiency has been overcome by the second generation of ERP.

Second-Generation ERP

ERP has traditionally excelled in the ability to manage administrative activities like payroll, inventory, and order processing. For example, an ERP system has the functionality of electronic ordering or the best way to bill the customer—but all it does is automate the transactions. The reports generated by ERP systems gave planners statistics about what happened in the company, costs, and financial performance. However, the planning systems with ERP were rudimentary. Reports from first-generation ERP systems provided a snapshot of the business *at a point in time*. But they did not support the *continuous* planning that is central to supply chain planning—planning that continues to refine and enhance the plan as changes and events occur, up to the very last minute before executing the plan. First-generation ERP systems did not support decision making either. To get such support for segments of the supply chain, companies used standalone (unintegrated) *supply chain management (SCM) software*.

SCM software.   Planning systems oriented toward *decision making* were provided by SCM software. To illustrate, consider how ERP and SCM approach an order-processing problem. There is a fundamental difference: The question in SCM becomes "Should I take your order?" instead of the ERP approach of "How can I best take or fulfill your order?" The following example demonstrates how SCM software works.

EXAMPLE

IBM links its global supply chain with SCM software.   IBM reengineered its global supply chain in order to achieve quick responsiveness to customers and to do so with minimal inventory. To support this effort, it developed a supply chain analysis tool called the Asset Management Tool (AMT). AMT integrates analytical performance optimization, simulation, activity-based costing, graphical process modeling, and enterprise database connectivity into a system that allows quantitative analysis of extended supply chains. IBM has used AMT to study such issues as inventory budgets, customer-service targets, and new-product introductions. The system was implemented at a number of IBM business units and their supply chain partners. AMT benefits include savings of over $750 million in material costs and reductions in administrative expenses each year. ●

However, SCM solutions need to be coordinated, and they sometimes require information provided by ERP software. Therefore, it makes sense to integrate ERP and SCM.

Integrating ERP and SCM.   How is ERP/SCM integration done? One approach is to work with different software products from different vendors. For example, a company might use SAP R/3 as an ERP and add to it Manugistics' manufacturing-oriented SCM software (as shown in the Warner-Lambert case). Such an approach, which is known as the *"best of breed"* approach, requires fitting different software, from different vendors, which may be a complex task unless special interfaces exist.

Table 10.2   Comparing SCM and SCI

Supply Chain Management (SCM)	Supply Chain Intelligence (SCI)
Largely about managing the procurement and production links of the supply chain.	Provides a broad view of an entire supply chain to reveal full product and component life cycle.
Transactional.	Analytical.
Tactical decision making.	Strategic decision making.
Helps reduce costs through improved operational efficiency.	Reveals opportunities for cost reduction, but also stimulates revenue growth.
Usually just the SCM application's data (as a vertical stovepipe).	Integrates supplier, manufacturing, and product data (horizontal).
Records one state of data, representing "now."	Keeps a historic record.
Assists in material and production planning.	Does what-if forecasting based on historic data.
Quantifies cost of some materials.	Enables an understanding of total cost.
Shows today's yield but cannot explain influences on it; thus provides no help for improvements.	Drills into yield figures to reveal what caused the performance level, so it can be improved.
Simple reporting.	Collaborative environment with personalized monitoring of metrics.

Source: P. Russom, "Increasing Manufacturing Performance Through Supply Chain Intelligence," *DM Review* (September 2000).

The second approach is for the ERP vendors to add SCM functionalities, such as decision support and *business intelligence* capabilities. **Business intelligence** refers to analysis performed by DSS, EIS, data mining, and intelligent systems (see Chapters 11 and 12). These added capabilities solve the integration problem. But as is the case with integration of database management systems and spreadsheets in Excel, the result can be a product with some not-so-strong functionalities. However, most ERP vendors are adding such functionalities for another reason: It is cheaper for the customers. Packages with these added functionalities represent the *second-generation ERP*, which includes not only decision support but also customer relationship management (CRM) (Chapter 8), e-commerce (Section 10.5), and data warehousing and mining (Chapter 11). Some second-generation systems include a *knowledge management* (Chapter 11) component as well.

Supply chain intelligence.   The inclusion of business intelligence in supply chain software solutions is referred to by some as **supply chain intelligence (SCI)**. SCI applications enable strategic decision making by analyzing data along the entire supply chain. To better understand SCI, it is worthwhile to compare it with SCM, as shown in Table 10.2 (page 335).

Before you go on . . .

1. Define ERP and its functionalities.

2. Describe SCM software.

3. Describe second-generation ERP (integrated ERP/SCM).

4. What is supply chain intelligence?

10.5   E-COMMERCE AND SUPPLY CHAIN MANAGEMENT

E-commerce is emerging as a superb approach for providing solutions to problems along the supply chain. As seen in the Dell example at the beginning of the chapter, many supply chain activities, from taking customers' orders to parts procurement, can be conducted as EC initiatives.

EC Activities Along the Supply Chain

A major role of EC is to facilitate buying, selling, and collaborating along the supply chain. Here we describe the types of EC activities along the supply chain.

Upstream activities.   Several innovative EC models can improve the upstream supply chain activities. These models are described generally as *e-procurement*. Three are presented in Chapter 9: reverse auctions, aggregation of vendors' catalogs at the buyer's site, and procurement via consortia and group purchasing.

Internal SCM activities.   Internal SCM activities include different *intrabusiness EC* activities. These activities range from entering orders of materials, to streamlining production, to recording sales, to tracking shipments. They are usually conducted over a corporate intranet. Details and examples are provided in Chapters 8 and 9.

Downstream activities.   Typical EC downstream activities are related to online selling as described in Chapters 8 and 9. Two popular models of downstream activities follow.

Selling on your own Web site.   Large companies such as Intel, Cisco, and IBM use this model. At the company's own Web site, buyers review electronic catalogs from which they buy. Large buyers are provided with their own Web pages and customized catalogs.

Auctions.   Large companies such as Dell conduct auctions of products or obsolete equipment on their Web sites. Electronic auctions can shorten cycle time and the supply chain and save on logistics and administrative expenses. One online auctioneer, for example, is Autodaq (*autodaq.com*). The buyers are car dealers who then resell the used cars (the transaction is B2B2C). Traditional car auctions are done on large lots, where the cars are displayed and physically auctioned. In the electronic auction, the autos do not need to be transported to a physical auction site, nor do buyers have to travel to an auction site. Savings of $500 per car can be realized.

Exchanges.   Considerable support to B2B supply chains can be provided by electronic exchanges (Chapter 9). Such exchanges are shown in Figure 10.5. Notice that in this example there are three separate exchanges. In other cases there may be only one exchange for the entire industry.

Restructuring the Supply Chain

E-commerce can introduce structural changes in the supply chain. For example, the creation of electronic markets drastically changes order processing and fulfillment. In many cases, linear supply chains are changed to hubs, as shown in the case of Orbis Corp. in IT's About Business 10.4.

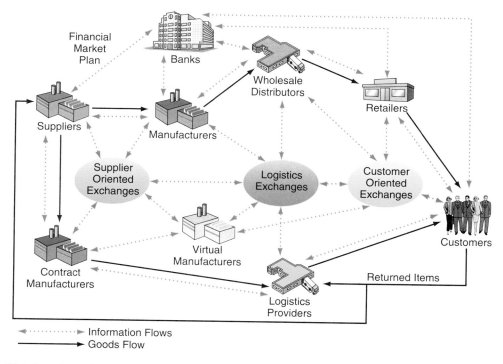

Figure 10.5   *Web-based supply chain involving trading exchanges.*

IT's About Business

productbank.com.au   POM   MKT

Box 10.4   Orbis changes a linear physical supply chain to an electronic hub

Retailer → Supplier (Sony) → Courier → Ad Agency → Scanning House → Digital Image → Catalog

Orbis.

Orbis Corp. is a small Australian company that provides Internet and EC services. One of its services is called ProductBank (*productbank.com.au*). This service revolutionized the flow of information and products in the B2B advertising field. In order to understand how the service works, let's look at how a retail catalog or brochure is put together. A catalog shows pictures of many products. These pictures are obtained from manufacturers such as Sony or Nokia. The traditional process is linear, as shown in the figure above.

The traditional process works like this: When retailers need a photo of a product they contact the manufacturers, who send the photos via a courier to an ad agency. The ad agency decides, in cooperation with the retailer, which photos to use and how to present them. The ad agency then rushes the photos to be scanned and converted into digital images, which are transferred to the printer. The cycle time for each photo is 4 to 6 weeks, and the total transaction cost of preparing one picture for the catalog is about $150 AU.

ProductBank simplifies this lengthy process. It has centralized the entire process by changing the linear flow of products and information to a digitized hub as shown in the figure below.

With the new system, manufacturers send digitized photos to Orbis, and Orbis enters and organizes the photos in a database. When retailers need pictures, they can view online the images in the database and decide which they want to include in their catalog. The retailers communicate electronically with their ad agency about what images they want to include in their catalogs. The ad agency makes suggestions and works on the design of the catalog. Once the design is complete, the catalog can be downloaded by the printer. The transaction cost per picture (usually paid by the manufacturer) is 30 to 40 percent lower, and the cycle time is 50 to 70 percent shorter than in the traditional catalog production method.

Questions

1. Identify the benefits to the supply chain participants.
2. Where does the cost reduction come from?
3. Where does the cycle time reduction come from?
4. Explain the benefits of electronic collaboration between the retailers and the ad agency.

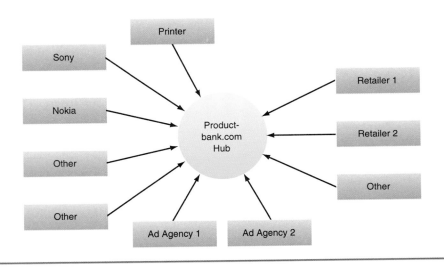

Integration of EC with ERP

Since many middle-sized and large companies already have an ERP system, and since e-commerce needs to *interface* with ERP, it makes sense to integrate the two. For example, SAP started building some EC interfaces in 1997, and in 1999 introduced mySAP.com as a major initiative. The mySAP initiative is a multifaceted Internet product that includes EC, online trading sites, an information portal, application hosting, and user-friendly graphical interfaces.

The logic behind integrating EC and ERP is that by extending the existing ERP system to support e-commerce, organizations not only leverage their investment in the ERP solution, but also speed up the development of EC applications. The problem with this approach is that the ERP software is very complex and inflexible (difficult to change), so it is difficult to achieve easy, smooth, and effective integration. One other potential problem is that ERP systems tend to focus on back-office (administrative) applications, whereas EC focuses on front-office applications such as sales and order taking, customer service, and other customer relationship management (CRM) activities. Ideally, one should attempt to achieve tight integration along the entire supply chain as done by McKesson, described in IT's About Business 10.5.

IT's About Business   *mckesson.com*

Box 10.5:   How McKesson integrates the pharmaceutical supply chain

McKesson Drug Company is the largest U.S. distributor of pharmaceuticals, healthcare products, medical supplies, and related products (*mckesson.com*). It is positioned between manufacturers and retailers and other business customers, such as hospitals. Its supply chain is shown in Figure 10.3a (page 323).

With annual sales of over $22 billion and close to 40,000 business customers, who generate over 2,000,000 purchasing orders every month for thousands of products, the supply chain and its management are rather complex.

Effectiveness and efficiency, which are needed for survival, can be achieved only with a tight integration with both the major customers and the suppliers. To enable such integration with its major customers (such as CVS drug chain and Rite Aid), McKesson assumed the responsibility of monitoring and replenishing the inventory of its major products at the store level. In other cases, virtually all purchasing orders are submitted to McKesson electronically. Once submitted, orders are organized by region and stored on a mainframe. Regional distribution centers pull the orders daily and make the necessary deliveries. In addition, all payments are made online.

McKesson provides its business customers with Web-based up-to-date sales data, by product and by store, enabling the customers to make better marketing, promotions, inventory, and pricing decisions. The tight software integration with the customers on the *downstream side* of the supply chain enables better demand forecast, which results in lower inventories and elimina-

tion of the bullwhip effect discussed earlier. On the *upstream side*, McKesson uses e-procurement with its major suppliers. It also collaborates with them electronically on demand forecasts by product. Finally, McKesson uses an elaborate intrabusiness e-commerce system between its headquarters, the distribution centers, and the transportation units (company owned and outsourced). All documentation flows electronically in the system. Also, warehouse management and order pickups are computerized to minimize pickers' efforts.

The benefits to McKesson of its integration of the supply chain include rapid, reliable, and cost-effective customer order processing. Sales personnel are no longer primarily order takers; they can do proactive marketing. Purchasing from suppliers has been reorganized to tightly match actual sales, and productivity of the warehouse staff has been significantly increased. Finally, customers are more loyal to McKesson because of the benefits they enjoy.

Questions

1. Enter *mckesson.com* and identify any new supply-chain related initiatives.

2. Identify the B2B2C activities used by McKesson.

3. In theory, manufacturers can sell direct to retailers, eliminating McKesson. Explain McKesson's strategy to protect itself. Is the company likely to be successful? Why or why not?

Manager's Checklist 10.2

How E-Commerce Activities Can
Improve SCM

- Digitized products (such as software) are much cheaper and faster to create and move than are physical products.
- Replacing paper documents with electronic documents improves speed and accuracy, and the cost of document transmission is much cheaper.
- Replacing faxes, telephone calls, and telegrams with an electronic messaging system streamlines communications and cuts communications costs.
- Restructuring the supply chain from linear to a hub (as shown in the Orbis case, in IT's About Business 10.4) enables faster, cheaper, and better communication, collaboration, and discovery of information.
- Enhancing collaboration and information sharing among the partners in the supply chain can improve cooperation, coordination, and demand forecasts.
- EC can shorten supply chains and minimize inventories. As a result of the build-to-order model provided by EC, the auto industry, for example, is expected to save billions of dollars annually in inventory reduction alone.
- Innovations such as FAQs and the self-tracking of shipments can reduce the need for information flow between companies and customers.
- E-marketplaces bring efficiencies into buying and selling, as shown in Chapter 9.

Other e-commerce activities can make significant contributions to SCM improvement, as suggested in Manager's Checklist 10.2.

Before you go on . . .

1. Describe how EC improves activities along the major segments of the supply chain.

2. Explain how EC changes the linear supply chain to a hub.

3. Describe the need for integrating EC with ERP.

10.6 ORDER FULFILLMENT IN E-COMMERCE

In the previous section we described how e-commerce tools can solve problems along the supply chain. However, some applications of EC, especially B2C and sometimes B2B, may have problems with their own supply chains. These problems usually occur in *order fulfillment* (Chapter 9, page 307). Let's explain.

Order Fulfillment and Logistics: An Overview

Order fulfillment refers not only to providing the customers with what they ordered and doing it on time, but also to providing all related customer service. To do so in e-tailing one must send small packages to a large number of customers. In contrast, in traditional retailing you ship large quantities to a small number of retail stores. Therefore, e-tailers face several problems in order fulfillment, especially during the holiday season. The problems occur in storage, picking up items, packaging, and shipping, all of which must be done effectively at a minimum cost. These problems result in inability to deliver on time, delivery of wrong items, paying too much for deliveries, and costly compensation of unhappy customers. Taking orders over the Internet could well be the easy part of B2C electronic commerce. Fulfillment to customers' door is the tricky part.

Several factors can be responsible for delays in deliveries. They range from inability to accurately forecast demand, to ineffective supply chains of the e-tailers. One factor that is typical of EC is that it is based on the concept of *pull* operations, which begin with an *order*, frequently a customized one. This is in contrast with traditional retailing that begins with *production to inventory*, which is then *pushed* to customers. In the pull case it is more difficult to forecast demand, due to the unique nature of customized orders.

Innovative Solutions to the Order Fulfillment Problem

During the last few years companies have developed innovative solutions to both B2C and B2B order fulfillment. Here are some examples.

Same-day, even same-hour delivery. In the digital age, next-morning delivery may not be fast enough. Today we talk about same-day delivery, and even delivery within an hour. Delivering groceries is an example where speed is important. Quick deliveries of pizzas have been practiced for a long time using telephone ordering. Many restaurants use the same approach, which is known as "dine online." Online ordering can be much more efficient.

EXAMPLE

Dialing for dinners. Some dine online companies offer aggregating services, which process orders for several restaurants (e.g., Campusfood.com and Dialadinner.com.hk) and also make the deliveries. Here is how it works in Hong Kong: Customers click on the online menu at *dialadinner.com.hk*, select the dishes they want, then submit their order electronically. Sometimes customers can even mix and match orders from two restaurants. For first-time customers, a Dialadinner staff member phones to check delivery details and to confirm that the order is genuine. The orders are then forwarded electronically from Dialadinner to the participating restaurants. Delivery staff receives a copy of the order by e-mail (SMS) on their mobile phones, telling them which restaurant to go to. There, they are handed the food and delivery details. Delivery is made in small cars or on motorcycles. Customers receive their meals and pay cash on delivery. Average time from order to delivery is 30 to 40 minutes. For other examples of quick delivery, see *4sameday.com* and *Xmessenger.com.* ●

Automated warehouses. Traditional warehouses are built to deliver *large quantities* to a *small number* of stores or manufacturing plants. In B2C EC, companies need to send *small quantities* to a *large number* of individual customers. The picking and packing process therefore is different, and usually more labor intensive. Therefore, large-volume EC fulfillment requires special, possibly automated, warehouses, which may include robots and other devices that expedite the pickup of products. Several large e-tailers, such as Amazon.com, operate their own warehouses. However, most order fulfillment is probably shipped via outsourcers. For a description of how a typical automated warehouse would work, see the book's Web site.

www.wiley.com/
college/turban

Dealing with Returns

Returning unwanted merchandise and providing for exchanges are necessary for maintaining customers' trust and loyalty. The Boston Consulting Group found that "absence of good return mechanism" was the second biggest reason that U.S. shoppers cited for refusing to buy on the Web. For their part, e-tailers face the major problem of how to deal with returns. Several options exist:

1. Return an item to the place where it was purchased. This is easy to do in a brick-and-mortar store, but not in a virtual one. To return an item to a virtual store, you need to get authorization, pack everything up, pay to ship it back, insure it, and wait up to two billing cycles for a credit to show up on your statement. The buyer is not happy. Neither is the seller, who must unpack the item, check the paperwork, and resell the item, usually at a loss. This solution is good only if the number of returns is small.

2. Separate the logistics of returns from the logistics of delivery. Returns are shipped to an independent unit and handled separately inside the company. This solution may be more efficient from the seller's point of view, but the buyer is still unhappy.

3. Allow the customer to physically drop the returned items at collection stations (such as at 7-Eleven stores or Mail Boxes Etc.), from which the returns can be picked up. For example, BP Australia Ltd. (operator of gasoline service stations) teamed up with Wishlist.com.au, to accept returns. Caltex Oil of Australia also provides such service at their convenience stores.

4. Completely outsource the logistics of returns. Several outsourcers, including United Postal Service (UPS), provide such services. The services they offer deal not only with returns, but also with the entire logistics process of deliveries.

Before you go on . . .

1. Describe the order fulfillment process.

2. Explain the same-day delivery process.

3. Describe the role of automated warehouses in the logistics of e-commerce.

4. List the difficulties of handling returns and describe the solutions.

www.wiley.com/
college/turban

WHAT'S IN IT FOR ME ?

  ACC

FOR THE ACCOUNTING MAJOR

The accounting information systems (part of the back-end systems) are a central component in any ERP package. As a matter of fact, all large CPA firms actively consult clients on ERP implementation, using thousands of specially trained accounting majors. Also, many supply chain issues ranging from inventory management and valuation to risk analysis are in the realm of accountants. Finally, many SCM software packages are available to support your job.

  FIN

FOR THE FINANCE MAJOR

Starting with MRP II and continuing with ERP, finance activities and modeling are integral portions of all such commercial software packages. Flows of funds (payments) are at the core of most supply chains, and they must be done efficiently and effectively. Financial arrangements are especially important along global supply chains where currency convention and financial regulations must be considered.

FOR THE MARKETING MAJOR

The downstream part of supply chains is where marketing, distribution channels, and customer service are conducted. An understanding of how this portion of the supply chain is related to the other portions in critical. Supply chain problems hurt customer satisfaction and marketing efforts, so you need to understand the nature of such problems and their solutions.

FOR THE PRODUCTION/OPERATIONS MANAGEMENT MAJOR

Supply chain management is usually the responsibility of the POM departments since it involves material handling, inventory control, logistics, and other activities done by that department. The POM department started the trend of software integration with MRP. Many of the SCM innovations are in the realm of the POM department. As a matter of fact, almost all POM majors will deal with supply chain issues and its software support once they are employed.

FOR THE HUMAN RESOURCES MANAGEMENT MAJOR

Interactions among employees along the supply chain, especially between business partners from different countries, are important for supply chain effectiveness. It is a necessity, therefore, for the HRM expert to understand the flows of information and the collaboration issues in SCM.

SUMMARY

❶ **Understand the concept of the supply chain, its importance, and its management.**
Supply chains connect suppliers to a manufacturing company, departments inside a company, and a company to its customers. To properly manage the supply chain, it is necessary to assure superb customer service, low cost, and short cycle time. The supply chain must be completely managed, from the raw material to the end customers.

❷ **Describe the various types of supply chains.**
The major types are: manufacture to inventory, build-to-order, and continuous replenishment. Each type can be global or local.

❸ **Describe the problems in managing supply chains.**
It is difficult to manage the supply chain due to the uncertainties in demand and supply and the need to coordinate several business partners' activities. One of the major problems is known as the bullwhip effect, where lack of coordination results in large, unnecessary inventories.

❹ **Describe the major categories of supply chain solutions.**
Solutions to SCM problems are provided via SCM functional software, ERP integrated software, and e-commerce applications. Innovative solutions also require cooperation and coordination with business partners, which are facilitated by IT innovations such as extranets that allow suppliers to view a company's inventories in real time.

❺ **Explain the need for software integration and describe the available software.**
Functional software is designed for departments, and it is difficult to integrate it for enterprisewide applications. Therefore, during the last 50 years, software integration has increased both in coverage and scope, from MRP to MRP II, to ERP, to enhanced ERP. Today, ERP software, which is designed to improve standard

business transactions, is enhanced with decision-support capabilities as well as Web interfaces.

❻ Explain how EC improves supply chain management.
Electronic commerce is able to provide new solutions to problems along the supply chain by automating processes and integrating the company's major business activities with both upstream and downstream entities via an electronic infrastructure.

❼ Describe EC order-fulfillment problems and solutions.
Order fulfillment in EC is difficult due to the need to ship small packages to many customers' doors. Outsourcing the logistics and delivery jobs is common, especially when same-day delivery is needed. Special large and automated warehouses also help in improving EC order fulfillment.

INTERACTIVE LEARNING SESSION

Go to the CD and access Chapter 10: Supply Chain Management and Integration. There you will find a video clip from the "Nightly Business Report" that presents a business problem involving the topics covered in this chapter. You will be asked to watch the video and answer questions about it.

www.wiley.com/
college/turban

For additional resources, go to the book's Web site for Chapter 10. There you will find Web resources for the chapter, including links to organizations, people, and technology; "IT's About Business" company links; "What's in IT for Me?" links; and a self-testing Web quiz for Chapter 10.

DISCUSSION QUESTIONS

1. What is the role of inventories in SCM, and why is it difficult to manage them?

2. Discuss what it would be like if the registration process and class scheduling process at your college or university were reengineered to an online, real-time, seamless basis with good connectivity and good empowerment in the organization. (If your registration is already online, find another manual process to reengineer.) Describe the supply chain in this situation.

3. Discuss how cooperation between a company that you are familiar with and its suppliers can reduce inventory costs.

4. Find examples of how organizations improve their supply chains in two of the following: manufacturing, hospitals, retailing, education, construction, or transportation.

5. Discuss the problem of reverse logistics in EC. What kind of companies may suffer the most?

6. Discuss the meaning of intelligence in "supply chain intelligence."

7. Explain the bullwhip effect. In which type of business is it likely to occur most? How can the effect be controlled?

PROBLEM-SOLVING ACTIVITIES

1. Draw the supply chain of Dell and a supply chain of a competitor that sells in retail stores. Comment on the differences.

2. Review the Warner-Lambert Listerine case in IT's About Business 10.2 (page 332) and draw W-L's supply chain. How was W-L's supply chain improved with IT?

3. It is said that supply chains are essentially "a series of linked suppliers and customers; every customer is in turn a supplier to the next downstream organiza-

tion, until the ultimate end user." Explain. Use of a diagram is recommended.

4. Go to a bank and find out the process and steps of obtaining a mortgage for a house. Draw the supply chain. Now assume that some of the needed information, such as the value of the house and the financial status of the applicant, is found in a publicly available database (such a database exists in Hong Kong, for example). Draw the supply chain in this case. By how much can the cycle time be reduced?

INTERNET ACTIVITIES

1. Enter *ups.com*. Examine some of the IT-supported customer services and tools provided by the company. Write a report on how UPS contributes to supply chain improvements.

2. Enter *supply-chain.org* and *cio.com*, and identify recent issues in supply chain management. Also find information about SCOR and CPFR (try *cpfr.org*).

3. Enter *isourceonline.com*, *supplychaintoday.com*, and *tilion.com*. Find information on the bullwhip effect and on the strategies and tools used to lessen the effect.

4. Enter *coca-colastore.com*. Examine the delivery and return options available there.

5. Enter *oracle.com* and identify the solutions offered there for supply chain problems.

6. The U.S. post office is entering the EC logistics business. Examine its services and tracking systems at *uspsprioritymail.com*. What are the potential advantages for EC shippers?

7. Enter *brio.com* and identify Brio's solution to SCM integration as it relates to decision making for EC. View the demo.

8. Enter *mySap.com*. Identify its major components. Also review the Advanced Planning and Optimization tool. How can each benefit the management of a supply chain?

9. Enter *kewill.com*. Examine the various products offered there, including Commander WMS. Relate this to SCM.

10. Enter *frictionless.com* and find how Frictionless Sourcing eliminates supply chain inefficiencies. Follow the demo. Submit a report.

11. Enter *i2.com* and review its SCM products that go beyond ERP. Examine the OCN Network and Rhythm. Write a report.

TEAM ACTIVITIES AND ROLE PLAYING

1. Each team will be assigned to a major ERP vendor such as SAP, PeopleSoft, Oracle, J.D. Edwards, etc. Members of the groups will investigate topics such as:

   a. Web connections.

   b. Use of business intelligence tools.

   c. Relationship to CRM and to EC.

   d. Major capabilities.

   e. Availability of ASP services.

   Each group will prepare a presentation for the class, trying to convince the class why its software is best for a local company known to the students (e.g., a supermarket chain).

2. Assign each team to one type of supply chain, such as build-to-order or continuous replenishment. The team should find two examples of the assigned type, draw the supply chains, and explain the IT and EC solutions used.

REAL-WORLD CASE   *quantum.com*

Quantum Corporation Streamlines Its Supply Chain

The Business Problem Quantum Corporation (*quantum.com*) is a major U.S. manufacturer of hard-disk drives and other high-technology storage components. Quantum faced two key challenges in its manufacturing process.

The first challenge was streamlining Quantum's component supply process in order to lower on-hand inventory. Quantum's traditional ordering process was labor intensive, involving numerous phone calls and manual inventory checks. To ensure that production would not be interrupted, the process required high levels of inventory. Quantum needed a solution that would automate the ordering process to increase accuracy and efficiency, reduce needed inventory to 3 days, and provide the company's purchasing agents with more time for nontransactional tasks.

Quantum's second challenge was to improve the quality of the component data in its material requirements planning (MRP) system. Incomplete and inaccurate data caused delays in production. Quantum's solution of manually reviewing reports to identify errors was labor-intensive and occurred too late; problems in production were experienced before the reports were even reviewed. Quantum needed a technology solution that would enable it to operate proactively to catch problems before they caused production delays.

The IT Solution   The solution that Quantum chose to automate its component supply process was an inter-enterprise system that automatically e-mails reorders to suppliers. Initiated in 1999, the system uses an innovative event detection and notification solution from Categoric Software (*categoric.com*). It scans Quantum's databases twice daily, assessing material requirements from one application module against inventory levels tracked in another. Orders are automatically generated and sent to suppliers as needed, allowing suppliers to make regular deliveries that match Quantum's production schedule.

The system also provided other improvements. It enabled Quantum to tap into multiple data sources to identify critical business events. To elevate data quality, Quantum implemented Xalerts to proactively catch any data errors or omissions in its MRP database. The systems' notifications are now sent whenever any critical MRP data fall outside the existing operational parameters (see the screen).

The Results   The system has produced the desired results. For example, the estimated value of the improved ordering process using the new system is millions of dollars in inventory reductions each year. The buyers

have reduced transaction tasks and costs, and both Quantum and its buyers get a lot more information with a lot less work. Before the implementation of Xalerts, Quantum's analysts would search massive reports for MRP data errors. Now that the new system is implemented, exceptions are identified as they occur. This new process has freed the analysts from the drudgery of scanning reports and has greatly increased employee satisfaction.

Data integrity of the MRP increased from 10 percent to almost 100 percent, and Quantum is now able to quickly respond to changing customer demand. The system paid for itself in the first year.

Sources: Compiled from an advertising supplement in *CIO Magazine* (October 1, 1999), and from information at *categoric.com* (November 2001).

Questions

1. Identify the internal and external parts of the supply chain that were enhanced with the system.
2. Enter *categoric.com* and find information about supply-chain products, especially on Xalerts. Describe the capability of the product (review the screen).
3. Explain how purchasing was improved.
4. Describe how Quantum's customers are now being better served.

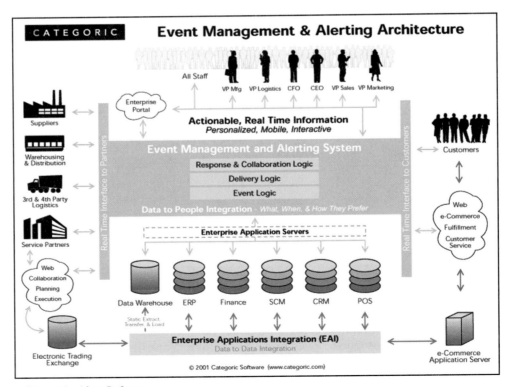

Categoric Alert Software.

VIRTUAL COMPANY ASSIGNMENT

wiley.com/college/turban

Extreme Descent Snowboards

Background   Jacob March greets you as you enter the conference room. This is the first monthly managers' meeting you have been invited to attend. Jacob escorts you to a chair beside Wolf Ludwig, Assistant Director of Development. Ludwig continues his conversation, stating that a potential supplier from China can provide high-quality material at a reasonable price.

www.wiley.com/
college/turban

Jacob interrupts Wolf, saying, "We have not done business with a supplier outside the United States. We'll need to explore the issue before committing the company to this supplier relationship. The supplier is willing to support an electronic data interchange (EDI) application between us."

Jacob turns to you, and says, "For your next assignment, we need you to study these issues and prepare a report for our next meeting." He hands you his handwritten notes.

Assignment

Visit the *Dell Computer* e-commerce site *(www.dell.com)*, and click on "online shopping for the home computer," in order to research information for this assignment.

Jacob's paper contains the following notes.

- Are there any procedures that EDS can implement to better serve our customers? Outline the procedures and support your answer.
- What is supply chain management? How can Extreme Descent Snowboards incorporate an EDI system for supply chain management?
- Should Extreme Descent Snowboards develop an EDI system using Web-based technology? What are the advantages and disadvantages associated with using this technology?

As you leave the meeting, you think to yourself that one of the Web search engines would be a good place to start to find out more about companies doing business with China.

Do the research that is necessary, and prepare a report for the next meeting.

11 DATA, KNOWLEDGE, AND DECISION SUPPORT

CHAPTER PREVIEW

A manager's primary function is making decisions, and decision makers *must* have data, information, and knowledge. The quality of these, and the manner in which they are used, determine the quality of the decisions and consequently the welfare of organizations. It is not surprising that many organizations describe themselves as *information corporations*. Today, Web technologies and digitization are increasing the creation, dissemination, storage, and use of information. Unfortunately, the amount of information is increasing so rapidly that organizations sometimes feel as if they are drowning in it. In this chapter we describe how modern organizations handle the information overload, and how data, information, and knowledge are used in supporting decision making.

This chapter covers some of the most important new concepts in IT support of decision making, including knowledge management, decision support systems, data warehousing, business intelligence, data mining, and electronic document management. All in all, these concepts are critical for modern organizations as they tackle the many problems that result from global competition and business pressures.

CHAPTER OUTLINE

11.1 Management and Decision Making
11.2 Data Transformation and Management
11.3 Decision Support Systems
11.4 Enterprise Decision Support
11.5 Data and Information Analysis and Mining
11.6 Data Visualization Technologies
11.7 Knowledge Management and Organizational Knowledge Bases

LEARNING OBJECTIVES

1. Describe the concepts of managerial decision making and computerized support for decision making.
2. Understand the process of converting data into information and knowledge for use in decision support.
3. Describe the framework for computerized decision support and the concept of decision support systems.
4. Describe executive information systems and group support systems, and analyze their roles in management support.
5. Describe online analytical processing and data mining.
6. Describe data-visualization methods and explain geographical information systems as a decision support tool.
7. Explain the concepts of knowledge management and organizational knowledge base.
8. Describe IT support for idea generation.

MANAGING GLOBAL BUSINESS AT 3M CORPORATION

The Business Problem

3M is a multinational corporation headquartered in St. Paul, Minnesota. It produces and sells more than 50,000 products (actually 500,000 products, if variations in size, package, language, and customized features are considered). The company is decentralized, and each of its 50 business units maintains separate sales, marketing, manufacturing, and research and development data. Each business unit also tracks its customers, products, and suppliers.

Although corporate-level transaction processing systems supported corporatewide sales, the business units kept separate databases and conducted independent decision support activities. As a result the company had difficulties responding to new customers and markets in the global economy. For example, customers who purchased from several business units had to deal with several salespeople. Sometimes the sale of one product required the involvement of two units. This usually meant redundancy in supplying pricing and product information. Tracking the inventories, sales, and profitability of each product was extremely difficult. The company also had trouble connecting with its suppliers to solve logistics problems.

Popular office products from 3M.

The IT Solution

The company created a global enterprise data warehouse (GEDW), which consists of four primary sections: goods and services, trading partners, global sales, and digital media repository. As defined in Chapter 5, a data warehouse is a centralized repository of corporate data extracted from the transaction processing system, the corporate raw data, and external databases. It mainly contains data needed for internally oriented decision support, such as scheduling. The GEDW includes the latest information technologies such as Web-based data query tools and high-power parallel processing servers. The GEDW can be viewed as a huge data storage and distribution center, with data collected and repackaged according to the needs of the users.

Recipients of the data include 3M's customers, employees, and other business partners. The customers receive access to all their own sales data accumulated from point-of-sale terminals. They also can access 3M's electronic catalogs. 3M also constructed a dynamic Web site that allows customers (retailers and wholesalers) not only to access information, but also to generate their own customized dynamic Web pages easily and quickly from the data warehouse. Corporate data video clip-pictures, drawings, and brochures were digitized and stored in the data warehouse and electronic catalogs. The video gives both distributors and customers vivid views of the company's products.

Finally, using browser technology and Web-based decision support tools, end users can easily create applications or retrieve information. Also, end users can use their own PCs to do most of the analytical processing they need, and heavy-duty processing can be done using centralized processing servers and the intranet.

The Results

Using the GEDW the company was able to achieve the following results:

- Distributors and retailers, as well as end users, now receive information in minutes instead of weeks or months, including the delivery of rich multimedia.
- Customers can find all their information in one place.
- Inventories are lower, and better and quicker inventory decisions are made, even in globally remote locations.

The data warehouse enabled 3M to expand its customer base in many countries in order to exploit the opportunities created by globalization, technological developments, and e-commerce. In addition, the company increased its growth rate by being able to easily introduce to distributors and customers many products and their variations. The Web also enables business partners and salespeople to easily communicate and to generate ideas for new and improved products. Finally, the data warehouse integrates information about sales, finance, and logistics, enabling accurate supply chain management and demand forecasting.

Overall, the company was able to create customer-focused marketing, to increase collaboration with and among business partners, and to get closer to its customers. All of these improvements in access to corporate data and its processing have translated into significantly larger revenues and profits.

Sources: B. Francis, "Open Door Policy," *PC Week* (May 25, 1998), and 3m.com (press releases, 2001).

What We Learned from This Case

The 3M case demonstrates the vast amount of data in organizations and the importance of organizing that data for optimal use. The case shows the company's need to share data both internally and with business partners and customers and to make the data available in a format that enables end users to process them quickly. The case also demonstrates the concept of a data warehouse and its role in supporting managerial decision making. Finally it shows how all this is done with the support of Web-based applications.

11.1 MANAGEMENT AND DECISION MAKING

Management is a process by which certain goals are achieved through the use of resources (people, money, energy, materials, space, time). Appropriate use of these resources requires managers to make decisions in planning, organizing, motivating, and control. These resources are considered to be *inputs*, and the attainment of the manager's goals is viewed as the *output* of the management process. A manager's success is often measured by the ratio between outputs and inputs for which he or she is responsible. This ratio is an indication of the organization's *productivity*. Information systems, as discussed in Chapter 1, are intended to help companies properly manage their businesses and continuously increase productivity.

The Manager's Job

To understand how information systems support managers, it is necessary first to briefly describe the manager's job. Managers do many things, depending on their position in the organization, the type and size of the organization, organizational policies and culture, and the personalities of the managers themselves. Despite this variety, managers have three basic roles:

1. *Interpersonal roles:* figurehead, leader, liaison
2. *Informational roles:* monitor, disseminator, spokesperson
3. *Decisional roles:* entrepreneur, disturbance handler, resource allocator, negotiator

Early information systems mainly supported the informational roles. In recent years, information systems have been developed that support all three roles. In this chapter, we are mainly interested in the support that IT can provide for *decisional* roles.

350

To begin with, it is useful to emphasize that in making any decision, one must select among two or more alternatives. We divide the manager's work as it relates to decisional roles into two phases: Phase I is the identification of problems and opportunities. Phase II deals with the decisions of what to do about them. Figure 11.1 provides a flowchart of the two-phase decision-making process and the flow of data and information in it. There we see that information comes from both internal and external environments. Internal information is generated mostly from the functional areas. External information comes from sources such as newspapers, industry newsletters, government reports, personal contacts, the Internet, and online databases. Given the large amount of data available, managers must find the *relevant* information and then evaluate its importance. Whenever appropriate, information is channeled to quantitative and qualitative analysis, for interpretation. Then the manager, or a group of managers, decides whether a problem or a business opportunity exists. If so, then the problem/opportunity is transferred as an input to Phase II. In Phase II, managers evaluate alternatives and choose one for solving the problem or pursuing the business opportunity.

Why Managers Need IT Support

It is difficult to make good decisions without processing data or information in each activity and phase of the decision-making process. However, making decisions with manually processed data and information is increasingly difficult due to the following trends:

- ***The increasing number of alternatives to be evaluated*** in each decision. These are a result of innovations in technology, improved communication, the development of global markets, and the use of the Internet and e-commerce.

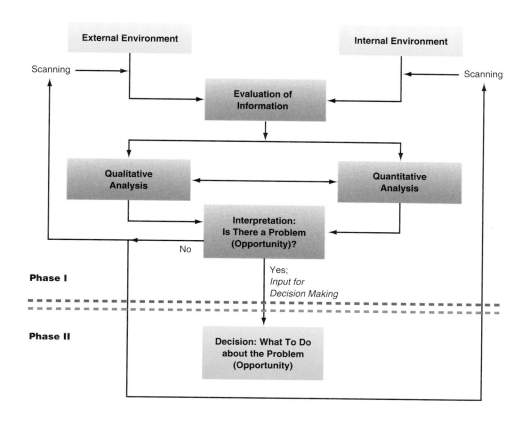

Figure 11.1   *Two phases of a manager's decision role and the flow of information in the decision process.*

- **Time pressure.** Frequently, it is not possible to manually process the needed information fast enough to be effective.
- **Decision complexity.** Decisions are getting complex due to increased interrelationships and uncertainty in the decision environment. This complexity frequently makes it necessary to conduct a sophisticated analysis in order to make a good decision, and such analysis usually requires the support of IT.
- **Cost of making wrong decisions.** Due to the complexity and interdependencies of business processes and supply chains, the cost of making an error, even in one place, can be very high.
- **The need to access remote information and expertise.** Decision makers often must quickly gather information that is not right at hand, and they sometimes need to consult with experts or have a group decision-making session when the participants are in different locations.

These trends complicate decision making, but computerized support can be of enormous help. For example, computerized modeling can examine numerous alternatives very quickly, can provide a systematic risk analysis, can be integrated with communication systems and databases, and can be used to support group work. How all this is accomplished will be shown in the remainder of this chapter.

Several information technologies can be used to support the activities shown in Figure 11.1, as well as to support the three managerial roles described earlier. In this chapter, we look at several such management support system technologies. We also will see what kinds of data, information, and knowledge are used by decision makers and how they are used.

Before you go on . . .

1. Define the manager's job and list the three key managerial roles.
2. Explain the two phases of managerial decision making.
3. Explain why managers need IT support.

11.2   DATA TRANSFORMATION AND MANAGEMENT

Remember, from Chapter 1, that **data** are raw facts, not organized to convey specific meaning; **information** is a collection of facts organized for meaning; and **knowledge** is information that has been organized and processed to convey expertise as it applies to a business problem. In any organization, a major goal of gathering and processing data, information, and knowledge is to provide support to decision makers. These decision makers are scattered throughout the organization and make various kinds of decisions. For example, when a marketing manager wants to determine the selling price of a product, he or she needs to have *information* about the competitor's pricing, *data* on historical price levels and sales volume, and *knowledge* about the dynamics of the market and how a competitor may react to a change in price. Similarly, when a production manager needs to assign employees to jobs, he or she needs *data* about how long it takes to process each job on each machine, *information* about when certain jobs must be completed, and *knowledge* that will help find the least expensive, yet effective schedule. To meet the different needs of different managers, the management of data, information, and knowledge within organizations must be flexible and adaptable, yet powerful. The process of transforming data and information into knowledge for organizational decision making is described next.

The Data Transformation Process

Businesses do not run on just raw data. They run on information and the knowledge of how to put that information to use. Knowledge is not readily available, however, especially in today's rapidly changing world. In many cases it is continuously constructed from data and/or information, in a process that may not be simple or easy.

The transformation of data into knowledge may be accomplished in several ways. In general, it starts with data collection from various sources (see Figure 11.2). The acquired data (shown in the upper-left corner of the figure) are usually stored in simple databases. From there data can be used directly by end users for decision support. Or they can be processed, organized, and stored in a *data warehouse* and then analyzed (e.g., by using analytical processing) by end users for decision support. Some of the data are converted to information prior to storage in the data warehouse, and some of the data and/or information can be analyzed to generate knowledge. For example, by using **data mining**, a process that looks for unknown relationships and patterns in the data, knowledge regarding the impact of advertising on a specific group of customers can be generated.

Experiences elicited directly from end users can also be used to generate knowledge (orange box in the upper-right corner in Figure 11.2 to the purple box below it). This generated knowledge is stored in an **organizational knowledge base**, a repository of accumulated corporate knowledge and of purchased knowledge. The knowledge in the knowledge base (brown box) can be used to support less experienced end users, or to support complex decision making. Both the data and the information, at various times during the process, and the knowledge derived at the end of the process, may need to be presented to users. Such a presentation can be enhanced by various presentation tools.

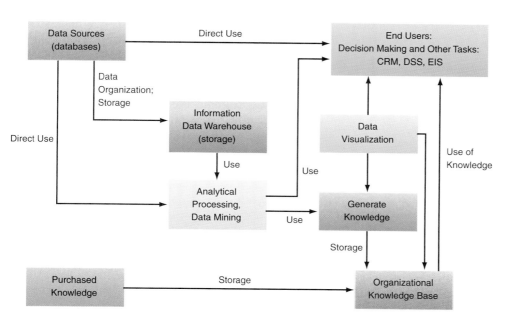

Figure 11.2 *Data, knowledge, and decision making.*

Data Sources and Collection

As we've seen in earlier chapters, data can include documents, pictures, maps, sound, and animation. They also include concepts, thoughts, and opinions and can be raw (not processed) or summarized. Many IS applications use summary or extracted data. Data may be changing continuously, such as stock prices or temperature. These are referred to as **dynamic data**, as opposed to **static data**, which do not change.

Data sources. Data can also be classified by their source—as internal, personal, and external. There are many sources for external data, ranging from commercial databases to sensors and satellites. Data are available on CD-ROMs, as films, and as music or voices. Pictures, diagrams, maps, and television are also sources of data.

Internal data. All the data generated by the corporate transaction processing systems, functional user information systems, and other functions and individuals are considered to be *internal*. Such data include the company's records for payroll, production, sales, and so forth. These data are organized in one or several databases.

Personal data. Employees may document their own expertise by creating *personal* data. These include, for example, subjective estimates of sales, opinions about what competitors are likely to do, and certain rules and formulas developed by the users. These data can reside on the user's PC or be placed in databases or knowledge bases that can be accessed by others in the company. Some personal data are not documented at all, but are kept in people's memories.

External data. *External* data are generated outside an organization, but relevant portions of it flow into the organization. Government reports constitute a major source for external data. Another major source of external data is the Internet. Hundreds of thousands of organizations worldwide place publicly accessible data on their Web servers, flooding us with data. A user can access Web sites of vendors, clients, and competitors.

Some external data flow to an organization on a regular basis through electronic data interchange (EDI), extranets, or other traditional company-to-company links. The rest of the data come as a result of searches. However, since most of the external data are irrelevant to a specific application, one needs to continuously monitor the external environment to ensure that important data are not overlooked.

Methods for collecting raw data. The diversity of data, especially when it comes from a multiplicity of sources, makes the task of data collection fairly complex, creating quality and integrity problems. *Raw data* (data that have not been processed) can be collected manually or by instruments and sensors. Data can also be scanned and transferred electronically. **Clickstream data** are those that can be collected automatically from a company's Web site, reflecting what visitors are doing on the site. Sometimes needed data are not at hand and must be collected in the field. Some examples of manual data collection methods are time studies, surveys, and observations. In some cases it is necessary to elicit data from people.

Search engines are frequently used to collect external data. However, using search engines may be time consuming and may even be ineffective (search engines find only 3% to 30% of all relevant Internet information). An alternative approach is to use *push technology*, in which engines automatically collect data on the topic that a user is interested in and periodically deliver the results to the user. This method saves time and may cover more sources than do other methods.

Data Quality

Regardless of how they are collected, data need to be validated. A classic expression that sums up the situation is "garbage in, garbage out" (GIGO). Therefore, safeguards on data quality are designed to prevent data problems.

Data quality (DQ) refers to the accuracy, completeness, and integrity of data. It is an extremely important issue since data quality determines the data's usefulness as well as the quality of the decisions based on these data. Data are frequently found to be inaccurate, incomplete, or ambiguous. The economic and social damages from poor-quality data costs organizations billions of dollars every year. Therefore, organizations must take active steps to ensure that data are accurate, secure, relevant, timely, complete, and consistent. Several methods for ensuring data quality are available, and DQ is interrelated with security (Chapter 15). Once quality is assured, those data are stored in some organized way.

Data Storage and Management

As was shown in Figure 11.2, data and information can be stored in databases, in *data warehouses*, and in *data marts* (discussed in Chapter 5). End users use the stored data in several ways. For example, end users may make queries, create a report, conduct a trend analysis, compare data, or present the data graphically. Basically, the stored data are processed and transformed to create information or knowledge.

Before, during, and after the transformation, these data need to be managed (as do the resulting information and knowledge). Data management may be a difficult task for the following reasons:

- The amount of data increases exponentially with time. Much past data must be kept for a long time for legal reasons and for analysis such as forecasting, and new data are added rapidly.

- Data are collected by many individuals in an organization, using several methods and devices.

- Raw data may be stored in different computing systems, databases, formats, and human and computer languages.

- Only small portions of an organization's data are relevant for any specific decision.

- An ever-increasing amount of external data need to be considered in making organizational decisions.

- Legal requirements relating to data differ among countries and change frequently.

- Selecting data management tools can be a problem because of the large number of commercial products available.

- Data security, quality, and integrity are critical, yet are easily jeopardized.

Data management can be more efficient and effective if electronic document management is used.

Electronic Document Management Systems

Organizations face the problem that a large portion of their corporate data and information exists only in paper format and so cannot be processed directly by computers. The need for greater efficiency in handling business documents to gain an edge on the competition has fueled the increased availability of *document management systems*, also known as *electronic document management*.

A **document management system (DMS)** automates the management and control of electronic documents through their entire life cycle within an organization, from initial creation to final archiving. It retains an image of an electronic document, creates an index of keywords, may put the entire document into computer-readable format, and manages (and limits) distribution. Physical paper need not be passed from employee to employee. The major tools of document management are *workflow software, authoring tools, digital cameras, scanners*, and *databases*.

Document management systems allow organizations to exert greater control over creation, storage, and distribution of documents, yielding greater efficiency in the access and reuse of information, the control of documents through a workflow process, and the reduction of processing times. The full range of functions that a DMS may perform includes document identification, digitization, storage, and retrieval; tracking; variation control; workflow management; and presentation. Document management systems usually include computerized *imaging systems* that can result in substantial savings, as IT's About Business W11.1 on the Web site shows.

www.wiley.com/
college/turban

In many organizations, documents are now stored as multimedia objects with hyperlinks. The Web provides easy access to pages of information; and DMSs excel in this area. Web-enabled DMSs that provide instantaneous conversion of documents to HTML also make it easy to put information on an intranet. BellSouth, for example, saves an estimated $17.5 million each year through its intranet-enabled forms management system. Another example is the Massachusetts Department of Revenue, which has used imaging systems to increase productivity of tax return processing by about 80 percent.

Electronic delivery of documents has been around since 1999, with UPS and the U.S. Post Office playing a major role in such service. They deliver documents electronically over a secured system (e-mail is not secured), and they are able to deliver complex "documents" such as large files and multimedia videos (which can be difficult to send via e-mail). (See *exchange.ups.com* and take the test drive.)

One of the major vendors of document management systems is Lotus Development Corporation (now owned by IBM). Its *document databases* and their replication property provide many advantages for group work and information sharing (see *lotus.com*). The following example demonstrates the use of document management for group work.

EXAMPLE

Motorola creates virtual communities for knowledge sharing.   Motorola uses DMS not only for document storage and retrieval, but also for small group collaboration and companywide knowledge sharing. The system enables employees to develop virtual communities where they can discuss and publish information, all with Web-enabled DMS. ●

Business Intelligence

One ultimate use of the data gathered and processed in the data life cycle is for business intelligence. In general, the broad term **business intelligence** describes a variety of activities to pull together all the data required to make sound business decisions, regardless of where the data originate. Business intelligence generally involves the creation or use of a data warehouse and/or data mart for storage of data, and the use of front-end analytical tools such as Oracle's Sales Analyzer and Financial Analyzer or MicroStrategy's Microstrategy Web. Such tools can be employed by end users to access data, ask queries, request ad hoc (special) reports, examine scenarios, create CRM activities, devise pricing strategies, and much more.

How business intelligence works.   A typical business intelligence process is shown in Figure 11.3. The process starts with raw data which are usually kept in *corporate databases*. For example, a national retail chain that sells everything from grills and patio furniture to plastic utensils has data about inventory, customer information, data about past promotions, and sales numbers in various databases. Though all this information may be scattered across multiple systems—and may seem unrelated—business intelligence software can bring it together. This is done by using a *data warehouse*. In the data warehouse (or mart) tables can be linked, and data cubes are formed. For instance, inventory information is linked to sales numbers and customer databases, allowing for deep analysis of information. Some data warehouses have a dynamic link to the databases; others are static.

Using the business intelligence software the user can ask queries, request ad-hoc reports, or conduct any other analysis. For example, deep analysis can be carried out by performing multilayer queries. Because all the databases are linked, you can search for what products a store has too much of. You can then determine which of these products commonly sell with popular items, based on previous sales. After planning a promotion to move the excess stock along with the popular products (by bundling them together, for example), you can dig deeper to see where this promotion would be most popular (and most profitable). The *results* of your request can be reports, predictions, alerts, and/or graphical presentations. These can be disseminated to decision makers to help them in their decision-making tasks.

More advanced applications of business intelligence include outputs such as financial modeling, budgeting, resource allocation, and competitive intelligence. Later in this chapter we will explore tools such as analytical processing and data mining, which are used to generate advanced outputs for business intelligence. Advanced business

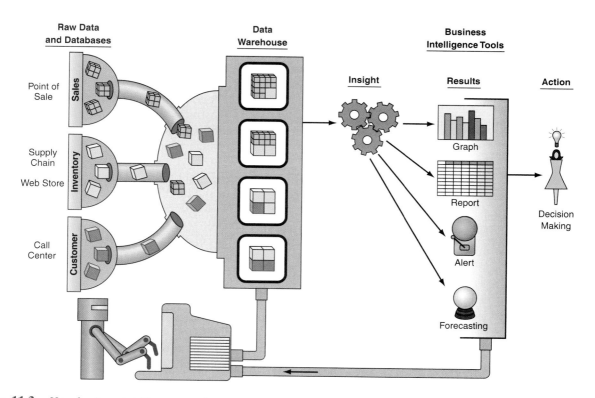

Figure 11.3   *How business intelligence works.*

intelligence systems include components such as decision models, metrics, data profiling and reengineering tools, and much more. (For details see *dmreview.com*.)

Once data are collected, refined, and stored they are ready for use by end users. If the data are used for supporting the decisional role of managers, they are likely to be transferred to a decision support system (DSS), which is the topic of the next section.

Before you go on . . .

1. Describe the data-to-knowledge transformation process.

2. Outline data sources and acquisition.

3. Describe the issue of data quality.

4. Describe an electronic document management system.

5. Describe the concept of business intelligence.

11.3   DECISION SUPPORT SYSTEMS

Decision making can be a complicated process because decision makers are faced with an ever-increasing number of alternatives, the relationships between the variables involved are complex, and frequent changes are occurring. Decisions often must be made under time pressure, and several decisions may be interrelated. These factors have created a need for computer support of decision making by an approach known as *decision support systems*.

The Decision-Making Process

When making a decision, either organizational or personal, the decision maker typically goes through a fairly systematic process composed of four major phases: *intelligence, design, choice*, and *implementation*. A conceptual presentation of the four-stage process is shown in Figure 11.4, which illustrates the tasks included in each phase. Note that there is a continuous flow of information from intelligence to design to choice (bold lines), but at any phase there may be a return to a previous phase (broken lines).

The phases can be used to explain the approach of decision support systems (DSSs). A user with a problem starts with the **intelligence phase**, where reality is examined and the problem is defined. In the **design phase**, a *model*, or simplified representation of reality, is constructed. This is done by making assumptions that simplify reality and by quantitatively expressing the relationships among all relevant variables. The model is then validated, and criteria are set for how to evaluate potential solutions. The evaluation involves using the criteria to compare the alternatives, and it attempts to forecast how well a solution will solve the original problem. This step may generate several attractive solutions to the problems. The **choice phase** involves selecting the best solution. The solution is then tested "on paper." A testing may involve experimenting with different scenarios. Once the selected solution seems to be economically feasible, the last phase—**implementation**—occurs. Successful implementation results in resolving the original problem.

A **decision support system (DSS)** attempts to automate several tasks in this decision-making process. This automation centers around the use of models to simulate the real-life situation.

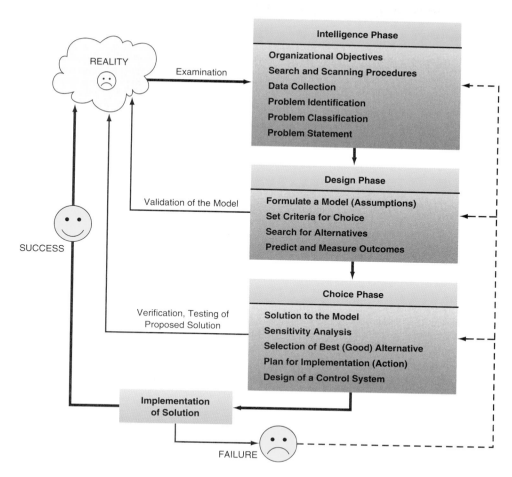

Figure 11.4   *The process and phases in decision making/modeling.* [*Source: Based on H. Simon,* The New Science of Management Decisions, *rev. ed., Englewood Cliffs, NJ: Prentice-Hall, 1977.*]

Modeling in Decision Making

A **model** is a *simplified* representation or abstraction of reality. A simplification is used because reality is too complex to copy exactly, and because much of its complexity is actually irrelevant to a specific problem. With DSS modeling, experiments and analyses are performed on the model rather than on the reality that it represents. The benefits of modeling are listed in Manager's Checklist 11.1 (page 360). Representation through models can be done at various degrees of abstraction. Models are classified into four groups according to their degree of abstraction: iconic, analog, mathematical, and mental.

Iconic (scale) models.   An *iconic model*—the least abstract model—is a physical replica of a system, usually based on a different scale from the original. Iconic models may appear to scale in three dimensions, such as models of an airplane, car, bridge, or production line. Photographs are another type of iconic model, but in only two dimensions.

Analog models.   An *analog model* does not look like the real system but behaves like it. An analog model could be a physical model, but the shape of the model differs from that of the actual system. Some examples are organizational charts that depict structure, authority, and responsibility relationships; maps where different colors represent water or mountains; stock charts; blueprints of a machine or a house; and a thermometer.

The Benefits of Modeling Decision Support Systems

- Manipulating decision models, by changing variables and evaluating possible solutions, is much easier than manipulating the real systems. Modeling does not interfere with the daily operation of the organization.
- Models allow for the compression of time. Years of operation can be simulated in seconds of computer time.
- The cost of modeling is much lower than the cost of examining alternatives on the real system itself.
- The cost of making mistakes during simulated trial-and-error experiments is much lower than if real systems were used.
- Today's business environment holds considerable uncertainty. Modeling allows a manager to evaluate the risks involved in specific actions.
- Mathematical models allow the analysis of a very large, sometimes infinite, number of possible alternatives and solutions.
- Models can provide clear views of complex phenomena, and thus enhance and reinforce learning and support training.

Mathematical (quantitative) models.   Iconic and analog models may not be suitable for modeling complex relationships and/or for conducting experiments with them. A more abstract model is possible with the aid of mathematics. Most DSS analysis is executed numerically using *mathematical*, statistical, financial, or other *quantitative models*. With recent advances in computer graphics, there is a tendency to use iconic and analog models to complement mathematical modeling in decision support systems. For example, visual simulation (see Section 11.6) combines the three types of models.

Mental models.   In addition to the explicit models just described, people frequently use a behavioral mental model. A *mental model* provides a description of how a person thinks about a situation. The model includes beliefs, assumptions, relationships, and flows of work as perceived by an individual. For example, a manager's mental model might say that it is better to promote older workers than younger ones and that such a policy would be preferred by most employees. Mental models determine the information we use and the manner in which people interpret (or ignore) information.

Developing a mental model is usually the first step in modeling. Once people perceive a situation, they may then model it more precisely using another type of model. Mental models are subjective and frequently change, so it is difficult to document them. They are important not only for decision making, but also for human–computer interaction.

A Framework for Computerized Decision Support

To better understand decision support systems it helps if we classify decisions along two major dimensions—problem structure and the nature of the decision.

Problem structure.   The first dimension is *problem structure*. It is based on the idea that decision-making processes fall along a continuum ranging from highly structured to highly unstructured decisions. (See the left column in Figure 11.5.) *Structured* decisions refer to routine and repetitive problems for which standard solutions exist. In a structured problem, the first three of the key decision-process phases (intelligence, design, and choice) are laid out in a particular sequence, and the procedures for obtain-

Type of Control				
Type of Decision	**Operational Control**	**Management Control**	**Strategic Planning**	**Support Needed**
Structured	Accounts receivable, order entry `1`	Budget analysis, short-term forecasting, personnel reports, make-or-buy analysis `2`	Financial management (investment), warehouse location, distribution systems `3`	MIS, management science models, financial and statistical models
Semistructured	Production scheduling, inventory control `4`	Credit evaluation, budget preparation, plant layout, project scheduling, reward systems design `5`	Building new plant, mergers and acquisitions, new product planning, compensation planning, quality assurance planning `6`	DSS
Unstructured	Selecting a cover for a magazine, buying software, approving loans `7`	Negotiating, recruiting an executive, buying hardware, lobbying `8`	R & D planning, new technology development, social responsibility planning `9`	DSS ES neural networks
Support Needed	MIS, management science	Management science, DSS, EIS, ES	EIS, ES, neural networks	

Figure 11.5 *Decision support framework. Technology is used to support the decisions shown in the column at the far right and in the bottom row.*

ing the best (or at least a good enough) solution are known. Whether the solution means finding an appropriate inventory level or deciding on an optimal investment strategy, the solution's criteria are clearly defined. Common solution criteria are cost minimization or profit maximization.

At the other extreme of problem complexity are *unstructured* processes. These are "fuzzy," complex problems for which there are no cut-and-dried solutions. An *unstructured problem* is one in which intelligence, design, and choice are not organized in a particular sequence. In such a problem, human intuition is frequently the basis for decision making. Typical unstructured problems include planning new service offerings, hiring an executive, or choosing a set of research and development projects for the next year.

In between structured and unstructured problems are *semistructured* problems, in which only some of the decision process phases are structured. They require a combination of standard solution procedures and individual judgment. Examples of semistructured problems would be annual evaluation of employees, setting marketing budgets for consumer products, and performing capital acquisition analysis.

The nature of decisions.   The second dimension of decision support deals with the *nature of decisions*. We can define three broad categories that encompass all managerial decisions: (1) *operational control*—the efficient and effective execution of specific tasks, (2) *management control*—the acquisition and efficient use of resources in accomplishing organizational goals, and (3) *strategic planning*—the long-range goals and policies for growth and resource allocation. These are shown on the top row of Figure 11.5.

The decision matrix.   The three primary classes of decision structure and the three broad categories of decisions can be combined in a nine-cell decision support matrix, which is in the center of Figure 11.5. Low-level managers usually perform the structured and operational control-oriented tasks (cells 1, 2, and 4). Tasks in cells 6, 8, and 9 are mainly the responsibility of top executives. The tasks in cells 3, 5, and 7 are usually the responsibility of middle managers and professional staff.

Computer support for structured decisions.   Computer support to the nine cells in the matrix is shown in the right-hand column and in the bottom row of Figure 11.5. Structured and some semistructured decisions, especially of the operational and management control type, have been supported by computers since the 1950s. Decisions of this type are made in all functional areas, but especially in finance and operations management.

Problems that lower-level managers encounter on a regular basis typically have a high level of structure. It is therefore possible to abstract, analyze, and classify them into standard classes. For example, a "make-or-buy" decision belongs to this category. Other examples are *capital budgeting* (e.g., replacement of equipment), allocation of resources, distribution of merchandise, and inventory control. For each standard class, prescribed solutions have been developed through the use of mathematical formulas. This approach is called *management science* or *operations research*, and it is also executed with the aid of computers.

Management science.   The management science approach takes the view that managers can follow a fairly systematic process for solving certain categories of semistructured problems and therefore it is possible to use a scientific approach to managerial decision making. This approach, which also centers on modeling, requires the following steps:

1. *Define* the problem (a decision situation that may deal with a setback or with an opportunity).
2. *Classify* the problem into a standard category.
3. *Construct* a standard mathematical model that describes the real-life problem.
4. *Find* potential solutions to the modeled problem and evaluate them.
5. *Choose* and recommend a specific solution to the problem.

For each standard category, such as resource allocation, there is a standard procedure, such as linear programming, that can be used to find a solution to problems in that category. Such procedures are usually computerized and are available in commercial software. Unfortunately, standard models cannot solve managerial problems that are not structured. Such problems require the use of a methodology known as decision support systems (DSSs).

Computer Support for Unstructured Decisions

The concepts involved in **decision support systems (DSSs)** were first articulated in the early 1970s. Unfortunately, the term DSS, like the terms MIS and IT, means different things to different people, and there is no universally accepted definition. DSSs can be viewed as an approach or a philosophy rather than a precise methodology. To begin to get a feel for what such a system can do for an organization, let's look at a typical case of a successfully implemented DSS, presented in IT's About Business 11.1.

This case involving Houston Oil and Minerals (now part of Tenneco Automotive) demonstrates some of the major characteristics of a DSS. The risk analysis performed first was based on the decision maker's initial definition of the situation, using a management science approach. Then, the executive vice president, using his experience, judgment, and intuition, decided that the model should be modified. The initial model, although mathematically correct, was incomplete. With a regular simulation

IT's About Business

tenneco-automotive.com   **FIN**

Box 11.1: Using a DSS to determine risk

Houston Oil and Minerals Corporation (now part of Tenneco Automotive) was interested in a proposed joint venture with a petrochemicals company to develop a chemical plant. Houston's executive vice president responsible for the decision wanted analysis of the risks involved in areas of supplies, demands, and prices. Bob Sampson, manager of planning and administration, and his staff built a DSS in a few days. The results strongly suggested that the project should be accepted.

Then came the real test. Although the executive vice president accepted the validity and value of the results, he was worried about the potential downside risk of the project, the chance of a catastrophic outcome. The executive vice president said something like this: "I realize the amount of work you have already done, and I am 99

percent confident of it. But I would like to see this in a different light. I know we are short of time, and we have to get back to our partners with our yes- or-no decision."

Sampson replied that the executive could have the risk analysis he needed in less than one hour. "Within 20 minutes, there in the executive boardroom, we were reviewing the results of his what-if questions. Those results led to the eventual dismissal of the project, which we otherwise would probably have accepted."

Questions

1. Why was it necessary to make a quick analysis?
2. Why might the DSS have reversed the initial decision?

system, a modification of the computer program would have taken a long time, but the DSS was able to provide a very quick analysis. Furthermore, the DSS was flexible and responsive enough to allow managerial intuition and judgment to be incorporated into the analysis.

The characteristics and capabilities of DSS.   There is no consensus on exactly what characteristics and capabilities constitute a DSS. But we can outline a set of characteristics and capabilities that can be considered ideal and comprehensive. Most decision support systems have some of the following attributes:

1. Support is provided for decision makers at all management levels, whether individuals or groups, by bringing together human judgment and computerized information. Such support applies mainly to semistructured and unstructured problems, which cannot be solved (or cannot be solved conveniently) by other computerized systems or by management science.

2. The DSS can support several interdependent and/or sequential decisions.

3. The DSS can support all phases of the decision-making process—intelligence, design, choice, and implementation—as well as a variety of decision-making processes and styles.

4. The user can adapt it over time to deal with changing conditions.

5. Many of the systems are relatively easy to construct. Small DSSs are built by end users, using tools such as Excel.

6. The systems usually utilize models (some of which are seamlessly standard, such as management science, statistical, or financial models; others are custom made). Advanced DSSs are equipped with a knowledge management component that allows the efficient and effective solution of very complex problems.

7. In the case of larger-scale DSSs, systems are integrated with enterprise information systems, data warehouses, and the Internet.

8. Sensitivity analysis is frequently easily executed.

Sensitivity analysis.   **Sensitivity analysis** is the investigation of the effect that changes in one or more parts of a model have on other parts of the model. Usually, we check the effect that changes in input variables have on output variables. Sensitivity analysis is extremely valuable in a DSS because it makes the system adaptable to changing conditions and to the varying requirements of different decision-making situations. It offers a better understanding of the model and the problem it purports to describe. It may increase the confidence of the users in the model, especially when the model is not so sensitive to changes. A *sensitive model* means that small changes in conditions dictate a significantly different solution. A *nonsensitive model* is one in which changes in conditions do not significantly change the recommended solution. The chances for a particular solution to succeed are very high in a nonsensitive model. Two popular types of sensitivity analysis are *what-if* and *goal-seeking analyses*.

What-if analysis.   A model builder must make predictions and assumptions regarding the input data, many of which are based on the assessment of uncertain futures. When the model is solved, the results depend on these assumptions, which are frequently subjective, made by one or a few people. **What-if analysis** attempts to check the impact of a change in the assumptions (input data) on the proposed solution. For example, *what* will happen to the total inventory cost *if* the originally assumed cost of carrying inventories is not 10 percent but 12 percent? Or, *what* will be the market share *if* the initially assumed advertising budget is overspent by 5 percent? In a well-designed DSS, managers themselves can interactively ask the computer these types of questions as many times as needed.

Goal-seeking analysis.   **Goal-seeking analysis** represents a "backward" solution approach: It attempts to find the value of the inputs necessary to achieve a desired level of output. For example, let us say that a DSS initial solution yielded a profit of $2 million. Management may want to know what sales volume and additional advertising would be necessary to generate a profit of $2.7 million. This is a goal-seeking problem.

Components and Structure of a DSS

Every DSS contains at least three components: *data management, user interface,* and *model management*. A few advanced DSSs also contain a *knowledge management* component. What does each component (subsystem) consist of?

1. **Data management.** The data management component includes a specially constructed *database* or set of *files* that contains relevant data for the decision situation and is managed by a *database management system (DBMS)*. Data can also be obtained directly from the corporate *data warehouse*, from regular databases, or from other sources.

2. **User interface (or human–machine communication).** The user interface subsystem enables the user to communicate with and command the DSS. Most DSSs have graphical user interfaces.

3. **Model management.** Model management components include software with financial, statistical, management science, or other quantitative models. These provide the system's analytical capabilities and an appropriate software management program to manage the models. Some of the models are preprogrammed; others are built by the DSS builder or end user.

4. **Knowledge management.** The knowledge management subsystem can support any of the other subsystems or act as an independent component, providing knowledge for the solution of the specific problem. This subsystem is available in only some DSSs.

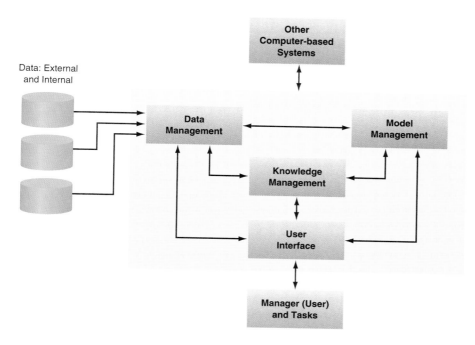

Figure 11.6 *Conceptual model of a DSS, showing four main software components facilitated by other parts of the system.*

These components constitute the software portion of the DSS (see Figure 11.6). They can be facilitated by additional software. DSSs run on standard hardware ranging from PCs to mainframes. The components of the DSS are put together either by programming them from scratch, by "gluing" together existing components, or by using integrated DSS building tools. Some DSSs are commercially available for specific applications in certain industries such as banks, hospitals, and manufacturing. End user–constructed DSSs are usually built with integrated tools, which include word processors, spreadsheets, graphics, and database management systems.

There is a fifth component of the DSS that is not included in the list of software components above—and that is *the user*. The user can be an individual, a group, or several independent users. The end user is considered an integral part of the DSS since he, she, or they interact with and contribute to the development and use of the system.

DSS and the Web

Many of today's DSSs are built as Web-based systems. As such they can be easily and inexpensively used by many people throughout the organization. Web-based DSSs offer the following capabilities:

- The DSS builder can access Web pages and view organizational data that are related to the DSS project, thus saving time.

- The Web supports interactive DSS-related queries and ad hoc report generation. Users can select a list of variables from a pull-down menu when executing a predefined query or report. This gives the builder the ability to customize the DSS output.

- Users have the capabilities of advanced DSS applications without requiring special software. All users really need is a Web browser.

Most vendors of decision support applications have modified their tools to make them work across the Web. Web-based DSSs facilitate the use of these systems and are especially suitable to organizational and enterprisewide executive information systems.

Before you go on . . .

1. Describe the typical decision-making process.

2. Explain modeling and its benefits.

3. Using the nine-cell decision support framework, explain the relationship between problem structure and the nature of decisions.

4. Define DSS and describe its major characteristics/capabilities.

5. List the major DSS components.

6. Relate the DSS to the Web.

11.4 ENTERPRISE DECISION SUPPORT

Decision support applications can be segregated into two broad categories: those that support individuals, and those that support users working as members of groups. The first category usually provides support to functional analysts and to low-level managers. The second category provides support to groups and to upper management. Because users in the second category typically have a broad view of organizational issues and decisions, these systems are classified as *enterprise decision support systems*. We focus here on two types of enterprise support systems: (1) executive information systems and (2) group DSSs.

Executive Information and Decision Support

The majority of personal DSSs support the work of professionals and middle-level managers. Rarely have DSSs been used directly by top- or even middle-level executives. Why is this? The primary reason is that these systems were not designed to meet executives' needs. System designers have developed decision support systems to fill the gap. An **executive information system (EIS)**, also known as an **executive support system (ESS)**, is a tool designed to support the information needs of top executives.

EISs provide rapid access to timely information and direct access to management reports. An EIS is very user friendly, is supported by graphics, and (as we'll see in more detail shortly) provides "exception reporting" and "drill down" capabilities. It is also easily connected with online information services and electronic mail. EISs may include modules for analysis support, communications, office automation, and intelligence. Some of the newer EISs are Web-based, and they are embedded in business intelligence software. IT's About Business 11.2 demonstrates what an EIS is and why it is sometimes needed.

Capabilities of EISs. Executive information systems vary in their capabilities and benefits. The following capabilities are common to most EISs.

Drill down. The **drill down** capability provides details behind any given information. For example, an executive may notice a decline in corporate sales in a weekly report. To find the reason, he or she may want to view a detail such as sales in each region. If one region looks problematic, the executive may want to drill down to see further details (sales by product or by salesperson). In certain cases, this drill-down process may continue through several layers of detail. An EIS makes it possible for

IT's About Business

hertz.com

Box 11.2: An enterprisewide information system at Hertz

Hertz Corporation, the largest company in the car rental industry, competes against dozens of companies in hundreds of locations worldwide. Several marketing decisions must be made almost instantaneously (such as whether to follow a competitor's price discount). The company's marketing decisions are decentralized and are based on information about cities, climates, holidays, business cycles, tourist activities, past promotions, competitors' actions, and customers' behavior. The amount of such information is huge, and the only way to process it is to use computers. The problem faced by Hertz was how to provide accessibility to such information and use it properly. A mainframe-based DSS was developed as early as 1987 to allow fast analysis by executives and managers. But a marketing manager who had a question had to go through a staff assistant, which made the process lengthy and cumbersome. The need for a better system was obvious.

In 1988, Hertz decided to add a PC-based EIS as a companion to the DSS. The combined system gave executives tools to analyze the mountains of stored information and make real-time decisions without the help of assistants. The system was migrated to a Web-based en-

terprise system in 2001. It is extremely user-friendly and is maintained by the marketing staff. Since its assimilation into the corporate culture conformed to the manner in which Hertz executives were used to working, implementation and extensive use were no problem. Hertz managers say that the enterprise system creates synergy in decision making. It triggers questions, a greater influx of creative ideas, and more cost-effective marketing decisions. In the late 1990s, the system was integrated with a *data warehouse* and connected to the corporate intranets and the Internet. Now local managers know all competitors' prices, in real time. By using supply-demand models, they can assess the impact of price changes on the demand for cars. In 2001 the system was connected to the corporate ERP and expanded to include e-commerce capabilities.

Questions

1. Why was the DSS insufficient by itself, and how did the addition of the EIS make it effective?
2. Why is the data warehouse useful?
3. Why was an integration to e-commerce needed?

the executive to search for this information, through layers of detail if necessary, without needing to consult programmers to serve as intermediaries.

Drill down in an EIS can be achieved by direct query of databases, and by using a browser. Just starting to appear are intelligent systems that provide automatic answers to questions such as "Why did sales decline?"

Critical success factors and key performance indicators.   The factors that *must* go right in order for the organization to achieve its goals are called **critical success factors (CSFs)**. Such factors can exist at the corporate level as well as at the division, plant, and department levels. Critical success factors, once identified, can be monitored, measured, and compared to standards. One or more key performance indicators, a sample of which is provided in Table 11.1, can measure each CSF. The left side of the table lists CSFs; the right side lists the indicators.

Status access.   In the *status access mode* of an EIS, an executive can access at any time the latest data or reports on the status of key indicators or other factors. The *relevance* of information is important here. The *latest data* may require daily or even hourly operational tracking and reporting. In some cases, real-time reporting may be required.

Trend analysis.   In analyzing data, it is extremely important to identify trends. Are sales increasing over time? Is market share decreasing? Is the competitor's share of the market declining against ours? The executive likes to examine the trends

Table 11.1   Illustrative Key Performance Indicators for Typical Critical Success Factors

CSF	Key Performance Indicators
Profitability	Profitability measures for each department, product, region, etc.; comparisons among departments, and product comparisons with those of competitors
Financial	Financial ratios, balance sheet analysis, cash reserve position, rate of return on investment
Marketing	Market share, advertisement analysis, product pricing, weekly (daily) sales results, customer sales potential
Human resources	Turnover rates, skills analysis, absenteeism rate
Planning	Corporate partnership ventures, growth/share analysis
Economic analysis	Market trends, foreign exchange values, industry trends, labor cost trends
Consumer trend	Consumer confidence level, purchasing habits, demographical data

represented by changes in data. *Trend analysis* can be done using forecasting models, which are included in many executive support systems.

Ad hoc analysis.   Executive information systems provide for *ad hoc analysis* capabilities, with which executives can make specific requests for data analysis. Instead of merely having access to existing reports, the executives can do creative analysis on their own. They may even select the programming tools to be used, the outputs, and the desired presentation of information. Several end-user tools provide for ad hoc analysis, which is part of online analytical processing (Section 11.5).

Exception reporting.   *Exception reporting* is based on the concept of *management by exception*, in which an executive gives attention only to significant deviations from standards. In exception reporting, an executive's attention is directed only to cases of very bad (or very good) performance. This approach saves considerable time for both producers and readers of reports.

Intelligent EIS.   To save the executive's time in conducting a drill down, finding exceptions, and identifying trends, an intelligent EIS has been developed. Automating these activities not only saves time but also ensures that the executive will not miss any important indications in a large amount of data. Intelligent EIS may include an intelligent agent for alerting management to exceptions.

Integration with DSSs.   Executive information systems are useful in identifying problems and opportunities. Such identification can be facilitated by an intelligent component. In addition, it is necessary to do something if a problem or an opportunity has been discovered. Therefore, many software vendors provide integrated EIS/DSS tools in their business intelligence packages, as was illustrated in IT's About Business 11.2 (page 367).

Web-based enterprise systems.   In recent years, the EIS has been enhanced with relational and multidimensional analysis and presentation, user-friendly data access, user-friendly graphical interface, imaging capabilities, hypertext, intranet access

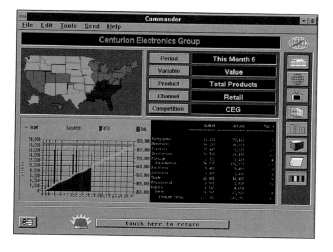
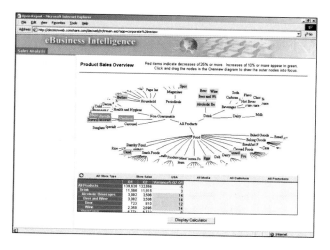
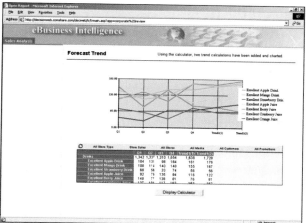
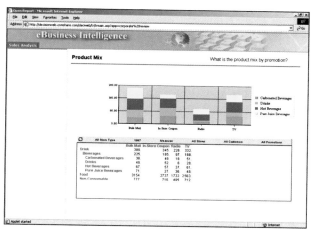

Sample screens from Comshare's Decision—a modular system for generating business intelligence reports.

e-mail, Internet access, and modeling. In large corporations EISs are linked to data warehouses and the intranet. Such systems are no longer referred to as executive information systems, but as **enterprise support systems**, which indicates that they can be used not only by executives but also by other managers.

Group Decision Support Systems

A **group decision support system (GDSS)** is an interactive computer-based system that facilitates the solution of semistructured and unstructured problems by a group of decision makers. It is a type of *groupware* software (Chapter 4). The goal of the GDSS is to improve the productivity of decision-making meetings, either by speeding up the decision-making process or by improving the quality of the resulting decisions, or both. This is accomplished by providing support for the exchange of ideas, opinions, and preferences within the group. The GDSS encourages generation of ideas, resolution of conflicts, and freedom of expression. It contains built-in mechanisms that discourage development of negative group behaviors, such as destructive conflict, miscommunication, and "groupthink."

The GDSS can be designed for one type of problem or for a variety of group-level organizational decisions. Because it must accommodate users with varying levels of

Manager's Checklist 11.2

How a GDSS Benefits Group
Decision Making

- Supports parallel processing of information and facilitates idea generation by participants.
- Enables larger groups, with more complete information, knowledge, and skills, to participate in the same meeting.
- Offers rapid and easy access to external information.
- Allows nonsequential computer discussion. (Unlike oral discussions, computer discussions do not have to be serial or sequential.)
- Produces instant, anonymous voting results.
- Provides structure to the planning process, which keeps the group on track.
- Enables several users to interact simultaneously.
- Automatically records all information that passes through the system for future analysis (develops organizational memory).

knowledge regarding computing and decision support, a GDSS generally is easy to learn and use. The GDSS can increase the benefits of the group decision-making process, as listed in Manager's Checklist 11.2. It also can reduce the losses (from group dysfunctions) that are possible in that process.

Supporting face-to-face meetings.   Initially GDSSs were designed to support face-to-face meetings in what is called a *decision room*. For example, the room at City University of Hong Kong is equipped with state-of-the-art workstations, a local-area network, a server, and a "facilitator station," which controls a multiple-screen projector (see Figure 11.7, part *a*). An electronic decision room requires a trained facilitator.

Corporate "war rooms."   Following the examples of the military, corporations are creating decision rooms in which top executives can plan and simulate strategies. One such room, created and developed by Professor Patrick M. Georges at HEC School of Management in Paris, and promoted by SAP, is the *Management Cockpit* (*management-cockpit.net*). The Management Cockpit is a strategic management room that enables managers to pilot their businesses better (see Figure 11.7, part *b*). Key

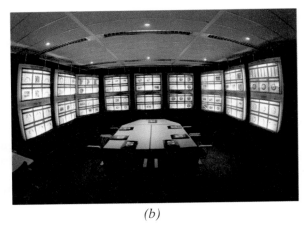

(a)   (b)

Figure 11.7   *(A) Decision room at City University of Hong Kong. (B) Management Cockpit© created by Patrick M. Georges and developed by the N.E.T. company. The Management Cockpit is a trademark of SAP.*

performance indicators and information relating to critical success factors are displayed graphically on the walls of the meeting room. Executives could call up this information on their laptops, of course, but a key element of the concept is a cockpit-like arrangement of instrument panels and displays, which users manipulate as they conduct what-if scenarios using the graphic displays. There, on the four walls—Black, Red, Blue, and White—ergonomically designed graphics depict different areas of corporate performance as reflected in mission-critical factors (see Figure 11.7, part *b*). A major advantage of the Management Cockpit is that it provides a common basis for information and communication among participants. At the same time, it supports efforts to translate a corporate strategy into concrete activities by identifying and monitoring performance indicators. The Cockpit environment is integrated with SAP's ERP products and reporting systems. External information can be easily imported to the room to allow competitive analysis.

Supporting virtual teams.   However, GDSSs are no longer limited to use in physical decision rooms. With capabilities similar to those offered in a decision room, GDSSs are now available for distributed groups over the Internet, over intranets, or over private networks. Thousand of companies use such software, ranging from industry giants such as Ford Motor to small retailers. Of special interest are Eroom.com and NetMeeting (*videofrog.com*) which offer collaborative environments for teams (with discussion, database, linking, polls, calendar, and more).

Before you go on . . .

1. Define EIS and describe its major characteristics.

2. Define GDSS and list its benefits.

3. Distinguish between supporting a group in one room and supporting a virtual team.

11.5   DATA AND INFORMATION ANALYSIS AND MINING

Both individual and organization decision support systems involve some data and/or information analysis. Two popular approaches—analytical processing and data mining—are described in this section.

Analytical Processing

Analytical processing refers to the activity of analyzing accumulated data, such as for projections, comparisons, statistical inferences, and decision analysis. Placing information that has undergone analysis in the hands of decision makers empowers them to make better and faster decisions, leading to greater competitive advantage. Analytical processing can be done offline, or it can be done on the Web.

Online analytical processsing.   **Online analytical processing (OLAP)** refers to such end-user activities as DSS modeling using spreadsheets and graphics that are done online. Unlike online transaction processing (OLTP) applications, OLAP involves many different data items in complex relationships. One objective of OLAP is to analyze these relationships and look for patterns, trends, and exceptions. (Note that the word *online* in the term *OLAP* refers to *online processing*, discussed in Chapter 4, and not to the Internet.)

An example of data analyzed by OLAP would be sales data that have been aggregated by region, product type, and sales channel. A typical OLAP query might access a large sales database or marketing data mart to find all product sales in each region for each product type. After reviewing the results, an analyst might further refine the query to find sales volume for each sales channel within region or product classifications. As a last step, the analyst might want to perform year-to-year or quarter-to-quarter comparisons for each sales channel. This whole process would be carried out online, with rapid response time that enables the analysis process to proceed undisturbed.

OLAP queries can be characterized as online queries that do the following:

- Access very large amounts of data—as many as several years of sales data, for example.
- Analyze the relationships between many types of business elements, such as sales, products, regions, and channels.
- Involve aggregated data, such as sales volumes, budgeted dollars, and dollars spent.
- Compare aggregated data over hierarchical time periods—monthly, quarterly, yearly.
- Present data in different perspectives, such as sales by region versus sales by product or by product within each region.
- Involve complex calculations between data elements, such as expected profit calculated as a function of sales revenue for each type of sales channel in a particular region.
- Respond quickly to user requests so that users can pursue an analytical thought process without being stymied by the system.

Today it is possible to access an OLAP database from the Web or a corporate intranet. There are several tools for OLAP mostly available from vendors such as *brio.com*, *cognus.com*, *crystaldecisions.com*, and *microstrategy.com*.

Although OLAP is very useful in many cases, it is retrospective in nature and cannot provide automatic or prospective complex analysis. This can be better done by data mining techniques.

Data Mining for Decision Support

Data mining was introduced in Chapter 5 as a data management technique used with data warehouses and data marts. In this section, we reexamine data mining as a form of decision support. It derives its name from the similarities between searching for valuable business information in a large database and mining a mountain for a vein of valuable ore. Both processes require either sifting through an immense amount of material or intelligently probing that material to find exactly where the value resides. Given databases of sufficient size and quality, data mining technology can generate new business opportunities by providing these two capabilities:

- *Automated prediction of trends and behaviors.* Data mining automates the process of finding predictive information in large databases. Questions that traditionally required extensive hands-on analysis can now be answered directly and quickly from the data. A typical example of a predictive problem is targeted marketing. Data mining can use data about past promotional mailings to identify the targets most likely to respond favorably to future mailings.

- **Automated discovery of previously unknown patterns.** Data mining tools also identify previously hidden patterns. An example of pattern discovery is the analysis of retail sales data to identify seemingly unrelated products that are often purchased together, such as baby diapers and beer. (Yes, this is true.) Other pattern discovery problems include detecting fraudulent credit card transactions and identifying anomalous data that may represent data entry–keying errors.

When data mining tools are implemented on high-performance parallel processing systems, they can analyze massive databases in minutes.

Data mining can be conducted by nonprogrammers. In organizations it appears under different names, such as knowledge extraction, data dipping, data archeology, data exploration, data pattern processing, data dredging, and information harvesting.

Characteristics of data mining.   The following are the major characteristics of data mining:

1. The relevant data are often difficult to locate because they are in very large databases, such as data warehouses, data marts, or in Internet and intranet servers. Data mining tools are needed to extract the buried information "ore."
2. The "miner" is often an end user, empowered by "data drills" and other power query tools to ask ad hoc questions and get answers quickly, with little or no programming skill.
3. The data mining environment usually has a client/server architecture.
4. Because of the large amounts of data, it is sometimes necessary to use parallel processing for data mining.
5. Data mining tools are easily combined with spreadsheets and other end-user software development tools, enabling the mined data to be analyzed and processed quickly and easily.
6. Data mining yields five types of information: (a) associations, (b) sequences, (c) classifications, (d) clusters, and (e) forecasting.
7. "Striking it rich" often involves finding unexpected, valuable results.

Data mining tools.   Data miners can use several IT-based tools and techniques. The most well-known tools are neural computing, intelligent agents, and association analysis:

- **Neural computing.** Neural computing is a machine-learning approach by which historical data can be examined for patterns (details are given in Chapter 12). Using neural computing tools, users can go through huge databases and, for example, identify potential customers of a new product or search for companies whose profiles suggest that they are heading for bankruptcy.
- **Intelligent agents.** One of the most promising approaches to retrieving information from the Internet or from intranet-based databases is the use of intelligent agents (see Chapter 12).
- **Association analysis.** This is an approach that uses a specialized set of algorithms that sort through large data sets and expresses statistical rules among items.

Mining the Web.   While the concept of data mining started with mining data warehouses, today the tool can be used with other collections of data, notably the Web. Known as *Web mining*, this technique enables management to analyze, for example, what visitors are doing on its Web pages. It is form of market research.

*"With over 1.5 billion pages on the Web, just be happy you find **anything**."*

www.wiley.com/
college/turban

A sampler of data mining applications.   According to a GartnerGroup estimation (*gartnergroup.com*), during 2001 at least half of all the Fortune 1000 companies world-wide used data mining technology. As shown by the representative examples in Table W11.1 and the Ocean Spray Company example, both on the book's Web site, data mining can be very helpful. Note that the intent of many of these examples is to identify a business opportunity in order to create a sustainable competitive advantage.

Ethical and Legal Issues

Several ethical and legal issues are related to data analysis and mining. Representative issues include data security, copyright infringement, proper use of accumulated data, and discrimination.

Ethical issues related to data analysis and mining.   Using data mining, it is possible not only to discover information that has been buried in remote databases, but also to manipulate and cross-index it. In 1996 Lexis-Nexis, the online information service, was accused of permitting lawyers and law enforcement personnel access to sensitive information about individuals, which it had mined from information buried in distant courthouses. This had a potential benefit for law enforcement but could invade individuals' privacy. The company argued that the firm was criticized unfairly, since it provided only basic residential data (who lived where) for lawyers and law enforcement personnel. The question remains open to debate, though: Should companies that have valuable data-mined information be prohibited from allowing others access to such information? Even companies that use data mining for purposes not connected with law enforcement can face this issue. Corporations with decision support systems of various types may need to address some other ethical issues, such as accountability. For example, a company developed a DSS to help people compute the financial implications of early retirement. However, the DSS developer did not include the tax implications, which could result in incorrect retirement decisions, yet the company provided the DSS results to employees.

Another important ethical issue is human judgment, which is frequently used in DSS. Human judgment is subjective, and may therefore lead to unethical decision making. Companies may wish to provide some ethical guidelines for DSS builders. Finally, the possibility of automating managers' jobs could lead to layoffs and related social and family dislocations. Some may ask whether automated decision making should be done, and if so, to what extent.

Legal issues related to data analysis and mining.   The key legal issues surrounding use of data analysis and mining are potential discrimination, data security, and data ownership. Findings of data analysis or mining may suggest to a company to send catalogs or promotions to only one age group or one gender, which might be deemed discriminatory. For example, a man sued Victoria's Secret for discrimination because his female neighbor received a catalog with deeply discounted items and he received only the regular catalog. Since the discount was given for volume purchasing and not as a result of gender, he lost the case. However, lawsuits can be very expensive for companies to contend with, even when they win them.

Another issue with possible legal repercussions is data security. Are the company's competitive data safe from external snooping or sabotage? Are confidential data, such as personnel details, safe from improper or illegal access and alteration? This is true for all confidential personnel data, whether it comes from an organization's database or from more intense data mining efforts.

A related question is who owns such personal data. Compilers of public-domain information such as Lexis-Nexis may face a problem of people lifting large sections of their work without first paying royalties. The Collection of Information Anti-Piracy Act provides greater protection from online piracy.

> **Before you go on . . .**
>
> 1. Define OLAP and describe its characteristics.
>
> 2. Define data mining and list some typical characteristics.
>
> 3. Relate data mining to the Web.
>
> 4. Describe some legal and ethical issues related to data analysis and mining.

11.6   DATA VISUALIZATION TECHNOLOGIES

Once data (information) have been processed by a DSS, EIS, or GDSS, the results can be presented to users as text or as tables, and via several data-visualization technologies. Data-visualization is important for better understanding of data relationships and compression of information.

Data Visualization

Visual technologies "make pictures worth a thousand words (or numbers)" and make IT applications more attractive and understandable to users. **Data visualization** refers to presentation of data by technologies such as digital images, geographical information systems, graphical user interfaces, multidimensional tables and graphs, virtual reality, three-dimensional presentations, and animation. Visualization software packages offer users capabilities for self-guided exploration and visual analysis of large amounts of data. By using visual analysis technologies, people may spot problems that have existed for years undetected by standard analysis methods. Visualization technologies can also be integrated among themselves to create a variety of presentations.

Data visualization is easier to implement when the necessary data are stored in a data warehouse. Our discussion here focuses mainly on the data-visualization techniques of visual simulation and geographical information systems. Related topics, such as multimedia, hypermedia, and multidimensionality are presented in Chapters 4 and 5, and virtual reality is presented in Chapter 12.

Visual Interactive Decision Making

Computers can help people visualize something before it actually exists by simulating what that thing would look like. In general, to *simulate* means to assume the appearance or characteristics of reality. *Simulation* has many applications. When applied to decision support systems, simulation generally refers to a technique for conducting experiments (such as what-if analysis) with a digital computer on a model of a management system. **Visual interactive modeling (VIM)** uses computer graphic displays to represent the impact of different management or operational decisions on goals such as profit or market share. VIM differs from regular simulation in that the user can intervene in the decision-making process, see the results of the intervention, and interact with and manipulate the system.

One of the most developed areas in VIM is **visual interactive simulation (VIS)**, a decision simulation in which the end user watches the progress of the simulation model in an animated form using graphics terminals. The user may interact with the simulation and try different decision strategies. Therefore, VIM can be used for training, as shown in IT's About Business 11.3.

Geographical Information Systems

A **geographical information system (GIS)** is a data-visualization technology that captures, stores, checks, integrates, manipulates, and displays data using *digitized maps*. Its most distinguishing characteristic is that every record or digital object has an identified geographical location. By integrating maps with spatially oriented (geographical

IT's About Business

partekforest.com

Box 11.3: Computer training in complex logging machines

In the forest industry, countries with high labor costs must automate tasks such as moving, cutting, delimbing, and piling logs in order to be price-competitive. A new machine, called the "Harvester," can replace 25 lumberjacks. The Harvester is a highly complex machine that takes six months to learn how to operate. The trainee would destroy a sizeable amount of forest in the process, and terrain suitable to practice on is decreasing. In unskilled hands, this expensive machine can also be damaged. Therefore, extensive and expensive training is needed. Sisu Logging of Finland (a subsidiary of Partek Forest) found a solution to the training problem by using a real-time simulation. In such simulations, the chassis, suspension, and wheels of the vehicles have to be modeled together with the forces acting on them (inertia and friction), and the movement equations linked with them have to be solved in real time. This type of simulation is mathematically complex, and until 1997 required equipment investment running into millions or tens of millions of dollars. However, with the help of a visual simulation program, training can now be carried out for only 1 percent of the cost of the traditional method.

Inside the simulator are the Harvester's actual controls, which are used to control a virtual model of a Harvester plowing its way through a virtual forest. The machine sways back and forth on uneven terrains, and the grapple of the Harvester grips the trunk of a tree, fells it, delimbs it, and cuts it into pieces very realistically in real time.

The simulated picture is very sharp: Even the structures of the bark and annual growth rings are clearly visible where the tree has been cut. In traditional simulators, the traveling path is quite limited, but in this Harvester simulator, you are free to move in a stretch of

Logging—an important industry in Finland.

forest covering two hectares (about 25,000 square yards).

The system can be used to simulate different kinds of forests in different parts of the world, together with different tree species and climatic conditions. An additional advantage of this simulator is that the operations can be videotaped so that training sessions can be carefully studied afterward. Moreover, it is possible to practice certain dangerous situations. A similar system is currently used by many major forest companies worldwide.

Questions

1. Why is the simulated training time shorter?
2. Why is visualization beneficial here?

location) and other databases, users can generate information for planning, problem solving, and decision making. A GIS can help increase an organization's productivity and the quality of its decisions. Data can be superimposed on a map using bullets and colors. For example, location of branch offices and percentage of overlapping among branches could be mapped, showing in one picture what might take thousands of words to describe.

GIS categories.   The field of GIS can be divided into two major categories: functions and applications. There are four major functions: spatial imaging (such as electronic maps), design and planning, database management, and decision modeling. These functions support different areas of applications, namely surveying and mapping, design and engineering, demographics and market analysis, transportation and logistics, facilities management, and strategic planning and decision making. GIS is particularly helpful in decision support.

Most major GIS software vendors are providing Web access via browsers or a Web/Internet/intranet server that hooks directly into their software. Thus, users can access dynamic maps and data via the Internet or a corporate intranet.

GIS and decision making.   GIS provides a large amount of extremely useful information that can be analyzed and utilized in decision making. For example, as one market researcher explained: "I can put 80-page spreadsheets with thousands of rows into a single map. It would take a couple of weeks to comprehend all of the information

Table 11.2   GIS Applications

Company	What the Application Does
PepsiCo, Inc.	Helps select new locations for Taco Bell and Pizza Hut restaurants by combining demographic data and traffic patterns
CIGNA (health insurance)	Answers such questions as "How many CIGNA-affiliated physicians are within an 8-mile radius of a business?"
Western Auto (a subsidiary of Sears)	Creates a detailed demographic profile of store's neighborhood to determine the store's best product mix
Sears, Roebuck & Co.	Supports planning of truck routes
Health maintenance organizations (HMOs)	Tracks cancer rate to determine clinics' expansion strategy and allocation of expensive equipment
Wood Personnel Services (employment agency)	Maps neighborhoods where temporary workers live; used for locating marketing and recruiting cities
Wilkening & Co. (consulting services)	Designs optimal sales territories and routes for clients, reducing travel costs by 15 percent
CellularOne Corp.	Maps company's entire cellular network to identify clusters of call disconnects and to dispatch technicians accordingly
Sun Microsystems	Manages leased property in dozens of places worldwide
Consolidated Rail Corp.	Monitors the condition of 20,000 miles of railroad track and thousands of parcels of adjoining land
Federal Emergency Management Agency (FEMA)	Assesses the damage of natural disasters by relating videotapes of the damage to digitized maps of properties
Toyota, GM, and other automakers	Combines GISs and GPSs as a navigation tool to direct drivers to destinations.

from the spreadsheet; but in a map, the story can be told in seconds." For many companies, the intelligent organization of data within a GIS can provide a framework to support the process of decision making and of designing alternative strategies. There are countless applications of GIS to improve decision making in the public or private sector, as shown in Table 11.2 (on page 377).

Emerging GIS applications.   The integration of GISs and global positioning systems (GPSs) has the potential to help restructure the aviation, transportation, and shipping industries. It enables vehicles or aircraft equipped with a GPS receiver to pinpoint their location as they move. Emerging business applications of GPSs include railroad car tracking and earth-moving equipment tracking. A special personal-interest application is the mapping systems installed in cars, which allow you to find how to go from where you are to a desired address, to well-known locations, or to the nearest gasoline station or restaurants. So far, these systems are available in various models of luxury cars. Recently such systems were introduced to location-based e-commerce (l-commerce, Chapter 9).

Before you go on . . .

1. Define data visualization and list some of its technologies.

2. Describe visual simulation and list its advantages.

3. Define GIS and explain its use as a decision support tool.

11.7   KNOWLEDGE MANAGEMENT AND ORGANIZATIONAL KNOWLEDGE BASES

So far we described how data are processed into information required in decision support. But, data and information can sometimes be transformed into knowledge, which can be very useful in supporting decision making. For example, we have demonstrated how knowledge is derived for problem solving, such as forecasting or predicting customer behavior. It makes sense that the knowledge created for solving a specific problem will be reused whenever the organization faces the same or a similar problem. ("Why reinvent the wheel?") This simple idea is the basis for a challenging concept called **knowledge management (KM)**. A major purpose of knowledge management is to allow for *knowledge sharing*. Knowledge sharing with customers, among employees, and with business partners has a huge potential payoff in improved customer service, shorter delivery cycle times, and increased collaboration within the company and with business partners. Furthermore, some knowledge can be sold to others or traded for other knowledge.

Knowledge management is still an emerging field. A 1999 national U.S. study by Omni Tech Consulting Group indicated that KM is in the early stages of development, having at most only a moderate effect on today's organizations. However, over 80 percent of top executives expect KM will have a *significant* and major impact on their organizations by 2003–2005. Executives recognize KM as a trump card with which they can distance themselves from the competition. Many executives have called KM "the most significant strategic process developing in the past 20 years."

What Is Knowledge Management?

Because knowledge management is still a developing field, there is no settled definition as yet. However, a good working definition of knowledge management is this: KM is the process of accumulating and creating knowledge efficiently, managing an organizational knowledge base for storing the knowledge, and facilitating the sharing of knowledge so that it can be applied effectively throughout the organization.

Related concepts. Several valuable concepts are closely related to knowledge management:

- **Knowledge assets.** The knowledge regarding markets, products, technologies, and organizations that a business owns or needs to own, and that enables its business process to generate profit or improve operations.

- **Tacit and implicit knowledge.** Knowledge appears in two forms: tacit and explicit. **Tacit knowledge** is the result of subjective, experiential learning, and is frequently not documented. **Explicit knowledge** deals with objective, rational, and technical knowledge, and it is usually documented.

- **Best practices.** A collection of the most successful solutions and/or case studies related to a specific problem or situation in a particular industry or in the business world generally.

- **Intellectual capital.** The collection of knowledge, documents, research, and internal discussion amassed by an organization over the years.

- **Knowledge system.** A comprehensive corporatewide system that collects knowledge, stores it in a database, maintains the database, and disseminates the knowledge to users.

- **Organizational knowledge base.** The captured knowledge of an organization, stored in one place and structured so that it is accessible to decision makers within the organization.

- **Competitive intelligence.** The various activities conducted by companies, usually with IT tools, to collect competitive information (about competitors, products, and markets).

The following examples demonstrate the use of knowledge management in businesses.

EXAMPLES

3M uses KM to develop new products. A strong culture of knowledge management permeates 3M Corporation's operations. The company actively encourages new product development by requiring that 30 percent of annual sales come from products less than four years old. It has a history of using its organizational knowledge base to spin off new businesses from existing technical platforms, and of sharing technical knowledge to communicate about current product activities and status. 3M is also using KM to make discoveries that can lead to new products.

BP repair specialists share knowledge.   British Petroleum (BP) uses desktop teleconferencing to connect its repair specialists around the world, enabling them to view, discuss, and assess malfunctioning drilling parts and recommend solutions. The solutions are then captured and sorted for later analysis to guide future repairs. The company saves millions of dollars annually on travel, as well as on quicker and better repairs.

Motorola employees share documents and ideas.   Motorola is using KM to link its virtual communities of employees. Via a Web-enabled document management system, employees can publish and discuss information with their peers, no matter where in the world they are. The extensive idea sharing improves products and services. A similar system is used by IBM to identify the knowledge needed for problem solving. ●

IT Support of KM Activities

In order for organizations to take advantage of knowledge management, information systems departments must provide systems that support KM. The major KM activities that must be supported are as follows:

- *Knowledge identification.* Determines what knowledge information is critical to decision making.
- *Knowledge discovery and analysis.* By use of search engines, databases, and data mining, the proper knowledge must be found, analyzed, and put into proper context.
- *Knowledge acquisition.* Much knowledge resides in experts' minds. Knowledge engineers and special software tools are able to gather and organize this knowledge to make it useful to others.
- *Knowledge creation via idea generation.* Some knowledge is created by using idea-generation techniques.
- *Establishment of organizational knowledge bases.* Organizational knowledge and best practices need to be stored in a knowledge base, which is indexed and properly maintained. An *organizational knowledge base* should not be confused with *knowledge bases* of an intelligent system (see Chapter 12), which contain limited knowledge used for solving a very specific problem. An organizational knowledge base is much broader, containing accumulated corporate knowledge for solving many problems.
- *Knowledge distribution and use.* Target audiences are defined and technologies are put into place to enable knowledge delivery when needed.

Building and maintaining organizational knowledge bases involve many activities. We can see some of what is involved by looking at the example of Accenture, a company whose pioneering efforts in organizational knowledge bases have set a standard, as described in IT's About Business 11.4.

Implementing Knowledge Management

Implementing KM is not a simple project. The cost of building and maintaining the organizational knowledge base can be very high, and the benefits sometimes are difficult to justify. Some implementation issues are: Who will decide on what to include in the knowledge base and how? Who will extract the knowledge from its sources? How will managers and professionals be trained to make effective use of the knowledge? Who will keep the knowledge up-to-date, and how? What portion of the knowledge base should be open to outsiders, and how can proprietary and sensitive information be secured? How will the firm integrate the knowledge base with existing databases? And finally, how will managers validate the quality of the knowledge?

Depending on the answers to these and similar questions, the activities and processes of KM can be supported by the following technologies: data warehousing and data marts, databases (and especially marketing databases), data mining, case-based reasoning, neural computing, Web-based search and retrieval tools, informa-

IT's About Business

knowledgespace.com,
knowledgespace.arthurandersen.com

Box 11.4: Accenture's knowledge base leapfrogs the competition

For a large consulting company whose very product is knowledge, there is considerable motivation to create a knowledge base to share accumulated know-how. For this reason, the international accounting firm Arthur Andersen and its sister company, Accenture, began in the early 1990s to create a "Global Best Practices" (GBP) knowledge base, a central repository of knowledge about world-class business practices. The GBP knowledge base contains quantitative and qualitative information about how companies achieve best-in-the-world standards of performance in activities that are common to most companies. Andersen's consultants use this information to provide clients with an ever-growing body of knowledge that can be used for performance improvement. Being able to provide such knowledge to its customers gives the company a competitive edge. Here is how the company gathers knowledge:

- The GBP hotline receives requests from its consultants' employees each month, which are sorted into business practice categories.

- These requests, combined with ongoing research into emerging areas, are used to determine which process areas are to be developed or enhanced for an upcoming release.

- Teams are created to develop best practices context and diagnostic tools in specific areas. The teams consist of research analysts, along with content experts who serve specific clients.

- Qualitative and quantitative information and tools are stored on the corporate intranet and on a CD-ROM and can be accessed by all Andersen professionals worldwide.

- Use of the knowledge base in the field with clients generates suggestions, which are received by the hotline or captured through formal or informal surveys for further improving the knowledge base.

The knowledge base contains information such as best companies' profiles, relevant Andersen engagement experience, top-10 case studies and articles, world-class performance measures, diagnostic tools, customizable presentations, process definitions and directory of internal experts, best-control practices, and even tax implications. Four years after the GBP was created, it was so successful that it had fundamentally shifted the company's culture and the way it did business. As a matter of fact, Arthur Andersen developed several other knowledge bases, each dedicated to an important topic. One other corporate knowledge base is the Proposal Toolbox, which contains detailed information on all proposals submitted by Andersen's employees, worldwide. It includes names of which employees have worked on which projects, resources used, and so on. This knowledge base is used to cut the time for preparing new proposals from weeks to days. Certain portions of the knowledge base are open to the public (*knowledgespace.com*). Users can get 30 days' free trial. The site includes some of the GBP, current business issues, an intelligent search engine using "push" technology, experts' opinions, links, references, and much more.

Questions

1. What was the justification for the company to invest in this project?

2. Why is the knowledge base open to clients?

3. Does it make sense to sell GBP to the public, when such information may be purchased by a competing consultant?

tion personalization, data visualization, intranets and the Web (which are becoming the KM infrastructure), document management and text retrieval, help-desk software, and intelligent agents. These technologies have been discussed in this and in other chapters of the book. Their deployment is related to the specific KM activities. For example, data mining would most likely be used for knowledge discovery.

Because of the potential for big payoffs from KM, companies not only are creating organizational knowledge bases, but also are completely reorganizing themselves as **knowledge-based organizations**. Even a new position of **chief knowledge officer (CKO)** has been created, whose role is to capture and leverage knowledge using IT.

CKOs have three responsibilities: creating knowledge management infrastructure, building a knowledge culture, and making it all pay off.

Appointing a CKO may be the first step toward fulfilling management guru Peter Drucker's prediction that the typical business will be a knowledge-based organization composed largely of specialists who direct and discipline their own performance through organized feedback from colleagues, customers, and headquarters. Drucker claimed that to remain competitive, and maybe even to survive, businesses will have to convert themselves into organizations of knowledge specialists.

Sharing knowledge also means facilitating organizational learning. **Organizational learning** is an important approach that advocates that organizations must *learn* from their experiences in order to survive. Failure to learn can be fatal for organizations. Because knowledge bases enable companies to learn faster than their competitors, they give those who use them a sustainable competitive advantage. People can learn from the experience of others when this experience is documented in a knowledge base.

Supporting Idea Generation and Creativity

As mentioned above, knowledge creation in many cases requires *creativity* and *idea generation*. This is especially important in generating alternative DSS solutions.

Some people believe that an individual's creative ability stems primarily from personality traits such as inventiveness, independence, individuality, enthusiasm, and flexibility. However, several studies have found that creativity is not so much a function of individual traits as was once believed, and that individual creativity can be learned and improved. This understanding has led innovative companies to recognize that the key to fostering creativity may be the development of an idea-nurturing work environment. Idea-generation methods and techniques, to be used by individuals or in groups, are consequently being developed.

Manual methods for supporting idea generation (such as brainstorming in a group) can be very successful in certain situations. However, in other situations, such an approach is either not economically feasible or not possible. For example, manual methods in group creativity sessions will not work or will not be effective when: (1) there is no time to conduct a proper idea-generation session; (2) there is a poor facilitator (or no facilitator at all); (3) it is too expensive to conduct an idea-generation session; (4) the subject matter is too sensitive for a face-to-face session; or (5) there are not enough participants, the mix of participants is not optimal, or there is no climate for idea generation. In such cases, computerized idea-generation methods have been tried, with frequent success.

Idea-generation software.   **Idea-generation software** is designed to help stimulate a single user or a group to produce new ideas, options, and choices. The user does all the work, but the software encourages and pushes, something like a personal trainer. Although idea-generation software is still relatively new, there are several packages on the market.

Various approaches are used by idea-generating software to increase the flow of ideas to the user. IdeaFisher, for example, has an associative lexicon of the English language that cross-references words and phrases. These associative links, based on analogies and metaphors, make it easy for the user to be fed words related to a given theme. Some software packages use questions to prompt the user toward new, unexplored patterns of thought. This helps users to break out of cyclical thinking patterns, conquer mental blocks, or deal with bouts of procrastination. Creative Think *(creativethink.com)* provides techniques to move the user out of habitual thought patterns.

Idea-generation software for groups works somewhat differently from such software for individuals. Participants in groups simultaneously create ideas that are shown to other participants, stimulating electronic discussion or generating more ideas. A large number of ideas is usually generated in a short time. These ideas are then organized, debated, and prioritized by the group, all electronically. (Group decision support systems, discussed earlier, may incorporate group idea-generation software.)

The benefits of creativity enhancement afforded by idea-generating software are numerous. A competitive advantage can be realized across all industry spectrums because of the many new ideas and approaches that can be facilitated electronically. Here are a few examples.

EXAMPLES

CEC found new markets. CEC Instruments, of San Dimas, California, used idea-generation software to cope with shrinking military contracts. In order to survive, the company had been looking to the commercial market. After using IdeaFisher, CEC's contract manager realized that the company had overlooked an expanding market for its technical instruments in the commercial aviation market.

Inventor saw ways to cut costs. Clayton Lee, an inventor in Houston, Texas, used IdeaFisher to reduce the manufacturing costs of a new product from $2,000 to $100 per unit. As a result, the market for the product widened enormously. In addition, the software was used to modify some of Lee's existing products. ●

Before you go on . . .

1. Provide a working definition of knowledge management.

2. List the major information technologies that support knowledge management.

3. Describe an organizational knowledge base and how it is used.

4. Describe how idea generation is supported by IT.

WHAT'S IN IT FOR ME?

www.wiley.com/
college/turban

FOR THE ACCOUNTING MAJOR

An accountant can play a major role in justifying the creation of a knowledge base and in its auditing. In addition, if you work for a large CPA company that provides management services or sells knowledge, you will most likely use some of your company's best practices that are stored in a knowledge base.

FOR THE FINANCE MAJOR

The finance department is responsible for justifying major investments such as an organizational knowledge base and enterprise systems. In addition, DSS applications are found mostly in financial management and analysis. Spreadsheet technology, which is a common tool of decision support, is used extensively in the finance department.

MKT FOR THE MARKETING MAJOR
Knowledge about customers can make the difference between success and failure. In many data warehouses and knowledge bases the vast majority of information and knowledge is about customers, products, sales, and marketing. Marketers will certainly use an organization's knowledge base and will probably participate in its creation. Numerous DSS models are used in topics ranging from allocating advertising budgets to evaluating alternative routings of salespeople.

POM FOR THE PRODUCTION/OPERATIONS MANAGEMENT MAJOR
Knowledge management is extremely important for running complex operations. The accumulated knowledge regarding scheduling, logistics, maintenance, and so on is extremely valuable. Innovative ideas are necessary for improving operations and can be supported by KM. Complex production and operations decisions, in areas ranging from inventory to production planning, are supported by DSSs.

HRM FOR THE HUMAN RESOURCES MANAGEMENT MAJOR
HRM people need to use a knowledge base frequently to find out how past cases were handled. Consistency in how employees are treated is important and is a protection against legal actions. Also, training for building, maintaining, and using the knowledge system could be the responsibility of the HRM department. Finally, the HRM department might resolve the issue of compensating employees for contributing their knowledge.

SUMMARY

❶ **Describe the concepts of managerial decision making and computerized support for decision making.**
Managerial decision making is synonymous with management. It can be viewed as a process involving four major phases: intelligence, design, choice, and implementation. These processes can serve as a guide for the design of computerized decision support systems.

❷ **Understand the process of converting data into information and knowledge for use in decision support.**
Data are the foundation of any information system. They exist in internal and external sources, including the Internet. Many factors that impact the quality of data must be recognized and controlled. Data frequently are transformed into information or knowledge via data warehouses. Information can be transformed into useful knowledge through analysis or data mining and can be stored in an organization's knowledge base.

❸ **Describe the framework for computerized decision support and the concept of decision support systems.**
Decisions can be classified along a continuum from structured to unstructured. They can also be classified as strategic, operational, or managerial. This creates a nine-cell matrix of decision support against which problems can be mapped. DSS is a methodology that models situations for a quick computerized analysis of semi-structured and unstructured complex problems. The major components of a DSS are the database and its management system, the model base and its management system, and a user-friendly interface. A knowledge (intelligent) component can be added.

❹ Describe executive information systems and group support systems, and analyze their roles in management support.

An EIS is a corporatewide decision support system designed for executives but used by others as well. It allows quick and easy analysis, communication, ad hoc report generation, and detailed inquiries (drill down). Group DSS is a methodology for supporting the process of making decisions in a group. The group members can be in one room or in several locations. The method facilitates idea generation and collaboration and lessens negative aspects of face-to-face meetings.

❺ Describe online analytical processing and data mining.

OLAP allows sophisticated querying of specialized databases. Data mining refers to a family of tools based on different algorithms that can be used to discover otherwise-unnoticed relationships among data in large databases.

❻ Describe data-visualization methods and explain geographical information systems as a decision support tool.

Data visualization is important for better understanding of data relationships and for compression of information. A geographical information system (GIS) captures, stores, manipulates, and displays data using digitized maps. A GIS can support decisions related to mapping, such as where to open a store or where to advertise.

❼ Explain the concepts of knowledge management and organizational knowledge base.

Knowledge management refers to a process of discovering knowledge and preserving it in an organizational knowledge base for future sharing among company employees (and sometimes externally). An organizational knowledge base contains all the relevant know-how and best practices and can be reused by employees when needed.

❽ Describe IT support for idea generation.

Idea generation is frequently necessary for finding solutions to problems. Using IT, it is possible to significantly increase the number of ideas and to facilitate brainstorming.

INTERACTIVE LEARNING SESSION

Go to the CD and access Chapter 11: Data, Knowledge, and Decision Support. There you will be given choices to make about designing a groupware system to achieve particular objectives. You will be given a variety of cases and then will place the various components together to make a group DSS. You will be given feedback about the efficacy of your choices.

www.wiley.com/ college/turban

For additional resources, go to the book's Web site for Chapter 11. There you will find Web resources for the chapter, including links to organizations, people, and technology; "IT's About Business" company links; "What's in IT for Me?" links; and a self-testing Web quiz for Chapter 11.

DISCUSSION QUESTIONS

1. Your company is considering opening a branch in China (yes- or-no decision). List several typical activities in each phase of the decision process (intelligence, design, choice, and implementation).

2. A hospital desires to know what level of demand for its services will guarantee an 85 percent bed occupancy. What type of sensitivity analysis should the hospital use, and why?

3. Describe both internal and external data that may be needed in a DSS for a company's selection of an investment stock portfolio.

4. American Can Company announced that it was investigating the acquisition of a company in the health maintenance organization (HMO) field. Two decisions were involved in this act: (1) the decision to acquire an HMO, and (2) the decision of which one to acquire. How can a DSS and an EIS be used in each decision?

5. Discuss how critical success factors are measured in your company, in a company with which you are familiar, or in your university.

6. Discuss the opportunities that an organizational knowledge base can provide to a pharmaceutical company such as Merck or Johnson & Johnson.

7. Discuss the factors that make document management valuable. What capabilities are particularly valuable?

8. Describe the process of knowledge discovery using data mining.

9. Relate the 3M case at the beginning of this chapter to the phases of the data and transformation process.

PROBLEM-SOLVING ACTIVITIES

1. Susan Lopez was promoted to director of the transportation department in a medium-size university. She controlled the following vehicles: 17 sedans, 9 vans, and 3 trucks. The previous director was fired because there were too many complaints about not getting vehicles when needed. Susan is told not to expect any increase in budget for the next two years, which means there will be no replacement or additional vehicles. Susan's major job was to schedule vehicles for employees, and to schedule maintenance and repair of the vehicles.

   You have been asked to advise Susan regarding the possibility of using a DSS to improve her manually done job. Susan has the latest vintage PC and Microsoft Office software, but currently she is using the computer only for word processing and e-mail.

   a. Justify use of the proposed DSS. What can this DSS do to improve Susan's job?

   b. Which of the Microsoft Office components may be used for the DSS, and for what?

2. Interview a knowledge worker in a company you work for or to which you have access. Find out what data problems they have encountered and the measures they have taken to solve them.

INTERNET ACTIVITIES

1. Enter *eroam.com*, *banxia.com*, *facilitators.com*, and *videofrog.com*. Find information on their GDSS products.

2. Online analytical processing (OLAP) is becoming an important business intelligence tool. Browse the Web in search of the latest developments.

3. Find five customer success stories related to use of DSSs. Try *microstrategy.com*, *cognos.com*, *crystaldecisions.com*, and *dssresources.com*. Analyze the cases for DSS characteristics.

4. Conduct a survey and prepare a report on document management tools and applications by visiting *dataware.com*, *documentum.com*, and *aiim.org/aim/publications*.

5. Access the Web sites of one or two of the major data management (or data warehouse) vendors, such as Oracle, NCR, SAS, and Sybase. Trace the capabilities of their latest products, including Web connections.

6. Visit *brint.com*, *kmworld.com*, and *cio.com*. Review recent information on knowledge management. Write a report on your findings.

7. Identify the latest DSS activities. Start with *dssresources.com* and *support2000.com/dss.htm*.

8. Enter *microstrategy.com* and take the following tours: (1) "What is business intelligence" and (2) "Quick tour of Microstrategy 7." Prepare a report on your findings.

TEAM ACTIVITIES AND ROLE PLAYING

1. Prepare a report regarding Web-based DSSs that support investment and profitability analysis. Assign each team to a major vendor. As a start, go to *dssresources.com*. Also view Comshare

   Decision Web (*comshare.com*) and DSS Web (*microstrategy.com*).

2. Prepare a report on the topic of knowledge management and intranets. Pay specific attention to the role

of the data warehouse, the use of browsers for query, and data mining. Each team can concentrate on one IT support tool. Also explore the issue of text retrieval and document management.

Finally, describe the role of extranets in support of KM. Each team should also visit one or two vendors' sites, read the white papers, and examine products.

REAL-WORLD CASE   *dell.com*

Database Marketing Increases Dell's Sales

The Business Problem   Dell Computer Corporation has been the world's largest direct-sale vendor of personal computers. The company was having difficulty in acting quickly on the masses of data it gathers from customers. Many of the 50,000 phone calls and e-mail messages received by Dell daily are from potential customers who dial 800 numbers or send e-mail to reach the company's sales representatives. The rest are from current users of Dell machines, asking the technical support staff for help. There was simply too much information to process, and it was difficult to do it on time.

The IT Solution   The company created a customers' data mart. The employees who take customer calls work on PCs linked to a computer that contains the company's customer database, which in 2001 had well over 2 million customer entries. The sales representatives enter information about each call as they receive it, recording names and addresses along with product preferences and/or technical problems. The company stores all this information and much more in a data mart shared by employees in various departments, from marketing to product development to customer service.

The Results   The company uses analytical processing, data mining, and statistical tools to analyze the data. The data yield significant marketing and sales guidelines. Says Tom Martin, Dell's chief marketer, "We know that if we use a yellow background on a catalog cover, we'll get a 30 percent lower response rate than with gray." The company tailors its mailings even more precisely to each recipient. The rate of response to its mailings to small businesses rose 250 percent once Dell used customer feedback to refine its pitch. At a mailing price of 50¢ to $3 per piece, the benefits of accurate targeting add up quickly. In 1999 Dell was moving to cus-

tomized electronic catalogs for its major business customers. This move saves mailing expenses and enables the company to provide up-to-the-minute catalogs.

Experience from the database also guides the sales representatives who receive calls. As they enter information about each caller, sales suggestions automatically pop up on their computer screens. Dell had a tenfold increase in sales of three-year warranties after prompting representatives to pitch them to all callers buying systems costing more than a certain dollar amount.

Routine analysis of customer and sales data allows Dell to spot consumer trends such as a shift to larger hard-disk drives. At one time, when Dell was shipping most of its systems with drives capable of storing 120 MB, the customer database alerted management to the fact that new orders for drives with nearly twice the storage capability were rapidly climbing. Dell buyers rushed out and negotiated volume discounts from large disk-drive manufacturers, and locked in deliveries before their competitors.

"Know your customer" is a tried-and-true business rule, and Dell gets the most it can out of it through customer databases.

Questions

1. What role does the data mart play in Dell's marketing strategies?
2. Can you identify any data mining and analytical processing necessary for the information described in the case?
3. Is there any possibility of invasion of privacy of Dell's customers? If so, how can this privacy be protected?
4. Do you think the paper catalog is eventually going to disappear?

VIRTUAL COMPANY ASSIGNMENT

wiley.com/college/turban

Extreme Descent Snowboards

Background You knock at the door of Jacob's office as he sets down the phone, and he greets you with, "Welcome, I have been expecting you." Jacob explains that he just returned from an IT Management seminar in Atlanta. One session of the seminar was on knowledge management. He thinks this is a topic the company should explore.

www.wiley.com/
college/turban

Jacob smiles and proceeds to tell you about your next assignment: "I need you to prepare a report on knowledge management." Then he hands you a memo outlining the topics he wanted included in the report. As you head back to your cubicle, you read the following from the memo:

Assignment

There were two Web sites that were introduced at the seminar. These sites are an excellent starting point for your research:

www.brint.com   This site devotes a channel to knowledge management.
www.kmresourse.com   This site is devoted totally to knowledge management.

Answer the following questions as part of your report.

- What is knowledge management?
- In what areas could EDS benefit from a system like this?
- What kinds of information would be contained in the knowledge management system?
- Who would benefit most from this system?
- How could EDS justify the investment for a knowledge management system?

INTELLIGENT SYSTEMS IN BUSINESS

12

CHAPTER PREVIEW

For generations people have attempted to make smart machines to perform tasks that require intelligence. In this chapter we present the achievement of this goal as it is related to the world of business. Available intelligent systems range from expert systems to industrial robots. These systems can be used by themselves or in conjunction with other systems, to increase productivity, quality, and customer service, and to reduce cycle time. They can also be integrated among themselves or embedded in other information, electrical, or mechanical systems to improve the functionality of those systems. Intelligent systems also can be used to facilitate communication and collaboration among people within and between organizations, expanding the capabilities of the latter. Intelligent systems help us to communicate better with people who speak other languages as well as to communicate with computers. In addition, intelligent systems help us to overcome the information overload, enabling us to quickly find, compare, and analyze data and to better conduct electronic commerce and customer service. Finally, such systems can act as advisers and tutors to people.

CHAPTER OUTLINE

LEARNING OBJECTIVES

1. Describe artificial intelligence and compare it to conventional computing.
2. Identify the characteristics, structure, benefits, and limitations of expert systems.
3. Describe the major characteristics of natural language processing and voice technologies.
4. Describe neural computing and its capabilities.
5. Define intelligent agents and their role in IT.
6. Describe virtual reality.

ANALOG DEVICES USES INTELLIGENT SYSTEMS TO SUPPORT COLLABORATION WITH CUSTOMERS

analog.com

The Business Problem

Analog Devices Inc. designs, manufactures, and markets a broad line of precision integrated circuits (ICs) used in analog and digital signal-processing applications. The products are sold to various manufacturers that use ICs in their own products. The market for such ICs is very competitive.

With thousands of products, Analog Devices had been printing new catalogs and data sheets each year, some of which measured up to two feet thick. The cost of printing and shipping catalogs to 50,000 customers worldwide reached about $3 million each year.

Analog's sales engineers used to take customer requirements by phone and try to manually find a match in the company's product range. This complex process involves considering dozens of constraints while interacting with customers (usually design engineers) to ascertain their needs and priorities. Only well-trained engineers are successful in this lengthy process. Since it is very difficult to find and retain such engineers, there were problems with matching products to customers.

Web site of semiconductor manufacturer Analog Devices.

Analog Devices, like its competitors, tried to find a better way to service its customers. Initially, projects were developed using an algorithm-based search engine combined with a standard database management system. This approach failed because this type of search returns a value only when *all* conditions are exactly met. When customers provided an incomplete set of specifications, the answer was "no match"; when the customers relaxed some specifications, hundreds of matches were found. Thus, the process was lengthy, expensive, and error-prone.

The IT Solution

Analog Devices decided to change the process by improving the customer–company communication. Using an IT-based intelligent system called *case-based reasoning*, which derives conclusions from historical cases, and combining it with a decision-support optimization model, the company allows customers to specify product requirements interactively, online, in order to find the right product, or the one closest to their needs, *by themselves*.

With this system the customer enters specifications directly on the screen. Values can be numbers or information such as "the best," "sort of," or "less than." The system always provides an answer, a list of the top-ten Analog Devices products that most closely meet the specified requirements. The customer then examines the products online. If the customer is not satisfied, another search begins with new specifications and priorities. This process can continue until the right product is identified.

The system was initially delivered to customers with the entire catalog on a CD-ROM. Today, the system is accessible to customers through an extranet, so they can use the inexpensive Internet to save money on communication and collaboration. The company's engineers can also use the system on the company's intranet.

The Results

Analog Devices saved initially about $2 million a year, because the cost to produce and ship 120,000 CD-ROMs was far less expensive than the paper version of the catalog.

The extranet savings are much larger since there is no need to make and ship the CD-ROMs whenever significant changes are made. In addition, the quality of the service provided by Web-based intelligent systems makes a difference in this competitive market. Now, when customers call sales support they usually know exactly what they want, and what they order is exactly what they need. The company's support engineers now have time to accommodate more complex customer requirements.

As the system tracks customers' requests, a future extension will use data collected to analyze this information and input them to an improved design of new products.

Sources: Compiled from D. Kress, "AI at Work," *PC AI* (March/April 1998), and from *analogdevices.com* (2002).

What We Learned from This Case

The opening case demonstrates how an intelligent system solved a difficult business problem by improving and expediting communication and collaboration between the company and its customers. The system facilitated the work of the sales engineers. Previously, only well-trained engineers were successful, but it took them a considerable amount of time. Now much of the search is done by the customers themselves, freeing the sales engineers to do other tasks. The opening case also demonstrates that the intelligent system solution was integrated with other information technologies (CD-ROM, Internet, extranet, search engine) as well as with a DSS. Case-based reasoning is one of several intelligent systems that businesses can use to improve their operations. This case is also an example of *collaborative commerce* (Chapter 9).

The fundamentals of the major intelligent systems and the support they provide for problem solving and seizing business opportunities are the subjects of this chapter. We will also discuss a related application, virtual reality.

12.1 ARTIFICIAL INTELLIGENCE AND INTELLIGENT SYSTEMS

As the opening case illustrated, the introduction of an intelligent system enabled non-experts to perform a task previously done by experts. This is only one benefit of *intelligent systems*, which are the commerical applications of artificial intelligence (AI).

Artificial Intelligence and Intelligent Behavior

Artificial intelligence (AI) is a term that encompasses many definitions. Most experts agree that AI is concerned with two basic ideas. First, it involves studying the thought processes of humans; second, it deals with representing those processes via machines (computers, robots, and so on). One well-publicized definition of AI is "behavior by a machine that, if performed by a human being, would be called *intelligent*." The three objectives of artificial intelligence are (1) to make machines smarter, (2) to understand what intelligence is, and (3) to make machines more useful.

What is the meaning of the term *intelligent behavior*? Several capabilities are considered to be signs of intelligence:

- Learning or understanding from experience
- Making sense of ambiguous or contradictory messages
- Responding quickly and successfully to a new situation
- Using reasoning to solve problems and direct actions effectively
- Dealing with complex situations

- Understanding and inferring in ordinary, rational ways
- Applying knowledge to manipulate the environment
- Recognizing the relative importance of different elements in a situation

Although AI's ultimate goal is to build machines that will mimic human intelligence, current intelligent systems found in commercial AI products are far from exhibiting any significant intelligence. Nevertheless, intelligent systems are currently conducting many tasks that require some human intelligence, for a *significant improvement* of productivity, quality, and cycle time.

An interesting test to determine whether a computer exhibits intelligent behavior was designed by Alan Turing, a British AI pioneer. According to the **Turing test**, a computer could be considered "smart" only when a human interviewer, conversing with both an unseen human being and an unseen computer, cannot determine which is which.

So far we have concentrated on the notion of intelligence. According to another definition, artificial intelligence is the branch of computer science that deals with ways of representing *knowledge* using symbols in addition to numbers and using *heuristics* (rules of thumb) rather than just algorithms for processing information.

Knowledge and AI.   AI is frequently associated with the concept of *knowledge*. The computer cannot have experiences or study and learn as the human mind can, but it can use knowledge given to it by human experts. Such knowledge consists of facts, concepts, theories, heuristic methods, procedures, and relationships. As defined in Chapters 1 and 11, knowledge is information organized and analyzed to make it *understandable* and *applicable* to problem solving or decision making, and to incorporate procedures, ideas, and human experience. The collection of knowledge related to a problem (or an opportunity) to be used in an intelligent system is organized and stored in what we call a **knowledge base**, and it is specific to a problem.

Comparing Artificial and Natural Intelligence

The potential value of AI can be better understood by contrasting it with natural (human) intelligence. AI has several *commercial advantages* over natural intelligence:

- AI is more *permanent*. Natural intelligence is perishable from a commercial standpoint, because workers may take knowledge with them when they leave their place of employment, or they may forget their knowledge. AI, however, is permanent as long as the computer systems and programs remain unchanged.

- AI can be *less expensive* than natural intelligence. There are many circumstances in which developing or buying an intelligent system costs less than having human beings carry out the same tasks, as was shown in the opening case.

- AI is *consistent and thorough*. Natural intelligence is erratic because people are erratic; they may not perform consistently.

- AI can be *documented*. Decisions made by a computer can be *easily documented* by tracing the activities of the system. Natural intelligence is difficult to document.

- AI offers *ease of duplication and dissemination*. Transferring a body of knowledge from one person to another usually requires a lengthy process of apprenticeship; some expertise can never be duplicated completely. Knowledge embodied in a computer system can be copied and easily moved to another computer, anywhere and any time. For example, the knowledge needed to match customers' needs with Analog Devices' products is now available on the extranet for the company's customers to use when needed; knowledge distribution can be made rapidly and inexpensively to thousands of customers worldwide.

On the other hand, natural intelligence has *several advantages* over AI:

- Natural intelligence is *creative*, whereas AI is rather uninspired. The ability to acquire knowledge is inherent in human beings. But with AI, tailored knowledge must be built into a carefully constructed system.

- Natural intelligence enables people to benefit from and *directly use sensory experiences*. Many AI systems must first interpret information collected by sensors, thus providing users with indirect sensory experiences.

- Natural intelligence enables people to *recognize relationships* between things, to *sense qualities*, and to *spot patterns* that explain how various items interrelate.

- Perhaps most important, human reasoning is always able to make use of a wide *context of experiences* and bring that to bear on individual problems. In contrast, AI systems typically gain their power by having a very narrow focus.

"IT FIGURES. IF THERE'S ARTIFICIAL INTELLIGENCE THERE'S BOUND TO BE ARTIFICIAL STUPIDITY."

Despite their limitations, AI methods can be extremely valuable. They can make computers easier to use and make knowledge more widely available. Furthermore, with the passage of time, the magnitude of these limitations is decreasing. The major potential benefits of AI are shown in Manager's Checklist 12.1.

Conventional versus AI Computing

Conventional computer programs are based on *algorithms* (mathematical formulas or sequential procedures that lead to a solution). An algorithm is converted into a computer program that tells the computer exactly what operations to carry out in order to solve problems. Conventional computing is therefore done by *numerical processing*. AI programs go beyond conventional computing by including *heuristics*, or rules of thumb that express knowledge.

AI software also uses **symbolic processing** of knowledge. In AI, a symbol can be a letter, word, or number that represents objects, processes, and their relationships. Objects can be people, things, ideas, concepts, events, or statements of facts. Using symbols, it is possible to create a knowledge base of facts and concepts, and the

Manager's Checklist 12.1

- Makes the use of some computer applications very friendly.
- Significantly increases the speed and consistency of problem solving.
- Helps solve problems that cannot be solved by conventional computing.
- Helps solve problems that have incomplete or unclear data.
- Helps in handling the information overload (by summarizing or interpreting information).
- Significantly increases the productivity of performing many tasks.
- Helps in searching and finding relationships among large amounts of data.
- Facilitates the delivery of fast customer service at a low cost.

The Potential Benefits of Artificial Intelligence

Table 12.1   Conventional versus AI Computing

Dimension	Conventional	AI
Processing	Primarily algorithmic	Includes symbolic conceptualization
Nature of input	Must be complete	Can be incomplete
Search approach	Frequently based on algorithms	Frequently uses rules and heuristics (rules of thumb)
Explanation	Usually not provided	Provided
Focus	Data, information	Knowledge
Maintenance and update	Usually difficult	Relatively easy changes can be made in self-contained modules
Reasoning capability	No	Yes

relationships that exist among them. The major differences between AI computing and conventional computing are shown in Table 12.1.

Does a computer really think?   Knowledge bases and search techniques certainly make computers more useful, but can they really make computers more intelligent? The fact that most AI programs are implemented by search and pattern-matching techniques leads to the conclusion that computers *are not really intelligent*. You give the computer a lot of information and some guidelines about how to use this information. The computer can then come up with a solution. But all it does is test the various alternatives and attempt to find some combination that meets the designated criteria. The computer appears to be "thinking'" and often gives a satisfactory solution. However, the human mind is just too complex to duplicate. *Computers certainly cannot think* in the same way humans do, but they can be very useful for increasing our productivity. This is done by several commercial AI technologies.

Commercial Artificial Intelligence Systems

The development of machines that exhibit intelligent characteristics draws on several sciences and technologies, ranging from linguistics to mathematics. The major intelligent systems are: expert systems, natural language processing, speech understanding, robotics and sensory systems, computer vision and scene recognition, intelligent computer-aided instruction, fuzzy logic, neural computing, and case-based reasoning. A combination of two or more of the above is considered a *hybrid intelligent system*. An overview of some of these intelligent systems follows.

Expert systems.   Expert systems (ESs) are computerized advisory programs that attempt to imitate the reasoning processes of experts in solving difficult problems. Expert systems are of great interest to organizations because they can increase productivity and augment workforces in specialty areas where it is becoming increasingly difficult to find and retain human experts. Expert systems are further discussed in Section 12.2.

Natural language technology.   Natural language processing (NLP) gives computer users the ability to communicate with computers in human languages. The field of natural language processing is discussed in detail in Section 12.3.

Speech (voice) understanding.   Speech understanding is the recognition and understanding by a computer of a *spoken* language. Details are given in Section 12.3.

Robotics and sensory systems.   Sensory systems such as vision recognition combined with AI define a broad category of systems generally referred to as robotics. A *robot* is an electromechanical device that can be programmed and reprogrammed to automate manual tasks.

Robots combine sensory systems with intelligent systems and mechanical motions to produce machines of widely varying abilities. Robotics is used mainly in welding, painting, cleaning, and simple material handling. Assembly-line operations, particularly those that are highly repetitive or hazardous, are also beginning to be performed by robots. Robots are used for finding, moving, and packing items in automated e-commerce warehouses, for example. Robots are getting more and more capable. They are being put to use in ways that ease life by performing tasks in hazardous environments and by performing household tasks ranging from cutting the grass in your backyard, to cooking, to cleaning the floor.

Some nonbusiness uses for robots: In August 1997, the first World Cup Robot Soccer Competition was conducted in Nagoya, Japan. Competing robots included several AI technologies. (See robocup.org.)

Computer vision and scene recognition.   Visual recognition has been defined as the addition of some form of computer intelligence and decision making to digitized visual information received from a machine sensor. The resultant information is then used to perform or control such operations as robotics movement, conveyor speeds, and production-line quality control. The basic objective of computer vision is to *interpret* scenarios. Computer vision is used extensively in performing industrial-quality control tasks (such as inspection of products). Would you believe that *every* Tylenol or other brand-name pill is checked by computer vision for defects? Defective pills are removed.

Intelligent computer-assisted instruction.   Computer-assisted instruction (CAI), which has been in use for several decades and now is the base of *e-learning*, brings the power of the computer to the educational process. Now CAI methods are being applied to the development of intelligent computer-assisted instruction (ICAI) systems that can tutor humans by shaping their teaching techniques to fit the learning patterns of individual students. To a certain extent, such a machine can be viewed as an expert system. However, the major objective of an expert system is to render advice, whereas the purpose of ICAI is to teach.

ICAI applications are not limited to schools. As a matter of fact, they have found a sizable niche in the military and corporate sectors. ICAI systems are being used today for various tasks such as problem solving, simulation, discovery, learning, drill and practice, games, and testing. Such systems are also used to support people with physical or learning impairments. An increasing number of ICAI programs are now offered on the Internet and intranet, supporting virtual schools and universities. ICAI can be combined with distance learning, learning situations in which teachers and students are in different locations. Another application of ICAI is *interpretive testing*. Using this approach, GMAT (the MBA admission test) and other infamously long tests have shortened their length of testing time. By being able to better interpret the answers, the test can more accurately pinpoint the strengths and weaknesses of the test takers by asking fewer but more relevant questions.

Machine learning.   Conventional computerized problem-solving techniques cannot solve complex problems where specialized knowledge is needed. Such knowledge can be provided, in some cases, by an expert system (ES). However, the use of an ES is limited by factors such as its rule structure, difficulties in knowledge acquisition, and the inability of the ES to learn from experiences. For situations where an ES is inappropriate, machine learning can be used. **Machine learning** refers to a set of methods that attempt to teach computers to solve problems or to support problem solving by analyzing (learning from) historical and current cases. This task, however, is not simple. One problem is that there are many models of learning, and sometimes it is difficult to match a learning model with the type of problem that needs to be solved. Three methods of machine learning—*neural computing, case-based reasoning*, and *fuzzy logic*—are described in Section 12.3.

Handwriting recognizers.   The dream of every post office in the world is to be able to automate the reading of all handwritten address characters, regardless of their shape. Today's scanners are good at "reading" typed or printed material, but they are not very good at handwriting recognition. Handwriting recognition is supported by technologies such as expert systems and neural computing and is available in some pen-based computers. Handwriting interfaces are especially popular with nontypists because they can convert handwritten text into typed digital text. Of special interest are products such as Pen Computing (see Chapter 3 and *Palm.com*).

Intelligent agents.   One of the most interesting applications of intelligent systems is their inclusion in **intelligent agents**, which perform a variety of tasks for their masters much like a human agent does. Intelligent agents, as we will see in Section 12.4 and as demonstrated in Chapter 9, are extremely important for e-commerce and other Web-based applications.

Other applications.   Artificial intelligence can be applied to several other tasks such as *automatic programming*, which automatically writes computer programs in response to and in accordance with the specifications of a program developer. Recently,

IT's About Business

ge.com

Box 12.1:   General Electric's SCISOR analyzes financial news

General Electric's Research and Development Center has developed a natural language system called SCISOR (System for Conceptual Information Summarization, Organization, and Retrieval) that performs text analysis and question-answering in a limited, predefined subject area (called a *constrained domain*). One application of this system deals with analyzing financial news. For example, SCISOR automatically selects and analyzes stories about corporate mergers and acquisitions from the online financial service of Dow Jones. It is able to process news in less than 10 seconds per story. First, it determines whether the story is about a corporate merger or acquisition. Then, it selects information such as the target, suitor, and price per share. The system allows the user to browse and ask questions such as, "What price was offered for Polaroid?" or "How much was Bruck Plastics sold for?"

The system's effectiveness was demonstrated in testing, when it proved to be 100 percent accurate in identifying all 31 mergers and acquisitions stories that were included in a universe of 731 financial news releases from the newswire service.

A similar application is a Web-based personalized news system that was developed in Singapore to track business news available in English, Chinese, and Malay, summarize it, and extract desired personalized news in any of these languages.

Questions

1. What are the benefits of analyzing financial news via a machine?

2. What other applications might be developed with this type of system?

3. How could such a system be combined with an Internet news dissemination portal such as *money.cnn.com*?

an *automatic translation of Web pages* to other languages has become very popular. Other applications are preparation of news summaries and translation from one human or computer language to another. Some computer programs, for example, "read" stories in newspapers or other documents, including those available on the Internet, and make summaries in English or other languages. This capability helps handle the problem of information overload, as described in IT's About Business 12.1.

Before you go on . . .

1. List the major advantages that artificial intelligence has over natural intelligence.

2. List the major disadvantages of artificial intelligence compared with natural intelligence.

3. List and briefly define the commercial AI application tools.

12.2   EXPERT SYSTEMS

Of all the intelligent systems, the one with the most business applications is the expert system. When an organization has a complex decision to make or a problem to solve, it often turns to experts for advice. These experts have specific knowledge and experience in the problem area. They are aware of alternative solutions, chances of success, and costs that the organization may incur if the problem is not solved. Companies engage experts for advice on many matters, ranging from mergers and acquisitions to advertising strategy. Experts can diagnose problems correctly and solve them satisfactorily within a reasonable time frame. The more unstructured the situation, the more specialized is the advice. However, human experts are expensive, and they may not be readily available. Expert systems (ES) are an attempt to mimic human experts.

Concepts of Expert Systems

In order to explore the concepts involved in ES, read IT's About Business 12.2 (page 398), which describes a well-known application case at General Electric. The case of GE's David Smith demonstrates that the basic idea behind an ES is simple: Expertise is transferred from an expert, or other sources of expertise, to a computer and is stored there. *Expertise* is the extensive, task-specific knowledge acquired from training, learning, and experience. It enables experts to make better and faster decisions than non-experts in solving complex problems. Expertise takes a long time (usually years) to acquire. Users can call on the computer's stored expertise for specific advice as needed. The computer can make inferences and arrive at a conclusion. Then, like a human expert, the computer program advises the nonexperts and explains, if necessary, the logic behind the advice. When they contain the wisdom of several experts, expert systems can sometimes perform better than any single expert can.

The goal of an expert system is to transfer expertise from an expert and documented sources to a computer and then to the user. This process involves four activities: *knowledge acquisition* (from experts or other sources), *knowledge representation* (in the computer), *knowledge inferencing*, and *knowledge transfer and use* to solve a problem. Through the activity of knowledge representation, acquired knowledge is organized as rules or objects, and is stored electronically in a knowledge base.

IT's About Business   ge.com

Box 12.2:   GE's expert system models human troubleshooters

General Electric's top locomotive field service engineer, David I. Smith, had been with the company for more than 40 years and was expert at troubleshooting diesel electric locomotive engines. Smith traveled throughout the country to places where locomotives were in need of repair to determine what was wrong and to advise young engineers. The company was dependent on Smith. There was just one problem: Smith was nearing retirement.

GE's traditional approach to such a situation was to set up apprenticeship teams that paired senior and junior engineers for several months or even years. By the time the older engineers retired, the younger engineers had absorbed enough of their expertise to carry on. It was a good short-term solution, but GE still wanted a more effective and dependable way of disseminating expertise among its engineers and preventing valuable knowledge from retiring with people like David Smith.

GE decided to build an expert system to solve the problem by modeling the way a human troubleshooter works. The system builders spent several months interviewing Smith and transferring his knowledge to a computer. The computer program was developed over a three-year period, slowly increasing the knowledge and number of decision rules stored in the computer. The resulting diagnostic technology enables a novice engineer or even a technician to uncover a fault by spending only a few minutes at the computer terminal. The system can also explain to the user the logic of its advice, serving as a teacher. Furthermore, the system can lead users through the required repair procedures, presenting detailed, computer-aided drawings of parts and subsystems and providing specific how-to instruction demonstrations. It is based on a flexible, humanlike thought process, rather than rigid procedures expressed in flowcharts or decision trees.

The system is currently installed at every railroad repair shop served by GE, thus eliminating delays, preserving Smith's expertise, and boosting maintenance productivity. After his retirement, Smith was hired as a consultant to help in updating and maintaining the system's knowledge.

Questions

1. Why was this application ideal for an expert system approach?
2. What are the major advantages of the computerized ES?
3. How can GE keep the knowledge in the system up to date after Smith stops his consultancy?

A unique feature of an expert system is its ability to "reason." Given the necessary expertise stored in the knowledge base and accessibility to databases, the computer is programmed so that it can make inferences, based on a search-and-match process. Knowledge inferencing is performed in a component called the **inference engine** and results in advice or a recommendation for novices. ES can explain its recommendation through a subsystem called the *justifier* or the *explanation facility*.

During the past few years, the technology of expert systems has been successfully applied in thousands of organizations worldwide to problems ranging from identifying credit card fraud to medical diagnosis to the analysis of dust in mines. Two illustrative applications are listed next.

EXAMPLES

Helping the Navajo Nation.   The states of Arizona, New Mexico, and Utah are transferring management of the welfare program to the Navajo Nation, which now self-administers the program for its own people. The program provides financial and human services to approximately 30,000 Navajo clients. An expert system facilitates self-management of the welfare program. The interactive solution Case Worker Advisor (from *exsys.com*) integrates the tribe's unique cultural heritage while following complex tribal, federal, and state guidelines.

Carrier configures equipment orders.   Carrier Corporation, a major air conditioning manufacturer, introduced expert systems into its operations. For each customized order, Carrier must procure all the parts and subsystems so that orders can be filled on time. The ES configures a set of part numbers for each customer's equipment order. Using the ES, Carrier was able to minimize both pricing and configuration errors, reduce cycle time, and increase customer satisfaction as well as profitability (*carrier.com*). In summer 2001, Carrier teamed up with IBM to create a Web-enabled air conditioner that allows customers to turn on their home air conditioners before they reach home. Commands are given from cellphones or PCs, through *myappliance.com*. The system also can monitor performance for early detection of problems. ●

Benefits	Limitations	Manager's Checklist 12.2
• *Increased output and productivity:* Many tasks (e.g., diagnosis) can be performed much faster. • *Increased quality and reliability:* Consistent output, lower error rate, important data not overlooked. • *Capture of scarce expertise:* Top experts' knowledge is captured for dissemination to many. • *Ability to operate in hazardous environment:* ES can be installed on robots that operate in toxic and other dangerous environments. • *Improved customer service:* Fast access to information and to FAQs facilitates customer service by help-desk employees. • *Humanlike intelligence:* Can make other computer systems smarter and more powerful when embedded in them. • *Facilitated fault tolerance:* Can work with incomplete input information and generate good conclusions even if some input data are missing. • *Complex problem solving and decision making:* Can integrate multiple opinions, quickly analyze data, and suggest solutions. • *Training capabilities:* Can simulate decisions and explain reasoning behind the decisions. • *Reduction of cycle time and downtime:* Advice is available anywhere, at any time, and analysis can be performed quickly. • *Embedded systems*: ESs are easily embedded in thousands of electrical, mechanical, and IT systems.	• *Limited expertise:* Knowledge to be captured is not always readily available; expertise can be hard to extract from humans. In some instances, experts may refuse to contribute their knowledge, or may contribute incorrect or incomplete knowledge. • *No single correct solution:* The approach of each expert to a given situation may be different, yet correct. • *Natural cognitive limits:* Users of expert systems may not use the benefits of the system to the fullest extent because of limited understanding. • *Narrowly defined subject areas:* ES works well only for certain tasks such as diagnosing a malfunction in a machine. • *Occasional incorrect recommendations:* Many expert systems have no independent means of checking whether their conclusions are reasonable or correct. • *Limited vocabulary, or jargon:* The terminology that experts use for expressing facts and relations is frequently not understood by others. • *Cost*: Help in building ESs is frequently required from knowledge engineers who are rare and expensive. • *Lack of trust by end users:* Users may not trust a machine. • *Bias*: Knowledge transfer is subject to perceptual and judgmental biases. • *Liability issues:* Liability for bad advice provided by an ES is difficult to assess.	The Benefits and Limitations of Expert Systems

Benefits and Limitations of Expert Systems

Why have ESs become popular? Because of the large number of capabilities and benefits they provide at a reasonable cost. However, available ES methodologies are not always straightforward and effective, and some problems have slowed the commercial spread of ES. Despite some limitations, though, the use of ES is growing rapidly. The major benefits and limitations are compiled in Manager's Checklist 12.2 (on page 399).

The Process and Components of Expert Systems

The process in which expert systems are constructed and used is indicated in Figure 12.1 and described here. The major component parts of expert systems shown in the figure are also discussed.

The process of ES.   The process of ES can be divided into two parts: the system development environment and the consultation environment. The *development environment* (shown on the left side of Figure 12.1) is the part in which the ES is constructed. The *consultation environment* (shown on the right side of Figure 12.1) describes how advice is rendered to the users.

The development process starts with a knowledge engineer, who can also be the system builder, acquiring knowledge from experts and/or documented sources. This knowledge is programmed in the system's knowledge base together with facts about the subject area (domain), usually in terms of "if–then" rules.

In the consultation environment, the user contacts the system via the user interface to ask for advice. The ES collects information from the user, usually by asking questions about symptoms and conditions, and then activates the inference engine, which searches the knowledge base for recommended actions. An example of a consultation is provided in IT's About Business 12.3.

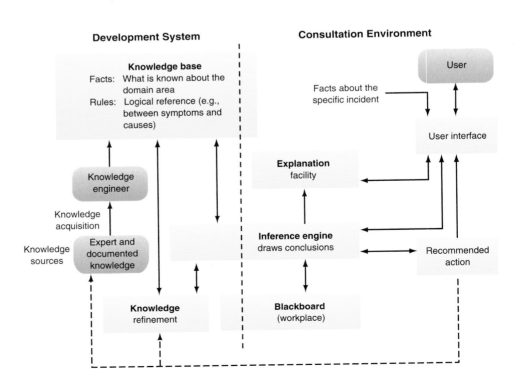

Figure 12.1 *Structure and process of expert systems.*

IT's About Business

exsys.com   **MKT**

Box 12.3:   How to select an advertising medium—a sample of an ES consultation

This prototype system will attempt to provide recommendation(s) on the advertising mix so as to maximize the client's product exposure in the market. Currently, the system makes recommendations on only two types of advertising media: television and newspaper.

Sample Printout of Consultation: The system will ask the user several questions, such as the one shown below, to find the requirements and/or symptoms of the problem.

```
EXSYS Pro ══════ You may select ONLY ONE value ══════

      Client prefer
      1    Only TV media
      2    Only Newspaper media
      3    More TV media
      4    More Newspaper media
      5    No preference indicated




                    ↕ ►► Why
```
Enter the value number<s> or select with arrow keys and press <ENTER>
WHY QUIT <H>-help Memo <F10>

The user asks the computer "Why do you need this information?" The computer answers by displaying the pertinent rule (Rule #1).

```
EXSYS Pro ═══════ RULE NUMBER: 1 ═══════

   IF:
       <1> Client prefer ONLY TV media
   THEN:
        All budget on TV - Confidence=8/10

   NOTE:  The client is always right. We should always try to meet the
   client's expectations. If the client prefers only TV as the
   advertising medium for product exposure, we should accommodate it.



```
IF line # for derivation <K>-known data <C>-choices
↑or↓ - prev. or next rule <J>-jump <H>-help <F10>-Memo <ENTER>-Done:

The computer continues with questions such as:

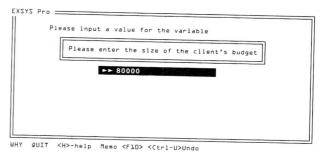

```
EXSYS Pro ═══

      Please input a value for the variable

      ┌─────────────────────────────────────────┐
      │ Please enter the size of the client's budget │
      └─────────────────────────────────────────┘
           ►► 80000


```
WHY   QUIT   <H>-help   Memo <F10> <Ctrl-U>Undo

After the user has answered all questions, the ES displays the recommendations:

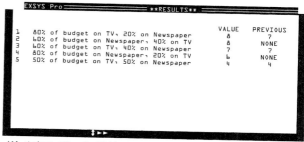

```
EXSYS Pro══════════════════ **RESULTS** ═══════════════

                                              VALUE   PREVIOUS
   1    80% of budget on TV, 20% on Newspaper     8        7
   2    60% of budget on Newspaper, 40% on TV     8      NONE
   3    60% of budget on TV, 40% on Newspaper     7        7
   4    80% of budget on Newspaper, 20% on TV     6      NONE
   5    50% of budget on TV, 50% on Newspaper     4        4


                    ↕ ►►
```
All choices <A> only if >1 <G> Print <P>   Change/rerun <C>
Rules used <line #> Quit/save <Q> Help <H> Memo <F10> Done <D>

Source: Printouts were generated with software from Exsys Inc. (*exsys.com*).

Questions

1. How can this system be adapted for electronic commerce?

2. Would you trust the recommendations of this system more than those offered by human experts? Why or why not?

The components of ES.   The following major components exist in an expert system: a knowledge base, a memory area called the blackboard, an inference engine, a user interface, and an explanation facility. The functions of these components are briefly described here.

- The *knowledge base* contains knowledge necessary for understanding, formulating, and solving a specific class of problems. It includes two basic elements: (1) facts, such as the problem and its various states, and (2) rules, that direct the use of knowledge to solve the specific class of problems.

- The *blackboard* is an area of working memory set aside for the description of a current problem, as specified by the input data; it is also used for storing intermediate results. It is a temporary database used by the inference engine to execute its tasks.

- The "brain" of the ES is the *inference engine*, which is essentially a computer program that provides a methodology for reasoning and formulating conclusions.
- The *user interface* in ES allows for user–computer dialogue, which can be best carried out in a natural language, usually presented as questions and answers, and sometimes supplemented by graphics. The question-and-answer dialogue triggers the inference engine to match the problem symptoms with the knowledge in the knowledge base and to generate advice.
- The *explanation subsystem* can trace responsibility for conclusions to their source, which is crucial both in the transfer of expertise and in problem solving. This subsystem explains the ES's behavior by interactively answering questions such as the following: Why was a certain question asked by the expert system? How was a certain conclusion reached? Why was a certain alternative rejected? What is the plan to reach the solution?

Human experts have a kind of *knowledge-refining* system with which they analyze their own performance, learn from it, and improve it for future consultations. Similarly, such evaluation is necessary in computerized learning so that the program will be able to improve by analyzing the reasons for its success or failure. Such a component is not currently available in commercial expert systems, but it is being developed in experimental expert systems.

Illustrative Applications

Expert systems are in use today in all types of organizations. They are especially useful in certain generic categories, displayed in Table 12.2. The following examples illustrate the diversity and nature of ES applications.

Table 12. 2   Generic Categories of Expert Systems

Category	Task or Problem Addressed
1. Interpretation	Inferring situation descriptions from observations
2. Prediction	Inferring likely consequences of given situations
3. Diagnosis	Inferring system malfunctions from observations
4. Design/configuration	Configuring objects under constraints
5. Planning	Developing plans to achieve goal(s)
6. Monitoring	Comparing observations to plans and flagging exceptions
7. Debugging	Detecting problems and inconsistencies and prescribing remedies for malfunctions
8. Repair	Executing a plan to administer a prescribed remedy
9. Instruction	Monitoring performance, diagnosing, debugging, and correcting learning
10. Control	Monitoring system behavior; interpreting, predicting, repairing, and sometimes alerting operators
11. Data analysis	Quantitiative and qualitative analysis of complex data
12. Customer/product support	Solving help-desk problems
13. Decision support	Interactive advisory systems

EXAMPLES

The U.S. Treasury fights criminals with an expert system.   One of the major tasks of the U.S. Financial Crime Enforcement Network (FinCEN), an agency of the U.S. Department of the Treasury, is to prevent and detect money laundering. One area of investigation is cash transactions over $10,000, which all banks must report. The problem is that there are more than 200,000 such transactions every week (more than 12,000,000 per year). FinCEN does not have the budget or the staff to conduct the analysis necessary to manually examine all of these transactions.

The practical solution is the use of a rule-based expert system that contains the expertise of FinCEN's top experts. The expert system is used to automatically detect suspicious transactions and changes in transaction patterns. Then, these are checked manually. Since its inception in 1993, the expert system has helped to uncover cases of money-laundering activities valued at over $250 million annually.

Ticket auditing at Northwest Airlines.   When Northwest Airlines (NWA) acquired Republic Airlines, its volume of operations increased to 70,000 tickets per day. These tickets needed to be audited by comparing a copy of each ticket against fare information, including travel agent commissions. Manual comparison was slow and expensive. Therefore, only *samples* of the tickets (about 1%) were audited. The sample indicated an error rate of about 10 percent (usually a loss to the airline).

NWA's solution to this problem was to build a ticket-auditing ES that scans all tickets electronically and stores the information in a database. Another database stores all the fares and commission agreements. Then the expert system goes to work. The ES first determines the correct fare, using only 250 rules. The most favorable commission to travel agents is determined, and any discrepancy results in a report to the agent with a debit or credit and an appropriate explanation. The system also provides information for marketing, contract management, planning, and control. The reduction in agent errors saves NWA about $10 million annually. ●

Expert Systems and the Internet/Intranets

The relationship between expert systems and the Internet and intranets is a two-way street. The Net supports ES (and other AI) applications, and expert systems support the Net.

One of the justifications for an ES is the potential to provide knowledge and advice to large numbers of users. The widespread use of the Internet and intranets provides the opportunity to disseminate expertise and knowledge to mass audiences. By disseminating knowledge to many users, the cost per user becomes small, making an ES very attractive. Implementing expert systems (and other intelligent systems) as knowledge servers, it becomes economically feasible and profitable to publish expertise on the Net, as the following examples demonstrate.

EXAMPLES

OSHA uses an expert system.   The U.S. Department of Labor Occupational Safety and Health Administration (OSHA) has an up-and-running Web-based ES. The system provides guidance to help employers protect workers from the hazards of entry into permit-required confined spaces. The system helps determine if a space is covered by OSHA's regulation on such spaces. For example, by going to the site (*osha.gov*) and using the Web browser interface, you can see if you need a special government permit to work in your room. (See Problem-Solving Activity 2 at the end of the chapter.)

Customer service online in Japan. Ebara Manufacturing, a Japanese pump manufacturer, produces several thousand kinds of pumps for many industries. Traditionally, customers would just ask for a pump. Sales personnel had to figure out what kind was really needed. As products got more numerous and sophisticated, this manual system started to break down. Ebara fixed this problem with an online expert system. The system takes customers through a series of questions that connect their needs to specific products, often in less than a minute. ●

Before you go on . . .

1. List and briefly describe the major components of an ES.

2. What are the potential advantages of an ES?

3. List the 13 generic categories of an ES.

12.3 OTHER INTELLIGENT SYSTEMS

An expert system's major objective is to provide expert advice. However, expert systems can be used only for the special situations for which they have been developed. Other intelligent systems can broaden the range of applications. Four such technologies are described next.

Natural Language Processing and Voice Technology

Typically, when you want to tell a computer what to do, you type commands on the keyboard using predetermined commands, or you click on an icon. In responding to your commands, the computer outputs message symbols or other short, cryptic notes of information. Many problems would be minimized or even eliminated if we could communicate with the computer in our own languages, rather than the command-language that at this point is the necessary intermediary. We would simply type in directions, instructions, or information in our natural language. Better yet, we would converse with the computer using voice. The computer would be smart enough to interpret the input, regardless of its format. *Natural language processing (NLP)* refers to communicating with a computer in English or whatever language you speak.

To understand a natural language inquiry, a computer must have the knowledge to analyze and then interpret the input. This may include linguistic knowledge about words, domain (subject area) knowledge, common-sense knowledge, and even knowledge about the users and their goals. Once the computer understands the input, it can take the desired action. In this section we briefly discuss applications of NLP programs, voice recognition, voice portals, and voice generation.

Applications of natural language processing. Natural language processing programs have been applied in several areas. The most important are human–computer interfaces (mainly to databases), abstracting and summarizing text, grammar analysis, translation of a natural language to another natural language, translation of a computer language to another computer language, speech understanding, and letter composition. By far the most dominant use of NLP is in interfaces, or "front-ends," to other software packages, especially databases.

Voice (speech) recognition and understanding. Voice (or speech) recognition is a process that allows users to communicate with a computer by speaking to it. The term *speech recognition* is sometimes applied only to the first part of the process—recognizing words that have been spoken without necessarily interpreting their meanings. The other part of the process, wherein the meaning of speech is ascertained, is called *speech understanding*. It may be possible to understand the meaning of a spoken sentence without actually recognizing every word, and vice versa. When a speech recognition system is combined with a natural language processing system, the result is an overall system that not only recognizes voice input but also understands it.

The ultimate goal of voice recognition is to allow a computer to understand the natural speech of any human speaker at least as well as a human listener could understand it. In addition to the fact that this is the most natural method of communication, voice recognition offers several other advantages, as shown in Manager's Checklist 12.3.

There are a few limitations to voice recognition. The major limitation is the inability to recognize long sentences, or to recognize speech fast enough. The better the system in this respect, the higher the cost. An additional limitation of speech recognition systems is that they do not (yet) interface well with icons and windows, so speech may need to be combined with the keyboard operation, which slows down the system.

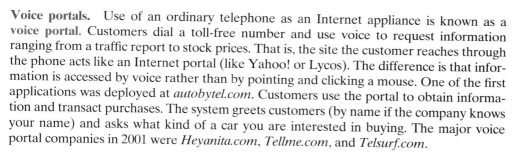

Voice portals. Use of an ordinary telephone as an Internet appliance is known as a **voice portal**. Customers dial a toll-free number and use voice to request information ranging from a traffic report to stock prices. That is, the site the customer reaches through the phone acts like an Internet portal (like Yahoo! or Lycos). The difference is that information is accessed by voice rather than by pointing and clicking a mouse. One of the first applications was deployed at *autobytel.com*. Customers use the portal to obtain information and transact purchases. The system greets customers (by name if the company knows your name) and asks what kind of a car you are interested in buying. The major voice portal companies in 2001 were *Heyanita.com*, *Tellme.com*, and *Telsurf.com*.

Voice generation (voice synthesis). Natural language *generation* strives to allow computers to produce ordinary English language, on the screen or by voice so that people

---

Manager's Checklist 12.3

Benefits of Voice Recognition

- *Ease of access:* Many more people can speak than can type. As long as communication with a computer depends on developing typing skills, many people may not be able to use computers effectively.
- *Speed:* Even the most competent typists speak more quickly than they type. It is estimated that the average person can speak twice as quickly as a proficient typist can type.
- *Manual freedom:* There are many situations in which computers might be useful to people whose hands are otherwise occupied, such as product assemblers, pilots of military aircraft, and busy executives.
- *Remote access:* Many computers are set up to be accessed remotely by telephone. If a remote database includes speech recognition capabilities, you could retrieve information by issuing oral commands into a telephone.
- *Accuracy:* In typing information, people are prone to make mistakes, especially in spelling. These are minimized with voice input.

can understand computers more easily. The technology by which computers speak is known as **voice synthesis**. The synthesis of voice by computer differs from the simple playback of a prerecorded voice by either analog or digital means. As the term *synthesis* implies, sounds that make up words and phrases are constructed electronically from basic sound components and can be made to form any desired voice pattern.

In July 2001, AT&T Labs started selling speech software called Natural Voices that is so good at reproducing the sound, inflections, and intonations of a human voice that it can recreate voices—even the voices of long-dead celebrities or any one for which a sample voice is available. Priced at thousands of dollars, the software is selling to producers of animated movies, publishers of video games, car manufacturers that provide voice driving directions, and books-on-tape publishers.

Applications of voice technology.   As voice recognition and synthesis technology has improved in recent years, many applications have been developed for commercial use. Table 12.3 lists a sampling of such applications via input or output devices; two more are presented in more detail below.

Table 12.3   Sample of Voice Technology Applications

Company	Application
Scandinavian Airlines, other airlines	Answering inquiries about reservations, schedules, lost baggage, etc.[a]
Citibank, many other banks	Informing credit card holders about balances and credits, providing bank account balances and other information to customers[a]
Delta Dental Plan (CA)	Verifying coverage information[a]
Federal Express	Requesting pickups, responding to inquiries about delivery of specific shipments[a,b]
Illinois Bell, other telephone companies	Giving information about services, receiving orders[a,b]
Domino's Pizza	Enabling stores to order supplies, providing price information[a,b]
General Electric, Rockwell International, Austin Rover, Westpoint Pepperell, Eastman Kodak	Allowing inspectors to report results of quality assurance tests[b]
Cara Donna Provisions	Allowing receivers of shipments to report weights and inventory levels of various meats and cheeses[b]
Weidner Insurance, AT&T	Conducting market research and telemarketing[b]
U.S. Department of Energy, Idaho National Engineering Laboratory, Honeywell	Notifying people of emergencies detected by sensors[a]
New Jersey Department of Education	Notifying parents when students are absent and about cancellation of classes[a]
Kaiser-Permanente Health Foundation (HMO)	Calling patients to remind them of appointments, summarizing and reporting results[a]
Car manufacturers	Activating radios, heaters, and so on, by voice[b]
Texoma Medical Center	Logging in and out by voice to payroll department[b]
St. Elizabeth's Hospital	Prompting doctors in the emergency room to conduct all necessary tests, reporting results by doctors[a,b]
Hospital Corporation of America	Sending and receiving patient data by voice, searching for doctors, preparing schedules and medical records[a,b]

[a]Via an output device.

[b]Via an input device.

EXAMPLES

Minnesota wrestles with tax inquiries.   With limited staffing and many Minnesota residents without touch-tone dialing service, the Department of Revenue needed to find an innovative solution to meet its increasing tax inquiry phone load and expand its service. The department put speech recognition technology into place with an interactive voice system via the telephone. As a result, it was able to respond immediately to an additional 100,000 taxpayer phone inquiries per year that could not have been handled otherwise.

American Express books flights.   American Express Travel Related Services (AETRS) uses a voice recognition system that allows its customers to check and book domestic flights by talking to a computer over the phone. The system asks customers questions such as: Where do you want to travel to? From where? When? and so on. The system can recognize 350 city and airport names, and it lets callers use more than 10,000 different ways to identify a location. Compared to telephone service by an operator, reservation transaction cost is reduced by 50 percent. The average transaction time is reduced from 7 to 2 minutes. AETRS offers a similar service on the Web. ●

Neural Computing

The tools of AI described so far have been mostly restricted to *stored* knowledge and logic. A different approach is intelligent systems that use architecture that mimics certain processing capabilities of the brain. The results are knowledge representations and processing based on *massive parallel processing* (executing multiple processing instructions simultaneously) rather than sequential information processing, fast retrieval of large amounts of information, and the ability to recognize patterns based on experiences. One technology that attempts to achieve such results is called **neural computing** or **artificial neural networks (ANNs)**.

An artificial neural network is a computer model that emulates a biological neural network. Today's neural computing uses a very limited set of concepts from biological

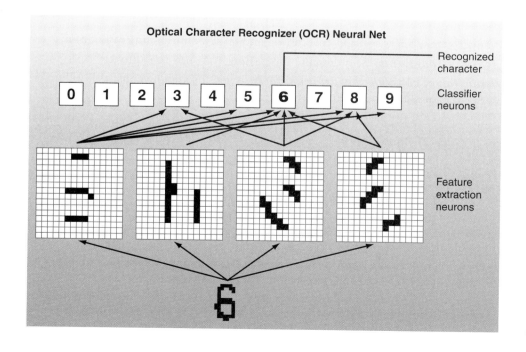

Figure 12.2 *Neural Internet-based optical character recognizer. It analyzes locations of input images to identify the number 6.*

neural systems to implement software simulations of massively parallel processes. An artificial neuron receives inputs analogous to the electrochemical impulses that biological neurons receive from other neurons. The neurons in an ANN receive information from other neurons or from external sources, transform the information, and pass it on to other neurons or as external outputs.

The value of neural network technology includes its usefulness for **pattern recognition**, learning, and the interpretation of incomplete inputs. Figure 12.2 (page 407) is a simplified explanation of how a neural network can recognize characters. Sets of neurons extract features from the input images. (Here, neurons extract the locations of vertical, horizontal, and diagonal strokes.) The locations of these features indicate possible choices of the character class. Most of the evidence shows that 6 is the best choice.

Neural networks have the potential to provide some of the human characteristics of problem solving that are difficult to simulate using the logical, analytical techniques of DSSs or even expert systems. For example, neural networks can analyze large quantities of data to discover patterns and characteristics in situations where the logic or rules are not known. An example would be *loan applications*. By reviewing many historical cases of applicants' responses to questionnaires and the granting decisions (yes or no), the ANN can create "patterns" or "profiles" of applications that should be approved, or those that should be denied. A new application is matched against the pattern. If it comes close enough, the computer classifies it as a "yes" or "no"; otherwise it goes to a human to decide. Applications can thus be processed more rapidly. The benefits of neural networks are summarized in Manager's Checklist 12.4.

Specific business areas that are well-suited to the use of ANNs are:

- *Data mining:* Finding data in large and complex databases, as explained in Chapter 11
- *Tax fraud:* Identifying, enhancing, and finding irregularities
- *Financial services:* Identification of patterns in stock market data and assistance in bond trading strategies, mortgage underwriting, and foreign rate exchange forecast
- *Loan application evaluation:* Judging worthiness of loan applications based on patterns in previous application information (e.g., customer credit scoring)
- *Solvency prediction:* Assessing the strengths and weaknesses of corporations and predicting possible failures
- *New product analysis:* Sales forecasting and targeted marketing evaluation
- *Airline management:* Seat demand forecasting and crew scheduling
- *Prediction of consumer behavior on the Internet:* Predicting consumer behavior in order to plan e-commerce advertising

Manager's Checklist 12.4

Benefits of Neural Networks

- *Pattern recognition:* Can analyze large quantities of data to establish patterns and characteristics in situations where the logic or rules are not known.
- *Fault tolerance:* Since there are many processing nodes, damage to a few nodes or links does not bring the system to a halt.
- *Generalization:* When a neural network is presented with an incomplete or previously unseen input, it can generalize to produce a reasonable response.
- *Adaptability:* The network learns in new environments. New cases are used immediately to retrain the program and keep it updated.
- *Forecasting capabilities:* Similar to statistics, predictions can be made based on historical data.

- **Evaluation of personnel and job candidates:** Matching personnel data to job requirements and performance criteria
- **Resource allocation based on historical, experiential data:** Finding allocations that will maximize outputs
- **Foreign exchange rate evaluation:** Evaluating exchange rates of various currencies, including country risk rating
- **Identifying takeover targets:** Predicting which companies are most likely to be acquired by other companies
- **Stocks, bonds, and commodity selection and trading:** Analyzing various investment alternatives, including pricing of initial public offerings
- **Signature validation:** Matching against previous signatures
- **Human resources prediction:** Predicting employee performance and behavior and analyzing personnel requirements
- **Credit card fraud detection:** Detecting fraud by analyzing purchasing patterns.

For a more specific example of the use of neural network technology in a credit card fraud detection application, see IT's About Business 12.4.

Case-based Reasoning

The idea of **case-based reasoning (CBR)** is to adapt successful solutions used in the past in order to solve new problems. Case-based reasoning first finds the solutions that solved problems similar to the current problem. It then adapts the previous solution

---

IT's About Business   visa.com   ACC   FIN

Box 12.4:   Visa cracks down on credit card fraud

Only 0.2% of Visa International's revenues in 1995 were lost to fraud, but when that percentage means a loss of $655 million, it is well worth addressing. In 1996, Visa began using neural network technology in order to reverse the number of fraudulent transactions. By 2002 the company was using the system globally.

Most people stick to well-established patterns of card use and only rarely splurge on expensive nonessentials. Neural networks are designed to notice when a card that is usually used to buy gasoline once a week is suddenly used to buy a number of tickets to the latest theater premiere on Broadway.

Bank of America field-tested Visa's cardholder risk identification system (CRIS) and believes that the system cuts fraudulent card use by up to two-thirds. The Toronto Dominion Bank found that losses were reduced, and overall customer service improved, with the introduction of neural computing. Another bank recorded savings of $5.5 million in six months. Visa member banks cut their losses by more than 16 percent in the first year of the system's use. With numbers like that, the $2 million Visa spent to implement CRIS certainly seems worth the investment. In fact, Visa says, CRIS paid for itself in less than a year.

In 1995, CRIS conducted more than 16 billion transactions. In 2002, VisaNet (a data warehouse and e-mail operation) and CRIS handled more than 210 billion transactions.

The only downside to CRIS is that occasionally the system prompts a call to a cardholder's spouse when an out-of-the-ordinary item, such as a surprise vacation trip or a diamond ring, is charged. After all, no one wants to spoil surprises for loved ones.

Questions

1. How does the system detect fraud?
2. What is the advantage of CRIS over an automatic check against the balance in the account and against a set of rules such as "Call a human authorizer when the purchase price is more than 200 percent of the average previous bill"?
3. Why do you think neural networks were used but not expert systems?

to fit the current problem, taking into account any differences between the current and previous situations. Finding relevant cases involves several steps: (1) characterizing the input problem by assigning appropriate features to it, (2) retrieving from memory the cases with those features, and (3) picking the case or cases that best match the input.

Case-based reasoning has proved to be an extremely effective approach in complex cases. The basic justification for the use of CBR is that it processes the right information retrieved at the right time. Case-based reasoning can be used by itself or can be combined with other reasoning paradigms. Target applications include tactical planning, political analysis, situation assessment, legal planning, diagnosis, fraud detection, design/configuration, message classification, and complex searches. Analog Devices' IT system described in the opening case is an example of case-based reasoning.

Fuzzy Logic

Fuzzy logic deals with uncertainties by simulating the process of qualitative human reasoning, allowing the computer to behave less precisely and logically than do conventional computers. The rationale behind this approach is that decision making is not always a matter of true or false, black and white. It often involves gray areas where the terms *approximately*, *possible,* and *similar* are more appropriate.

Take, for example, the variable "height." Most people would agree that if you are above 6 feet, you are tall. Similarly, if your height is less than 5 feet, you are short. But between 6 feet and 5.75 feet, there is less probability that you will be considered tall. Similarly, between 5 and 5.25 feet some will consider you short. Notice that in the area between 5.25 and 5.75 feet you have a chance for being considered either short or tall.

Currently there are only a few examples of fuzzy logic applications in business, but the results are significant improvements in productivity. More often, fuzzy logic is used together with other intelligent systems, as illustrated in the following example.

EXAMPLE

Developing marketing strategy.   An international investment firm used IT systems to develop marketing strategy. Developing marketing strategy is a complex process performed sequentially, with contributions from corporate experts. Numerous marketing strategy models were developed over the years to support the process. Unfortunately, most of the models supported only one goal (e.g., to perform forecasting). However, one firm developed a system that integrates expert systems, fuzzy logic, and ANN, shown in Figure 12.3, to solve this problem. The systems components are:

- *Neural networks.* These are used to predict future market share and growth.
- *Expert systems.* These provide intelligent advice on developing market strategy to individuals and to a planning team.
- *Fuzzy logic.* This helps managers handle uncertainties and fuzziness of data and information.

The integration of the technologies helps in sharing information, coordination, and evaluation. The system is designed to support both individuals and groups. ●

Any of the intelligent systems described in this and the previous sections can also be used as a knowledge component of an *intelligent agent,* the topic we turn to in the next section.

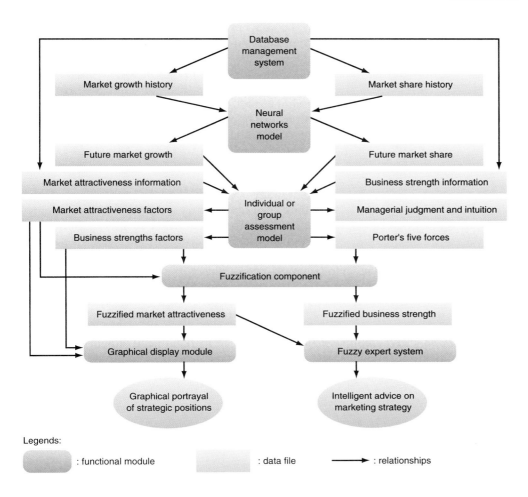

Figure 12.3 *The architecture of hybrid intelligent systems.* [Source: *S. Li, "The Development of a Hybrid Intelligent System for Developing Marketing Decision Strategy,"* Decision Support Systems, *January 2000, Fig. 1, p.399. Reprinted with permission from Elsevier Science.*]

Before you go on . . .

1. Describe natural language processing and its major benefits.

2. List the major benefits of voice recognition.

3. What are the major benefits of neural computing? What are some popular applications of ANNs?

4. Define case-based reasoning and fuzzy logic.

12.4   INTELLIGENT AGENTS

Intelligent agents (IAs) have the potential to become one of the most important tools of information technology in the twenty-first century. IAs can alleviate the most critical limitation of the Internet—information glut or overload—and can facilitate electronic commerce. Before we look at their capabilities, let's determine what we mean by IAs.

The term *agent* is derived from the concept of agency, which means employing someone to act on your behalf. A computerized agent represents a person and interacts with others to accomplish a predefined task. Several names are used to describe intelligent agents: *software agents, wizards, knowbots,* and *softbots.* The names reflect the nature of the agent. A good working definition is this: An **intelligent agent** is a software entity that senses its environment and then carries out some operations on behalf of a user (or a program), with a certain degree of autonomy, and in so doing employs knowledge or representation of the user's goals or desires.

Characteristics of Intelligent Agents

There are several traits or abilities that many people think of when they discuss intelligent agents: capability to work on their own (autonomy); exhibition of goal-oriented behavior; mobility (transportable over networks); dedication to a single repetitive task; ability to interact with humans, systems, and other agents; inclusion of a knowledge base; and ability to learn. Although not all intelligent agents have all of these capabilities, they are very useful in facilitating tasks such as the following.

Information access and navigation.   Information access is today's major application of intelligent agents, and it is done by use of different search engines.

Decision support and empowerment.   Knowledge workers need support, especially in decision-making. Intelligent agents can facilitate decision making and empower employees, as shown in IT's About Business 12.5.

Repetitive office activities.   There is a pressing need to automate repetitive tasks performed by administrative and clerical personnel in functional areas, such as sales or customer support, in order to reduce labor costs and increase office productivity.

IT's About Business   *edify.com*

Box 12.5:   Empowering employees by using intelligent agents

Fringe benefits are frequently likened to a cafeteria— people mix and match what they like within the constraints of what is available and how much they can use. The management of fringe benefits is a very resource-intensive process, especially when thousands of employees are involved. Nike and Signet Bank both installed intelligent agent software that empowers employees to manage their own fringe benefits selections online. Employees access the human resources databases and conduct activities such as selecting and changing benefits or making charitable contributions through payroll deductions.

The software agent that supports these activities is called Electronic Workforce (from Edify Corp.). It enables employers to delegate to employees some time-consuming and repetitive tasks that were previously conducted by human resources (HR) employees. Employees enter and delete data, command the computer to perform certain transactions, and interpret information.

If they make mistakes or request benefits for which they are not eligible, the agent immediately alerts them to the problem. Previously, paperwork would have to be routed to an employee for corrections and then back to the HR department. The use of the agent enables companies to increase benefits options and employee satisfaction, with the same or even fewer human resources employees. Some new applications involve speech recognition capabilities and enhanced customer e-mail.

Questions

1. Can you imagine what would happen if there were no agents in this case?

2. How can an agent know that an employee made a mistake?

3. Enter *edify.com* and examine the new capabilities of Electronic Workforce and other agent-based products.

Today, labor costs are estimated to be as much as 60 percent of the total cost of information delivery.

Mundane personal activities.   In our fast-paced society, time-strapped individuals need new ways to minimize the time spent on routine personal tasks like booking airline tickets. One specific form of intelligent agents is the *voice-activated interface agent* that reduces the burden on the user of having to explicitly command the computer.

Search and retrieval.   It is not economically possible to directly manipulate a database system in a business setting that involves millions of data objects. Users have to delegate to agents the tasks of searching and cost comparison. These agents perform the tedious, time-consuming, and repetitive tasks of searching databases, retrieving and filtering information, and delivering results to the user.

Electronic commerce agents.   Some of the agents described earlier are used in various EC activities (see Chapter 9).

Domain experts.   It is advisable to capture costly expertise, model it, and make it widely available. "Expert" software agents can be models of real-world experts, such as translators, lawyers, diplomats, union negotiators, and even clergy.

Management activities.   Intelligent agents can even be used to assist managers in performing their activities. Some management-oriented tasks that an agent can do are: advise, alert, broadcast, browse, critique, distribute, enlist, empower, explain, filter, guide, identify, match, monitor, navigate, negotiate, organize, present, query, report, remind, retrieve, schedule, search, secure, solicit, store, suggest, summarize, teach, translate, and watch.

Mobile Agents

Agents may be either static, residing on the client machine to manage a user interace, for instance, or mobile. *Mobility* is the degree to which the agents travel through networks. **Mobile agents** can move from one Internet site to another and can send data to and retrieve data from the user, who can focus on other work in the meantime. This can be very helpful to users. For example, if users want to continuously monitor an electronic auction that takes a few days, they essentially would have to be online continuously for days.

Table 12.4   Applications of Intelligent Agents (Non-Internet)

Application	Description
User interface agents	Monitor usage and suggest improvement. Example: Microsoft's wizards.
Operating systems agents	Add accounts, do group management, manage access, add/remove programs and devices, monitor licenses.
Spreadsheet agents	Offer suggestions for improvements. Can tutor novice users. Sometimes called *wizards*.
Workflow and task management agents	Administer workflow management—monitor activities, alert, and remind. Example: Ginkgo from IBM. (See *networking.ibm.com/iag/iaghome*, and IBM's intelligent agent custom services.)
Software development agents	Assist in routine activities such as data filtering.

Mobile agents that automatically watch auctions and stocks for you are readily available. Another example of a mobile agent is one that travels from site to site, looking for information on a certain stock as instructed by the user. When the stock price hits a certain level, or if there is news about the stock, the agent alerts the user.

Applications of Intelligent Agents

Most intelligent agent applications can be classified into three categories: (1) Internet agents, (2) electronic commerce agents, and (3) other agents. The first two categories are illustrated in Chapters 7 and 9. "Other agents" are shown in Table 12.4 (page 413).

Before you go on . . .

1. Define intelligent agents.

2. List the major characteristics of intelligent agents.

3. List some typical applications of intelligent agents.

12.5   VIRTUAL REALITY: AN EMERGING TECHNOLOGY

What Is Virtual Reality?

There is no universal definition of **virtual reality (VR)**. The most common definitions imply that virtual reality is interactive, uses computer-generated, three-dimensional graphics, and is delivered to the user through a head-mounted display. Defined technically, VR is an "environment and/or technology that provides artificially generated *sensory cues* sufficient to engender in the user some willing suspension of disbelief." The user gets the feeling of physically being in an environment by interacting with a simulation of it.

The benefits of virtual reality are obvious: More than one person and even a large group can share and interact in the same environment. VR thus can be a powerful medium for communication, collaborative entertainment, and learning. The user can grasp and move virtual objects. In VR a person "believes" that what he or she is doing is real, even though it is artificially created. This capability can be utilized for gaining a competitive business advantage.

Sophisticated VR systems simulate sight, sound, and touch and combine these senses with computer-generated input to users' eyes, ears, and skin. By using a head-mounted display, gloves, and a bodysuit, or by means of large projected images in simulator cabs, users can "enter" and interact with artificially generated environments. For example, Figure 12.4 shows a skier in the NEC Corporation (Japan) Lab. NEC used the laboratory to develop a ski simulator, which is available in amusement centers and and is also used for training.

Business Applications of Virtual Reality

Extensive use of virtual reality is expected in marketing. For example, Tower Records *(towerrecords.com)* offers a virtual music store on the Internet; customers can "meet" in front of the store, go inside, and preview CDs and videos. They select and purchase their choices electronically and interactively from a sales associate. Similarly, virtual supermarkets could spark interest in home grocery shopping. In the future, shoppers

Figure 12.4   *Developing virtual skiing in Japan.*

Table 12.5   Examples of Virtual Reality Applications

Industry	Applications
Manufacturing	• Worker training • Design, testing, and virtual prototyping of products and processes • Engineering and ergonomic analysis • Simulation of assembly, production, and maintenance
Transportation	• Virtual aircraft mockups • New-car design and testing of cars in virtual accidents • Simulation of flying first class in airplanes
Finance	• View stock prices and characteristics
Architecture	• Display of building and other structures
Military	• Training (pilots, astronauts, drivers) and battlefield simulation
Medicine	• Training of surgeons (with simulators) and planning surgeries • Planning physical therapy
Marketing	• Store and product display • Electronic shopping

will enter a virtual supermarket, walk through the virtual aisles, select virtual products, and put them in a virtual cart; actual groceries will later be delivered to customers' homes. Several real estate companies use VR to present properties even before they are built. Applications in these and other areas are shown in Table 12.5.

Virtual reality is just beginning to move into many business applications. Three-dimensional worlds on the Internet should prove popular because they provide metaphors to which everyone can relate.

Before you go on . . .

1. Define virtual reality.

2. List the advantages of virtual reality.

3. Describe some business applications of virtual reality.

12.6 ETHICAL AND GLOBAL ISSUES OF INTELLIGENT SYSTEMS

There are many issues related to the implementation of intelligent systems. We'll discuss three of these issues here: ethical and societal issues, legal issues, and global issues.

Ethical and Societal Issues

In general, scientists and managers are concerned with the possibility of power misuse and harm to people from the use of intelligent systems. Professor Rheingold, a virtual reality pioneer, raised the issue of behavior in a world where the distinction between the real and the virtual is unclear. For example, when the line between reality and virtual reality is blurred, some people might use real weapons with as little thought for the actual consequences as they use virtual ones. Several of the ethical issues discussed in Chapter 15 are directly related to intelligent systems. For example, privacy is a major concern in knowledge bases (who will have access to information stored in the knowledge base?), and experts' knowledge is related to intellectual property.

If you have watched or read any science fiction, you no doubt have found scenarios in which robots turn against humans. Isaac Asimov, a famous science fiction writer, suggested that the following **laws of robotics** be followed in developing robotic applications:

1. A robot may not injure a human being or, through inaction, allow a human to be harmed.

2. A robot must obey orders given by humans except when that conflicts with the first law.

3. A robot must protect its own existence unless that conflicts with the first or second laws.

EXAMPLE

2001: A Space Odyssey's
*HAL computer with friend
Dave.*

Movie Robots.   If you saw the classic science fiction film *2001: A Space Odyssey*, you might remember the astronaut, Dave, saying to the robot (which was named HAL), "Open the pod bay door, HAL." HAL replies, "I'm sorry, Dave, I can't do that." A similar scenario occurred with a robot named David in the movie *Artificial Intelligence (AI)*. As these scenes make clear, computers with intelligent systems might be able to refuse human orders, and they might hurt people. This example relates to the issue of how much decision-making power to delegate to computers and how to guard against malfunctions. ●

The knowledge embedded in intelligent systems is often acquired from human experts. This knowledge is frequently available in terms of rules, some of which are difficult to explain whereas others have not even been tested. Therefore, an ES based on such rules may not be accurate. Furthermore, the use of such rules may damage not only property, but people as well. Like any other knowledge, computerized rules must be tested before they are used and then must be constantly updated and maintained.

Legal Issues

The use of intelligent systems raises interesting legal issues such as:

- What happens if a manager or expert enters an incorrect judgment value into an ES and the result is damage or a disaster?

- Who is liable for wrong advice (or information) provided by an ES? For example, what happens if a physician accepts an incorrect diagnosis made by a computer and performs an act, based on this diagnosis, that results in the death of a patient? Is it the fault of the physician, the knowledge engineer that solicited the expertise, the knowledge contributor, the software manufacturer, the system builder, or some combination of them?

- Who owns the knowledge in a knowledge base?

- Who is an expert? What if several experts disagree?

- Can management force experts to contribute their expertise?

- Should royalties be paid to experts who provide the knowledge to ES, and if so, in what amount?

- What is the value of an expert opinion in court when the expertise is encoded in a computer?

These legal issues are largely not addressed by current laws. There are many pending lawsuits related to IT, the Internet, and e-commerce, some of which are directly related to intelligent systems.

Global Aspects of Intelligent Systems

Intelligent systems are used in many applications related to global trade. Although most intelligent systems, whether used domestically or globally, are similar to any other information system, some do have unique global aspects. The following examples demonstrate the variety of global applications.

Foreign trade.   An expert system that advises companies on how to exploit opportunities related to the NAFTA agreement (which promotes trade among the United States, Mexico, and Canada) is available online (*corporateinformation.com*). For example, the system determines whether a finished product qualifies for preferential tariff treatment, and it helps companies set up buying policies.

Foreign exchange transactions.   An application called the *FS System* advises on foreign exchange trading—trading of the currencies of various nations as their values rise and fall in relation to each other. It contains trading, hedging, and risk-control strategies (*athenagroup.com*). Similarly, *TARA* is an intelligent assistant for traders making foreign exchange transactions. Foreign exchange traders need to consider historical trends, a country's risks, economic directions, and more. Manufacturers Hanover Trust is using this system to facilitate its traders' investment decisions. (For more see *afexco.com*, and *forex-trc.com*.)

Employee training.   Many companies train their employees online before they go to a foreign country. The intelligent systems cut the training time by as much as 50 percent, and employees can be trained anywhere.

Weather forecasting.   *Climatic expert systems* provide long-range climate forecasts for the North Pacific, North Atlantic, North America, Europe, and the European Arctic seas. Such forecasts are critical for global commodity traders. The service is provided for free on the Internet (*onlineweather.com*).

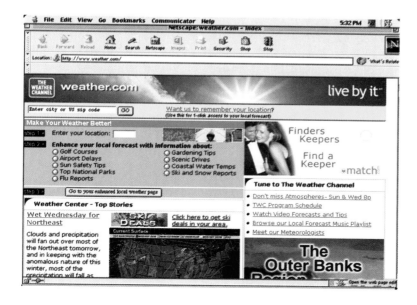

A specialized expert system for weather forecasting.

Automatic language translations.   As countries' borders begin to disappear in global trading, language translation is becoming very important. This topic is very important in e-commerce, where appropriate translation of Web pages is a critical success factor. The use of intelligent systems in language translation has been progressing rapidly since the mid-1990s.

Many other systems and applications are used to facilitate international trade. Several examples were provided earlier (e.g., the use of ES to fight money laundering across international borders, and the use of a hybrid intelligent system for developing global marketing strategy). As international trade is expanding, mainly due to the Internet and trading blocks like the European Union and NAFTA, expertise will be needed in many areas, ranging from legal issues to export and import licenses. Such expertise can be provided to a global audience online. Also, expert systems can provide to users in developing countries the advice of top experts in the fields of medicine, safety, agriculture, and crime fighting.

Before you go on . . .

1. List the laws of robotics.
2. Describe some major legal issues in intelligent systems.
3. Relate intelligent systems to global trade.

www.wiley.com/
college/turban

FOR THE ACCOUNTING MAJOR

Intelligent systems are used extensively in auditing to uncover irregularities. They are also used to uncover and prevent fraud. Today's CPAs use intelligent systems for many of their duties, ranging from risk analysis to cost control. Intelligent agents are also used for several mundane tasks such as managing accounts in operating systems or monitoring employees' Internet usage.

FOR THE FINANCE MAJOR

People have been using computers for decades to solve financially oriented problems. Innovative applications exist in stock market decisions, bond refinancing, debt risk assessment, analysis of financial conditions, business failure prediction, financial forecasting, investment in global markets, and more. Intelligent systems were found to be superior to other computerized methods in many instances. Intelligent agents can facilitate the use of spreadsheets and other computerized systems used in finance. Finally, intelligent systems can help in reducing fraud in credit cards, stocks, and other financial services.

FOR THE MARKETING MAJOR

New marketing approaches such as *targeted marketing* and *marketing transaction databases* are heavily dependent on IT in general and on intelligent systems in particular. Intelligent systems are partially useful in mining customer databases and predicting customer behavior. Successful applications are noted in almost any area of marketing and sales, from analyzing the success of one-to-one advertisement to supporting customer help desks. With the increased importance of customer service, the use of intelligent agents is becoming critical for the provision of fast response.

FOR THE PRODUCTION/OPERATIONS MANAGEMENT MAJOR

Many of the early expert systems were developed in the production/operations management field for tasks ranging from diagnosis of machine failures and prescription of repairs to complex production scheduling and inventory control. Some companies, such as DuPont and Kodak, have deployed hundreds of expert systems in the planning, organizing, and control of their operational systems.

FOR THE HUMAN RESOURCES MANAGEMENT MAJOR

HRM departments use intelligent systems for many applications. For example, intelligent agents can find resumes of applicants posted on the Web and sort them to match needed skills. Expert systems are used in evaluating candidates (tests, interviews). Intelligent systems are used to facilitate training and to support self-management of fringe benefits. Neural computing is used to predict employee performance on the job as well as to predict labor needs. Voice recognition systems provide benefits information to employees.

SUMMARY

❶ Describe artificial intelligence and compare it to conventional computing.
The primary objective of AI is to build computers that will perform tasks that can be characterized as intelligent. The major characteristics of AI are symbolic processing (in contrast with numerical processing in conventional systems), use of heuristics (instead of algorithms), and the application of inference techniques.

❷ Identify the characteristics, structure, benefits, and limitations of expert systems.
Expert systems technology attempts to transfer knowledge from experts and documented sources to the computer's knowledge base, in order to make the knowledge available to nonexperts for the purpose of solving problems quickly and effectively. The inference engine, or thinking mechanism, is a program that uses the knowledge base to solve problems. Expert systems can provide many benefits. The most important are improvement in productivity and/or quality, preservation of scarce expertise, enhancing other systems, coping with incomplete information, and providing training. Limitations of expert systems include the inability to learn from mistakes, the development cost, and legal/ethical issues in their applications.

❸ Describe the major characteristics of natural language processing and voice technologies.
Natural language processing (NLP) provides an opportunity for a user to communicate with a computer in day-to-day spoken language. Speech recognition enables people to communicate with computers by voice. Voice-synthesis technology enables computers to reply in a humanlike voice. Voice portals provide access to the Internet by using voice via telephone. There are many applications and benefits of these emerging technologies.

❹ Describe neural computing and its capabilities.
Neural systems are organized and operated in a way similar to biological neural networks. Artificial neurons receive, process, and deliver information. A group of connected neurons forms an artificial neural network that can be used to discover patterns in historical data and make predictions accordingly. Neural networks are especially useful in data and Web mining in e-commerce.

❺ Define intelligent agents and their role in IT.
Intelligent agents are software entities that can sense the environment and carry out a set of operations with some degree of autonomy, using a knowledge base in

the process. They can perform many mundane tasks, saving a considerable amount of time and improving quality.

❻ **Describe virtual reality.**
Virtual reality is a 3-D interactive computing environment that is beginning to support business simulation applications.

INTERACTIVE LEARNING SESSION

Go to the CD and access Chapter 12: Intelligent Systems in Business. There you will be given a case scenario in which you must interact with an expert system that will make a loan decision. You will have the opportunity to change the parameters based on various economic forecasts and then see the outcomes. You then will choose how much "leeway" you would give the human over the expert system.

www.wiley.com/
college/turban

For additional resources, go to the book's Web site for Chapter 12. There you will find Web resources for the chapter, including links to organizations, people, and technology; "IT's About Business" company links; "What's in IT for Me?" links; and a self-testing Web quiz for Chapter 12.

DISCUSSION QUESTIONS

1. Explain how an ES can distribute (or redistribute) the available knowledge in an organization.

2. What is the difference between voice recognition and voice understanding?

3. Compare and contrast neural computing and conventional computing.

4. Compare and contrast conventional processing with artificial intelligence processing.

5. Review the various tasks that intelligent agents can perform. Do these tasks have anything in common?

6. Deep Blue of IBM defeated the world chess champion, Gary Kasparov, in 1997. If computers cannot think, how is such a defeat possible? Find some recent information about machines playing against humans.

7. Why are neural computing and case-based reasoning viewed as machine learning?

8. How is e-learning related to AI?

9. How is virtual reality related to AI?

PROBLEM-SOLVING ACTIVITIES

1. Lance Eliot made the following comment in *AI Expert* (August 1994, p. 9): "When you log-on to the network, a slew of agents might start watching. If you download a file about plant life, a seed company agent might submit your name for a company mailing. Besides sending junk mail, such spying agents could pick up your habits and preferences and perhaps make assumptions about your private life. It could note what days you get onto the system, how long you stay on, and what part of the country you live in. Is this an invasion of your privacy? Should legislation prevent such usage of intelligent agents? Perhaps a network police (more intelligent agents) could enforce proper network usage."

   a. Prepare arguments to support your perspective on this issue.

   b. Prepare counterarguments on the same issue.

2. Access the U.S. Department of Labor Web site on safety (*osha.gov*). Go to "OSHA etools."

   a. Examine the expert systems available.

   b. Write a report on the capabilities of two of the systems.

3. Airline gate assignment, the responsibility of gate controllers and their assistants, is a complex and demanding task. At O'Hare Airport in Chicago, for example, two gate controllers typically plan berthing for about 400 flights a day at some 50 gates. Flights arrive in clusters for the convenience of customers who must transfer to connecting flights, so the controllers must sometimes accommodate a cluster of 30 or 40 planes in 20 or 30 minutes. To complicate the matter, each flight is scheduled to remain at its gate a different length of time, depending on the

schedules of connecting flights and the amount of servicing needed. Mix those problems with the need to juggle gates constantly because of flight delays caused by weather and other factors, and you get some idea of the challenges.

a. Based on what you learned in this chapter, what is the most appropriate intelligent system that can be used to support the work of the controllers?

b. Why? How could the support be given?

INTERNET ACTIVITIES

1. Prepare a report on the use of ES in a help desk. Review products and customer cases at *4helpdesk.com*, *exsys.com*, and *ebehelpdesk.com*.

2. There is considerable interest in intelligent agents at MIT (*ai.mit.edu*). Find the latest activities on IA from that site. What projects deal with crime prevention?

3. Enter the site of Tower Records (*towerrecords.com*) and examine the use of virtual reality in 3-D presentations. Also, visit *mindflyx.com/au*, *sgi.com*, and *liquidimage.com/ca* and examine the VR products. Finally, join a VR newsgroup and try to locate new business applications.

4. Visit *sas.com*, *egz.com* and *hnc.com*. Identify links to real-world applications of neural computing in fi-nance, manufacturing, health care, crime fighting, and transportation. Prepare a report on current applications.

5. Enter *google.com*, *pcai.com*, and *cio.com*, and identify the latest managerial trends and issues related to applied AI technologies.

6. Enter *botspot.com/newsletter*, *pcai.com*, and *agent-land.com*, and identify electronic commerce intelligent agents for helping shoppers. (Use the most recent 3 months.)

7. Enter *worldpoint.com* and check the capabilities of language translation. Find a competing vendor and compare.

TEAM ACTIVITIES AND ROLE PLAYING

1. Assign each team a major functional area (accounting, finance, etc).

   a. Using a literature search, material from vendors, or industry contacts, each team finds recent applications (within the last year) of intelligent systems.

   b. The team will submit a report about the applications found in each functional area.

   c. The class will conduct an analysis of the similarities and differences among the applications across the functional areas. A possible arrangement is to look at the underlying technology. (For example, compare the use of ANN in marketing versus finance or management.)

2. Each team composes a list of mundane tasks he or she would like an intelligent software agent to execute. Are intelligent agents available today to do the tasks on your lists? Consult *botspot.com* and *agent-land.com*.

3. Enter *pcai.com/pcai* and find the AI information categories. Assign each team to one or two categories. Search for recent (last 6 months) news items and interesting applications.

4. Integrated systems are being heavily utilized to fight terrorist threats. Assign each team one area, such as airports, sports stadiums, or large buildings. What technologies are used for each purpose?

REAL-WORLD CASE

Rules of Thumb Schedule Trains in Paris

The Business Problem   One of France's busiest train stations is the Gare de l'Est in Paris. Trains are parked at 30 platform tracks and then funneled onto six mainline tracks. More than 1,100 trains come and go every day, including some that cruise at close to 200 miles per hour! That's a train every 30 seconds during busy periods.

Scheduling local and long-distance trains at the 30 platforms is a complex logistics problem. Traffic levels are near the theoretical maximum. Each train must be assigned one of 640 possible routes into and out of the station. Local and long-distance trains share the same platform assignments. One single delayed train can cause a chain reaction that reverberates through the schedule for as long as four hours afterward. When a track or platform must be taken out of service for repairs, as many as 250 trains each day may have to be diverted. Only specialists at the Gare de l'Est have the skills to reroute these trains without creating major delays—skills they have derived from 10 to 15 years of experience working at the station.

The number of possible solutions to such problems is astronomical. As in chess, the moves and countermoves are so numerous that there is no satisfactory algorithmic solution to this problem. To enumerate all possible solutions using even a powerful computer may take days to execute. Yet, in the real world of railroading, a solution is needed in minutes.

Dispatchers who have solved daily problems manually for scores of years handle the scheduling. Until now, the solution for these human experts has been to use rules of thumb—heuristics. These rules are enunciated as constraints that say what may and may not be done in terms of train routes; they also consider the effects of any change on all the other routes. A basic rule in railroading, for example, is that two trains may not occupy the same track at the same time. The first corollary is that, on a single track, no train may pass another from either direction. These are rules that *must never* be violated. Other rules can be relaxed to solve pressing problems, such as "Don't assign a train to a platform until the previous debarkees have fully cleared the platform."

The deficiencies of a manual system are the following:

1. When a dispatcher is out sick, an extreme amount of pressure is placed on the remaining dispatchers.

2. Due to time constraints, dispatchers can run through only a limited number of possible arrangements for both planning and rerouting, so the best ones may be missed.

3. On holidays, when extra trains are needed, it is necessary to relax some rules. Working under time pressure, dispatchers do not always relax the most appropriate rules.

4. Employees fill out paper documents manually, a time-consuming process.

5. Less experienced dispatchers make mistakes, which may cause significant delays.

6. Daily planning and preparation of the semiannual timetable takes a great deal of time.

7. The scheduling issue creates a limit on the flow of traffic that is much lower than the physical limit.

8. Unnecessary delays may develop when the dispatchers cannot work fast enough to handle emergencies.

The IT Solution   Adding more dispatchers is an expensive solution that does not resolve all of the above deficiencies. In late 1988, it became clear to management that computerized support was needed. One proposal suggested the use of an expert system.

Such a system was built in 1989 and has run successfully since. Today, it is interactive, runs on an intranet, and works with a combination of rules and object-oriented programming. When a problem develops, the ES divides it into subproblems. Possible routes are quickly examined. If a potential conflict between trains is indicated, appropriate recommendations for its resolution are automatically provided by the ES. The program applies its rule base automatically, listing any situation it cannot solve. Then the dispatcher, in an interactive mode, attempts to solve the problem with the aid of the computer.

The Results   The system is especially useful for the less experienced dispatchers, but even experienced dispatchers use it to save time. Overall, the ES increased the productivity of the dispatchers by up to 100 percent, reduced errors, and solved most of the deficiencies listed above.

Source: Based on information provided by Texas Instruments, the builder of the system.

Questions

1. A preliminary study concluded that DSS or MIS would not be correct solution approaches. Why?

2. The possibility of using neural computing was examined but quickly discarded. Why?

3. Which of the deficiencies listed earlier cannot be removed by an expert system? Why?

4. Can this system be transferred to train stations in other countries? Why or why not?

5. Explain how the improvements are achieved. What is the role of dispatchers now? Are dispatchers needed at all?

6. The ES output was designed so that the electronic forms and information flow would look exactly the same as those of the manual system. What is the logic of such a design?

VIRTUAL COMPANY ASSIGNMENT

wiley.com/college/turban

Extreme Descent Snowboards

Background Jacob stops by your cubicle after the weekly management meeting. As usual, he greets you with a smile and a handshake, and he takes a seat across from your desk.

Jacob explains that to order a snowboard from EDS, the customer enters the

www.wiley.com/
college/turban

required information into an online form. Based on the answers to questions on that form, EDS can build a customized snowboard. But, says Jacob, "Many customers do not know exactly what features they want in a snowboard. Sometimes they have bought a board that does not match their expertise or riding requirements. We would like to customize the selection process, making it easier for the customer. Then we could recommend a snowboard best suited for them. Eventually, we could implement an expert system."

For your next assignment, Jacob asks you to prepare a report on whether the company would benefit by installing an expert system that could support the customer when choosing a snowboard.

Assignment

Jacob asks that you do the following research and answer the related questions in a report on expert systems.

1. Visit Native Minds *(http://nicole-sfl. nativeminds.com/demos_default.html)*. Native Minds is a virtual workforce for the Web. Experience the virtual sales representative. Try the Telecom Industries Demo, "Ask Celly." How could EDS implement a virtual workforce like this? Support your answer.

2. Can implementing expert systems in the EDS Web site provide a competitive advantage over our competitors?

3. Is this a sustainable advantage?

4. Should the customer have the option of choosing his or her own snowboard or using the expert system to choose an appropriate snowboard?

5. What are the advantages of having the expert system to choose a snowboard for every customer?

6. Could this expert system support any other area(s) within EDS? If so, which area(s)?

13 STRATEGIC SYSTEMS AND REORGANIZATION

LEARNING OBJECTIVES

1. Describe strategic information systems and explain their advantages.
2. Describe Porter's competitive forces model and how IT improves competitiveness.
3. Describe representative strategic information systems and the advantage they provide with the support of IT.
4. Understand the role of business processes in organizations and the reasons why reengineering is necessary.
5. Demonstrate the role of IT in supporting BPR and especially mass customization, cycle time reduction, self-directed teams, and empowerment.
6. Describe virtual corporations and their IT support.

BRITISH AIRWAYS GAINS STRATEGIC ADVANTAGE KEEPING MOBILE CUSTOMERS INFORMED

The Business Problem

British Airways' customers are, by definition, on the move. Given the heavy competition within the travel industry, customer satisfaction and loyalty have become increasingly important to British Airways. This focus on customer loyalty drives British Airways to continually look for new ways to improve the "complete" flight experience—from reservation, through the journey to the airport, check-in, the flight itself, and completion of arrival procedures at the destination airport. As one of the biggest international airlines in the world, British Airways strives to stay ahead of competitors and to turn customer satisfaction into profit.

British Airways wanted to extend its existing e-commerce program to an additional channel—providing its customer base with flight information and the ability to check in while on the move, from their mobile phones or PDAs. Giving customers access to check-in and flight information facilities from mobile phones was an extension of service that British Airways knew customers would appreciate. What better way to enhance passengers' travel experience than to make the journey simpler, faster, and more convenient?

British Airways passenger checks in wirelessly with her mobile phone.

The IT Solution

Together, IBM and British Airways have implemented the technology, infrastructure, and services to extend British Airways' highly successful e-commerce platform to the mobile channel. The resultant mobile service—the first of its kind in the United Kingdom—allows passengers to check flight availability and view British Airways' flight arrival and departure information from around the world, using the convenience of a mobile Internet-enabled phone. In addition, Executive Club members on selected departures from the U.K. can check in for their flights and pick a seat from mobile devices.

As part of the British Airways e-commerce platform, customers now have simple and personalized access to the British Airways Web site via the My TravelSpace feature. This feature also links in with outbound e-mail marketing programs. For British Airways, the e-commerce platform seamlessly integrates the airline's systems and processes to provide multichannel customer facilities and a greatly increased capacity to manage the requests and transactions of its customer base. Working with IBM on the initial integrated platform, British Airways was able to add the mobile phone as one further channel through which customers can gain access to a truly personalized service—on the Web, via self-service check-in kiosks, and through other planned digital channels. All of these will offer a familiar and consistent user experience to loyal customers.

The Results

A total of 4,500 British Airways passengers now check in for their flights via the Web site or their mobile devices each month—in addition to the 50,000 a week who check in with British Airways' IBM kiosks, 160 of which are installed at over 40 airports. While greatly improving the customer experience, the addition of the mobile channel allows British Airways to improve the efficiency of its check-in process, reducing staff costs and freeing customers from unnecessary queuing. The advent of mobile data capability also gives British Airways an opportunity to understand and test the capability of mobile devices, particularly for transactions. Furthermore, for British

Airways, the mobile service promised true business value through reductions in customer call center and service costs, alongside brand enhancement and first-mover advantage in a highly competitive environment. The real benefit to British Airways and its passengers involves being able to extend the benefits of British Airways' e-commerce platform, to bring convenience, choice, and control to the mobile e-business experience.

What We Learned from This Case

This case demonstrates the following points:

1. Industries with slim profit margins, like airlines, must compete on several strategic fronts, customer service being an important one.

2. Those companies in an industry who do not compete on the basis of low cost are often the most innovative with customer service. Using conventional strategies, such as cutting prices, may not be sufficient to gain a competitive edge and market share, or may not allow sufficient profits.

3. A *fundamental change* in the manner in which business is done is sometimes the only way to succeed, or even to survive.

4. Those firms that can successfully implement an IT-driven innovation can gain a significant competitive advantage as first movers.

These points are the major topics of this chapter, which concentrates on strategic information systems. Strategic information systems can be used by themselves as a change mechanism, or they can be used as enablers of fundamental structural changes known as *business process reengineering*.

13.1 STRATEGIC ADVANTAGE AND INFORMATION TECHNOLOGY

Strategic Information Systems

Strategic information systems (SISs) are systems that *support* or *shape* an organization's competitive strategy. An SIS is characterized by its ability to *significantly* change the manner in which business is done, as in the case of British Airways. The system does so through its contribution to achievement of the strategic goals of an organization and/or its ability to increase performance and productivity significantly. For example, British Airways, like its competitors, understands that customers need access to their travel information 24/7. However, the great strategic insight is that customers also need this access from wherever they are. Knowing that the majority of its customers are equipped with mobile phones and PDAs, British Airways made it a strategic priority to provide the desired information via these channels. Although competitors can duplicate this strategic advantage in customer service, they cannot do so quickly, easily, or cheaply.

Originally, strategic systems were considered to be *outwardly focused*, aiming at direct competition in their industry, for example, by providing new services to customers and/or suppliers, with the specific objective of beating competitors. But since the late 1980s, strategic systems are also being viewed *inwardly*: They are focused on enhancing the competitive position of the firm by increasing employees' productivity, improving teamwork, and enhancing communication. British Airways combined both outward and inward orientations to its advantage.

In addition to the inward and outward approaches, there is another dimension to SIS—**strategic alliances**—wherein two or more companies share an interorganizational system. For example, GM, Ford and Chrysler have an *extranet* that enables them to compete against Toyota and other car manufacturers.

The Role of IT in Strategic Systems

Information technology contributes to strategic systems in several ways. Consider these four:

1. Information technology creates *applications* that provide direct strategic advantage to organizations. For example, Federal Express was the first company in its industry to use information technology for tracking the location of every package in its system.

2. IT supports strategic changes such as *reengineering*. For example, IT allows efficient decentralization by providing high-speed communication lines, and it streamlines and shortens product design time with computer-aided engineering tools.

3. IT provides for technological *innovations* or acts as an enabler of innovation. These can be incorporated in the firm's goods or services, or affect how those are provided.

4. IT provides *competitive intelligence* by collecting and analyzing information about innovations, markets, competitors, and environmental changes. Such information provides strategic advantage: If a company knows something important before its competitors, or if it can make the correct interpretation of information before its competitors, then it can introduce changes first and benefit from them.

Competitive Intelligence

Information about the competition can mean the difference between winning and losing a business battle. Many companies continuously monitor the activities of their competitors. For example, Hertz monitors car rental prices of its competitors on a daily basis, and Kraft, the giant food maker, closely monitors the performance of its competitors. Such activities to gather information on competitors are part of **competitive intelligence**. Information about markets, technologies, and government's actions is also collected by competitive intelligence. Competitive intelligence drives business performance by increasing market knowledge and raising the quality of strategic planning.

| EXAMPLE |

How Frito Lay chips away at its competition.   Frito Lay, the world's largest snack food producer and distributor, is known for its extensive use of IT. Its strategic information system is a central nervous system within the business that integrates marketing, sales, manufacturing, logistics, and finance, and it provides managers with information about suppliers, customers, and competitors. Frito's employees in the field collect sales and inventory level information daily, by store and by product, across the United States and in some other countries. They feed this information electronically to the company. The employees also collect information about the quantities of competing products available in each store, sales and promotions of competing products, and new products launched by competitors. By combining the data with internal information, Frito's managers can better target local demand patterns, plan sales promotions, and determine pricing strategy. ●

fritolay.com

Table 13.1   Competitive Intelligence on the Internet

Intelligence Search Strategy	Description
Review competitor's Web sites.	Such visits can reveal information about new products or projects, potential alliances, trends in budgeting, advertising strategies used, financial strength, and more.
Analyze related newsgroups.	Internet newsgroups help uncover what people think about a company and its products. For example, newsgroup participants may state what they like or dislike about a company's products or those of its competitors. You can also examine people's reactions to a new idea by posting a question.
Examine publicly available financial documents of competitors.	This can be accomplished by entering a number of databases. While some databases charge nominal fees, others are free. The most notable is the Securities and Exchange Commission's EDGAR database (sec.gov/edgarhp.htm).
Do market research at your own Web site.	You can pose questions to Web site visitors. Some companies even give prizes to those visitors who best describe the strengths and weaknesses of various products (your own or competitors').
Use an information delivery service to gather news on competitors.	Information delivery services (such as Info Wizard, My Yahoo, or PointCast) find what is published on the Internet, including newsgroup correspondence, about competitors and their products. Known as *push technologies*, these services provide any desired information, including news, some in real-time, for free or a nominal fee.
Use corporate research companies.	Corporate research and ratings companies such as Dun & Bradstreet and Standard and Poor's provide information ranging from risk analysis to stock market analysts' reports about competitors, for a fee. These reports are available electronically.

Competitive intelligence can be enhanced by several information technologies, including intelligent agents. Research indicates that the percentage of companies using IT to support competitive intelligence increased from 31 percent in 1993 to about 50 percent in 1999. This increase is due primarily to the use of the Internet. The Internet plays an increasingly important role in supporting competitive intelligence. Using Internet tools, a company can implement specific search strategies to gather competitive intelligence easily, quickly, and relatively inexpensively, as illustrated in Table 13.1.

There is another aspect to competitive intelligence: *industrial espionage.* Corporate spies are looking for marketing plans, cost analyses, new products/services, and strategic plans. Such espionage can sometimes be unethical or illegal. Another problem is the theft of portable computers at conferences, which is spreading all over the world. Many of the thieves are interested in the information stored in the computers, not in the computers themselves. Protecting against such activities is important and is discussed in Chapter 15.

Before you go on . . .

1. Define strategic information systems (SISs).
2. Describe the role of IT in SIS.
3. Describe IT-based business intelligence.

13.2   PORTER'S COMPETITIVE FORCES MODEL AND IT

Some studies show that more than 90 percent of executives surveyed strongly agree that IT can facilitate a strategic advantage that has a significant impact on profitability and even survival of their organizations. In this section we will examine some of the theories related to competition and strategic advantage.

Porter's Model

Competition is at the core of a firm's success or failure. One of the most well-known frameworks for analyzing competitiveness is Porter's **competitive forces model**. This model (mentioned briefly in Chapter 1) has been used to develop strategies for companies to increase their competitive edge. The model recognizes five major forces that could endanger a company's position in a given industry. Although the details of the model differ from one industry to another, its general structure is universal (see Figure 13.1). The five major forces can be generalized as follows.

1. The threat of entry of new competitors
2. The bargaining power of suppliers

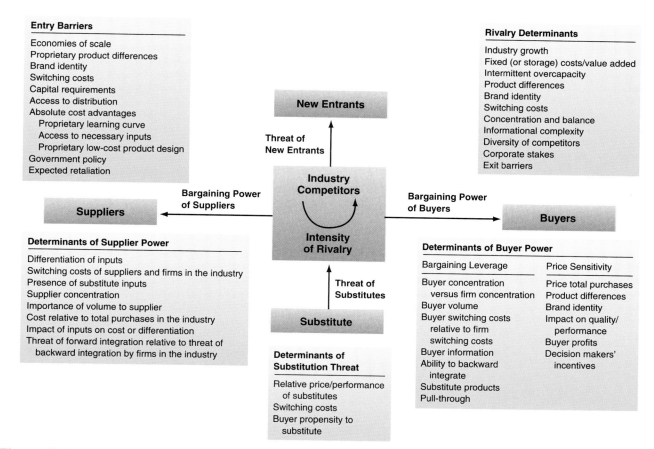

Figure 13.1   *Porter's five forces model (including the major determinant of each force).* [*Source: M. E. Porter,* Competitive Advantage: Creating and Sustaining Superior Performance. *Copyright 1985–1988 by Michael E. Porter. Reprinted with permission from the Free Press, a division of Simon & Schuster, Inc.*]

3. The bargaining power of customers (buyers)

4. The threat of substitute products or services

5. The rivalry among existing firms in the industry

The strength of each force is determined by several factors in the industry structure, examples of which are also cited in Figure 13.1. Most of the forces and the determining factors are related to the business pressures identified in Chapter 1.

Response Strategies

The purpose of identifying competitive forces is to enable an organization to develop a *strategy* aimed at establishing a profitable and sustainable position *against* these five forces. To do so, a company needs to develop a strategy of performing activities differently from its competitors. Porter proposed the following three response strategies to competitive forces.

1. *Cost leadership strategy:* Producing products and/or services at the lowest cost in the industry. An example is Wal-Mart, which through business alliances supported by computers and by computerized purchasing and inventory management is able to provide low-cost products at its stores.

2. *Differentiation strategy:* Being unique in the industry, such as providing high-quality products at a competitive price. For example, using an extranet and a computerized inventory system, Caterpillar provides its customers with a product maintenance service that no other competitor can match.

3. *Focus strategy:* Selecting a narrow-scope segment (*niche market*) and achieving either a cost leadership or a differentiation strategy in this segment. For example, several computer chip manufacturers make customized chips for specific industries or companies. Another example is frequent flyer programs that allow airlines to identify frequent travelers and offer them special incentives. Some airlines have several million customers registered in the programs, which can be managed efficiently only with the help of computers.

Over the years, Porter and others have added to the list of response strategies. The major extensions are the following.

- *Growth strategy:* Increasing market share, acquiring more customers, or selling more products by using electronic commerce to strengthen a company and increase profitability in the long run.

- *Alliances strategy:* Working with business partners. Facilitated by EDI, extranets, and groupware, this strategy creates synergy, allows companies to concentrate on their core business, and provides opportunities for growth.

- *Innovation strategy:* Developing new products and services, new features in existing products and services, and new ways to produce or sell them (for example, via the Internet). Also included are innovative information systems applications.

- *Internal efficiency strategy:* Improving the manner in which business processes are executed (for example, by using CAD/CAM). Such improvements increase employee and customer satisfaction, quality, and productivity, while decreasing time to market. Improved decision making and management activities also contribute to improved efficiency.

- *Customer-oriented strategy:* Concentrating on making customers happy. Strong competition and the realization that the customer is king/queen is the basis of this approach. IT contributions to this strategy include improved customer service facilitated by e-mail or computerized catalogs, for example.

These strategies may be interrelated. For example, some innovations are achieved through alliances that reduce cost and increase growth. Cost leadership improves customer satisfaction and may lead to growth.

Examples of IT-supported competitive strategies can be found in Section 13.3. (Indeed, examples can be found throughout the entire book.) In certain industries there may be a greater emphasis on one strategy than another. For example, in the trucking industry, cost leadership is critical, and companies are using innovative techniques to achieve it, as illustrated in IT's About Business 13.1.

Before we describe specific applications of how IT supports Porter's strategies, though, let us first explore in more detail how the model works.

How the Model Is Used

Porter's model is industry related, assessing the position of a company relative to competitors in its industry. The specific actions suggested by use of the model do not necessarily relate to IT. However, in most cases, response strategies these days do involve the use of IT. We'll use Wal-Mart (see Figure 13.2 on page 432) as an example to demonstrate the four steps involved in using Porter's model.

Step 1: List the players in each competitive force. An illustration of a competitive threat, for example, is electronic shopping via the Internet, which may be a substitute for going shopping at a Wal-Mart store.

IT's About Business   *jbhunt.com, roadway.com*   **POM**

Box 13.1:   Trucking companies use IT for gaining cost leadership

The trucking business is very competitive. Here are some examples of how IT helps in significant cost savings.

J.B. Hunt of Lowell, Arkansas, is a large truckload carrier. Its corporate PCs are connected to the fuel commodity market for minute-by-minute monitoring of the greatly fluctuating fuel prices. They can trigger the purchase of fuel at the lowest possible prices, which can result in significant savings since fuel costs represent 18 to 35 percent of the company's total operating costs. In addition, the system allows J.B. Hunt to pass on a very accurate fuel surcharge to its customers every week.

Roadway Express, another trucking company, owns several hundred gas pumps nationwide. Using computers, the company continuously compares six vendors' prices and related expenses to purchase the least expensive gas available at any given time.

Leaseway Trucking does not own pumps, but it centrally controls the purchasing of gas by over 10,000 drivers. Using geographical positioning systems (GPSs), the company knows where its trucks are at any given time. Knowing where the nearest, least expensive gas station is

located, corporate headquarters instructs drivers, in real time, where to buy gas. This strategy has reduced fuel costs by 10 percent.

Computers are also used by large companies to monitor drivers' and trucks' productivity. Using telecommunications and GPS, companies can monitor the exact location of trucks, study their performance, and thereby improve it. In addition, large trucking companies use DSS and EIS to optimize their operations. IT provides large companies with a competitive edge against the small companies and allows truckers to survive in an extremely competitive business.

Questions

1. Why do large truckers have the competitive edge?

2. Which of Porter's response strategies can be used by small truckers? Can IT be of any help?

3. A small trucking company can afford GPS (cost is less than $200 per unit). What is the advantage of using GPS?

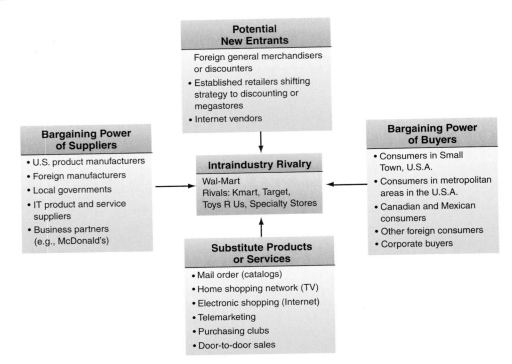

Figure 13.2 *Porter's model for Wal-Mart.* [*Source: Based on J. D. Callon,* Competitive Advantage Through Information Technology *(New York: McGraw Hill, 1996), pp. 40, 141.*]

Step 2: Relate the major determinants of each force (shown in the model in Figure 13.1) to each player listed in Figure 13.2. For example, with respect to electronic shopping, we can check the switching cost of the buyers, the buyers' propensity to substitute, the price advantage of electronic shopping, and so forth.

Step 3: Devise a strategy with which Wal-Mart can defend itself against these forces, based on the specific players and the determinants. For example, to counter electronic shopping, Wal-Mart could provide playgrounds for children, hand out free samples of products, and recognize frequent shoppers personally. Wal-Mart could also respond by imitating the competition; the company actually did just that by introducing Wal-Mart Online.

Step 4: Look for supportive information technologies. An illustration of this step for Wal-Mart's online shopping is a technology for managing frequent shoppers. It will be necessary to use a gigantic database and an online processing system with a good database management system and analytical capability to assess shoppers' activities accurately.

Of course, a similar process using Porter's model can be employed by Wal-Mart's competitors. A competitor can portray all the determinants and then look for response strategies and information technologies to increase the competitive pressure on Wal-Mart.

Table 13.2 summarizes the role of IT in relation to each competitive force. Strategic advantage must be sustained in order for organizations to survive and thrive. While the expense required to establish IT systems may prohibit some competitors from imitating successful systems, other competitors will follow suit. Therefore constant innovations are required. Also, inward systems can be helpful in providing competitive advantage. Specific examples of IT facilitating additional competitive strategies are presented in the next section.

Table 13.2   Impact of Competitive Forces and the Role of IT

Key Force Affecting the Industry	Business Implications	Potential IT Respones
Threat of new entrants	Additional capacity Reduced prices New basis for competition	Provide entry barriers/reduce access by exploiting existing economies of scale, differentiating products/services, controlling distribution channels, segmenting markets.
Supplier power high	Raises prices/costs Reduces quality of supply Reduces availability	Implement supplier sourcing systems. Extend quality control into suppliers' operations. Use forward planning with supplier.
Buyer power high	Forces prices down Higher quality demanded Service flexibility required Encourages competition	Differentiate products/services and improve price/performance. Increase switching costs of buyers. Facilitate buyer product selection.
Substitute products treatened	Limits potential market and profit Imposes price ceilings	Use differentiation strategy. Incorporate IT into product, service, or method of provision.
Intense competition from rivals	Price competition Need to develop new products and services Distribution and service become critical Customer loyalty required	Improve price/performance. Redefine products and services to increase value. Redefine market segments. Improve price/performance. Differentiate products and services in distribution channel and to consumer. Get closer to the end consumer—understand the use requirements.

Source: J. Ward and P. Griffiths, *Strategic Planning for Information Systems*, 2nd ed. (Chichester, England: Wiley, 1997), p. 86.

Before you go on . . .

1. Describe Porter's competitive forces and response strategies.
2. Explain how Porter's model is used and what role IT plays in the model.

13.3   STRATEGIC INFORMATION SYSTEMS: SOME EXAMPLES

In this section we present several examples of how IT has successfully supported the competitive response strategies presented in the previous section. Several of the cases illustrate support for more than one strategy.

EXAMPLES

Intranet gives Geisinger a shot in the arm.   Health maintenance organizations (HMOs) are growing very rapidly in the United States as an approach to containing health care costs. The rapid growth of some HMOs creates problems of inefficient operations and poor customer service, as in the case of Geisinger, a rural HMO in Danville, Pennsylvania.

The company, which grew through mergers and acquisitions, had 40 different IT legacy systems that needed to be upgraded and integrated. An innovative approach required use of an intranet to deal with the complexity of this integration. Not only does its intranet allow Geisinger to integrate its systems, but it also allows the HMO to offer innovative services such as "Tel-a-Nurse," which enables patients to communicate comfortably with nurses by asking medical questions over the intranet. Moreover, Geisinger installed a clinical management information system to work with its intranet. Doctors use digital cameras to take pictures of patients' injuries. Stored in a database, the pictures are accessible through the intranet for specialist consultation and for insurance processing.

The HMO's intranet is also used for patient education, human resources management, routine paperwork, and library systems. Geisinger's radiology department, for example, which performs diagnostic procedures such as X-rays, mammograms, and MRIs, has placed an electronic information kiosk in its waiting rooms for patients' education.

ibm.com

Image management software cuts PC setup, maintenance costs. A PC image is made up of the hardware and software loaded on a personal computer. Most large companies maintain many different PC images to support a variety of hardware configurations, operating systems, languages, network drivers, and business applications. Each one of these separate images has to be developed, tested, managed, maintained, backed up, and documented—all of which takes time and money. When this process is applied to thousands of individual PCs, it quickly becomes a costly and time-consuming problem that drains IT resources and budgets. Industry analysts say most companies report that managing PC images represents as much as 50 percent of their total hardware support costs, and that they need to dedicate at least 30 percent of their internal computing staffs to deal with this problem. New ImageUltra software from IBM can reduce the number of PC images from hundreds or thousands to a single "super-image" for all PCs in an enterprise network. IBM estimates the new technology and related services can save businesses an average of $100 per PC, per year, over the life of the system, establishing a new benchmark for the PC industry in long-term affordability and manageability.

dnb.com

Dun & Bradstreet evaluates credit. Dun & Bradstreet (D&B) is a credit clearinghouse that provides risk analysis to manufacturers, wholesalers, jobbers, and marketers in various industries. D&B maintains and updates a database of credit ratings on approximately 220,000 businesses. Customers who pay D&B for the credit analysis used to complain about long waiting periods and inaccuracies (it is difficult to update the material constantly), inconsistencies (such as different interpretations by different risk analysts), and slow response time. An expert system is now capable of handling more than 95 percent of all requests. As a result, response time has been reduced from about three days to a few seconds, and the credit recommendations are more accurate and consistent. As soon as there are changes in a company's data, the expert system reevaluates the implications for creditworthiness and informs its clients if needed. The system has helped the company maintain its position as a leading information provider. Clients communicate with D&B via the Internet or a value-added network. Once a client purchases a report from D&B, it can be placed on the buyer's intranet and accessed by all authorized employees.

national.com

National Car Rental makes a quick and satisfactory car pickup. National Car Rental has been an innovator in using IT to become competitive in the car rental business. Market research revealed that car rental customers were tired of long delays, waiting in line, and providing the same information again and again (driver's license, car preferences, features in rental cars, and so on). Customers were also frustrated because cars were randomly assigned to them; they were unable to select the exact model, color, or features they wanted. Customers who tried to specify car model or color caused delays, which upset other customers waiting in line.

National Car Rental came up with an innovation called the Emerald Card. The Emerald Card prequalifies customers; they simply make a reservation, skip the line, and select a car of their choice from the rental lot. When they leave the lot, they use the Emerald Card as documentation to show that they rented a car and are leaving with it. When they return the car, they again use the Emerald Card to indicate the return, and an invoice is generated automatically. Advertising the card, National was able to attract some competitors' customers who value this service, as well as retaining their own customers.

Dialing up Coca-Cola.   Coca-Cola has always faced fierce competition around the world. By using a radical new SIS that marries "smart" Coke machines with cellular telephone technology, Coca-Cola has a strong competitive advantage in Singapore. There, people can now buy drinks from vending machines by using their mobile telephones. As a result of a joint venture between Singapore Telecommunications, Ltd. and F&N Coca Cola Pte. Ltd. of Singapore, subscribers to the SingTel cellular network interact with the Coke machine via their mobile phones by punching in an ID number and pressing the call button or by sending a short mail message. The machine receives the call or mail, identifies the user, and enables the user to then make the desired selection from the machine. The charge is transferred to the user's telephone bill. The telephone company does not collect a commission from Coke, but does make money on the phone call or electronic message sent. Many of the machines in Singapore also accept electronic money cards. ●

coca-cola.com
singtel.com

Sustaining a Competitive Advantage

The SISs of the 1970s and 1980s were primarily *outward systems*, which are visible to competitors and can now be duplicated quickly (in months rather than years). Also, innovations in technology may make even new systems obsolete very quickly. Therefore, the major problem that companies face now is how to *sustain* their competitive advantage. Porter's extension of his classical model includes strategies such as growth and internal efficiency that help facilitate sustainability.

When SISs are combined with structural changes in the organization, they can provide a *sustainable strategic advantage*. For example, Federal Express uses a comprehensive strategic information system (called PRISM) to manage its human resources and increase the effectiveness and efficiency of its operations. The system does not compete directly with any company, but it does provide a strategic advantage by building and maintaining a first-class personnel system. (For an application of the shift of corporate operations to a *strategic* orientation, see IT's About Business W13.1 at the Web site.

Another popular approach to sustaining a competitive advantage is the use of *inward systems* that are not visible to competitors. Companies such as General Motors and American Airlines, for example, use inward intelligent systems in a number of ways, but the details are secret. It is known that several investment companies are using neural computing, but again the details are not known. Such inward systems can provide a sustainable advantage as long as they remain a secret, or as long as competitors do not develop similar or better systems using their own creativity.

Yet another approach to sustaining a competitive advantage is to install a comprehensive, innovative, and expensive system that is very difficult to duplicate. This is basically what Caterpillar has done to fend off its Japanese competitors. Federal Express's online package tracking systems is another example of this strategy, although any system that is outwardly visible and seen as a source of competitive advantage will eventually be duplicated by competitors (as FedEx's system was).

www.wiley.com/ college/turban

A Framework for Global Competition

Many companies are operating in a global environment. First, there are the truly global or multinational corporations. Second are the companies engaged in export or import. Third, a large number of companies face competition from products created in countries where labor and other costs are low, or where there is an abundance of natural resources. Finally, other companies have low-cost production facilities in these same countries. Doing business in a global environment is becoming more and more challenging as the political environment improves (more opportunities become available) and as telecommunications and the Internet open the door to a large number of buyers, sellers, and competitors worldwide. The increased competition forces companies to look for better ways to do business, and they frequently evaluate IT as a potential solution.

According to the *global business drivers framework*, the success of companies doing business in a competitive global environment depends on the alignment of their global business strategy and their information systems. This connection can be seen in multinational companies such as Caterpillar, where a business strategy of strong support to dealers and customers worldwide is accomplished by developing an effective global information system. Information managers must be innovative in identifying the IT systems that a firm needs in order to be competitive worldwide and must tie them to strategic business imperatives. The global business drivers framework provides a tool for identifying the business entities such as customers, suppliers, projects, and orders that will benefit most from an integrated global IT management system. These entities are the business pressures—the "drivers"—that form the basis for the strategic information systems. Advances in e-commerce are of special interest to global traders. Many of the business drivers can be facilitated by the Internet, which is much cheaper and more accessible than private communication networks.

Before you go on . . .

1. Describe the issue of sustainability and list solutions.

2. Describe the global business drivers framework.

13.4   INEFFECTIVE ORGANIZATIONS IN THE INFORMATION AGE

As indicated earlier, one of the strategies used to sustain competitive advantage is to combine IT with *structural change*. A fundamental change in the manner in which business is conducted is frequently referred to as *reorganization* or *business process reengineering (BPR)*. Information technology is usually the major enabler of such reorganization, as will be illustrated in this and the following sections.

The Need for a Fundamental Change

Organizations are managed today by a set of principles that have evolved since the beginning of the Industrial Revolution. This revolution started with the concept of division of labor, conceived by Adam Smith in 1776. According to this concept, instead of one craftsman making an entire product (such as a shoe or a pin), several people would make the product, each specializing in one task. Each task would be relatively simple, so it would be easy to learn. This would reduce the long apprenticeship periods. In addition, when people specialize in these simple tasks, output can increase. This situation led to cheaper products and consequently higher demand. Because the tasks were simple, they were easy to automate when machines were introduced. Automation reduced the price of products further and further, and factories became larger and larger. Instead of producing for customers after an order was placed, products were produced in large quantities and then sold in the marketplace. Several principles and methods were created over the years that enhanced the development of the Industrial Revolution. The most important ones are:

- Specialization of labor
- Mass production (producing large quantities, storing them, selling them at a later time)
- Hierarchical organizational structure following functional specialties with top-down lines of authority
- Assembly lines that bring the work to the worker whenever possible
- Complex support systems for planning and budgeting, resource allocation, coordination, and control

These principles and methods were successful in developing world-class organizations, moving nations to a developed status, and significantly increasing standards of living.

However, these principles and methods are not working as they used to for many companies because the world has moved into a competitive global environment with continuous and unpredictable change. Significant change in the environment or in any component of the organization results in an organization's *disequilibrium*. Unless the structure, processes, strategy, management, and technology are adjusted in response to the disequilibrium, organizations will not function well. As long as the pace of the change was slow, it was possible to deal with change by using *continuous improvement* programs, which included automation of existing processes, small structural modifications, quality and productivity improvement programs, and modifications in management procedures. But as the pace and the magnitude of business pressures and changes have accelerated, continuous improvement programs have become inappropriate in many cases.

Research shows that it is five to six times more difficult and expensive to obtain a new customer than it is to retain an existing one. So keeping customers should be one of an organization's most basic concerns. Yet during the 1980s and early 1990s, customers in almost every area of business became disillusioned with the types of services they were receiving from most organizations. When customers tried to get service, they often got answers like: "We have them on order." "I'll have to check with the other department and get back to you." "I'll get to you when I can." "It's not my job." "You can have any color as long as it's black." "I don't care what she told you, it can't be returned." "We'll need more people if we do that." What went wrong with these organizations? The answer is simple: Companies continued with their old structures and processes while the business environment was changing. The result was ineffective organizations.

The Problem of the Stovepipe

One fundamental problem that makes organizations ineffective is that the ways they do things do not keep up with technology. Many of the traditional approaches used by organizations were developed before computing technology and, more recently, network technology. Organizations typically have used what is called the **hierarchical organization.** This is a pyramidal structure in which the ultimate authority and responsibility reside at the top, and authority and responsibility flow down through successions of levels to the bottom of the organization. However, all organizations have both *horizontal* and *vertical* dimensions. The organization's layers (usually top, middle, and supervisory management) define the horizontal dimensions; the organization's functional departments define the vertical dimensions.

The vertical dimension of the organization, which is primarily focused on functional specialization, has caused many problems in organizations as they have tried to move into the information-based economy. Such problems are sometimes referred to as "stovepipes" in recognition of their vertical nature. Interaction among vertical functions—across the stovepipes—turns out to be crucial in order for organizations to operate efficiently and effectively.

Here is an example of a stovepipe problem: A customer places an order with the sales department. After a few days, she calls Sales to find out the status of the order. To answer the customer's questions, Sales starts to call various departments. Frequently, it is difficult to trace the order. People push the order from place to place and feel only a small sense of responsibility and accountability, so Sales may not be able to give the customer an answer in time, or may even give an incorrect answer.

As this simple example illustrates, the difference between duties of functional units and business processes in an organization often is confused. In the stovepipe-problem example, for instance, the business processes involved in filling an order could be considered the responsibility of the selling department or the distribution department; finance personnel may also be involved depending on how the payment for the product is to be made. Figure 13.3 illustrates that an organization can have vertical functions but also have processes that transcend departmental boundaries horizontally. These are sometimes referred to as *cross-functional activities*. Product development, order processing, planning, resourcing, control, and customer service are examples of business processes that can transcend the functional boundaries of distribution, purchasing, research and development, production, and sales.

The problem of the stovepipe can intensify if the supporting information systems are structured improperly. As we've seen earlier in the book, organizations generally have operated and built information systems along functional boundaries. For example, a budgeting system was perceived to be primarily that of the finance department, even though all functional areas of the organization do budgeting. A net effect of focusing on vertical functions has been fragmented, piecemeal information systems that operate so that the "left hand doesn't know what the right hand is doing."

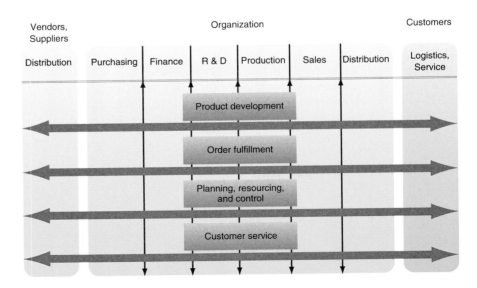

Figure 13.3 *Business processes across functional areas and organizational boundaries. [Source: E. Turban et al.,* Information Technology for Management *(New York: Wiley, 1999), p. 119.]*

The Need for Integration

Besides creating inefficient redundancies, the vertical structure with its functional in-formation systems causes difficulties in the *integration* of information that is required for decision making. For example, account numbers in an information system devel-oped along departmental lines may not be logically related and so cannot be used for cross-referencing a customer's accounts. This seriously limits reporting capabilities. A loan officer, for instance, may want to check information pertaining to a loan appli-cant's savings accounts. However, there may be no linkage to these data from the loan system. Indeed, the loan officer may even have to ask the loan applicant if he or she has a savings account with the bank and what the account number is.

Consider a case where the management of the bank wants to increase the offering of mortgage loans. Management decides to send letters encouraging specific cus-tomers to consider buying homes, using convenient financing available through the bank. Management also decides that the best customers to whom to send such letters are the following.

1. Customers who do not currently have mortgage loans or who have loans for a very small percentage of the value of their homes

2. Customers who have good checking account records (i.e., few or no overdrafts)

3. Customers with sufficient funds in their savings accounts to make a down payment on a home

4. Customers who have good payment records on any installment loans with the bank

Because the data necessary to identify such customers may be available in differ-ent files of different databases, there may be no convenient or economical way to

IT's About Business   zeiss.de   **POM**

Box 13.2:   Carl Zeiss and its suppliers integrate business processes

The Carl Zeiss Group, well known as the manufacturer of some of the world's finest optical equipment, relies heavily on its supply chain. Through consignment arrangements, the supply chain partners provide Carl Zeiss with a wide variety of manufactured parts that are then incorporated into the company's products.

Much of the responsibility for making the consign-ment arrangement work rests on the shoulders of Zeiss's suppliers. They have the task of ensuring that their sup-ply matches the manufacturing demand and is delivered when needed. While in theory this arrangement made Carl Zeiss's internal operations simpler by delegating the responsibility for filling the supply pipeline to its sup-pliers, in practice it required a great deal of coordination between Zeiss's IT systems and those of its suppliers. Different suppliers needed different data, and it all had to be collated more or less manually; suppliers had no di-rect access to the Zeiss systems.

Carl Zeiss saw the potential for making the process far more efficient by leveraging its internal systems through an extended ERP solution. By giving access to critical SAP R/3 data to suppliers, Zeiss could eliminate the time- and labor-intensive routine of coordinating data between members of the supply chain. All partners are now connected via an extranet to relevant manufac-turing demand data at Zeiss. Access to the Carl Zeiss data is controlled through user authorization, so each member of the supply chain sees only the data that are relevant to them. At the same time, Carl Zeiss's employ-ees are able to interact with all suppliers. The same data drives all of the processes, from shipping to inventory management to forecasting.

Questions

1. How does this system impact a supplier's inven-tory management?

2. What competitive advantage is realized through improved data sharing?

3. How does the integrated software help?

integrate them. Management is understandably disappointed and unable to function effectively.

For optimum use of information, integration should cross not only departmental boundaries, but also organizational ones, reaching suppliers and customers. An example of an integration of a firm with its suppliers is provided in IT's About Business 13.2 (page 439).

All too often, however, organizations have failed to integrate information systems. Nonintegrated information systems and the conflict between the horizontal nature of business processes and the vertical (functional) structure of businesses are the primary reasons for organizational problems that necessitate business process reengineering, the topic of the next section.

Before you go on . . .

1. Explain the need for a fundamental change in the way organizations are organized and operated.

2. What is the stovepipe problem?

13.5   BUSINESS PROCESS REENGINEERING

One popular approach to improving organizational effectiveness is referred to as **business process reengineering (BPR).** BPR is a holistic process that can lead to a complete organizational transformation and stabilization. As described earlier, an organization's *business processes* are the activities that use various kinds of inputs to create an output of value to the customer. For example, accepting an application for a loan, processing it, and approving (or rejecting) it is a business process in a bank. An organization operates *numerous* business processes to attain its goals. In business process reengineering (BPR), an organization fundamentally rethinks and radically redesigns its business processes to achieve *dramatic improvements* in such measures of performance as quality, cost, speed, and services. BPR can be introduced in one, several, or all organizational processes. As shown in Figure 13.4, information technology supports most BPR projects.

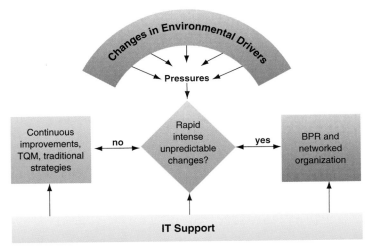

Figure 13.4 *BPR, continuous improvement programs, and IT support.*

The implementation of BPR involves many concepts, some of which have been known for several decades. The approach was formalized in the late 1980s and early 1990s, when the term "BPR" was coined. When BPR was first implemented, it usually involved a significant break with past business rules and practices—almost requiring an organization to start over from scratch. This extreme view of BPR has modified somewhat. It is no longer considered necessary to destroy everything and start anew; BPR now can be implemented using a more flexible approach.

Principles of BPR

Certain common principles exist in business process reengineering, and most of them are facilitated by IT. The major principles are as follows.

- Several jobs are combined into one.
- Employees make decisions (empowerment of employees). Decision making becomes part of the job.
- Steps in the business process are performed in a natural order, and several jobs get done simultaneously.
- Processes to manufacture similar products or provide similar services can be structured so that only slight variations will permit provision of "customized" goods or services. This makes possible the economies of scale that result from mass production, yet allows customization of products and services.

IT's About Business   *ibm.com*

Box 13.3:   IBM Credit Corporation reduced cycle time by 90 percent

IBM Credit Corporation provides credit to customers who purchase IBM computers. The process of credit approval used to take an average of seven days. Because of the long processing time, salespeople felt that they were losing many potential customers. Therefore, reducing processing time became critical.

In the old process, the IBM salesperson telephoned in, requesting credit approval for a customer. A clerk logged the call on paper, and a messenger took it to the credit department. Next, a specialist entered the data into the computer, checked creditworthiness of the potential customer, and prepared a report. The report was physically moved to the Business Practices department, and the Business Practices department modified a standard loan to fit the customer's needs. Using a spreadsheet, a pricer then determined the appropriate interest rate and payment schedule, adding another piece of paper to the application. An administrator used the information to develop a quote letter, which was delivered to the salesperson, who submitted it to the customer. Incremental attempts to increase productivity improved some of these activities, but the overall time reduction was minimal.

IBM reengineered the credit approval process. In the new process, one person, called a deal structurer, conducts all the above steps. This one generalist replaces four specialists. To enable one person to execute the above steps, a simple DSS provides the deal structurer with the guidance needed. The program guides the generalist in finding information in the databases, plugging numbers into an evaluation model, and pulling standardized clauses (boilerplate) from a file. For difficult situations, the generalist can get help from a specialist.

The results have been phenomenal: Turnaround time on orders has been slashed from seven days to four hours. Furthermore, IBM Credit can now handle a volume of business up to 100 times larger.

Questions

1. Why is this change considered a BPR?
2. What role did IT play in supporting the BPR?
3. What is the role of the deal structurer?

- Work is performed where it makes the most sense, including at the customer's or supplier's sites. Thus, work is shifted, if necessary, across organizational and even international boundaries.
- Controls and checks and other non-value-added work are minimized.
- Reconciliation—checking a product against a purchase order, for example—is minimized by cutting back the number of external contact points and by creating business alliances.
- A hybrid centralized/decentralized operation is used.
- A single point of contact (called a "case manager" or a deal structurer) is provided to customers.

An example of how BPR is done using such principles is provided in IT's About Business 13.3 (page 441).

The Enabling Role of Information Technology

IT has been used for several decades to improve productivity and quality by automating existing processes. However, when it comes to reengineering, the traditional process of looking at problems first and then seeking technology solutions for them needs to be reversed. Instead, organizations can first recognize that BPR makes powerful solutions possible, and then seek the processes that can be helped by it.

IT can break old rules that limit the way work is performed. Some typical rules are presented in Table 13.3.

The IT tools for BPR.   A large variety of IT tools can be used to support BPR. The major categories of support tools are as follows.

- *Simulation and visual simulation tools.* Simulation is essential to support the modeling activities of BPR. In addition to conventional simulation and visual simulation tools, there are simulation tools that are specifically oriented for BPR.
- *Flow diagrams.* Flow diagrams can be made with CASE tools or other systems development charting tools. They can also be made by specialized BPR tools that are usually integrated with other tools.
- *Work analysis.* Analyzing both existing processes and proposed solutions can be accomplished with tools that conduct forecasting, risk analysis, and optimization.
- *Workflow software.* In redesigning business processes, it is usually necessary to analyze the work to be done and the manner in which it flows from one place to another. A workflow system is a powerful business process automation tool that places system controls in the hands of end-user departments. There are three types of workflow software: *administrative*—expense reports, travel requests and messages; *ad hoc*—product brochures, sales proposals, and strategic plans; and *production*—credit card mailings, mortgage loans, and insurance claims.
- *Other tools.* Several special tools plan and manage the BPR process and the organization transformation. Information tools and technologies can also be part of the BPR solution itself. For example, CAD/CAM and imaging technologies contribute to cycle time reduction, EDI supports virtual corporations and other interorganizational systems, and expert systems support case managers and mass customization.
- *Integrated tool kits.* Several integrated tool kits are available to support BPR. The most well-known tool is SAP R/3.

Table 13.3   Changes in Work Rules Brought by IT

Old Rule	Intervening Technology	New Rule
Information appears in only one place at one time.	Shared databases, client/server architecture, electronic mail	Information appears simultaneously wherever needed.
Only an expert can perform complex work.	Expert systems, neural computing	Novices can perform complex work.
Managers make all decisions.	Decision support systems, enterprise support systems, expert systems	Decision making is part of everyone's job.
Field personnel need offices to receive, send, store, and process information.	Wireless communication and portable computers, information highways, electronic mail	Field personnel can manage information from any location.
You have to locate items manually.	Tracking technology, groupware, workflow software, client/server	Items are located automatically.
Plans get revised periodically.	High-performance computing systems	Plans get revised instantaneously whenever needed.
People must come to one place to work together.	Groupware and group support systems, telecommunications, electronic mail, client/server	People can work together from different locations.
Customized products and services are expensive and take a long time to develop.	CAD-CAM, CASE tools, online systems for JIT decision making, expert systems	Customized products can be made quickly and inexpensively (mass customization).
A long period of time is spanned between the inception of an idea and its implementation (time-to-market).	CAD-CAM, electronic data interchange, groupware, imaging (document) processing	Time-to-market can be reduced by 90 percent.
Work should be moved to countries where labor is inexpensive (off-shore production).	Robots, imaging technologies, object-oriented programming, expert systems	Work can be done in countries with high wages and salaries.

Source: Compiled from M. Hammer and J. Champy, *Re-engineering the Corporation* (New York: Harper Business, 1993).

- **Internet and intranet infrastructures.** The role of IT in business process reengineering is increasing due to new applications based on Internet and intranet infrastructure.

The Major Reengineering Activities

Reengineering efforts involve many activities. We describe the major ones in this section and also show the support given by IT to BPR.

Redesign of processes.   One of the most publicized examples of process redesign is the accounts payable process at Ford Motor Company, described in IT's About Business 13.4 (page 444). This case illustrates how IT can help in redesigning a process to result in dramatic cost reduction.

From mass production to mass customization.   One of the most innovative concepts of the Industrial Revolution was *mass production*, in which a company produces a large quantity of an identical, standard product. The product is then placed in a warehouse for future distribution to many customers. Because mass production results in

IT's About Business

ford.com   **ACC**

Box 13.4:   Reengineering processes at Ford Motor Company

As part of its productivity improvement efforts, Ford management thought that by streamlining processes and installing new computer systems it could reduce the head count of its accounts payable department by some 20 percent, to 400 people.

But after visiting Mazda's payables department (Ford is part owner of Mazda), Ford managers increased their goal: Perform the accounts payable process with only 125 clerks. Why did they think this could be done? Analysis of the existing system revealed that when the purchasing department wrote a purchase order, it sent a copy to Accounts Payable. Later, when Materials Control received the goods, it sent a copy of the receiving document to Accounts Payable. Meanwhile, the vendor also sent an invoice to Accounts Payable. If the purchase order, receiving document, and invoice matched, then Accounts Payable issued a payment. Unfortunately, the department spent most of its time on the many mismatches. To prevent them, Ford instituted "invoiceless processing." Now, when the purchasing department initiates an order, it enters the information into an online database. It does not send a copy of the purchase order to anyone. The vendor receives notification through an EDI (see the figure).

When the goods arrive at the receiving dock, the receiving clerk checks the database to see whether the goods correspond to an outstanding purchase order. If so, he or she accepts them and enters the transaction into the computer system. (If there is no database entry for the received goods, or if there is a mismatch, the clerk returns the goods.)

Under the old procedures, the accounting department had to match 14 data items among the receipt record, the purchase order, and the invoice before it could issue payment to the vendor. The new approach requires matching only four items—part number, amount, unit of measure, and supplier code—between the purchase order and the receipt record. The matching is done automatically, and the computer prepares the check, which Accounts Payable sends to the vendor (or an electronic transfer is done). There are no invoices to worry about since Ford has asked its vendors not to send them.

Questions

1. What support was provided by IT?
2. How did IT contribute to improved quality?
3. Why was invoicing abolished?
4. Why is this a BPR?

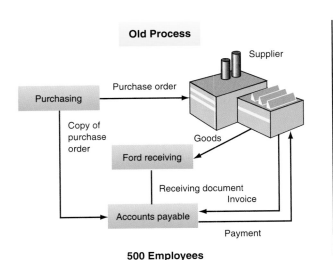

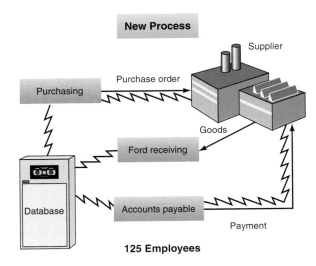

Comparison of old and reengineered processes at Ford Motor Company. [*Source: E. Turban et al.,* Information Technology for Management *(New York: Wiley, 1999), p. 128. Reengineering accounts payable processes at Ford.*]

low costs, products are relatively inexpensive, and many customers purchase identical products. The concept of mass production was adapted to thousands of products, ranging from simple watches to major appliances, vehicles, and computers.

A major change in marketing started about 30 years ago with the increased competition between automobile manufacturers. Customers were able to select "options," such as an air conditioner or automatic transmission. Manufacturers collected the customized orders. Once they accumulated enough similar orders to justify the economic manufacturing of identical customized products, they produced the items. The result was a waiting time of several months. A similar strategy was developed in other relatively expensive products. However, today's customers are not willing to wait so long. The solution was found in mass customization.

The basic idea of **mass customization** is to enable a company to produce large volumes, yet to customize the products to the specifications of individual customers. Mass customization enables a company to provide flexible and quick responsiveness to a customer's needs, at a low cost and with high quality. It is made possible by allowing fast and inexpensive production changes, by reducing the ordering and sales process costs, by shortening the production time, and by using prefabricated parts and modules. An important point is that mass customization involves not only the operations function but also marketing and sales, personnel, and finance. (For an example of how reengineering enabled mass customization, see IT's About Business W13.2 at the book's Web site.)

www.wiley.com/college/turban

Mass customization will likely increase with the spread of e-commerce, which transforms the supply chain from a traditional *push model* to a *pull model*. In the push model, the business process starts with manufacturing and ends with consumers buying the products or services. In the pull model, the process starts with the consumer ordering the product (or service) and ends with the manufacturer making it. E-commerce is especially helpful in developing one-to-one relationships with customers, taking orders electronically, and learning about customers' needs, which are then fulfilled economically.

Cycle time reduction.   Cycle time refers to the time it takes to complete a business process from beginning to end. Because speed is recognized as a major element that provides competitive advantage, **cycle time reduction** is a major business objective. IT makes a major contribution in shortening cycle times by allowing companies to combine or eliminate steps, and to expedite various activities in the business process.

The success of Federal Express, for example, is clearly attributable to its ability to reduce the delivery time of packages by using complex computer-supported systems that allow flexible planning, organization, and control. The comeback of Chrysler Corporation and its success in the 1990s can be attributed largely to its "technology center," which brought about a more than 30 percent reduction in its time to market (the time from beginning the design of a new model to the delivery of the car). Boeing Corporation reengineered its design of airplanes by moving to total computerization, in which an electronic rather than a physical prototype was built. In addition to reducing the cycle time, the process redesign has improved quality and reduced costs. Because of this, Boeing was able to compete successfully with Airbus Industries. Notice that both in Boeing's and Chrysler's cases the change was fundamental and dramatic. First, the role of the computer was changed from a tool to a platform for the total design. Second, it was not just a process change, but a cultural change relative to the role of the computer and the design engineers. Computing also played a major communications role during the entire design process.

There is an old (and true) saying that "time is money," so saving time saves money. But cycle time reduction does more than just save money. If you beat your

IT's About Business

ibm.com/solutions/lifesciences
phaseforward.com   MKT

Box 13.5:   IT-based BPR speeds new pharmaceuticals to market

Phase Forward Inc. and IBM are offering solutions to help drug makers reduce the number of years and millions of dollars in costs involved in the development cycle of lifesaving medicines. The two companies are collaborating on solutions that automate the clinical trial process of testing and reporting on the safety and effectiveness of new drug targets.

Getting a new drug to market can cost as much as $500 million and take up to 15 years. Nearly half of the time is expended on clinical trials, and data from more than 95 percent of the thousands of clinical trials conducted annually are captured using a pen-and-paper approach, which often results in mistakes. Phase Forward's Internet-based solutions are joined with IBM's hosting and consulting services to automate the process—from clinicians entering patient data via a Web browser to electronic report submissions to the U.S. Food and Drug Administration. Dr. Caroline Kovac, general manager of IBM Life Sciences, said, "This is an area that is ripe for e-business. Phase Forward is the market leader in Web-based applications for clinical trials. By working together, we can bring the clinical trial process into the twenty-first century and enable drug makers to get needed treatments to patients faster."

Questions

1. What support was provided by IT?
2. What benefit does the Internet provide?
3. How will this new process provide competitive advantage to adopters?

competitors to the market with a new product, a product improvement, or a new service, you can gain a substantial market share. Pharmaceutical companies, for example, are desperately trying to reduce the cycle time of new drugs. If successful, they will be the first on the market, they may receive a patent on the innovation, and revenues will begin flowing sooner to repay their huge investments. Finally, telecommunications and especially the Internet and intranets provide a means of economically reducing cycle time by cutting communications time through the use of e-mail and EDI, and by allowing collaboration in design and operations of products and services. IT's About Business 13.5 illustrates how IT can help in redesigning a process to result in dramatic cycle time reduction.

Cycle time reduction can be very beneficial, but to obtain maximum results from reengineering efforts it may be necessary to restructure not just one or a few processes, but the entire organization, as we describe next.

Restructuring Entire Organizations

We've seen that a current problem in many organizations is vertical structures. The fundamental problem with the hierarchical approach is that any time a decision needs to be made, it must climb up and down the hierarchy. All it takes to bring everything to a screeching halt is for one person who does not understand an issue to say "no." Also, if information is required from several "functions," getting all the right information coordinated can be a time-consuming and frustrating process for employees and customers alike.

In response, some businesses have felt the need to restructure the entire organization. How is organizational restructuring done? It all depends. In some cases, providing each customer with a single point of contact can solve the fundamental problem just described. For example, in a traditional bank, each department views the same customer as a separate customer. The customer interacts with each department separately, filling in duplicate applications and dealing with many contact people in the bank.

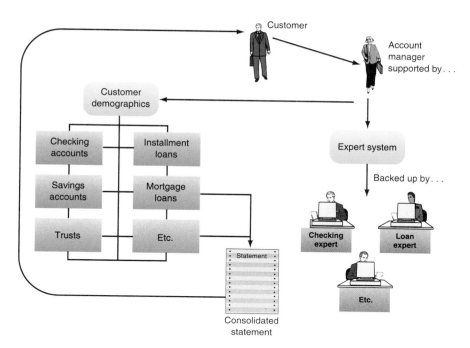

Figure 13.5 *Reengineered bank with integrated system.* [*Source: E. Turban et al.,* Information Technology for Management *(New York: Wiley, 1999), p. 134.*]

Figure 13.5 depicts the alternative—a reengineered bank. The customer deals with a single point of contact, an account manager. The account manager is responsible for *all* bank services and provides all services to the customer, who receives a single statement for all his or her accounts. Notice that the role of IT is to back up the account manager by providing expert advice on specialized topics, such as loans. Also, by allowing easy access to the different databases, the account manager can answer queries, plan, and organize the work with customers. Although in concept this is reengineering of a business process, the process is so integral to the bank's operation that changing it essentially changes the entire organization.

One of the most interesting forms of a restructured organization is the networked organization.

The networked organization.   **Networked organizations** refer to organizational structures that resemble computer networks and are supported by computerized systems. The major characteristics of the networked organization are shown in Figure 13.6 (page 448) and are compared to the characteristics of the hierarchical organization.

Today there is a clear trend away from the hierarchical organization toward the networked organization. This trend is being brought about by the evolution from an industrial-based economy to an information-based economy. Today, most people do *knowledge work*, in which the intellectual context of the work increases to the point where the subordinate often has more expertise than the "hierarchical" supervisor. If managers know "everything," they can use hierarchical methods to tell employees what to do, how to do it, and when to do it. But physicians, scientists, engineers, and similar employees in an organizational network are not just cogs in a hierarchical machine. Each employee has special expertise and information. Therefore, it is better to view the information-based organization as a client/server network. The best "node" should be used to solve the problem.

Figure 13.7 (page 448) portrays a continuum from the hierarchical approach to the networked approach. The nodes in the network can be individuals or teams, as will be described later. Note that in the middle, between the hierarchical and networked

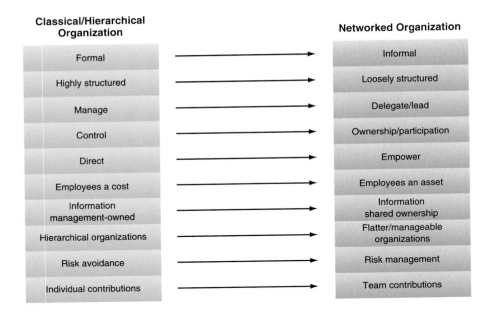

Figure 13.6 *Networked versus hierarchical organization.* [*Source: E. Turban et al.,* Information Technology for Management *(New York: Wiley, 1999), p. 136.*]

approaches, is the **flattened organization**. It has fewer layers of management and a broader span of control than the hierarchical organization, and can be considered to be an improved structure over a hierarchy.

As a straightforward example of a network approach to problem solving, let us say a student in class begins to have cardiac arrest. What should happen? If one student in the class knows CPR, he or she should become a situational leader and configure a team to solve the problem. That person is the best-equipped node in the

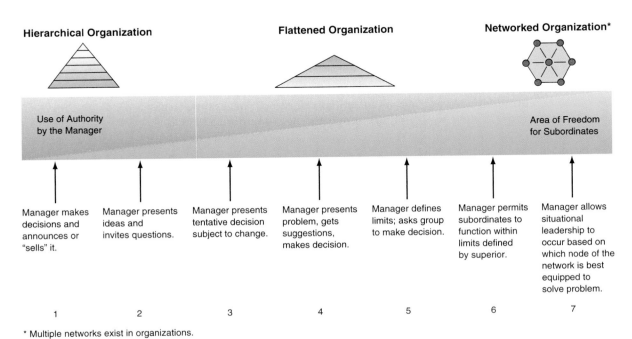

Figure 13.7 *The roles of managers and subordinates in the different types of organizations.* [*Source: E. Turban et al.,* Information Technology for Management *(New York: Wiley, 1999), p. 137.*]

network. Note that the situational leader might be temporarily hierarchical in behavior. For example, he or she might tell one person to call 911, another to get some blankets, and another to keep the hallways clear for the ambulance personnel. The professor should relinquish authority, and those people assigned tasks by the CPR expert should not argue about who should call 911! The goal is to recognize the most important task. In this case, saving a life preempts teaching, and the situational leader needs to emerge from the network.

Figure 13.8 provides a graphic portrait of the network organization for a division of British Petroleum. Note the *standing teams* of Engineering Resources, Technology Development, and Business Services. The 16 independent clusters represent *pickup teams* (yellow) assigned to solve problems that develop.

Empowerment.   *Empowerment* is the vesting of decision-making or approval authority in employees in instances where such authority traditionally was a managerial prerogative. As a philosophy and set of behavioral practices, empowerment means allowing self-managing teams and individuals to be in charge of their own tasks, as they meet company goals. As an organizational program, empowerment means giving permission to the workforce to develop and utilize their skills and knowledge to their fullest potential for the good of the organization as well as for themselves, and it means providing the framework in which this can be done.

Empowerment's relationship to IT.   Empowerment can be enhanced through IT. One of IT's most important contributions is the provision of the right information, at the right time. Information is necessary, but it may not be sufficient. To be fully empowered means to be *able to make decisions,* and these require *knowledge*. Knowledge is scarce in organizations, and specialists usually hold it. To empower employees means to increase the availability of such knowledge. Expert systems and other intelligent systems can play a major role in providing knowledge, as can the Internet, intranets, and knowledge bases. Finally, group DSS can be used to enhance the decision-making capabilities of employees working in teams.

Information technology also can provide tools that will enhance the creativity and productivity of employees, as well as the quality of their work. These tools can be special applications for increasing creativity, spreadsheets for increasing productivity, and handheld computers to improve communication.

Finally, empowerment may require training. People may need more skills and higher levels of skills. Self-directed teams, for example, are supposed to have all the necessary skills to achieve their goals. Once organized, teams will require training, which can be enhanced by IT. For example, many companies provide online training,

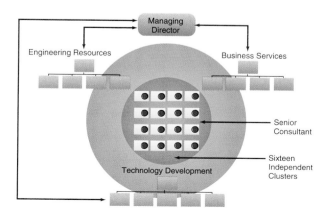

Figure 13.8 *British Petroleum Engineering networked with self-directed teams.* [*Source: Quinn D. Mills,* Rebirth of the Corporation *(New York: Wiley, 1991). Copyright © 1991 John Wiley & Sons, Inc. Reprinted by permission of John Wiley & Sons, Inc.*]

use multimedia, and even apply intelligent computer-aided instruction. Many companies are using intranets to provide training. Levi Strauss & Company uses a program called Training for Technology, which aims at training people to use the skills and tools they need in order to be able to find information and use it properly.

Empowerment of customers, suppliers, and business partners.   In addition to empowering employees, some companies are empowering their customers, suppliers, and other business partners. For example, Levi Strauss allows its textile suppliers to access its database, so they know exactly what Levi Strauss is producing and can ship supplies just-in-time. The company is using a similar approach with all its suppliers. Federal Express uses the Internet to empower its customers to check prices, prepare shipping labels, find the location of the nearest drop box, and trace the status of packages. Finally, Dell empowers its customers to track orders and troubleshoot problems. Extranets, a combination of the Internet and intranets, allow companies to empower their business partners.

Teams.   Many of the largest U.S. corporations are using **self-directed teams**. Types of teams include the following:

- *Permanent or workgroup teams*, usually multiskilled, which conduct the routine work of the organization

- *Problem-solving teams*, usually multidisciplinary and multiskilled, which are established for the purpose of solving a specific problem and then are dismantled

- *Quality circles*, which meet intermittently to find and solve workplace-related problems

- *Management teams* consisting mainly of managers from different functional areas, whose major objective is to coordinate the work of other teams

- *Virtual teams*, whose members are in different places, frequently belong to different organizations, and communicate electronically

In all of these teams, IT plays a critical role in empowering team members and providing the necessary communication links among teams.

The networked organization and self-directed teams are related to another BPR innovation—the virtual corporation—which is presented in Section 13.6.

Ethical and Societal Issues

Gaining competitive advantage through the use of IT may sometimes involve the temptation to commit unethical or even illegal actions. Companies use IT to monitor the activities of other companies and may invade the privacy of individuals, for instance. In using business intelligence (for example, spying on competitors), companies may engage in unethical tactics such as pressuring a competitor's employees to reveal information or using software that is the intellectual property of other companies (frequently without the knowledge of these other companies). Finally, companies may need to use IT to monitor the activities of their employees and customers, and in so doing they may invade the privacy of individuals.

Conducting BPR may result in the need to lay off, retrain, or transfer employees. Should management notify the employees in advance regarding such possibilities? And what about older employees who may be more difficult to retrain? Should they be offered the choice between an early retirement package and retraining? Other ethical issues may involve the need to share sensitive or personal information. Finally, individuals may have to share computer programs that they designed for their personal use in doing their jobs. Such programs may be considered the intellectual property of the individuals.

Reengineering efforts involve dramatic changes in people's jobs and working relationships. Often jobs are eliminated. Remaining competitive often does involve pain. However, the pain of reengineering is much less than the pain of being completely eliminated as a viable business. A statement by the artist Pablo Picasso puts into perspective the meaning of reengineering: "Every act of creation is first of all an act of destruction."

Before you go on . . .

1. List the major BPR principles.

2. List the major IT tools for BPR.

3. Describe mass customization, cycle time reduction, restructuring, networked organizations, empowerment, and teams.

4. Describe the role of IT in each of the above.

13.6 VIRTUAL CORPORATIONS AND INFORMATION TECHNOLOGY

One of the most interesting reengineered organizational structures is the virtual organization, usually referred to as a *virtual corporation (VC)*. The creation, operation, and management of a VC are heavily dependent on IT, and virtual corporations are especially facilitated by the Internet and extranets.

Characteristics of Virtual Corporations

A **virtual corporation (VC)** is an organization composed of several business partners sharing costs and resources for the purpose of producing a product or service. The VC can be temporary, with a onetime mission such as launching a satellite, or it can be permanent. Permanent virtual corporations are designed to create or assemble a broad range of productive resources rapidly, frequently, and concurrently. VCs include several partners, each creating a portion of a product or service, in an area in which they have special advantage such as expertise or low cost.

The concept of VCs is not new, but recent developments in IT allow new implementations that exploit its capabilities. The modern VC can be viewed as a *network* of creative people, resources, and ideas connected via online services and/or the Internet, who band together to produce products or services. A typical structure of a VC is shown in Figure 13.9 (page 452).

The major characteristics of virtual corporations are:

- *Excellence.* Each partner brings its core competence (area of excellence), thus creating an all-star winning team. No single company can match what the virtual corporation can achieve.

- *Full utilization of resources.* Some resources of the business partners are sometimes underutilized; such resources can be put to use in the VC, providing a competitive advantage.

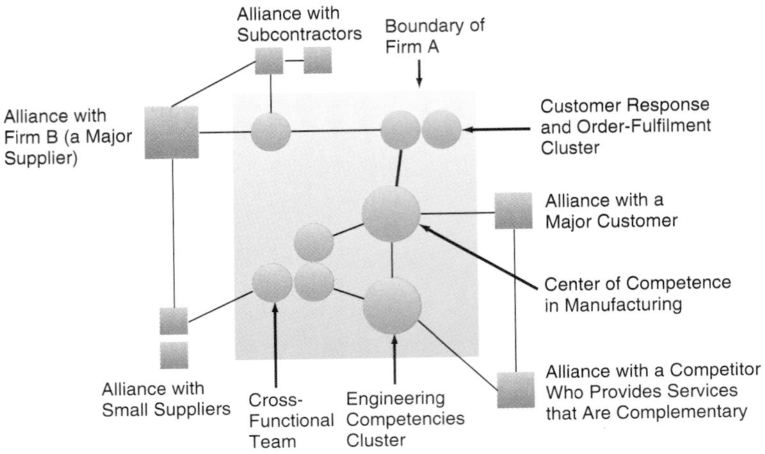

Figure 13.9 *A network structure facilitates the creation of virtual companies.* [*Source: J. Cash, Jr. et al.,* Building the Information Age Organizations: Structures, Control and Information Technology *(Burr Ridge, IL: R. D. Irwin, 1994), p. 34.*]

- *Opportunism.* The partnership is opportunistic. A VC is organized to seize a market opportunity. For example, if one of the partners is in a different country, the VC has access to more customers and/or to inexpensive resources.
- *Lack of borders.* It is difficult to identify the boundaries of a VC. For example, close cooperation among competitors, suppliers, and customers makes it difficult to determine where one company ends and another begins in the VC partnership.
- *Trust.* Business partners in a VC must be far more reliant on each other and more trusting than ever before. Their business destinies are intertwined.
- *Adaptability to change.* The VC can adapt quickly to the environmental changes discussed in Chapter 1 because its structure is relatively simple.
- *Technology.* Information technology makes the VC possible. A networked information system is a must.

How IT Supports Virtual Corporations

In a VC the resources of the business partners remain in their original locations but are integrated for the VC's use. Because the partners are in different locations, they need information systems for supporting communication and collaboration. Such systems are a special case of interorganizational information systems (IOSs), as described in Chapter 8.

IT can support virtual corporations in several ways. The most obvious are those that allow communication and collaboration among the dispersed business partners. For example, e-mail, desktop videoconferencing, screen sharing, and several other groupware technologies support VCs. Standard transactions are supported by EDI and EFT. The Internet is the infrastructure for these and other technologies. Virtual office systems, for example, can be supported by intelligent agents. Modern database technologies and networking permit business partners to access each other's databases. Lotus Notes and similar integrated groupware tools permit diversified interorganizational collaboration. In general, most VCs cannot exist without information technology.

EXAMPLES

ambra.com

Five companies join in IBM's Ambra.   IBM's Ambra was formed to produce and market a PC clone. Ambra's headquarters are in Raleigh, North Carolina. There, 80 employees use global telecommunications networks to coordinate the activities of five companies that are business partners in the virtual company.

Wearnes Technology of Singapore is doing engineering design and subsystem development services and manufacture for Ambra PC components. SCI Systems assembles the Ambra microcomputers in its assembly plants on a build-to-order basis from order data received by its computers from AI Incorporated. AI, a subsidiary of Insight Direct, a national telemarketing company based in Tempe, Arizona, receives orders for Ambra computers from customers over its 800-number telephone lines or its Web site. Merisel Enterprises provides the product and delivery database used by AI and handles Ambra order fulfillment and customer delivery. Finally, another IBM subsidiary provides field service and customer support.

No need to buy office furniture for Turnstone.   Steelcase Inc. is a major U.S. maker   *steelcase.com*
of office furniture. It formed a virtual corporation subsidiary called Turnstone that sells its products through catalogs designed and printed by a third-party company (and now also available on the Web). Turnstone customers e-mail or phone in credit card orders to a telemarketing company based in Denver, Colorado, which transmits the order data to computers at warehouses operated by Excel Logistics, Inc. in Westerville, Ohio. From there the products are shipped to customers by subcontracted carriers. Excel's computer systems handle all order processing, shipment tracking, and inventory control applications. Marketing, financial management, and coordinating the virtual company's business partners are the only major functions left to Turnstone's managers. ●

Before you go on . . .

1. Define virtual corporations (VCs).

2. Describe VC benefits and IT support.

WHAT'S IN **IT** FOR ME ?

www.wiley.com/
college/turban

FOR THE ACCOUNTING MAJOR   ACC

One of the major issues in both strategic information systems and business process reengineering is the justification of the investment, which can be substantial. In order to collect the data for such a justification the accountant must understand these technologies and the role of IT. Also, the auditing of the supporting information systems, reengineered organizations, and virtual corporations may be more complex.

FOR THE FINANCE MAJOR   FIN

Investments in both SIS and BPR can be substantial. The finance department needs to conduct a cost–benefit analysis of proposed investments in either. Also, budgets for SIS and BPR projects need to be prepared and funds secured. To do an appropriate job, finance people must understand the nature of these technologies and the manner in which they enable organizations to seize opportunities and solve problems.

FOR THE MARKETING MAJOR   MKT

SIS and/or BPR are likely to change distribution channels, order fulfillment, customer service, and many tasks that are under the control of marketing and sales. SIS and BPR provide a chance for marketing and sales to significantly improve their productivity by seizing many technology-related opportunities. Paperless environments, virtual organizations, mass customization, and Internet-based customer service are some of the new features that BPR and SIS bring to organizations. It is difficult to imagine a modern marketing department that does not strive to use SIS these days to increase competitiveness.

POM

FOR THE PRODUCTION/OPERATIONS MANAGEMENT MAJOR

BPR is most likely to completely change existing business processes including production lines, materials handling, design, and inventory systems. The changes could be so significant that POM methods may need to be reengineered, too. The operations people are most likely to be responsible for the implementation of BPR, and they must work closely with the information systems department, which provides the IT support. Without such cooperation, BPR efforts are likely to fail at an extremely large cost.

HRM

FOR THE HUMAN RESOURCES MANAGEMENT MAJOR

Major organizational changes brought by BPR may have significant impacts on people, their jobs, their career ladders, and their behavior in the organization. Concepts such as empowerment, networked organizations, and virtual teams are revolutionary. What makes SIS and BPR different is the *magnitude* of the organizational changes that could disrupt the operation of the organization if not handled properly by management and HRM. HRM will be involved in layoffs if needed. Finally, BPR and new IT may require substantial training or retraining.

SUMMARY

❶ Describe strategic information systems and explain their advantages.
Strategic information systems (SISs) support or shape competitive strategy. They can be outward (customer) oriented or inward (organization) oriented. They provide an organization with a competitive edge in its industry.

❷ Describe Porter's competitive forces model and how IT improves competitiveness.
Porter's model of competitive industry forces is frequently used to explain how companies can increase their competitiveness. It lists five forces that shape competition. Response strategies and related SIS can be used to lessen these forces. To counter the forces one can use strategies such as cost leadership, differentiation, and focus, which can be facilitated by SIS.

❸ Describe representative strategic information systems and the advantage they provide with the support of IT.
SIS can be used by both suppliers of goods and suppliers of services. A variety of companies use SIS to compete in their respective industries in cost leadership, quality, speed, growth, innovation, internal efficiency, and customer orientation. An SIS may provide support for more than one strategy. Today companies use the Internet, intranets, EDI, global ISDN networks, decision support systems, and intelligent systems to increase quality, productivity, and speed.

❹ **Understand the role of business processes in organizations and the reasons why reengineering is necessary.**
Continual incremental improvements in business processes are necessary but are frequently insufficient to deal with today's business pressures. One reason is that hierarchical organizations tend to be bureaucratic and inflexible and have difficulty in responding to cross-functional needs. BPR is the fundamental rethinking and radical redesign of business processes to achieve dramatic improvements. IT is the major enabler of BPR.

❺ **Demonstrate the role of IT in supporting BPR and especially mass customization, cycle time reduction, self-directed teams, and empowerment.**
The trend is for organizations that are reengineered to behave like networks and operate in an online, real-time, empowered mode of operation. BPR applications include: (a) *mass customization*, which enables production of customized goods by methods of mass production at a low cost; (b) *cycle time reduction*, which is an essential part of many BPR projects and is usually attainable only by IT support; (c) *self-directed teams*, which can be permanent teams or quickly configured teams that solve specific problems and are then dissolved; and (d) *empowerment* of employees, which is done by providing them with IT-supported information and knowledge so they can work autonomously to make the necessary decisions.

❻ **Describe virtual corporations and their IT support.**
One of the most innovative BPR strategies is the creation of business alliances and virtual corporations. A virtual corporation is an organization composed of several business partners sharing costs and resources for the purpose of producing a product or service. The VC can be temporary or it can be permanent. It is supported by telecommunications, extranets, EDI, and groupware software.

INTERACTIVE LEARNING SESSION

Go to the CD and access Chapter 13: Strategic Systems and Reorganization. There you will find a video clip from the "Nightly Business Report" that presents a business problem involving the topics covered in this chapter. You will be asked to watch the video and answer questions about it.

www.wiley.com/
college/turban

For additional resources, go to the book's Web site for Chapter 13. There you will find Web resources for the chapter, including links to organizations, people, and technology; "IT's About Business" company links; "What's in IT for Me?" links; and a self-testing Web quiz for Chapter 13.

DISCUSSION QUESTIONS

1. Review the opening case. Explain how the use of IT helped the firm reengineer its core business process and how it will change delivery of its service.

2. Provide three examples of IT being used to build a barrier to entry for new competitors and new products.

3. Discuss the idea that IT by itself can rarely provide a sustainable competitive advantage.

4. What is the importance of business intelligence in strategic information systems?

5. Explain the role an intranet can play in lessening the stovepipe problem.

6. Relate virtual corporations to networked organizations. Why is a VC considered to be business process reengineering?

7. Discuss what it would be like if the registration process and class scheduling process were reengineered to an online, real-time basis with good connectivity and good empowerment in the university organization.

PROBLEM-SOLVING ACTIVITIES

1. Study the Web sites of Amazon.com and Barnes & Noble (*barnesandnoble.com*) and find some information about the competition between the two. Analyze Barnes & Noble's defense strategy using Porter's five forces model and its extensions. Prepare a report.

2. The normal way to collect fees from travelers on expressways is to use tollbooths. Automatic coin-collecting baskets can expedite the process, but do not eliminate the long waiting lines during rush hours. About 80 percent of the travelers are frequent users of the expressways near their homes, and they complain bitterly. The money collection process in some highways has been reengineered, reducing travelers' waiting time by 90 percent and money processing cost by 80 percent. Several new information technologies including *smart cards* are used in the process. Find information on how IT is used to expedite toll collection.

3. Carlson Travel Network of Minneapolis is the second largest travel agency in the country. To save time and money for its customers it provides an agentless service to corporate clients, the first of which was General Electric Company. A computerized system allows GE employees to book trips by filling out a form on their PCs. The system is available 24 hours a day. It is connected with the computer reservation systems of major airlines, car rental companies, and hotel chains. The automated system generates detailed spending reports, enabling GE to negotiate special rates for their employees. Complex travel itineraries are still handled manually, but they account for less than 5 percent of the total trips. The system saves GE several million dollars each year.

   a. Identify the process reengineering activities.

   b. Describe the support provided by IT.

   c. Find other companies that allow their employees to book trips by themselves.

INTERNET ACTIVITIES

1. Enter SEC's EDGAR database (*http://freeedgar.com*). Prepare a list of the documents that are available, and discuss the benefits one can derive in using this database for conducting a competitive intelligence.

2. Access the site of Levi Strauss or J.C. Penney. Find information about how to order their customized clothes. E-mail either company to find out more about their mass customization plan.

3. Surf the Internet to find some recent material on the role IT plays in supporting BPR. Search for products and vendors and download an available demo.

4. Enter *ets.org*. Find the ways you can download software for GMAT preparation. Compare the services provided to those you get in a regular bookstore. What competitive advantage does ETS have? How is it supported by IT?

TEAM ACTIVITES AND ROLE PLAYING

1. Assign group members to each of the major car rental companies. Find out their latest strategies regarding customer service. Visit their Web sites, compare the findings, and prepare a report on competitiveness in the car rental industry and the role of IT. Prepare a Porter's forces model to substantiate your findings.

2. Assign members to UPS, FedEx, and the United States Postal Service. Each group will study the strategies of one company with respect to overnight delivery and the use of the Internet as a transport medium.

3. Explore the concept of *virtual classrooms* and universities. (Start by visiting *cs.unc.edu* and *arpa.mil/sbir*.) Each member will explore an actual case. Summarize the findings. What competitive advantage is provided to universities that are offering virtual classes?

REAL-WORLD CASE   *mfrpc.com*

Reengineering Professional Work with IT

The Business Problem   Mir Fox & Rodriguez P.C. is a 60-person Houston-based professional accounting firm that was experiencing a problem common to many professional services firms: stiff competition for qualified employees. The firm's managers were spending more and more time supervising the staff. Work was getting bogged down in the process, and the firm's bottom line began to suffer. That's when Carolyne Fox, one of the firm's founders, and her partners began looking for technology that could help them reengineer the actual process of one of their most common services, conducting an accounting audit. At the end of 1994, the principals at Mir Fox & Rodriguez embarked on a five-year plan to automate their business using new technology. Their initial goal was to work faster. "When we first started this process we had our blinders on," Fox comments. "We were just focused on working faster, which we did. But we had simply automated what was designed to be a paper-intensive process. Then we realized we needed to completely change what we do and how we do it."

The IT Solution   Mir Fox & Rodriguez chose Lotus Notes as the format to reengineer their business, run a virtually paperless office, and create new opportunities. Fox and her team created Virtual AuditorSM, a custom application developed using Lotus Notes R5. Virtual AuditorSM is comprised of 17 different Lotus Notes forms, programs within the application that automate the audit process. The heart and soul of the application is RiskmasterSM, a complex form that walks the auditor through a series of questions about the client's business. Using mathematical formulas, RiskmasterSM evaluates answers to the questions and helps the auditor make the right decisions about what to do next. Fox says the firm chose Lotus Notes because it offers the advanced functions they needed, yet was not difficult to learn. "That was the real value," Fox says. "With Lotus Notes, we could learn how to create these programs ourselves. We didn't need to hire developers."

While managers still need to review the audits, the staff is able to provide higher-quality work with minimal supervision because the application is providing the guidance that a senior person would offer. "We've taken our intellectual capital and encapsulated it in this application," says Fox. "The program asks the right questions and then executes the judgment that a very senior person would."

The Results.   With Virtual AuditorSM, the firm is now operating in a virtually paperless environment. Fox says the staff is working at a higher level because no one is wasting time doing menial tasks such as photocopying. The technology helps the firm remain extremely profitable while keeping hourly rates down. "After the first year using Virtual AuditorSM our effective rate per hour went up $11 per hour, and we expect it to go up more this year," Fox reports. "There's no measure more critical than that." Mir Fox & Rodriguez was so successful with Virtual AuditorSM, the firm is using the technology to create new business opportunities. After its consulting practice merged with another firm in January 2001, the firm launched Your Corner Office. The new company will offer financial and business advisory services over the Web to small and mid-size businesses—a market Fox says is often priced out of traditional professional services.

Source: SmallBusinessSchool.org and *mfrpc.com.*

Questions

1. Most examples of reengineering of business processes deal with manufacturing and service provision, and relatively few deal with redesign of knowledge work of professionals. Should we assume that highly trained professionals have already designed their work processes to be as efficient and as effective as possible?

2. Which of the five forces of Porter are countered by the new systems at Mir Fox & Rodriguez?

3. Which competitive strategies of those suggested in the chapter are noticeable in this case?

4. Which of the business pressures discussed in Chapter 1 are evident in this case?

5. Which of the corporate response activities of Chapter 1 are evident in this case?

VIRTUAL COMPANY ASSIGNMENT

wiley.com/college/turban

Extreme Descent Snowboards

Background As you stride confidently into the suite of executive offices at EDS, an administrative assistant smiles at you and tells you that Matt Brandy, one of the co-founders of EDS, is expecting you. The door to Matt Brandy's office is open, but you knock anyway since you see Matt working at his personal computer. Matt stands and walks around his desk to greet you. As you take a seat in front of the large oak desk, you look around the office and think to yourself that being a successful executive certainly has its advantages.

www.wiley.com/college/turban

After a few moments of casual conversation about your internship, Matt explains that your next assignment will be extremely important in determining the future direction of EDS. He hands you a folder containing instructions for your assignment. You thank Matt for his time. He then stands and walks around this desk to shake your hand as you leave his office. After you leave the suite of executive offices, you read your next assignment.

Assignment

Using an Internet search engine of your choice, identify, visit, and explore the Web sites of three companies that sell "customized" snowboards over the Internet. You can use the same companies you used in the assignment for Chapter 9.

You will then prepare and submit a report that addresses the following questions and issues. You may want to use a spreadsheet package (such as Microsoft Excel) to answer questions 1 and 2.

1. Compare the three companies you have identified to EDS. Make the comparison with respect to products, pricing, service, and warranty.

2. Using Porter's competitive forces model, identify and describe the competitive forces that can impact the snowboard industry.

3. Using the competitive forces model, identify and describe the strategy or combination of strategies that each of the three competitors uses. Recommend a strategy or combination of strategies for EDS to follow. What organizational changes, resources, and technology would be required to carry out your recommendation?

INFORMATION SYSTEMS DEVELOPMENT

CHAPTER PREVIEW

Planning and developing large information systems is akin to a multilevel chess game—it is a very demanding task for even the most experienced professionals. Information systems tend to grow in complexity as they grow in size. *Systems development* is the entire set of activities needed to construct an information systems solution to a business problem or opportunity. This chapter discusses a variety of approaches to systems development. We begin with planning. Next we present the concept of the systems development life cycle (SDLC), which provides the framework for all activities in the development process. Third, we discuss other methods for systems development that organizations may use in standalone fashion or in conjunction with the SDLC, including prototyping, rapid application development, and object-oriented development. The next section examines alternatives to in-house development, including end-user development, acquisition of systems from vendors, and use of application service providers (ASPs). The chapter closes with a look at Internet- and intranet-based systems development.

CHAPTER OUTLINE

LEARNING OBJECTIVES

1. Describe the information systems planning process.
2. Discuss the concept of a systems development life cycle (SDLC).
3. Discuss the advantages and disadvantages of the traditional development, prototyping, rapid application development, object-oriented development, and end-user development life cycles.
4. Identify the advantages and disadvantages of CASE tools.
5. Evaluate the alternatives to in-house systems development.
6. Discuss the key features of Internet and intranet development.

EVEN IN TOUGH TIMES, IT PROJECTS AND PEOPLE REMAIN A PRIORITY FOR BOISE CASCADE

bc.com

The Business Problem

With revenue down about 5 percent, Boise Cascade Corp. was having a difficult year, but that didn't mean the $7.81 billion forest-products and office-supplies company would be shelving important IT projects, said company chairman and CEO George Harad. In fact, the Boise, Idaho, company increased its IT budget slightly for the year, to about $60 million, and the IT department had several initiatives in the works. The company is convinced its IT projects will help it achieve two key goals: increased efficiency and greater responsiveness to customers. In an industry that generally takes a wait-and-see approach to IT, Boise Cascade stands out for its early identification and pursuit of strategic IT projects it believes will yield measurable improvements in its business.

The IT Solution

Among the projects in progress is One Boise, an initiative to unify databases used by Boise Cascade's office-products-distribution business. The project reflects the company's overall philosophy of keeping its data and IT systems and processes "clean and simple," as Bob Egan, VP of IT, describes it. The company tackles IT projects methodically, from the ground up, so that it has a solid base on which to build top-level user applications and services, which are more flexible as a result. For instance, the

underlying organization of its databases and its company-wide use of applications and shared utilities mean Boise Cascade can more easily change its user interfaces and make applications available via the Web. "We're conservative in approach but not in outcomes," Egan says.

Another tactic of the IT department is to work with executives from all the company's business units. For instance, for each major application it implements, the IT staff works with a senior-level executive from the affected operating unit to identify priorities and ensure that the new technologies will be cost effective.

In the IT department itself, Egan's own priorities are clear: He treats Boise's IT staff as a top asset. The department maintains a healthy attitude about work-life balance, including an emphasis on 40-hour work weeks, with rare exceptions for major projects. The biggest project the department took on in the past year was an overhaul of Boise Cascade's network services. The project included implementing new directory services based on Microsoft Active Directory, putting in new firewalls, installing a virtual private network, and building a subnetwork for the e-commerce sites it operates for its paper and wood-products divisions.

At the same time, Boise upgraded the groupware tools it uses, including Lotus Notes, Exchange 2000, and NetMeeting. It also installed quality-of-service software that will let it monitor and control how the company uses its network bandwidth. The upgrade, whose goal was to prepare for anticipated increases in traffic from wireless devices (such as pagers, handhelds, notebooks equipped with wireless modems, and wireless LANs) and e-commerce, gives Boise a load-balanced network for its e-commerce sites and hosted applications. In the future, it will supply authentication and security services that will provide essential access controls as the company establishes more connections among its network, the Internet, and customer networks.

460

The company has managed to minimize IT turnover rate to an unusually low 3 percent annually for the past five years, has achieved its major IT development goals, and is achieving the business goals that the IT supports. In implementing e-commerce systems for its major businesses, Boise Cascade set out to provide customers with Web-based, real-time access to the same product-ordering and delivery systems Boise Cascade uses internally. Customers can do some custom product configuration, create and save catalog templates, customize their views of product data, and arrange for deliveries, Egan says. "All the business logic needed for custom product configuration and delivery is available over the Web," adds Egan, "and three-fourths of customer inquiries can be handled through self-service over the Web."

Source: John Rendleman and Diane Rezendes Khirallah, *informationweek.com* (September 17, 2001).

What We Learned from This Case

Because information systems are so critical to competitive advantage in so many companies, their timely and careful development are very high priorities. Just how much of a priority becomes more clear when development budgets are threatened in tough economic circumstances. This strong prioritization of IT shows that Boise Cascade understands the major role IT plays in achievement of its goals of increased efficiency and enhanced customer relations. In addition, the company also has an enlightened perspective on how to manage its IT personnel, who represent crucial knowledge resources that are not easily duplicated or substituted for. The case also demonstrates the increasing importance of Web and e-commerce application development, paying benefits of increased customer service and customer retention. Finally, we see that the firm anticipates that mobile computing will be an important aspect of how it interacts with its customers, and how this new communication channel should interface with its other e-commerce platforms.

14.1 INFORMATION SYSTEMS PLANNING

Planning an information system doesn't start with bits and bytes, mips, or a Web site. Rather, it starts with gaining a holistic perspective on what the firm aims to achieve and how it will do so. **Systems development** is the entire set of activities needed to construct an information systems solution to a business problem or opportunity. A key component is information systems planning, which begins with the strategic plan of the organization, as shown in Figure 14.1 (page 462). The organization's strategic plan states the firm's overall mission, the goals that follow from the mission, and the broad steps necessary to reach these goals. An essential input into the organization's strategic plan is an assessment of the current state of the organization, in which the current performance of the firm is compared to the previous strategic plan. The mission states what the organization ideally wants to become or to create at some future point in time. The strategic planning process matches the organization's objectives and resources to its changing markets and opportunities.

The organizational strategic plan and the existing IT architecture provide the inputs in developing the information systems strategic plan. The **IT architecture** delineates the way an organization's information resources should be used to accomplish its mission. It encompasses both technical and managerial aspects of information resources. The technical aspects include hardware and operating systems, networking, data and data management systems, and applications software. The managerial

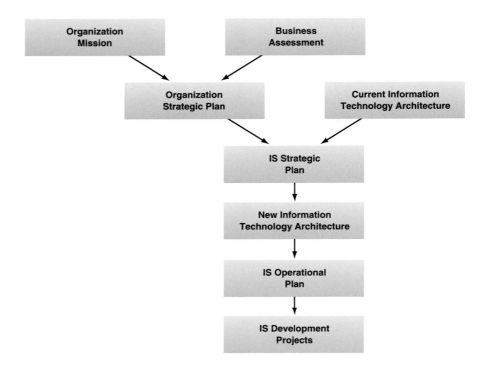

Figure 14.1 *The infor-mation systems planning process.*

aspects specify how managing the IS department will be accomplished, how functional area managers will be involved, and how IS decisions will be made.

The IS Strategic Plan

The **IS strategic plan** is a set of long-range goals that describe the IT architecture and major IS initiatives needed to achieve the goals of the organization. The IS strategic plan must meet three objectives:

- It must be aligned with the organization's strategic plan.
- It must provide for an IT architecture that enables users, applications, and databases to be seamlessly networked and integrated.
- It must efficiently allocate IS development resources among competing projects, so the projects can be completed on time, within budget, and have the required functionality.

The IS strategic plan states the *mission* of the IS department, which defines the department's underlying purpose. The mission helps to answer questions relating to three major issues:

- ***Efficiency.*** Does the IS function help the organization reach its goals with minimum resources?
- ***Effectiveness.*** Does the IS function help the functional area managers (and executives) do the right things?
- ***Competitiveness.*** Does the IS function engage in projects that will enhance the organization's competitive position?

The mission of the IS department requires a great deal of input from *all* of the organization's functional area managers, and often from higher organizational officers as well. This input will help to define the appropriate role of the IS department in accomplishing the organization's goals.

The IS Operational Plan

The IS strategic plan may require a new IT architecture, or the existing IT architecture may be sufficient. In either case, the IS strategic plan leads to the **IS operational plan**, which is a clear set of projects that will be executed by the IS department and by functional area managers in support of the IS strategic plan.

A typical IS operational plan contains the following elements:

- *Mission:* The mission of the IS function
- *IS environment:* A summary of the information needs of the functional areas and of the organization as a whole
- *Objectives of the IS function:* The IS function's current best estimate of its goals
- *Constraints on the IS function:* Technological, financial, and personnel limitations on the IS function
- *Long-term systems needs:* A summary of the systems needed by the company and the IS projects selected to reach organizational goals
- *Short-range plan:* An inventory of present projects, and a detailed plan of projects to be developed or continued during the current year

Before you go on . . .

1. Where does information systems planning begin?

2. What is the relationship of the IS strategic plan to the organization's strategic plan?

14.2 THE TRADITIONAL SYSTEMS DEVELOPMENT LIFE CYCLE (SDLC)

The **systems development life cycle (SDLC)** is the traditional systems development method used by most organizations today. The SDLC is a structured framework that consists of sequential processes by which information systems are developed. As shown in Figure 14.2 (page 464), these include systems investigation, systems analysis, systems design, programming, testing, implementation, operation, and maintenance. These processes, in turn, consist of well-defined tasks. Some of these tasks are present in most projects, whereas others are present in only certain types of projects. That is, large projects typically require all the tasks, whereas smaller development projects may require only a subset of the tasks.

Other models for the SDLC may contain more or fewer than the eight stages we present here. The flow of tasks, however, remains largely the same, regardless of the number of stages. In the past, developers used the **waterfall approach** to the SDLC, in which tasks in one stage were completed before the work proceeded to the next stage. Today, systems developers go back and forth among the stages as necessary.

Systems development projects produce desired results through team efforts. Development teams typically include users, systems analysts, programmers, and

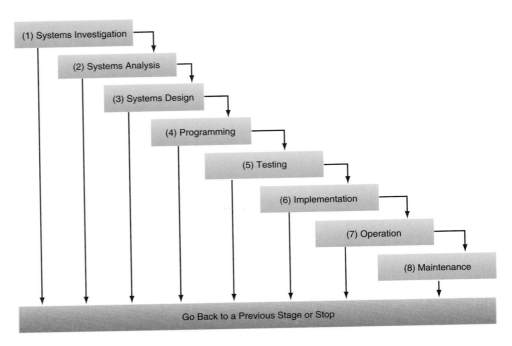

Figure 14.2 *An eight-stage systems development life cycle (SDLC).*

technical specialists. *Users* are employees from all functional areas and levels of the organization who will interact with the system, either directly or indirectly. Direct interaction means that users will make hands-on use of the system, and indirect interaction means that users will use the outputs from the system. **Systems analysts** are information systems professionals who specialize in analyzing and designing information systems. **Programmers** are information systems professionals who modify existing computer programs or write new computer programs to satisfy user requirements. **Technical specialists** are experts on a certain type of technology, such as databases or telecommunications. All people who are affected by changes in information systems (users and managers, for example) are known as **systems stakeholders**, and are typically involved by varying degrees and at various times in the systems development.

In the remainder of this section we will look at each of the processes in the SDLC.

Systems Investigation

Systems development professionals agree that the more time invested in understanding the business problem to be solved, in understanding technical options for systems, and in understanding problems that are likely to occur during development, the greater the chance of actually successfully solving the (correct) problem. For these reasons, systems investigation begins with the business problem. Problems (and opportunities) often require not only understanding them from the internal point of view, but also seeing them as organizational partners (suppliers or customers) would see them. Another useful perspective is that of competitors. How have they responded to similar situations, and what outcomes and additional opportunities have materialized? Creativity and out-of-the-box thinking can pay big dividends when isolated problems can be recognized as systemic failures whose causes cross organizational boundaries. Once these perspectives can be gained, those involved can also begin to better see the true scope of the project and propose possible solutions. Then an initial assessment of these proposed system solutions can begin.

Feasibility studies.   The next task in the systems investigation stage is the feasibility study. The **feasibility study** determines the probability of success of the proposed systems development project and assesses the project's technical, economic, and behavioral feasibility. The feasibility study is critically important to the systems development process because, done properly, the study can prevent organizations from making costly mistakes (like creating systems that will not work, will not work efficiently, or that people can't or won't use). The various feasibility analyses also give the stakeholders an opportunity to decide what metrics to use to measure how a proposed system (and later, a completed system) meets their various objectives.

Technical feasibility.   **Technical feasibility** determines if the hardware, software, and communications components can be developed and/or acquired to solve the business problem. Technical feasibility also determines if the organization's existing technology can be used to achieve the project's performance objectives.

Economic feasibility.   **Economic feasibility** determines if the project is an acceptable financial risk and if the organization can afford the expense and time needed to complete the project. Economic feasibility addresses two primary questions: Do the benefits outweigh the costs of the project? Can the project be completed as scheduled?

Three commonly used methods to determine economic feasibility are breakeven analysis, return on investment (ROI), and net present value (NPV). **Breakeven analysis** determines the amount of time required for the cumulative cash flow from a development project to equal its initial and ongoing investment. **Return on investment** is the ratio of the net cash inflows from a project divided by the cash outflows of the project.

The **net present value** is the net amount by which project savings exceed project expenses, after allowing for the cost of capital and the time value of money. The *cost of capital* is the minimum desired rate of return on an investment and is the average cost of funds used to finance the operations of the business. NPV also takes the time value of money into account. The *time value of money* means that a sum received at a future date is not worth as much as a sum received today, because a sum of money you have today can be invested to earn interest. (For more details on how to compute NPV, see the Web site.)

www.wiley.com/
college/turban

Determining return on investment in IT projects is rarely straightforward, but it often is essential. Part of the difficulty stems from the fact that the proposed system or technology may be "cutting edge," and there may be no previous evidence of what sort of ROI is to be expected. IT's About Business Box 14.1 (page 466) gives a good example of both the organizational necessity and the inherent challenges of ROI analysis of IT projects.

Behavioral feasibility.   **Behavioral feasibility** addresses the human issues of the project. All systems development projects introduce change into the organization, and people generally fear change. In fact, employees may overtly or covertly resist a new system. Overt resistance may take the form of sabotaging the new system (e.g., entering data incorrectly) or deriding the new system to anyone who will listen. Covert resistance typically occurs when employees quietly refuse to use the new system. They simply do their jobs using their old methods.

A primary manifestation of change brought about by the introduction of new systems is changes in organizational information flows. These changes affect the *information gatekeepers*, who are the stakeholders with responsibility for information that is important to the organization or one of its units. Because "knowledge is power," these gatekeepers want to remain in control of collecting, processing, and disseminating this information.

IT's About Business

sears.com   FIN

Box 14.1   Sears demands ROI analysis for hand-held computer system

Dennis Honan, an IS executive at retailer Sears, Roebuck & Co., is a veteran of what he calls the company's "ROI culture." Honan, VP of Information Systems for Sears's Home Services business, got approval to spend some $20 million to equip the unit's 14,000-person service staff with handheld PCs. The overriding goal of the project was to improve the efficiency of Sears's service technicians. Not only were they to be given handheld computers, but the devices would also be linked by wireless WANs to Sears's databases. Honan projected an average 6 to 8 percent gain in the technicians' productivity, mainly because the setup would let them request price estimates, check availability for appliance parts, place orders, receive software upgrades, and get job-schedule updates from wherever they were working. That, in turn, would let technicians complete more calls a day.

Also, when customers cancel or reschedule service calls—something that happens up to 100 times a day in some districts—technicians and dispatchers could learn about the changes and make schedule adjustments almost immediately. In the past, they'd be paged, have to find a pay phone, then wait for instructions. "Here was an opportunity to computerize everything, eliminate paper service orders, and have the ability to communicate almost instantaneously with the technicians," says Vince Accardi, director of process management.

The project sounded good enough to go, but presenting a formal ROI analysis was "absolutely essential" to the approval process, Honan says. Adds Joseph Smialowski, Sears's senior VP and CIO and a key player in the approval of all types of investments at the retailer, "All our projects—whether it's opening new stores or buying new systems—have to compete for the capital that's available. There are really no projects that can slip through without going through a quantitative analysis."

To justify the handheld PC initiative, Home Services managers used a cost–benefit measure to determine net annual savings. To illustrate the longer-term benefits of the investment, they also calculated the net present value (NPV) of cash flows over a five-year period.

Home Services presented the expected benefits in terms of expected annual savings for Sears. The project proposal then went through a multilevel evaluation process: first within Home Services, and next at the Company's strategic planning level. The plan was evaluated for technical soundness, accuracy of the cost estimates, and to see if it fit Sears's business model and enterprise architecture.

The proposal then went to Sears's finance committee, which includes the company's CEO, the chief financial officer (CFO), the CIO, and two business presidents. They approved the project. It was then rolled out, first in test markets, then district by district.

Source: B. Violino, "Sears, Roebuck, & Co. Productivity Gains from Mobile Computing," *http://www.informationweek.com/679/79iuro6.htm* (1998).

Questions

1. IS projects at Sears are not exempt from demanding ROI analysis. Why would they be, or why should they be, at any other business organization?

2. Given the enormous expense of the project—which is just one small part of the overall IT infrastructure—what would you estimate the yearly IT budget to be at a firm like Sears?

A more positive and pragmatic concern of behavioral feasibility is assessing the skills and training needs that often accompany a new information system. In some organizations, a proposed system may require mathematical or linguistic skills beyond what the workforce currently possesses. In others, a workforce may simply need additional skill building rather than remedial education. Behavioral feasibility is as much about "can they use it" as it is about "will they use it."

After the feasibility analysis, a "Go/No-Go" decision is reached. The functional area manager for whom the system is to be developed and the project manager sign off on the decision. If the decision is "No-Go," the project is put on the shelf until conditions are more favorable, or the project is discarded. If the decision is "Go," then the systems development project proceeds and the systems analysis phase begins.

As noted above, although originally conceived to be discrete consecutive steps, current thinking holds that certain activities in the SDLC should be repeated as necessary. The most common of these are feasibility analyses, often repeated at the ends of the analysis, design, programming, and testing phases. The reason is simply that the accuracy of any feasibility study substantially increases as developers learn more about all aspects of the project.

Systems Analysis

Once a development project has the necessary approvals from all participants, the systems analysis stage begins. **Systems analysis** is the examination of the business problem that the organization plans to solve with an information system. This stage defines the business problem, identifies its causes, specifies the solution, and identifies the information requirements that the solution must satisfy. Understanding the business problem requires understanding the various processes involved. These can often be quite complicated and interdependent. Analysts have a variety of tools that support this analysis. (For an example of a modern process modeling tool and how it is used, see IT's About Business W14.1 at the book's Web site.)

www.wiley.com/college/turban

Organizations have three basic solutions to any business problem: (1) Do nothing and continue to use the existing system unchanged. (2) Modify or enhance the existing system. (3) Develop a new system. The main purpose of the systems analysis stage is to gather information about the existing system, to determine which of the three basic solutions to pursue, and to determine the requirements for an enhanced or new system. The end product (the "deliverable") of this stage is a set of systems requirements.

Arguably the most difficult task in systems analysis is to identify the specific *information requirements* that the system must satisfy. Information requirements specify what information, how much information, for whom, when, and in what format. Systems analysts use many different techniques to obtain the information requirements for the new system. These techniques include structured and unstructured interviews with users, and direct observation. Structured interviews have questions written in advance. In unstructured interviews, the analyst does not have predefined questions but uses experience to elicit the problems of the existing system from the user. With direct observation, analysts observe users interacting with the existing system.

In developing information requirements, analysts must be careful not to let any preconceived ideas they have interfere with their objectivity. Further, analysts must be unobtrusive, so that users will interact with the system as they normally would.

There are problems associated with eliciting information requirements, regardless of the method used by the analyst. First, the business problem may be poorly defined. Second, the users may not know exactly what the problem is, what they want, or what they need. Third, users may disagree with each other about business procedures or even about the business problem. Finally, the problem may not be information related, but may require other solutions, such as a change in management or additional training.

The systems analysis stage produces the following information:

- Strengths and weaknesses of the existing system
- Functions that the new system must have to solve the business problem
- User information requirements for the new system

Armed with this information, systems developers can proceed to the systems design stage.

Systems Design

Systems analysis describes *what* a system must do to solve the business problem, and **systems design** describes *how* the system will accomplish this task. The deliverable of the systems design phase is the technical design that specifies the following:

- System outputs, inputs, and user interfaces
- Hardware, software, databases, telecommunications, personnel, and procedures
- How these components are integrated

This output is the set of system specifications.

Systems design encompasses two major aspects of the new system:

- **Logical systems design** states *what* the system will do, with abstract specifications.
- **Physical systems design** states *how* the system will perform its functions, with actual physical specifications.

Logical design specifications include the design of outputs, inputs, processing, databases, telecommunications, controls, security, and IS jobs. Physical design specifications include the design of hardware, software, database, telecommunications, and procedures. For example, the logical telecommunications design may call for a wide-area network connecting the company's plants. The physical telecommunications design will specify the types of communications hardware (e.g., computers and routers), software (e.g., the network operating system), media (e.g., fiber optics and satellite), and bandwidth (e.g., 100 Mbps).

When both these aspects of system specifications are approved by all participants, they are "frozen." That is, once the specifications are agreed upon, they should not be changed. However, users typically ask for added functionality in the system (called **scope creep**), for several reasons. First, as users more clearly understand how the system will work and what their information and processing needs are, they see additional functions that they would like the system to have. Also, as time passes after the design specifications are frozen, business conditions often change, and users ask for added functionality. Because scope creep is expensive, project managers place controls on changes requested by users. These controls help to prevent **runaway projects**—systems development projects that are so far over budget and past deadline that they must be abandoned, typically with large monetary loss.

Programming

Systems developers utilize the design specifications to acquire the software needed for the system to meet its functional objectives and solve the business problem. As discussed in Chapter 4, organizations may buy the software or construct it in-house.

Although many organizations tend to purchase packaged software, many other firms continue to develop custom software in-house. For example, Wal-Mart and Eli Lilly build practically all their software in-house. The chief benefit of custom development is systems that are better suited than packaged applications to an organization's new and existing business processes. For many organizations, custom software is more expensive than packaged applications. However, if a package does not closely fit the company needs, the savings are often diluted when the information systems staff or consultants must extend the functionality of the purchased packages.

If the organization decides to construct the software in-house, then **programming** involves the translation of the design specifications into computer code. This process can be lengthy and time-consuming, because writing computer code remains as much an art as a science. Large systems development projects can require hundreds of thousands of lines of computer code and hundreds of computer programmers. In such projects, programming teams are used. These teams often include functional area users to help the programmers focus on the business problem at hand.

In an attempt to add rigor (and some uniformity) to the programming process, programmers use structured programming techniques. These techniques improve the logical flow of the program by decomposing the computer code into *modules*, which are sections of code (subsets of the entire program). This modular structure allows for more efficient and effective testing, because each module can be tested by itself. These structured programming techniques include the following restrictions:

- Each module has one, and only one, function.
- Each module has only one entrance and one exit. That is, the logic in the computer program enters a module in only one place and exits in only one place.
- There are no GO TO statements allowed.

For example, a flowchart for a simple payroll application might look like the one shown in Figure 14.3. The figure shows the only three types of structures that are used in structured programming: sequence, decision, and loop. In the *sequence* structure, program statements are executed one after another until all the statements in the sequence have been executed. The *decision* structure allows the logic flow to branch, depending on certain conditions being met. The *loop* structure enables the software to

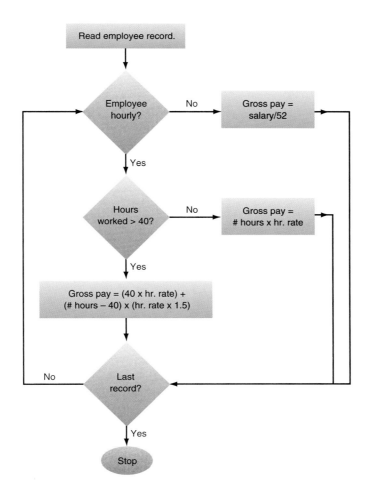

Figure 14.3 *Flowchart diagram of a payroll application of structured programming.*

execute the same program, or parts of a program, until certain conditions are met (e.g., until the end of the file is reached, or until all records have been processed).

As already noted, structured programming enforces some standards about how program code is written. This approach and some others were developed not only to improve programming, but also to standardize how a firm's various programmers do their work. This helps ensure that all the code developed by different programmers will work together. Even with these advances, however, programming can be difficult to manage. IT's About Business 14.2 gives an example of these sorts of challenges and current approaches for dealing with them.

Testing

Thorough and continuous testing occurs throughout the programming stage. Testing checks to see if the computer code will produce the expected and desired results under certain conditions. Testing requires a large amount of time, effort, and expense to do properly. However, the costs of improper testing, which could possibly lead to a system that does not meet its objectives, are enormous.

Testing is designed to detect errors ("bugs") in the computer code. These errors are of two types: syntax errors and logic errors. **Syntax errors** (e.g., a misspelled word or a misplaced comma) are easier to find and will not permit the program to run. **Logic errors** permit the program to run, but result in incorrect output. Logic errors are more

---

IT's About Business   belk.com

Box 14.2:   Belk Inc. tracks development progress, reaps rewards

With limited management resources available and the pressure to deploy new business solutions quickly, measuring productivity in systems development often becomes a low priority for many organizations. IT departments at smaller companies in particular seem reluctant to institute policies to track the performance of development projects. Some companies, however, have been forced to adopt productivity measurement methods, and are reaping rewards for doing so.

For example, national retailer Belk Inc. had to adopt productivity metrics as a means of reducing devastating system failures. Conda Lashley, the veteran IT consultant that Belk hired, was used to nursing client organizations through crashes that periodically downed their systems. But nothing had prepared Lashley for the failure rate at Belk. Soon after joining the company as senior VP for systems development, Lashley discovered that Belk's batch systems went down an astounding 800 times a month. The Charlotte, North Carolina, outfit, a private company with estimated annual revenue of $1.7 billion, paid a heavy price for the constant bandaging: In 1997, Belk spent $1.1 million of its $30 million IT budget on unplanned maintenance.

To steady the systems, Lashley instituted a series of tracking measures. Programmers began logging their time. Required software functions were carefully counted in application development projects. Belk compared its cycle time, defect rates, and productivity with competitors' figures. And systems managers were required to draw up blueprints for reducing the crashes—with the results reviewed in their performance evaluations.

The transition to tracking the IT department's performance was painful but worthwhile. Belk's systems became more stable—monthly disruptions dropped to 480 incidents, a figure Lashley hopes to slash by another 30 percent. Unplanned maintenance costs also have been brought under control, with initial cuts in unplanned maintenance expenses of $800,000.

Questions

1. Why do you think IT departments are reluctant to use productivity measures, beyond the basic reason of resource scarcity?

2. What is it about the software development process that makes its progress difficult to measure or estimate?

3. What do you think about the notion that one cannot truly understand something that one cannot measure?

difficult to detect, because the cause is not obvious. The programmer must follow the flow of logic in the program to determine the source of the error in the output.

As software increases in complexity, the number of errors increases, making it almost impossible to find them all. This situation has led to the idea of **good-enough software**, software that developers release knowing that errors remain in the code. However, the developers feel that the software will still meet its functional objectives. That is, they have found all the **show-stopper bugs**, errors that will cause the system to shut down or will cause catastrophic loss of data.

Implementation

Implementation is the process of converting from the old system to the new system. Organizations use four major conversion strategies: parallel, direct, pilot, and phased.

In a **parallel conversion** process, the old system and the new system operate simultaneously for a period of time. That is, both systems process the same data at the same time, and the outputs are compared. This type of conversion is the most expensive, but also the least risky. Most large systems have a parallel conversion process to lessen the risk.

In a **direct conversion** process, the old system is cut off and the new system is turned on at a certain point in time. This type of conversion is the least expensive, but the most risky if the new system doesn't work as planned. Few systems are implemented using this type of conversion, due to the risk involved.

The **pilot conversion** process introduces the new system in one part of the organization, such as in one plant or in one functional area. The new system runs for a period of time and is assessed. After the new system works properly, it is introduced in other parts of the organization.

The **phased conversion** process introduces components of the new system, such as individual modules, in stages. Each module is assessed, and, when it works properly, other modules are introduced until the entire new system is operational.

Operation and Maintenance

After conversion, the new system will operate for a period of time, until (like the old system it replaced) it no longer meets its objectives. Once the new system's operations are stabilized, audits are performed during operation to assess the system's capabilities and determine if it is being used correctly.

Systems need several types of *maintenance*. The first type is *debugging* the program, a process that continues throughout the life of the system. The second type is *updating* the system to accommodate changes in business conditions. Examples here include adjusting to new governmental regulations and managing the Y2K problem. These corrections and upgrades usually do not add any new functionality; they are necessary in order for the system to continue meeting its objectives. The third type of maintenance adds *new functionality* to the system. This process involves adding new features to the existing system without disturbing its operation.

Before you go on . . .

1. What are the basic steps in the traditional systems development life cycle?

2. What is the purpose of structured programming?

3. What are the common strategies for implementing new systems?

14.3   ALTERNATIVE METHODS FOR SYSTEMS DEVELOPMENT

Most organizations use the traditional systems development life cycle because it has three major advantages: control, accountability, and error detection. An important issue in systems development is that the later in the development process that errors are detected, the more expensive they are to correct. The structured sequence of tasks and milestones in the SDLC thus makes error detection easier and saves money in the long run.

However, the SDLC does have disadvantages. By its structured nature, it is relatively inflexible. It is also time-consuming, expensive, and discourages changes to user requirements once they have been established. Development managers who must develop large, enterprisewide applications therefore find it useful to mix and match development methods and tools in order to reduce development time, complexity, and costs. These methods and tools include prototyping, rapid application development, integrated computer-assisted software engineering (ICASE) tools, and object-oriented development. Although all these methods and tools can reduce development time, none can consistently deliver in all cases. They are perhaps best considered as options to complement or replace portions of the SDLC. This section discusses each of these methods and tools.

Prototyping

Using the **prototyping** approach, systems developers first obtain only a general idea of user requirements. That is, the developers do not try to obtain a complete set of user specifications for the system and do not plan to develop the system all at once. Instead, they quickly develop a **prototype**, which either contains parts of the new system of most interest to the users, or is a small-scale working model of the entire system. The prototype is given to the users, who are able to use it and make suggestions for improving it. The developers review the prototype with the users and use the suggestions to refine the prototype. This process continues through several iterations until either the users approve the system or it becomes apparent that the system cannot meet users' needs. If the system is viable, the developers can use the prototype on which to build the full system. Developing screens that a user will see and interact with is a typical use of prototyping. (See Figure W14.1 at the book's Web site for a model that shows the prototyping process.)

www.wiley.com/
college/turban

The main advantage of prototyping is that this approach speeds up the development process. In addition, prototyping gives users the opportunity to clarify their information requirements as they review iterations of the new system. Prototyping is useful in the development of decision support systems and executive information systems, where user interaction is particularly important.

Prototyping also has disadvantages. It can largely replace the analysis and design stages of the SDLC in some projects. As a result, systems analysts may not produce adequate documentation for the programmers. This lack of documentation can lead to problems after the system becomes operational and needs maintenance. In addition, prototyping can result in an excess of iterations, which can consume the time that prototyping should be saving.

Joint Application Design (JAD)

Joint application design (JAD) is a group-based method for collecting user requirements and creating system designs. JAD is most often used within the systems analysis and systems design stages of the SDLC.

In the traditional SDLC, systems analysts interview or directly observe potential users of the new information system individually to understand each user's needs. The analysts will obtain many similar requests from users, but also many conflicting requests. The analysts must then consolidate all requests and go back to the users to resolve the conflicts, a process that usually requires a great deal of time.

In contrast to the SDLC requirements analysis, JAD has a group meeting in which all users meet simultaneously with analysts. During this meeting, all users jointly define and agree upon systems requirements. This process saves a tremendous amount of time.

The JAD approach to systems development has several advantages. First, the group process involves more users in the development process while still saving time. This involvement leads to greater support for, and acceptance of, the new system and can produce a system of higher quality. This involvement also may lead to easier implementation of the new system and lower training costs.

The JAD approach also has disadvantages. First, it is very difficult to get all users to the JAD meeting. For example, large organizations may have users literally all over the world; to have all of them attend a JAD meeting would be prohibitively expensive. Second, the JAD approach has all the problems caused by any group process (e.g., one person can dominate the meeting, some participants may be shy and not contribute in a group setting, or some participants may sit back and let others do the work). To alleviate these problems, JAD sessions usually have a facilitator, who is skilled in systems analysis and design as well as in managing group meetings and processes.

Rapid Application Development (RAD)

Rapid application development (RAD) is a systems development method that can combine JAD, prototyping, and integrated CASE tools (described below) to rapidly produce a high-quality system. RAD is an iterative approach similar to prototyping, in which requirements, designs, and the system itself are developed with sequential refinements. RAD and prototyping are iterative and emphasize speed of development. However, prototyping typically uses specialized languages, such as fourth-generation languages (4GLs) and screen generators, whereas RAD packages include different tools with similar capabilities. With RAD tools, developers enhance and extend the initial version through multiple iterations until it is suitable for operational use. The tools work together as part of an integrated package. RAD produces functional components of a final system, rather than limited-scale versions.

With RAD, users are intensively involved early in the development process. Initially, JAD sessions are used to collect system requirements. ICASE tools (discussed next) are then used to quickly structure requirements and develop prototypes. As the prototypes are developed and refined, users review them in additional JAD sessions.

Rapid application development methods and tools enable systems developers to build applications faster, such as systems where the user interface is important or systems that involve rewriting legacy applications. Typical RAD packages include:

- *Graphical user development environment:* The ability to create many aspects of an application by drag-and-drop applications.
- *Reusable components:* A library of common, standard "objects" such as buttons and dialog boxes. The developer drags and drops these items into the application.
- *Code generator:* After the developer drags and drops components into the design, the package *automatically* writes computer programs to implement the reports, input screens, buttons, and dialog boxes.

- **Programming language:** Such as Visual Basic or C++. This package includes an integrated development environment (IDE) for creating, testing, and debugging computer code.

The main advantage of RAD is the active involvement of users in the development process. Active user involvement means that the new system has a better chance of meeting user needs, eases implementation of the new system, and can reduce training costs. RAD also speeds the development process, reduces development costs, and can create applications that are easier to maintain and modify.

Like other methods, RAD does have disadvantages. The method's accelerated approach to systems analysis may result in systems with limited functionality and flexibility for change. The system, therefore, may not be able to respond to changing business conditions and may have a limited useful life span. RAD's accelerated development process may produce systems that are not of the highest quality. RAD packages can result in an endless iterative process. RAD packages do provide features that enable developers to document the system, but developers may ignore these features in the accelerated process.

www.wiley.com/
college/turban

Like many methodologies, RAD can be used to develop enterprisewide applications. See IT's About Business W14.2 at the book's Web site for an example of RAD in this role in a large corporation.

Integrated Computer-Assisted Software Engineering (ICASE) Tools

Computer-aided software engineering (CASE) tools automate many of the tasks in the SDLC. The tools used to automate the early stages of the SDLC (systems investigation, analysis, and design) are called *upper CASE* tools. The tools used to automate later stages in the SDLC (programming, testing, operation, and maintenance) are called *lower CASE* tools. CASE tools that provide links between upper CASE and lower CASE tools are called **integrated CASE (ICASE)** tools. (For more on CASE tools, see the Web site.)

www.wiley.com/
college/turban

CASE tools provide advantages and disadvantages for systems developers. These tools can produce systems with a longer effective operational life that more closely meet user requirements. CASE tools can speed up the development process and result in systems that are more flexible and adaptable to changing business conditions. Finally, systems produced using CASE tools typically have excellent documentation.

On the other hand, CASE tools can produce initial systems that are more expensive to build and maintain. CASE tools do require more extensive and accurate definition of user needs and requirements. Also, CASE tools are difficult to customize and may be difficult to use with existing systems.

Object-Oriented Development

Object-oriented development is based on a fundamentally different view of computer systems than that found in traditional SDLC development approaches. Traditional approaches provide specific step-by-step instructions in the form of computer programs, in which programmers must specify every procedural detail. These programs usually result in a system that performs the original task but may not be suited for handling other tasks, even when the other tasks involve the same real-world entities. For example, a billing system will handle billing but probably will not be adaptable to handle mailings for the marketing department or generate leads for the sales force, even though the billing, marketing, and sales functions all use similar data such as customer names, addresses, and current and past purchases.

An object-oriented (OO) system begins not with the task to be performed, but with the aspects of the real world that must be modeled to perform that task. Therefore, in the example above, if the firm has a good model of its customers and its interactions with them, this model can be used equally well for billings, mailings, and sales leads.

Advantages of the object-oriented approach.   The OO approach to software development offers many advantages:

1. It reduces the complexity of systems development and leads to systems that are easier and quicker to build and maintain, because each object is relatively small and self-contained.
2. It improves programmers' productivity and quality. Once an object has been defined, implemented, and tested, it can be reused in other systems.
3. Systems developed with the OO approach are more flexible. These systems can be modified and enhanced easily, by changing some types of objects or by adding new types.
4. The OO approach allows the systems analyst to think at the level of the real-world systems (as users do) and not at the level of the programming language. The basic operations of an enterprise change much more slowly than the information needs of specific groups or individuals. Therefore, software based on generic models (which the OO approach is) will have a longer life span than programs written to solve specific, immediate problems.
5. The OO approach is also ideal for developing Web applications.
6. The OO approach depicts the various elements of an information system in user terms (i.e., business or real-world terms), and therefore, the users have a better understanding of what the new system does and how it meets its objectives.

The OO approach does have disadvantages. OO systems, especially those written in Java, generally run more slowly than those developed in other programming languages. Also, many programmers have little skill and experience with OO languages, necessitating retraining.

Object-oriented analysis and design (OOA&D).   The development process for an object-oriented system begins with a feasibility study and analysis of the existing system. At this point, systems developers identify the objects in the new system.

The *object* is the fundamental element in OOA&D. It represents a tangible real-world entity, such as a customer, bank account, student, or course. Objects have properties. For example, a customer has an identification number, name, address, account number(s), and so on. Objects also contain the operations that can be performed on their properties. For example, customer object's operations may include obtain-account-balance, open-account, withdraw-funds, and so on.

Therefore, OOA&D analysts define all the relevant objects needed for the new system, including their properties (called *data values*) and their operations (called *behaviors*). The analysts then model how the objects interact to meet the objectives of the new system. In some cases, analysts can reuse existing objects from other applications (or from a library of objects) in the new system, saving time spent coding. In most cases, however, even with object reuse, some coding will be necessary to customize the objects and their interactions for the new system.

Before you go on . . .

1. What are some common disadvantages of the SDLC approach?

2. What alternative analysis and design methodologies does RAD typically encompass?

3. How is object-oriented systems development fundamentally different from the SDLC approach?

14.4 SYSTEMS DEVELOPMENT OUTSIDE THE IS DEPARTMENT

The information systems department usually employs the methods discussed in the two previous sections. These methods require highly skilled employees and are complex, resulting in a backlog in application development and a relatively high failure rate. Therefore, in-house software development is not always a feasible solution. Organizations consider alternatives to in-house development for various reasons: The IS staff may not be large enough, the IS staff may not have necessary skills (e.g., Web applications), the IS staff may have too many systems development projects scheduled, or the IS staff may exhibit poor performance due to turnover or rapid changes in technology.

The four main methods for developing systems outside the information systems department are end-user development, external acquisition, use of application service providers, and outsourcing.

End-User Development

For the first two decades of computer applications in the business world (early 1950s to mid-1970s), users worked in a mainframe computing environment and were totally dependent on the IS staff. Since that time, an enormous shift has taken place, with users now making direct, hands-on use of computers to solve their business problems, a phenomenon called **end-user computing**. Users are also performing more and more **end-user development** of their own systems.

Today, IS professionals still manage and control the hardware, software, databases, and networks needed to support the modern computing environment. Professional IS programmers still develop and maintain complex software systems, while users will continue to do more ad-hoc programming.

Many factors are driving the trends toward increased end-user computing and end-user development—increasingly powerful hardware at declining cost, increasingly diverse software capabilities, a demand for the IS projects and accompanying backlog in IS departments, and ability of a computer-literate workforce to develop small applications at little extra cost. Many of these factors represent continuing trends, meaning that end-user computing and end-user development will become even more important in the future. For more on end-user computing, see the book's Web site.

www.wiley.com/
college/turban

External Acquisition of Software

The choice between developing proprietary software in-house and purchasing existing software is called the **make-or-buy decision**. Proprietary application software gives the organization exactly what it needs and wants, as well as a high level of control in the development process. In addition, the organization has more flexibility in modifying the software during the development process to meet new requirements. On the other hand, proprietary software requires a large amount of resources (time, money, personnel) that the in-house staff may have trouble providing. The large quantity of resources needed for this software increases the risk of making the software in-house.

The initial cost of off-the-shelf software is often lower because the software development firm can spread the cost over a number of customers. There is lower risk that the software will fail to meet the firm's business needs, because the software can be examined prior to purchase. The software should be of high quality, because many customers have used and helped debug it. However, buying off-the-shelf software may mean that an organization has to pay for features and functions that are not needed. The software may lack necessary features, causing the buyer to have to make expensive modifications to customize the package. Finally, the buyer's particular IT infrastructure may differ from what the software was designed for, and require some additional modification to run properly. (Advantages of external aquisition of software are discussed at the Web site.)

www.wiley.com/
college/turban

Criteria that may be used to select an application package to purchase include:

- Cost and financial terms
- Upgrade policy and cost
- Vendor's reputation and availability for help
- Vendor's past customers (check references)
- Ease of Internet interface
- Availability and quality of documentation
- Necessary hardware and networking resources
- Required training (does vendor provide?)
- Security
- Speed of learning for developers/users
- Graphical presentation
- Data management capabilities

Application Service Providers (ASPs)

Application service providers (ASPs) provide applications to organizations on a subscription basis. The packaged application is not sold or licensed to the organization and does not reside on the user's system. Instead, it is hosted on the ASP's data center and is accessed remotely by the customer. The concept is not new, having been offered by EDS, IBM, and others for over 30 years.

Customers today typically access applications over an Internet-based or carrier-operated virtual private network. The growth in ASP popularity comes from the increased availability and reliability of such networks, the widespread use of Web browsers as a client interface, and the increased difficulty and cost of installing licensed or purchased software on one's own network. Many ASPs offer basic services consisting of access to standard versions of applications, and also offer more complex services including upgrades and updates, network and server monitoring, and basic help-desk support.

Application service is part of a general trend away from selling software toward providing software services. Such services can range from simple applications all the way through customer relationship planning systems to enterprise resource planning systems. For an example of the how one company uses the services of an ASP to connect with suppliers, see IT's About Business 14.3 (page 478). Although there are numerous independent ASPs, many famous large firms such as Compaq, Pricewater-house-Coopers, Intel, Oracle, SAP, and others also provide application service (often through collaboration with one or more other firms). Using ASPs (rather than

IT's About Business

metallicpower.com

Box 14.3:   Leased application helps product developers meet milestones

A small West Coast manufacturer is expecting big benefits if the promise of new online workflow software pans out. Startup fuel-cell developer Metallic Power Inc. has begun testing a design-sharing application from Bom.com Inc. to avoid mistakes like the one that happened about a year ago. The company nearly missed a deadline because a supplier hadn't seen the data for an updated design drawing of the zinc-air fuel-cell frame Metallic is developing and sent a part built on the wrong specifications.

The Carlsbad, California, manufacturer—which is designing the zinc-air fuel cell for computer power backup and to replace conventional engine batteries in electric vehicles—says staying on schedule builds investor confidence. "If we don't make a milestone, then investors don't look so highly at us," says Metallic design engineer Bret Lobree. The parts mistake wasn't serious, Lobree says, but it could have been worse if the company were closer to the 2003 deadline for shipping its first zinc-air fuel-cell product. "It could have meant making a milestone or not, and at this point in our lives, completing milestones is important," he says.

Last month, Metallic started using Bom's hosted Supplier Access application, which lets companies lease bills-of-materials management software. Bills of materials contain the data associated with a component offered to suppliers for bid. The application lets manufacturers share product development information with suppliers, who will be able to respond to the information online. Metallic uploads its designs of plastic or metal parts for its backup systems to Bom. Users can send an e-mail that delivers their supplier a link to Bom's Web page, where the file is viewed. "I don't have to fill out a fax form or a separate e-mail," Lobree says. "If I make a change to the part, I can update it and then inform them there's been a change." Metallic Power pays about $100 per seat monthly or $1,000 per seat (computer) annually for the service. There's no installation charge, since users only need a Web browser to upload and view files.

Source: Antone Gonsalves, *http://www.informationweek.com* (September 10, 2001).

Questions

1. Why might leasing this software from the ASP be more cost-effective for Metallic Power Inc.?

2. Would leasing also be attractive for Metallic Power's customers? Why or why not?

3. How does the leased software impact the company's bottom-line financial standing?

the old model of licensing or purchase) is also part of a shift toward outsourcing, discussed below.

Outsourcing

Information technology is now an integral organizational resource. However, IT is not the primary business of many organizations. *Core competencies,* the areas in which an organization performs best and that represent its competitive advantage, are in other functions, such as manufacturing, logistics, or services. IT is complex, expensive, and constantly changing, making it difficult for organizations to manage. Organizations may not be able to manage their information technology as well as firms that specialize in managing IT. For these organizations, outsourcing IT may be the best strategy.

Outsourcing, in its broadest sense, is the purchase of any product or service from another company. For example, all major automobile companies outsource the manufacture of many components, such as sound systems and air conditioners. Also, many firms outsource their cafeterias to food service companies, and many organizations outsource their entire human resources departments to outside firms. In general, companies outsource the products and services they do not want to or are unable to produce themselves.

Information systems departments have outsourced computer hardware, telecommunications services, and systems software (such as operating systems) for some time. These departments also purchase end-user software (e.g., Microsoft Office) because there is no reason to reinvent tools that a software company specializing in these products can provide more cheaply.

Recently, information technology has involved hiring outside organizations to perform functions that in the past have been performed internally by information systems departments. Common areas for outsourcing have included maintaining computer centers and telecommunications networks. Some companies, however, outsource most of the IT functions—including systems and applications development—leaving only a very small internal information systems department. This department develops IS plans and negotiates with the vendors performing the outsourced functions.

Firms that provide outsourcing cite numerous benefits that establish their claim that they can provide IT services at 10 to 40 percent lower cost, with higher quality. They note these reasons:

- **Hardware economies of scale.** With multiple customers, outsourcers can use more cost-efficient larger computers or obtain discounts on volume purchases of hardware. They also can operate their computers with less excess capacity because peak loads from different customers will not all occur at the same time.
- **Staffing economies of scale.** A larger customer base also makes it possible for outsourcers to hire highly skilled, specialized technical personnel whose salaries would be hard to justify in smaller IS groups.
- **Specialization.** Providing computer services is one of the core competencies of the outsourcing firm, rather than an incidental part of its business.
- **Tax benefits.** Organizations can deduct outsourcing fees from current income, in contrast to depreciating computer hardware purchases over three to five years.

However, outsourcing can create problems for companies, which include:

- **Limited economies of scale.** Although outsourcers can negotiate larger discounts on hardware, the advantage may not be significant, especially over a five-year life of a mainframe.
- **Staffing.** Typically, former employees, rather than the highly skilled vendor staff, serve customers. In some cases, the outsourcer shifts the better former employees to other accounts.
- **Lack of business expertise.** In addition to losing former employees to other accounts, the remaining staff members tend to become more technically oriented and have less knowledge of the business issues in the customer's industry.
- **Contract problems.** Some customers fail to adequately specify service levels in their contract with the outsourcer and so must pay excess fees for services not in the contract, or for volumes greater than the averages written into the contract.
- **Internal cost reduction opportunities.** Organizations can achieve many of the cost savings of outsourcing by improving their own IT management. For example, these firms can achieve economies of scale by consolidating multiple data centers into one location.

Outsourcing can benefit public as well as private organizations. For example, government IT organizations are beginning to adopt outsourcing practices. Federal agencies, states, and local municipalities are hiring outside services firms for more than just specific system-integration projects. Some are outsourcing parts of their daily IT operations such as desktop and LAN management. Others are even more aggressive, turning over major IT functions to outside companies.

EXAMPLE

brinker.com,
cognizant.com

Brinker looks offshore for Web app solutions.   When $3 billion Dallas restaurant owner Brinker International wanted to improve its gift-card program at more than 850 restaurants a few years ago, it looked offshore to Cognizant Technology Solutions to find a service provider that could turn a good idea into a good product under a tight deadline. Recently, Robert Hess, Brinker's director of software services, said his company has its sights set on developing a new Web-based application that will create a competitive advantage by aggregating data from its restaurants and making that information available via the Web. And it has again tapped Cognizant Technology Solutions to get the project done on time and on budget. In the highly competitive restaurant business, Brinker's philosophy is that the key to improving each restaurant's performance lies in understanding point-of-sale and inventory data collected at each location. Hess says the number of developers he needed to complete the project, as well as the urgency of the project, led him to outsource much of the work to Cognizant. About 70 percent of the development work is done at facilities in India, keeping costs down, while the rest is done in conjunction with Brinker personnel, primarily in Dallas. ●

There are a variety of guidelines to help organizations as they outsource some or all of their IT function. These guidelines include:

- ***Short-period contracts.*** Outsourcing contracts are often written for five-to ten-year terms. Because IT and the competitive environment change so rapidly, it is probable that some of the terms will not be in the customer's best interests after five years. If a longer-term contract is used, it needs to include adequate mechanisms for negotiating revisions where necessary.

- ***Subcontracting.*** Vendors may subcontract some of the service to other vendors. The contract should give the customer some control over the circumstances, including choice of vendors, and any subcontract arrangements.

- ***Selective outsourcing.*** This strategy is used by many organizations that prefer not to outsource the majority of their IT functions, but rather to outsource only certain areas (such as network management).

www.wiley.com/
college/turban

For more on out-sourcing, see the example about Connecticut and also Manager's Checklist W14.1 at the book's Web site.

As we can see from this section and from Sections 14.2 and 14.3, there are a number of ways to develop information systems. Each of these represents a basic approach, but there can be a number of variations. Given that no two organizations or systems are exactly alike or affected by the same constraints, systems developers face a complex decision when choosing a development methodology. Also, they may switch from one methodology to another for different parts of a large system, depending on a variety of considerations. To better illustrate how such a decision might be made, Manager's Checklist 14.1 summarizes the advantages and disadvantages of these methodologies.

Even the appropriate systems development methodology cannot ensure success in all cases. Organizational factors such as culture, bureaucracy, and budget can make or break a development project. See IT's About Business W14.3 at the book's Web site for an example of an organization facing systems development challenges.

www.wiley.com/
college/turban

Advantages	Disadvantages	Manager's Checklist 14.1

Advantages and Disadvantages of Systems Development Methodologies

Traditional Systems Development (SDLC)

Advantages	Disadvantages
• Forces staff to be systematic by going through every step in a structured process. • Enforces quality by maintaining standards. • Has lower probability of missing important issues in collecting user requirements.	• May produce excessive documentation. • Users are often unwilling or unable to study the specifications they approve. • Takes too long to go from the original ideas to a working system. • Users have trouble describing requirements for a proposed system.

Prototyping

Advantages	Disadvantages
• Helps clarify user requirements. • Helps verify the feasibility of the design. • Promotes genuine user participation in the development process. • Promotes close working relationship between systems developers and users. • Works well for ill-defined problems. • May produce part of the final system.	• May encourage inadequate problem analysis. • Not practical with large number of users. • User may not give up the prototype when the system is completed. • May generate confusion about whether or not the information system is complete and maintainable. • System may be built quickly, which may result in lower quality.

Joint Application Development (JAD)

Advantages	Disadvantages
• Easy for senior management to understand. • Provides needed structure to the user requirements collection process.	• Difficult and expensive to get all people to the same place at the same time. • Potential to have dysfunctional groups.

Rapid Application Development (RAD)

Advantages	Disadvantages
• Active user involvement in analysis and design stages. • Easier implementation due to user involvement.	• System often narrowly focused, which limits future evolution, flexibility, and adaptability to changing business conditions. • System may be built quickly, which may result in lower quality.

Object-Oriented Development (OO)

Advantages	Disadvantages
• Integration of data and processing during analysis and design should lead to higher-quality systems. • Reuse of common objects and classes makes development and maintenance easier.	• Very difficult to train analysts and programmers on the OO approach. • Limited use of common objects and classes.

End-User Development

Advantages	Disadvantages
• Bypasses the information systems department and avoids delays	• Creates lower-quality systems because an amateur does the programming.

(continued on page 482)

Manager's Checklist 14.1

Advantages and Disadvantages of Systems Development Methodologies *(Continued)*

Advantages	*Disadvantages*
End-User Development	
• User controls the application and can change it as needed. • Directly meets user requirements. • Increased user acceptance of new system. • Frees up IT resources and may reduce application development backlog.	• May eventually require consulting and maintenance assistance from the IT department. • System may not have adequate documentation. • Poor quality control. • System may not have adequate interfaces to existing systems.
External Acquisition of Application Package or Services	
• Software exists and can be tried out. • Software has been used for similar problems in other organizations. • Reduces time spent for analysis, design, and programming. • Has good documentation that will be maintained.	• Controlled by another company that has its own priorities and business considerations. • Package's limitations may prevent desired business processes. • May be difficult to get needed enhancements if other companies using the package do not need those enhancements. • Lack of intimate knowledge about how the software works and why it works that way.

Before you go on . . .

1. Why do companies seek alternatives to having their IS department develop systems?

2. What are the advantages and disadvantages of end-user-developed systems?

3. What factors are considered in a make-or-buy decision?

14.5   BUILDING INTERNET AND INTRANET APPLICATIONS

Web browsers and Internet communications use open, nonproprietary standards, making it easy to adapt them to any operating system and to any personal computer hardware. Open standards eliminate most of the incompatibility problems and integration difficulties that have always been problems for systems developers.

The *Web browser* is a highly intuitive and nearly universal interface that is easy to learn to use. The hyperlinks feature of Web pages represents an extremely powerful capability for organizing information into a usable and accessible form. It requires less skill to develop Web pages in *hypertext markup language (HTML)*, or using Web page development tools, than it takes to write code in programming languages such as C or COBOL. This simplicity means that applications can be developed rapidly. Implementations are easy because most users already know how to work with a browser. Although there are some major potential security problems, the simplicity of the browser and the HTML language reduce the risks of failure in development.

These considerations suggest that developing Internet (and intranet) applications should be fast and inexpensive.

An Internet and Intranet Development Strategy

Because the Web browser technology is so new yet so simple, most organizations do not use the SDLC approach for Internet/intranet development. Much of the activity has been on a low-budget, experimental basis to gain experience with the technologies. However, most organizations have now gained some experience, so it is appropriate for them to start implementing more formal planning and development policies.

The first planning issue is to identify the objectives for organizational Web sites. These should align with and support organizational strategies. The objectives will vary depending on whether the sites are on: (1) the Internet, which represents the organization to the general public; (2) an extranet, for use with business partners; or (3) an intranet, to serve the needs of organizational employees.

This initial planning also needs to adequately cover infrastructure requirements as well as security and legal issues. Organizational servers and communications links need to have capabilities consistent with the importance of the site to the organization's activities and business strategies. If the site is critical, it needs to have enough capacity to avoid breakdowns or delays during peak periods. The organization also needs to have specialized personnel (e.g., *Webmasters*) to operate and maintain Web sites, and it may want to establish a steering committee to develop and monitor compliance with policies regarding organizational sites.

Security provisions need to be appropriate to the intended use of each site, with adequate *firewalls* (see Chapter 15) to protect data and programs, and with mechanisms to protect the security of customer transactions. The legal department needs to address potential liability issues related to the sites and set policies to prevent improper use of intellectual property.

After the planning issues have been resolved, the organization can identify and prioritize potential projects. Management may choose to fund the more promising applications, leaving the others to be developed later or by end users. The steering committee should monitor end-user projects to make sure that they comply with organizational standards in relation to communications with external customers, and with internal security requirements.

JAVA — A Promising Tool

Internet and intranet Web pages are coded primarily in HTML, a simple language that is most useful for displaying static content to viewers. HTML has very limited capabilities for interacting with viewers or for providing information that is continually being updated. It is not suitable for collecting information, such as names and addresses, for providing animation, or for changing information such as stock quotes. To do these types of things it is necessary to add programs written in some form of programming language to the HTML for a Web site.

As discussed in Chapter 4, **Java** is relatively new, but it has already established itself as the most important programming language for putting extra features into Web pages. Java was specifically designed to work over networks: Java programs can be sent from a Web server over the Internet and then run on the computer that is viewing the Web page. It has numerous security features to prevent these downloaded programs from damaging files or creating other problems on the receiving computer.

Java is an object-oriented language, so the concepts of object-oriented development are relevant to its use. However, the Java Web page programs, called *applets*, need to be relatively small to avoid delays in transmitting them over the Internet. Java programs run more slowly than other languages, such as C, which is another reason to keep them small. Because Java programs tend to be small, it is not necessary that Java developers use the very formal development methodologies appropriate for large system projects. Prototyping is probably the most suitable approach for developing Java applets, because it provides for a high level of interaction between the developers and users in regard to the critical issues of the appearance and ease-of-use of the Web page.

Before you go on . . .

1. Why is creating Internet-based systems often easier than other types of systems?

2. Why does the Java language play so important a role in Internet-based systems?

www.wiley.com/
college/turban

WHAT'S IN IT FOR ME ?

FOR THE ACCOUNTING MAJOR

Accounting personnel help perform the cost–benefit analyses on proposed projects to assess their economic feasibility. They may also monitor ongoing project costs to keep the budget on track. Both of these business functions are traditionally data intensive. Because of this, their information systems are continually being developed and refined. Accounting personnel undoubtedly will find themselves involved with systems development at various points throughout their careers.

FOR THE FINANCE MAJOR

Finance personnel are frequently involved with the financial issues that accompany any large-scale systems development project. They need to stay abreast of the emerging techniques used to determine project costs and return on investment. Due to the intensity of data and information in their various functions, finance departments themselves are also common recipients of new systems. Finance personnel who are acquainted with systems development methodologies are better equipped to assist in getting the right system developed in the right way.

FOR THE MARKETING MAJOR

Marketing, in most organizations, is becoming data- and information-intensive, so the marketing function is also a hotbed of systems development. Marketing personnel, like their cohorts in other functional areas, will find themselves participating on systems development teams. This will involve development of in-house systems, but it increasingly means aiding in the development of systems—such as Internet and WWW-based systems—that reach out directly from the organization to the customer.

FOR THE PRODUCTION/OPERATIONS MANAGEMENT MAJOR

Participation on development teams is also a common role for production/operations people. Manufacturing is becoming increasingly computer controlled and integrated with other allied systems, from design to logistics to inventory control to customer support. Every link in this value chain requires expert input to develop effective systems that can seamlessly integrate with other parts of the larger, enterprisewide system.

FOR THE HUMAN RESOURCES MAJOR

The human resources department is closely involved with several aspects of the systems development project. New systems may require terminating employees, hiring new employees, or changing job descriptions, tasks that are handled by the human resources department. The organization may hire consultants for the development project, and the human resources department handles contracts with these consultants. If the organization outsources the entire development project, the human resources department may still handle some of the HR-related contractual issues with the other company.

SUMMARY

❶ Describe the information systems planning process.

Information systems planning begins with the strategic plan of the organization, which states the firm's overall mission, the goals that follow from the mission, and the broad steps necessary to reach these goals. The organizational strategic plan and the existing IT architecture provide the inputs in developing the information systems strategic plan. The *IS strategic plan* is a set of long-range goals that describe the IT architecture and major IS initiatives needed to achieve the goals of the organization. The IS strategic plan states the mission of the IS department, which defines its underlying purpose. The IS strategic plan may require a new IT architecture, or the existing IT architecture may be sufficient. In either case, the IS strategic plan leads to the *IS operational plan*, which is a clear set of projects that will be executed by the IS/IT department and by functional area managers in support of the IS strategic plan.

❷ Discuss the concept of a systems development life cycle (SDLC).

The systems development life cycle is the traditional systems development method used by most organizations today. The SDLC is a structured framework that consists of distinct sequential processes: systems investigation, systems analysis, systems design, programming, testing, implementation, operation, and maintenance. These processes, in turn, consist of well-defined tasks. Some of these tasks are present in most projects, while others are present in only certain types of projects. That is, smaller development projects may require only a subset of the tasks, and large projects typically require all tasks.

❸ Discuss the advantages and disadvantages of the traditional development, prototyping, rapid application development, object-oriented development, and end-user development life cycles.

Development managers who must develop large applications find it useful to mix and match development methods and tools in order to reduce development time, costs, and complexity. Also, they may switch from one methodology to another for different parts of a large system, depending on a variety of considerations. Manager's Checklist 14.1 summarizes the specific advantages and disadvantages of the various alternative methods of systems development.

❹ Identify the advantages and disadvantages of CASE tools.

The advantages of CASE tools are that they can produce systems with a longer effective operational life that more closely meet user requirements, can speed up the development process and result in systems that are more flexible and adaptable to changing business conditions, and can produce systems with excellent documentation. The disadvantages are that CASE tools can produce initial systems that are more expensive to build and maintain, require more extensive and accurate definition of user needs and requirements, are difficult to customize, and may be difficult to use with existing systems.

❺ Evaluate the alternatives to in-house systems development.

In-house systems development requires highly skilled employees to undertake a complex process, which results in a backlog in application development and a relatively high failure rate. Organizations may sometimes find it preferable to purchase already-existing applications packages than to develop them. The three main methods for developing systems outside the information systems department are end-user development, external acquisition, and outsourcing. In addition, application service providers (ASPs) are becoming popular. The advantages and disadvantages of these three alternatives are summarized in Manager's Checklist 14.1.

❻ Discuss the key features of Internet and intranet development.

Internet and intranet development uses Web browsers with open, nonproprietary standards, making it easy to adapt to any operating system and to any personal computer hardware. Web browsers are nearly universal and the interface is easy to learn to use, so applications can be developed rapidly. The simplicity of the browser and the HTML language reduce the risks of failure in development, so most organizations do not use the SDLC approach for Internet/intranet development. But they should have specialized Webmasters to operate and maintain Web sites, and these sites must have adequate security. Internet and intranet development often uses the Java programming language and applets.

INTERACTIVE LEARNING SESSION

Go to the CD and access Chapter 14: Information Systems Development. There you will be given several case scenarios. You will be asked which combination of systems development tools would make the most sense to use. You also will be asked about the management practices and techniques that could be employed to successfully manage the development project. You will be given feedback on your choices and allowed to refine your responses.

For additional resources, go to the book's Web site for Chapter 13. There you will find Web resources for the chapter, including links to organizations, people, and technology; "IT's About Business" company links; "What's in IT for Me?" links; and a self-testing Web quiz for Chapter 13.

www.wiley.com/
college/turban

DISCUSSION QUESTIONS

1. Why is it important for everyone to have a basic understanding of the systems development process?

2. Should prototyping be used on every systems development project? Why or why not?

3. What can be done to prevent a runaway systems development project?

4. What are the characteristics of structured programming? Why is structured programming so important?

5. How can an organization control end-user development? Should an organization be strict in this control or loose? Support your answer.

PROBLEM-SOLVING ACTIVITIES

1. Develop a hybrid systems development methodology, using the SDLC as the framework, and adding prototyping, joint application design, rapid application development, and CASE tools where appropriate. Point out the advantages of your new methodology.

2. Develop guidelines for deciding when a system should be scrapped and a new system developed. Include cost, maintenance, and systems effectiveness in your answer.

3. Research the viability of using the Java language as a basis for an enterprisewide IS.

INTERNET ACTIVITIES

1. Use an Internet search engine to obtain information on CASE and ICASE tools. Select several vendors and compare and contrast their offerings.

2. Use the World Wide Web to find consulting firms that specialize in systems analysis and design. Compare the size, reputation/history, and degree of specialization.

3. Use the Web to learn about analysis and design of intranets. What sort of sites have the most (and the most useful) information?

TEAM ACTIVITIES AND ROLE PLAYING

1. Divide into groups, with each group visiting a local company (include your university). At each firm, study the systems development process. Find out the methodology or methodologies used by each organization and the type of application each methodology applies. Prepare a report and present it to the class.

2. As a group, design an information system for a startup business of your choice. Describe your chosen systems development methodologies, and justify your choices of hardware, software, telecommunications support, and other aspects of the proposed system.

REAL-WORLD CASE *lehman.com*   FIN

Lehman Brothers Traders Are Instantly Informed Thanks to Java-based Applications

The Business Problem   Lehman Brothers, founded in 1850, provides a wide menu of research, distribution, trading, and financing services to businesses, institutions, governments, and high-net-worth individual investors. For several years, the firm has been building client/server applications that use a Visual Basic client to access databases and a custom-developed UNIX analytics engine through Common Object Request Broker Architecture (CORBA). This aging architecture provided a lot of functionality to Lehman's traders and operations, but as market volatility increased, the firm needed more current market intelligence. The fat-client application didn't scale well and required too much support.

Lehman Brothers Inc. set itself this goal: Make it possible for financial traders to provide clients with an immediate sense of how their portfolios are doing, as well as the tools to better advise clients on various investment scenarios based on projected market changes. But Robert Okin, the Lehman executive heading the project, didn't want to sacrifice the current application's strengths. "We were asked to extend the reach of our app, yet maintain the rich client interface," says Okin, Lehman's VP of structured credit trading technology.

The IT Solution   "Embrace and extend" is a marketing phrase that characterizes what the New York global investment bank is accomplishing, using commercial software components from Infragistics Inc. Graphical user interface components are being used to retrofit an aging client/server application for doing portfolio management and scenario analysis. With the Infragistics toolkit, developers can deliver the look and feel of Microsoft Office, Outlook, or Windows 2000 (Windows XP is in the offing). The presentation components include grids, charts, Outlook bars, calendaring components, and data explorers, which deliver the familiar look and feel of Microsoft applications. Using these off-the-shelf components, developers can more quickly deliver a professional-looking application with maximum code reuse.

The Results   Lehman had been depending on analytics engines that ran at the end of the day to value a trader's portfolio. It was only on the following morning that traders could see where they stood. The Infragistics components let Lehman create a front-end trading application that hooks into its existing middleware. This lets traders access the most current company and market data. "The Java-based version we're working on now is going to allow traders to bring up their portfolios in real time as they enter trades," Okin says. "They can also play around with the various [market dynamics] that affect the valuation of those trades." When traders click on the page, Sun Microsystems' Java WebStart application-management tool in the background brings up the application on the user's desktop. Java WebStart lets users launch applications simply by clicking on a Web-page link.

Lehman was able to bring the application from planning to working code within three months with four developers—a month of specification and design and two months of coding put them close to beta testing. Certainly, the fact that they already had a client/server application in place that delivered significant functionality, as well as the server-based middleware interfaced with their back-end systems and real-time data, gave the Lehman developers a solid platform upon which to build. Okin credits the use of commercial components for letting Lehman deliver the application sooner than if it had needed to build a JavaServer Page screen that could handle more than 50 deals, and provide the rich client/server capabilities that one expects from a desktop application. A future goal is to support mobility among traders so they can access the application while traveling.

Questions

1. What is the significance of the type of legacy system in place at Lehman Brothers?

2. Why would the company prefer to go with commercially available components instead of developing its own in-house?

3. Why would Java be important for a system that supports remote access? (*Hint*: The Web.)

VIRTUAL COMPANY ASSIGNMENT

wiley.com/college/turban

Extreme Descent Snowboards

www.wiley.com/
college/turban

Background   Matt Brandy and Jacob March were already seated at the small conference table when you entered Jacob's office. Jacob waves for you to join them. After a few minutes of small talk, Matt resumes his conversation to include you.

Matt indicated that there are many reasons to initiate a systems development project. This is exactly what Matt had in mind when he and Kellie decided to expand their sales globally using the Internet. Matt said he is interested in seeing how their competitors are expanding on the Internet.

Jacob said, "This would be a project for an intern." As you leave the office, Jacob follows and gives you some ideas to get started with.

Assignment

1. Choose one of EDS's competitors that you used in the assignment for Chapter 9. Compare its site to the EDS e-commerce site. provide the complete URL for both sites. Write a report describing the strengths and weakness of both sites.

2. In your opinion, what are the most important steps in the systems development process that could be used to improve the EDS e-commerce site? (refer to Figure 14.2 in the text for the traditional development stages.)

IMPLEMENTING IT: ETHICS, IMPACTS, AND SECURITY

CHAPTER PREVIEW

Now that you are acquainted with the major capabilities of IT and the substantial benefits it can provide to organizations, we will explore some of the major issues that are involved in putting these systems to work for you, no matter what function you perform in your company. Specifically, the issues can be of ethical, behavioral, organizational, societal, or technical nature. Of the many implemenation issues, we will look here at the those that are most frequently encountered, and view them from several perspectives: What are these issues? Why do they appear? Why are they important? What can we do about them? Answers to these and other questions can be found in this chapter. Finally, information systems *security* must be practiced by all people at home, at school, and at work. Therefore we conclude the chapter and the book with a look at that topic.

CHAPTER OUTLINE

15.1 Ethical Issues
15.2 Impact of IT on Organizations and Jobs
15.3 Impacts on Individuals at Work
15.4 Societal Impacts and Internet Communities
15.5 Security Is a Concern for Everyone
15.6 Protecting Information Systems

LEARNING OBJECTIVES

1. Describe the major ethical issues related to information technology and identify situations in which they occur.

2. Identify the major impacts of information technology on organizational structure, power, jobs, supervision, and decision making.

3. Understand the potential dehumanization of people by computers and other potential negative impacts of information technology.

4. Identify some of the major societal effects of information technology.

5. Describe the many threats to information security.

6. Understand the various defense mechanisms used to protect information systems.

7. Explain IT auditing and planning for disaster recovery.

DISASTER RECOVERY PLANS IMPLEMENTED AFTER TERRORIST ATTACK

The Business Problem

When the World Trade Center towers were attacked by terrorists on September 11, 2001, every business located in the twin towers faced an immediate business problem—first, find surviving employees, and second, recover data in order to get the business back up and running. Singapore-based Overseas Union Bank (OUB) was one such business. The bank had its New York office on the 39th floor of the World Trade Center. As soon as the CNN news reached Singapore (at 9:30 P.M. there) of the disaster, the bank's *business continuity* plan was put into action. A recovery team in New York was mobilized in minutes. The first concern was for the bank's employees, and an immediate attempt was made to find survivors. Fortunately, all 13 employees survived. Second, it was necessary to recover as soon as possible and resume operations.

The IT Solution

The OUB employees and the recovery team were drilled for a disaster beforehand, so they knew that they needed to move to the backup site outside New York. But given the devastation of the day, this was not possible because bridges and tunnels out of New York were closed and transportation was nearly at a standstill. So, OUB solicited the help of a business partner, and a new business recovery plan was drafted in hours. Using borrowed computers and phone lines, OUB employees extracted data from their computer backup system and reconstructed the business two miles from Wall Street by the end of the day.

The WTC catastrophe made many organizations aware of the importance of disaster recovery planning.

The Results

With the new recovery plan, a temporary site, and the reconstructed data files, it took a relatively short time for Overseas Union Bank to resume normal operations. The financial damage was minimal.

But, many small businesses had no disaster planning, and some did not even have backup files. An example was Jan He Law office of China, which operated from the 77th floor of the WTC. Fortunately, all of its employees survived, but all of the firm's client files stored in computers were gone. The firm was unable even to contact its clients, since all the telephone numbers were filed on the computers, without off-site backup. The damage was enormous.

What We Learned from This Case

The WTC disaster highlighted the need for data storage and backup, for disaster recovery planning, and for operational communication systems. Large companies tend to have sophisticated disaster recovery plans as well as backup sites that enable them to roll the applications over in real time. Smaller firms may need to rely on backing up data to tape and sending the tapes off site.

In this chapter we will cover the topic of IT security and protection, which is critical to the success of networked computing and of electronic commerce. Before we do so, we begin with a presentation of ethical issues, which were emphasized in previous chapters. Then we take a bird's-eye view of the overall impacts of IT—on individuals, groups, organizations, and society.

15.1   ETHICAL ISSUES

Some marketers attemped to use the WTC tragedy to increase their sales, a perfectly legal act but one that many considered to be unethical. **Ethics** is a branch of philosophy that deals with what is considered to be right and wrong. There are many definitions of ethics, such as "codes of morals of a particular profession," "the standards of conduct of a given profession," and "agreement among people to do right and to avoid wrong." In one of the oldest codes of ethics, the Ten Commandments, clear specifications are given about what an individual should and should not do. Over the years, philosophers have proposed many ethical guidelines. It is important to realize that what is unethical is not necessarily illegal. Thus, in most instances, an individual or organization faced with an ethical decision is not considering whether to break the law. In today's complex environment, the definitions of "right" and "wrong" are not always clear.

The spread of IT has created many new ethical situations. For example, the issue of a company legally monitoring employees' e-mail is very controversial; 47 percent of the readers of *InformationWeek* believe it is acceptable for companies to do so, 53 percent disagree. Obviously, there are major differences among companies and individuals with respect to what is ethical.

A Framework for Ethics

Many companies and professional organizations develop their own codes of ethics. A **code of ethics** is a collection of principles intended as a guide for the members of a company or an organization. The diversity of IT applications and the increased use of the technology have created a variety of ethical issues, as illustrated throughout this text. An attempt to organize these issues into a framework was undertaken by R. O. Mason and others, who categorized ethical issues into four kinds: privacy, accuracy, property, and accessibility.

- *Privacy issues:* Collection, storage, and dissemination of information about individuals
- *Accuracy issues:* Authenticity, fidelity, and accuracy of information collected and processed
- *Property issues:* Ownership and value of information (intellectual property)
- *Accessibility issues:* Right to access information and payment of fees to access it

Representative questions and issues in each category are listed in Table 15.1 (page 492). Of these, we focus here on the issues of privacy and intellectual property.

Protecting Privacy

Privacy means different things to different people. In general, *privacy* is the right to be left alone and the right to be free of unreasonable personal intrusions. *Information privacy* is the right to determine when, and to what extent, information about oneself can be communicated to others. This right applies to individuals, groups, and institutions.

The definition of privacy can be interpreted quite broadly. However, the following two rules have been followed fairly closely in past court decisions in many countries:

1. The right of privacy is not absolute. Privacy must be balanced against the needs of society.

2. The public's right to know is superior to the individual's right of privacy.

Table 15.1   A Framework for Ethical Issues

Privacy issues	• What information about oneself should an individual be required to reveal to others? • What kind of surveillance can an employer use on its employees? • What things can people keep to themselves and not be forced to reveal to others? • What information about individuals should be kept in databases, and how secure is the information there?
Accuracy issues	• Who is responsible for the authenticity, fidelity, and accuracy of information collected? • How can we ensure that information will be processed properly and presented accurately to users? • How can we ensure that errors in databases, data transmissions, and data processing are accidental and not intentional? • Who is to be held accountable for errors in information, and how should the injured party be compensated?
Property issues	• Who owns the information? • What are the just and fair prices for its exchange? • How should one handle software piracy (copying copyrighted software)? • Under what circumstances can one use proprietary databases? • Can corporate computers be used for private purposes? • How should experts who contribute their knowledge to create expert systems be compensated? • How should access to information channels be allocated?
Accessibility issues	• Who is allowed to access information? • How much should be charged for permitting accessibility to information? • How can accessibility to computers be provided for employees with disabilities? • Who will be provided with equipment needed for accessing information? • What information does a person or an organization have a right or a privilege to obtain, and under what conditions and with what safeguards?

Source: Compiled from R.O. Mason et al., *Ethics of Information Management* (Thousand Oaks, CA: Sage Publishers, 1995).

www.wiley.com/
college/turban

These two rules show why it is difficult in some cases to determine and enforce privacy regulations. The right to privacy is recognized today in all U.S. states and by the federal government, either by statute or common law. For a representative list of federal privacy legislation related to IT, see Table W15.1 on the book's Web site. Some representative issues of privacy are discussed next.

Electronic surveillance.   According to the American Civil Liberties Union (ACLU), monitoring computer users—**electronic surveillance**—is a major problem. The ACLU estimates that tens of millions of computer users are being monitored, most without their knowledge. Employees have very limited protection against employers' surveillance. Although several legal challenges are now underway, the law appears to support employers' rights to read electronic mail and other electronic documents. Surveillance is also a concern for private individuals (via personal e-mail, for example), whether done by corporations, government bodies, or criminal elements. Many Americans are pondering the right balance between personal privacy and electronic surveillance in terms of threats to national security. The World Trade Center disaster and the anthrax attack made many Americans change their positions, moving toward more government surveillance.

Personal information in databases.   Information about individuals is being kept in many databases. Perhaps the most visible locations of such records are credit reporting agencies. Other places where personal information might be stored are banks and financial institutions; cable TV, telephone, and utilities companies; employers;

apartments and mortgage companies; equipment rental companies; hospitals; schools and universities; supermarkets, retail establishments, and mail-order houses; government agencies (Internal Revenue Service, Census Bureau, your municipality, your state); libraries; and insurance companies. Also, any questionnaires you fill out on the Internet (e.g., when you try to win a prize) usually end up in some database. For an example of how one large company collects and uses customer information, see IT's About Business 15.1.

There are several concerns about the information you provide to these record-keepers. Do you know where the records are? Are the records accurate? Can you change inaccurate data? How long will it take to make a change? Under what circumstances will personal data be released? How are the data used? To whom are they given or sold? How secure are the data against access by unauthorized people?

IT's About Business

americanexpress.com MKT

Box 15.1:   American Express uses customer information for marketing decisions: Is privacy protected?

American Express was one of the first financial services companies to adopt a formal privacy policy regarding information about its customers. These policies restrict disclosure of data to those with a "business need" to see it. American Express also gives its customers the choice not to receive promotional material.

However, American Express is using its vast database internally to generate lists for its own mass mailings and specialized promotions. Stephen Cone, senior vice president for direct marketing, uses *data mining*, employing sophisticated mathematical models to sift through billions of bits of data to predict what products a person might be interested in. For example, all information—from the original application to each card transaction—is accessed to build individual profiles. These profiles can be used to determine marketing strategies and to generate a list of potential customers.

From purchased lists, American Express compiles a list of many potential cardholders in the United States, including college students. The records note every solicitation American Express has ever sent to each person. The lists also contain demographic data and lifestyle indicators. American Express produces many specialized models from this data. For example, American Express has a "who's moving" model that is extremely valuable because people who are relocating tend to make several other changes at the same time. The company also has a "lifestyle" model that decides which solicitation letters to send to a prospect. The effect of this selective, direct marketing tool is that response rates are up 7 to 10 percent over previous methods.

Even though American Express does not rent out its list, it does enter into joint ventures with merchandising companies that conduct several thousand promotions a year. They offer everything from invitations to local pizzerias to solicitations for potential buyers of luxury cars. American Express can pinpoint the cardholders most likely to respond to each offer. American Express has realized that information about actual consumer behavior is extremely valuable. How consumers spend their money is a better measure of their needs and desires than any marketing survey could ever be.

Questions

1. American Express is making connections with business partners to exploit opportunities to increase sales and profit by using customers' information in its databases. If agreement is reached, customer data are shared. Do you think that what American Express is doing is ethical?

2. How would you feel about this privacy issue if you were an American Express customer? How well do you think your privacy is being protected?

3. Enter the Web site of American Express (*americanexpress.com*) to find out about the privacy assurances provided to customers. For added information, you can send an e-mail to the corporation's public relations department.

Some commercial companies offer services to assist individuals in the control of personal records. For example, Privacy Guard Corporation advises individuals about how to protect their rights, and it monitors several databases.

Information on Internet bulletin boards and newsgroups.   Every day there are more and more *electronic bulletin boards, newsgroups*, and *electronic discussion arrangements* such as chat rooms, both on the Internet and within corporate intranets. It is estimated that in 2001 there were 45 million users of more than 220,000 public bulletin boards of all types. How does society keep owners of bulletin boards from disseminating information that may be offensive to readers or simply untrue? The difficulty we have addressing this problem highlights the conflict among freedom of speech, privacy, and ethics, a continuing dynamic in American society.

Privacy codes and policies.   One way to protect privacy is to develop **privacy policies** or **codes**, which can help organizations avoid legal problems. In many corporations, senior management has begun to understand that with the ability to collect vast amounts of personal information on customers, clients, and employees comes an obligation to ensure that the collected information—and, therefore, the individual—is protected. A sampling of privacy policy guidelines is given in Table 15.2.

International aspects of privacy.   There are major differences among countries with respect to privacy regulations. Some countries, like Sweden and Canada, have very strict laws; others have little regulation. For example, in 2001, Italy, Spain, Portugal, and Greece were still developing legislation protecting an individual's right to control personal data in governmental or commercial databases, and other privacy and ethics-related laws. The existing inconsistency of standards could obstruct the flow of information among countries in the European Community. To overcome this problem, the European Community Commission (ECC) has issued guidelines to all its country

Table 15.2   Privacy Policy Guidelines—A Sampler

Data collection	• Data should be collected on individuals only for the purpose of accomplishing a legitimate business objective. • Data should be adequate, relevant, and not excessive in relation to the business objective. • Individuals must give their consent before data pertaining to them can be gathered. Such consent may be implied from the individual's actions (e.g., applications for credit, insurance, or employment).
Data accuracy	• Sensitive data gathered on individuals should be verified before it is entered into the database. • Data should be accurate and, where and when necessary, kept current. • The file should be made available so the individual can ensure that the data are correct. • If there is disagreement about the accuracy of the data, the individual's version should be noted and included with any disclosure of the file.
Data confidentiality	• Computer security procedures should be implemented to provide reasonable assurance against unauthorized disclosure of data. They should include physical, technical, and administrative security measures. • Third parties should not be given access to data without the individual's knowledge or permission, except as required by law. • Disclosures of data, other than the most routine, should be noted and maintained for as long as the data are maintained. • Data should not be disclosed for reasons incompatible with the business objective for which they are collected.

members regarding the rights of individuals to access information about themselves and to correct errors. The ECC data protection laws that took effect on October 2, 1998, are stricter than U.S. laws and therefore may create problems for multinational corporations such as American Express and EDS, which may face lawsuits for privacy violation.

The transfer of data in and out of a nation without knowledge of the authorities or individuals involved raises a number of privacy issues. Whose laws have jurisdiction when records are in a different country for reprocessing or retransmission purposes? For example, if data are transmitted by a Polish company through a U.S. satellite to a British corporation, which country's privacy laws control what data and when? Questions like these will become increasingly more complicated and more common as time goes on. Governments must make an effort to develop laws and standards to cope with the rapidly increasing rate of information technology in order to solve some of these privacy issues.

The Organization for Economic Cooperation and Development (OECD) in Europe has probably provided the best-known set of guidelines intended to protect individuals' privacy in the electronic age. A sample of principles related to data collection are listed in Manager's Checklist 15.1.

Protecting Intellectual Property

The issue of privacy receives much publicity because it affects almost every individual. In contrast, the issue of protecting intellectual property is discussed less frequently because it affects only some individuals and corporations. Yet the issue is an important one for those who make their livelihoods in knowledge fields. **Intellectual property** is the intangible property created by individuals or corporations, which is protected under *trade secret, patent*, and *copyright* laws.

A **trade secret** is intellectual work, such as a business plan, that is a company secret and is not based on public information. An example is a corporate strategic plan. Laws about trade secrets are legislated at the state level in the United States.

A **patent** is a document that grants the holder exclusive rights on an invention for 20 years. Thousands of patents related to IT have been granted during the years. Examples of IT-related patents are "A method and system for natural-language

---

Manager's Checklist 15.1

Data Collection Principles

1. ***Collection limitation.*** Data should be obtained lawfully and fairly; some very sensitive data should not be collected at all.

2. ***Data quality.*** Data should be relevant to the stated purposes, accurate, complete, and up to date; proper precautions should be taken to ensure this accuracy.

3. ***Purpose specification.*** The purposes for which data will be used should be identified, and the data should be destroyed if they no longer serve the given purpose.

4. ***Use limitation.*** Use of data for purposes other than specified is forbidden, except with the consent of the data subject or by authority of the law.

5. ***Security safeguards.*** Agencies should establish procedures to guard against loss, corruption, destruction, or misuse of data.

6. ***Openness.*** It must be possible to acquire information about the collection, storage, and use of personal data.

7. ***Individual participation.*** The data subject has the right to access and challenge personal data.

"NO ROYALTY THIS QUARTER. MY BOOK GOT ON THE INTERNET, AND NOW IT'S A FREEBIE."

translation" (#5477451) and "Expert-based systems and methods for managing error events on a local area network" (#5483637). Open Market Corporation obtained several patents regarding electronic commerce. Juno received patent #5809242 for displaying and updating interactive ads on the Internet.

Copyright is a statutory grant that provides the creators of intellectual property with ownership of it for the life of the creator plus 50 years. Owners are entitled to collect fees from anyone who wants to copy the property. The U.S. Federal Computer Software Copyright Act (1980) provides protection for *source* and *object code* (see the definitions in Chapter 4), but one problem is that it is not clear what is eligible to be protected. For example, similar concepts, functions, and general features (such as pull-down menus, colors, or icons) are not protected by copyright law. One of the most interesting Web-related copyright cases is that of Napster. Napster allowed music swapping via P2P file-sharing technology. The company was sued by music publishers for copyright violation and was closed down. In September 2001, the company reached a licensing agreement with several music publishers, including Bertelsmann, that enables Napster to continue operations but requires that Napster collect fees from customers, using special software to do so. For another example of copyright-infringement issues, see IT's About Business W15.1 on the Web site.

www.wiley.com/college/turban

The most common intellectual property related to IT deals with software. The copying of software without making payment to the owner (such as giving a disk to a friend to install on his or her computer) is a copyright violation, and a major problem for software vendors.

International aspects of intellectual property.   Copyright laws in the digital age are being challenged, and international agreements are needed. In 1996, the World Intellectual Property Organization began to discuss the need for copyright protection of intellectual property delivered on the Internet. More than 60 member countries are still trying to bridge cultural and political differences and come up with an international treaty. Part of the agreement being worked on is called the "database treaty," and its aim is to protect the investment of firms that collect and arrange information in databases.

> ### Before you go on . . .
>
> 1. Define ethics and list its four categories as they apply to IT.
>
> 2. Describe the issue of privacy as it is affected by IT.
>
> 3. What does a code of ethics contain?
>
> 4. Describe the issue of intellectual property protection.

15.2   IMPACTS OF IT ON ORGANIZATIONS AND JOBS

The use of information technologies, and most recently the Web, has brought many organizational changes that are being felt in areas like structure, authority, power, job content, employee career ladders, supervision, and the manager's job. In this section we look at how IT is changing organizational structure and jobs.

How Will Organizations Change?

IT may cause a nearly complete change in organizations, including their structure, supervision, and power distribution.

Flatter organizational hierarchies.   IT allows for the increased productivity of managers, an increased *span of control* (more employees per supervisor), and a decreased number of managers and experts. It is reasonable to assume, then, that fewer managerial levels will exist in many organizations, and there will be fewer staff and line managers. This trend is already evidenced by the continuing phenomenon of the "shrinking of middle management."

Flatter organizational hierarchies will also result from reduction in the total number of employees, reengineering of business processes, increased productivity of employees, and the ability of lower-level employees to perform higher-level jobs with the support of information systems. Starting in the late 1980s and accelerating since then, many organizations are getting smaller and leaner.

Changes in supervision.   The fact that an employee's work is performed online and stored electronically introduces the possibility for greater electronic supervision. For professional employees whose work is often measured by their completion of projects, "remote supervision" implies greater emphasis on completed work and less on personal contacts and office politics. This emphasis is especially true if employees work in geographically dispersed locations, including homes, away from their supervisors.

Power and status.   Knowledge is power—this fact has been recognized for generations. The latest developments in computerized systems are changing the power structure within organizations. The struggle over who will control the computers, the company intranet, and the information resources has become one of the most visible conflicts in many organizations, both private and public. Expert systems, for example, may reduce the power of certain professional groups because the employee's knowledge will be in the public domain. On the other hand, individuals who control electronic commerce applications may gain considerable prestige, knowledge, power, and status. As a result, a power redistribution is underway in many organizations.

How Will Jobs Change?

One issue of concern to all employees is the impact of IT on their jobs. The content of jobs, career ladders, functional areas, and managerial duties will undoubtedly be affected. Changes will occur particularly in jobs of intermediaries, such as insurance and real estate agents. Many jobs will be eliminated. Many other changes will take place that we can only speculate about at this point.

Job content.   Job content is important not only because it is related to organizational structure, but also because it is interrelated with employee satisfaction, compensation, status, and productivity. Changes in job content occur when work is redesigned, for example, when business process restructuring is attempted, or when electronic commerce changes the marketing distribution system. Certainly many jobs will be redesigned to take advantage of the Web and emerging information technologies. These will, in turn, require higher levels of computing literacy from workers and need for retraining.

Employee career ladders.   Increased use of IT in organizations could have a significant and somewhat unexpected impact on career ladders. Today, many highly skilled professionals have developed their abilities through years of experience, holding a series of positions that expose them to progressively more difficult and complex situations. The use of e-learning and intelligent tutoring systems may shortcut a portion of this learning curve by capturing and more efficiently managing the use of knowledge.

However, several questions relating to employee career paths are subject to thought and debate: How will high-level human expertise be acquired with minimal experience in lower-level tasks? What will be the effect on compensation at all levels of employment? How will human resources development programs be structured? What career paths will be offered to employees in a rapidly changing technological environment?

Impacts on the functional areas.   As seen in Chapter 8, technological changes are affecting all functional areas. For example, the move to build-to-order strategy changes not only production lines but also marketing and distribution.

The manager's job.   The manager's job may be affected by IT. For example, one of the most important tasks of managers is making decisions. As seen in Chapter 11, IT can change the manner in which many decisions are made, and consequently change managers' jobs.

Many managers have reported that information technology has finally given them time to get out of the office and into the field. They also have found that they can spend more time planning activities instead of putting out fires. Information gathering for decision making can now be done much more quickly with search engines and intranets. Managers used to work on a large number of problems simultaneously, moving from one to another as they waited for more information on their current problem or until some external event interrupted them. IT tends to reduce the time necessary to complete any step in the decision-making process. Therefore, managers can work today on fewer tasks during each day but complete more of them.

Another possible impact on the manager's job could be a change in leadership requirements. What are generally considered to be good qualities of leadership may be significantly altered with the use of IT. For example, when face-to-face communication is replaced by electronic mail and computerized conferencing, leadership qualities attributed to physical presence may be lessened, and effective leadership may be perceived to be more closely linked to effective computer-based communication.

Before you go on . . .

1. List the major organizational impacts of IT.

2. How will jobs change?

3. How is the manager's job likely to change?

15.3   IMPACTS ON INDIVIDUALS AT WORK

IT may have a variety of impacts on individuals. Here we consider some that are of concern to many people.

Will My Job Be Eliminated?

IT can significantly increase the productivity of employees, restructuring job content and changing the skill requirements of many jobs. Therefore, one of the major concerns of every employee, part-time or full-time, is job security. This issue is not new; it has frequently been brought to the attention of the public since the beginning of the Industrial Revolution and the introduction of automation.

For years unemployment has been a major concern of countries that use little automation (developing countries). However, since the 1990s, this concern has spread to industrialized countries as well. Due to difficult economic times, increased global competition, demands for customization, and increased consumer sophistication, many companies have had no choice but to increase their investments in IT. The United Nations and other organizations are conducting investigations to study unemployment, which continues to increase in several countries into the twenty-first century (for example, it was recently 20 percent in Egypt).

Because computers are becoming smarter and more capable as time passes, the competitive advantage of replacing people with machines is increasing rapidly. For this reason, some people believe that society is heading toward massive unemployment; others disagree. The major arguments of the two opposing factions—those who believe that massive unemployment is coming (led by Nobel Prize–winner Wassily Leontief) and those who believe that this is not going to happen (led by Nobel Prize–winner Herbert Simon)—are presented in Table W15.2 at the book's Web site.

www.wiley.com/college/turban

The debate about how IT will affect employment raises a few other questions. Is unemployment really socially undesirable? (People could have more leisure time; in Europe, the work week is already less than 35 hours.) Should the government intervene more in the distribution of income and in the determination of the employment level? Can the "invisible hand" in the economy, which has worked so well in the past, continue to be successful in the future? Will IT make most of us idle but wealthy? (Robots will do the work, and people will enjoy life, goes this argument.) Should the issue of income be completely separated from that of employment? The answers to these questions will be provided in part by future developments of IT and by government policies.

Which specific jobs will be eliminated and which are created depend on many factors. The more technically oriented your job is, the better the chance that it will not be eliminated. However, it may be changed.

Dehumanization and Psychological Impacts

Some of the ways that IT may affect the perceptions and behaviors of individuals are considered next.

Dehumanization.   A frequent criticism of traditional data processing systems has been their negative effect on people's individuality. Such systems have long been criticized as being impersonal; they *dehumanized* and *depersonalized* the human activities that had been computerized. Many people feel a loss of identity; they feel like "just another number" because computers reduce or eliminate the human element that was present in the noncomputerized systems.

However, although the major objective of newer IT technologies (such as collaborative commerce) is to increase productivity, they can also create flexible systems that

allow individuals to include their opinions and knowledge in the system. These technologies attempt to be people-oriented and user-friendly. When they succeed at being people-friendly, they can counter dehumanization.

Psychological impacts.   Home computers threaten to have an even more isolating influence than that of television. If people are encouraged to work and shop from their living rooms, some unfortunate psychological effects—such as depression and loneliness—could develop. Another example is distance learning. Children can be schooled at home through IT, but the lack of social contact could be damaging to their development. Recently, some people have been reported to spend too much time on the Internet, being almost addicted to being online. Studies indicate that people who spend more time on the Net spend less time with their friends and families.

Impacts on Health and Safety

Computers and information systems are a part of the job environment that may adversely affect our health and safety. To illustrate, we will discuss several potential hazards.

Job stress and anxiety.   An increase in workload and/or responsibilities can trigger *job stress*. Although computerization has benefited organizations by increasing productivity, it has also created an ever-increasing workload on many employees. Workers feel overwhelmed and start feeling frustrated and anxious about their jobs and their performances. Many employees feel *information anxiety* because other people are better than they in using computers, because they are slow in learning new technologies, and because of the need to continuously learn new things. These feelings of *anxiety* can adversely affect workers' health and productivity. Management's responsibility is to help alleviate these feelings by redistributing the workload among workers, hiring more employees, and/or redesigning jobs and training.

Video display terminals.   Exposure to *video display terminals (VDTs)* raises the issue of the risk of radiation exposure, which has been associated with cancer and other health-related problems. For example, lengthy exposure to VDTs has been blamed for miscarriages in pregnant women. However, results of the research done to investigate this charge have been inconclusive. It is known that exposure to VDTs for long periods of time can affect an individual's eyesight.

Repetitive strain injuries.   Other potential hazards are backaches and muscle tension in the wrists and fingers resulting from working many hours a day with computers. *Carpal tunnel syndrome* is a pernicious and painful form of repetitive strain injury that affects the wrists and hands. It has been associated with the long-term use of keyboards. Repetitive strain injuries can be very costly to corporations. Thousands of lawsuits have been filed against computer manufacturers and employers. For example, a lawsuit was filed against IBM requesting $11.5 million because of the inappropriate design of a keyboard that supposedly caused carpal tunnel syndrome.

Lessening the negative impact on health and safety.   Designers are aware of the potential problems associated with prolonged use of computers and other IT devices. Consequently, they have attempted to design a better computing environment. Research in the area of **ergonomics** (human factors) provides guidance for these designers.

(a)

(b)

(c)

(d)

Ergonomic products protect computer users: (a) Wrist support. (b) Back support. (c) Eye-protection filter (optically coated glass). (d) Adjustable foot rest.

For instance, ergonomic techniques focus on creating an environment for the worker that is well lit and comfortable. Devices such as antiglare screens have helped alleviate problems of fatigued or damaged eyesight, and chairs that contour to the human body have helped decrease backaches. Some sample ergonomic products are shown in the nearby photos.

Before you go on . . .

1. List the major potential impacts of IT on the individual's job.

2. List potential impacts on an individual's health and safety.

15.4   SOCIETAL IMPACTS AND INTERNET COMMUNITIES

The social implications of IT are far reaching. Most are positive, but some may be negative. The next section describes several representative effects. Others may exist or develop in the future.

Improved Quality of Life

Many improvements in **quality of life** can be attributed to IT. An increase in organizational efficiency may result in more leisure time for workers. The workplace can be expanded from the traditional nine-to-five job at a central location to 24 hours a day from any location. This expansion provides a flexibility that can significantly improve the quality of leisure time, even if the total amount of leisure time is not increased. Here are some major areas of improvement.

Opportunities for people with disabilities.   The integration of intelligent systems, such as speech and vision recognition, into a computer-based information system can create new employment opportunities for people with disabilities. For example, those who cannot type are able to use voice-operated typewriters, and those who cannot travel can work at home.

Adaptive equipment for computers permits people with disabilities to perform tasks they would not normally be able to do. Figure 15.1 shows a PC for a blind user, a PC for a deaf user, and a PC for a motor-disabled user. Since the summer of 1994, companies with 15 employees or more have been required to comply with the Americans with Disabilities Act. This act requires companies to take reasonable steps to ensure that employees with disabilities will be able to work using specially adapted computers as well as with other equipment.

IT provides many devices for people with disabilities. Examples include a bilingual notebook computer for blind students, a two-way writing telephone, a robotic page-turner, a hair-brusher, and a hospital-bedside video trip to the zoo. When the

(a)   (b)   (c)

Figure 15.1   *Enabling people with disabilities to work with computers. [Source: J. J. Lazzaro, "Computers for the Disabled," Byte (June 1993).]*
(a) A PC for a blind user, equipped with an Oscar optical scanner and a Braille printer, both by TeleSensory. The optical scanner converts text into ASCII code or into proprietary word processing format. Files saved on disk can then be translated into Braille and sent to the printer. Visually impaired users can also enlarge the text on the screen by loading a TSR software magnification program.
(b) The deaf user's PC is connected to a telephone via an Ultratec Intele-Modem Baudot/ASCII modem. The user is sending and receiving messages to and from someone at a remote site who is using a telecommunications device for deaf people (right).
(c) This motor-disabled person is communicating with a PC using a Pointer Systems optical head pointer to access all keyboard functions on a virtual keyboard shown on the PC's display. The user can "strike" a key in one of two ways. He can focus on the desired key for a user-definable time period (which causes the key to be highlighted), or he can click an adapted switch when he chooses the desired key.

Web emerged, so did special arrangements to accommodate disabilities. For example, blind people can navigate the Web by using a special screen that dictates text from Web sites, word processors, and other applications. The problem is that many electronic commerce sites, such as home banking and stock purchasing online, do not work yet with the special screen reader for the blind. Only about 1 percent of Web sites were designed to be used by people with disabilities in 2001. To do so, according to *w3.org/wai*, a Web site should: (1) provide alternative text for images; (2) provide text equivalents for audio information; (3) ensure that text and graphics are perceivable when viewed without color; and (4) format tables so they can be understood by text-to-speech or Braille software for the blind.

This one-handed keyboard helps employees with disabilities to interact with their computer.

Improvements in health care. IT has brought about major improvements in health care delivery, ranging from better and faster diagnoses, to expedited research and development of new drugs, to more accurate monitoring of critically ill patients. One technology that has made a special contribution is intelligent systems. Of special interest are expert systems that support diagnosis of diseases, and the use of virtual reality in the planning of complex surgeries. On the drawing board are plans for vending-like machines that will dispense prescription drugs. The patient will enter the prescription in the machine, which will verify the prescription and the payment and will dispense the drug (*instymeds.com*). The following examples demonstrate some IT-enabled improvements in health care.

EXAMPLES

Internet sites bring information. The Internet cancer sites (*cancer.med.upenn.edu* and *cancernet.nci.nih.gov*) feature tens of thousands of documents written by experts. They offer information on the latest research studies and cancer pain management. They also help families cope with emotional and financial burdens. The sites have several million visitors each day from over 150 countries.

Small-town emergency services use an intranet. Residents of Maryville, Kansas, a community of 12,000, enjoy a townwide intranet that ties the town's hospital, health clinics, schools, county health department, and emergency services into a seamless data network. The system provides access to medical records in seconds, which enables health care workers to handle emergencies quickly. ●

Help for the consumer. Several IT systems are in place, and many more will be developed, to help the lay person perform tasks that require expertise. For example, TaxCut (*nysscpa.org*) is an expert system that can help in tax preparation; Legaldocs.com is an ES that helps a lay person with legal forms and advice, and Mysimon.com provides consumers with product information. Intelligent robots may some day clean the house and cook for us.

Robots performing hard labor. Robots can work in uncomfortable or dangerous environments. For example, the California Transportation Department and the University of California at Davis have developed robotic road-maintenance systems that save money, reduce congestion, and prevent worker accidents. The robo-repairer uses lasers to spot cracks between the pavement and the shoulder and then dispenses the right amount of patch material. Incidentally, farmers use a similar machine that dispenses fertilizers and/or pesticides after a robot "sees" the crop and soil and analyzes them. Caltrans Corporation is using an unmanned machine, based on technology developed for the military, that combines a hovercraft and a video camera to inspect bridges. Other highway robots inspect traffic lanes and identify hazardous materials from a safe distance. Managers at Caltrans say such machines are critical to keeping roads in good shape to handle the ever-increasing volume of traffic.

More than any other country, Japan has made extensive use of robots. The Central Japan Railway Company is using robots to vacuum rubbish. The robots, which are capable of doing the work of 15 people each, have been operating at the Sizuko station in central Japan. Japan also uses robots to assist the blind and the elderly as well as to diagnose some illnesses and even to clean cemeteries.

Crime fighting and other benefits.   Computer applications can benefit society in crime fighting as well. Here are some examples:

- AI-based systems monitor buildings by taking pictures of people, cars, and any other moving object. The system tries to find unusual movements and alert management, thus increasing security.

- A geographical information system helps the San Bernadino Sheriff's Department to visualize crime patterns and allocate resources.

- Since 1997, information about sex offenders has been put on the Internet.

- Los Angeles County has a sophisticated computer program for tracking over 150,000 gang members in the county. The program significantly helps reduce gang crime.

- A computerized voice mail system is used in Rochester, New York, so that homeless and other needy people can find jobs, access health care resources, and gain independent living skills.

- Electronic imaging and faxing enhance searches for missing children. High-quality photos plus text can be sent from the Center for Missing and Exploited Children (*missingkids.com*) to many fax machines and to portable machines in police cars. Of special interest is the support given by computers in a California kidnapping case, in IT's About Business W15.2 at our Web site.

www.wiley.com/
college/turban

The Digital Divide

The term **digital divide** refers to the gap in computer technology in general, and now in Web technology in particular, between those who have such technology and those who do not. A digital divide exists both within and among countries. The problem, from a societal point of view, is that the gap is increasing rapidly. In 2001, for example, only 5 percent of the world's population used the Web, and the vast majority of this 5 percent was located in the developed economies of North America, Europe, South East and East Asia, and Australia. The issue is how to close the gap.

As technologies develop and become less expensive, the speed at which the gap can be closed will accelerate. Cell phones will increase inexpensive access to the Internet as well as to Web TV.

According to Narayana Murthy, CEO of Infosys Technologies of India, IT and the Web can turn poor countries such as India into economic powerhouses. They can also help dissolve rigid social barriers. One of the developments that can close the digital divide is the Internet kiosks in public places and cybercafés. Most PC producers are donating computers to schools in developing countries, which will help close the digital divide for future generations of young people.

Internet Communities

H. Rheingold, in his 1993 book *The Virtual Community: Homesteading on the Electronic Frontier*, proposes that every Web site should incorporate a place for people to chat and congregate. He initiated the concept of a *virtual community center*—a place where discussions cover many controversial topics, but mostly the impact of technology on life. This center evolved to the concept of an Internet community. **Internet communities** are online communities of people with shared interests. They are quickly spreading over the Internet.

Researchers have identified the following five types of Internet communities:

1. ***Communities of interest.*** Here, people have the chance to interact with each other on a specific topic. For example, if you are interested in gardening, try *gardenweb.com*. The Motley Fool (*fool.com*) is a forum for individual investors. City 411 (*city411.com*) provides comprehensive information about local communities where many topics such as entertainment, traffic, and weather reports are displayed.

   Geocities (*geocities.com*) is the largest Internet community. It is organized into several dozen communities of interest. Millions of members are organized in communities such as MotorCity (car lovers) and Nashville (country music). Members have a "marketplace" for buying and selling goods and services.

   Thousands of other communities of interest exist on the Web. Of special interest are China.com, which caters to the Chinese-speaking community; ivillage.com, which caters to women; and elcito.com, which serves the Spanish-speaking community.

2. ***Communities of relations.*** These communities are organized around certain life experiences. For example, the cancer forum on CompuServe contains information and an exchange of opinions regarding cancer. Parent Soup is a favorite gathering spot for parents, and seniors like to visit SeniorNet.org.

3. ***Communities of fantasy.*** Here, participants create imaginary environments. For example, AOL subscribers can pretend to be a medieval baron at the Red Dragon Inn. On *espn.com* and *games.yahoo.com*, participants can create competing fantasy sport teams. Similarly, there are a number of games that thousands of people play simultaneously (*see/ea.com*, go to pogo). In Aliens online (*scifi.com*), you can win only if you join a team for $10/month; and Kingdom of Drakkar (I, II) allows you to play various roles (see *cgonline.com* and *adellion.com*).

4. ***Communities of transactions.*** These communities facilitate buying and selling. Members include buyers, sellers, intermediaries, and so on. In Chapter 9, we provided examples, such as Virtual Vineyard, which sells wines and provides experts' information on wines. Electronic games vendor Wizards.com created a community where members can chat, trade cards, and discuss tournaments. A fishing enthusiast's community can be found at *ausfish.com*.

5. ***Communities of professionals.*** These communities are established to support professional communication and the exchange of valuable work or research-related information. For example, Analog Devices (*analog.com*) created a community giving chip design engineers online access to its technical experts.

Electronic communities can create value for their organizers in the following ways: They charge usage fees; they charge users content fees for downloading articles, music, or pictures; they draw revenues from transactions and advertisements; and they may take advantage of synergies by reducing the cost of customer service.

Electronic communities are also related to electronic commerce. Electronic communities will eventually have a massive impact on almost every company that produces consumer goods and services. The electronic communities will change the nature of corporate strategy and the manner in which business is done.

Telecommuting

By **telecommuting**, or *teleworking*, employees can work at home, at a customer's premises, or while traveling, using a computer linked to their place of employment. A growing number of professionals do a significant portion of their work at home or on the road. Telecommuting, which is used by many corporations in large cities, is also appealing to small entrepreneurs. Almost all groupware technologies (Chapters 4, 6, 11) can be used to support telecommuting. Regular and overnight mail, special messengers, and fax are still used to support telecommuting, but the Internet is gradually replacing them.

Telecommuting has a number of potential advantages for employees, employers, and society, as presented in Manager's Checklist 15.2. However, there are also potential disadvantages. The major disadvantages for employees are increased feelings of isolation, loss of social interactions, lower pay (in some cases), and no workplace visibility (which may contribute to slower promotions). The major disadvantages to employers are difficulties in supervising work, potential data security problems, training costs, and the high cost of purchasing and maintaining telecommuters' equipment.

 Manager's Checklist 15.2

The Benefits of Telecommuting

Benefits to the employee	• Less stress (no driving, no office pressure).
	• Ability to go to school while working.
	• Improved family life (fewer job vs. family conflicts).
	• Money saved on lunches, clothes, gas, parking, and car maintenance.
	• Commuting time saved.
	• Ability to control schedule and manage time better.
	• Employment opportunities for housebound people (single parents, disabled).
Benefits to the organization	• Increased productivity (15 to 50 percent is claimed).
	• Reduced real estate (rental) cost.
	• Reduced cost of parking lots.
	• Ability to retain skilled employees.
	• Ability to tap remote labor pool. Greater staffing flexibility.
	• Lower labor and absenteeism cost. (Some people will take lower wages in order to stay home.)
	• Better interaction of employees with clients and suppliers. (Work can be done at the customers' sites.)
Benefits to society	• Less use of fossil fuels.
	• Fewer traffic problems, including less air pollution.
	• More business for suburbs and rural areas.

Nevertheless, the advantages evidently outweigh the disadvantages; the use of telecommuting is on the increase. Overall, most companies that have attempted telecommuting are very happy with it. (For an example of telecommuting, see IT's About Business 15.2.) Some experts predict that in 15 to 25 years, 50 percent of all work will be done at home, on the road, or at the customer's site.

Telecommuting and productivity. Why would productivity go up if people work at home? Strangely enough, reduced absenteeism has been cited by more than one organization as a major reason for increased productivity. Paul Ruper, Associate Director of New Ways to Work, claims absenteeism can be reduced by telecommuting because it eliminates "sort-of" illnesses. He refers to those mornings when an employee wakes up and just feels sort of "blah." The trip to work and a whole day at the office is not going to make him feel any better, so he stays home. The telecommuter, on the other hand, might rest in bed a bit longer or relax a bit in the morning and then feel ready to get to work. Or, the freedom to stay in jeans for the day, instead of dressing up for work, might be all that is needed to ease the "blah" feeling.

IT's About Business

pcfvirtual.com

Box 15.2: Virtual ad agency in Hawaii

Peterson, Cheng, and Fleishman (PCF) Advertising Agency in Hawaii has no central office, receptionists, secretaries, or parking hassles. All their employees work out of their homes. Most of the employees are in their 30s and perform their jobs individually, without much consultation with others. The employees are organized into teams of four, but they rarely meet. Communication is done via the Internet, faxes, and cellular phones. The agency, which started in 1996, has grown rapidly (from $2.5 million in 1996, to $8 million in 2000). How did it do so?

First, because the agency's expenses are very low, it can charge its clients much less than the competition. But in addition, it taught clients to save time by reducing the number of meetings and to use IT. The company is also using an innovative approach to advertising: instead of focusing on the traditional "creative" side of advertising, PCF takes an integrated approach, blending creative, media, promotional, and public relations efforts into a holistic approach to advertising and marketing.

Founding partner Ginger Peterson attributes the success to high-tech services, in combination with "the art of customer service." Jon Cheng, the high-tech guru at the agency, said that the virtual office helped the company to attract a high-tech staff. Traffic to and from Honolulu takes hours, so "commuting" on the Internet really saves time. "People do not have to sacrifice their families," Cheng said.

Is there any limitation? "Yes." Cheng said. "You need to learn not to do distracting things, such as turning on the TV or playing with the family dog. Telecommuters must be skilled, goal-oriented, self-motivated, disciplined, and have good time management skills."

Peterson feels that the virtual office will be perfect for any service-oriented business that does most of its work behind the scenes. Telecommuting makes the connection among team members more efficient. Time is saved and quality is improved because all communications are documented. Furthermore, the lower expenses enable the company to cut costs and seize opportunities to increase its market share.

Source: Deborah Brooker/*Honolulu Advertiser.*

Questions

1. PCF is one of the few companies that is truly virtual. It does not have an office. How is this possible? (Visit *pcfvirtual.com*.)

2. Cheng advised: "Choose your employees carefully.... Some people would be lost if they were left on their own at home." Why?

3. During the period of PCF's phenomenal growth, the economy in Hawaii was declining. How would you explain its success?

Telecommuting forces managers to manage by *results* instead of by *overseeing*. This process, although difficult, can help both the manager and the employee reduce misunderstandings about work. The employee will have a clear understanding of his or her responsibilities and thereby be accountable for his or her actions and results. For an example of one company's experience with telecommuting, see IT's About Business 15.2 (page 507).

Even though many employees are attracted to telecommuting, it is not for everybody and should not be mandatory. Some employees need to work face-to-face with others, and for those employees, telecommuting may not be an option. Also, not all jobs can be done while telecommuting, and not all managers can participate. One of the issues that affects the expansion of telecommuting is information systems security, the topic of the next section.

Before you go on . . .

1. List some societal activities improved by IT.

2. List improvements to health and safety as a result of IT.

3. Define and classify Internet communities.

4. Describe telecommuting and its major benefits.

15.5   SECURITY IS A CONCERN FOR EVERYONE

Information resources are scattered throughout the organization. Furthermore, employees travel with and take home corporate computers and data. Information is transmitted to and from the organization and among the organization's components. IT physical resources, data, software, procedures, and any other information resource may therefore be vulnerable to security risks in many places at any time.

Threats to Information Systems

Information systems face many dangers, as exemplified by the following incidents.

Incident 1.   During the late summer and early fall of 2001, there appeared several deadly viruses: Code Red and Code Red II, Offensive, Magistr.B, Invalid SSL, APost, Vote worm, and Nimda. The viruses are getting more and more destructive. For example, Nimda arrives by e-mail as an attachment or with random text in the subject line. The virus will attach itself to all the user's e-mail addresses in the address book. The infection may cause e-mail servers to run slowly or shut down. (For details of worms and their prevention, see *scmagazine.com/scmagazine/sc-online/2001/article/015/article.html).*

Incident 2.   On Sunday, May 8, 1988, a fire disabled a major Illinois Bell switching center in Hinsdale, Illinois. The outage affected the voice and data telecommunications of more than one-half million residents and hundreds of businesses, over a period ranging from two days to three weeks. Dozens of banks were hindered in cashing checks and transferring funds; at least 150 travel agencies were hindered in their ability to make reservations and print tickets; about 300 automated teller machines were shut down; most of the cellular phone and paging systems in the area were disrupted, as were the communications of hundreds of companies, both inside and outside the immediate area. The business cost was conservatively estimated to be $300 million.

Incident 3.   In 1996, the *Los Angeles Times* reported that computers made an $850 million error in Social Security. The glitch shortchanged about 700,000 Americans in retirement benefits and had been undetected for almost 23 years until it was discovered during an audit in 1994. Although the newspaper blamed the computer, the fault was actually that of the programmers who were unable to automate properly the complex computations of the benefits. It took more than three years to fix the problem.

Incident 4.   There are 250,000 annual attempts to crack the U.S. Pentagon's security system. In April 1998, a teenage Israeli hacker was arrested on suspicion of hacking his way into the Pentagon and 700 other sensitive computer systems worldwide. He used the name of a real company, NetDex, as a launch pad for his attacks. The hacker broke into unclassified computer networks to examine and possibly alter personnel data. This most successful break sent a wake-up call to the Pentagon's security officials, who started bolstering security immediately.

Incident 5.   In July 1998, the opening of Hong Kong's new international airport, the world's most expensive airport, was plagued with computer glitches. For example, a computer bug erased inventory records, bringing cargo operations to a halt. (Hong Kong airport ranks third in the world in terms of cargo.) A problem with the software erased flight information from monitors, preventing passengers from finding flights. The computerized baggage system caused lost luggage; as a result, as many as 10,000 bags were left behind, in just one day.

These incidents illustrate the **vulnerability** (susceptibility to harm) of information systems, the diversity of causes of computer security problems, and the substantial damage that can be done to organizations.

Systems Vulnerability

Information systems are made up of many components in several locations. Thus, each information system is vulnerable to many potential **hazards**. (See Figure W15.1 on the Web site for a summary of the major threats to the security of an information system.) The vulnerability of information systems is increasing as we move to a world of networked computing. Theoretically, there are hundreds of points in a corporate information system that can be subject to some threat. These threats can be classified as *unintentional* or *intentional*.

www.wiley.com/
college/turban

Unintentional threats.   Unintentional threats can be divided into three major categories: *human errors, environmental hazards*, and *computer systems failures*.

Several computer problems result from *human error*. Errors can occur in the design of the hardware or the information system. They can also occur in the programming, testing, data collection, data entry, authorization, and instructions. Human errors contribute to the vast majority of control- and security-related problems in many organizations.

Environmental hazards include earthquakes, hurricanes, severe snow, sand, storms, floods, tornadoes, power failures or strong fluctuations, fires (the most common hazard), defective air-conditioning, explosions, radioactive fallout, and water-cooling system failures. Such hazards may disrupt normal computer operations and result in long waiting periods and exorbitant costs while computer programs and data files are recreated. *Computer systems failures* can be the result of poor manufacturing or defective materials. Unintentional malfunctions can happen for other reasons, ranging from lack of experience to incompatibility of software.

The following examples demonstrate systems vulnerability due to human error.

EXAMPLES

Corrupt data blitz the London Stock Exchange. On April 30, 2000, the London Stock Exchange was paralyzed by its worst computer system failure, before finally opening nearly eight hours late. A spokesman for the exchange said the problem, which crippled the supply of prices and firm information, was caused by corrupt data. He gave no further details. Dealers were outraged by the fault, which came on the last day of the tax year and just hours after violent price swings in the U.S. stock markets. The British Financial Services Authority said it viewed the failure seriously, adding it would insist any necessary changes to systems would be made immediately and that lessons would be "learned rapidly" to ensure the breakdown would not be repeated.

Leap year takes Japan by surprise. On February 29, 2000, in Japan, hundreds of ATMs were shut down, a computer system at a nuclear plant seized up, weather-monitoring devices malfunctioned, display screens for interest rates at the post offices failed, seismographs provided wrong information, and there were many other problems related to programming for "leap year." The problem was that years that end in "00" do not get the extra day, added every four years, unless they are divisible by 400 (2000 is a leap year, but not 1900, or 2100). This rule was not programmed properly in some old programs in Japan, thus creating the problems. ●

Intentional threats. Computer systems may be damaged as a result of intentional actions. Examples include: theft of data; inappropriate use of data (e.g., manipulating inputs); theft of mainframe computer time; theft of equipment or programs; deliberate manipulation in handling, entering, processing, transferring, or programming data; labor strikes, riots, or sabotage; malicious damage to computer resources; destruction from viruses and similar attacks; and miscellaneous computer abuse and crimes. Most intentional threats, when executed, are viewed as computer crimes.

Computer Crimes

The number, magnitude, and diversity of computer crimes and abuse are increasing rapidly. Lately, increased fraud related to the Internet and electronic commerce is in evidence. To learn how to protect yourself from computer crime, see Chapter 9, *ftc.gov, fraud.org,* and *consumersworld.org.*

Types of computer crimes and criminals. Computer crimes can occur in four ways. First, the computer can be the *target* of the crime. For example, a computer may be stolen or destroyed, or a virus may destroy data. Second, the computer can be the *medium* of the attack by creating an environment in which a crime or fraud can occur. For example, false data are entered into a computer system to mislead individuals examining the financial condition of a company. Third, the computer can be the *tool* by which the crime is perpetrated. For example, a computer is used to plan a crime, but the crime does not involve a computer. Fourth, the computer can be used to *intimidate* or *deceive*. For instance, a stockbroker stole $50 million by convincing his clients that he had a computer program with which he could increase their earnings by 60 percent per month.

Crimes can be performed by *outsiders* who penetrate a computer system (frequently via communication lines) or by *insiders* who are authorized to use the computer system but are misusing their authorization. A **hacker** is the term often used to describe outside people who penetrate a computer system. A **cracker** is a *malicious hacker* who may represent a serious problem for a corporation.

Computer criminals, whether insiders or outsiders, have a distinct profile and are driven by several common motives. For example, the criminals are mostly white males, ages 19 to 35, who work with computers, and are usually very bright. The major motives are economic, ideological, psychological, and egocentric. Ironically, many employees fit this profile, but only a few of them are criminals. Therefore, it is difficult to predict who will be a computer criminal.

Methods of attack.   Two basic approaches are used in deliberate attacks on computer systems: data tampering and programming techniques.

Data tampering ("data diddling") is the most common approach and is often used by insiders. It refers to entering false, fabricated, or fraudulent data into the computer or changing or deleting existing data. For example, to pay for his wife's drug purchases, a savings and loan programmer transferred $5,000 into his personal account and tried to cover up the transfer with phony debit and credit transactions.

Computer criminals also use *programming techniques* to modify a computer program, either directly or indirectly. For this crime, programming skills and knowledge of the targeted systems are essential. **Programming fraud** schemes appear in many forms, such as viruses. Due to their frequency, viruses merit special mention here.

Viruses.   The most publicized attack method, the **virus**, receives its name from the program's ability to attach itself to ("infect") other computer programs, causing them to become viruses themselves. A virus can spread throughout a computer system (see Figure 15.2). Due to the availability of public domain software, widely used telecommunications networks, and the Internet, viruses can also easily spread to many organizations. Viruses are known to spread all over the world. Some of the most notorious viruses are "international," such as I Love You, Melissa, Michelangelo, Pakistani Brain, Jerusalem, and Red Code.

When a virus is attached to a legitimate software program, the program becomes infected without the owner of the program being aware of the infection. Therefore, when the software is used, the virus spreads, causing damage to that program and possibly to others. In Section 15.6, we'll look at protection against viruses.

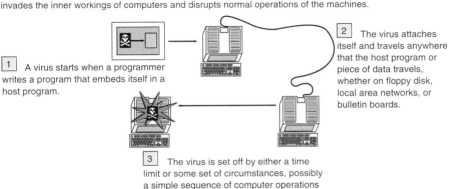

Just as a biological virus disrupts living cells to cause disease, a computer virus—introduced maliciously— invades the inner workings of computers and disrupts normal operations of the machines.

1   A virus starts when a programmer writes a program that embeds itself in a host program.

2   The virus attaches itself and travels anywhere that the host program or piece of data travels, whether on floppy disk, local area networks, or bulletin boards.

3   The virus is set off by either a time limit or some set of circumstances, possibly a simple sequence of computer operations by the user. Then it does whatever the virus programmer intended, whether it is to print "Have a nice day" or erase data.

Figure 15.2   *How a computer virus can spread.* [*Source: Courtesy of Thumbscan.*]

Other methods: denial of service.   On February 6, 2000, the biggest e-commerce sites were falling like dominos. First was Yahoo!, which was forced to close down for three hours. Next were eBay, Amazon.com, E*Trade, and several other major EC and Internet sites that had gone dark.

The attacker(s) used a method called **denial of service (DOS)**. By hammering a Web site's equipment with too many requests for information, an attacker can effectively clog a system, slowing performance or even crashing a site. All one needs to do is to get the DOS software (available for free in many hacking sites), break into unrelated, unprotected computers and plant some software there, select a target site, and instruct the unprotected computers to repeatedly send a request for information to the target site. It is like constantly dialing a telephone number so that no one else can get through. It takes time for the attacked site to identify the sending computers and to block e-mails from them. Thus, the attacked site may be out-of-service for a few hours.

Representative federal laws dealing with computer crime.   According to the FBI, an average robbery involves $3,000; an average white-collar crime involves $23,000; but an average computer crime involves about $600,000. A number of U.S. federal laws make it possible for law enforcement officials to pursue and prosecute those who engage in computer crime. (For a list of federal statutes dealing with computer crime, see the book's Web site.)

www.wiley.com/
college/turban

Before you go on . . .

1. Define controls, threats, vulnerability, computer crime, viruses, hackers, denial of service, and backup.

2. Provide examples of intentional and unintentional threats to computer users (both idividuals and organizations).

3. How can high-tech criminals pose threats to society?

4. Describe viruses. Why can their damage be very high?

15.6 PROTECTING INFORMATION SYSTEMS

The large number of potential threats to information systems has resulted in a great number of defensive strategies and tools. Before we present the major ones, it is necessary to describe some general issues related to IT protection. Defending information systems is neither simple nor an inexpensive task.

Defense Strategies: How Do We Protect IT?

Protection of IT is accomplished by inserting *controls*—defense mechanisms that are designed to protect all the components of an information system, specifically, data, software, hardware, and networks. Their implementation requires a defense strategy. The following are the major types of *defense strategies*:

1. *Controls for prevention and deterrence.* Properly designed controls may prevent errors from occurring, deter criminals from attacking the system, and better yet,

deny access to unauthorized people. Prevention and deterrence are especially important where the potential for damage is very high.

2. **Detection.** It may not be economically feasible to prevent all hazards, and preventive measures may not always work. Therefore, unprotected systems are vulnerable to attack. Like a fire, the earlier it is detected, the easier it is to combat and the less damage. Detection can be performed in many cases by using special diagnostic software.

3. **Damage control.** This means minimizing losses once a malfunction has occurred. Users typically want their systems back in operation as quickly as possible. This can be accomplished by including a *fault-tolerant system* that permits operation in a degraded mode until full recovery is made.

4. **Recovery.** A recovery plan explains how to fix a damaged information system as quickly as possible. Replacing rather than repairing components can be a route for fast recovery.

5. **Correction.** Correcting damaged systems can prevent the problem from occurring again.

Information system controls can be divided into two major groups: general (system) controls and application controls. **General controls** are established to protect the system regardless of the specific application. For example, protecting hardware and controlling access to a data center are independent of the specific application. **Application controls** are safeguards that are intended to protect specific applications.

General controls.   The major categories of general controls are physical controls, access controls, data security controls, communications (networks) controls, and administrative controls.

Physical controls.   *Physical* controls constitute the physical protection of computer facilities and resources. This includes protecting physical property such as computers, data centers, software, manuals, and networks. Physical security provides protection against most natural hazards as well as against some human hazards. Appropriate physical security may include several controls such as human guards and locked doors.

Access control.   *Access control* is the restriction of unauthorized user access to a portion of a computer system or to the entire system. To gain access, a user must first be *authorized*. Then, when the user attempts to gain access, he or she must be *authenticated*. Access control software is commercially available for large mainframes, minicomputers, personal computers, local area networks, and dial-in communications networks. Access control to the network is executed through firewalls, which will be discussed later in this section.

Access to a computer system basically consists of three steps: (1) physical access to a terminal, (2) access to the system, and (3) access to specific commands, transactions, privileges, programs, and data within the system. The defense strategy may involve the use of several types of access controls. A typical secured system is shown in Figure 15.3 (page 514). Insiders who want to access the computer follow the footsteps until they reach a computer. The outsiders access via the telephone or networks. Note the physical shield (the locked door) that the user must pass through (follow the footsteps). Solid lines with arrows show the nonphysical (logical, administrative) controls.

Access procedures match every valid user with a unique *user identifier* (*UID*). They also provide authentication methods to verify that users requesting access to the

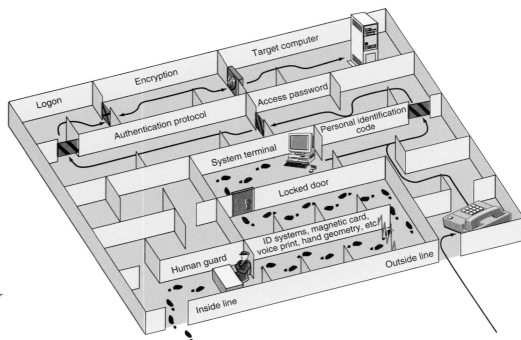

Figure 15.3 *Computer defenses.* [*Source: Joe Lertolaq 1983 Discover Magazine.*]

computer system are really who they claim to be. You may recall that authenticity, privacy, integrity, and nonrepudiation are the cornerstones of security of electronic commerce. User identification can be accomplished by using biometric controls.

Biometric controls. A **biometric control** is an automated method of verifying the identity of a person, based on physiological or behavioral characteristics. The most common biometric controls are the following:

- ***Hand geometry.*** Similar to fingerprints except the verifier uses a television-like camera to take a picture of the user's hand. Ninety characteristics of the hand (e.g., finger length and thickness) are electronically compared against the information stored in the computer.

- ***Blood vessel pattern in the retina of an eye.*** A match is attempted between the pattern of the blood vessels in the back-of-the-eye retina that is being scanned and a prestored picture of the authorized individual's retina.

- ***Voice.*** A match is attempted between the user's voice and the voice pattern (e.g., distinctive highs and lows in a person's speech) stored on templates.

- ***Signature.*** Signatures are matched against the prestored authentic signature. This method can supplement a photo-card ID system.

- ***Keystroke dynamics.*** The person's keyboard pressure and speed is matched against prestored information.

- ***Facial recognition.*** The face is captured on video so the system can encode measurements between distinctive facial features.

- ***Facial thermography.*** An infared camera captures a portrait of the face and registers the different temperatures emanating from underlying blood vessels. The picture is stored. When you use the computer another picture is taken and matched with the prestored one.

- **Fingerprints (finger imaging).** Each time a user wants access, matching a fingerprint against a template containing the authorized person's fingerprint (see attached photo) identifies him or her.
- **Iris scan.** A video image of the eye is captured, and unique features such as iris pattern and color are encoded and prestored. Scanning the iris and matching it against prestored information is considered the most reliable biometric.

Biometic controls received considerable attention after the WTC disaster. They can be helpful in preventing some terrorist attacks (see *msnbc.com/news/630735. asp?<p1=1#BODY*).

Modern fingerprint identification systems aid security efforts.

Data security controls.   *Data security* is concerned with protecting data from accidental or intentional disclosure to unauthorized persons, or from unauthorized modification or destruction. Data security functions are implemented through operating systems, security access control programs, database/data communications products, recommended backup/recovery procedures, application programs, and external control procedures. Data security must address the following issues: confidentiality of data, access control, critical nature of data, and integrity of data. **Data integrity** is the condition that exists as long as accidental or intentional destruction, alteration, or loss of data *does not* occur. It is the preservation of data for its intended use.

Other general controls.   Several other types of controls are considered general. These include programming controls, controls to prevent misunderstanding or misinterpretation, and system development controls. Of special interest are *administrative controls*, which deal with issuing guidelines and monitoring compliance with the guidelines, and *communications (network) controls*, which are discussed later.

Application controls.   General controls do not protect the *content* of each specific application. Therefore, controls are frequently built into the applications (i.e., they are part of the software) and are usually written as validation rules. They can be classified into three major categories: *input controls*, *processing controls*, and *output controls*.

Input controls.   Input controls are designed to prevent data alteration or loss. Data are checked for accuracy, completeness, and consistency. Input controls are very important; they prevent the GIGO (garbage-in, garbage-out) situation.

Processing controls.   Processing controls ensure that data are complete, valid, and accurate when being processed and that programs have been properly executed. These programs allow only authorized users to access certain programs or facilities, and they monitor the computer's use by individuals.

Output controls.   Output controls ensure that the results of computer processing are accurate, valid, complete, and consistent. By studying the nature of common output errors and the causes of such errors, management can evaluate possible controls to deal with problems. Also, control ensures that outputs are sent only to authorized personnel.

Network protections and firewalls.   On April 13, 1998, an AT&T maintenance problem that resulted from a software bug sent large portions of the Internet into a gridlock. The outage lasted a full day and was not completely diagnosed for more than a week. It prevented many consumers from completing credit card purchases, halted withdrawals at many Wells Fargo bank ATMs, and even caused some cash registers to malfunction at Starbucks. AT&T's officials admitted their security procedures were inadequate. It is estimated that AT&T lost $40 million in revenue as a result.

High-speed public data networks, such as AT&T's, have become an increasingly popular way for banks, airlines, retailers, and other businesses to relay customer information and other data to their branch offices. Such public networks, which are about 50 percent cheaper than private lines, are called *frame relay networks*. The AT&T incident demonstrates the increased importance of the Internet and intranets for business. Therefore, we discuss network protection here in some more detail. Security issues regarding electronic commerce are discussed in Chapter 9.

Many measures can be employed to protect networks. The most common are access controls that include authentication and passwords, encryption, cable testers, intrusion detection, and firewalls.

Access control.   As noted earlier, an access control system guards against unauthorized dial-in attempts. Most of the methods discussed earlier, such as authentication and passwords, are valid for network protection, too.

Encryption.   Another network protection device is **encryption**, which encodes regular text into unreadable scrambled text or numbers for transmission. As explained in Chapter 9, the encypted text is then *decrypted* (decoded) upon receipt. Encryption accomplishes three purposes: (1) identification (helps identify legitimate senders and receivers), (2) control (prevents changing a transaction or message), and (3) privacy (impedes eavesdropping).

Cable testers.   A popular defense of LANs is troubleshooting. For example, a *cable tester* can quickly find almost any fault that can occur with LAN cabling.

Intrusion detection.   Because protection against *denial of service* is difficult, the sooner one can detect an usual activity, the better. Therefore, it is worthwhile to place an *intrusion detection* device near the entrance point of the Internet to the intranet (close to a firewall, discussed next). The objective is early detection, and this can be done by several devices. Examples of such devices are SilentRunner (from Raytheon), Praesidium (from HP), and IDS (from Cisco).

Firewalls.   A **firewall** is a system, or a group of systems, that enforces an access control policy between two networks. It is commonly used as a barrier between the secure corporate intranet, or other internal networks, and the Internet, which is assumed to be unsecured.

Firewalls are necessary because of hacking, which is a growing phenomenon. It is believed that hacking costs U.S. industry several billion dollars each year. Hacking is such a popular activity that more than 80,000 Web sites are dedicated to it, and anyone can download, at no cost, tools that are needed to break into computerized systems. Firewalls provide the most cost-effective solution to the problem of hacking, though they are by no means 100% effective.

Firewalls are used to implement control access policies. The firewall follows strict guidelines that either permit or block traffic. Several firewalls may exist in one information system. IT's About Business 15.3 details the use of firewalls at Fidelity Investment.

IT's About Business

fidelity.com **FIN**

Box 15.3:　Firewalls at Fidelity Investments

Fidelity Investments is the largest mutual fund company in the U.S. and a stockbroker. The company allows its customers and prospective customers to personalize their access to information available on Fidelity's Web site. This service, called Web Express, was pioneered by Fidelity and includes information about balances and stock positions, historical transactions, online registration for new accounts, secure log-ins, real-time quotes on various securities (stocks, mutual funds, options, and indices), and trading capabilities. A major concern is the protection of security and privacy, a difficult task because even simple transactions require complex operations, including dynamically generated HTML.

The architecture of the highly secure system works like this: When the customer enters the Web site, his or her information is encrypted (using SSL encryption), and the encrypted information passes through the fire-wall to the Netscape commerce server. The server, acting as a client, sends a transaction remote procedure call (RPC) to a second firewall in a replication server. This server generates a second RPC that goes to a transaction dispatcher that connects it to the mainframe servers and databases.

Questions

1. Visit Fidelity Investment's Web site (*fidelity.com*). What accounting-related information is provided by the services offered to individuals?

2. What bookkeeping services are provided to individual investors?

3. Explain how firewalls improve the connections between Fidelity and its customers.

Auditing Information Systems

Controls are established to ensure that information systems work properly. Controls can be installed in the original system, or they can be added once a system is in operation. Installing controls is necessary but not sufficient. In addition, it is also necessary to answer questions such as the following: Are controls installed as intended? Are they effective? Has any breach of security occurred? If so, what actions are required to prevent reoccurrence? These questions need to be answered by independent and unbiased observers. Such observers perform the task of information system *auditing*.

An **audit** is an important part of any control system. In an organizational setting, it is usually referred to as a regular *examination and check* of financial and accounting records and procedures. Specially trained professionals, who may be either internal employees or external consultants, execute auditing. In the information systems environment, auditing can be viewed as an additional layer of controls or safeguards.

Types of auditors and audits.　There are two types of auditors and audits: internal and external. Information system auditing is usually a part of the accounting *internal auditing* and is frequently done by corporate internal auditors. An *external auditor* is a corporate outsider. This type of auditor reviews the findings of the internal audit and the inputs, processing, and outputs of information systems. The external audit of information systems is frequently a part of the overall external auditing performed by a certified public accounting (CPA) firm.

Information systems auditing can be very broad, so we present only its essentials here. Auditing looks at all potential hazards and controls in information systems. It focuses attention on topics such as new systems development, operations, maintenance, data integrity, software application, security and privacy, disaster planning and recovery, purchasing, budgets and expenditures, chargebacks, vendor management, documentation, insurance and bonding, training, cost control, and productivity.

Several guidelines are available to assist auditors in their jobs, such as those from the Institute of Internal Auditors, Orlando, Florida (*theiia.org*).

How is auditing executed?   IS auditing procedures can be classified into three categories: auditing *around* the computer, auditing *through* the computer, and auditing *with* the computer.

Auditing around the computer means verifying processing by checking for known outputs using specific inputs. The best application of this approach is in systems that produce a limited range of outputs. The approach is fast and inexpensive, but it may give false results. For example, two errors may compensate for each other, resulting in seemingly correct output. In *auditing through the computer*, inputs, outputs, and processing are checked. Auditors review program logic, test data, and controlling processing and reprocessing. *Auditing with the computer* means using a combination of client data, auditor software, and client and auditor hardware. It allows the auditor to perform tasks such as simulating payroll program logic using live data.

Auditors use several tools to increase their effectiveness and efficiency in all the above areas. Typical tools are checklists, formulas, and charts. These can be executed manually or can be computerized.

Auditors and security consultants may try to break into a computer system in what is called a *simulated attack*, in order to find weak points in the system, as the example below demonstrates. In some cases, companies hire famous hackers to do the job.

EXAMPLE

Auditors break into Illinois system.   Auditors for the State of Illinois issued a public statement in which they notified the State that they were successful in their mission of breaking into the Central Computer Facility that serves 159 state agencies. The auditors pulled off their mission with "disturbing ease." An authorized hacker, operating from a remote location, was able to break into the system and read, modify, and delete data such as payroll and prison records. Real hackers could have altered the security structure and violated system integrity. The security system, which had been thought to be satisfactory, was enhanced immediately, and all known security flaws were fixed. ●

Disaster Recovery Planning

The best defense is to be prepared for various eventualities. An important element in any security system is a disaster recovery plan. Destruction of all (or most) of an organization's computing facilities can cause significant damage. Therefore, it is difficult for many organizations to obtain insurance for their businesses without showing a satisfactory disaster prevention and recovery plan for the information systems.

Disaster recovery is the chain of events linking planning to protection to recovery. The purpose of a recovery plan is to keep the business running after a disaster occurs (*business continuity*). Both the IS department and line management should be involved in preparation of the plan. Recovery planning is part of *asset protection*. Planning should focus first on recovery from a total loss of all computing capabilities. Proof of capability usually involves some kind of what-if analysis that shows that the recovery plan is current and effective. All critical applications must be identified in the plan and their recovery procedures addressed. The plan should be written so that it will be effective in case of disaster, not just in order to satisfy the auditors. The plan should be kept in a safe place; copies should be given to all key managers; and the plan should be audited periodically.

Disaster recovery planning can be very complex, and it may take several months to complete. Using special software, the planning job can be expedited. Consider the following example.

EXAMPLE

Cray showcases its security plan.   The Cray Research Data Center (Eagan, Minnesota) is used not only for its own needs but also as a showcase and demonstration site for customers and researchers. Cray is best known for producing the world's most powerful supercomputers. Cray's corporate security and disaster recovery plan covers various building systems in addition to Cray's information systems: electrical power (protection, backup), air-conditioning, fire protection and alarms, and heating systems.

sgi.com

Corporate computers are monitored by sensors and controlled centrally. *Graphic displays* show both normal status and disturbances. All the devices controlled are represented as icons on floor-plan graphics. These icons can change colors (e.g., green means normal, red signifies a problem). The icons can flash as well. Corrective-action messages are displayed whenever appropriate. The alarm system includes over 1,500 alarms. Operators can be alerted, even at remote locations, in less than one second.

The security system is also integrated with a productivity monitoring and cost-effectiveness system concerning the buildings. Cost issues are addressed by looking at specific information, such as the possibility of reducing energy costs in the data center, reducing maintenance and operations costs, and assuring an optimal power usage. Thus, connections are made both to solve internal security problems and to recruit more customers. ●

Disaster avoidance is an approach oriented toward *prevention*. The idea is to minimize the chance of avoidable disasters (such as arson or other human-caused threats). For example, many companies use a device called *uninterrupted power supply (UPS)*, which provides power in case of a power outage. The Cray example also specifies some approaches toward fire control and cooling backups.

Back-up arrangements.   In the event of a major disaster, it is often necessary to move a centralized computing facility to a backup location, where an extra copy of data and/or programs are kept. At external hot-sites, vendors provide access to a fully configured backup data center. The WTC tragedy on September 11, 2001, illustrated the importance of backup arrangements, especially hot sites. Most of the large financial institutions such as Merrilll Lynch have hot sites to which they were able to shift their operation in a few minutes. But this was not the case for medium and small companies, as the chapter-opening story illustrated.

The potential for the disaster of a complete system failure is greater in systems that depend on the Internet. A complete shutdown due to Web-related failures has been a common event for stockbrokers, banks, retailers, and Internet service providers. For example, discount broker Schwab had eight failures in six months in late 1998 and early 1999. The consensus of IT professionals in 2001 is that data redundancy—keeping copies of data in various locations—is the best security solution.

Planning for disasters in the face of change.   The biggest challenge facing IT managers as they maintain disaster recovery plans is the constant change in the business. Some tips for dealing with constant change include the following:

- Isolate data that change frequently.
- Keep management and technical procedures separate.

Table 15.3   How Technologies Improved IT Security

Area of Security	IT Solution
Improved systems reliability	Fault tolerance systems (e.g., power supply), multiple disks.
Early or real-time detection of intrusion, failures, or noncompliance with rules	Intelligent agents monitor performance, compare to standards, analyze profiles.
Auditing information systems	Neural computer can detect fraud, and expert systems evaluate controls.
Troubleshooting	Quick diagnosis by expert systems, especially on networks and the Internet.
Disaster recovery planning	Internet-based expert systems for self-assessment including planning and disaster recovery.
Access protection	Smart cards.

 Manager's Checklist 15.3

Guidelines for How to Protect
Your PC and Data

- Always carry a scanner disk with you when accessing computers. Scan your hard drive for viruses every week (or install an automatic scanner).
- Scan and clear viruses whenever your disk contacts computers or leaves your hands (even for just a few minutes). Unlike Dustin Hoffman in *Outbreak*, you may not always be lucky enough to find an antivirus vaccine in time to save your fatally virus-infected homework files. Install a good antivirus program on your computer and keep it updated.
- Duplicate (back up) important information and store it in a safe place.
- Protect your campus and the community with a virus-free environment by cleaning and reporting virus-related activities.
- Don't spill coffee or other liquids on your computer.
- Write-protect your floppy disks until you need to write to them.
- Don't leave your password unattended.
- Use several passwords. You can get free software to store passwords securely, so that you do not need to memorize several passwords. Go to *advantagecom.net/nonags*, and look under "misc utilities" in the freeware section.
- You can create password protection to any software that does not offer such protection. Use "007 for Windows," for example. (It is available at the shareware library at *zdnet.com/swlib*.)
- When you delete files, they are still in your computer. To erase them permanently, consult your computer center, or at home use programs such as "eraser" or "mutilate" (available at *zdnet.com/swlib*).
- To keep your data private when you are away from your PC, you may use software such as "Megz Lock." This application performs a variety of tricks to keep your computer's data private (available at *zdnet.com/swlib*).
- To encrypt your e-mail use software such as "Pretty Good Privacy" (known as PGP). It is free at *pgp.com* and *nai.com/products/security/personal.asp*.
- If you do not have Windows XP, which has a firewell built into it, install one.

- Don't include data in the plan if they can be obtained elsewhere after the disaster.
- Write a plan that is independent of organization, positions, and personnel.
- Gather data on a daily basis.

IT Security in the Twenty-First Century

As we enter the third millennium, computer control and security are receiving increased attention. For example, according to a 2001 Dataquest survey, almost 80 percent of all U.S. corporations have battled computer viruses. Therefore, the latest technologies need to be employed to protect against viruses and computer crimes. Several examples are provided in Table 15.3.

How can I protect my PC and data? Your first step to protect your PC and data is to enter *nsca.com* and learn more about computer security. Then read and follow the guidelines presented in Manager's Checklist 15.3.

Self-healing computers. Using technology known as eliza, IBM is equipping its supercomputers with the ability to repair themselves and keep themselves running without human intervention. The computers will conduct diagnostics on themselves, fixing problems and keeping themselves running reliably.

Before you go on . . .

1. Describe prevention, deterrence, detection, limitation, recovery, and correction by IT security controls.

2. Distinguish between auditing around, through, and within the computer.

3. Define firewalls and explain their capabilities and importance.

4. Define and describe a disaster recovery plan.

www.wiley.com/
college/turban

FOR THE ACCOUNTING MAJOR

Auditing information systems is a growing area of special interest, as is Web-based auditing. Also, security of data is of major concern to the accountant. Accountants are also involved in fraud prevention and detection programs. Disaster recovery planning is usually done with the assistance of accountants.

FOR THE FINANCE MAJOR

The finance and banking industry is heavily dependent on computers and their networks. Security is one of the major requirements for the development of new technologies such as electronic (home) banking and smart cards. Also, payment systems are critical for e-commerce, and their security and auditing is of the utmost importance. Finally, banking and financial institutions are prime targets for computer criminals, as is fraud involving stocks and bonds sold over the Internet, which is increasing rapidly. Finance people must be aware of both the hazards and the available controls.

MKT **FOR THE MARKETING MAJOR**
Marketers clearly do not want to be sued because of invasion of privacy in data collected for the marketing database, nor do they want their innovative marketing strategies to fall into the hands of competitors. Also, since customers' privacy can easily be invaded while their data are kept in the marketing database or collected at the POS, marketers need to learn how to prevent such incidents.

POM **FOR THE PRODUCTION/OPERATIONS MANAGEMENT MAJOR**
Can telecommuting increase productivity? To what extent do security efforts reduce productivity? How can efficiency be increased with new organizational structures? The answers to these and other questions require the attention of production/operations management personnel to the topics discussed in this chapter.

HRM **FOR THE HUMAN RESOURCES MANAGEMENT MAJOR**
The impacts of IT on individuals, as discussed in this chapter, are especially important to HRM professionals. Motivation, supervision, career development, recruiting, and more are all affected by IT. Without an understanding of these issues, it is difficult to manage human resources. Also, HRM personnel should be interested in finding how to identify potential computer criminals in the recruiting process.

SUMMARY

❶ **Describe the major ethical issues related to information technology and identify situations in which they occur.**
The major ethical issues related to IT are privacy, accuracy, property (including intellectual property), and accessibility to information. Privacy may be violated when data are held in databases or are transmitted over networks. Privacy policies that address issues of data collection, data accuracy, and data confidentiality can help organizations avoid legal problems.

❷ **Identify the major impacts of information technology on organizational structure, power, jobs, supervision, and decision making.**
Information technology can make organizations flatter and change authority, job content, and status of employees. As a result, the manager's job and methods of supervision and decision making may drastically change. Also, many middle managers may lose their jobs.

❸ **Understand the potential dehumanization of people by computers and other potential negative impacts of information technology.**
The major negative impacts of IT are in the areas of job loss, invasion of privacy, and dehumanization. In terms of their impact on health and safety, computers can increase stress and health risks to eyes, back, bones, and muscles. Ergonomically designed computing facilities can greatly reduce the risks associated with computer use. Properly planned information systems can decrease the dehumanization, and shifts in workloads can reduce stress.

❹ **Identify some of the major societal effects of information technology.**
The major positive impacts of IT are its contribution to employment of the disabled, improvements in health care, delivery of education, crime fighting, and increased productivity. However, the effect on employment levels in general is debatable. In one view, IT will cause massive unemployment because of increased productivity. In another view, IT will increase employment levels because automation will

make products and services more affordable, thus increasing demand, and because the process of disseminating automation is slow enough to allow the economy to adjust to information technologies. Telecommuting options will lessen automobile traffic and pollution, as well as present certain managerial challenges in some organizations.

❺ Describe the many threats to information security.
Data, software, hardware, and networks can be threatened by many internal and external hazards. The damage to an information system can be caused either accidentally or intentionally. Also, computer criminals are driven by economic, ideological, egocentric, or psychological factors and are difficult to identify. Most computer criminals are insiders, but outsiders (such as hackers and crackers) can cause major damage as well.

❻ Understand the various defense mechanisms used to protect information systems.
Information systems are protected with controls such as security procedures, physical guards, or detecting software. These can be classified as controls used for *prevention, deterrence, detection, damage control, recovery,* and *correction* of information systems. Biometric controls are used to control access by checking physical characteristics (e.g., fingerprints and retinas) to identify authorized users.

❼ Explain IT auditing and planning for disaster recovery.
Auditing is done in a similar manner to accounting/finance auditing, around, through, and with the computer. A detailed internal and external IT audit may involve hundreds of issues and can be supported by both software and checklists. Related to IT auditing is the preparation for disaster recovery, which specifically addresses how to avoid, plan for, and quickly recover from a disaster.

DISCUSSION QUESTIONS

1. The Internal Revenue Service (IRS) buys demographic market research data from private companies. These data contain income statistics that could be compared to tax returns. Many U.S. citizens feel that their rights within the realm of the Privacy Act of 1974 are being violated by the agency's use of such information. Is this unethical behavior on the part of the IRS? Discuss.

2. Clerks at 7-Eleven stores enter data regarding customers (gender, approximate age, and so on) into the computer. These data are then processed for improved decision making. Customers are not informed about this, nor are they asked for permission. (Names are not keyed in.) Are the clerks' actions on behalf of 7-Eleven ethical?

3. Many hospitals, health maintenance organizations (HMOs), and federal agencies are converting, or plan to convert, all patients' medical records from paper to electronic storage (using imaging technology). Once the conversion is made, Web technology and electronic storage can enable quick access to most records. However, the availability of these records in a database and on networks may also enable unauthorized people to view one's private data. To protect privacy fully may cost too much money or result in much slower accessibility to the records. What policies could health care administrators use in such situations? Discuss.

4. Robots are used in California and Japan to support road maintenance. At the same time, they may take jobs away from people. Describe all the considerations that management will be faced with when it needs to decide whether to use robots.

5. Some insurance companies will not insure a business unless the firm has a computer disaster recovery plan. Explain why. What types of businesses are most likely to be included?

6. Discuss the role of IS auditors. How is this role related to traditional accounting auditing?

7. Describe how viruses can be used in wars between countries. (Check information about "vote virus" but **DO NOT OPEN** an attachment entitled WTC.exe.)

PROBLEM-SOLVING ACTIVITIES

1. An information security manager routinely monitored the contents of electronic correspondence among employees. She discovered that many employees were using the system for personal purposes. Some messages were love letters, and others related to a football betting pool. The security manager prepared a list of the employees, with samples of their messages, and gave them to management. Some managers punished their employees for having used the corporate e-mail for personal purposes. Some employees, in turn, objected to the monitoring, claiming that they should have the same right to privacy as they have using the company's interoffice mail system.

   a. Is monitoring of e-mail by managers ethical? (It is legal.) Why do you feel so?

   b. Is the use of e-mail by employees for personal communication ethical? Why or why not?

   c. Is the security manager's submission to management of a list of abusers ethical? Why?

   d. Is punishing the abusers ethical? Why or why not?

   e. What should the company do in order to rectify the situation?

2. Ms. I. M. Chancey (a fictitious name) worked as a customer support representative for a small software company in Palo Alto, California, until her employment was terminated. A few months later the company discovered that someone was logging onto its computers at night via a modem and had altered and copied files. During investigation, the police traced the calls to Ms. Chancey's home and found copies of proprietary information valued at several million dollars. It is interesting to note that Ms. Chancey's access code was canceled the day she was terminated. However, the company suspects that Ms. Chancey obtained an access code of another employee.

   a. How was the crime committed? Why were the controls ineffective? (State any relevant assumptions.)

   b. What can this company do to prevent similar incidents in the future?

3. Several years ago a massive computer crash caused the SABRE Passenger Reservation Service System of American Airlines to be idle for 13 hours. It was determined that the program was erroneously changed by another program. The altered information erased critical storage data on an IBM mainframe. Thus, the erroneous program "walked through" SABRE's memory, stripping away the digital labels on each disk volume. This resulted in the inability to address any of SABRE's disk drives.

   a. What kind of problem is described in this incident?

   b. The SABRE reservation system is one of the largest in the world. How is it possible that its controls were ineffective?

   c. How could this problem have been avoided?

4. Each year, 25,000 electronic messages arrive at an organization. Currently there are no firewalls. On the average there are 1.2 successful hackings at this organization each year. Each successful hacking costs $130,000.

   A firewall is proposed at a cost of $66,000. The estimated life is three years. The chance that an intruder will break through the firewall is 0.02 percent. In such a case, the damage will be $150,000 (30 percent) or $200,000 (50 percent), or no damage. There is annual maintenance cost of $20,000 for the firewall.

   a. Should management buy the firewall?

   b. An improved firewall is available. It is 99.9988 percent effective, costs $84,000, has a life of three years, and requires annual maintenance cost of $16,000. Should this one be purchased?

5. If you do not have Windows XP, which has a firewall, you can install a firewall for free. Your mission is to do just that. Use ZoneAlarm (*zonelabs.com*) or Tiny Personal Firewell (*fwnetwork.com*). For Apple users, use Open Door (*opendoor.com*).

INTERNET ACTIVITIES

1. The Internet and intranets are playing an important role in providing opportunities to people with disabilities. Find more about the topic by surfing the Internet. (try *google.com*)

2. Investigate the impact of the WTC disaster on information privacy. Start with *epic.org/privacy*.

3. Access the Web sites of the major antivirus vendors (*symantec.com* and *mcafee.com*). Find out what the vendors' research centers are doing. Also, check newsgroups (e.g., *virus, comp.virus, maous.comp.virus*). Find information on the most recently discovered viruses.

4. Many security software packages are available on the Internet (such as at *shareware.com*). Download a program such as McAfee's Virusscan. Unzip the program and use it to scan your hard drive. Prepare a short report.

5. Enter *privacyalliance.org* and find some of the privacy protection plans. Why do many think that these plans are insufficient?

6. Obtain a copy of PGP ("Pretty Good Privacy" at *pgp.com*) and learn how to encrypt your e-mail. Describe what you did, and submit a printout.

TEAM ACTIVITIES AND ROLE PLAYING

1. Internet communities are spreading very rapidly. Some concentrate on one activity (e.g., transactions, relations), while others are involved in several activities. Review the five types of communities. Each team should be assigned one type of community, and each student a specific community within the group's type.

   a. Identify the major services offered online. Do they conform with the goals of the type of community your team investigates?

   b. Do all communities in each of the five categories look similar to each other?

2. Divide the class into teams of two students. In each pair, one student will be a defender of a Web site and one will be an attacker. The defender creates a Web site on *Geocities.com* that the attacker tries to penetrate.

REAL-WORLD CASE

The World Trade Center Disaster: IT Reflections

The September 11, 2001, terrorist attack on the World Trade Center (WTC) brought to our attention the important role of the following IT topics:

The Role of the Internet, Search Engines, and Chat Rooms.   Immediately after the disaster, the use of the Internet increased by about 10-fold, with some sites (e.g., CNN) facing a volume increase of over 150-fold. The traffic overload made some sites unavailable for hours. The Internet and search engines were used to provide news and information to millions of people around the globe, and they also enabled people to find other people and/or public agencies, emergency services, and other important disaster relief information. In addition, survivors, relatives, and concerned individuals were helped by the Internet to feel somewhat encouraged that they were not suffering alone. People were trying to reach out to each other, to share with others in a community. Many special chat areas were created. Thus, the Internet was a convenient platform for Americans and people from many other nations to vent fears, frustrations, and anger to a virtual community.

Privacy vs. Security.   A dramatic shift in the debate over IT privacy was observed: Before the disaster, there had been a tug of war between protectors of civil liberties on one side and government intelligence gatherers on the other. Following the September 11 tragedies, the issue has become more of an emotional weighing of personal rights versus national security, with a shift in favor of stepping up government surveillance.

Some of the changes that occurred after the disaster are:

- A call was made for a global push for encryption software makers to let government authorities crack their tools. Similarly, ISPs were asked to provide traffic data to police, which previously had been considered an invasion of privacy.

- New antiterrorist legislation was introduced in the United States that would make it easier for the FBI to wiretap phones and e-mails.

- The use of disposable cell phones (preloaded with a finite number of calling minutes) and telephone cards was pointed to as a security risk since calls made with these devices are difficult to track.

- ID smart cards, which are very difficult to forge, are becoming mandatory in some countries. The U.S. Congress is deliberating the issue.

The Benefits of Disaster-Recovery Planning and Action.   The WTC disaster highlighted the need for data storage and backup, for disaster recovery planning, and for operational communication systems. Large companies tend to have sophisticated disaster recovery plans as well as backup sites that enable them to roll the applications over in real time. Smaller firms may rely on backing up data to tape and sending the tapes off site.

Online Crooks Exploit WTC Disaster. Several shameless con artists attempted to profit from the situation. Attempts were made to solicit donations for the survivors of the attacks and relatives of the victims. As an example, a widespread e-mail solicited donations for the Red Cross, but the link led to an imitation of the popular relief organization's Web site. There also were unethical and offensive uses of the Internet for spinning the attacks into marketing events, for example, selling life insurance. Some companies were even selling commemorative products related to the disaster.

Questions

1. Immediately after the attack, the MIT artificial intelligence lab (*ai.mit.com*) brainstormed ideas such as designing buildings that can heal themselves, creating personal black boxes that could help locate disaster survivors, and devising detectors to track suspects through nervous behavior or even smell. Go to the MIT Web site and report on any new specific ideas for security you find reported there.

2. This case demonstrates that the concept of information privacy can be examined from different points of view. What groups/organizations represent the various points of view? In general, where do you find yourself in the debate between privacy and security?

3. Even the most trying times apparently do not curb the impulse of some people to conduct fraud via the Internet. What steps would you recommend to organizations and to individuals to protect themselves from Internet crime?

VIRTUAL COMPANY ASSIGNMENT

wiley.com/college/turban

Extreme Descent Snowboards

www.wiley.com/
college/turban

Background   Kellie Onn, the Chief Executive Officer (CEO), of EDS, greets you with a warm smile and a firm handshake. She ushers you to a chair near her desk. As you look around her office, you notice that Jacob March is also there. Both of you greet each other.

Kellie expresses her concern of the lack of privacy after conducting business on the Internet. She wonders how this impacts the online customers when they enter their personal information on EDS e-commerce site.

As a result of her concern, Kellie says that she has begun reading about posting privacy policies on e-commerce site for the benefit of customers. She knows what a privacy policy is, but is unclear of all the data it should contain.

Kellie turns to Jacob and asks about some legal and ethical issues involving the employee use of email and the Internet. Jacob smiles and replies, "I think we have a new assignment for our intern."

At that moment, Kellie's administrative assistant knocks on the door and states that if Kellie does not leave immediately, she would keep their biggest supplier waiting.

Jacob hands you a tablet so you can take notes as he explains the assignment to you.

Assignment
Kellie wants a privacy policy strategy posted on the e-commerce site that will protect the integrity, privacy, and availability of the data that EDS exchanges electronically. Jacob suggests a good place to start would be a search engine to inquire about privacy policies. First, visit a site such as *TRUSTe* (*truste.com*) to learn more about privacy policies. Then prepare a report that answers the following questions and makes recommendations for a privacy policy at EDS.

1. What should be contained in a privacy policy?

2. Briefly outline a privacy policy for EDS so Kellie can recommend a privacy policy quickly at the next management meeting.

3. List advantages/disadvantages for putting employee reviews on the Internet.

4. What effect might this change in the review process have on the employees?

GLOSSARY

Active badge Clip-on badge that contains a microprocessor that transmits its location to a computer via sensors on the premises.

Ad hoc (demand) reports Management reports that are out of the routine and must be obtained by special request.

Agents Computer programs that conduct routing tasks, search and retrieve information, support decision making, and act as domain experts.

Alliances strategy Response to competitive pressures where a firm works with business partners via EDI, extranets, groupware; creates synergy; allows companies to concentrate on their core businesses; and provides opportunities for growth.

Analog model A model that does not look like the real system but behaves like it.

Analog signal Continuous waves that transmit information by altering the amplitude and frequency characteristics of the waves.

Analysis graphics software Software that provides the ability to convert previously analyzed data into graphic formats (bar charts, pie charts, etc.).

Analytical processing The activity of analyzing accumulated data, such as for projections, comparisons, statistical inferences, and decision analysis, done either online or offline.

Applets Small JAVA applications that can be included in an HTML page on the Internet.

Application controls Safeguards established to protect specific information system applications.

Application program An information system, usually a software program, developed for a specific purpose, such as executing the weekly payroll.

Application service providers Companies that provide applications to organizations on a subscription basis; the packaged application is not sold or licensed to the organization and does not reside on the user organization's system.

Application software The set of computer instructions that direct a computer system to perform specific information processing activities and provide functionality for users.

Application/data independence The storage of data apart from the applications in which the data will be used.

Archie Tool that enables users to regularly monitor external FTP sites, update a database on data files available for downloading, and search another computer system where relevant files are stored.

Arithmetic-logic unit (ALU) Portion of the CPU that performs the arithmetic calculations.

ARPANET A network, begun as an experiment by the U.S. government in packet-switched technology, that linked a largely technical audience of the military, government agencies, and academic researchers and scientists and formed the basis of the Internet.

Array The fundamental element of a multidimensional database that groups data in columns and rows; similar to a table in the relational database model.

Artificial intelligence (AI) The study of thought processes of humans and representation of those processes via machines (computers, robots, and so on).

Artificial neural networks (ANN) The technology that attempts to achieve knowledge representations and processing based on massive parallel processing, fast retrieval of large amounts of information, and the ability to recognize patterns based on experiences.

Assembler   Systems software that translates assembly language into machine language.

Assembly language   A lower-level programming language that is slightly more user-friendly than machine language; represents the second generation of programming languages.

Assured pipeline   A security device that examines an entire request for data to determine whether the request is valid.

Asynchronous transfer mode (ATM)   Data transmission technology that divides data into uniform cells, creates a virtual connection for the packet transmission, and eliminates the need for protocol conversion.

Asynchronous transmission   Data transmission of only one character at a time.

Attribute (in general)   Each characteristic or quality describing a particular entity.

Attribute (in relational database model)   A column of data in a relational database.

Auction   A market mechanism by which sellers place offers and buyers make sequential bids.

Audit   A regular examination or check of information systems, their inputs, outputs, and processing.

Automated teller machine (ATM)   Interactive input/output device that enables people to make bank transactions from remote locations.

Automatic number identification (ANI)   Service in which the number of an incoming call is identified and displayed to the person receiving the call; also known as *caller ID*.

Backbone network   The telecommunications network that connects backbone providers to one another and to access providers, with transmission traditionally on a reciprocal basis.

Backbone provider   A private company that provides long-distance, high-capacity telecommunications network service that links major Internet nodes; also referred to as an Internet service provider (ISP).

Backup   An extra copy of data and/or programs kept in a secured location(s).

Backward error correction (BEC)   Action taken to correct a transmission error by going "back" to the sender and requesting retransmission of the entire data stream or of a particular part, if it can be identified.

Bandwidth   The range of frequencies available in a communications channel, stated in bits per second; the greater the bandwidth, the greater the channel capacity.

Banner   An electronic "billboard" that typically contains a short text or graphical message to advertise a product or a vendor.

Barcode scanner   Optical scanner that reads the barcode label on merchandise.

Baseband transmission   Coaxial cable transmission that is analog and carries one signal at a time.

Batch processing   Transaction processing system that collects transactions as they occur, placing them in groups or batches that are prepared and processed at fixed intervals.

Baud rate   The amount of data that can be transmitted through a channel, measured in bits per second (bps).

Behavioral feasibility   Study that addresses the human issues of a proposed systems development project, including overt or covert resistance to change.

Binary form   Form in which data and instructions can be read by the CPU—only 0s and 1s.

Binary relationship   The conceptual linking of two entities in a database; can be either 1:1, 1:N, or N:N.

Biometric controls   Automated methods of verifying the identity of a person, based on unique physiological or behavioral characteristics, such as finger or retina prints, voice, or keystroke dynamics.

Bit   Short for binary digit (0s and 1s), the only data that CPUs can process.

Bluetooth   A wireless technology that allows digital devices to communicate with each other via low-power radio frequencies.

Breakeven analysis   Economic feasibility method that determines the amount of time required for the cumulative cash flow from a development project to equal its initial and ongoing investment.

Bridge   A communications processor that connects two networks of the same type.

Broadband   Communications channel bandwidth with the highest capacity, used by microwave, cable, and fiber-optic lines.

Broadband transmission   Coaxial cable transmission that is digital and carries multiple signals simultaneously.

Browsers   Software applications through which users access the Web; these applications communicate via HTTP, manage HTML, and display certain data types for graphics and sound.

Build-to-order   A supply chain model where the assembly of the customer's order begins immediately upon receipt of the order.

Bullwhip effect   Erratic shifts in orders along the supply chain.

Bus width   The size of the physical avenues down which data travel as electrical impulses on a computer chip.

Business intelligence   Analysis performed by DSS, EIS, data mining, and intelligent systems, designed to pull together all the data required to make sound business decisions.

Business process   A collection of activities that take one or more kinds of input and create an output for an organization; usually done in a single functional unit (department), but may cross functional units.

Business process reengineering (BPR)   The process of introducing a major innovation in an organization's structure or business processes, resulting in the possible overhaul of the organization's technological, human, or organizational dimensions.

Business-to-business EC (B2B)   Transactions conducted electronically between two businesses.

Business-to-consumer EC (B2C)   Transactions conducted electronically in which companies sell directly to consumers over the Internet.

Business-to-employee EC (B2E)   A special case of intrabusiness EC, with the organization using EC to provide products and services to its employees.

Buy-side marketplace (e-procurement)   A model in which electronic commerce technology is used to streamline the purchasing process in order to reduce the cost of items purchased, the administrative cost of procurement, and the purchasing cycle time.

Buyer's internal marketplace   A model where a company has many suppliers, but the quantities purchased are relatively small.

Byte   An 8-bit string of data, needed to represent any one alphanumeric character or simple mathematical operation.

Cable media   Communications channels that use physical wires or cables to transmit data and information—twisted-pair wire, coaxial cable, and fiber-optic cable.

Cache memory   A type of primary storage, closer to the CPU than is RAM, where the computer can temporarily store blocks of data used more often.

Camera   Input device that captures images (either still or in motion) and converts them into digital files.

Cascading style sheet (CSS)   Enhancement to HTML that adds page layout features to Web documents, by specifying a template for a graphic element that can be placed on the page.

Case-based reasoning (CBR)   The adaptation of solutions that were used to solve old problems to solve new problems, by finding cases in memory that solved problems similar to the current one and adapting the previous solution to fit the current problem, taking into account any differences between the two situations.

Cathode ray tube (CRT)   Technology, used in most monitors, in which beams of electrons illuminate pixels on a computer screen.

Cellular radio technology   Use of radio transmissions between cells in geographic service areas and a mobile telephone switching office, enabling wireless phone service.

Central processing unit (CPU)   The part of the computer that performs the actual computation or "number crunching"; also called microprocessor.

Centralized database   Database with all of the related data files stored in one location.

Channel assembly   A supply chain model where the parts of the product are gathered and assembled as the product moves through the distribution channel.

Channel conflict   When one method (or channel) of reaching customers hinders or impedes another method of reaching customers.

Channel systems   Networks that link the entities in a distribution channel.

Chatting   Real-time, interactive, written conversations of two or more people who are simultaneously connected to the Internet.

Chief information officer (CIO)   The director of a centralized information systems department (ISD); one of the top managers of an organization, analogous to the CEO, COO, and CFO.

Chief knowledge officer (CKO)   Organizational director whose role is to capture and leverage structured knowledge using IT in a knowledge-based organization.

Choice phase   In this phase of the decision-making process, the best solution is selected.

Class   Category that defines all the messages to which an object will respond, as well as the way in which identified objects are implemented; typically arranged in a tree-like structure.

Clickstream data   Data that can be collected automatically from a company's Web site.

Client/server architecture   A form of distributed processing in which several computers share resources and are able to communicate with many other computers; a client is a computer used to access shared network resources, and a server is a machine that is attached to the same network that provides clients with these services.

Clipping service   Service that tracks and retrieves articles on particular topics from electronic databases.

Clock speed   The preset speed of the clock on a computer chip that times all chip activities, measured in megahertz.

Coaxial cable   Insulated copper wire, used to carry high-speed data and television signals.

Code generator   Rapid application development (RAD) tool that *automatically* writes computer programs to implement the reports, input screens, buttons, and dialog boxes into the system design.

Code of ethics   A collection of principles intended as a guide for members of a company or an organization.

Collaborative commerce   A type of electronic commerce where business partners, usually along the supply chain, collaborate electronically.

Collaborate filtering   A personalization service available to Web users that polls their preferences on products, and then delivers customized information to the users based on their preferences.

Common carriers   Long-distance telephone companies.

Communications channels   Pathway or medium that enables data to be communicated from one location to another.

Communications processor   Hardware device that supports data transmission and reception across a telecommunications system.

Communications software   Software that allows computers to exchange data.

Compact disk read-only memory (CD-ROM)   A form of secondary storage that can be read only, not written on; offers high capacity and low cost.

Competitive advantage   An advantage over other business competitors in some measure such as cost, quality, or speed.

Competitive forces model   Analytical framework of M.E. Porter that depicts the five forces in a competitive market (entry of new competitors, bargaining power of suppliers, bargaining power of customers, threat of substitute products or services, rivalry among existing firms).

Competitive intelligence   The activities of an organization in gathering information on its competitors, markets, technologies, and government actions.

Compiler   A software program that translates a high-level language program to object code.

Componentware   A term used to describe component-based software applications.

Computer network   Communications media, devices, and software needed to connect two or more computer systems and/or devices.

Computer programs   Sequences of instructions for the computer.

Computer vision   The ability of a computer to see and interpret scenarios; used extensively in performing industrial quality control.

Computer-aided design (CAD)   The use of software to construct drawings on a computer screen and subsequently store, manipulate, and electronically update them, thus allowing for clearance testing and frequently reducing the cost of product prototyping.

Computer-aided design (CAD) software   Software that allows users to design, "build," and test prototypes in software and then transmit design specifications and instructions directly to machines.

Computer-aided manufacturing (CAM)   The use of software to plan and control a production facility.

Computer-aided software engineering (CASE)   Systems development approach that uses specialized tools, such as code generators and documentation generators, to automate many of the tasks in the SDLC.

Computer-based information system (CBIS)   An information system that uses computer and often telecommunications technology to perform some or all of its intended tasks.

Computer-integrated manufacturing (CIM)   The use of software to simplify, automate, integrate, and coordinate manufacturing technologies, techniques, and processes; integrates several systems such as CAD, CAM, MRP, and JIT.

Conceptual design   An abstract model of the database from the user or business perspective.

Connectivity   The ability of various computer resources to communicate through network devices without human intervention, allowing for portability, interoperability, and scalability.

Consumer-to-business EC (C2B)   Consumers make known a particular need for a product or service, and organizations compete to provide the product or service to consumers.

Consumer-to-consumer EC (C2C)   An individual sells products or services to other individuals electronically.

Continuous improvement   Programs conducted by organizations on a regular basis to improve operations, productivity, quality, and management procedures.

Continuous replenishment   Working closely with suppliers to establish a supply chain so flexible and efficient that inventory is continuously replenished.

Contract software   A specific software program developed for a particular company by a software vendor.

Control unit   Portion of the CPU that controls the flow of information.

Controls   Safeguards established to protect information systems; may be either general or application specific.

Cookie   A small data file placed on users' hard drives when they first visit a site that can exchange information automatically between a server and a browser and can be used to track users' actions and preferences.

Copyright   A statutory grant that provides the creator of intellectual property, including computer code, with ownership of it for the life of the creator plus 50 years.

Core competencies   The areas in which an organization performs best and that represent its competitive advantage.

Cost leadership strategy   Response to competitive forces whereby an organization produces products and/or services at the lowest cost in the industry.

Cracker   A malicious hacker who may represent a serious problem for an organization.

Cross-border data transfer   The flow of corporate data across national borders; laws regulating such transfers are inconsistent from country to country, though efforts at standardization are underway.

Customer-focused approach   A business approach that pays close attention to customers and their preferences.

Customer-oriented strategy   Response to competitive pressures where a firm concentrates on making customers happy.

Customer relationship management (CRM)   An approach that recognizes that customers are the core of the business and that the company's success depends on effectively managing relationships with them.

Customized catalog   Catalog assembled specifically for a particular company, usually a regular customer of the catalog owner.

Cyberbanking   (see Electronic banking)

Cybermall   (see Electronic mall)

Cycle time reduction   A shortening of the time it takes to complete a business process from beginning to end.

Data   Raw facts or elementary descriptions of things, events, activities, and transactions, that are captured, recorded, stored, and classified, but not organized to convey any specific meaning.

Data definition language (DDL)   Description of each data element in a database and the relationships among the records.

Data dictionary   List of definitions of data elements, characteristics that use the data elements, physical representation of the data elements, data ownership, and security.

Data inconsistency   Lack of agreement among various copies of a supposedly same piece of data in an organization's information systems.

Data integrity   Preservation of the accuracy, completeness, and reliability of data for its intended use. System integrity is provided by the integrity of its components and their integration.

Data isolation   Difficulty in accessing data from different applications in an organization's information systems.

Data management   The storage, retrieval, and manipulation of related data.

Data management software   Software that supports the storage, retrieval, and manipulation of related data; may be simple filing programs or more complex database management.

Data manipulation language (DML)   Instructions used with higher-level programming languages to query the contents of a database, store or update information therein, and develop database applications.

Data mart   A scaled-down version of a data warehouse that focuses on a particular subject area, usually a department or a business process.

Data mining   A process of looking for unknown relationships and patterns and extracting useful information from volumes of data, using tools such as neural computing or case-based reasoning.

Data model   Definition of the way data in a DBMS are conceptually structured.

Data quality (DQ)   A measure of accuracy, completeness, timeliness, consistency, accessibility, security, or other characteristics that describe useful data.

Data redundancy   A duplication of the same piece of information in several places in an organization's information systems.

Data tampering   Deliberately entering false, fabricated, or fraudulent data into an information system or changing or deleting existing data

Data visualization   Presentation and visual analysis of data by graphics, animation, or any other multimedia technology.

Data warehouse   A centralized repository of corporate data, needed mainly for internally oriented decision support, extracted from the transaction processing system, corporate suppliers' data, and external databases.

Database   A logical grouping of related files.

Database management system (DBMS)   The software program or group of programs that provide access to a database.

Debugging   The process of testing and correcting errors found in software.

Decision support system (DSS)   A computer-based information system that combines models and data to provide support for decision makers in solving semistructured or interdependent problems with extensive user involvement.

Decryption   Transformation of scrambled code into readable data after transmission.

Dedicated (leased) lines   Telephone lines that are continuously available for transmitting data between two devices, with no switching required.

Democratization of information   The result of using the Internet as a communications forum, in which an individual's communication is judged by the worth of the idea rather than one's social status, and access to information for all users is greatly increased.

Denial of service (DoS)   By hitting a Web site's equipment with too many requests for information, an attacker can effectively clog a system, slowing performance or even crashing a Web site.

Design phase   In this phase of the decision-making process, a model is constructed.

Desktop personal computer   The typical microcomputer system used as a standard tool in business and the home.

Desktop publishing software   Software that allows photographs and graphic images to be combined with text to produce a document ready for printing.

Differentiation strategy   Response to competitive forces whereby an organization finds a way to make itself unique in its industry (such as providing high quality products at a competitive price).

Digital certificates   Electronic identification cards that give access to an intranet.

Digital divide   The gap in computer technology in general, and now in Web technology in particular, between those who have such technology and those who do not.

Digital signal   Discrete pulses, either on or off, that convey information in a binary form that can be clearly interpreted by computers.

Digital signature   Authorizing signature added to electronic messages or electronic checks, usually in encrypted format.

Digital subscriber line (DSL)   A high-speed digital line that transmits data from homes and businesses over existing telephone lines, using modems.

Digital video disk (DVD)   An optical storage device used to store digital video or computer data.

Direct access   Data access in which any piece of data can be retrieved in a nonsequential manner by using the data's address to locate it.

Direct conversion   Implementation process in which the old information system is cut off and the new system is turned on at a certain point in time; the least expensive conversion but the most risky.

Direct file access method   Method that uses the key field to locate the physical address of a record in storage.

Disaster avoidance plan   Plan to prevent or avoid a controllable catastrophe in the corporate information system.

Disaster recovery plan   The plan to protect vital organizational data and to keep the IS and the business running in case a disaster occurs.

Discussion thread   Conversation or discussion on a particular subtopic in electronic newsgroups.

Disintermediation   The elimination of some of a company's employees as well as brokers and agents through use of electronic commerce.

Distance learning   The use of telecommunications technology to connect teachers and students outside the classroom, in either a point-to-point or an asynchronous setup.

Distributed (networked) processing   A type of traditional architecture that divides processing work between two or more computers, either mainframe or PCs, that are linked together in a network of some sort.

Distributed data management   Client/server structure in which all three application components are on the client, with database management distributed between the client and the server.

Distributed database   Database with all or part of the related data files stored in more than one location.

Distributed function   Client/server structure in which data management is on the server and presentation logic is on the client, with application logic distributed between the two.

Distributed presentation   Client/server structure in which all three application components are on the server, but presentation logic is distributed between the client and the server.

Distribution channels   The marketing organizations involved in getting a product or service from the manufacturer to customers, including manufacturers, sales representatives, wholesalers, and retailers.

Document management system (DMS)   System that automates the control of electronic documents through their entire life cycle within an organization, from initial creation to final archiving, by retaining an image of an electronic document, creating an index of keywords, and managing distribution.

Documentation   A written description of the functions of a computer program.

Domain name   The official name assigned to an Internet site, consisting of multiple parts, separated by dots, which are translated from right to left in locating the site.

Domain name system (DNS)   The system administered by Network Solutions Inc. (NSI) to assign names to each site on the Internet; originally administered on a first-come, first-served basis.

Dot pitch   The space between pixels on a computer screen; the finer the dot pitch (the less space between pixels), the finer the resolution on the screen.

Downstream supply chain   The part of the supply chain that includes all the processes involved in distributing and delivering the products to the final customers.

Drill down   The capability of an information system to provide, upon request, specific, additional detail on any given information.

Drill-down reports   Management reports that contain a greater-than-normal level of detail.

Dutch auction   A forward auction for multiple, identical items, but can be used for a single item; prices are set very high and slowly reduced, until a bid for a specific quantity is submitted; first bidder wins.

Dynamic data   Data that continuously change.

Dynamic HTML   A next step beyond HTML, which lets users interact with the content of richly formatted pages without having to download additional content from the server.

Dynamic pricing   Where prices continually change, based on the matching of supply and demand.

E-business   A broad definition of electronic commerce that refers not just to buying and selling, but also to servicing customers, collaborating with business partners, and conducting electronic transactions within an organization.

Economic feasibility   Study that determines if a proposed systems development project is an acceptable financial risk and if the organization can afford the expense and time needed to complete the project.

EFT/POS   A form of electronic funds transfer in which the purchaser is physically at the point of sale (POS); operates using either debit or credit cards.

Electronic banking   Various banking activities, from paying bills to securing loans, conducted over the Internet or private networks. (Also called *cyberbanking*, *virtual banking*, *home banking*, and *online banking*.)

Electronic bartering   The exchange of goods and/or services without a monetary transaction, arranged via online contacts.

Electronic benefits transfer (EBT)   A type of G2C electronic commerce, in which the government transfers Social Security, pension, and other benefits directly to recipients' bank accounts or to smart cards.

Electronic cash (e-cash)   Payment mechanism consisting of a computerized value of funds, stored on a smart card or customer's PC, that can be used as cash and is drawn down as used.

Electronic catalogs   Vendors' catalogs offered either on CD-ROM or on the Internet to advertise and promote products and services; many are now integrated with electronic order taking and payment capabilities. (Also called *online catalogs*.)

Electronic certificate   Verification provided by a trusted third party (a certificate authority) that a specific public key belongs to a specific individual.

Electronic checks (e-checks)   Payment mechanism similar to regular bank checks but transmitted electronically, with a signature in digital form, rather than as paper checks.

Electronic commerce (EC)   The buying and selling of products, services, and information via computer networks, primarily the Internet.

Electronic credit cards   Use of credit card numbers, transmitted electronically over the Internet, to pay for goods and services; can be unencrypted or encrypted, with coded or scrambled data readable by an intermediary between the buyer's and seller's banks.

Electronic data interchange (EDI)   Application that electronically transmits routine, repetitive business documents directly between the computer systems of separate companies doing business with each other.

Electronic exchanges (exchanges, e-hubs, portals)   Electronic marketplaces in which there are many sellers and many buyers.

Electronic funds transfer (EFT)   Application that electronically routes funds, debits and credits, and charges and payments among banks and between banks and customers using telecommunication networks.

Electronic government (e-government)   The use of Internet technology in general and electronic commerce in particular to deliver information and public services to citizens, business partners and suppliers, and those working in the public sector.

Electronic mail (e-mail)   Application that can electronically manipulate, store, and transmit computer-based messages through telephone wires or wireless networks.

Electronic mall   A collection of individual shops offering many products and services under one Internet address. (Also called *cybermall* and *e-mall*.)

Electronic purse   A wallet-sized, enhanced smart card that stores "money" for making small payments in any place where there is a card reader; can combine several credit cards, debit cards, and stored electronic cash; may also have the ability to transfer funds, pay bills, buy from vending machines, or pay for services.

Electronic retailing   Direct selling to consumers through electronic storefronts or malls, usually designed around an electronic catalog format.

Electronic solo storefronts   Electronic businesses that maintain their own Internet name and Web site; may be extensions of physical stores or may be new businesses started by entrepreneurs who saw a niche on the Web.

Electronic surveillance   The tracking of people's activities, online or offline, with the aid of computers.

Electronic wallet (e-wallet)   A software component that is downloaded to a user's PC and in which the user stores credit card numbers and other personal information.

Embedded computer   Computer placed inside another product to add features and capabilities.

Encapsulation   The process of creating an object in OOP.

Encryption   A process of making messages or data indecipherable prior to their transmission to protect them from unwarranted access. Those who have an authorized decryption key, which uses a code composed of a very large collection of letters, symbols, and numbers are able to decipher it.

End-user computing   The direct use or development of information systems by the principal users of the systems' outputs.

End-user development   The direct ad hoc programming and development of information systems by the principal users of a system or their staffs.

English auction   A forward auction where buyers bid on one item at a time; bidding price increases with additional bids; highest bidder wins.

Enhanced integrated drive electronics (EIDE)   An inexpensive interface to a computer's hard drive that offers good performance and supports up to four disks, tapes, or CD-ROM drives.

Enterprise information portal (EIP)   Web-based applications that enable companies to access internally and externally stored information and provide users a single point of access to personalized information needed for decision making.

Enterprise resource planning (ERP)   An integrated process of planning and managing *all* major business processes with a single client/server architecture in *real time*, including contacts with business partners and with customers.

Enterprise software   Programs that manage the vital operations of an organization (enterprise), such as inventory replenishment, human resource management, manufacturing, accounting, and financial management.

Enterprise storage systems An independent, external system with intelligence that includes two or more storage devices; the three major types are redundant arrays of independent disks (RAID), storage area network (SAN), and network-attached storage (NAS).

Enterprise support systems Systems where executive information systems are linked to data warehouses and the corporate intranet.

Enterprisewide computing A client/server architecture that connects data located in different areas within an entire organization, thus integrating departmental and corporate IS resources.

Enterprisewide network The interconnection of multiple LANs and WANs to form a network that completely spans an entire organization.

Entity A person, place, thing, or event on which an organization maintains information.

Entity class A grouping of entities of a given type.

Entity-relationship (ER) diagram Document that shows the entities, attributes, and relationships of a conceptual data model.

Entity-relationship modeling The process of designing a database by organizing data entities to be used and identifying the relationships among them.

Ergonomics The science of adapting machines and work environments to human factors.

Ethernet The most common protocol, used by more than three-fourths of all networks.

Ethics The branch of philosophy that deals with what is considered to be right and wrong.

Exception reports Management reports that alert managers to performance that exceeds certain threshold standards.

Executive information system (EIS) Information system that provides top executives with rapid access to timely information and direct access to management reports, especially exception reports and drill-down reports.

Executive support system (ESS) Comprehensive executive information system that may also include analytical, communication, and intelligent capabilities.

Expandable storage Removable disk cartridges used most often as backup storage for the internal hard drives of personal computers.

Expert systems (ESs) Intelligent computerized advisory programs that imitate the reasoning processes of experts in solving difficult problems.

Explicit knowledge Deals with objective, rational, and technical knowledge, and is usually documented.

Exposure The harm, loss, or damage that can result if something has gone wrong in an information system.

Extensible markup language (XML) A subset of SGML that describes a data format for structured document interchange on the Web; allows user-defined tags and attributes.

External data Data generated outside an organization.

Extranets Secure networks that link business partners and intranets over the Internet by providing access to areas of each other's corporate intranets; "extended intranets."

Extreme integration Integrating internal information systems (e.g., functional information systems and ERP systems) with supply chain management and sales-force automation systems that connect the organization to other business entities.

Facsimile (fax) Application that converts and sends the white and black areas of a page over telephone wires or wireless networks to a receiving machine that converts the coding back into white and black areas and prints the message.

Fault tolerance The ability of a computer system to produce correct results and continue to operate for a limited time even in the presence of certain faults, errors, or failures.

Feasibility study Critically important investigation that determines the probability of success of a proposed systems development project and assesses the project's technical, economic, and behavioral feasibility.

Fiber distributed data interface (FDDI) Data transmission technology that passes data around a ring at high speeds; based on speed and capacity of fiber optics but can use any transmission medium.

Fiber-optic cable Thousands of very thin filaments of glass fibers that conduct light pulses generated by lasers at high-speed frequencies.

Field A logical grouping of characters into a word, a small group of words, or a complete number.

Fifth-generation languages So far, the most advanced type of programming languages, mostly experimental.

File A logical grouping of related records.

File management The operating system's management of the files created and held in, and retrieved from, secondary storage.

File transfer protocol (FTP) Protocol that enables users to access a remote computer and retrieve files from it.

Filtering The narrowing down of options by using an intelligent agent that matches consumers' requirements and constraints with available product choices.

Firewall A security device located between a firm's intranet and external networks (e.g., the Internet); regulates access into and out of a company's network; commonly a barrier between a secure internal network and the Internet, which is assumed to be unsecured.

First-generation language Machine language; the level of programming languages actually understood by a computer.

Flash memory A form of read-only memory on a silicon computer chip that is compact, portable, has limited capacity, and requires little energy.

Flattened organization   An organizational structure midway between the hierarchical and networked organizations, with fewer layers of management and a broader span of control than the hierarchical organization.

Fluorescent multilayer disk (FMD-ROM)   An optical storage device used to store digital video or computer data with much greater storage capacity than DVDs.

Focus strategy   Response to competitive forces whereby an organization selects a narrow-scope segment (*niche market*) and achieves either a cost leadership or a differentiation strategy in this segment.

Forward auctions   Used mainly as a selling channel; a single seller auctions item(s) to many potential buyers.

Forward error correction (FEC)   Action taken to correct a transmission error that uses mathematical algorithms to correct the data stream without having to go back to the sender.

Fourth-generation languages (4GLs)   Another type of high-level programming languages, common in database applications, that do not require users to specify detailed procedures.

Frame relay   Data transmission technology that boosts bandwidth by breaking blocks of text into frames and sends them independently through the network but does not perform error correction.

Front-end processor   Specialized secondary computer that manages all routing communications with peripheral devices.

Functional exchanges   Needed services such as temporary help or space are traded on an "as needed" basis; prices are negotiable.

Fuzzy logic   Reasoning that deals with uncertainties or partial information, allowing the computer to behave less precisely and logically than conventional computers do.

Gateway   A communications processor that can connect dissimilar networks by translating from one set of protocols to another.

General controls   Safeguards established to protect an information system, both hardware and software, regardless of the specific application.

Geographical information database   Data model containing locational data for overlaying on maps or images.

Geographical information system (GIS)   A data visualization technology that captures, stores, checks, integrates, manipulates, and displays data using digitized maps.

Geostationary satellite (GEO)   Satellite placed in a stationary orbit 22,300 miles above the equator; maintains a fixed position above the earth's surface.

Gigabyte   Approximately 1 billion bytes.

Global information systems (GIS)   Interorganizational information systems that connect companies located in two or more countries. Companies connected by such systems may be multinational, international, or virtual.

Global positioning system (GPS)   A wireless system that uses satellites to enable users to determine their position anywhere on the earth.

Global supply chain   A supply chain that involves suppliers and/or customers in other countries.

Goal-seeking analysis   Study that attempts to find the value of the inputs necessary to achieve a desired level of output.

Good enough software   Software that developers release knowing that errors remain in the code but do not keep the software from meeting its functional objectives.

Gophers   Tool that enables users to locate information stored on Internet gopher servers through a series of hierarchical menus; users can move from site to site, narrowing their searches, and locating information anywhere in the world.

Government-to-business EC (G2B)   Governments performing business transactions via electronic commerce technologies.

Government-to-citizens EC (G2C)   The government provides services to its citizens via electronic commerce technologies.

Government-to-government EC (G2G)   Governments doing business with other governments via electronic commerce technologies.

Graphical user development environment   Development environment that offers the ability to create many aspects of an application by drag-and-drop applications.

Graphical user interface (GUI)   Systems software that allows users to have direct control of visible objects such as icons and actions that replace command syntax.

Graphics software   Software that allows users to create, store, display, and print charts, graphs, maps, and drawings.

Group decision support system (GDSS)   An interactive computer-based system that facilitates the solution of semi-structured and unstructured problems by a group of decision makers, either by speeding up the decision-making process or by improving the quality of the resulting decisions, or both.

Group purchasing   The requirements of many buyers are aggregated so that they make up a large volume.

Group support system (GSS)   An information system that supports the working processes of groups (e.g., communication and decision making).

Groupware   A class of software products that facilities communication and collaboration among people within an organization (workgroups), designed for use on all types of computer networks.

Growth strategy   Response to competitive forces where a firm increases market share, acquires more customers, or sells more products by using electronic commerce to strengthen itself and increase its profitability in the long run.

Hacker Person outside an organization who penetrates its computer system.

Hard drive A form of secondary storage that uses permanently mounted stacks of rigid magnetic disks for storage and read-write heads to read the stored data on these disks.

Hardware The physical equipment used for the input, processing, output, and storage activities of a computer system; consists of central processing unit (CPU), memory (primary and secondary storage), input technologies, output technologies, and communication technologies.

Help desk Organization unit that fields inquiries from customers by telephone, e-mail, faxes, and face-to-face interviews.

Hierarchical database model Data model that rigidly structures data into an inverted tree in which records contain two elements (one master field and a variable number of subfields).

Hierarchical organization An organizational structure in the shape of a pyramid, in which the ultimate authority and responsibility reside at the top and authority and responsibility flow down through successions of levels to the bottom of the organization.

Home page A text and graphical screen display that welcomes the user and explains the organization that has established the page; in most cases, will lead users to other pages.

Horizontal distributors Many-to-many electronic marketplaces for indirect materials, when systematic sourcing is used.

Hyperlinks The links that connect data nodes in hypertext.

Hypermedia database model Data model that stores chunks of information in nodes that can contain data in a variety of media; users can branch to related data in any organizational scheme.

Hypertext An approach to data management in which data are stored in a network of nodes connected by links and are accessed through interactive browsing.

Hypertext document The combination of nodes, links, and supporting indexes for any particular topic.

Hypertext Markup Language (HTML) The standard programming language used to create and recognize documents on the World Wide Web; lets users control visual elements without changing the original information; incorporates dynamic hypertext links to other documents stored on the same or different computers.

Hypertext Transport Protocol (HTTP) The communications standard used to transfer pages across the Web; defines how messages are formatted and transmitted.

Iconic model The least abstract model which is a physical replica of a system, usually based on a different scale from the original.

Idea-generation software Software designed to stimulate a single user or group to produce new ideas, options, and choices.

Identifier Attributes that identify entity instances.

Impact printer Output device that uses striking action to make impressions on paper.

Implementation The process of converting from an old information system to a new system.

Index Device that lists the key field of each record and where that record is located in storage.

Indexed sequential access method (ISAM) Arrangement of key fields that uses an index to locate individual records in sequential access.

Inference engine A component of an expert system that performs a reasoning function that results in advice to the user.

Information A collection of facts (data) organized in some way so that they are meaningful to a recipient.

Information architecture A high-level map of an organization's information requirements and the manner in which these requirements are being satisfied.

Information centers Facilities that train and support business users with end-user tools and technical support.

Information filter An automated method of sorting relevant from irrelevant information; the most publicized are those that screen out adult content from Web browsers.

Information gatekeepers The employees with responsibility for information that is important to the organization or one of its units.

Information infrastructure The physical facilities, services, and management that support all computing resources in an organization; consists of computer hardware, general-purpose software, communication facilities, databases, and information management personnel.

Information requirements Specific details on what items of information are needed by information system users, how much information, for whom, when, and in what format.

Information system (IS) A system that collects, processes, stores, and analyzes data, and disseminates information for a specific purpose.

Information system controls The procedures, devices, or software that attempt to ensure that the system performs as planned.

Information technology (IT) A particular component of a computer-based information system.

Infrared Red light not commonly visible to human eyes, modulated or pulsed for conveying information.

Inheritance A feature of OOP that replicates the properties of an object in succeeding subclasses of the object.

Inkjet printer Nonimpact printer that shoots fine streams of ink onto paper.

Innovation strategy Response to competitive pressures where a company develops new products or services, new features in existing products and services, and new ways to produce or sell them.

Instance   A particular entity within an entity class.

Instant messaging   Online, real-time communication between two or more people who are connected to the Internet.

Integrated computer-aided software engineering (ICASE)   Computer-aided software engineering (CASE) with automated links between the early stages of systems development (investigation, analysis, and design) and later stages (programming, testing, operation, and maintenance).

Integrated package   Spreadsheet software that contains both data management and graphical capabilities.

Integrated services digital network (ISDN)   High-speed transmission technology that allows users to simultaneously transfer voice, video, image, and other data at high speed.

Intellectual property   The intangible property created by individuals or corporations, which is protected under copyright, trade secret, and patent laws.

Intelligence phase   In this phase of the decision-making process, reality is examined and the problem is defined.

Intelligent agent   Uses expert, or knowledge-based, capabilities to do more than just "search and match."

Intelligent computer-assisted instruction (ICAI)   Systems that can tutor humans by using a knowledge component to shape their teaching techniques to fit the learning patterns of individual students.

Intelligent system   An information system typically employing artificial intelligence, whose output resembles that produced by human thought processes and is used to support decision making; examples are expert systems, natural language processing, speech understanding, robotics and sensory systems, fuzzy logic, neural computing, and case-based reasoning.

Integrated make-to-stock   Supply chain model focusing on tracking customer demand in real time, so that the production process can restock the finished-goods inventory efficiently.

Interactive marketing   A customized relationship between vendors and customers in which vendors present customized, one-on-one advertising, gather a customer's responses, and serve that customer based on his or her previous, unique responses.

Internal data   Data generated by the corporate transaction processing systems, functional user information systems, and other functions and individuals inside an organization.

Internal efficiency strategy   Response to competitive pressures, where a company improves the manner in which its business processes are executed.

Internal supply chain   The part of the supply chain that includes all the processes used by an organization in transforming the inputs shipped by the suppliers to outputs.

International Standards Organization Open Systems Interconnection protocol (ISO-OSI)   A file transfer protocol established by the International Standards Organization that defines how software on different systems interacts at seven different layers.

Internet   A massive electronic and telecommunications network connecting the computers of businesses, consumers, government agencies, schools, and other organizations worldwide, which exchanges information seamlessly using open, nonproprietary standards and protocols.

Internet communities   Online communities of people with shared interests.

Internet fax   Facsimile transmission of documents from a desktop computer on the sender's end to a standard fax machine on the receiver's end, through a fax server in an ISP's network.

Internet relay chat (IRC)   General chat program for the Internet, which divides chat groups into channels, each assigned its own topic of conversation.

Internet service provider (ISP)   Company whose primary business is to provide its customers with connections to the Internet.

Internet telephony   A service that lets users talk across the Internet to any personal computer equipped to receive the call—even around the world—for the price of only the Internet connection.

Internet (intranet) transaction processing   A broader form of online transaction processing conducted over the Internet or intranets.

Internet-based EDI   Electronic Data Interchange systems that use the TCP/IP protocol to run on the Internet (or intranets, extranets).

Internet2   A new communications network with access limited exclusively for research purposes and capable of transmitting gigabits (billions of bits) of information per second.

Interorganizational information systems (IOSs)   Electronic systems that involve information flow among two or more organizations in an ongoing relationship.

Interpreter   A compiler that translates and executes one source program statement at a time.

Intrabusiness (intraorganizational) EC   Electronic business transactions that take place *within* an organization, in an attempt to increase productivity, speed, and quality, and to cut costs.

Intranet   A private network that uses Internet software and TCP/IP protocols; in essence, a private Internet, or group of private segments of the public Internet network.

IP address   An assigned address for each computer on the Internet that distinguishes it from other computers; consists of four sets of numbers, separated by dots.

IS operational plan   A specified set of projects that will be executed by the IS department and by functional area managers in support of the IS strategic plan, including both long-term systems needs and short-range project plans.

IS strategic plan   A set of long-range goals that describe the IT architecture and major IS initiatives needed to achieve the goals of the organization.

IT architecture   Plan of the way an organization's information resources should be used to accomplish its mission, including both technical and managerial aspects of information resources.

Java   Object-oriented programming language, developed by Sun Microsystems, specifically designed to work over networks, with numerous security features to prevent downloaded programs from damaging files or creating other problems on the receiving computer; handles text, data, graphics, sound, and video and gives programmers the ability to develop applications that work across the Internet.

Java operating system (JavaOS)   Operating system designed to execute programs written in Java on hand-held products, network computers, and the Internet, without the need for a traditional operating system.

Join operation   Basic operation in a relational database that combines relational tables.

Joint application design (JAD)   A group-based method for collecting user requirements and creating system designs in which all users meet simultaneously with analysts to jointly define and agree upon systems requirements.

Joy stick   Input device that positions cursor on a screen, used primarily for dynamic graphics at workstations and for video games.

Just-in-time (JIT)   Inventory approach scheduling system that attempts to minimize in-process inventory, reduce inventory space and costs, and improve work flow by scheduling materials and parts to arrive at a workstation exactly when they are needed, minimizing inventory and idle production facilities.

Key-indicator reports   Management reports that summarize the performance of activities critical for the organization.

Keyboard   Most common input device, designed like a typewriter but with added function keys.

Keyword banners   Electronic advertisements that appear when a predetermined word is queried from the search engine; used to target customers with particular interests.

Kilobyte   Approximately 1,000 bytes (2^{10} bytes).

Knowledge   Information that has been organized and processed to convey understanding, experiences, accumulated learning, and expertise as it applies to a particular problem or process.

Knowledge base   A repository of accumulated knowledge, which can be used to support end users or to support complex decision making.

Knowledge database   Data model that stores decision rules that can be used for expert decision making.

Knowledge discovery   A process of looking for unknown relationships and patterns and extracting useful information from volumes of data.

Knowledge discovery in databases (KDD)   A process of looking for unknown relationships and patterns and extracting useful information from volumes of data.

Knowledge management (KM)   The process of accumulating and creating knowledge efficiently, managing a knowledge base, and facilitating the sharing of knowledge so that it can be applied effectively throughout an organization.

Knowledge workers   People who are responsible for finding or developing new knowledge and using it as a significant part of their work responsibility.

Knowledge-based organizations   Organizations designed as networks that capture, store, and utilize knowledge as a major activity, with the help of IT.

Language translator   Systems software that translates a high-level programming language into source code and language code.

Laptop computer   Transportable, lightweight microcomputer.

Laser printer   Nonimpact printer that uses laser beams to write information on photosensitive drums, over which paper and toner pass, making images on paper.

Learning agents   Software agents that exhibit some intelligent behavior.

Legacy system   An older information system, usually a mainframe system housed in a secured data center, operated by IS professional staff, and performing mainly repetitive transaction processing.

Line width   The distance between transistors on a computer chip.

Linux   A powerful version of UNIX that is completely free of charge and offers multitasking, virtual memory management, and TCP/IP networking.

LISTSERV   A public forum that allows discussions to be conducted through predefined groups; uses e-mail servers (rather than bulletin boards) for communications.

Local area network (LAN)   Network that connects communications devices within 2,000 feet so that every user device on the network can communicate with any other.

Location-based commerce (l-commerce)   Delivers information about goods and services based on where you (and your mobile device) are located.

Logic error   Programming error that permits the program to run but results in incorrect output; more difficult to detect than syntax errors.

Logical systems design   Abstract specification of what an information system will do, including the design of outputs, inputs, processing, databases, telecommunications, controls, security, and IS jobs.

Logical view   The user's view of a database management system, showing data in a meaningful format to the user and the software programs that process that data.

Low earth orbit satellite (LEO)   Satellite placed in orbit 400 to 1,000 miles above earth's surface.

Machine instruction cycle   The cycle of computer processing, whose speed is measured in terms of the number of instructions a computer chip processes per second.

Machine language   The lowest-level programming language, using binary digits, which is the only language the CPU understands; represents the first generation of programming languages.

Machine learning   A set of methods that attempt to teach computers to solve problems or to support problem solving by analyzing (learning from) historical cases.

Macintosh operating system   The operating system, featuring multitasking and graphics capabilities, available on Macintosh machines.

Macros   Sequences of commands used in spreadsheets that can be executed with one simple instruction.

Magnetic disk   A form of secondary storage on a magnetized disk divided into tracks and sectors that provide addresses for various pieces of data.

Magnetic diskette   A form of easily portable secondary storage on flexible Mylar disks; also called floppy disks.

Magnetic ink character reader   Optical scanner that reads magnetic ink printed on bank checks.

Magnetic tape   A form of secondary storage on large open reels or smaller cartridge or cassette.

Mainframe   Relatively large computer, used by corporations for centralized data processing and maintenance of large databases.

Maintenance   The final, and ongoing, stage of the system development life cycle, consisting of debugging a program, updating the system to accommodate changes in business conditions, and adding new functionality to the system.

Make-or-buy decision   The choice between developing proprietary software in-house and purchasing existing software from a software vendor.

Management by exception   Management system based on monitoring actual performance against preestablished standards and identifying the exceptions, which are then investigated and managed.

Management information system (MIS)   A system that accesses, organizes, and reports on organizational information needed for repetitive decision making in functional areas, usually by middle managers.

Manufacturing resource planning (MRP II)   A planning process that integrates a regular MRP system with other functional areas, especially finance and human resources.

Mass customization   Production of a large quantity of items that are custom manufactured to fit the specifications of individual customers.

Materials requirements planning (MRP)   A planning process that integrates production, purchasing, and inventory management of interrelated products.

Mathematical (quantitative) model   An abstract model used for modeling complex relationships and conducting experiments with these relationships using mathematics.

Medium earth orbit satellite (MEO)   Satellite placed in orbit about 6,000 miles above earth's surface.

Megabyte   Approximately 1 million bytes.

Memory button   Nickel-sized device, analogous to a barcode, that stores a small database.

Memory cards   Credit-card-sized devices used as storage devices in personal computers.

Mental model   A model that provides a description of how a person thinks about a situation.

Message   Instruction from another object that activates operations contained within the object receiving the message.

Metabrowser   Browser that allows surfers to select whatever content they want from anywhere on the Web and gather it all on one site.

Metadata   Data about data.

Metasearch engine   A search engine that automatically enters search queries into a number of other search engines and returns the results.

Method   An operation, action, or a behavior an object may undergo.

Microcomputer (personal computer, PC)   The smallest and least expensive category of general-purpose computers.

Microcontrollers   Computer chips embedded in products and technologies of various types and sizes (e.g., cell phones, toys, autos).

Micropayments   Payments of small dollar-amounts for goods and services.

Microphone   Input device for voice-recognition software.

Microprocessor   The CPU, made up of millions of microscopic transistors embedded in a circuit on a silicon wafer or "chip"; commonly referred to as chips.

Microwave   Wireless communications channel that uses microwave towers for high-volume, long-distance communication; must maintain line of sight from tower to tower.

Middleware   Software designed to link application modules developed in different computer languages and running on heterogeneous platforms whether on a single computer or over a network.

Minicomputer (midrange computer)   Relatively small, inexpensive, and compact computer that performs the same functions as a mainframe but to a limited extent.

Mobile agent   An agent that can move from one Internet site to another and can send data to or retrieve data from the user, who can focus on other work in the meantime.

Mobile commerce (m-commerce)   When electronic commerce is done in a wireless environment, such as using cell phones to access the Internet.

Mobile computing   Transmission of data to and from mobile computers on radio-based networks.

Mobile devices   Portable, lightweight devices for computing and communications, such as personal digital assistants.

Mobile Internet (wireless Web)   The use of wireless communications technologies to access network-based information and applications from mobile devices.

Model   A simplified representation or abstraction of reality which can be manipulated and the effects of such testing analyzed.

Modem   Device that converts signals from analog to digital and vice versa; contraction of the terms *modulate* and *demodulate*.

Monitor   The video screen used with most computers, which displays both input and output.

Moore's Law   The expectation that microprocessor complexity doubles approximately every two years.

Mouse   Hand-held device used to point a cursor at a desired place on a computer screen; a click instructs the computer to take some action.

MS-DOS   One of the original, text-based operating systems for the IBM PC and its clones.

Multidimensional database   Data model that consists of at least three views (dimensions) of the business data; often the core of data warehouses.

Multifunction output devices   Devices that combine a variety of output technologies, such as printer, fax, copier, and answering machine.

Multimedia database   Data model that can store data on many media.

Multimedia software   Software that combines spatially-based media (text and images) with time-based media (sound and video) for input or output of data.

Multimedia technology   The computer-based integration of text, sound, still images, animation, and digitized motion video.

Multiplexer   Device that allows a single communications channel to carry data transmissions simultaneously from many sources.

Multiprocessing   Simultaneous processing of more than one program by assigning it to run on different processors (CPUs).

Multitasking (Multiprogramming)   The operation of two or more programs running on a single processor (CPU) at the same time.

Multithreading   A form of multitasking that runs multiple tasks within a single application simultaneously.

Narrowband   Communications channel bandwidth with slow, low-capacity transmissions.

Natural language processing (NLP)   A knowledge-based user interface that gives computer users the ability to communicate with the computer in human languages.

Natural programming languages   Complex programming languages that are nonprocedural and that come closest to natural language instructions.

Net present value (NPV)   Economic feasibility method that calculates the net amount by which project savings or inflows exceed project expenses, after allowing for the cost of capital and the time value of money.

Network   A connecting system that permits the sharing of resources among different computers.

Network attached storage (NAS)   A special-purpose server that provides file storage to users who access the device over a network.

Network computer (thin client)   Computer without the full functionality of typical desktop PCs but that allows access to an organizational network.

Network database model   Data model that creates relationships among data through a linked-list structure in which subordinated records can be linked to more than one data record.

Network management software   Network software that reduces times spent on routine tasks and provides faster response to network problems, greater control, and remote diagnosing of problems.

Network operating system (NOS)   Systems software that controls the hardware, software, and communications media and channels across a network.

Networked organization   Organizational structure that resembles a computer network, characterized by looser organizational structure, empowerment of employees, situational leadership, shared information, and team contributions.

Neural computing   The technology that attempts to achieve knowledge representations and processing based on massive parallel processing, fast retrieval of large amounts of information, and the ability to recognize patterns based on experiences.

Newsgroup   Discussion group on the Internet in which an international audience is able to post on an electronic bulletin board ideas on a particular topic; some 30,000 newsgroups exist, on various topics; also called a forum.

Next-generation Internet   A group of very-high-bandwidth networks on the Internet that provide leading-edge network capability for research laboratories and universities.

Nonimpact printer   Output device that uses laser beams or streams of ink, rather than striking action, to make images on paper.

Nonprocedural languages   User-oriented programming languages that allow users to specify a desired result without having to specify the detailed procedures needed to achieve those results.

Nonvolatile   A characteristic of a storage medium that stored data will not be lost if there is no electricity flowing through the medium.

Normalization   A method for analyzing and reducing a relational database to its most streamlined form by eliminating redundant data elements; normalized data depend only on the primary key.

Notebook computer   Transportable, lightweight microcomputer that fits easily into a briefcase.

Object   In the object-oriented model, a combination of a small amount of data and instructions about what to do with that data when the object is selected or activated.

Object program   The set of programming instructions after source code has been translated into machine language.

Object-oriented database model   Data model based on the central idea of a small amount of data encapsulated with all the data needed in order to perform an operation with that data.

Object-oriented development   Fundamentally different development approach that uses interchangeable software components (objects) that model aspects of real-world things or concepts involved in performing a particular task.

Object-oriented programming (OOP) language   Programming language that encapsulates a small amount of data along with instructions about how to manipulate that data; inheritance and reusability features provide functional benefits.

Object-relational database model   Data model that adds object storage capabilities to relational databases.

Off-the-shelf application software   Software purchased, leased, or rented from a vendor that develops programs and sells them to many organizations.

Office automation system (OAS)   A support system that improves office efficiency through such functions as communications, word processing, and document management.

Offline browser   Browser that enables a user to retrieve pages automatically from Web sites at predetermined times, often during the night; a pull product.

One-to-one marketing   A new interactive style of marketing that uses marketing research gathered online to make one-to-one personal contact with customers, and that provides marketing organizations better understanding of consumers, the market, and the competition.

Online analytical processing (OLAP)   The activity of analyzing complex accumulated data, looking for patterns, trends, and exceptions, done online.

Online processing   Transaction processing system that processes data *as soon as* a transaction occurs.

Online service (OLS)   Company that offers Internet connection along with various services such as financial market information; may be targeted toward home computer users or toward businesses, depending on what services are offered.

Online transaction processing (OLTP)   Transaction processing system, operated on a client/server architecture, that allows an organization's suppliers to enter the TPS via an extranet and look at the firm's inventory level or production schedule.

Open source software   Software made available in source code form at no cost to developers.

Open systems   A model of computer products—hardware, operating system, and application software—that allow any computing device to be seamlessly connected to and interact with any other computing device.

Operating environment   A set of computer programs that add features enabling system developers to create applications without directly accessing the operating system; operating environments work only with an operating system.

Operating system   The main system control program, which supervises the overall operations of the computer, allocates memory to programs, and provides an interface between the user and the hardware. Categorized by number of users they support: desktop, departmental, and enterprise.

Optical character recognition (OCR)   Software used in conjuction with scanning technology that recognizes text and converts it into a digital form that can be manipulated by word processing applications.

Optical jukebox   A form of secondary storage that stores and reads many optical storage disks.

Optical mark reader   Optical scanner that reads pencil marks made on a predetermined grid.

Optical mouse   A mouse where a light, lens, and camera chip replace the ball, rollers, and wheels of the standard mechanical mouse; the optical mouse takes pictures of the surface it passes over and compares successive images to determine where it is going.

Optical networking   The use of fiber-optic filaments and related technology that transmits information as light rather than as electrical signals.

Optical storage device   A form of secondary storage on which data are recorded by tiny holes burned on the surface of a reflective platter and are read by another laser in computer's disk drive.

Order fulfillment   Providing customers what they ordered and doing so on time, as well as providing all related customer service.

Organic light-emitting diodes (OLEDs)   Provide computer displays that are brighter, thinner, lighter, and faster than liquid crystal displays (LCDs).

Organizational knowledge base   A repository of accumulated and purchased corporate knowledge, which can be used to support end users or to support complex decision making.

Organizational learning   The process of an organization applying and using a knowledge base to learn from its experiences and to gain competitive advantage in avoiding past mistakes.

Outsourcing   In a broad sense, the purchase of any product or service from another company. In a narrower sense, the purchase of computer services and software from computer vendors.

Outtasking   A new variant of outsourcing in which the responsibility for the performance of a particular function or the delivery of a particular service is assigned to an outside organization; done on a smaller scale than outsourcing, using multiple firms to perform specific tasks.

Package   Common term for a prepackaged computer program developed by a vendor and available for purchase.

Packet-switching   Data transmission technology that boosts bandwidth by breaking blocks of text into small, fixed bundles of data (packets) and sends each packet independently through the network.

Pages   Application programs or modules of fixed length, for use in virtual memory.

Palmtop computer   Hand-held microcomputer that is small enough to carry in one hand.

Parallel conversion   Implementation process in which the old system and the new system operate simultaneously for a period of time, during which both systems process the same data and the outputs are compared; costly but safe.

Parity bits   Accuracy controls that are added to characters at the sending end of an electrical line and verified at the receiving end of the line to determine whether bits were lost during transmission.

Partitioned database   Database whose data files are subdivided and distributed among various locations.

Patent   The grant of exclusive rights on an invention for 20 years.

Pattern recognition   The ability of a computer to classify an item by matching the item's characteristics with those of a stored category.

Peer-to-peer processing   A type of client/server, distributed processing that allows two or more computers to pool their resources, making each computer both a client and a server.

Pen mouse   A variant of the standard mouse, the pen mouse resembles an automobile stick shift in a gear box; moving the pen and pushing buttons on it move the cursor on the screen.

Permission marketing   Offers consumers incentives to accept advertising and e-mail voluntarily by asking people what they are interested in and asking them permission to send them marketing information.

Person-to-person (P2P) payment   Enables the transfer of funds between two individuals for a variety of purposes.

Personal application software   General-purpose, off-the-shelf application programs that are not linked to any specific business function but that support general types of processing.

Personal communication services (PCS)   Wireless communications using lower-power, higher-frequency radio waves than those used in cellular technology.

Personal digital assistant (PDA)   Hand-held palmtop computer that uses a pen rather than a keyboard.

Personalization   Customizing products, services, advertisements, and customer service at a reasonable cost.

Personalized Web services   Services that offer the ability to generate Web content that is personalized for individual Web site visitors.

Phantom stockouts   A problem with the supply chain that occurs when customers are told that a product they want is not available, though in fact the product is available.

Phased conversion   Implementation process that introduces components of the new system, such as individual modules, in stages, until the entire new system is operational.

Physical design   Layout that shows how the database is actually arranged on storage devices.

Physical systems design   Actual physical specifications for an information system, including the design of hardware, software, database, telecommunications, and procedures.

Physical view   The plan for the actual physical arrangement and location of data in a database management system.

Pilot conversion   Implementation process that introduces the new system in one part of the organization on a trial basis and after the new system works properly, introduces it in other parts of the organization.

Pixels   Tiny points on a computer screen that are illuminated by electrons.

Plotter   Output devices that use computer-directed pens to create complex, high-quality images.

Plug-and-play   A feature that enables the operating system to recognize new hardware and install the necessary software automatically.

Point-of-sale (POS) terminal   Computerized cash registers that allow the input of numerous data about the sales transaction.

Presentation graphics software   Graphics software with tools that enable users to assemble multiple text and graphic images into a complete presentation.

Primary key   The field that uniquely and completely identifies a record.

Primary storage   The main memory of a computer, in which small amounts of data that will be used immediately are stored.

Printer   Output device that transforms digital computer content into a printed, paper-based form.

Privacy policies   Codes that state an organization's guidelines with respect to protecting the privacy of customers, clients, and employees.

Private branch exchange (PBX)   A special-purpose computer that controls telephone switching at a company site; a type of LAN.

Private key One of two codes used in a public/private key encryption system; the private key is known only to its owner, but not to those who have the public key.

Procedural languages User-oriented programming languages that require programmers to specify step by step how the computer must accomplish a task; represent the third generation of programming languages.

Procedures The strategies, policies, methods, and rules for using an information system.

Process management Managing the program or programs running on a computer at a given time; a function of an operating system.

Procurement Purchasing and arranging inbound movement of materials, parts, and/or finished inventory from suppliers to manufacturing or assembly plants, warehouses, or retail stores.

Programmers Information systems professionals who modify existing computer programs or write new computer programs to satisfy user requirements.

Programming The translation of the design specifications into computer code; typically a time-consuming and costly process.

Programming fraud Use of programming techniques by computer criminals to modify a computer program, either directly or indirectly; viruses are an example.

Project operation Basic operation in a relational database that creates a subset consisting of columns in a table, to create new tables that contain only the information required.

Propagation delay Pause of a quarter of a second between sending and receiving transmissions from GEO satellites.

Proprietary application software Software that addresses a specific or unique business need for a company; may be developed in house or purchased from a software vendor.

Protocol The set of rules and procedures that govern transmission across a network, principally line access and collision avoidance.

Prototype Small-scale working model of a new, larger computer system.

Prototyping Alternative development approach in which systems developers first obtain only a general idea of user requirements, develop a prototype that is quickly put into use, and then refine the prototype based on users' suggestions and experiences with it.

Public key security The protection of intranets from outside intrusion and integration of them with the public network.

Public key One of two codes used in a public/private key encryption system; the public key is distributed to several authorized people for use in encrypting or decrypting messages.

Public key infrastructure (PKI) A security system based on use of two keys, and also including a digital signature and a certificate.

Public/private key encryption Security encryption system that uses two different keys, one public and the other private, one used for encryption and the other for decryption.

Push technology Applications that automatically supply (push) information from the Web to a user's desktop by a process running on either the user's desktop or a network server.

Quality of life The measure of how well we achieve a desirable standard of living.

Radio Wireless communications medium that sends electromagnetic data directly between transmitters and receivers over short distances via radio wave frequencies.

Random access memory (RAM) The part of primary storage that holds a software program (or a portion of it) and small amounts of data when they are brought from secondary storage.

Random banners Electronic advertisements that appear randomly; used to introduce new products to the widest possible audience, or to keep a brand in the public consciousness.

Rapid application development (RAD) A systems development method that uses special tools and an iterative approach in which requirements, design, and the system itself are developed with sequential refinements to rapidly produce a high-quality system.

Raw data Data that have not been processed.

Read-only memory (ROM) A type of primary storage where certain critical instructions are safeguarded because the storage is nonvolatile and the instructions can be read only by the computer and not changed by the user.

Real-time audio Audio transmission that travels so quickly over the Internet that its reception is delayed only so slightly as to be virtually "live."

Real-time video Video transmission that travels so quickly over the Internet that its reception is delayed only so slightly as to be virtually "live."

Record A logical grouping of related fields.

Redundant arrays of independent disks (RAID) A form of secondary storage that uses a large number of small hard drives to distribute data across all of the disk drives.

Registers Parts of the CPU that store very small amounts of data and instructions for short periods of time.

Relation The table of rows and columns used in a relational database.

Relational database model Data model based on the concept of tables, in which data are implicitly linked by the design of data into rows and columns, rather than physically linked together in storage.

Relationship The conceptual linking of entities in a database.

Remote data management   Client/server structure in data management is on the server and presentation and application logic are on the client.

Remote presentation   Client/server structure in which all three application components are on the server, but presentation logic is distributed between the client and the server.

Replicated database   Database with complete copies of the entire data files stored in many locations.

Repository   A computer-aided software engineering (CASE) tool that enables the integrated storage of specifications, diagrams, reports, data names, and data definitions.

Retinal scanning display   A technology that projects an image, pixel by pixel, directly onto a viewer's retina; used with mobile devices to improve the quality of the interface.

Return on investment (ROI)   An economic feasibility method calculated as the ratio of the net cash inflows from a project divided by the cash outflows of the project.

Reusability   A feature of OOP that allows objects created for one purpose to be used in a different OOP application.

Reusable components   In rapid application development (RAD), a library of common, standard "objects" such as buttons and dialog boxes that the developer drags and drops into the application.

Reverse auction   One buyer who wants to buy a product or a service; suppliers are invited to submit bids; lowest bid wins; several rounds can take place if the lowest bid is not satisfactory to the seller.

Reverse logistics   In a supply chain, when the flow of information and goods is reversed, as in the return of products.

Risk   The likelihood that a threat will materialize.

Robotics   The science of using electromechanical devices that can be programmed and reprogrammed to automate manual tasks.

Router   A communications processor that routes messages through several connected LANs or to a wide area network.

Runaway project   A systems development project that is so far over budget and past deadline that it must be abandoned, typically with large financial loss.

Sales automation software   Software used to automate the work of salespeople.

Sales force automation   Providing salespeople in the field with portable computers, access to databases, and so on to automate some of their tasks.

Satellite   Wireless communications channel that sends digital radio transmissions from point to point by means of communications satellites.

Schema   The logical description of an entire database and listing of all data items and the relationships among them.

Scope creep   Requests by users for added functionality in an information system after approval of the system design.

Search engine   Program that finds and lists Web sites or pages (designated by URLs) that match some user-selected criteria.

Second-generation languages   Lower-level programming languages that are still hardware-dependent but that are a step removed from machine language; they require that each statement be translated into machine language through use of an assembler.

Secondary key   A field that has some identifying information but does not identify a record with complete accuracy.

Secondary storage   Memory capacity that can store very large amounts of data for extended periods of time on a variety of media.

Secure Electronic Transaction (SET) protocol   More comprehensive protocol for credit card processing that incorporates digital signatures, certification, encryption, and an agreed-upon payment gateway to banks.

Secure Socket Layer (SSL)   Common protocol used in electronic commerce to encrypt messages.

Security   The operating system's control of access to files held in secondary storage.

Segmentation   Dividing markets into specific groups.

Select operation   Basic operation in a relational database that creates a subset consisting of all file records that meet stated criteria.

Self-directed teams   Organizational teams that make their own decisions and have authority and responsibility to execute specific tasks; may be permanent or temporary (problem-specific).

Sell-side marketplace   Organizations attempt to sell their products or services to other organizations electronically.

Sensitivity analysis   The study of the impact that changes in one or more parts of a model have on other parts of the model, usually the impact that changes in input variables have on output variables.

Sensor   Input device embedded in various technologies that collects data directly from the environment and inputs them into a computer system.

Sequential access   Data access in which the computer system must run through pieces of data in sequence in order to locate a particular piece.

Server farms   Large groups of servers maintained by an organization or by a commercial vendor and made available to customers.

Servers   Smaller types of midrange computers that support computer networks, enabling users to share files, software, peripheral devices, and other network resources.

Show-stopper error (or bug)   Programming errors that will cause a system to shut down or will cause catastrophic loss of data.

Single-key encryption   The sender of the electronic message encrypts the information with a key; receiver uses an identical key to decrypt the information.

Small computer systems interface (SCSI)   A relatively expensive interface to a computer that is fast and used for graphics workstations, server-based storage, and large databases.

Small-footprint database   Subsets of a database (i.e., certain types of data) provided for workers in the field using laptops and/or information appliances.

Smart cards   Plastic cards, like credit cards, that contain a microprocessor capable of storing and processing a considerable amount of information; can be used for electronic payments, storing a computerized value of funds that is drawn down as used.

Social interface   A user interface that guides the user through computer applications by using cartoon-like characters, graphics, animation, and voice commands.

Social responsibility   The willingness of corporations to take active measures to respond to social issues and to contribute toward social improvements.

Software   A set of computer programs that enables the hardware to process data.

Software agents   Software programs that conduct mundane tasks such as routing and search and retrieval of information, acting autonomously without human intervention.

Software components   The building blocks of applications that can be used many times in the same application or in different applications.

Software crisis   The inability of organizations to develop software applications fast enough to keep up with changing business conditions and evolving technologies.

Software suites   Collections of applications software packages that integrate the functions of those packages.

Source data automation   The use of various technologies to input data with minimal human intervention.

Source program   The set of programming instructions written in a user-oriented language (source code); must be "translated" into machine language in order for the computer to understand.

Spamming   Indiscriminate distribution of e-mail messages (junk e-mail).

Speech (voice) recognition   A process that allows users to communicate with a computer by speaking to it and having the computer recognize spoken words without necessarily interpreting their meanings.

Speech recognition software   Software that can recognize and interpret human speech, either one word at a time (discrete) or in a stream (continuous).

Speech understanding   The ability of a computer to recognize and understand *spoken* language (in sentences, rather than discrete words).

Spreadsheet software   Software that uses a grid of coded rows and columns to display numeric or textual data in cells.

Standard Generalized Markup Language (SGML)   Text-based language for describing the content and structure of digital documents, from which the simpler HTML was derived.

Static data   Data that do not change.

Storage area network (SAN)   An architecture for building special, dedicated networks that allow rapid and reliable access to storage devices by multiple servers.

Storage over IP   A technology that uses the Internet Protocol (IP) to transport stored data between devices within a SAN.

Storage service providers (SSPs)   Companies that provide their customers with storage capacity they require as well as professional storage services such as assessment, design, operations, and management.

Storage visualization software   Software used with SANs to graphically plot an entire network and allow storage administrators to view the properties of, and monitor, all devices from a single console.

Stored program concept   Modern hardware organization in which individual programs are executed in the computer's main memory, one after another.

Strategic alliances   Business alliances among two or more organizations that provide strategic benefits to the partners.

Strategic information system (SIS)   Information systems that support or shape an organization's competitive strategy, with both an outward and an inward focus.

Strategic plan   Statement of the firm's overall mission, the goals that follow from the mission, and the broad steps necessary to reach these goals.

Strategic systems   Systems that will provide strategic advantage in meeting organizational objectives, increasing market share, or preventing competitors from entering a market and so will significantly impact an organization's operations, success, or survival.

Streaming   Reception of data sent from a host server to an Internet user without waiting for the entire file to be downloaded.

Streaming audio   Streaming that enables the broadcast of radio programs, music, press conferences, speeches, and news programs over the Internet.

Streaming video   Streaming that enables the broadcast of video applications, including training, entertainment, communications, advertising, and marketing, over the Internet.

Structured decision   Routine and repetitive problems for which solutions exist.

Structured programming   Techniques used by programmers to improve the logical flow of a program by decomposing the computer code into *modules*, which are sections of code, or subsets of the entire program.

Structured query language (SQL)   A popular relational database language that enables users to perform complicated searches with relatively simple statements.

Stylus   A pen-style input device that the user touches to a menu of options or uses to handwrite information on a screen.

Subschema   The specific set of data from the database that is required by each application.

Supercomputer Computer with the most processing power, used in scientific and military work and increasingly in business, for simulation, modeling and other types of computation-intensive analysis.

Supply chain The flow of materials, information, payments, and services, from raw material suppliers, through factories and warehouses, to end customers.

Supply chain intelligence The inclusion of business intelligence in supply chain software solutions.

Supply chain management The planning and control of the flow of goods and materials from the original supplier through production and delivery operations to the ultimate consumer, in order to speed time to market, reduce inventory levels, lower costs, and enhance customer service.

Supply chain management (SCM) software Software that integrates the managerial and strategic tasks of supply chain management, helping companies plan, source, manufacture, and deliver their products in cost-effective and integrated ways.

Surfing The process of navigating around the Web by means of pointing and clicking a graphical Web browser.

Switched hub technologies Data transmission technology that can double bandwidth of existing LANs by the addition of a switching hub.

Switched lines Telephone lines for transmitting data, with the transmission being routed (switched) through paths to its destination.

Symbolic processing The use of symbols, rather than numbers, to process information and solve problems; the basis of artificial intelligence software.

Synchronous optical network (SONET) An interface standard for transporting digital signals over fiber-optic lines that allows the integration of transmissions from multiple vendors.

Synchronous transmission Data transmission of a group of characters in a continuous stream, controlled by a timing signal from the sending device.

Syntax error Programming errors such as a misspelled word or a misplaced comma that will not permit the program to run but are fairly easy to find and correct.

System control programs Programs that control the use of a computer system's hardware, software, and data resources.

System performance monitors Programs that monitor computer system performance and produce reports relating to the use of system resources.

System security monitors Programs that monitor the use of a computer system to protect it from unauthorized use, fraud, or destruction.

System support programs Programs that support the operations, management, and users of a computer system by providing various support services such as utilities, performance monitors, and security monitors.

System utility programs Programs that accomplish common tasks such as sorting records, creating directories, locating files, and managing memory usage.

Systematic sourcing Where organizations have long-term relationships in the trading of direct materials.

Systems analysis The examination of the business problem that the organization plans to solve with an information system; defines the business problem, identifies its causes, specifies a solution, and identifies the information requirements that the solution must satisfy.

Systems analysts Information systems professionals who specialize in analyzing and designing information systems.

Systems design Description of *how* an information system will accomplish the task identified in the systems analysis, including technical features such as system inputs, outputs, and user interfaces, and hardware, software, databases, and telecommunications.

Systems development The entire set of activities needed to construct an information systems solution to a business problem or opportunity.

Systems development life cycle (SDLC) The traditional structured framework that consists of sequential processes by which information systems are developed: investigation, analysis, design, programming, testing, implementation, operation, and maintenance.

Systems software The class of programs that acts primarily as an intermediary between computer hardware and application programs, controlling and supporting the computer system and its information processing activities.

Systems stakeholders All people who are affected by changes in information systems.

T-carrier system A digital transmission system that defines circuits that operate at different rates, all of which are multiples of the basic 64 Kbps used to transport a single voice call.

Tacit knowledge Knowledge that is the result of subjective, experiential learning, and is frequently not documented.

Teamware Intranet software, used for team building, sharing ideas and documents, brainstorming, scheduling, and archiving decisions.

Technical feasibility Study that determines if the hardware, software, and communications components of a proposed systems development project can be developed and/or acquired to solve the business problem, and whether the organization's existing technology can be used to achieve the project's performance objectives.

Technical specialists Experts on a certain type of technology, such as databases or telecommunications.

Telecommunications system Hardware and software that transmits information, including voice, text, graphics, and data, from one location to another.

Telecommuting   Generally refers to the ability of employees to work at home, at a customer's premises, or while traveling, by using a computer linked to their place of employment; also called *teleworking*.

Telematics system   Services powered by wireless communications, global positioning systems, and onboard electronics that provide location, navigation, traffic monitoring and control, toll collection, and travel information.

Telnet   Protocol that establishes an error-free link between the two computers and so allows users to be on one computer while doing work on another.

Terabyte   Approximately 1 trillion bytes.

Testing   An activity that occurs throughout programming and that is designed to detect errors ("bugs") in the computer code and to verify that the code will produce the expected and desired results.

Text mining   The application of data mining to nonstructured or less structured text files.

Thin-client systems   (see Network computer) Desktop computer systems that do not offer the full functionality of a personal computer.

Third-generation languages (3GLs)   The first generation of higher-level programming languages, which are closer to natural language and are therefore easier for programmers to use and in which one statement can be translated into a number of machine language instructions, making programming more efficient.

Threats (or hazards)   The various dangers to which an information system may be exposed.

Time value of money   Economic principle that recognizes that a sum received at a future date is not worth as much as a sum received today, because the sum received today can be invested to earn interest.

Time-sharing   An extension of multiprogramming that enables a number of users to operate online at the same time, as execution of programs rotates rapidly among the users.

Top-level specification   The rightmost part of an Internet domain name, such as com or edu; also called a zone.

Topology   The physical layout and connectivity of a network.

Total quality management (TQM)   A corporatewide organized effort to improve quality wherever and whenever possible.

Touch screen   Computer screen divided into different areas, which the user touches to trigger an action.

Trackball   Variant of a mouse, with which the user rotates a ball built into the device rather than moving the whole device.

Trade secret   Intellectual work that is a company secret and is not based on public information.

Transaction processing system (TPS)   A computerized information system that supports an organization's core operations, such as purchasing, billing, and payroll, by collecting, monitoring, storing, processing, and disseminating the organization's basic business transactions.

Transform algorithm   Mathematical formula that translates the key field directly into the record's storage location on disk.

Transmission Control Protocol/Internet Protocol (TCP/IP)   A file transfer protocol that can send large files of information across sometimes-unreliable networks; the protocol of the Internet.

Tuple   A row of data in a relational database.

Turing test   A test of whether a computer exhibits intelligent behavior: A computer is considered "smart" only when a human interviewer, conversing with both an unseen human being and an unseen computer, cannot determine which is which.

Twisted-pair wire   Strands of copper wire twisted together and used for almost all business telephone wiring.

Unified modeling language (UML)   A language for specifying, visualizing, constructing, and documenting the artifacts (such as classes, objects, etc.) in object-oriented software systems.

Uniform resource locator (URL)   The set of letters that points to the address of a specific resource on the Web.

UNIX   Operating system used by many business organizations because it provides many sophisticated desktop features on many different sizes and types of computers.

Unstructured decision   "Fuzzy," complex problems for which there are no cut-and-dried solutions.

Upstream supply chain   The part of the supply chain that includes the organization's first-tier suppliers and their suppliers, all the way to the origin of the material.

USENET   A protocol that gathers and stores e-mail messages categorized by topic and delineates how groups of messages can be stored on and sent between computers.

Value-added carriers   Companies that have developed private telecommunications systems and can provide more services than common carriers.

Value-added network (VAN)   Private, data-only wide area network used by multiple organizations that provides economies in the cost of service and network management, security, and high capacity.

Value chain   The primary activities of an organization (inbound logistics, operations, etc.) along with its support activities (infrastructure, human resources, technology, etc.), and the net value that is added to the organization's product or service by each primary activity, sequentially.

Value proposition   The value of goods and services perceived by customers.

Value system (integrated value chain)   When the value chain is extended to include suppliers, customers, etc.

Vendor-managed inventory   A service provided by large suppliers to large retailers, in which the vendor monitors and replenishes the inventory for the retailer.

Veronica (Very Easy Rodent-Oriented Netwide Index to Computer Archives)   Tool that enables users to search for text in gopher menus and places files on a temporary menu on the local server.

Vertical distributors   B2B marketplaces where direct materials (materials that are inputs to manufacturing) are traded in an environment of long-term relationship.

Vertical exchanges   Direct and indirect materials in one industry are purchased on an as-needed basis; buyers and sellers may not know each other.

Videoconferencing   Application that electronically enables two or more people to have face-to-face communications with a group in another location without having to be present in person.

Viral marketing (advocacy marketing)   Online word-of-mouth marketing where people forward messages to friends.

Virtual banks   As opposed to regular banks with added online services, virtual banks are dedicated solely to Internet transactions.

Virtual corporation (VC)   A reengineered organizational structure composed of several business partners, each with a special advantage, who share costs and resources for the purpose of producing a product or service; can be temporary or permanent.

Virtual memory   A feature that simulates more main memory than actually exists in the computer system by extending primary storage into secondary storage.

Virtual private network (VPN)   A wide area network operated by a common carrier; provides a gateway between a corporate LAN and the Internet.

Virtual reality (VR)   A three-dimensional computer-generated environment that provides artificially generated sensory cues sufficient to give the user a feeling that he or she is physically present in that environment.

Virtual Reality Modeling Language (VRML)   Language that can create three-dimensional worlds through which users can navigate within their Web browsers using a mouse or other device.

Virus   Software that can damage or destroy data or software by attaching itself to other computer programs.

Visual interactive marketing (VIM)   A method of modeling situations for decision making or problem solving that uses graphic displays to represent the impact of different management or operational decisions on goals.

Visual interactive simulation (VIS)   A decision simulation in which the end-user watches the progress of the simulation model in an animated form using graphics terminals and may interact with the simulation to try different decision strategies.

Visual programming languages   Programming languages used within a graphical environment.

Visual recognition   The combination of computer intelligence and digitized visual information received from a machine sensor, which is then used to perform or control such mechanical operations.

Voice output system   Computer system that uses synthesizer software to construct the sonic equivalent of textual words.

Voice over Internet Protocol (VoIP)   Voice calls carried over the Internet, either partially or completely bypassing the public switched telephone network.

Voice portal   The use of an ordinary telephone as an Internet appliance.

Voice recognition system   Computer system that uses microphones and special software to input speech into computers.

Voice synthesis   The technology by which computers "speak" by electronically constructing audio output from basic sound components.

Voiceband   Communications channel bandwidth capable of carrying voice transmissions.

Volatile   A characteristic of a storage medium that stored data will be lost when there is no electricity flowing through the medium.

Vulnerability   Given that a threat exists, the susceptibility of an information system to harm caused by the threat.

Waterfall approach   Traditional approach to the systems development life cycle, in which tasks in one stage were completed before the work proceeded to the next stage; today developers go back and forth among the stages as necessary.

Wearable computer   Computer that can be attached to users' clothing, to free their hands and movements.

Web authoring   Web page and site design.

Web crawler   A search engine that traverses the Web automatically, collecting index data; variously called spiders, ants, robots, bots, and agents.

Web site   All the pages of a particular company or individual.

Webmaster   The person in charge of an organization's Web site.

What-if analysis   The study of the impact of a change in the input data on the proposed solution.

Wide area information servers (WAIS)   Tool that enables users to locate files around the Internet by specifying names of database files they want to search.

Wide area network (WAN)   Networks that cover wide geographic areas and include regional networks such as telephone companies or international networks such as global communications service providers; may be commercial, privately owned, or public.

Wide-area telecommunications service (WATS)   A telephone service whereby companies pay for calls placed on toll-free voiceband lines.

Windows operating system   An operating system from Microsoft, in a variety of products, that provides a GUI using icons to provide instant access to common tasks.

Wireless local area networks (WLANs)   Provide LAN connectivity over short distances, typically less than 150 meters and in one building.

Wireless media   Communications channels that do not use physical wires or cables to transmit data and information, but that instead use the "airwaves."

Word length   The number of bits (0s and 1s) that a computer chip can process at any time.

Word processing software   Software that allows users to manipulate text; typically includes functions such as editing, formatting, printing, checks of spelling and grammar, some graphics capabilities, and so forth.

Workstation   Powerful desktop-sized computer that provides high-speed calculations and high-resolution graphics required by engineering applications.

World Wide Web   A portion of the Internet that uses the transport functions of the Internet, via a client/server architecture, to handle all types of digital information, including text, hypermedia, graphics, and sound.

WYSIWYG   Acronymn for "what you see is what you get," indicating that material is displayed on the computer screen just as it will look on the final printed page.

Yankee auction   A forward auction with multiple identical items offered; buyers bid on any number of items; bidding prices escalate.

Zone   The rightmost part of an Internet domain name; also called a top-level specification.

REFERENCES

"ABF Freight System," *Network World* (February 26, 2001).

Abramson, G., "Measuring Up" (ROI of KM), *CIO Magazine* (May 15, 1998).

Advertising Supplement, *CIO Magazine* (October 1, 1999).

Andersen, B., *Business Process Improvement Toolbox*, New York: American Society for Quality, 1999.

Andrews, W., "Global Commerce Forces Web Merchants to Find Ways to Handle Many Currencies," *Internet World* (February 23, 1998).

Anthony, R. N., *Planning and Control Systems: A Framework for Analysis*, Cambridge, MA: Harvard University Graduate School of Business Administration, 1965.

Arbib, M. A., *The Handbook of Brain Theory and Neural Networks*, Boston: MIT Press, 1998.

Armstrong, A., and J. Hagel III, "The Real Value of Online Communities," *Harvard Business Review* (May/June, 1996).

"Artificial Neural Networks," *Computerworld* (February 12, 2001).

Awad, E. M., *Building Expert Systems*, Minneapolis/St. Paul, MN: West Publishing Company, 1996.

Baker, R. H., *Extranets: The Complete Sourcebook*, New York: McGraw-Hill, 1997.

Barquin, R., and H. Edelstein, *Building, Using and Managing the Data Warehouse*, Upper Saddle River, NJ: Prentice-Hall, 1997.

"Behind BlueEyes," *MIT Technology Review* (May 2001), p. 32.

Bernard, R., *The Corporate Intranet*, New York: John Wiley & Sons, Inc., 1997.

Bidgoli, H., *Intelligent Management Support Systems*, Greenwood Pub. Group, 1998.

Bigus, J. P., *Data Mining with Neural Networks*, New York: McGraw Hill, 1996.

Birnbaum, J.H., "Unbelievable!" *Fortune* (April 13, 1998), pp. 98–110.

Bishop, M., *How to Build a Successful International Web Site*, Albany, NY: Coriolis Group Books, 1998.

Blackwell, R., *From Mind to Market: Reinventing the Retail Supply Chain*, New York: HarperCollins, 1997.

"Bluetooth Lets Gadgets Speak in One Language," *U.S. News & World Report* (May 15, 2000).

"Bollinger Shipyards," *ecompany.com*, (May 2001), pp. 119–120.

Bort J., and B. Felix, *Building an Extranet: Connect Your Internet with Vendors and Customers*, New York: John Wiley & Sons, Inc., 1997.

Boyett, J. H., and J. T. Boyett, *Beyond Workplace 2000: Essential Strategies for the New American Corporation*, New York: Dutton, 1995.

Bradley, S. P., et al. (eds.), *Globalization, Technology and Competition: The Fusion of Computers and Telecommunications in the 1990s*, Boston: Harvard Business School Press, 1993.

Bradshaw, J., ed., *Software Agents*, Boston: MIT Press, 1997.

Brancheau, J. C., et al., "Key Issues in Information Systems Management: 1994–95, SIM Delphi Results," *MIS Quarterly* (June 1996).

"Bricks and Clicks Make a Good Fit," *The Atlanta Journal-Constitution* (April 14, 2001).

"Broadband and Main," *BusinessWeek* (October 8, 2001), pp. 86–91.

Broadbent, M., and P. Weill, "Management by Maxim: How Business IT Managers Can Create IT Infrastructures," *Sloan Management Review* (Spring 1997).

Buchanan, S., and F. Gibb, "The Information Audit: An Integrated Strategic Approach," *Inter. Jour. of Info. Mgt.* (Feb. 1998).

"Burlington Coat Factory Warehouse Corporation," *Computerworld* (March 11, 2002).

Callon, J. D., *Competitive Advantage Through Information Technology*, New York: McGraw-Hill, 1996.

"Cars Will Let Motorists Drive and Surf," *Information Week* (January 8, 2001).

Cash, J., et al. *Building the Information Age Organization: Structures, Control and Information Technology*, Burr Ridge, IL: R. D. Irwin, 1994.

Cavoukian, A., and D. Tapscott, *Who Knows: Safeguarding Your Privacy in a Networked World*, New York: McGraw-Hill, 1997.

Chase, L., *Essential Business Tactics for the Net*, New York: John Wiley & Sons, 1998.

Chen, C. H., *Fuzzy Logic and Neural Network Handbook*, New York, McGraw Hill, 1996.

Choi, S. Y., et al., *The Economics of Electronic Commerce*, Macmillan, Technical pub., 1997.

Clarke, K. C., *Getting Started with Geographical Information Systems*, Upper Saddle River, NJ: Prentice-Hall, 1997.

Cleland, D. I., *Strategic Management of Teams*, New York: John Wiley & Sons, Inc., 1996.

Clinton, W. J., and A. Gore Jr., "A Framework for Global Electronic Commerce," *http://www.iitf.nist.gov/eleccomm/ecomm.htm*, July 1997.

Coleman, D., *Collaborative Strategies for Corporate LANs and Intranets*, Upper Saddle River, NJ: Prentice Hall, 1996.

Cox, E., *The Fuzzy Systems Handbook*, A Professional, 1998.

Cox, N., *Building and Managing a Web Services Team*, New York: Van Nostrand Reinhold, 1997.

"Crash-Landing Ahead?" *Information Week* (January 12, 1998), pp. 38–52

"CRM One Step at a Time," *Computerworld* (December 19, 2001).

Cronin, M. J., *Global Advantage on the Internet*, New York: Van Nostrand Reinhold, 1996.

"Cyberbanking at Wells Fargo," *Communications Week* (May 27, 1997), p. 44.

"DaimlerChrysler's Net Designs," *business2.com* (April 17, 2001), pp. 26–28.

Davenport, T. H., *Information Ecology: Mastering the Information Knowledge Environment*, New York: Oxford University Press, 1997.

Davenport, T., and P. Laurence, *Working Knowledge: How Organizations Manage What They Know*, Boston: Harvard Business School Press, 1997.

Davidow, W., and M. S. Malone, *The Virtual Corporation*, New York: HarperCollins, 1992.

Dennings, D.E., *Information Warfare and Security*, Reading MA: Addison Wesley, 1998.

Dertouzos, M., *What Will Be: How the New World of Information Will Change Our Lives*, San Francisco: Harper Edge, 1997.

Drucker, D. F., *Managing in a Time of Great Change*, New York: Truman Tally Books, 1995.

Earl M., and I. A. Scott, "What Is a Chief Knowledge Officer?" *Sloan Management Review*, Winter 1999.

El Sawy, O., *The BPR Workbook*, New York: McGraw Hill, 1999.

Ellsworth, J. H., and M. V. Ellsworth, *The Internet Business*, 2nd ed., New York: John Wiley & Sons, Inc., 1996.

Elofson, G., et al., "An Intelligent Agent Community Approach to Knowledge Sharing," *Decision Support Systems*, Vol. 20, No. 1 (1997).

Fayyad, U. M., ed., *Advances in Knowledge Discovery and Data Mining*, Boston: MIS Press, 1996.

"FBI Database Problem Halts Gun Checks," *Computerworld* (May 22, 2001).

"Fidelity Retrofits All Data for XML," *InternetWeek* (August 6, 2001).

"Five Patents to Watch," *MIT Technology Review* (May, 2001).

Fried, L., *Managing Information Technology in Turbulent Times*, New York: Wiley, 1995.

Garson, G. P., *Computer Technology and Societal Issues*, Harrisburg, PA: The Idea Group, 1995.

Gary, P., and H. J. Watson, *Decision Support in the Data Warehouse Systems*, Upper Saddle River, NJ: Prentice-Hall, 1998.

Gill, K. S. (ed.), *Information Society*, London: Springer Publishing, 1996.

Gill, P. J. "Business Modeling Tools Help Companies Align Their Business and Technology Goals," *Information Week* (April 19, 1999).

Gilmore, J. H., and B. J. Pine II, "The Four Faces of Mass Customization," *Harvard Business Review* (January/February 1997).

Goldman, S., et al., *Competitors and Virtual Organizations*, New York: Van Nostrand Reinhold, 1995.

Gollmann P., *Computer Security*, New York: John Wiley & Sons, Inc. 1999.

Gonsalves, A., "Bom.com Helps Product Developers Meet Milestones," *Information Week* (September 10, 2001).

Goralski, W. M., et al., *VRML: Exploring Virtual Worlds on the Internet*, Upper Saddle River, NJ: Prentice Hall, 1997.

Gorry, G. A., and M. S. Scott-Morton, "A Framework for Management Information Systems," *Sloan Management Review*, Vol. 13, No. 1 (Fall 1971).

"Ground Wars," *BusinessWeek* (May 21, 2001), pp. 64–68.

GVU: Graphics, Visualization & Usability Center at Georgia Institute of Technology, *www.cc.gatech.edu/gvu/user_ surveys.*

Hagel, J., and A. Armstrong, *Net Gain: Expanding Markets Through Virtual Communities,* Boston, MA: Harvard Business School Press, 1997.

Hammer, M., and J. Champy, *Reengineering the Corporation,* New York: Harper Business, 1993.

Hammer, M., and S. A. Stanton, *The Reengineering Revolution: A Handbook,* New York: Harper Collins, 1995.

Handfield, R., and E. Nicols, *Supply Chain Management,* Upper Saddle River, NJ: Prentice-Hall, 1999.

Hansen G. A., *Automating BPR: Using the Power of Visual Simulation to Improve Performance,* 2nd ed., Upper Saddle River, NJ: Prentice Hall International, 1997.

Haskin, D., "Leverage Your Knowledge Base" (Web-based document management systems), *Internet World* (Feb. 1998).

Hengl, T., *Artificial Intelligence on the Internet,* Knowledge Technology Inc., 1995.

"Hidden Treasure," *Business 2.0* (July 10, 2001), pp. 41, 43.

Hills, M., *Intranet Business Strategy,* New York: John Wiley & Sons, 1996.

Hiskurich, G. M., *An Organizational Guide to Telecommuting,* NewYork: American Society for Training and Development, 1998.

Hof, R. D., et al., *"Electronic Communities,"* Special report, *Business Week* (May 5, 1997).

Honwitt, E., "When Things Go Wrong" (Web disaster planning), *Computerworld* (Jan. 12, 1998), *www2.computerworld.com/ home/Emmerce.nsf/all/disaster.*

"How Business Intelligence Bridges Retail to e-Tail," *Knowledge Management Magazine* (June 2, 2000).

"How Marriott Never Forgets a Guest," *Business Week* (February 21, 2000).

Huber, G. P., "A Theory of the Effects of Advanced Information Technologies on Organizational Design, Intelligence, and Decision Making," *Academy of Management Review,* Vol. 15, No. 1 (1990).

Hubms, M. N., et al., *Readings in Agents,* Palo Alto: Morgan Kaufman, 1998.

"Increasing Manufacturing Performance Through Supply Chain Intelligence," *DM Review* (September 2000).

"Intel Goes E-Business," *InternetWeek* (November 23, 1998), pp. 1, 98.

"Intelligent Agents," A special issue of the *Communications of the ACM* (March 1999).

Ives, B., et al., "Global Business Drivers: Aligning IT to Global Business Strategy," *IBM Systems Journal,* Vol. 32, No. 1 (1993).

"Jackpot! Harrah's Entertainment," *CIO* (February 1, 2001).

Jackson, P., *Introduction to Expert Systems,* Reading, MA: Addison-Wesley, 1999.

James, F., "IT Helps HR Become Strategic," *Datamation* (April 1997).

Jamshididi, M., et al. (eds.), *Applications of Fuzzy Logic Towards High Machine Intelligent Quotient Systems,* Upper Saddle Road, NJ: Prentice Hall, 1997.

Jarvenpaa, S., and B. Ives, "The Global Network Organization of the Future: Information Management Opportunities and Challenges," *Journal of Management Information Systems* (Spring 1994).

Jessup, L. M., and J. Valacich (eds.), *Group Support Systems: New Perspectives,* New York: Macmillan, 1993.

Jilovec, N., *The A to Z of EDI: And its Role in E-Commerce,* DUKE Communication, 1998.

Johnsen, R., *Groupware: Computer Support for Business Teams,* New York: Free Press, 1988.

Jordan, E. "Supermarket Keeps It Fresh," Macquarie Graduate School of Management, Sydney, Australia.

Kalakota, R., and M. Robinson, *E-Business 2.0,* Reading, MA, Addison Wesley, 2000.

Kalman, E. A., and J. P. Grillo, *Ethical Decision Making and Information Technology,* 2nd ed., New York: McGraw-Hill, 1996.

Kanter, J., *Managing with Information,* 4th ed., Englewood Cliffs NJ: Prentice-Hall, 1992.

Kanter, R. M., *World Class: Thriving Locally in the Global Economy,* New York: Simon and Schuster, 1995.

Keen, P. G. W., *Shaping the Future: Business Design through Information Technology,* Cambridge, MA: Harvard Business School Press, 1991.

Kettinger, W. J., et al., "Business Process Change: A Study of Methodologies, Techniques and Tools," *MIS Quarterly* (March 1997).

Khama, R., *Distributed Computing Implementation and Management Strategy,* Englewood Cliffs, NJ: Prentice Hall, 1994.

Khoshafian, S., and M. Buckiewicz, *Introduction to Groupware, Workflow, and Workgroup Computing,* New York: Wiley Computer Publishing, August 1996.

Kirchmer, M., *Business Process Oriented Implementation of Standard Software: How to Achieve Competitive Advantage,* 2nd ed., Telos Press, 1999.

Knoke, W., *Bold New World: The Essential Road Map to the 21st Century,* New York: Rodensha America, 1996.

Kolonder, J., *Case-based Reasoning,* Mountain View, CA: Morgan Kaufman, 1993.

Komenar, M., *Electronic Marketing,* New York: John Wiley & Sons, 1997.

Kosiur, D., *Understanding Electronic Commerce,* Microsoft Press, 1997.

Kotler, J. P., *Leading Change,* Boston: Harvard Business School Press, 1996.

Kotler, P., and G. Armstrong, *Principles of Marketing,* 8 ed., Upper Saddle River, NJ: Prentice-Hall, 1999.

Krantz, S., *Building Intranets with Lotus Notes and Domino*, Gulf Breeze, FL: Maximum Press, 1998.

Kress, D., "AI at Work," *PC AI* (March/April, 1998).

Kugelmass, J., Telecommuting: *A Manager's Guide to Flexible Work*, New York: Lexington Press, 1995.

Lacity, M. C., and R. Hirschheim, "The Information Systems Outsourcing Bandwagon,"*Sloan Management Review* (Fall 1993), pp. 73–86.

Larson, T., "Global Information Technology Utilization Trends," *Journal of Global Information Management*, Spring, 1996.

Lawrence, P. (ed.), *Workflow Handbook*, New York: John Wiley & Sons, 1997.

Lazzaro, J. J., "Computers for the Disabled," *Byte* (June 1993).

Leontief, W., *The Future Impact of Automation on Workers*, Oxford: Oxford University Press, 1986.

Lertolaq, J., "Computer Defenses," *Discover* (1983).

"Lexis-Nexis Faces Database Purge in Wake of Copyright Ruling," *Information Week* (June 22, 2001).

Lindstone, H., and H. Turroff, *The Delphi Method: Technology and Applications*, Reading, MA: Addison-Wesley, 1975.

Lipnack, J., and J. Stamps, *Virtual Teams*, New York: John Wiley & Sons, Inc. 1997.

Li, S., "The Development of a Hybrid Intelligent System for Developing Marketing Decision Strategy," *Decision Support Systems* (January 2000), p. 399.

Liu, Z. "China's Information Superhighway: Its Goal, Architecture and Problems," *Electronic Markets*, Vol. 7, No. 4 (1997).

Maes, P., "Agents that Reduce Work and Information Overload," *Communications of the ACM* (July 1994).

Maes, P., et al., "Agents that Buy and Sell," *Communications of the ACM* (March 1999).

"Managing Customer Churn," *Information Week* (May 14, 2001).

"Managing Tons of Data," *Computerworld* (April 23, 2001).

Maitra, A. K., *Building a Corporate Internet Strategy: The IT Manager's Guide*, New York: Van Nostrand Reinhold, 1997.

Mankin, D., et al., *Teams and Technology*, Boston: Harvard Business School, 1996.

Marakas, G. M., and J. J. Elam, "Creativity Enhancement in Problem Solving: Through Software or Process," *Management Science* (August 1997).

Martin, J., *Cybercorp: The New Business Revolution*, New York: Amacom, 1996.

Martin, M. H., "Smart Managing" (ERP systems), *Fortune* (Feb. 2, 1998).

Mason, R. O., et al., *Ethics of Information Management*, Thousand Oaks: Sage Publishers, 1995.

Massetti., B., "An Empirical Examination of the Value of Creativity Support Systems in Idea Generation," *MIS Quarterly* (March 1996).

McKeown, P. G., and R. T. Watson, *Metamorphosis—A Guide to the WWW and Electronic Commerce*, 2nd ed., New York: John Wiley & Sons, 1998.

McKim, G. W., *Internet Research Companion*, Indianapolis, IN: Que, 1996.

McLeod, R., Jr., "Systems Theory and Information Resource Management: Integrating Key Concepts," *Information Resource Management Journal* (Spring 1995).

McNurlin, B., and R. Sprague, *Information Systems Management in Practice*, 5th ed., Upper Saddle River, NJ: Prentice Hall, 2001.

Meeker, N., *The Internet Advertising Report*, New York: Morgan Stanley, 1997.

Millet, I., and C. H. Mawhinney, "Executive Information Systems," *Information & Mangement*, Vol. 23 (1992).

Mills J. M., *Managing Telework: Strategies for Managing the Virtual Work Force*, New York: John Wiley & Sons, 1998.

Mills, Q. D., *Rebirth of the Corporation*, New York: John Wiley & Sons, 1991.

Mintzberg, H., *Mintzberg on Management*, New York: The Free Press, 1989.

Mintzberg, H., *The Nature of the Managerial Work*, New York: Harper & Row, 1973.

"More Employers Taking Advantage of New Cyber-Surveillance Software," *cnn.com*, July 11, 2000.

Naisbitt, J., *Global Paradox*, London: N. Breadly, 1994.

Naisbitt, James, *Megatrends*, Warner Books, 1982.

Negroponte, N., *Being Digital*, New York: Knopf, 1995.

Nelso, S. L., *The WWW for Busy People*, New York: Berkeley Osborne/McGraw Hill, 1996.

"Netscape: Inside the Big Software Giveaway," *Fortune* (March 30, 1998), pp. 150–151.

Neumann, S., *Strategic Information Systems—Competition Through Information Technologies*, New York: Macmillan, 1994.

O'Keefe, S., *Publicity on the Internet*, New York: John Wiley & Sons, 1997.

O'Leary, D., "Knowledge Management-Systems," *IEEE Intelligent Systems* (May/June 1998).

O'Leary, D., "AI and Navigation on the Internet and Intranet," *IEEE Expert* (April 1996).

"Olympic IT," *InfoWorld*, November 5, 2001, pp. 42–44.

"On-Target Marketing," *InformationWeek* (August 31, 1998), pp. 71–72.

"Open Door Policy," *PC Week* (May 25, 1998).

Oppliger, R., "Firewalls and Beyond," *Communications of the ACM* (May 1997).

Ouellette, T., "Notes Changes Name, Shifts Focus to Internet," *Computerworld,* Vol. 30, No. 45 (November 4, 1996).

Overly, M. R., *E-Policy: How to Develop Computer, E-Policy and Internet Guidelines to Protect your Company and Its Assets,* NewYork: AMACOM, 1998.

"PCs as Supercomputer," *Internet Week* (May 28, 2001), pp. 1, 45.

"Peer to Peer," *BusinessWeek 50* (Spring, 2001), pp. 194–196.

"Peer-to-Peer Grows Up and Gets a Real Job," *New York Times* (June 13, 2001).

Peppers, D., et al., *The One to One Fieldbook,* New York: Currency & Doubleday, 1999.

Perry, L. T., et al., *Real-time Strategy,* New York: John Wiley & Sons, 1993.

Petreley, N., "The Official Terminology Guide to Commercial Software Development," *Infoworld* (March 9, 1998), p. 140.

Pfaffenberger, B., *Building a Strategic Extranet,* IDG Books (1998).

Pine, J. B. II, *Mass Customization,* Boston: Harvard Business School Press, 1993.

Pinsonneault, A., and K. Kraemer, "The Impact of Information Technology on Middle Managers," *MIS Quarterly* (September 1993).

"Pipe Down," *business2.com* (May 29, 2001), pp. 38–39.

Pitkow, J. E., and G. M. Kethoe, "Emerging Trends in the WWW User Population," *Communications of the ACM* (June 1996).

Porter, M. E., *Competitive Advantage: Creating and Sustaining Superior Performance,* New York: Free Press, 1985–1989.

Porter, M. E., "What Is a Strategy?," *Harvard Business Review* (November/December 1996).

Power, B. S., and R. Sharda, "Obtaining Business Intelligence on the Internet," *Long Range Planning,* Vol. 30, No. 1 (April 1997).

"Predictions of the Death of PCs Were Exaggerated," *CIO* (June 1, 2001).

Preston, H. H., and U. Flohr, "Internationalizing Code from the Start Minimizes and Leads to Big Payoffs," *Byte* (March 1997).

"PriceWaterhouseCoopers 2001 Technology Forecast," PriceWaterhouseCoopers Technology Center, Menlo Park, CA.

"Privacy Worries Arise Over Spyware in Kids' Software," *U.S. News and World Report* (July 3, 2000), p. 55.

"Punching Holes in Internet Walls," *New York Times* (April 26, 2001).

Quelch, J. A., and L. R. Klein, "The Internet and International Marketing," *Sloan Management Review* (Spring 1996).

Radding, Alan, "Enterprise RAD Tools: Can They Do the Job?" *Information Week,* January 11, 1999.

Radding, A, "Rapid Development for Complex Apps," *Information Week* (December 21–28, 1998), pp. 67–70.

Ramarapu, N. K., and A. A. Lado, "Linking Information Technology to Global Business Strategy to Gain Competitive Advantage: An Integrative Model," *Journal of Information Technology,* Vol. 10 (1995).

Rayport, J. F., and J. J. Sviokla, "Exploring the Virtual Value Chain," *Harvard Business Review* (November/December 1996).

Rebstock, S., et al., "Group Support Systems, Power and Influence in Organizations: A Field Study," *Decision Sciences Journal* (Fall 1997).

Rendleman, J., and Khirallah, D. R., "Boise Cascade's IT Efforts Pursue Efficiency and the Customer," *InformationWeek* (September 17, 2001).

"Reverse Auctions Can Save Colleges Money on Big-Ticket Purchases, Users Say." *Chronicle of Higher Education* (August 10, 2001).

Roche, E. M., *Telecommunications and Business Strategy,* Chicago: Dryden Press, 1991.

Rockart, J. F., and Flannery, L. S., "The Management of End User Computing," *Communications of the ACM,* V. 26, No. 10, (1983), pp. 776–784.

"Schools Get Tool to Track Students' Internet Use," *nytimes.com* (May 21, 2001).

Scott-Morton, M., and T. J. Allen (eds.), *Information Technology and the Corporation of the 1990s,* New York: Oxford University Press, 1994.

Senge, P., *The Fifth Discipline: The Art and Practice of the Learning Organization,* New York: Currency/Doubleday, 1994.

Sethi, V., and W. R. King (eds.), *Organizational Transformation Through BPR,* 2nd ed., Upper Saddle River, NJ: Prentice Hall, 1998.

Simon, H., *The New Science of Management Decisions,* rev. ed., Englewood Cliffs, NJ, Prentice-Hall, 1977.

"Simultaneous Software," *Business Week* (August 27, 2001), pp. 146–147.

"Software Failure Halts Big Board Trading for Over an Hour," *nytimes.com* (June 9, 2001).

"Stop Moaning about Gripe Sites and Log On," *Fortune* (April 2, 2001), pp. 181–182.

Smith, G. S., and O. Rist, "Collaboration (Groupware)," *Internetweek* (January 19, 1998).

Special issue on Knowledge Management, *Journal of Business and Strategy* (Jan.–Feb., 1998).

Sprague, R. H., "Electronic Document Management: Challenges and Opportunities," *MIS Quarterly* (March 1995).

Stein, T., "Orders from Chaos" (supply chain systems), *InformationWeek* (June 23, 1997).

Sterne, J., *Customer Service on the Internet: Building Relationship, Increasing Loyalty, and Staying Competitive,* New York: John Wiley & Sons, 1997.

Sterne, J., *WWW Marketing,* 2nd ed., New York: John Wiley & Sons, 1999.

Stewart, T. A., *Intellectual Capital: The New Wealth of Organizations,* New York: Currency/Doubleday, 1997.

Strassman, P., "What Is the Best Defense? Being Prepared," *ComputerWorld* (March 31, 1997).

Stull, A. T., *Surfing for Success in Business: A Student Guide to the Internet,* Upper Saddle River, NJ: Prentice Hall, 1997.

Sullivan, D., *The New Computer User,* 2nd ed., Orlando, FL: Harcourt Brace, 1997.

Sullivan R. L., *Electronic Commerce with EDI,* Boston, Mass: Twain, 1998.

Suplee, C., "Robot Revolution," *National Geographic* (July 1997).

Sveiby, K. E., *The New Organizational Wealth: Managing and Measuring Knowledge-Based Assets,* San Francisco: Berrett-Koehler, 1997.

Synnott, W. R., *The Information Weapon,* New York: John Wiley & Sons, 1987.

Szuprowicz, B., *Extranets and Intranets: E-Commerce Business Strategies for the Future,* 5th ed., South Carolina: Computer Technology Research Group, 1998.

Tapscott, D., *The Digital Economy,* New York: McGraw-Hill, 1996.

Tapscott, D., and A. Caston, *Paradigm Shift: The New Promise of Information Technology,* New York: McGraw-Hill, 1993.

"Taxing Overhaul," *Internet Week* (April 23, 2001), pp. 50–51.

"The State of Software: Quality," *InformationWeek.com* (May 21, 2001).

"The Total Package," *ecompany.com* (June 2001), pp. 91–97.

"Thoroughly Modern Manufacturing," *Datamation* (February 1998).

"Trimac's Million Dollar Payback," *Internet Week* (December 3, 2001).

Trippi, R., and E. Turban (eds.), *Neural Computing Applications in Investment and Financial Services,* 2nd ed., Burr Ridge, IL: R. D. Irwin, 1996.

Trippi, R., and E. Turban, *Investment Management: Decision Support and Expert Systems,* New York: VNR Publishers, 1990.

Turban, E., et al., *Electronic Commerce: A Managerial Perspective,* Upper Saddle River, NJ: Prentice-Hall, 2000.

Turban, E., and J. Aronson, *Decision Support Systems and Intelligent Systems,* 6th ed., Upper Saddle River, NJ: Prentice Hall, 2001.

Turban, E., et al., *Information Technology for Management,* 3rd ed. New York: John Wiley & Sons, 2002.

Van Gigch, J. P., *Applied General Systems Theory,* 2nd ed., New York: Harper and Row, 1978.

Vassos, T., *Strategic Internet Marketing,* Indianapolis, IN: Que, 1996.

Violino, B., "Sears, Roebuck, & Company Productivity Gains from Mobile Computing," *Information Week* (April 27, 1998).

"Virginia Tech Brings Wireless to Appalachia and Beyond." *Mobile Computing & Communications* (September 2000), pp. 101–103.

"Virtual Reality," special issue of *Communications of the ACM* (May 1996).

Wang, R. Y., "Total Data Quality Management," *Communications of the ACM* (Feb. 1998).

Wang, S., "Analyzing Agents for Electronic Commerce," Information Systems Management (Winter 1999).

Ward, J., and P. Griffiths, *Strategic Planning for Information Systems,* 2nd ed., Chichester: John Wiley & Sons, 1997.

Wayner, P., *Digital Cash,* Boston: AP Professional, 1997.

"Web-Powered HR," *InternetWeek* (March 12, 2001), pp. 1, 14.

Wee, L. K., et al., "DeNews—A Personalized News System," *Expert Systems with Applications* (November 1997).

"Wells Fargo," *Datamation* (June 1997), pp. 91–93.

Wetherbe, J. C., *The World on Time,* Santa Monica, CA: Knowledge Exchange, 1996.

"Where Computers Meet the Road," *Business 2.0* (October 2001).

Whiteley, R. C., *The Customer Driven Company,* Reading, MA: Addison-Wesley, 1991.

Wigand, R., et al., *Information, Organization, and Management: Expanding Markets and Corporate Boundaries,* New York: John Wiley & Sons, 1997.

Wilson, C., *"Optical Networking,"* White Paper, *Interactive Week* (February 21, 1998).

"Wireless Delivery Drives Forward," *InfoWorld* (November 16, 2001).

Wong, F. S., et al., "Fuzzy Neural Systems for Stock Selection," *Financial Analysts Journal* (January/February, 1992).

Zimmenman J., *Doing Business with Government Using EDI: A Guide for Small Business,* New York, John Wiley & Sons, Inc., 1996.

Zwass, V., "Electronic Commerce: Structures and Issues." *International Journal of Electronic Commerce* (Fall 1996), p. 6.

3m.com (2001)

3com.com (U.S. Robotics)

abcnews.com (February 21, 2001)

abfs.com

adavi.com

a-dec.com

aetna.com

ambra.com

americanexpress.com

amica.com

analog.com

analogdevices.com (2002)

artstores.com

atip.or.jp/public/atip.reports.96/atip96.016.html

belk.com

bmil.com

bmw.com

boeing.com

boisecascade.com

bollingershipyards.com

British-Airways.com

canadiantire.com (2001)

categoric.com (November 2001)

chemconnect.com (2001)

cnn.com/2001/TECH/ptech/06/29/music.kiosks.idg/

coat.com

coca-cola.com.sg

colgate.com

comshare.com

condopronto.com

cydsa.com

daimlerchrysler.com

daiwa.com.jp

datamation.com/PlugIn/issues/1998/February/02son.html

dellauction.com

dnb.com

eddiebauer.com

edify.com

europcar.com

exchange.ups.com

exsys.com

fbi.gov

fidelity.com

ford.com

forrester.com

fritolay.com

ge.com

gm.com

hardware.ibm.com

harrahs.com

hertz.com

ibm.com

ibm.com/solutions/lifesciences

ibm1.com/businesscenter/us/smbusapub.nsf

.intel.com

intel.com/ebusiness (August 2001)

intel.com/eBusiness/enabling/ebusiness.htm

intelliseek.com

iomega.com

irs.gov

jbhunt.com

knowledgespace.com

knowledgespace.arthurandersen.com

lego.com

lexis-nexis.com

lilly.com.uk

linuxhq.com

llbean.com

marriott.com

mckesson.com

metallicpower.com

mfrpc.com

microsoft.com

missingkids.com

msnbc.com/news/630735.asp?<p1=1#BODY

muze.com

national.com

ncmec.com

nike.com

novell.com

nyse.com

oecd.org

oracle.com

oub.com.sg

pcfvirtual.com

pg.com

phaseforward.com

productbank.com.au

qualcomm.com

quantum.com

roadway.com

robocup.org

sap.com

sas.com

saturn.com

sgi.com

shopevanston.com

singtel.com

SmallBusinessSchool.org

software.ibm.com/speech

sonoco.com

sprint.com

steelcase.com

sun.com

syquest.com

tenneco-automotive.com

ti.com

tommyb2b.com

toysrus.com

transwave.com

trilogy.com

trimac.com

ups.com

us.dell.com/dell/media

visa.com

vt.edu

wellsfargo.com/com/comintro.jhtml (November 2001)

zeiss.de

INDEX

PHOTO CREDITS

CHAPTER 11
Page 349: Courtesy 3-M. Page 369: Courtesy Comshare, Inc. Page 370 (left): Courtesy of City University of Hong Kong. Page 370 (right): The Management Cockpit® is a registered trademark of SAP, created by Professor Patrick M. Georges and delivered by N.E.T. Research. Page 373: ©2000 by Sidney Harris. Page 376: Ponsse Oyj.

CHAPTER 12
Page 390: Courtesy Analog Devices. Page 393: ©2000 by Sidney Harris. Page 395: Kimimasa MayamaReuters/Kimimasa Mayama/Archive Photos. Page 405: ©2000 by Sidney Harris. Page 414: Courtesy NEC Corporation. Page 416: MGM/Archive Photos. Page 417: ©1995–2002. The Weather Channel Enterprises, Inc.

CHAPTER 13
Page 425: ©EyeWire/Getty Images.

CHAPTER 14
Page 460: ©CORBIS.

CHAPTER 15
Page: ©AP/Wide World Photos. Page 500: ©2000 by Sidney Harris. Page 501: Courtesy Worksmart. Page 503: Owen Franken/Corbis-Bettmann. Page 515: ©Telegraph Colour Library/FPG International/Getty Images.